D0024719

NAVIES OF EUROPE

To my mother, Marcella Sondhaus – my first teacher

359.0094
So 5

Hist.

Navies of Europe

1815–2002

LAWRENCE SONDHAUS

Longman

An imprint of **Pearson Education**

London · New York · Toronto · Sydney · Tokyo · Singapore · Hong Kong · Cape Town
New Delhi · Madrid · Paris · Amsterdam · Munich · Milan · Stockholm

Nvack College Library

PEARSON EDUCATION LIMITED

Head Office:
Edinburgh Gate
Harlow CM20 2JE
Tel: +44 (0)1279 623623
Fax: +44 (0)1279 431059

London Office:
128 Long Acre, London WC2E 9AN
Tel: +44 (0)207 447 2000
Fax: +44 (0)207 240 5771
Website: pearsoneduc.com www.history-minds.com

———————————

First published in Great Britain in 2002

© Pearson Education Limited 2002

The right of Lawrence Sondhaus to be indentified as Author
of this Work has been asserted by him in accordance
with the Copyright, Designs and Patents Act 1988.

ISBN 0 582 50613 1

British Library Cataloguing in Publication Data
A CIP catalogue record for this book can be obtained from the British Library

All rights reserved; no part of this publication may be reproduced, stored
in a retrieval system, or transmitted in any form or by any means, electronic,
mechanical, photocopying, recording, or otherwise without either the prior
written permission of the Publishers or a licence permitting restricted
copying in the United Kingdom issued by the Copyright Licensing Agency Ltd,
90 Tottenham Court Road, London W1P 0LP. This book may not be lent,
resold, hired out or otherwise disposed of by way of trade in any form
of binding or cover other than that in which it is published, without the
prior consent of the Publishers.

10 9 8 7 6 5 4 3 2 1

Typeset by Fakenham Photosetting Ltd, Fakenham, Norfolk
Printed and bound in China

The Publishers' policy is to use paper manufactured from sustainable forests.

#49641119

CONTENTS

LIST OF MAPS AND PLATES

Plate section, at centre of book

Plate 1   British ship of the line *Thunderer* (left) and Austrian frigate *Guerriera* (center) in the bombardment of Sidon (26 September 1840). *Naval Historical Center (US), Basic Collection.*

Plate 2   The German fleet of 1848–52. *Historische Sammlung der Marineschule Mürwik.*

Plate 3   British ship of the line *Agamemnon* in the bombardment of Sevastopol (17 October 1854). *Naval Historical Center (US), Basic Collection.*

Plate 4   The Anglo-French Baltic fleet (1854). *Naval Historical Center (US), Basic Collection.*

Plate 5   French armored frigate *Gloire* (1860). *Naval Historical Center (US), Basic Collection.*

Plate 6   British armored frigate *Warrior* (1861). *Naval Historical Center (US), Basic Collection.*

Plate 7   British turret ship *Captain* (1870). *Naval Historical Center (US), Basic Collection.*

Plate 8   Prussian paddle steamer *Loreley* (left) and screw corvette

Arcona (center) engage Danish warships at the Battle of Jasmund (17 March 1864). *Historische Sammlung der Marineschule Mürwik.*

Plate 9   Austrian screw ship of the line *Kaiser*, the day after engaging Italian ironclads at the Battle of Lissa (20 July 1866) *Naval Historical Center (US), Basic Collection.*

Plate 10   Italian battleship *Duilio* (1880). *Naval Historical Center (US), Basic Collection.*

Plate 11   German turret ship *Preussen* (1876) of the *Grosser Kurfürst* class, with casemate ship *Hansa* (1875) in background. *Historische Sammlung der Marineschule Mürwik.*

Plate 12   German *Sachsen*-class battleship (1878; pictured in 1895). *Naval Historical Center (US), Basic Collection.*

Plate 13   French protected cruiser *Milan* (1885). *Naval Historical Center (US), Basic Collection.*

Plate 14   French protected cruiser *Sfax* (1887). *Naval Historical Center (US), Basic Collection.*

Plate 15   British protected cruiser *Blake* (1892). *Naval Historical Center (US), Basic Collection.*

Plate 16   German torpedo boat (mid-1880s) with battleship *Sachsen* and rigged warships in background. *Historische Sammlung der Marineschule Mürwik.*

Plate 17   German *Siegfried*-class coastal battleship (pictured in early 1890s). *Naval Historical Center (US), Basic Collection.*

Plate 18   French submarine *Gymnote* (1888). *Naval Historical Center (US), Basic Collection.*

Plate 19   British pre-dreadnought *Royal Sovereign* (1891). *Naval Historical Center (US), Basic Collection.*

Plate 20   German *Gazelle*-class light cruiser (pictured circa 1900). *Naval Historical Center (US), Basic Collection.*

Plate 21   German pre-dreadnought *Kaiser Wilhelm II* (1900), of the *Kaiser Friedrich III* class. *Historische Sammlung der Marineschule Mürwik.*

Plate 22   German pre-dreadnought of the *Deutschland* class (1906). *Naval Historical Center (US), Basic Collection.*

Plate 23   German armored cruiser *Scharnhorst* (1907). *Naval Historical Center (US), Basic Collection.*

Plate 24   French submarine *Narval* (1900). *Naval Historical Center (US), Basic Collection.*

PREFACE

During the first decades of the modern era, as in the early modern period culminating in the wars of the French Revolution and Napoleon, the leading navies of Europe were the leading navies of the world. As industrialization revolutionized naval warfare, the navies of Europe continued to shape the international paradigm of sea power, as they had in the age of the wooden sailing ship. The first great non-European naval powers, the United States and Japan, emerged in the 1890s, and became the leading naval powers of the world by the late 1930s, but as they rose to prominence the organization, training, and matériel of their fleets continued to reflect models established in Europe. The operations of the navies of Europe are central to the stories of the First and Second World Wars as well as the post-1945 Cold War, when the Soviet Union built the most powerful navy ever assembled by a European country. At the onset of the twenty-first century, the navies of Europe remain a vital factor in the broader international arena. Some (the British, French, German, and Italian) have a greater significance than at any time in the past fifty or sixty years, while others (the Spanish and Dutch) enjoy a status relative to their peers that they have not known in 200 years.

This history will trace the rise of the modern navies of Europe, culminating in the First World War, and the subsequent decline, reconceptualization, and rebirth of European naval power in the decades since 1918. From the introduction of steam propulsion to the present era of high technology, an understanding of the success or failure of naval operations requires an understanding of the importance of technological developments in naval warfare. Thus the operational history of the navies of modern Europe will be presented with special attention to the evolving state of naval technology, from the breakthroughs of the nineteenth and early twentieth centuries (in steam power, armor, artillery and torpedoes) through the second half of the twentieth century (in aircraft carrier design and naval aviation in general) to the dawn of the twenty-first century (in naval stealth technology, propulsion systems, and warship design). Because the relative industrial capabilities of seafaring countries have been reflected in their naval building programs, a focus on industrial development will provide an important link between the matters investigated in this study and the broader history of the period.

The task of writing a general history of this length compels the author to make difficult decisions as to what to include, for it is not possible to provide complete coverage of the entire period. Matters related to naval personnel, including comparisons in training, education, and promotion policies, are omitted except when these factors have such a direct bearing on the operational effectiveness of a navy as to warrant inclusion as part of the explanation of its performance in wartime. Description of broader economic, political, and diplomatic factors affecting the navies of Europe has been kept to the minimum necessary to orient the reader.

ACKNOWLEDGMENTS

I would like to thank Heather McCallum for giving me the opportunity to publish this volume. I am grateful to the University of Indianapolis for a semester of leave to work on the manuscript, and to interlibrary loan staff of Krannert Memorial Library for facilitating much of my research. For their assistance in my quest to secure photographs, I would like to thank Jack Green, Robert Hanshew, and the staff of the Curator Branch, Naval Historical Center, Washington, DC, as well as Captain Michel de Monval of the French Navy and *Kapitänleutnant* Kraus of the German Federal Navy.

MAPS

+ *Hood* (1941)
Denmark Strait

Lusitania (1915) +

Bismarck (1941) +
• Brest
• Saint-Nazaire
• Bordeaux

• Ferrol

• Cadiz

• Halifax

Azores

Bermuda

Canary Islands

Santiago (1898) ✕

Cape Verde Islands

Martinique

• Dakar

Simonstown

+ *Dresden* (1915)

✕ Coronel (1914)   ✕ River Plate (1939)

✕ Falklands (1914, 1982)

✕ South Georgia (1982)

0	950	1900 miles
0	1500	3000 km

Map 1 Atlantic Ocean

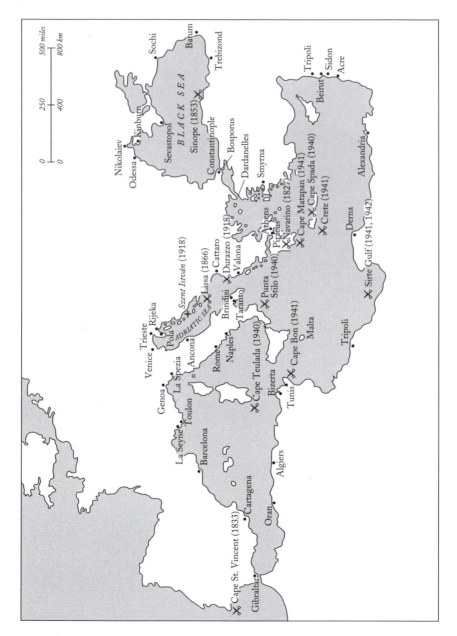

Map 2 Mediterranean Sea

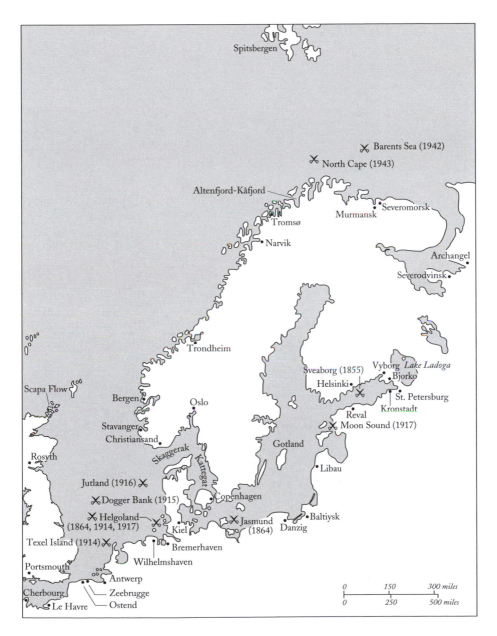

Map 3 Baltic Sea, North Sea and western Pacific Ocean

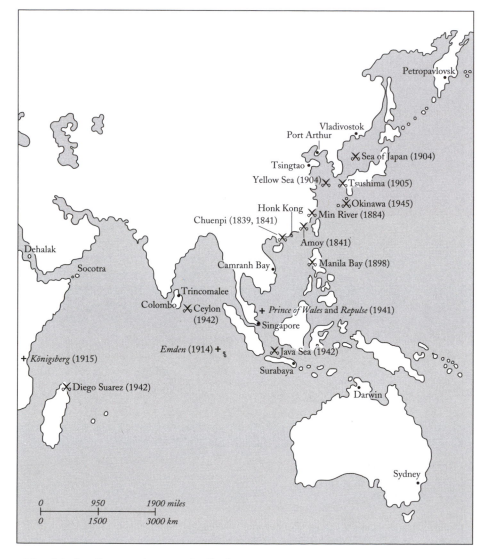

Map 4 Indian Ocean and western Pacific Ocean

1

FROM SAIL TO STEAM, 1815–40

When the Napoleonic wars ended in 1815, Europe's navies had more warships in service or under construction than ever before. In the decade between the battles of Trafalgar and Waterloo, an ambitious French shipbuilding program had compelled the British to construct unprecedented numbers of ships of the line and frigates in order to maintain their margin of superiority. As a consequence, the postwar British and French navies had many more warships than they needed for peacetime as well as a backlog of warships on the stocks, many· of which would remain there for years until being finished or scrapped. Reflecting Napoleon's effort to mobilize the shipbuilding resources of his satellite kingdoms, beyond Britain and France the maritime countries of postwar Europe inherited a variety of warships and warship projects, in shipyards from the Baltic to the Adriatic.

At least for capital ships, the pace of change remained slow for a quarter-century after 1815. As late as 1830 the British navy's reserve list still included a dozen ships of the line that had seen action at Trafalgar in 1805, among them Lord Nelson's *Victory*, launched in 1765. Another veteran of Trafalgar, the ship of the line *Revenge*, was still serving in the Mediterranean in 1841, while the battleships *Implacable* (ex-French *Duguay-Trouin*) and *Canopus* (ex-French *Franklin*), taken as prizes during the Napoleonic wars, were active in the British Mediterranean Fleet as late as 1841 and 1847, respectively.[1] But older vessels enjoying such long postwar careers typically were first- or second-rate ships of the line, or third-rates of extraordinarily sound construction, which could continue to provide service into an era in which most new wooden sailing battleships were significantly superior to traditional third-rate ships of 74 guns. As the wooden sailing warship types of the past evolved into their ultimate forms, innovations in propulsion and armament cast greater doubts over their future. While the first generation of steamships and shell guns did not bring a sudden transformation of naval warfare, proponents of these new technologies foresaw a day when the capital ships of a fleet would move under steam, and wooden hulls would be unable to withstand fire from the latest heavy artillery.

EUROPE'S SAILING FLEETS AFTER 1815

During the early modern period, the evolution of the standard sailing warship types – in descending order, from ships of the line to frigates, sloops or corvettes, brigs, schooners, and gunboats – had coincided with the conquest of the first European colonial empires. While the leading navies of Europe all maintained battle fleets of ships of the line, these were typically deployed in significant numbers only in European waters, or in American waters when European wars spread there. Most had even greater numbers of frigates, which in peacetime could patrol trade routes and defend colonies far more efficiently than battleships. Frigates were also important to the minor navies, which for financial reasons kept few, if any, ships of the line. Aside from Russia and Sweden, which had no overseas colonies, none of the naval powers had more battleships than frigates. The Napoleonic Wars left Britain as the only European country with an extensive overseas empire, yet afterward, France, Spain, and the Netherlands all still maintained more frigates than ships of the line.

It is difficult to compare the strength of navies in any era but especially for the age of sail. While different sources provide different figures for each ship type, the primary sources themselves – contemporary navy lists – often include aged warships in disrepair, new ones yet to be completed, others disarmed or adapted for auxiliary purposes. The number of warships kept in reserve ("in ordinary") likewise included many that would have been unfit for service in any event. According to one source, the British navy of 1815 had 520 active warships of all types and another 321 in reserve, down from the wartime high of 773 (206 in reserve) in 1809. Another account cites 218 ships of the line, 309 frigates, and 261 sloops or brigs on the navy list of 1815, including ships in reserve. All sources agree that the wartime battle fleet typically had around 100 ships of the line on active duty.[2]

Britain's postwar foreign secretary, Viscount Castlereagh, called for the navy to maintain a peacetime strength greater than the combined forces of the next two naval powers, France and Russia. Britain required naval power sufficient to confront such potential enemies in European waters, to defend its colonial empire, and to uphold moral and legal positions it had taken (and was persuading others to take) on a worldwide basis. Under the postwar Pax Britannica the navy led the way in keeping commercial sea lanes safe against piracy and in stopping the slave trade, which Parliament in 1807 had abolished throughout the empire. Nevertheless, the peacetime standard of the British navy after 1815 reverted to that of 1792, the last prewar year (100 ships of the line and 160 frigates), and did not account for the strength of other naval powers or the demands of new policies. Even the peacetime standard was not maintained, as each year relatively few new warships were completed while dozens of older ones were broken up or sold. By 1817 the British navy had 485 warships (including 98 ships of the line), of which 131 were active (including just 14 ships of the line). Counting vessels in reserve, by 1830 Britain had 106 ships of the line (of which 71 were deemed "in good order") and 144 frigates. Reflecting the fact that the navy's worldwide cruising presence depended upon frigates, in the postwar years some third-rate (74-gun) ships of the line were cut down and converted to fourth-rate (50-gun) "razee" frigates. But Britain faced the dilemma that such frigates were larger than necessary for normal peacetime cruising duties; indeed, the type was more suitable for the navies of France or the United States, which would use them as commerce raiders in case of war against Britain.[3] The dramatic postwar reduction of the active fleet left only 19,000 seamen on duty as of 1817, down from 140,000 in 1814, and almost 90 percent of the officer corps unemployed, on half-pay. Under the circumstances there was plenty of manpower for the warships in service, and a seaman's service remained irregular, on the traditional hire-and-discharge system. Impressment (which had provided at least half of British warship crews late in the Napoleonic era) was not used after 1815. Twenty years later an Act of Parliament established the Register of Seamen, to identify men for naval service in time of war, but decisive change did not come until after a serious manning crisis during the Crimean War.[4]

To offset the numbers of battleships leaving the navy list, 21 under construction as of 1815 were completed by 1828. Another 37 new ships of the line were commissioned between then and 1849. Britain built no 74-gun third-rates after the *Carnatic* (launched 1832), instead favoring the 84-gun two-decker and constructing a number of 120-gun three-deckers. By employing covered slips and using seasoned timber, the dockyards were able to build ships that lasted for decades without rotting. Imported Italian oak, Indian teak, and African teak supplemented domestic oak stocks. The East India Company also built some teak warships for the navy in Indian shipyards, including seven ships of the line completed between 1815 and 1848. The last of these, the 80-gun *Meeanee*, launched in November 1848, was Britain's last new sailing ship of the line.[5]

Postwar Britain failed to build new ships of the line and frigates fast enough to replace those being sold or scrapped, yet its gradually shrinking fleet easily remained larger than its nearest competitors. Under the Bourbon restoration, France remained the second naval power but had few colonies and harbored no pretensions of maritime greatness. By one account the French navy in 1815 had 69 ships of the line, but most were built of unseasoned timber in the years after Trafalgar or, rushed to completion, did not measure up to the traditional high standards of French naval construction. As early as 1819, just 31 were considered seaworthy. New commissionings down to 1830 (when the French navy list included 53 battleships) were of ships laid down before 1815 and completed gradually as funding permitted. The only three-decker ordered after the Napoleonic wars, the 120-gun *Valmy*, was not launched until 1847. Lacking a battle fleet capable of taking on the British, in the event of war the French planned a commerce-raiding *guerre de course* strategy hinging on frigates. Between 1815 and 1830 a building program increased the number of French frigates from 38 to 67, including some powerful 60-gun vessels, but still left France with less than half as many frigates as Britain. In 1815 King Louis XVIII reappointed as navy minister the ultraroyalist François-Joseph Gratet du Bouchage, the last man to hold the post before the establishment of the republic in 1792. Bouchage discharged veteran Napoleonic officers and replaced them with royalists, few of whom were fit for active duty after years in exile. The appointment of Captain Hugues de Chaumareys to command a mission in 1816 to reassert French control over Senegal finally brought matters to a head. The incompetence of Chaumareys, who had not been to sea in a generation, led to the stranding of the frigate *Méduse* on the coast of Mauretania and the loss of almost half the men aboard. The disaster prompted the dismissal of hundreds of royalist officers whose commissions had been recently restored. In the summer of 1817 one of Napoleon's old marshals, Laurent de Gouvion Saint-Cyr, replaced Bouchage as navy minister; thereafter, Napoleonic veterans returned to dominate the postwar officer corps for the years to come. In 1835, the same year in which the British finally copied the traditional French *Inscription Maritime* by introducing their Register of Seamen, France went a step further by instituting formal naval conscription, calling up all seamen automatically at age twenty.[6]

In 1815 the third-largest battle fleet belonged to Russia, which emerged from the Napoleonic era with at least 48 ships of the line and 21 frigates. The distribution of warship types reflected Russia's strategic emphasis on coastal defense and maintaining a regional naval strength in the Baltic and the Black Sea, rather than the defense of an overseas empire or protecting a large merchant marine. The wartime peak of Russian naval strength came earlier than that of Britain or France; indeed, as of 1800 Russia had over 80 ships of the line and 40 frigates, having temporarily surpassed France to become the second naval power after Britain. The size of the Russian fleet remained relatively constant in the postwar years, as did its internal distribution of forces (roughly two-thirds to the Baltic Fleet and most of the rest to the Black Sea Fleet, with only token forces in the Pacific). In 1830 the Russians had no less than 47 ships of the line and 26 frigates.[7] The battleships included a small number of three-deckers, but the need for shallower-draught ships of the line, especially in the Baltic, led Russia to continue building 74s after Britain and France abandoned the type in favor of larger two-deckers. For the age of the wooden warship, estimations of Russia's naval strength must be viewed in light of the fact that the country's vast fir forests provided most of the timber for its shipyards, and that larger warships built of fir usually had a service life of just eight to ten years (although the navy tried to keep them "afloat," at least on the navy list, for much longer). During the 1830s, long before other European navies adopted the annual tradition of summer maneuvers, both Russian fleets put large numbers of ships to sea every summer.[8] In expending so much effort in training, Russia acknowledged the fact that most of its seamen were conscripts from the interior, unfamiliar with the sea.

Spain emerged from the Napoleonic wars with 21 ships of the line, less than half as many as Russia. But the numbers are deceiving, as the Spanish navy list of 1815 still included 3 battleships build in the 1750s. Spain had not constructed a ship of the line of its own since 1798, and its only battleships newer than that were 4 taken from the French in 1808 by Spanish loyalists at Cadiz. Tsar Alexander I supported Spain's effort to reconquer its rebellious American colonies by transferring 5 ships of the line and 6 frigates from the Russian navy in 1818–19, but these acquisitions were of little use owing to their rotten fir hulls, and none of the battleships lasted past 1823. With an aging fleet and no program of new construction, Spain had no hope of recovering its colonial empire and ceased to be a relevant factor in the European naval balance of power. Even with the Russian purchases, the number of ships of the line fell to 15 by 1820, then declined further to 4 by 1830 and 2 by 1840. Spain had 15 frigates in 1815, only 5 in 1830.[9]

None of the minor European naval powers maintained a significant battle fleet after 1815. Having inheriting a number of vessels built by the French at Antwerp, the Dutch navy at least momentarily included more ships of the line (19) than frigates (14). In the years that followed the Netherlands became Europe's fourth naval power, though only because its fleet of battleships deteriorated at a slightly less alarming rate than Spain's. Like other French warships laid down in the years between Trafalgar and Waterloo, those built at Antwerp were less seaworthy owing to shoddy construction from unseasoned timber. By 1830 only 5 of the Dutch ships of the line remained. The frigates were another matter, as a country that still had a colonial empire in the East Indies and a large merchant marine, active worldwide, could not afford to be short of cruising warships. New construction more than replaced frigates sold or scrapped, leaving the Dutch with 17 in 1830. Other countries trailed far behind. Sweden had 13 ships of the line and 7 frigates in 1815, 8 ships of the line and five frigates in 1830. The Danish navy, twice destroyed by Britain during the Napoleonic wars (in 1801 and 1807), recovered by 1830 to include 3 ships of the line and 7 frigates.[10] Because the Russian Baltic Fleet (their most likely future adversary) dwarfed the combined fleets of Sweden and Denmark, the two countries developed coastal defense flotillas consisting of several dozen gunboats, each armed with one or two cannon, which could be either rowed or sailed. The Danes employed such vessels against the British, with some success, after the second (1807) destruction of their battle fleet. Postwar Prussia considered a similar system, and King Frederick William III joined some of Prussia's leading generals in advocating the creation of a Prussian navy, but until the early 1840s the largest Prussian warship was a schooner usually employed as a training ship for the Danzig merchant marine academy.[11] Austria's postwar reacquisition of Venice brought with it the navy of the Napoleonic kingdom of Italy, a windfall surpassed only by the Dutch inheritance at Antwerp. But at the time, the financially troubled Habsburg regime had no use for such a large fleet (10 ships of the line and 8 frigates, including vessels still under construction) and Prince Clemens von Metternich attempted to sell the lot. In a postwar Europe not short of warships, he found no buyers. By 1830 two of the ships of the line had entered service as razee frigates; the rest either burned in dockyard accidents or were scrapped. Austria eventually commissioned all eight of the frigates, usually keeping four in service at a time, leaving those still unfinished as of 1815 on the stocks until they were needed as replacements for their sister-ships. The most extreme case was the 44-gun *Venere*, which was laid down in 1813, launched in 1832, and served (after 1849 as *Venus*) until 1860.[12] In the years 1815–30 the two largest Italian kingdoms each maintained a navy larger than the Austrian. In 1815 the restored Bourbon regime of Naples inherited two ships of the line and six frigates from the deposed King Joachim Murat, Napoleon's brother-in-law. Meanwhile, in Sardinia–Piedmont, the talented Admiral Giorgio Des Geneys took advantage of the patronage of pro-navy King Charles Felix to build a force of eight frigates (including three of 60 guns) by 1829.[13]

NAVAL ACTIONS IN MEDITERRANEAN AND IBERIAN WATERS (1816–29)

In the twilight of the age of sail, European naval activity focused on Mediterranean and Iberian waters. During the summer of 1816 the British sent Admiral Edward Pellew, Lord Exmouth, to the North African coast with a fleet of 5 ships of the line, 5 frigates, 7 sloops and

4 bomb vessels, supplemented by a Dutch force of 5 frigates and 1 corvette. Exmouth's punitive attack on the pirate fleet of Algiers in August 1816 provided the first dramatic example of the sort of naval action that became common under the Pax Britannica. In what historian Andrew Lambert has called "a spectacular reassertion of power in support of European ideals," the Anglo–Dutch force destroyed the Algerian fleet and harbor defenses, bombarded the city of Algiers, and forced the local bey to accept allied demands for an end to piracy. Tunis and Tripoli subsequently acceded to the same terms without resistance, but the expedition as a whole was not without cost. While none of Exmouth's ships was sunk at Algiers, few of them emerged unscathed and their crews sustained 818 casualties, a sobering reminder of the sort of punishment formidable shore batteries could inflict upon wooden warships.[14] Three years later a British squadron returned to Algiers, Tunis, and Tripoli to encourage their leaders to suppress the slave trade. For the North African ports the traffic in slaves had generated profits second only to piracy, because they served as the northern termini of Saharan caravan routes that linked the coast with Timbuktu and other northern outposts of black Africa. A French ship of the line and frigate supplemented the British expedition of 1819. It was the first case of postwar Anglo–French naval cooperation, ironically at a time when French vessels remained active in the transatlantic slave trade.[15]

As a consequence of Exmouth's 1816 expedition, the North Africans promised a general cessation of piracy but largely ignored the commitment when it came to the vessels of the weaker Mediterranean states. Italian and Austrian merchantmen continued to be victimized by North African pirates, even after the navies of these states attempted to face the threat themselves. Sardinian expeditions led by Des Geneys failed to bring Morocco (1822) or Tripoli (1825) to terms. A Neapolitan squadron appeared off Tripoli the same year but made such a poor showing that the local bey subsequently doubled his tribute rate for Naples.[16] Austria achieved greater success in an expedition against Morocco (1828–30), if only because of greater persistence. A relatively weak squadron under Captain Francesco Bandiera (two corvettes, a brig, and a schooner) launched a daring raid to free the crew of a captured Austrian merchant brig, then bombarded the port of El Araisch (Larache) in July 1829. Reinforced by a frigate, Bandiera remained on station until the sultan agreed to reinstate the Austro–Moroccan treaty he had broken at the onset of the crisis.[17]

Under the Concert of Europe established at the Congress of Vienna (1814–15), Britain, Russia, Austria, and Prussia pledged to preserve the new postwar order against future threats, but a series of liberal revolutions in 1820–21 exposed serious differences among the great powers. The British sympathized with constitutionalist revolts against the absolute monarchs of Spain, Portugal, Naples, and Sardinia–Piedmont, and considered their Vienna obligations to include only the preservation of national borders, not the governments within them. Under the leadership of Prince Metternich, the eastern absolute monarchies – Austria, Prussia, and Russia – interpreted the commitment to include the preservation of individual ruling families and their systems of government. Britain rejected the demands of the eastern powers for military intervention against the four revolutions, and safeguarded the constitutionalist cause in Portugal by sending a squadron to Lisbon. Armies deputized by the Concert, minus Britain, crushed the remaining revolutions. The operation against Naples involved Austria's navy as well as its army, but while the army easily defeated the Neapolitan rebels on land, occupying the city of Naples in March 1821, the 2 Austrian frigates sent to support the advance were blockaded in the central Adriatic, at the island of Lissa, by the Neapolitan ship of the line *Capri* and a frigate, and were freed only after word arrived that the Austrian army was in Naples. The revolution in Sardinia–Piedmont broke out during the Austrian campaign against Naples. Hoping to make a show of force off Genoa (and now painfully aware that frigates alone would not suffice), Austria planned to arm two of the ships of the line it had inherited from the French at Venice. In April 1821, Austrian troops defeated the Sardinian rebels, before the ships ever left port.[18]

France resumed active participation as a European great power by volunteering to intervene against the liberal revolution in Spain. French troops reached Madrid in May 1823, just one month after crossing the Pyrenees. Members of the liberal Cortes forced King Ferdinand VII to retreat with them to Cadiz, where a strong French squadron (3 ships of the line and 10 frigates) under Rear Admiral Guy Duperré set up a blockade until the French army arrived to lay siege to the city. Recognizing that (unlike in Portugal) a demonstration of naval power alone would not suffice to save the constitutional cause in Spain, Britain elected not to challenge the French operation. After Cadiz fell in September 1823, Ferdinand VII returned to absolute power.[19] His restoration came too late for Spain to recover its position in Latin America, where the Iberian chaos of 1820–23 ensured the ultimate success of independence movements. Of the eleven warships Alexander I sold to Spain just one frigate made it to the New World, where (after being captured by patriots) it became flagship of the Chilean navy.[20]

The beginning of Greece's war for independence against the Ottoman Empire coincided with the other southern European revolutions but divided the Concert of Europe along different lines. While Romantic-era philhellenism spawned strong pro-Greek sentiments in both Britain and France, Russia supported the Greek movement in its traditional role as patron of Orthodox Christians under Turkish rule. Among the great powers of Europe, Austria alone supported the Ottoman Empire, and not just because of Metternich's conservative principles. Greece's undisciplined fleet of privateers victimized Austrian and Italian merchantmen as well as ships flying the Turkish flag, making it impossible for Austria to sympathize with the Greek cause. In addition to sending a squadron to the Eastern Mediterranean (where its ships were involved in a number of skirmishes with the Greeks), Austria built a frigate in Venice for Sultan Mahmut II's ally, Mehemet Ali of Egypt, and offered to sell some of its own warships to the Egyptians.[21]

Neither the Greeks nor the Turks made decisive use of naval power. The privateer captains nominally subordinate to Admiral Andreas Miaoulis were bold in pursuit of booty but reluctant to risk their ships against Ottoman naval vessels. Thus, the Greeks disrupted Turkish trade but left the Ottoman fleet in overall command of the sea. Early in the conflict the Greeks employed fireships successfully enough to make the Ottoman navy overly cautious when operating near Greek vessels or ports, despite its overwhelming superiority. After his isolated garrisons in Greece fell to the rebels, the desperate Mahmut II turned for help to the pasha of Egypt, Mehemet Ali. In recent years the ambitious pasha had built a respectable army and navy of his own with the help of foreign advisers, mostly from France. After entering the war in 1824, the Egyptians quickly reconquered the island of Crete for the sultan, then in February 1825 moved on to the Morea to continue their offensive.[22]

Mehemet Ali's victories forced Greek rebel leaders to acknowledge the need to replace their privateer fleet with a disciplined regular navy of formidable warships. In August 1825 they hired a British officer, Thomas, Lord Cochrane, to replace Miaoulis. Cochrane (later Earl of Dundonald), one of the most talented British commanders of the war against France, had lost his commission after being disgraced in a stock market scandal in 1814. During the Latin American wars for independence, he employed scores of British officers and seamen idled by the end of the Napoleonic wars to lead the navies of Chile (1818–22) and Brazil (1823–25) to decisive victories. His new Greek fleet was to have as its core two 64-gun frigates ordered in the United States and six paddle steamers built in Britain. Cochrane remained in Britain until the latter were ready, thus delaying his arrival in Greece for nineteen months. The first of the steamers reached Greek waters in September 1826, the frigate *Hellas* in December 1826, and another three steamers by the following spring. The remaining two steamers were never completed, and the Greeks had to sell the second American frigate to the United States navy to cover the cost of the first. Cochrane arrived in Greece in March 1827, bringing with him several veteran British officers from the Latin American wars. Miaoulis stayed on as second in command and, along with the notoriously independent Greek ship captains, found it difficult to get along with the foreigners. Even with the addition of the *Hellas* and the four steamers, the Greek navy remained woefully inferior to the combined Turco–Egyptian fleet. Cochrane's boldest move, a raid on Alexandria in June 1827, failed owing to a combination of steamship engine trouble, unfavorable winds for his sailing ships, and the refusal of some of his Greek captains to obey orders.[23]

During the same month as Cochrane's failure at Alexandria, Turkish and Egyptian troops stormed the Acropolis. The defeat left the Greek revolution on the verge of being crushed, and stirred pro-Greek public and political opinion across Europe. To save the Greek cause (and to head off unilateral Russian action, a distinct possibility under the new tsar, Nicholas I, who had succeeded Alexander I in 1825), the British and French intervened in the war. In July 1827, they joined the Russians in concluding the Treaty of London, committing themselves to a policy of armed mediation in which naval power would be used to force the Turks and Egyptians to evacuate the Morea. A Russian squadron of four ships of the line and four frigates had to come from the Baltic, as the Black Sea Fleet could not pass through the Turkish straits. France contributed four ships of the line and one frigate, while Britain added three ships of the line and four frigates. Six smaller warships completed the allied fleet, which Britain's Vice Admiral Sir Edward Codrington led into Navarino Bay, chief anchorage of the Turco–Egyptian fleet, on 20 October 1827. The Turco–Egyptian commander, Mehemet Ali's son Ibrahim, had around 65 warships at his disposal, among them 7 ships of the line and 15 frigates. Ibrahim's ships were anchored along the shore in three concentric semicircles, against which Codrington's line formed a semicircle of its own, blocking the route of escape. Codrington did not have specific instructions to destroy Ibrahim's fleet if the allied demands were not accepted; nevertheless, a battle erupted just before the last of the allied ships took their positions. Turco–Egyptian warships apparently opened fired on small boats sent out by the British and French, after which the entire allied line returned fire. For two and a half hours Codrington's ships pounded away at Ibrahim's fleet, ultimately sinking a ship of the line, 12 frigates, 22 corvettes, and 19 brigs, killing 7,000 Turkish and Egyptian sailors. The allies suffered casualties of 177 killed and almost 500 wounded, but lost no ships.[24]

Navarino made naval history on two accounts, as the first action since the 1670s in which the British and French navies fought as allies, and the last major battle at which no steamships were present. The decisive defeat of the Turco–Egyptian fleet also made it impossible for the sultan to reconquer Greece. In January 1828 Count Ioannis Capodistrias, formerly foreign minister of Russia, became president of a Greek republic, recognized as an independent state by international treaty in 1830. With the three leading naval powers standing behind Greece, Cochrane's services were no longer needed. In any event, he clashed repeatedly with Capodistrias and other "double-dealing knaves" in the Greek leadership. He resigned his Greek commission in November 1828 and returned to Britain, where the victory of his Whig friends in the election of 1830 led to the restoration of his British commission two years later. His career at sea lasted until 1851 when, at seventy-six, he completed a tour as commander of the British South American and West Indian station.[25] Meanwhile, in Greece, Miaoulis again became commanding admiral. He, too, had a stormy relationship with Capodistrias and, unfortunately for the Greek navy, became involved in intrigues against the new regime.

In the months after Navarino, Britain and France sought to mend their broken relations with the Ottoman Empire. Russia steered an opposite course, finally declaring war on Turkey in April 1828, following a winter of rising tensions. The Turkish fleet had only the six ships of the line and three frigates not destroyed at Navarino, a force clearly inferior to the nine ships of the line and four frigates of the Russian Black Sea Fleet.[26] Taking full advantage of its complete command of the Black Sea – something Peter the Great and subsequent tsars had only dreamed of in their many wars with Turkey – the Russian navy kept the army supplied from captured coastal ports during its march southward toward Constantinople. Along the way, Nicholas I took personal command of the blockade and siege of Varna (October 1828), which he directed from the three-decker *Parizh*. The Turks captured a Russian frigate in May 1829, during their first fleet sortie out of the Bosporus, but the Ottoman navy attempted just one more sortie, the following month, before spending the rest of the war at anchor. The Turkish army finally stopped the Russian offensive at Adrianople. A treaty of peace signed in September 1829 extended Russia's western Black Sea border to the mouth of the Danube.[27]

THE INTRODUCTION OF THE STEAM WARSHIP (TO 1840)

As the industrial revolution began to affect naval construction, Britain, like any true hegemon, did not take the lead in developing technologies that promised only to negate its own considerable advantages. When it came to steam propulsion the Admiralty let the British private sector shoulder the burden of early research and development. As a result, during years in which maritime technology began a fundamental transformation, the navy's share of Britain's annual budget actually declined from just over 20 percent in 1815 to less than 10 percent by the 1830s. The French navy took the opposite approach, as at least some of its leaders came to view new technologies as the means to overturn British naval superiority at some time in the future. After 1815

France became the center of innovative naval thinking, with the government rather than the private sector funding the experimentation.[28]

After 1815 Britain and France sought to expand their coastal colonial footholds in western Africa, and both navies tested their first steamships with the intention of using them as transports for expeditions up African rivers. In 1816 a British paddle steamer designed for such duty on the Congo River was such a disappointment that it was rebuilt as a sailing ship before leaving home waters. The French had better luck with two small paddle steamers, which passed their trials and in 1818 were deployed on the Senegal River.[29] The technology spread quickly to other navies but for years it remained strictly a novelty. Most European navies commissioned a single small steamer, nominally armed or unarmed, for use as a yacht for dignitaries. The first steamers typically were purchased from private British shipyards or, if built in other countries, fitted out with engines ordered from British firms. The Russians commissioned their first naval steamship in 1817, two years after building a small river steamer. The steamship made its Mediterranean debut in 1818 when one was launched at Naples, but the Neapolitan navy waited until the 1830s to commission its first steam warships. In 1819 Denmark purchased James Watt Jr's *Caledonia* for use as a royal steam yacht, but the Danish navy did not acquire its first armed steamers until years later.[30] Most historians agree that Greece's 400-ton *Karteria*, the first of the four British-built steamships commissioned under Lord Cochrane's command, was the first steam-powered vessel to see combat, in February 1827. Armed with four 68-pounders, the *Karteria* had its greatest success with red-hot shot, firing 18,000 rounds of it during 1827 alone. The four Greek steamers were plagued by engine trouble, and despite their heavy armament were little more than a nuisance to the Turco–Egyptian fleet. Nevertheless, enough British officers either served aboard the ships or saw them in action while serving with the British Mediterranean Fleet to generate interest in their further development.[31]

Apart from its experimentation with a river steamer for African colonial service, the British navy initially valued steamers as tugs and towboats for its sailing warships. In 1821 the navy purchased the small steam tug *Monkey*, and the following year activated the *Comet*, a larger, brig-sized tug built specifically for naval service.[32] Even the navy's most skeptical commanders recognized the utility of steamers to tow warships into and out of ports in times of calm winds or unfavorable tides, and fell into the habit of leasing private steamers for such duties. This practice became so common (and so expensive) that the Admiralty acquired several more steam tugs of its own, all of which were unarmed, operated by civilian contractors, and not entered on the navy list. In 1824 the British navy deployed its first steamship outside of home waters, sending the unarmed *Lightning* to Algiers as a towboat for small mortar vessels, as part of a British squadron responding to Algerian violations of the 1816 anti-piracy treaty. The *Lightning* subsequently saw duty as a yacht for the dockyard tours of the Duke of Clarence, appointed Lord High Admiral in 1827. Clarence, younger brother of (and, as William IV, eventual successor to) King George IV, later that year ruled that British navy steamers should be commanded by naval officers and included in the navy list. The following year, during Britain's initial intervention in Portugal's Miguelist War, the paddle steamer *Echo* became the first to serve abroad under the new conditions, employed as a dispatch boat. In 1829 the British navy finally armed one of its steamships, fitting the 500-ton *Columbia* with two light cannon. The navy's first purpose-built steam warship, the 900-ton *Dee*, received its commission in 1830, and by the following year several of the navy's older and smaller steamers, including the *Comet*, had been armed with at least two guns. Four paddle steamers modeled after the *Dee* were completed by 1833, but all of them suffered from weaknesses attributable to the Admiralty's policy of deferring to the private sector in steamship development. In particular, their side lever engines featured a large, heavy power plant that was less than ideal for warships.[33]

The deployment of the British navy's *Lightning* to Algiers in 1824 caught the attention of the French, who soon placed the armed steamer *Caroline* on their navy list, three years before the British did the same for the *Lightning*. Later in 1824 the First Lord of the Admiralty, Lord Melville, warned the Duke of Wellington that France might build a steam-powered navy.[34] But the British had little to fear, as the French navy did not have a successful steam warship until 1829, when it commissioned the 910-ton *Sphinx* – a vessel fitted with imported British engines. In June 1830 the *Sphinx* and its sister-ship, the *Nageur*, supported the French assault on Algiers, an operation ordered by King Charles X in part to distract public opinion away from domestic troubles. The Algerians (and the other powers of Europe) initially took it to be a typical punitive action, especially as the pretext – Algerian disrespect for French merchants and consular personnel – hardly warranted more. But the sheer size of Vice Admiral Duperré's fleet, which included 103 warships of various sizes to convoy 575 transports with 35,000 troops, indicated otherwise. The *Sphinx* and *Nageur* participated in the initial bombardment of Algiers, then carried messages to and from Toulon during the subsequent invasion and occupation of the territory.[35] Algiers provided the North African foothold which France later expanded into a vast empire, but the initial conquest failed to serve its domestic political purpose. Three weeks later a revolution toppled Charles X, paving the way for his more liberal cousin, Louis Philippe, to take the throne. Meanwhile, Britain and the other naval powers with Mediterranean interests did not oppose France's actions, since the example of what had happened to Algiers encouraged better behavior by the other North African states. Indeed, the French conquest of Algiers, on the heels of the successful Austrian operation against Morocco (1828–30), emboldened the Mediterranean states traditionally most vulnerable to piracy. In 1833 Sardinia–Piedmont and Naples sent a joint squadron led by four frigates to Tunis, forcing the Tunisians to pay an indemnity for losses suffered by Sardinian merchants. The following year, a demonstration by three Neapolitan warships forced a considerable reduction in the tribute Naples paid to the sultan of Morocco.[36]

In their common support of the cause of Greek independence, Britain and France forged a partnership which strengthened after 1830. For most of the decade Louis Philippe's government was an active supporter of the policies of Lord Palmerston, then in his first term as British foreign secretary, helping to enforce the Pax Britannica in the littoral of western Europe. The two countries cosponsored the creation of an independent, neutral Belgium after it seceded from the Netherlands in 1830, deploying a joint squadron to blockade the Dutch coast after Dutch troops intervened against the rebellious Belgians. Britain even countenanced the intervention of French troops in Belgium, as the most expedient way to get the Dutch army to withdraw. The Dutch decided not to risk their navy for the sake of Belgium, keeping all 7 of their ships of the line and several of their 25 frigates in the Scheldt while the much smaller Anglo–French force blockaded their coast. The blockade continued until 1833, by which time the allied fleet included armed British paddle steamers, employed for the first time in a war zone. Coinciding with the campaign in the Low Countries, France threw its support behind Britain's intervention in Portugal, under way since 1828. Battling the forces of the conservative usurper Dom Miguel, in 1831 Rear Admiral Albin-Reine Roussin forced the mouth of the Tagus with six ships of the line and nine smaller sailing warships. The following summer, Dom Pedro I returned to Portugal from Brazil to support the rights to the throne of his daughter, Maria. Having earlier employed Cochrane to command the Brazilian navy, Dom Pedro hired Britain's Sir Charles Napier to lead the Portuguese loyalist fleet. Napier helped secure the throne for Maria by winning a decisive victory over the Miguelist squadron in 1833 off Cape St Vincent. After the defeat of the Miguelists, Britain and France intervened in a similar situation in Spain, where the death of Ferdinand VII in 1833 touched off a civil war between conservatives loyal to Don Carlos, brother of the late king, and liberals loyal to the legitimate heir, Ferdinand VII's daughter Isabella. In 1834 the Anglo–French cooperation in the Iberian peninsula was formalized in a "Quadruple Alliance" including the legitimate governments of Spain and Portugal. But the pair of divisive civil wars, coming less than a decade after the two countries lost their Latin American colonies, dealt a severe blow to those in Portugal and Spain who hoped for a revival of their navies and maritime interests. Portugal never recovered its long-lost place among naval powers of the second rank. The situation was slightly better in Spain, where the loyalist navy had acquired and armed several paddle steamers during the Carlist War, among them the *Isabel II* (ex-*Royal William*), a former British Atlantic packet steamer.[37]

Elsewhere in southern Europe, Britain and France both opposed Austria's decision to crush liberal revolutions in the Papal States in 1831-32. While the British navy did not intervene, the French landed troops at Ancona and throughout the 1830s kept a squadron in the Adriatic, eventually including steamships.[38] The Anglo–French partnership showed strain only in North Africa, where Britain recognized the conquest of Algiers but did not want more territory added to France's colonial empire. Palmerston sent British squadrons to Tunis in 1836 and again in 1837, as much to deter Louis Philippe from annexing additional land as to intimidate the local ruler. In 1836 the British first mapped a canal route across the isthmus of Suez, evidence that they already were starting to view the Gibraltar–Malta–Alexandria route as the key to their communications with India. At the same time, of course, control of the route from Toulon to Algiers took on an increasing importance to the French. Owing to the growing significance of these interests, both Britain and France stationed their strongest fleets in the Mediterranean throughout the 1830s.[39]

In the meantime, Russia's brief partnership with Britain and France in support of Greek independence came to an end shortly after the Battle of Navarino. One of its legacies, a Russian squadron in the Eastern Mediterranean, remained a factor into the early 1830s. It is no small irony that most of the Greek warships left behind by Cochrane ultimately fell victim to this Russian squadron, after Admiral Miaoulis involved the navy in an 1831 uprising against Capodistrias. When the Greek president appealed to the Russians for help, they obligingly destroyed most of Miaoulis's fleet in its anchorage at Poros, where the surviving Greek warships (including the American-built frigate *Hellas*) were sunk or burned by their own crews to prevent capture.[40] Later the same year the Egyptians rebelled against the Turks, and by 1832 the army and navy of Mehemet Ali were threatening Asia Minor itself. Palmerston rejected the sultan's pleas for British help, on the grounds that the British navy was busy enough with its Dutch and Portuguese interventions. At the time, the foreign secretary also did not want to upset his partnership with France, which, in the Near East, supported Egypt against the Ottoman Empire. In desperation the Turks turned for help to the Russians. In March 1833 Admiral Mikhail Lazarev appeared in the Bosporus with most of the Black Sea Fleet (led by ten ships of the line and four frigates) escorting transports carrying 11,000 troops. Lazarev's force included the paddle steamer *Meteor*, the first Russian steamship to participate in a naval operation. The show of force prompted Mehemet Ali to stop his march on the Ottoman capital, but the Turks paid dearly for it. The subsequent Treaty of Unkiar-Skelessi (Hünkar Iskelesi) made the Ottoman Empire a Russian protectorate and guaranteed Russian warships free passage of the Bosporus and Dardanelles.[41] Thus, the Russian fleet could enter the Mediterranean whenever it wished, and in case of danger withdraw to the safety of the Black Sea, with the Turks obligated to close the straits behind them.

The Russian Black Sea Fleet of the 1830s typically included 12 ships of the line. Its main base, at Sevastopol, had been fortified recently with the help of British engineers. Its larger warships were built at Nikolaiev on the Bug River, some forty miles from the sea, the only Russian ship-yard outside of the Baltic other than a small one at Sevastopol. The fact that Nikolaiev had no dry dock until the late 1840s further shortened the service lives of Russia's Black Sea warships. During the 1830s additions to the Black Sea Fleet included 11 ships of the line, three dozen smaller sailing warships, and 14 steamships. Of the latter, six were built at Nikolaiev (all fitted with imported British machinery) and eight purchased from British builders. In addition to the absence of essential supporting facilities, the projection of Russia's naval power in the region suffered from the limits of its leader's strategic vision. Nicholas I and his advisers considered the Black Sea Fleet's primary role to be local, supplying, transporting, and providing fire support for the troops of the Russian army. The fact that it played this role very well against the Turks in 1828–29, in their defense in 1833, and against rebels in Georgia throughout the 1830s only served to reinforce the rather limited Russian perception of what the Black Sea Fleet could do. Nevertheless, the mere presence of such a large Russian force in the Black Sea required Britain and France to maintain more warships in the Eastern Mediterranean. Though it was hardly by design, Admiral Lazarev commanded a classic "fleet in being."[42]

As Europe's navies built or acquired paddle steamers with genuine fighting potential, they had difficulty rating them under the same systems traditionally used for sailing warships. The British ultimately classified armed steamships according to their displacement, not their number of guns. As a result, the 1,610-ton *Gorgon* (commissioned in 1837) was rated a first-class sloop and the 1,960-ton *Cyclops* (1839) a second-class frigate, even though both carried just six guns.[43] France initially placed its faith in somewhat smaller armed steamers, building 22 paddle steamers on the model of the 910-ton *Sphinx* over the decade after the warship made its successful debut off Algiers. The *Sphinx* class steamers eventually supported the French sailing fleet on almost all of its stations worldwide. In the first transatlantic deployment of armed steamers by a European power, Rear Admiral Charles Baudin took the *Phaeton* and *Météore* along with four frigates and ten smaller sailing warships to Veracruz during the brief Franco–Mexican "Pastry War" of 1838.[44]

Among the minor naval powers of southern Europe, Naples finally added its first armed steamship in 1833. A greater commitment to steam followed a decade later, after pro-navy King Ferdinand II took the throne. In the years 1842–47 the Neapolitan navy added 19 paddle steamers, 6 built in Naples and 13 purchased in Britain or France. In contrast, the Sardinian navy suffered hard times after the naval enthusiast King Charles Felix died in 1831. Sardinia–Piedmont purchased its first paddle steamer from Britain in 1834 and had five by 1847. As in sailing warships, in steamship strength the leading Italian fleets were far ahead of the Austrian navy, which launched its first steamer at Porto Ré (Kraljevica) in 1836 but added just one more before 1848. Meanwhile, in 1843 Spain commissioned its first domestically built naval steamer, after purchasing additional steamships from Britain and the United States in the years since the end of the Carlist War. The Italian, Austrian, and Spanish programs remained dependent upon Britain and other leading naval powers, for engineers, steam engines, or entire warships.[45]

The minor naval powers of northern Europe were slow to embrace steam propulsion, and none did so on the scale of Naples. The Netherlands elected not to construct a large steam fleet despite the fact that it could have, on its own resources. The Dutch marine engineering industry initially was second only to the British, and used as a resource by the French and Russian fleets. But when Anglo–Dutch relations returned to normal after Belgium achieved its independence, the Netherlands took advantage of the fact that, under the Pax Britannica, it was not in Britain's strategic interests to see another naval power gain possession of either the Dutch coast or the Dutch East Indies. Even without a formal alliance, the Dutch enjoyed de facto British protection and had no need to expend the resources necessary to maintain their position as a second-rate naval power into the age of steam. Like the Netherlands, Sweden had the engineering expertise and the industrial base essential for the construction of a modern steam navy. Furthermore, in contrast to the Dutch, the Swedes had a clear potential enemy to build against: the Russian Baltic Fleet. Nevertheless, the Swedish navy commissioned just three paddle steamers and used them mostly to tow its old sailing warships and flotilla of oared coastal gunboats. Adopting a similar posture on steam, the Danish navy commissioned only four paddle steamers before 1848, which were employed in much the same way. Both of the minor Baltic navies thus became relatively weaker vis-à-vis the Russians, who continued to acquire British-built steamships for the Baltic and Black Sea fleets right up to the breakdown of Anglo–Russian relations on the eve of the Crimean War. The 1,500-ton *Vladimir* (completed in 1848) was the largest and best of the Russian navy's British paddle steamers.[46]

The commissioning of ever increasing numbers of armed paddle steamers during the 1830s did nothing to change the balance of power among the leading navies, all of which continued to value steamships primarily for their auxiliary roles as tugs, towboats, and dispatch vessels. Late in the decade British naval authorities theorized that, in combat conditions, a steamship would be liable to destruction if it came within 3,000 yards of a ship of the line. The disadvantage of being able to carry only a limited number of guns was not offset by a steamer's added mobility, which in any event came from machinery carried above the waterline, turning large side paddles likely to be destroyed by the first enemy broadside.[47] Taking into account the number and quality of armed steamships, the ranking of the leading naval powers of Europe (Britain first, France second, Russia third) remained unchanged. Among second- and third-rate naval powers, steam propulsion had an impact most notably in the rise of Naples, which used the new technology to surpass Spain, the Netherlands, Sweden, and Denmark by the mid-1840s. Later in the decade, the acquisition of steamships would figure significantly in the Frankfurt Parliament's plans for a fleet for a united Germany, in Sardinia–Piedmont's hopes for a united Italy, and in the survival of Austria as a regional naval power.

Among the factors transforming naval warfare, in the years after 1815 innovations in ordnance ranked second only to the slow rise of the steamship. Paddle steamers could not carry a standard broadside of guns, leading navies to arm them with fewer, heavier guns, such as the 68-pounders mounted in Cochrane's Greek navy steamers. The trend toward larger guns affected sailing ship armament as well, only not so dramatically. During the war of 1812, large American frigates such as the *Constitution* and *United States*, armed with 24-pounders, had easily defeated British frigates armed with 18-pounders, impressing the British navy enough to cause it to move toward heavier ordnance. In 1826 British ships of the line received a uniform broadside of 32-pounders, in place of the mixed battery carried during and immediately after the Napoleonic wars. The change was vindicated the following year at Navarino, where close-range broadsides from Codrington's flagship *Asia* riddled the hull of its Turkish opponent. The 32-pounder soon became standard for British frigates and paddle steamers, and was retained into the mid-1840s, even after the French navy introduced a 36-pounder and the Russians a 42-pounder.[48]

Coinciding with the move toward larger smooth-bore cannon capable of firing heavier solid shot, the French pioneered exploding shells and the shell guns needed to fire them. The artillerist Henri-Joseph Paixhans began experimenting with shell guns as early as 1809, and soon concluded that the new ordnance needed a new type of ship to carry it. Thereafter, the French saw a clear connection between the introduction of heavier naval artillery (shell or otherwise) and the paddle steam warship as an ideal platform for it. In 1821 Paixhans wrote the visionary *Idées pour le blindage du batteries flottantes*, advocating warships that would carry a small number of heavy guns in hulls plated with iron. He soon abandoned the notion of armor but in *Nouvelle force maritime* (1822) called for a steam-powered French fleet armed with shell guns, arguing that such a force would render all sailing battle fleets irrelevant and thus eliminate Britain's naval superiority.[49] French navy leaders, skeptical of Paixhans's ideas, nevertheless placed the old ship of the line *Pacificateur* at his disposal in 1824, enabling him to conduct trials which demonstrated the potential of his new guns.[50] Later that year the navy purchased some of his shell guns for its first armed paddle steamer, the *Caroline*. But Paixhans's vision of combining the two new technologies to produce the capital ship of the future, replacing the sailing battleship, remained a dream. His early shell guns were notoriously unreliable, and French industry could not produce the sufficient quality or quantity of steam engines to enable the French navy to rule the waves. It came as no surprise that the most successful of the early French naval steamers (the *Sphinx* included) had imported British engines.[51]

The British navy purchased its first shell guns in 1838, 68-pounders mounted aboard ships of the line, frigates, and paddle steamers to supplement their primary armament of 32-pounders. Around the same time, Admiral Lazarev ordered the first shell guns for the Russian Black Sea Fleet. The British in particular remained skeptical of the new ordnance, even after the guns were mounted aboard their own ships. While the destructive power of shell guns could not be denied and, as time when on, their design became more reliable, critics cited their limited range as a distinct liability. Shells, being lighter than solid shot, simply could not be fired as far by the standard smooth bore guns of the time. For example, the British 32-pounder had a range of 1,300 yards, an 8-inch shell gun just 800 yards. Of course, until such time as naval battles were actually fought at such distances, the question of range remained purely academic.[52]

CONCLUSION

By 1830 it had become clear that steam propulsion would change the way European navies fought wars in the future, but the extent of the change remained open to debate. By 1840 the first regularly scheduled service by transatlantic packet lines had provided further evidence of the sort of utility that steam propulsion could have for European navies beyond European waters. The logistical problems of supporting a global steam navy remained discouraging, however, as the needs of packet steamers offering point-to-point service were modest compared to those of cruising warships, which the leading navies had to be able to deploy anywhere in the world.

Even though France, in the 1820s and 1830s, failed to take advantage of steam power in the manner proposed by Paixhans, many French naval officers embraced his notion that technology would be the key to any future successful challenge to Britain's naval position. Paixhans is perhaps most significant for his role in helping to make such thinking a part of the culture of the French navy, shown later in its pioneering of the screw-propelled battleship in the late 1840s, the ironclad warship in the late 1850s, the torpedo boat in the early 1880s, and the submarine in the late 1890s. Thus, as the industrial revolution continued to transform European navies, France provided most of the stimuli in the modernization process, while Britain's stronger industry enabled it to preserve its naval superiority through every challenge.

NOTES

[1] Andrew Lambert, *The Last Sailing Battlefleet: Maintaining Naval Mastery, 1815–1850* (London, 1991), 7, 38, 54.

[2] Cf. Hans Busk, *The Navies of the World; Their Present State, and Future Capabilities* (London, 1859), 75; Michael Lewis, *The Navy in Transition, 1814–1864: A Social History* (London, 1965), 64–9; and Richard Harding, *Seapower and Naval Warfare, 1650–1830* (London, 1999), 294.

[3] Lambert, *The Last Sailing Battlefleet*, viii, 148–51; *idem, Battleships in Transition: The Creation of the Steam Battlefleet, 1815–1860* (Annapolis, MD, 1984), 26; Busk, *Navies of the World*, 75; Fred T. Jane, *The British Battle Fleet*, 2 vols (London, 1915; reprint, London, 1990), 1:211; Lewis, *The Navy in Transition*, 64–9, *passim*. Harding, *Seapower and Naval Warfare*, 294, gives figures of 82 ships of the line and 100 frigates in 1830.

[4] Michael Lewis, *A Social History of the Navy, 1793–1815* (London, 1960), 139; *idem, The Navy in Transition*, 64–9, *passim*; Colin White, *Victoria's Navy: The End of the Sailing Navy* (Annapolis, MD, 1981), 68–9.

[5] Lambert, *The Last Sailing Battlefleet*, viii-ix, 108–10, 180–9.

[6] Michèle Battesti, *La Marine au XIXe siècle: Interventions extérieures et colonies* (Paris, 1993), 16–17; Henri Legohérel, *Histoire de la Marine française* (Paris, 1999), 80–1; Busk, *Navies of the World*, 75; Lambert, *The Last Sailing Battlefleet*, 10, 40, 142–3; *idem, Battleships in Transition*, 97; Lewis, *The Navy in Transition*, 184. Legohérel, *Histoire de la Marine française*, 75–6, gives figures of 103 ships of the line and 54 frigates in 1815 (which must include warships still on the stocks), declining to 71 ships of the line and 41 frigates in 1817. Harding, *Seapower and Naval Warfare*, 294, gives figures of 33 ships of the line and 40 frigates in 1830.

[7] Fred T. Jane, *The Imperial Russian Navy*, 2nd edn (London, 1904; reprint, London, 1983), 114; Harding, *Seapower and Naval Warfare*, 293–5.

[8] George Sydenham Clarke, *Russia's Sea-Power Past and Present, or The Rise of the Russian Navy* (London, 1898), 80; Lambert, *The Last Sailing Battlefleet*, 12, 143; Jane, *The Imperial Russian Navy*, 133.

[9] John D. Harbron, *Trafalgar and the Spanish Navy* (London, 1988), 169–73; Harding,

Seapower and Naval Warfare, 294. The latter gives slightly lower figures for Spanish ships of the line.

[10] Harding, *Seapower and Naval Warfare*, 294.

[11] Lawrence Sondhaus, *Preparing for Weltpolitik: German Sea Power before the Tirpitz Era* (Annapolis, MD, 1997), 4–8.

[12] Lawrence Sondhaus, *The Habsburg Empire and the Sea: Austrian Naval Policy, 1797–1866* (West Lafayette, IN, 1989), 40–6, 275–6.

[13] Carlo Randaccio, *Le marinerie militari italiane nei tempi moderni, 1750–1850* (Turin, 1864), 26–34 *passim*, 86, 90; Lamberto Radogna, *Storia della Marina Militare delle Due Sicilie, 1734–1860* (Turin, 1978), 78, 90–3.

[14] Lambert, *The Last Sailing Battlefleet*, 8, 99.

[15] C. I. Hamilton, *Anglo–French Naval Rivalry, 1840–1870* (Oxford, 1993), 3. On France's position regarding the slave trade, 1815–48, see Basil Lubbock, *Cruisers, Corsairs & Slavers: An Account of the Suppression of the Picaroon, Pirate & Slaver by the Royal Navy during the 19th Century* (Glasgow, 1993), 100–24 *passim*.

[16] Randaccio, *Le marinerie militari italiane*, 28–32, 90–2; Radogna, *Storia della Marina Militare*, 93–5.

[17] Sondhaus, *The Habsburg Empire and the Sea*, 74–5.

[18] Ibid., 59–61.

[19] Hamilton, *Anglo–French Naval Rivalry*, 3; Maurice Dupont and Étienne Taillemite, *Les guerres navales françaises: du Moyen Age à la guerre du Golfe* (Paris, 1995), 227.

[20] On the naval dimension of the Latin American Wars for Independence see Lawrence Sondhaus, *Naval Warfare, 1815–1914* (London, 2001), 8–15.

[21] Sondhaus, *The Habsburg Empire and the Sea*, 70–1.

[22] Douglas Dakin, *The Greek Struggle for Independence* (Berkeley, CA, 1973), 74–7, 123, 132–8.

[23] Ibid., 169–72, 202–3, 215–17.

[24] John C. K. Daly, *Russian Seapower and "the Eastern Question", 1827–41* (Annapolis, MD, 1991), 1–13; Anthony J. Watts, *The Imperial Russian Navy* (London, 1990), 11–12; Jane, *The Imperial Russian Navy*, 128–30.

[25] Dakin, *The Greek Struggle for Independence*, 255–6; Lewis, *A Social History of the Navy*, 190.

[26] F. N. Gromov, Vladimir Gribovskii, and Boris Rodionov, *Tri Veka Rossiiskogo Flota*, 3 vols (St Petersburg, 1996), 1:172–3.

[27] Daly, *Russian Seapower and "the Eastern Question"*, 18–34; Clarke, *Russia's Sea-Power*, 76–7; Bernd Langensiepen and Ahmet Güleryüz, *The Ottoman Steam Navy, 1828–1923*, ed. and trans. James Cooper (Annapolis, MD, 1995), 1–3.

[28] Andrew Lambert, "Introduction of Steam," in *Steam, Steel, and Shellfire: The Steam Warship, 1815–1905*, ed. Robert Gardiner (London, 1992), 14–15; John F. Beeler, *British Naval Policy in the Gladstone–Disraeli Era, 1866–1880* (Palo Alto, CA, 1997), 58.

[29] Lambert, "Introduction of Steam," 15–19.

[30] Ibid., 27–8; V. M. Tomitch, *Warships of the Imperial Russian Navy* (London, 1968), 101; Radogna, *Storia della Marina Militare*, 85; David K. Brown, *Paddle Warships: The Earliest Steam Powered Fighting Ships, 1815–1850* (London, 1993), 19.

[31] Douglas Dakin, *British and American Philhellenes during the War of Greek Independence,1821–1833* (Thessaloniki, 1955), 124–6, 137; Lambert, "Introduction of Steam," 19–20.

[32] White, *Victoria's Navy: The End of the Sailing Navy*, 12.

[33] Lambert, "Introduction of Steam," 17–23, 29; Busk, *Navies of the World*, 37–9; Denis Griffiths, "Warship Machinery," in *Steam, Steel and Shellfire: The Steam Warship 1815–1905*, ed. Robert Gardiner (London, 1992), 170. According to Brown, *Paddle Warships*, 12, Dee was completed in 1832.

[34] Lambert, "Introduction of Steam," 18–21.

[35] Ibid., 19; Dupont and Taillemite, *Les guerres navales françaises*, 227–33; François Ferdinand d'Orleans, Prince de Joinville, *De l'etat des forces navales de la France* (Frankfurt, 1844), 29.

[36] Radogna, *Storia della Marina Militare*, 97–100.

[37] Hamilton, *Anglo–French Naval Rivalry*, 4, 9; Lambert, "Introduction of Steam," 23, 27; Dupont and Taillemite, *Les guerres navales françaises*, 233–4; Lewis, *The Navy in Transition*, 82.

[38] Sondhaus, *The Habsburg Empire and the Sea*, 78–9.

[39] Hamilton, *Anglo–French Naval Rivalry*, 4–10.

[40] David Woodward, *The Russians at Sea: A History of the Russian Navy* (New York, 1966), 97; Dakin, *The Greek Struggle for Independence*, 296–7.

[41] Daly, *Russian Seapower and "the Eastern Question"*, 66–99, 196–9; Woodward, *The Russians at Sea*, 97; Gromov *et al.*, *Tri Veka Rossiiskogo Flota*, 1:177.

[42] Daly, *Russian Seapower and "the Eastern Question"*, 46, 100–39 *passim*, 196–8; Jane, *The Imperial Russian Navy*, 134; Andrew Lambert, *The Crimean War: British Grand Strategy against Russia, 1853–56* (Manchester, 1991), 2.

[43] Lambert, "Introduction of Steam," 20–1, 29.

[44] The French went to war after Mexico refused to pay compensation for depredations against French citizens, the latter including a baker whose shop had been pillaged by Mexican soldiers. See Dupont and Taillemite, *Les guerres navales françaises*, 235–6; Sondhaus, *Naval Warfare, 1815–1914*, 30.

[45] Radogna, *Storia della Marina Militare*, 109–12; Sondhaus, *The Habsburg Empire and the Sea*, 91, 130–1, 173; Lambert, "Introduction of Steam," 28; Randaccio, *Le marinerie militari italiane*, 36–40. In some countries the capabilities of domestic industry remained primitive for decades to come; Spain, for example, did not even build a railway locomotive of its own until 1884. See Agustín Ramón Rodríguez González, *Politica naval de la Restauracion, 1875–1898* (Madrid, 1988), 126.

[46] Lambert, "Introduction of Steam," 27–8.

[47] Ibid., 21, 23.

[48] Lambert, *The Last Sailing Battlefleet*, ix, 98; *idem*, "Iron Hulls and Armour Plate," in *Steam, Steel and Shellfire: The Steam Warship 1815–1905*, ed. Robert Gardiner (London, 1992), 50.

[49] Donald L. Canney, *The Old Steam Navy*, 2 vols (Annapolis, MD, 1993), 2:2; James J. Tritten, "Navy and Military Doctrine in France," in *A Doctrine Reader: The Navies of United States, Great Britain, France, Italy, and Spain*, ed. James J. Tritten and Luigi Donolo (Newport, RI, 1995), 52.

[50] Lambert, "Iron Hulls and Armour Plate," 50; John Campbell, "Naval Armaments and Armour," in *Steam, Steel and Shellfire: The Steam Warship 1815–1905*, ed. Robert Gardiner (London, 1992), 158.

[51] Lambert, "Introduction of Steam," 19–20.

[52] Lambert, *The Last Sailing Battlefleet*, 105; Hamilton, *Anglo–French Naval Rivalry*, 24; D. Bonner-Smith and A. C. Dewar (eds), *Russian War, 1854, Baltic and Black Sea: Official Correspondence* (London, 1943), 211.

2

MIDCENTURY TRANSITIONS, 1840–55

By the late 1840s the navies of Europe included an unprecedented variety of warships, as the introduction of the screw propeller added another series of steamship types to the largest fleets. By the early 1850s technological developments included the spread of screw propulsion beyond the navies of the first rank, and the death of both the line-of-battle sailing ship and the paddle steamer as warships. The changes steam power brought to naval warfare were reflected first in the Near Eastern Crisis and the First Opium War, then in the Adriatic, Baltic, and North Sea campaigns of the revolutions of 1848–49. Finally, the Crimean War provided an opportunity for the three leading naval powers to demonstrate the state of the art in technology, tactics, and strategy, and in the process revealed the extent to which a country's level of industrialization now shaped its naval capabilities.

THE NEAR EASTERN CRISIS (1839–41)

In April 1839 war resumed between the Ottoman Empire and Egypt. Mehemet Ali's Egyptian forces soon threatened Asia Minor as they had six years earlier, leaving Russia poised to invoke its 1833 treaty rights and again "save" the Ottoman Empire. Britain and France shared fears of Russian domination in the Balkans and Near East but favored very different solutions, Palmerston championing Ottoman independence and territorial integrity, the French supporting a strong Egypt as the best hedge against the further expansion of Russian influence in the region. Two months into the renewed Turco-Egyptian conflict the Turkish throne passed to Sultan Abdul Mecid, amid the sort of division and intrigue typical of the Ottoman succession. Shortly after Abdul Mecid's accession the derya kaptan (fleet commander), Firari Ahmet Fevzi Pasha, deserted to the Egyptians with most of the Ottoman navy, including 8 ships of the line and 12 frigates. His treachery gave Mehemet Ali (whose fleet already included 11 ships of the line built since 1831) an overwhelming naval superiority over the Turks. Abdul Mecid entrusted the loyal remnants of the Ottoman fleet to Captain Baldwin Walker, a British officer who had been serving as the derya kaptan's adviser. Meanwhile, Palmerston, regretting his failure to intervene in the Turco–Egyptian conflict of the early 1830s, demanded that Mehemet Ali return his Syrian conquests to the sultan. When France openly supported the pasha's refusal to comply, the near decade-long Anglo–French entente came to an end.[1]

Both countries reinforced their Levantine squadrons, and by the end of 1839 France's Admiral Lalande commanded a force led by 13 ships of the line. His frigate captains included Louis Philippe's son, François Ferdinand d'Orléans, Prince de Joinville, who had commanded a corvette in Baudin's squadron the previous year, during the Franco–Mexican "Pastry War." As tensions escalated into a general European war scare, French nationalism reached levels not seen since the Napoleonic wars. Over the winter of 1839–40 Louis Philippe fanned the flames with patriotic pronouncements and symbolic gestures, including the renaming of a number of ships of the line after Napoleon's victorious battles, such as Austerlitz and Wagram. A more blatant bid to associate his regime with the glorious Napoleonic past followed early in 1840, when the king decided to send Joinville and his frigate Belle-Poule to St Helena to bring back the body of the late emperor. The British agreed to the request, in the knowledge that denying it would only have incited French nationalism still more. In March 1840 the king appointed a new cabinet including Adolphe Thiers as both premier and foreign minister, and the charismatic Admiral Roussin as navy minister. As their policy became increasingly aggressive, the French reinforced their Eastern Mediterranean fleet to include 20 ships of the line.[2]

Such posturing by France revived the Napoleonic-era coalition of Britain, Russia, Austria, and Prussia. In the Treaty of London (15 July 1840) the four powers agreed to intervene in the Near Eastern war, with the British navy providing most of the pressure in an armed mediation against Mehemet Ali. The allies offered to recognize him as hereditary pasha of Egypt and ruler for life over southern Syria (Lebanon) in exchange for returning the rest of Syria, some other conquered Arab lands, Crete, and the derya kaptan's mutinous warships to Turkish control. Britain almost doubled its number of ships of the line in commission to 26, the most since 1815. The commander of the British Mediterranean Fleet, Admiral Robert Stopford, served as allied commander. Austria and the Ottoman Empire contributed token forces to the cause, the former two frigates, two corvettes, and several brigs under Rear Admiral Bandiera, the latter a ship of the line and several smaller warships under Baldwin Walker, serving as a Turkish rear admiral. Russia did not lend ships to the operation, as the Black Sea Fleet at the time was fully occupied supporting the Russian army against another rebellion in Georgia. Prussia made its contribution along the Rhine, where its army served as the allies' first line of defense.[3]

Mehemet Ali defied the allies and continued to use his fleet to sustain the Egyptian occupation of Palestine and Syria. In August 1840 Stopford's armada arrived to force him out. Each of his coastal strongholds was bombarded, then occupied by an allied landing party. On 26 September Archduke Frederick, nineteen-year-old captain of the Austrian frigate *Guerriera*, personally led the landing that secured Sidon (see Plate 1). In the month of October, Beirut, Tripoli, Haifa, and Tyre fell in turn, leaving only Acre in Egyptian hands. During the bombardment of Acre (3 November 1840) Stopford's fleet enjoyed such favorable winds that his steamers were released from towboat duty to serve as autonomous warships. The *Gorgon*, *Vesuvius*, *Stromboli*, and *Phoenix* (the latter serving as Stopford's temporary flagship) supplemented the fire of British, Austrian, and Turkish sailing warships, the fleet as a whole pouring some 40,000 rounds into the city. During the night the Egyptians abandoned Acre, and the following morning Archduke Frederick led the Anglo–Austrian party that took possession of its citadel for the allies.[4]

In late October 1840, after opting not to go to war in support of Mehemet Ali, Louis Philippe sacked Thiers, Roussin, and the rest of the French cabinet. In defeat, Mehemet Ali faced stiffer terms than those offered in July 1840, losing all of his territorial conquests but emerging with international recognition as hereditary pasha of Egypt. He had to return the sultan's mutinous warships, and in the future could build no new warships of his own without the consent of Constantinople. In July 1841 France joined the allies in signing the Straits Convention, which made the Ottoman Empire a de facto protectorate of all five great powers. Henceforth the Bosporus and Dardanelles were to remain closed to foreign warships whenever the Turks were at peace. Britain won a clear diplomatic victory, as Palmerston made good use of naval power to resolve the Near Eastern crisis on his own terms. Without a shot being fired against either Russia or France, the Russians lost the position they had achieved in 1833, as sole protectors of the Ottoman Empire, and the French were forced to abandon Egypt. The allied naval campaign also advanced the careers of two of its most prominent officers. In 1844, at age twenty-three, Archduke Frederick became commander of the Austrian navy after a mutiny by Venetian Italian officers, led by two sons of Francesco Bandiera, ruined the career of Austria's leading admiral. That same year, after being knighted by Queen Victoria for his service in the Near East, Walker returned home to continue his career as one of the most influential officers of the British navy.[5]

THE FIRST OPIUM WAR (1839–42)

Coinciding with the Near Eastern crisis, Britain also brought its naval power to bear in East Asia, in a cause far more controversial than opposing the ambitions of the pasha of Egypt. Indeed, the First Opium War was perhaps the most domestically divisive British foreign adventure up to that time. Palmerston's resolve to wage war to preserve the opium trade touched off bitter debate in Parliament and in the press. In particular, the war aroused the ire of church leaders, some of whom wanted to evangelize China, all of whom objected to the campaign on moral grounds. While the official position held that the issues at hand were British honor and general trading rights, it could not be denied that the war was being fought to keep China open to opium. In the end, the same naval power that upheld the Pax Britannica, safeguarding the general peace and promoting British values, rendered decisive service in the preservation of a clearly immoral business interest.

The shipping of opium from India to China aboard British vessels dated from the early years of the British East India Company. China first tried to ban the imports in 1729. In the early 1820s the Chinese temporarily suspended tea exports in an attempt to compel the British to stop the opium trade, only to see it quadruple during the remainder of the decade. During the 1830s the trade nearly doubled again. The Chinese emperor finally moved decisively in May 1839, instructing his high commissioner at Canton (then China's entrepôt for all foreign trade) to destroy all the opium on hand, some 20,000 chests, worth over £2 million (or $20 million) in the currency of the day. In September the first British warships arrived on the scene, a small frigate and a sloop under Captain (later Rear Admiral) George Elliot. In the end the war began not specifically over the dumping of the opium, but after Elliot refused to turn over a British seaman suspected of murdering a Chinese man ashore. In the Battle of Chuenpi (3 November 1839) Elliot's warships dispersed a fleet of 29 armed junks, sinking 4 of them. Hostilities were well under way by the time Palmerston, in February 1840, formally demanded that the Chinese government pay for the destroyed opium, cede territory in compensation for the insult to British honor, and grant British merchants trading rights in ports other than Canton.[6]

By the summer of 1840 Elliot had received considerable reinforcements: 3 ships of the line, 14 other sailing warships, 4 armed paddle steamers (from the East India Company's Indian navy), and an Anglo–

Indian expeditionary force of 3,600 men aboard 27 transports.[7] He blockaded Canton, and in July 1840 detached warships to secure Chusan Island, strategically located near the mouth of the Yangzte River. The following month Elliot concluded a treaty with the Chinese requiring only the payment for the opium, release of all British prisoners, and cession of the island of Hong Kong. Palmerston sacked him upon learning of the deal (some eight months later, in April 1841), sending Rear Admiral Sir William Parker to China as his replacement. In the meantime, the Chinese reneged on the August 1840 treaty, and in January 1841 the British again attacked at Chuenpi, key to the Pearl River approach to Canton. The 700-ton iron-hulled Indian paddle steamer *Nemesis* led the successful assault, sinking 11 armed junks. The ship's commander, W. H. Hall, later recalled that its mobility and firepower caused "astonishment [among] the Chinese, who were unacquainted with this engine of destruction." The victory left the way open for Elliot to occupy Canton but, lacking the means to hold the city, instead he took possession of Hong Kong, at the time a sparsely populated island.[8]

In August 1841 Parker assumed command and quickly organized an attack on Amoy, where a force led by 2 ships of the line sank 26 armed junks and bombarded Chinese shore batteries. Two months later, his forces took Chen-hai with the city of Ningpo, securing the mouth of the Yangzte River.[9] During the spring of 1842 further reinforcements arrived, strengthening the expeditionary corps to 12,000 men and the fleet to 25 sailing warships and 6 troopships, supported by 12 Indian and 2 British steamers. The additional forces enabled Parker to put troops ashore at Shanghai and other key coastal cities. In July, his ship of the line *Cornwallis* led 11 frigates and sloops, 10 paddle steamers, and several transports up the Yangzte River to Nanking, which Parker vowed to destroy unless the Chinese capitulated. In the Treaty of Nanking (29 August 1842) China accepted Palmerston's terms of February 1840 – ironically so, since largely because of the Opium War, Palmerston and the rest of the Liberal government had fallen twelve months earlier. The British received Hong Kong, a generous indemnity for the opium lost in 1839, and trading rights in Canton, Shanghai, and three other ports. The Chinese lowered their duty on British imports but did not formally legalize the opium trade until suffering a further defeat in the Second Opium War (1856–60).[10] In the meantime, other powers hastened to exploit the weakness of China, which in 1844 granted comparable trading concessions to France and the United States.

The First Opium War signaled the extent to which industrialization had made European naval technology superior to that of the non-Western world. As in the Near Eastern crisis, the firepower of sailing ships of the line remained paramount, especially against fortifications ashore, but in contrast to the campaign against Mehemet Ali, in China steam played a decisive role. From Elliot's ascent of the Pearl River to Canton, to Parker's ultimate expedition up the Yangzte River to Nanking, the *Nemesis* and the other steamships made the British victory possible.

THE TRANSITION TO SCREW PROPULSION (1841–50)

Early in the steamship era the ancient concept of moving a vessel by means of a screw propeller lost out to the more easily achievable paddle wheel. Pioneers such as the American John Stevens (in 1804) and the Austrian Josef Ressel (in 1827) constructed vessels equipped with screw propellers, but the performance of their steamers failed to impress potential investors. In 1836 Francis Pettit Smith of Britain patented the placement of a screw propeller between the sternpost and the rudder. Two years later he built the 200-ton *Archimedes*, which, like most early screw steamers, was slower than contemporary paddle steamers (with a top speed of 7.75 knots), vibrated excessively, and leaked at the stern. John Ericsson of Sweden made it to the Admiralty before Smith, in 1837 staging a demonstration in which his screw-propelled launch *Francis B. Ogden*, named after his patron, the US consul in Liverpool, towed the Admiralty barge. While some British naval leaders soon recognized the potential of screw propulsion as an auxiliary to sail, the commercial sector embraced the technology much faster. A turning point came in October 1840, when renowned shipbuilder Isambard Brunel opted for screw propulsion for the iron-hulled *Great Britain*, originally designed as a paddle steamer.[11]

Stormy Anglo–French relations in the wake of the Near Eastern crisis of 1839–41 added a sense of urgency to the technological transition. In 1842 Admiral A. A. Dupetit-Thouars imprisoned the British consul in Tahiti, after landing parties from his ships seized the island. Louis Philippe's government subsequently reprimanded the admiral and also disavowed his proclamation annexing Tahiti (which became a de facto French protectorate in any event). By the following year relations had healed enough to enable Queen Victoria to make a state visit to France, but the storm broke in 1844, when the Prince de Joinville, by now France's most influential admiral, publicly advocated that France build a steam battle fleet to challenge Britain's naval supremacy. In his *De l'état des forces navales de la France* (1844), the prince contended that steamships already were the true measure of a country's naval strength, in addition to being the capital ships of the future. Joinville advocated a steam-powered battle fleet for European waters and a sailing frigate fleet which would defend French interests elsewhere. Like Paixhans earlier, he believed that technology was the key to the French navy catching up with its traditional rival, arguing that a steam battle fleet would make Britain's lead over France in ships of the line (88 to 46, as of 1845) irrelevant. Undeterred by the fact that Britain enjoyed an even greater advantage over France in naval steamships (125 to 43), Joinville observed that the French navy had another 18 steamers under construction, and cited reports that just 76 British navy steamers were actually armed. He concluded that the French would "reign as masters" in the Mediterranean as soon as naval resources were reallocated to build the steam fleet and new strategies devised to use it effectively.[12]

Skeptics questioned whether France could afford the expense of constructing such a fleet in the first place, and of maintaining it once it was built. Answering the latter criticism, Joinville contended that it cost no more per year to operate four paddle steamers than to maintain a single 74-gun ship of the line.[13] There was plenty of evidence that this was not the case. Indeed, the larger steamers of the British navy had proven to be very expensive both to build and to operate. The 3,190-ton *Terrible* of 1845 cost £94,650, ten times more than the *Comet* of 1822, and its primitive twin-cylinder ("Siamese") Maudslay engines came close to their top speed of 11 knots only by consuming extraordinary amounts of coal. The *Terrible* was larger than a 74-gun ship of the line but mounted just 19 guns, owing to a problem common to all paddle steam warships: its paddle boxes took up too much of the broadside.[14] Facing such realities of cost versus firepower, the British rejected the notion that the paddle steamer could ever function as a capital ship. Instead, in 1846 – a full quarter-century after purchasing its first steam tug – the British navy reaffirmed what it considered to be the primary function of paddle steamers by providing one as a partner for each of its operational sailing ships of the line, to serve as its towboat or tug. By the following year the Pacific flagship *Collingwood* was the only active British ship of the line lacking a paddle escort.[15]

Amid the furor over Joinville's book, Britain and France did not shrink from provocative displays of naval power. During the summer of 1844 the British sent an intimidating squadron to Tahiti, including the *Collingwood*, and criticized the French for an operation in which Joinville led three ships of the line and six paddle steamers on a punitive bombardment of Tangier. By the following summer, for the first time since the Napoleonic wars, the British public and politicians were expressing doubts about the adequacy of their country's naval power. Palmerston, as a member of the opposition, heightened anxieties in July 1845 with a speech in the House of Commons in which he called the Channel a "steam bridge," an avenue for a French invasion of Britain rather than a barrier to it. Relations worsened still more in 1846, when Louis Philippe arranged the marriage of one of Joinville's brothers to a Spanish princess, in violation of a previous Anglo–French understanding. The French navy minister, Admiral Ange-René-Armand de Mackau, exploited the rising Anglophobia of the French chamber, securing its support for a program including 93 million francs for new warship construction.[16]

The financial windfall came at a fortuitous moment in the technological transition, for in 1845 Joinville had become a convert to the cause of screw propulsion.[17] The advantage of the screw over the paddle was obvious enough: it could be adapted to conventional designs of sailing frigates and ships of the line without disrupting the broadside of guns, and (in contrast to side paddles) it did not handicap a ship's ability to move under sail. But Joinville's epiphany came too late for France to take the lead in embracing the new technology, as the British navy had already launched the 1,110-ton screw sloop *Rattler* in April 1843. The *Rattler* exceeded 9 knots in its trials, vindicating the design. Nevertheless, the Admiralty handed the French an opportunity to catch up by refusing to commit wholly to screw propulsion. During 1843 the British completed the radical conversion of the sailing frigate *Penelope* to a paddle steamer, as late as 1846 ordered a new paddle frigate, and throughout the mid-1840s continued to build large sailing warships.[18] The French did not launch their first larger screw warship, the 2,010-ton converted sailing frigate *Pomone*, until October 1845. By then, they had laid down the full-powered screw frigate *Isly* and also the *Mogador*, a paddle frigate of roughly the same dimensions, in order to placate paddle advocates with an eventual performance test of the two types. Joinville's sentiments notwithstanding, Admiral Mackau's program of 1846 included more sailing ships than steamships and, among the steamers, more paddle than screw. But advocates of screw propulsion were heartened by the inclusion of funds to convert sailing ships of the line to screw, and to lay down the world's first purpose-built screw ship of the line, the future *Napoléon*. The 5,120-ton battleship was designed by thirty-year-old Stanislas Dupuy de Lôme, soon to become France's leading naval architect, and ordered on Bastille Day, 1847.[19]

In response to the French *Pomone* and *Isly*, in 1846 the British launched their first screw frigate, the *Amphion*, converted the paddle steamer *Phoenix* to a screw sloop, and made a commitment to build additional screw frigates (some as full-powered steamers, others with auxiliary propulsion). All sailing frigates under construction as of 1847 were completed as screw steamers. The Admiralty at first rejected the idea of a screw ship of the line but in 1847 completed the conversion to screw of the first of four old Napoleonic-era 74s designated for service as "blockships." Armed with a reduced battery of 60 guns and capable of just 7 knots, the blockships were conceived specifically to support a British war plan against the French, the so-called "Cherbourg Strategy," which centered around an attack on France's Channel naval base. The same attacking fleet was projected to include a number of small screw gunboats on the model of the iron-hulled 310-ton *Fairy* (completed in

1845). For the time being the British constructed no additional screw gunboats, on the assumption that, in an emergency, dozens could be built at short notice. At the onset of the Crimean War, this proved to be the case.[20]

Four years after returning home from Turkey, Captain Sir Baldwin Walker became Surveyor of the Navy and founder of Britain's wooden screw battle fleet. Under his direction, in April 1848 the *Agamemnon*, just laid down as a sailing warship, was designated for completion as Britain's first purpose-built screw liner. While Dupuy de Lôme conceptualized the *Napoléon* as a steamship with the ability to sail, the design of the *Agamemnon* emphasized sailing qualities. Nevertheless, when completed, the 5,080-ton warship would be capable of steaming at 12 knots. In 1849 the Admiralty ordered the conversion of the *Sans Pareil*, a sailing ship of the line laid down four years earlier, and by 1850 the British had begun to build another screw battleship from the keel up, the *James Watt*. That same year, Walker inherited the powers of the Office of Comptroller of Steam, foreshadowing the future direction of British naval construction. Meanwhile, in France, the *Napoléon* was laid down at Toulon in February 1848, only to fall victim to the revolution which broke out in Paris seventeen days later. The Prince de Joinville was forced into exile along with his father, Louis Philippe, and the naval program of 1846 became a dead letter. Under the new Second Republic, six different men served as navy minister during 1848 alone, no new larger warships were begun, and fiscal constraints limited work on the *Napoléon* and other projects then under way. By January 1849 mounting financial troubles prompted the French to propose a mutual reduction of naval spending. The British rejected the overture and spent almost as much on their fleet in 1849 as in 1847, when the navy had accounted for over 13 percent of state expenditure, a thirty-year high. The French finally launched the *Napoléon* in May 1850 but waited until 1853 to begin work on their next new screw ship of the line. In the meantime, the French navy continued to modernize by converting sailing ships of the line to screw. Notwithstanding their lack of progress when compared to the British, in the race to acquire screw ships of the line the French easily remained ahead of everyone else. Before 1852, no other country laid down a new warship of the type or began a conversion.[21]

After first providing their screw-propelled ships of the line with the same sort of heavy upper deck guns as paddle steamers, the British quickly adopted a conventional armament for all decks. The British and French navies alike believed that the first screw ships of the line would fight in line-ahead formation along with sailing battleships. When their telescopic funnels were down, screw liners could be distinguished from their sailing counterparts only by their greater length, and by the greater distance between the fore and mainmast, where the engines were located.[22] Critics of the screw-propelled warship contended that the location of the mainmast in relation to the length of the ship harmed its sailing qualities, but trials matching new screw steamers against sailing warships – the screw schooner *Renard* versus brigs and sailing schooners in 1848, then the screw frigate *Arrogant* against a sailing frigate in 1850 – demonstrated that properly constructed screw steamers could sail as well as sailing warships of the same types. Indeed, paddle steamers could not match the sailing abilities of screw steamers, and this fact secured the triumph of the screw propeller over the paddle wheel. Improved steam power plants further helped the cause. The first British screw warships had two-cylinder engines manufactured by Maudslay, but John Penn pioneered the trunk engine in time for its installation in the *Arrogant* in 1848.[23]

THE REVOLUTIONS OF 1848–49

The establishment of the Second Republic in France sparked a series of liberal revolutions throughout Europe. By December 1848 French presidential elections had brought to power Louis Napoleon Bonaparte, nephew of the late emperor. In the meantime, Germans elected a constituent assembly, the Frankfurt Parliament, which attempted to unify Germany under a constitutional monarchy. The prospect of German unification threatened the multinational Austrian Empire, which was also plagued by the coinciding campaign for Italian unification and the nationalist aspirations of Hungary.

The threat Italian nationalism posed to Austria's predominantly Italian navy had been made clear in the failed mutiny of 1844, led by the sons of Admiral Bandiera. When the revolution reached Venice in March 1848, it came as no surprise that most Austrian naval personnel deserted to the Venetian Republic. Fortunately for Austria, the naval commander, Archduke Frederick, before his death in 1847 had transferred most of the active warships away from the main base at Venice to more secure harbors such as Trieste and Pola. Thanks to this redeployment, in 1848 the Austrians saved all three of their frigates, two corvettes, six brigs, and one paddle steamer. The new Venetian navy inherited four corvettes, five brigs, and one steamer, but most of the vessels had been in reserve or in disrepair in the Venice Arsenal; indeed, the rebels from the start had more officers and seamen than they needed for the handful of truly seaworthy ships at their disposal. In contrast, owing to the massive desertion of ethnic Italians, the Austrian navy had more ships than it could man. As a stalemate loomed, Sardinia–Piedmont helped the rebel cause by declaring war on Austria. Naples, in the hands of rebels since early 1848, soon followed suit.[24]

During the spring and summer of 1848, while the Austrian army slowly reconquered northern Italy, the naval balance in the upper Adriatic changed almost monthly. In April, Captain Ludwig Kudriaffsky imposed an Austrian blockade on Venice with two frigates, two brigs, and four paddle steamers, three of which were leased from the Austrian Lloyd. In May, Naples sent two frigates, one brig, and five paddle steamers to the waters off Venice, forcing Kudriaffsky to withdraw to Trieste. The Sardinians contributed three frigates, one brig, and one schooner, which joined the Neapolitans and a Venetian contingent of one corvette and two brigs in blockading the Austrians at Trieste. In June, a counterrevolution in Naples restored the absolute power of King Ferdinand II, who promptly ordered the Neapolitan squadron home, leaving the active Sardinian-Venetian fleet with no steamships and barely more sailing warships than Kudriaffsky's squadron. The Sardinians salvaged the situation by sending their entire navy to maintain the blockade of Trieste; their fleet commander, Vice Admiral Giuseppe Albini, soon had at his disposal four frigates, two corvettes, two brigs, and eight steamers, in addition to the small Venetian squadron. But in late July the Austrian army defeated the Sardinians at the Battle of Custoza, after which an armistice compelled Albini to leave the Adriatic. By August the Austrians had reoccupied all of their northern Italian territories except for the city of Venice.

Other than the corvette and two brigs activated in late spring, the Venetians had fitted out no warships, trusting their security at sea to the Neapolitan and Sardinian navies. Once the latter withdrew, Kudriaffsky once again blockaded Venice, only to be chased off in September 1848 by a French squadron, sent to the upper Adriatic in a demonstration of solidarity with the Venetians. Their arrival prompted Albini to bring the Sardinian fleet back into the Adriatic, in violation of the armistice. While his ships spent the winter of 1848–49 at Ancona in the Papal States, Austria sent agents abroad to recruit foreign officers and purchase warships. Hans Birch von Dahlerup of Denmark received command of the navy with the rank of vice admiral, taking the job out of patriotism, as the Danes at the time were at war with the German states over Schleswig–Holstein and eager to separate the Austrians from the northern Germans. The new warships included the British yacht *Waterlily*, armed as the Austrian navy's first screw steamer. Sardinia–Piedmont repudiated the armistice in March 1849, but Albini's fleet was still at Ancona when the Austrian army routed the Sardinians at the Battle of Novara, later in the month. A new armistice required all Sardinian warships to leave the Adriatic once again.

The French continued to maintain their squadron in the Adriatic, but it ceased to be a factor after the election of President Bonaparte in December 1848. To appease conservative French Catholics, Bonaparte reversed the republic's Italian policy and, in the Papal States, actively opposed Giuseppe Garibaldi's Roman Republic. In April 1849 the French navy transported over 7,500 men, almost 350 horses, and three batteries of artillery from Toulon to Civitavecchia. It was the first significant use of a steam-powered fleet to ferry troops in European waters, and it impressed the British enough to rekindle their fears of a French invasion across the "steam bridge" of the Channel. The bold stroke enabled the French army quickly to overthrow Garibaldi and restore the temporal powers of Pope Pius IX. Thereafter, the pope's position was safeguarded (at least for the next 21 years) by a French garrison in Rome.[25] Meanwhile, Dahlerup reimposed the blockade of Venice and, when Austrian troops moved southward into the Papal States, blockaded Ancona as well. In June Ancona fell, and in July the Austrian army moved heavy siege guns into place around the Venice lagoon. While waiting for their arrival, the Austrian navy had tried unsuccessfully to bomb the city from balloons launched from its warships. The army's subsequent shelling was destructive enough to turn the populace against the rebel leadership, which placed its last hopes on the Venetian navy breaking the blockade. A former Austrian officer, Captain Achille Bucchia, led several sorties against Dahlerup's forces, but his squadron of four corvettes, three brigs, and one steamer was no match for the Austrian frigates *Guerriera*, *Venere*, and *Bellona*, three steamers, a corvette and two brigs. During a series of skirmishes, Dahlerup paired his three steamers with his frigates, copying the British tactic of pairing steamers with sailing ships of the line. Serving as tugs or towboats when needed, the steamers enabled the frigates to hold their positions through changes in the wind and tides, leaving their challengers in a hopeless position. To make matters worse for the Venetians, by mid-August cholera had struck both the city and its navy. At the same time, the Austrian army, with Russian assistance, suppressed the Hungarian revolution, leaving Venice as the last enclave of rebellion in the Austrian Empire. The city surrendered on 22 August 1849.[26]

The other significant naval conflict of 1848–49 stemmed from the German–Danish dispute over the fate of Schleswig–Holstein. The German duchy of Holstein and predominantly German duchy of Schleswig were long ruled by Denmark as separate possessions, but in January 1848 King Frederick VII declared them integral territories of the Danish kingdom. When the German population of the duchies rejected incorporation into Denmark, their cause became caught up in the tide of liberal nationalism that engulfed the German states during the revolutions of March. After Prussia sent an army into Schleswig–Holstein, Denmark retaliated by blockading the north German ports. For patriotic Germans, the blockade came to symbolize the weakness of their divided nation. As tiny Denmark brought German maritime commerce to a standstill, it became clear to German nationalists that the future united Germany would require a strong navy to defend its maritime interests.[27]

The city of Hamburg armed the sailing frigate *Deutschland* and three paddle steamers to serve as a makeshift squadron until the Frankfurt Parliament (convened in May to write a constitution for the lands which, since 1815, had constituted the German Confederation) created a German navy. But the parliament focused more on the long term, debating the naval needs of a future united Germany while doing nothing to resolve the immediate problems of defending the coast and breaking the blockade. To make matters worse, the navy question exacerbated regional divisions among the German states. After a majority of the representatives rejected the Austrian delegation's plan to have the parliament pay for a "German" Adriatic squadron (proposed on the logic that the German Confederation included Trieste, then under Italian blockade), Austria withheld its funding for the overall project. Enough of the landlocked states then joined the boycott to eliminate half of the navy's financial support. Austria understandably could not contribute to the defense of northern Germany at a time when it faced a number of revolutionary challenges to its own existence. The Austrians remained firm in their policy even though it weakened the position of Archduke John, the Habsburg prince chosen by the Frankfurt Parliament as imperial regent (*Reichsverweser*). Their position enabled Prince Adalbert of Prussia to take the lead in the quest for a German navy. On hiatus from organizing his own country's coastal defenses against the Danes, Adalbert spent the winter of 1848–49 in Frankfurt supervising the formulation of a German fleet plan. Others involved included Saxon-born Captain Karl Rudolf Bromme (or Brommy), formerly of the Greek navy. They worked against a deadline of March 1849, when the German–Danish Armistice of Malmö (concluded in August 1848) was scheduled to expire unless the Schleswig–Holstein question was resolved. During the deliberations, north German shipyards began work on 27 small sailing gunboats which joined the German navy by early 1849.

Prince Adalbert's report to the Frankfurt Parliament, in February 1849, envisaged a two-part fleet similar conceptually to the one Joinville had proposed for France in 1844. German overseas interests would be safeguarded by a sailing force including a fleet of 15 frigates and 5 schooners, while the home fleet would consist of 5 steam frigates and 20 steam corvettes. The plan added a coast guard in which 10 steam tugs would tow 80 small coastal gunboats, in imitation of the Danish and Swedish coastal defense systems. Adalbert also argued for the development of naval bases in the Baltic and North Sea, and for a canal across Holstein deep enough for warships to use. (Since 1784 the Eider Canal had linked Kiel on the Baltic with the Eider River, which flowed westward into the North Sea, but the waterway had an average depth of just 3.5 meters and could only be used by small craft.) The canal Adalbert wanted finally opened in 1895, and the rest of the fleet plan remained a dream as well. In lieu of a formal naval base, the German navy established an anchorage at Bremerhaven on the Weser. During the armistice the ships armed earlier by Hamburg were joined by five paddle steamers purchased in Britain, including the 1,300-ton former Cunard passenger liners *Barbarossa* and *Erzherzog Johann*. Guns were purchased from Britain's Woolwich Arsenal to arm them. In February 1849 the navy bought the 1,650-ton transatlantic paddle steamer *Hansa* (ex-*United States*) from the Black Ball Line, but it did not reach Bremerhaven until August, too late to see action in the war (see Plate 2).

Recognizing that years would pass before a German naval academy could train an officer corps for the fleet, Adalbert looked abroad for officers, focusing on the United States and Belgium, the only countries to grant diplomatic recognition to the Frankfurt Parliament. During the armistice Prussian midshipmen served aboard the frigate USS *St Lawrence*, then cruising in European waters, and Commodore Foxhall Parker visited Frankfurt in January 1849 to explore the possibility of becoming German navy commander. He arrived in time to witness the tide turning against the parliament, as in the last weeks of 1848 the revolution had been crushed in both Berlin and Vienna. Parker declined the offer of a German commission and advised his fellow officers to do likewise. Two Austrian naval officers subsequently refused the German navy command, leaving the post to Captain Brommy. Brommy filled the highest ranks of his officer corps with Belgians and Britons, the lower ranks mostly with veteran German merchant captains. Most of his cadets were patriotic schoolboys with no prior exposure to the sea. His crews consisted of German volunteers, supplemented by foreigners (mostly British) who had elected to stay with the steamships the Frankfurt Parliament had purchased.

After the armistice lapsed Brommy's fleet added a second sailing frigate, captured from the Danes by local Schleswig–Holstein forces at Eckernförde. On 5 April 1849 a Danish squadron consisting of the 84-gun ship of the line *Christian VIII*, the 48-gun frigate *Gefion*, and two small paddle steamers attacked the port, intending to land troops from three transports. At the climax of a long artillery exchange, contrary winds drove the *Christian VIII* and *Gefion* into the crossfire of two shore batteries. After red-hot shot destroyed the *Christian VIII*, the captain of the *Gefion* surrendered his ship. The battle provided further evidence of the vulnerability of wooden warships to shore batteries mounting the latest artillery. While the Germans ashore lost 21 men killed and wounded, the Danes suffered 201 casualties (and lost 943 prisoners). The Germans commissioned the captured frigate as *Eckernförde* but left it in the port as a harbor watch, lacking a crew to sail it to join the rest of the fleet in the North Sea, a voyage that would have been a suicide run in any event, through Danish waters.

Two months later Brommy finally went on his first sortie from Bremerhaven. On 4 June his flagship *Barbarossa* and two smaller steamers chased off the Danish blockaders at the mouth of the Weser, then pursued them into the North Sea, almost capturing the sailing corvette *Valkyrien*, which sought refuge at the island of Helgoland (then a British possession, acquired by Germany in 1890). Ten days later the same German warships engaged the Danish paddle steamer *Hekla* and two sailing frigates at the mouth of the Elbe. The German navy saw no further action before the Armistice of Berlin (19 July) ended the war. Prussia concluded the truce with Denmark (and the definitive Treaty of Berlin, 2 July 1850) on behalf of the German states, as the Frankfurt Parliament had disbanded in June 1849, after floundering ever since late March, when King Frederick William IV of Prussia rejected its offer to become constitutional monarch of a united Germany.

Over the next three years, the German navy remained in existence, its ships anchored at Bremerhaven, while Austria, Prussia, and the other German states debated its fate. Until the German Confederation was restored in May 1851, Archduke John continued to serve as *Reichsverweser* and Brommy remained loyal to him. In the autumn of 1850 the struggle for hegemony within Germany almost led to war, but a show of strength by the Austrian army, supported by Russian diplomacy, forced Prussia to abandon plans to unify the rest of the northern states around itself. After the revival of the old confederation, the member states considered preserving Brommy's force as a German federal navy, then decided to liquidate it. Many conservatives considered the fleet an unpleasant reminder of the revolutionary upheaval; Prussia's minister–president, Otto von Manteuffel, labeled it the "illegitimate child" of the Frankfurt Parliament. In April 1852 Prussia received the paddle steamer *Barbarossa* and frigate *Eckernförde* as compensation for its funding of the navy in the years 1848–51. German merchants bought the *Hansa*, the *Erzherzog Johann*, and the frigate *Deutschland*, and a British company purchased the six smaller steamships. Brommy refused to strike his flag until March 1853, when the last steamer was transferred to its buyer.

Throughout the life of the German navy of 1848, both Schleswig–Holstein and Prussia maintained naval forces of their own. The Schleswig–Holstein navy, formed in June 1848, had a peak strength of 1 schooner and 11 sailing gunboats, 3 paddle steamers, and the screw gunboat *Von der Tann*, the first screw-propeller warship built in Germany. Lieutenant Johann Ernst Kjer commanded the force during its most active months, from March to July 1849, and from July 1850 to its ultimate surrender in January 1851. During the second phase of the fighting, the Schleswig–Holstein government stood alone against Denmark, refusing to accept the Prusso–Danish treaty which restored the status quo ante in the duchies. The tiny navy managed to harass the Danes but never sank an enemy warship, while losing the *Von der Tann* and one sailing gunboat. After the duchies surrendered, the Danes raised these sunken vessels and added them to their own navy, along with the rest of the former Schleswig–Holstein warships, the last of which were taken to Copenhagen in April 1852.[28] The Prussian navy of 1848 had just two seagoing vessels, the 350-ton training corvette *Amazone* and an armed postal steamer, neither of which engaged the enemy before the Armistice of Malmö. Expansion began in earnest only after Prince Adalbert returned from Frankfurt in February 1849, realizing that his German fleet plan would never come to fruition. In any event, Brommy's navy was stationed at Bremerhaven for action in the North Sea, and could do nothing to protect Prussia's long Baltic coast. By the time the armistice lapsed in March, Adalbert had armed a second postal steamer and a merchant paddle steamer, established a new base at Stettin, and hired a former Dutch officer, Captain Jan Schröder, to serve as operational commander. Schröder rushed his crews (mostly volunteer seamen or soldiers transferred from the Prussian army) through a training course, only to see his warships remain largely idle after hostilities resumed. During 1849 the Danish navy did not maintain a close blockade of the Prussian coast, instead concentrating on bottling up Brommy's fleet and skirmishing with the Schleswig–Holstein navy. The only action in the Baltic came on 27 June, when Schröder's steamer *Preussischer Adler* exchanged fire with the Danish sailing brig *St Croix*.[29] During the immediate postwar years, Adalbert and Schröder continued to expand and train the tiny Prussian fleet. British shipyards laid down another two paddle steamers, and in 1850–51 the new sailing corvette *Mercur* went on a training cruise to Brazil. After Brommy's fleet was disbanded, the 1,300-ton paddle steamer *Barbarossa* and 1,400-ton frigate *Eckernförde* (the latter under its pre-revolutionary Danish name *Gefion*) became the largest warships in the Prussian navy.[30]

While the naval forces of France were observers of, rather than participants in, the dramatic events of 1848–49, the French naval revival of the 1850s came as a direct result of the revolutionary upheaval and the rise to power of Louis Napoleon Bonaparte. The new president kept naval spending in check until 1851, when the French assembly called for further construction of screw ships of the line. He then seized upon the idea of making naval expansion an important part of a nationalist program to mobilize public support behind his personal rule. His agenda included various schemes to reconfigure the mainland of Europe along lines of nationality, and he considered a stronger fleet essential to prevent Britain from standing in his way. The French navy received generous funding, first under his dictatorship of the Second Republic (established December 1851), then during his reign as Emperor Napoleon III (from December 1852), yet it could not recover the ground it had lost to its British rival during the revolution of 1848 and the three years that followed. Dupuy de Lôme's screw ship of the line *Napoléon*, ordered in 1847, was launched in 1850 but not commissioned until 1852. Additional screw battleships were finally ordered during the spring of 1852.[31] By the end of the following year, Britain had three new screw ships of the line and seven conversions in service, while France had the *Napoléon* and eight conversions. Russia lagged far behind, with two new screw battleships under construction and two conversions under way, none of which would be ready before 1855. Having started the new arms race, then fallen behind, the French struggled to catch up with the British. During the Crimean War France would complete another five new screw battleships and seven conversions, while Britain completed two and eleven, respectively, to remain slightly ahead. In the conflict against Russia the British also deployed a total of nine former sailing 74s as steam blockships, all in the Baltic. Among naval powers of the second rank only neutral Sweden had a screw ship of the line in commission during the Crimean War, the *Carl XIV Johan*, converted in 1852–54.[32]

By the time of the revolutions of 1848–49 both the British and French had decided to construct all of their larger warships as screw steamers, yet other navies continued to add large paddle frigates well into 1850s, either instead of screw steamers or alongside them. By 1852 Grand Duke Constantine's campaign to modernize the Russian navy swelled its paddle fleet to 34 steamers, but as late as 1853 the Black Sea Fleet had no screw steamers at all and the Baltic Fleet nothing larger than a screw corvette.[33] Naples, which in the mid-1840s developed the leading European navy of the second rank by embracing the paddle steamer wholeheartedly, clung to the type too long, launching its last in 1856 before laying down its first screw frigates the following year. The Neapolitan navy of the late 1850s included 12 large paddle frigates and several more smaller paddle steamers, none of which had much fighting value by the standards of the time.[34] The Austrian navy, which after 1851 had Emperor Francis Joseph's brother, Archduke Ferdinand Max, as one of its senior officers, in 1854 commissioned two British-built steam frigates, one paddle and one screw. The following year two screw frigates and two screw corvettes were laid down in Venice and Trieste. Austria continued to commission paddle steamers throughout the decade, adding another twenty in all, but never considered them frontline warships.[35] Under the direction of Prince Adalbert, Prussia also began work on its first screw warships in 1855, a pair of corvettes laid down at Danzig.[36]

THE CRIMEAN WAR (1853–56)

In his quest to rally conservative French Catholics behind his regime, Louis Napoleon followed his military intervention at Rome in 1849 by contesting Russia's traditional protectorate over Near Eastern Christian shrines in 1850. His campaign only grew more aggressive after he assumed the crown as Napoleon III. When the Russians reacted by placing fresh demands on the Turks, the British (after initially refusing to support the claims) decided to back the French. After an Anglo–French fleet anchored off the Dardanelles in June 1853, a Russian army occupied the Turkish Danubian Principalities (Romania) in July, and prepared to cross the Danube into the province of Bulgaria. Formal Russian and Turkish declarations of war followed in October, at which time the Anglo–French fleet passed through the Dardanelles into the Sea of Marmara.[37]

The Russian Black Sea Fleet of 1853 included at least a dozen seaworthy ships of the line. Of its 20 paddle steamers, at least 7 were armed as warships. Egyptian reinforcements strengthened the Ottoman navy to 5 ships of the line, 13 frigates, 18 smaller sailing ships, and 8 paddle steamers. The Russians had no screw steamers in the Black Sea; the sultan's only one was a former sailing frigate recently converted to screw in Britain. At the Battle of Sinope (30 November 1853), the first decisive naval action of the war, six ships of the line, two frigates, and three paddle steamers under Vice Admiral Pavel Nakhimov attacked a Turco–Egyptian squadron of seven frigates, three corvettes, and three paddle steamers under Vice Admiral Osman Pasha. Copying British practice, the Russians used their steamers as tugs and towboats for their three largest ships of the line, the 120-gun three-deckers *Imperatritsa Maria*, *Tri Sviatitelia*, and *Rostislav*. They also made good use of their thirty-eight heavy Paixhans, against an opponent with no shell guns. Nakhimov destroyed the entire Turco–Egyptian squadron except for one paddle steamer, which escaped to Constantinople with news of the disaster. The Russians lost no ships of their own.[38]

The Russian triumph at Sinope had a profound impact on the future of battleship design, mostly because the shell gun received credit for the destruction of Osman Pasha's fleet, causing Napoleon III to question the future viability of wooden warships. This conclusion overlooked the fact that competent solid-shot gunnery would have brought the same result, at least over the six hours it had taken for Nakhimov to sink the Turco–Egyptian squadron, even though he had six ships of the line with over 600 guns against an opponent whose largest ships were frigates.[39] In any event, the sinking of the Turco–Egyptian squadron left the way clear for the Russian navy to attack Constantinople. To defend the Ottoman capital, early in the new year the Anglo–French fleet left the Sea of Marmara and passed through the Bosporus into the Black

Sea. In March 1854, Britain and France finally declared war on Russia, and made plans to land troops at Varna on the Bulgarian coast. By then, the allied fleet in the Black Sea included 19 ships of the line (10 British and 9 French), most of them sailing ships. Those able to steam included Britain's *Sans Pareil* and *Agamemnon*, sent to the Mediterranean in 1853 upon their completion. The allies enjoyed such an overwhelming advantage at sea that the sultan's fleet (5 ships of the line, 6 frigates, 15 smaller sailing ships, and 6 paddle steamers) remained largely idle for the duration of the war.

Veterans of the Napoleonic wars served as senior commanders in the navies of the allies as well as in their armies. The allied Black Sea commanders in 1854 were sixty-eight-year-old Vice Admiral James Deans Dundas and fifty-eight-year-old Vice Admiral Ferdinand-Alphonse Hamelin. In contrast, Russia's Nakhimov had received his baptism of fire much later, in 1827, as a junior officer at the Battle of Navarino.[40] But youth did not equate to boldness, at least once the Russians found themselves opposing the British and French navies instead of just the Ottoman fleet. Outnumbered in ships of the line and lacking screw steamers, Nakhimov and the commander in chief at Sevastopol, Admiral Vladimir Kornilov, kept their fleet safely in port, attempting only occasional paddle steamer sorties. It became increasingly clear that Russia was not prepared to fight against other European powers, either on land or at sea. Indeed, the British and French declarations of war surprised the Russians. Their wars with the Turks were common enough (the war of 1853 was the eighth since the 1690s) but such involvement by the Western powers was unprecedented. In the spring of 1854 the Russians would have accepted a return to the status quo ante, as demonstrated in the withdrawal of their fleet to Sevastopol and of their army from the Ottoman Balkan and Danubian provinces. It was the allies who chose war over diplomatic negotiation, in the hope that a decisive victory would end the Russian threat to the Ottoman Empire and, by extension, the Near East as a whole.

The British paddle steamer *Furious* was the first allied ship to come under fire in the war, when Russian shore batteries at Odessa foiled its mission to evacuate the local British consul. Outraged that the Russians had fired upon the *Furious* while it was flying a flag of truce, in retaliation Dundas sent nine paddle steamers (five British, four French) to bombard Odessa in late April 1854. During the assault, red-hot shot set ablaze the French *Vauban*, which was saved; the rest of the squadron emerged unscathed, as did the Russian shore batteries. In May, in the course of another raid on Odessa, the allies lost their first warship, the British paddle steamer *Tiger*, which had to be abandoned after it ran aground.[41] During June the Russian army retreated from Bulgaria back across the Danube, enabling the British and French to redeploy the army they had assembled at Varna to the Crimea, to attack Sevastopol.

During two weeks in September, 89 warships and over 100 transports landed 55,000 troops at Eupatoria (Evpatorii), up the coast from the Russian stronghold. The Russian navy made no attempt to disrupt the operation. Afterward, Kornilov removed guns and men from idle ships to bolster the defenses of Sevastopol, and blocked the entrance to its harbor by scuttling five ships of the line. The Russians adopted a siege mentality even though the city, strictly speaking, was never under siege, as the allies never managed to block the roads connecting Sevastopol to the north.[42]

The deliberate destruction of almost half of its ships of the line eliminated the Russian Black Sea Fleet as a factor in the war. When the allied fleet bombarded Sevastopol on 17 October 1854, shore batteries provided the only opposition, but the battle demonstrated once again the vulnerability of wooden warships facing good fortress artillery. The allied force of 30 warships included 13 ships of the line (5 screw and 8 sailing), which took a beating from heavy Russian guns firing shells and red-hot shot. The latter was particularly lethal, setting afire the *Agamemnon*, three other ships of the line and a frigate (see Plate 3). Other mishaps included the grounding of the ship of the line *Rodney*. Ultimately all of these ships were saved, but the allies suffered 520 killed and wounded in the six-hour battle. Russian casualties ashore were light but included Admiral Kornilov, whose death left Nakhimov the senior naval officer in Sevastopol. The allied fleet sustained further, even greater damage in a mid-November gale. The destruction of the French ship of the line *Henri IV* and 25 other ships closed a disappointing 1854 Black Sea campaign for the allies.[43]

The frustrations of the Crimea paled in signficance to those the allies experienced in the Baltic theater during 1854. The British Baltic command went to another aged veteran of the Napoleonic wars, sixty-eight year-old-Vice Admiral Sir Charles Napier. Because Russia's Baltic Fleet was roughly twice the size of the Black Sea Fleet (including 25 ships of the line, of which 17 were fit for action), the Admiralty gave Napier more ships of the line than his Black Sea counterpart, Dundas, including all but two of the screw battleships in commission at the start of the war. In March 1854 Napier took 15 ships of the line (9 screw and 6 sailing), 4 blockships, and a host of smaller warships into the Baltic. In contrast, the French sent most of their best warships to the Black Sea, leaving little to spare for the Baltic. When Vice Admiral A. F. Parseval-Deschênes joined Napier much later in the spring, his French Baltic squadron initially included just one screw ship of the line (see Plate 4). While the opposing fleets in the Baltic were more evenly matched than their counterparts in the Black Sea, the large number of British screw battleships gave the allies a distinct advantage and ensured that, here, too, the Russians would stand on the defensive. They sowed the approaches to St Petersburg with primitive Jacobi mines (caulked wooden kegs filled with explosives), and placed their faith in the heavy guns of Kronstadt and other fortified coastal strongholds.[44]

Because the allied armies sent most of their available manpower to the Crimea, the allies in the Baltic did not have the troops necessary to assault large, fortified Russian ports. Smaller outposts fell easily, including Libau (Liepaja) in May 1854 and Bomarsund, in the Åland Islands, in August.[45] By late summer Napier had been reinforced to a strength of 29 ships of the line (13 screw and 16 sailing), most of the screw liners being new conversions rushed to the Baltic straight from the dockyards. Pressured to attempt an attack on Sveaborg, the fortress guarding the approaches to Helsinki, Napier protested that his fleet was still too weak. While he certainly did not lack the warships, many of them arrived in the Baltic manned by skeleton crews, reflecting the weakness of the British system of manning warships. With the public and politicians unwilling to accept either a return to past impressment or the introduction of modern conscription, the Admiralty could only appeal to the quarter-million men on the Register of Seamen, of whom just 400 volunteered for naval service in 1854. At the start of the campaign the First Lord of the Admiralty, Sir James Graham, proposed that Napier "pick up some Norwegian sailors" on his way to the Baltic. A number of Scandinavians ended up serving in the British fleet, but Napier's ships were still undermanned.[46] The allies accomplished little before the onset of winter conditions forced them to withdraw their fleets in October. Upon his return to Britain, Napier defended himself by claiming that he had not engaged "the very powerful fleet of the enemy" because of the risk involved: if he had lost such a battle, "in three weeks from that time a Russian fleet, full of troops, might be on our coasts. . . ." Napier failed to mention the fact that the Russians had no screw ships of the line and had no intention of leaving the security of their base at Kronstadt. After his dismissal in December ended his naval career, he entered politics and as a postwar MP was instrumental in convening a "Royal Commission on Manning the Navy," which led to significant reform.[47]

Napier was not the only British admiral sacked in December 1854. In the Black Sea, Admiral Dundas turned over his command to Rear Admiral Sir Edmund Lyons. At sixty-five, Lyons was almost as old as his predecessor. Before being appointed to serve as Dundas's second in command at the start of the war, he had spent thirteen years in the diplomatic service, experience which would serve him well in the waging of coalition warfare. In January 1855 the Turks sent 40,000 troops to Eupatoria and Sardinia–Piedmont declared war on Russia; the Sardinians soon sent a squadron to the Black Sea and 15,500 troops to the Crimea. Palmerston, appointed prime minister in January 1855, saw to it that British forces were better equipped for the upcoming campaigns in both theaters of action. By the spring of 1855 screw battleships had replaced most of the sailing ships of the line in the British Black Sea force. The new vessels included the *Royal Albert*, Lyons's flagship.[48]

In the spring and summer of 1855 the allies deployed a flotilla of gunboats to secure the Sea of Azov and close Sevastopol's supply line from the Don River basin. During the summer the Russian army failed in several attempts to break the allied lines around Sevastopol. Meanwhile, the Russian navy remained inactive, further paralysed by the deaths of Nakhimov and the third senior admiral in the city, Vladimir Istomin, during July. The final battle for Sevastopol began on 7 September with an allied bombardment. On the 8th, French and British troops stormed the city's defenses. That night, the Russians used the road still open to the north to evacuate the city; as they withdrew, the dockyard was set ablaze. On the morning of 9 September Lyons reported that "the six remaining ships of the line had been sunk at their moorings, leaving afloat no more of the late Russian Black Sea Fleet than two dismasted corvettes and nine steamers, most of which are very small." Some Russian naval personnel stayed in the harbor until 12 September, when they scuttled the remaining steamships.[49]

The allies next focused on the Russian fortress at Kinburn, which guarded the mouths of the Bug and Dnieper rivers. On 17 October 1855 Lyons and France's Vice Admiral A. J. Bruat directed an allied bombardment of Kinburn including eight ships of the line (four British and four French), supported by several paddle steamers, mortar vessels, and screw gunboats, the last modeled on the type first proposed for Britain's "Cherbourg Strategy" a decade earlier. Bruat's ships also included the 1,575-ton armor-plated wooden floating batteries *Dévastation*, *Lave*, and *Tonnante*, flat-bottomed vessels that could not sail and had engines capable of just 4 knots, sufficient only for minor maneuvering. Because they could not move under their own power, steamships had towed them from France to the Black Sea, to their anchorage 1,000 yards from the fort at Kinburn. Napoleon III had authorized the construction of the batteries after the outcome of the Battle of Sinope and the initial bombardment of Sevastopol caused him to lose faith in wooden battleships. The emperor was pleased with their contribution to the destruction of the fortress at Kinburn, during which they fired 3,000 rounds. The 4-inch wrought-iron plates of the batteries had not been damaged by enemy fire, and the only casualties aboard any of the three vessels came when a lucky shot passed through one of the *Dévastation*'s open gunports, killing two French sailors.[50] In the wake of the fall of Kinburn, the last significant Russian fortress on the Black Sea, the growing strength of the allies underscored the hopelessness of the Russian cause. After entering the war the Sardinians had deployed an all-steam fleet in the Black Sea, including the new screw frigate *Carlo Alberto*. Austria did not enter the war, but with the consent of the Turks and approval of the British and French, its army had occupied the Danubian Principalities in 1854, after the Russian withdrawal. In 1855 Archduke Ferdinand Max, newly appointed commander of the Austrian navy, cruised the Eastern Mediterranean with two paddle steamers, four sailing frigates, and four sailing corvettes. Over the winter of 1855–56, Austrian diplomacy would lay the foundation for the negotiations which brought an end to the war.[51]

As in the Black Sea, in the Baltic the British gave the fleet command for 1855 to a younger rear admiral. Richard Saunders Dundas (no relation to the 1854 Black Sea commander), son of the former First Lord of the Admiralty, Lord Melville, in 1853 became the first British naval officer commissioned after the Napoleonic wars to reach flag rank.[52] The French also turned to a younger Baltic commander for 1855, Rear Admiral Charles Pénaud. Dundas arrived in the Gulf of Finland in May, and Pénaud followed in June. The British deployed an all-steam fleet in the Baltic in 1855, adding 5 newly converted blockships, 16 mortar vessels, and 16 screw gunboats. The French also added 10 screw gunboats. For half the summer Dundas hesitated to attack Sveaborg, but Pénaud finally persuaded him to act. The British supplied most of the naval units for the assault on 9–10 August: a screw-propelled fleet of two ships of the line, three frigates, one corvette, one sloop, four blockships, several gunboats and mortar vessels, supported by nine paddle steamers. In contrast to the naval bombardment of Sevastopol in October 1854, this time the attackers inflicted far more damage than they sustained, destroying 6 Russian ships of the line and 17 smaller warships in the harbor. The lone British sloop was the only allied warship damaged in the battle, and the allies suffered just 16 casualties against 2,000 for the Russians. The difference stemmed from the allied decision not to attack with a force consisting primarily of ships of the line, opting instead for smaller craft which the batteries ashore had greater difficulty targeting. The allies applied the lesson two months later in their attack on Kinburn, where screw gunboats, mortar vessels, and shallow-draught paddle steamers joined the armored batteries in firing most of the shots. In preparation for the 1856 Baltic campaign, which had as its goal the reduction of Kronstadt and occupation of St Petersburg, the British ordered 200 screw gunboats and 100 mortar vessels, and in 1855–56 completed eight armored batteries modeled after those used by the French at Kinburn. Meanwhile, during 1855 the Russians commissioned the converted screw ships of the line *Orel* and *Vyborg*, along with 23 screw gunboats, and laid up most of their sailing battleships to free manpower for the gunboats. The only Russian Baltic sortie of the war came on 2 September 1855, when the *Vyborg* came out of Kronstadt but turned back when met by the British screw ship of the line *Colossus*. The allies' Baltic plans for 1856 were cancelled when the Congress of Paris convened to negotiate an end to the war.[53]

CONCLUSION

The threat of a massive Anglo–French assault on Kronstadt and St Petersburg in 1856 combined with the possible addition of Austria and Sweden to the allied coalition to bring Russia's new tsar, Alexander II, to the peace table. The Treaty of Paris (30 March 1856) required Russia to cede only a small piece of territory at the mouth of the Danube to the Turks, but prohibited the Russians from having either fortifications or a fleet in the Black Sea. Russia also had to destroy its fortifications in the Åland Islands, off the coast of Finland. The treaty allowed the screw ships of the line *Sinop* and *Tsesarevich*, then under construction at Nikolaiev, to be removed from the Black Sea to the Baltic. By the time they were launched and fit to sail, the first armored frigate was already under construction in France, and the days of the wooden battleship were numbered.[54]

By the end of the Crimean War the midcentury transition in warship design and technology had ended with the screw-propelled steamship as the new standard. Indeed, a dozen years after the British and French navies introduced their first screw steamers, every warship that was not a screw steamer was considered obsolete or fit only for auxiliary duties. Except for the brig, which was too stout to be practical as a steamer, every traditional sailing ship type had its life extended by screw propulsion, from the ship of the line down to the schooner and gunboat. After its performance in the Crimean War, the screw gunboat, an inexpensive design that could be built very quickly, far surpassed its sailing predecessor in numbers and popularity. Although they were not designed for overseas duty, eventually screw gunboats were employed so extensively by the great powers of Europe in the claiming of colonies and bullying of less powerful (usually non-European) adversaries that the term "gunboat diplomacy" was coined to describe such activity.[55] After the 1850s, paddle steamers and sailing ships continued to serve alongside screw steamers, but mostly in non-European settings. Europe's navies found small, fast paddle steamers useful as dispatch vessels or for colonial service, and as late as 1860 sailing ships of the line still served as flagships of the British South African and Pacific stations. Into the late 1800s most navies continued to use sailing vessels for warm-water training cruises for cadets and apprentice seamen.

But no sooner than the new screw-steamer paradigm was established, doubts about the durability of the wooden screw steamship as a battleship led to the development of the first armored floating batteries. While screw frigates and smaller screw steamer types would survive for another twenty years, after barely a decade screw ships of the line were destined to be rendered obsolete by the first ironclad capital ships. The deployment of the French armored batteries against Kinburn in 1855 sparked the long developmental spiral of ever more powerful guns and ever stronger armor, a contest in which the competitors' level of industrial development mattered more than anything else. While the First Opium War had demonstrated what the navy of the leading industrialized Western power could do to the world's strongest pre-industrial non-Western state, the Crimean War provided the first example of the difference industrial technology could make in a conflict among the leading European powers. Having few railroads (and none at all, south of Moscow), Russia could not keep its coastal strongholds supplied as well as Britain and France, using steamships, could sustain the forces blockading and assaulting them. Henceforth the state of a country's industrial and technological development would determine its overall rank as a European power, and would be crucial to its development and maintenance of a modern navy.

NOTES

[1] Hamilton, *Anglo–French Naval Rivalry*, 11; Langensiepen and Güleryüz, *The Ottoman Steam Navy*, 3; Daly, *Russian Seapower and "the Eastern Question"*, 143.

[2] Hamilton, *Anglo–French Naval Rivalry*, 11; François Ferdinand d'Orléans, Prince de Joinville, *Essais sur la marine française* (Paris, 1853), 10.

[3] Hamilton, *Anglo–French Naval Rivalry*, 21; Sondhaus, *The Habsburg Empire and the Sea*, 102–3; Lambert, *The Last Sailing Battlefleet*, 38; Daly, *Russian Seapower and "the Eastern Question"*, 159–63; Bonner-Smith and Dewar (eds), *Russian War, 1854*, 212.

[4] Sondhaus, *The Habsburg Empire and the Sea*, 103–4; Lambert, "Introduction of Steam," 23; Langensiepen and Güleryüz, *The Ottoman Steam Navy*, 3.

[5] Daly, *Russian Seapower and "the Eastern Question"*, 171–3; Lambert, *The Last Sailing Battlefleet*, 87; Sondhaus, *The Habsburg Empire and the Sea*, 127–36.

[6] Jack Beeching, *The Chinese Opium Wars* (New York, 1975), 84–104; Jasper Ridley, *Lord Palmerston* (New York, 1971), 250–4.

[7] Beeching, *The Chinese Opium Wars*, 111–12; Lambert, "Introduction of Steam," 28.

[8] Ridley, *Lord Palmerston*, 257; W. H. Hall, *Narrative of the Voyages and Services of the Nemesis, from 1840 to 1843*, 2nd edn (London, 1845), 2, 121.

[9] Beeching, *The Chinese Opium Wars*, 115, 124–35.

[10] Ibid., 144–56; Hall, *Narrative of the Voyages and Services of the Nemesis*, 478–549 and *passim*; Ridley, *Lord Palmerston*, 258. The Second Opium War (1856–60), sparked by the Chinese seizure of the small British merchantman *Arrow*, ended with an Anglo–French army of 30,000 being deployed for a march on Beijing, where the Summer Palace was sacked and burned. China's defeat brought the opening of more ports to foreign commerce, the opening of the interior of China to foreign merchants and missionaries, and the legalization of the opium trade. See J. Y. Wong, *Deadly Dreams: Opium, Imperialism, and the Arrow War (1856–1860) in China* (Cambridge, 1998), 99, 280, 487–9 and *passim*; Beeching, *The Chinese Opium Wars*, 246–325; Dupont and Taillemite, *Les guerres navales françaises*, 244–5.

[11] Andrew Lambert, "The Screw Propeller Warship," in *Steam, Steel and Shellfire: The Steam Warship 1815–1905*, ed. Robert Gardiner (London, 1992), 31–2; Brown, *Paddle Warships*, 80.

[12] Joinville, *De l'état des forces navales de la France*, 14–15, 25–6, 38–41; Busk, *Navies of the World*, 75.

[13] Joinville, *De l'état des forces navales de la France*, 35.

[14] Lambert, "Introduction of Steam," 23–4; *idem, Battleships in Transition*, 19; Brown, *Paddle Warships*, 79; Griffiths, "Warship Machinery," 170.

[15] Lambert, "Introduction of Steam," 26; *idem, The Last Sailing Battlefleet*, 54.

[16] Hamilton, *Anglo–French Naval Rivalry*, 17–20; Lambert, *The Last Sailing Battlefleet*, 41; Dupont and Taillemite, *Les guerres navales françaises*, 237, 239; Battesi, *La Marine au XIXe siècle*, 29, 33; Legohérel, *Histoire de la Marine française*, 83. The 1845 bombardment of Tangier forced Morocco to conclude a treaty recognizing French sovereignty over Algeria.

[17] Lambert, "Introduction of Steam," 26.

[18] Lambert, "The Screw Propeller Warship," 33–5; Brown, *Paddle Warships*, 48.

[19] Hamilton, *Anglo–French Naval Rivalry*, 37, 43; Lambert, "The Screw Propeller Warship," 36–9. The French navy's first screw steamer, the small dispatch vessel *Napoléon* (later renamed *Corse*), was laid down by Normand in 1841 and completed in 1843.

[20] Lambert, *Battleships in Transition*, 139; *idem*, "The Screw Propeller Warship," 38, 42–4; Brown, *Paddle Warships*, 16; Busk, *Navies of the World*, 42.

[21] Hamilton, *Anglo–French Naval Rivalry*, 42–3, 51–3; James Phinney Baxter, *The Introduction of the Ironclad Warship* (Cambridge, MA, 1933), 67; Beeler, *British Naval Policy*, 58; Lambert, "The Screw Propeller Warship," 40; *idem, Battleships in Transition*, 124, 138, 140; idem, *The Last Sailing Battlefleet*, 90.

[22] Lambert, "The Screw Propeller Warship," 37; *idem, Battleships in Transition*, 32–3.

[23] Griffiths, "Warship Machinery," 173; Lambert, "The Screw Propeller Warship," 35; *idem, Battleships in Transition*, 31–2.

[24] Unless otherwise noted, the source for material below on Austria and the Italian navies of 1848–49 is Sondhaus, *The Habsburg Empire and the Sea*, 150–60, 175.

[25] Hamilton, *Anglo–French Naval Rivalry*, 53.

[26] Sondhaus, *The Habsburg Empire and the Sea*, 160–2.

[27] Unless otherwise noted, the source for material below on the German navy of 1848–52 is Sondhaus, *Preparing for Weltpolitik*, 19–32.

[28] Gerd Stolz, *Die Schleswig-Holsteinische Marine, 1848–1852* (Heide in Holstein, 1978), *passim*.

[29] Sondhaus, *Preparing for Weltpolitik*, 37–41.

[30] Ibid., 41–5.

[31] Lambert, *Battleships in Transition*, 99, 140; *idem*, "The Screw Propeller Warship," 37–40.

[32] Lambert, *Battleships in Transition*, 122–47; *idem*, "The Screw-Propeller Warship," 40–1.

[33] Lambert, "Introduction of Steam," 27–8.

[34] Radogna, *Storia della Marina Militare*, 133–40; Lodovico Bianchini, *Della storia delle finanze del regno di Napoli* (Naples, 1859), 504.

[35] Karl Gogg, *Österreichs Kriegsmarine, 1848–1918* (Salzburg, 1967), 28–33.

[36] Sondhaus, *Preparing for Weltpolitik*, 55.

[37] Unless otherwise noted, the sources for this section are Lambert, *The Crimean War*, 3, 9–22, 60, 102–6, 135–40, 146, 218, 230–4, 246–8, 296–8; Gromov *et al.*, *Tri Veka Rossiiskogo Flota*, 1:191–6; Woodward, *The Russians at Sea*, 99–104, 109; Watts, *The Imperial Russian Navy*, 12–13.

[38] Langensiepen and Güleryüz, *The Ottoman Steam Navy*, 4, 193.

[39] Lambert, "Iron Hulls and Armour Plate," 52; *idem*, *Battleships in Transition*, 92.

[40] Bonner-Smith and Dewar (eds), *Russian War, 1854*, 206–7.

[41] Lambert, "Introduction of Steam," 23; *idem*, *Battleships in Transition*, 95.

[42] Bonner-Smith and Dewar (eds), *Russian War, 1854*, 219–20; Clarke, *Russia's Sea-Power*, 89–90.

[43] Bonner-Smith and Dewar (eds), *Russian War, 1854*, 210–27; Lambert, *Battleships in Transition*, 95–6.

[44] Lambert, *Battleships in Transition*, 41; Campbell, "Naval Armaments and Armour," 167; Clarke, *Russia's Sea-Power*, 93; Bonner-Smith and Dewar (eds), *Russian War, 1854*, 3–5.

[45] Captain Astley Cooper Key to Napier, HMS *Amphion*, 18 May 1854, text in Bonner-Smith and Dewar (eds), *Russian War, 1854*, 56–7; see also ibid., 11–12.

[46] White, *Victoria's Navy: The End of the Sailing Navy*, 69; Graham quoted in Lewis, *The Navy in Transition*, 186.

[47] Napier to W. A. B. Hamilton, Secretary of the Admiralty, Merchiston, 5 January 1855, in Bonner-Smith and Dewar (eds), *Russian War, 1854*, 189–91; Eugene L. Rasor, *Reform in the Royal Navy: A Social History of the Lower Deck, 1850 to 1880* (Hamden, CT, 1976), 26.

[48] Bonner-Smith and Dewar (eds), *Russian War, 1854*, 227–8; A. C. Dewar (ed.), *Russian War, 1855, Black Sea: Official Correspondence* (London, 1945), 3, 6–8.

[49] Lyons to Secretary of the Admiralty Thomas Phinn, *Royal Albert*, 10 September 1855, in Dewar (ed.), *Russian War, 1855, Black Sea*, 291.

[50] Lambert, "Iron Hulls and Armour Plate," 52; Baxter, *Introduction of the Ironclad Warship*, 78–86.

[51] Sondhaus, *The Habsburg Empire and the Sea*, 183–4.

[52] Lewis, *The Navy in Transition*, 79.

[53] Dundas to Secretary of the Admiralty, HMS *Duke of Wellington*, 13 August 1855, in D. Bonner-Smith (ed.), *Russian War, 1855, Baltic: Official Correspondence* (London, 1944), 184; see also ibid., 8–12; Hamilton, *Anglo–French Naval Rivalry*, 77; Clarke, *Russia's Sea-Power*, 94; Watts, *The Imperial Russian Navy*, 13; Lambert, *Battleships in Transition*, 50–2, 113; *idem*, "The Screw Propeller Warship," 44; Dupont and Taillemite, *Les guerres navales françaises*, 241.

[54] Watts, *The Imperial Russian Navy*, 14; Lambert, *Battleships in Transition*, 144.

[55] By 1859 Britain had 161 screw gunboats, most displacing under 240 tons, carrying two to four heavy guns. Other countries investing heavily in the new type included Prussia, which laid down 23 between 1859 and 1861, and Austria, which laid down 22 between 1857 and 1860. Lambert, "Introduction of Steam," 23–5; Busk, *Navies of the World*, 49–50; Gogg, *Österreichs Kriegsmarine*, 30; Sondhaus, *Preparing for Weltpolitik*, 65–6.

3

THE EMERGENCE OF THE ARMORED WARSHIP, 1855–78

In November 1854, a month after the allied fleet took a pounding from Russian fortress artillery at Sevastopol, Napoleon III proposed to his navy minister, Théodore Ducos, that ships of the line be fitted with armor plate. The following autumn, the performance of the French armored floating batteries in the Battle of Kinburn confirmed the French emperor's belief that ironclad warships would be the capital ships of the future. While historians continue to disagree over whether the batteries really were a decisive factor at Kinburn, at the time the French assumed they were, so much that after October 1855, the French navy placed no orders for new wooden screw ships of the line. Admiral Lyons, the British commander at Kinburn, likewise was impressed enough with the floating batteries to recommend to the Admiralty that the British navy have "as many good ones as the French."[1] The sailing ship of the line, slowly evolving and improving, had been the capital ship of Western navies for some two hundred years, but the screw propeller extended its life only for another decade after the commissioning of the *Napoléon* in 1852. Even then, its last years were overshadowed by the dawning ironclad revolution, in which the frigate, in armored form, became the new standard capital ship.

FROM THE WOODEN SCREW LINER TO THE ARMORED FRIGATE

In January 1857, Napoleon III ordered the new director of construction for the French navy, Stanislas Dupuy de Lôme, to design an armored frigate. Even though Dupuy de Lôme himself had drawn up the plans for the *Napoléon* just ten years earlier, after Kinburn he agreed that the screw liner had no future. In November 1857 he completed the drawings of the future *Gloire*, which was laid down at Toulon four months later. In March 1858 Napoleon III ordered five additional armored frigates of the same type, prompting the British to devise an ironclad program of their own. A mere two years after their victory over Russia in the Crimean War, Europe's two leading naval powers were embroiled in a new arms race.[2]

By the time the *Gloire* was laid down, France and Britain each had commissioned 6 purpose-built and 21 converted screw ships of the line, but because the French had ordered no new screw liners since 1855, the British had many more on the stocks or under conversion. Britain also enjoyed a qualitative advantage in the type; its 121-gun, 6,960-ton three-decker *Victoria* (launched in 1859) was the largest and, at over £150,000, also the most expensive screw ship of the line ever built. By 1861, when the leading navies commissioned their last ships of the type, Britain had 17 purpose-built screw liners, 41 conversions, and the 9 blockships used during the Crimean War, while France had 9 purpose-built screw liners and 28 conversions. The British also had another nine on the stocks, laid down in 1859–60, six of which were eventually completed as ironclads. Europe's other navies did not invest heavily in screw ships of the line. Russia completed its fourth and last new screw liner in 1860, and converted a total of five. Sweden had one purpose-built ship of the line and one conversion. Austria built one, and Denmark and Naples each converted one.[3]

The armored frigate *Gloire* had approximately the same dimensions as a wooden screw ship of the line. The 5,630-ton, three-masted warship initially had a barquentine rig, later replaced with a conventional full rig, and armor plate 4.5 inches thick. Its armament consisted of thirty-six 6.4-inch rifled muzzle loaders, two on the upper deck and the rest divided between two broadsides on the gun deck below. When the ship was fully loaded, the *Gloire*'s gunports were just six feet above the waterline, reflecting the fact that Dupuy de Lôme had designed it not for the traditional cruising life of a frigate, but for service as a battleship in European waters (see Plate 5). Its coal capacity (just 700 tons) limited its cruising range in any event. Because French industry at the time could produce only enough iron for one *Gloire*-sized hull per year, the ship had to be built of wood and plated with armor. The five other ironclads ordered by Napoleon III in 1858 included two identical copies of the *Gloire*, one copy with an iron hull, and two 6,715-ton, wooden-hulled two-deckers, the future *Magenta* and *Solferino*. The *Gloire* was launched in November 1859 and completed in August 1860. The others were commissioned in 1862. By then, Napoleon III had authorized another ten near-duplicates of the *Gloire*, ranging in displacement from

5,700 to 6,120 tons. All were laid down during 1861 and, owing to the limitations of French industry, all but one had wooden hulls. They were commissioned in the years 1865–67.[4]

Britain, in its role as naval hegemon, understandably did not take the initiative in a new technology that promised to erase its own considerable advantage in capital ships. After Kinburn, the surveyor of the navy, Baldwin Walker, did not jump to the same conclusions as Napoleon III and Dupuy de Lôme. Indeed, by the end of the Crimean War the British navy had more armored floating batteries than the French but considered the type a dead-end rather than an evolutionary step to a new capital ship. After limited postwar experiments with armor plate at the Woolwich Arsenal, in February 1858 Walker proposed construction of an experimental armored corvette. The onset of construction on the *Gloire* one month later, followed by word that Napoleon III had ordered another five armored frigates, demanded a more decisive response. In April 1858 Walker submitted a revised proposal, matching the French program with six British armored frigates. He served as surveyor of the navy for another three years, long enough to claim the honor of being founder of the British ironclad fleet. Nevertheless, in contrast to Dupuy de Lôme, Walker at first doubted the wooden ship of the line would be completely replaced by the armored frigate. More so than his French counterpart, he recognized the weakness of the first generation of wrought iron armor plate and doubted it could stand up to the latest rifled artillery. Lancaster developed a heavy muzzle-loading rifle in the mid-1850s, and late in the decade Armstrong produced a 7-inch breech-loading rifle which Walker wanted to adopt as the British navy's new heavy gun. He became a stronger advocate of armored warships only after the Armstrong rifle failed to pierce a standard thickness of armor plate in its trials.[5]

The design concept for the *Warrior*, Britain's first armored frigate, came from a class of unusually large wooden screw frigates Walker had ordered two years earlier, in reaction to the US navy's construction of the *Merrimack* (4,635 tons) and its five larger half-sisters during the mid-1850s. The 5,640-ton *Mersey* and *Orlando*, the largest of the six so-called "response" frigates, carried twenty-eight 10-inch guns and twelve 68-pounders, and were capable of 13 knots.[6] The fact that Walker wanted his armored frigates to be ironclad versions of the *Mersey* and *Orlando* was reflected in the *Warrior*'s design, completed in January 1859 by his assistant surveyor (chief constructor), Isaac Watts. Thus, it bore little resemblance to the *Gloire* other than in its most basic characteristics. Both ships were three-masted broadside battery frigates with 4.5 inches of armor and 36 guns, but the *Warrior* had an iron hull and was 125 feet longer than its French counterpart (see Plate 6). Furthermore, its sailing ability (setting twice as much canvas as the *Gloire*), coal bunker capacity (200 tons more than the *Gloire*), and Penn trunk engines (capable of over 14 knots, still a respectable speed twenty years later) all reflected Walker's desire that it should be able to cruise overseas like a traditional frigate.[7]

With a hull made of iron rather than wood, completely plated with armor, the *Warrior* displaced an unprecedented 9,140 tons, 60 percent more than the *Gloire*. The Thames Iron Works of Blackwall laid down the ship in May 1859, fourteen months after the *Gloire*, and launched it in December 1860. It was completed in October 1861, by which time the British navy had nine more iron-hulled armored frigates under construction and was converting six screw ships of the line to armored frigates. Thus Britain matched France's total of 16 ironclads built or building by the end of 1861, but because the smallest of Walker's ships were similar in displacement to the largest French ironclads, the British force was clearly superior. Had the two fleets ever met in battle, the sole advantage for the French might have been the near homogeneity of their line, as 14 of their 16 armored frigates were of the basic *Gloire* design. In contrast, on the British side only the second ironclad, the *Black Prince*, was a near-identical sister-ship of the *Warrior*. The six wooden-hulled conversions were much smaller, displacing 6,000–7,000 tons, as were four of the other eight iron-hulled frigates, the smallest of which was the 6,070-ton *Defence*. The remaining four iron-hulled frigates were larger than the *Warrior* and reflected considerable experimentation in design. The 9,830-ton *Achilles* had four masts, the 10,780-ton *Northumberland* and its half-sisters, *Minotaur* and *Agincourt*, five masts. Like the *Warrior* and *Black Prince*, they were designed as cruising frigates but spent most of their service lives as battleships in European waters. Aside from the *Minotaur* and *Northumberland* (completed in 1868) all were in service by 1867.[8]

Shortly after the Anglo–French ironclad race began, Sardinia–Piedmont went to war with Austria, hoping (as in 1848) to become the catalyst for the unification of Italy. The French soon intervened against the Austrians, and in May 1859 deployed a fleet in the Adriatic. Because work had only recently begun on the *Gloire* and its initial sister-ships, the French battle fleet was led by six screw ships of the line, and also included the three armored floating batteries deployed during the Crimean War. Such overwhelming force sufficed to keep the Austrian navy in port. Britain remained neutral in the conflict, despite concerns that a united Italy might become a French ally or satellite. In July 1859 the Austrians sued for peace, ceding Lombardy to Sardinia–Piedmont. They continued to rule Venetia but could do nothing to save their conservative Italian client states. These collapsed one by one during the following year, under pressure from local nationalists supported in the north by Sardinian troops and in the south by Garibaldi's army of "Red Shirts." Garibaldi assembled a fleet of paddle steamers, some armed as warships, others used as troop transports, and in May 1860 landed his troops on Sicily. As he conquered the island and moved on to the Neapolitan mainland, Admiral Count Carlo Pellion de Persano block-aded Naples with the Sardinian fleet. After the entire Neapolitan navy deserted to Persano in September 1860, Garibaldi also agreed to place his steamers under the Sardinian admiral; thus, the de facto birth of the Italian navy preceded the formal proclamation of Italian unification by several months. Early the following year Persano provided fire support off Gaeta, the last royal Neapolitan garrison, which capitulated in February 1861. Garibaldi's troops advanced from the south to meet Sardinian forces moving down from the north, and in March, Sardinia–Piedmont's Victor Emmanuel II was proclaimed king of a united Italy, despite the fact that the pope still ruled in Rome (ironi-cally, protected by a French garrison) and the Austrians in Venetia.[9]

The Royal Italian navy inherited from its Sardinian predecessor two 2,700-ton armored corvettes, begun in June and December 1860 by the La Seyne shipyard in France. Austria matched them with two small 2,800-ton armored frigates, laid down in December 1860 by the Cantiere Navale Adriatico of Trieste. In August 1861 Italy raised the stakes by ordering two 5,700-ton armored frigates from William Webb of New York. Austria responded with three 3,600-ton armored frigates, ordered in Trieste in October 1861. At a time when almost all of the early French ironclads had wooden hulls, the La Seyne shipyard built the two Italian armored corvettes entirely of iron. Otherwise, all of the ships laid down in the incipient Adriatic naval race had wooden hulls. Meanwhile, during 1861 Spain became the fifth country to join the ironclad competition, laying down the 6,200-ton wooden-hulled *Tetuán* in the navy yard at Ferrol and ordering the 7,190-ton iron-hulled *Numancia* from La Seyne. Both ships were launched in 1863.[10]

During 1861 Russia also began its first three ironclad projects. The Thames Iron Works delivered the 3,280-ton armored frigate *Pervenetz* in 1863, while Russian shipyards completed the 6,130-ton *Sevastopol* in 1865 and the 6,040-ton *Petropavlovsk* in 1867. The latter pair were both converted from wooden screw frigates.[11] The experience of the Crimean War made the Russians hesitant to construct greater numbers of armored frigates. The wooden screw fleet built in the late 1850s under the direction of Tsar Alexander II's brother, Grand Duke Constantine, ultimately included just nine ships of the line, as Constantine acknowledged the likelihood that, in the event of war, any Russian battleships would only be blockaded in the Gulf of Finland.[12] Russian naval leaders felt the same way about large ironclads, and instead developed a strategy for war in which their unarmored frigates and corvettes or "clippers" would wage a *guerre de course* against enemy (presumably British) commerce. Indeed, the new Russian Pacific squadron – based at Petropavlovsk until 1860, when work began on the new port of Vladivostok – consisted entirely of fast wooden screw steamers intended for cruiser warfare.[13] Thus, Russia adopted the commerce raiding strategy at the same time that France discontinued it, despite the fact that, after 1856, international law placed new limits on such campaigns. Twenty years would pass before the Russian navy again committed to a program of capital ship construction.[14]

Historians often date the onset of the ironclad age from the American Civil War battle at Hampton Roads (9 March 1862) between the USS *Monitor* and the CSS *Virginia* (ex-USS *Merrimack*). By then, however, four years had passed since the onset of construction on the *Gloire*, during which six European navies had laid down a total of 46 armored broadside battery warships. This figure does not include the ironclad floating batteries built during the Crimean War, or others like them constructed in the early 1860s, all of which had limited value as warships. As of March 1862 Britain had 2 armored frigates completed and 14 under construction. France had 4 completed and 12 under construction. Austria had five ironclads, Italy four, Russia three, and Spain two; aside from the Italian *Terribile*, commissioned in September 1861, all were still under construction. The Battle of Hampton Roads did not start the ironclad revolution, but news of the first clash of armored warships altered the parameters of the ironclad debate in Europe. Navies of the first and second rank took for granted that they needed armored warships, and turned their attention to the question of which types to build.

EUROPEAN NAVIES DURING THE AMERICAN CIVIL WAR (1861–65)

Britain never came close to intervening in the American Civil War, but Palmerston's flirtation with the Confederacy early in the conflict, combined with the construction of Confederate warships in private British shipyards, strained Anglo–American relations to breaking point. Britain kept its squadrons at Bermuda and Halifax reinforced throughout the war but did not send the *Warrior* or any of its new armored frigates across the Atlantic. The obsolete floating battery *Terror*, sent to Bermuda in 1859 after being completed too late to see action in the Crimean War, was the only British ironclad to serve in either force.[15]

Facing the dilemma of whether to build "monitors" instead of armored frigates, the British navy added both types. Long before the *Monitor* made its appearance, the idea for a turret ship had been championed in Britain by Captain Cowper Coles, who in 1859 patented a turret which turned on rollers just below deck level. In contrast, the turret designed by John Ericsson for the *Monitor* turned on a spindle and was mounted on top of the deck. A month before the Battle of Hampton Roads, the Admiralty ordered the *Prince Albert*, a mastless coastal ironclad with Coles turrets. Whereas the *Monitor* had an armor-plated wooden hull, displaced 990 tons, carried its two 11-inch guns in a single turret, and rode so low in the water that its decks were awash in all but the calmest seas, the *Prince Albert* had an iron hull, displaced 3,690 tons, carried four 9-inch guns in four centerline turrets, and had seven feet of freeboard. In contrast to the short life of the *Monitor*, which sank in a storm off Cape Hatteras in December 1862, the *Prince Albert* (laid down April 1862, completed February 1866) survived until the turn of the century. It was the first British "monitor" ordered but not the first to enter service; that honor went to the *Royal Sovereign*, a former screw ship of the line which, in August 1864, emerged from a radical rebuilding as a mastless turret ship. Similar in design to the *Prince Albert*, it had four centerline turrets, but with 10.5-inch ordnance and a second gun in the bow turret. The only other British turret ships built during the American Civil War were the 2,570-ton rams *Scorpion* and *Wivern*, commissioned in 1865. Originally laid down for the Confederate States, they were completed for the British navy after being seized at Laird in October 1863, when Palmerston's government decided to ban the construction of Confederate warships by private British shipbuilders. After the war, the British navy laid down another eight coastal defense monitors, ranging in size from the 2,900-ton *Abyssinia* (built 1868–70) to the 4,910-ton *Glatton* (1868–72). Other warships tailored for coastal defense included the 4,330-ton ram *Hotspur* (1868–71), the 5,440-ton ram *Rupert* (1870–74), and the three 1,230-ton armored gunboats of the *Vixen* class (1864–67). Meanwhile, two turret ships, the 8,320-ton *Monarch* (1866–69) and 7,770-ton *Captain* (1867–70) were built for high seas duty. Both were three-masted, fully rigged warships with the general appearance of large armored frigates; they carried their primary armament of four 12-inch guns paired in two centerline turrets amidships (see Plate 7). Unfortunately the *Captain* had a freeboard of just 6.5 feet, a feature which contributed to its sinking in a gale off Cape Finisterre in September 1870. Coles was among the 472 men lost in the disaster.[16]

Edward Reed, appointed chief constructor in 1863 under Walker's successor, Spencer Robinson, introduced the central battery or casemate ship as a solution to the dilemma posed by the requirements of ever more powerful guns and ever thicker armor. Like the *Monarch* and the *Captain*, the central battery ship was superficially similar to an armored broadside frigate but carried a smaller battery of heavier guns. Instead of mounting the guns in turrets, Reed placed them on pivots in a heavily armored casemate amidships, which also protected the ship's engines. Before building a casemate battleship, Reed first tested the design in four smaller vessels converted from wooden screw warships: the sloops *Research* (completed April 1864) and *Enterprise* (June 1864) and the corvettes *Favourite* and *Pallas* (March 1866). All had recessed freeboard fore and aft of the casemate to allow the end guns to fire ahead and astern. Reed repeated this feature in a fifth small casemate ironclad, the 4,470-ton *Penelope* (June 1868), but not in his first casemate battleship, the 7,550-ton *Bellerophon* (April 1866), which had ten 9-inch guns in its casemate, supplemented by single bow and stern guns for end-on fire. Seventeen of the 18 warships of the type built for the British navy were begun before 1870. Aside from the four experimental ships and three ship of the line conversions, all were built with iron hulls, and a total of 12 were capable of end-on fire from the casemate. In his first experimental casemate ships, Reed used the same 4.5 inch thickness of armor fitted to the *Warrior* and other early British armored frigates. Reflecting ever increasing concerns over the armor-piercing power of the latest rifled artillery, the *Bellerophon* had 6 inches of armor plating covering its central battery, the last of the casemate ships 12 inches.[17]

Given the technological and operational parameters of the mid- to late 1860s, the British navy considered the central battery ship the best possible capital ship design. Nevertheless, even Reed himself continued to experiment with other armored warship types. His two armored frigates, the 7,750-ton *Lord Clyde* (built 1863–66) and 7,840-ton *Lord Warden* (1863–67), were Britain's last broadside ironclads and last purpose-built wooden-hulled battleships. Despite his opposition to Coles and the turret ship, Reed also designed the last large turret ships of his era, the revolutionary 9,330-ton battleships *Devastation* (1869–73) and *Thunderer* (1869–77), and their slightly larger half-sister, the 10,890-ton *Dreadnought* (1870–79). The trio foreshadowed the later "pre-dreadnoughts" of the quarter-century preceding the all big-gun *Dreadnought* of 1906. They had no masts and carried their primary armament of four 12-inch guns in centerline turrets fore and aft of a central superstructure.[18]

After work began on the last of the *Gloire*'s half-sisters in 1861, the French waited until 1865 to lay down another armored warship. In the interim, Napoleon III was preoccupied with other matters, in particular his project to establish a satellite empire in Mexico. In 1862–63 the armored frigate *Normandie* served in the French squadron off Veracruz; discounting the British battery *Terror* at Bermuda, it was the first armored warship to cross the Atlantic and the only European ironclad sent to the New World during the American Civil War. For five years the French navy supported Napoleon III's involvement in Mexico, facing no opposition and losing just one vessel, the 750-ton screw gunboat *Amphion*, which was wrecked off Veracruz just before the French withdrawal in 1866.[19] France further antagonized the United States by allowing its shipyards to build vessels for the Confederacy, none of which, ultimately, was delivered. In 1865 French battleship construction finally resumed, and by 1870 seven casemate ships had been laid down. All lacked the recessed freeboard fore and aft of the central battery which would have permitted the end guns of the casemate to fire ahead and astern. Dupuy de Lôme chose instead to top the casemate with two or four heavy pivoting guns in barbettes, revolving turrets ringed by heavy armor. Departing from the philosophy of their armored frigate program, the French did not build their casemate battleships on a single design; nevertheless, they were generally similar, ranging in displacement from the 7,580-ton *Océan*, the first completed (built 1865–70), to the 8,980-ton *Richelieu* (1869–76).[20] Rather than use battle fleet ironclads overseas, the French built smaller armored vessels for cruising duties: the 3,720-ton broadside ironclad *Belliqueuse* (built 1863–66), the seven casemate ships of the *Alma* class, ranging in size from the 3,510-ton *Thetis* to the 3,830-ton *Montcalm* (laid down 1865, completed 1867–69), and the three casemate ships of the 4,585-ton *Galissonnière* class (laid down 1868–69, completed 1874–79). Like the French casemate battleships, the casemate cruisers were not capable of end-on fire from the central battery.[21]

Early in the ironclad era, French shipyards held their own in the competition with the British. The *Gloire* took two years, five months to complete, exactly the same length of time as the *Warrior*, and the 16 French armored frigates begun in the years 1858–61 took an average of just over four years to complete, the same as the average for 16 British armored frigates begun in 1859–61. But by the late 1860s France's inferior industrial capacity had doomed its latest challenge to Britain's naval supremacy. For the seven French central battery ships laid down in 1865–70 building times averaged well over seven years, compared to just over three years for the 11 British central battery ships laid down in 1863–68. Britain's ironclads not only were built faster, but most were also larger and structurally sounder ships, owing to their iron construction. Indeed, the only British armored frigates or casemate ships with wooden hulls were those converted from wooden screw steamers. In contrast, owing to persistent shortcomings in domestic iron production, 14 of France's 16 armored frigates were of wood construction, as were six of its seven central battery battleships (all but the *Friedland*) and all ten of its casemate cruisers. Britain further enhanced its advantage by developing vastly superior naval artillery. Experiments conducted in the years 1863–65 led to the adoption of 9 to 12-inch muzzle-loading rifles constructed of steel encased in wrought iron, capable of piercing 9 to 12 inches of wrought-iron plate at 1,000 yards. France had manufactured similar, smaller guns since the mid-1850s, including the 6.4-inch muzzle-loading rifles mounted in the *Gloire* and its sister-ships, which lacked the firepower to penetrate the armor of most ironclads of the early 1860s. As of 1870 the British navy's heavy artillery was still clearly superior to the latest French product, a respectable 10.8-inch rifled muzzle loader.[22]

Anglo–American tensions during the American Civil War ultimately gave the British navy an advantage over the French in yet another area, unarmored cruising warships. In 1864 the United States Congress approved a program of fast wooden screw steamers intended for use as commerce raiders against the British Empire. The 4,215-ton sloop *Wampanoag*, one of four ships in the program not cancelled when the war ended, averaged over 17 knots during trials in 1868. Although these ships were laid up shortly after their trials, never to serve again, they inspired a British program of unarmored iron-hulled frigates and corvettes in response. Edward Reed's frigate *Inconstant* (built 1866–69) displaced 5,780 tons and made 16.2 knots on its trials. His 3,080-ton corvettes *Volage* and *Active* (built 1867–70) also impressed critics. The end of the Anglo–American war scare brought the cancellation of the last half of the program, as the cost of the ships could not be justified (for example, £300,000 for the *Inconstant*, compared to £377,000 for the *Warrior*, a much larger frigate plated with armor).[23] Nevertheless, the fast iron-hulled cruisers set a new standard for unarmored cruising warships. After the late 1860s few navies laid down new wooden-hulled frigates; the 3,200-ton *Endymion* (built 1860–66) was the last begun by the British navy, the 4,020-ton *Newcastle* (built 1858–74) the last completed. Smaller wooden screw warships were built into the 1870s.[24]

Europe's third naval power, Russia, was the only one to embrace the monitor type, owing to its predominantly coastal naval warfare needs, which were similar to those of the United States navy during the civil war. During a war scare following a Polish rebellion in 1863, the Russian navy ordered ten near-identical copies of the single-turret USS *Monitor*, two of which were built in Belgium by the Cockerill firm, the rest in St Petersburg shipyards. Work also started on the armored frigate *Ne Tron Menia*, a 3,340-ton Russian copy of the British-built *Pervenetz*, and the 1,460-ton coastal turret ship *Smerch*. All of these warships were in service by 1866, along with the 4,000-ton armored frigate *Kreml* (laid down in 1864). They were followed on to the stocks by a pair of triple-turret and four double-turret monitors, the armored frigates *General Admiral, Gerzog Edinburski,* and *Minin,* the casemate ship *Kniaz Pozharski,* and the mastless turret battleship *Petr Veliki.* The last, a near-identical copy of the British *Devastation,* was laid down in 1869; at 9,665 tons, it remained the largest Russian warship for thirteen years after its completion in 1876. Counting all warships built and building, by 1870 Russia had a formidable force of 27 ironclads. Owing to the limitations of domestic industry, the Russian navy tended to copy others rather than pioneer technologies of its own. Exceptions came in the areas of mine warfare, where the Russians in 1868 developed the first glass tube battery electrolyte denotator, and in submarine craft, which were valued as potential blockade-breakers.[25]

The minor naval powers of northern Europe shared a defensive focus similar to that of Russia, similarly reflected in the number and types of ironclads they built. Twelve of the first 13 armored warships in the Dutch navy were small coastal ironclads, including seven monitors. The lone exception, the armored frigate *De Ruyter*, underwent more radical transformations than any other larger warship in history. Laid down in 1831 as a 74-gun sailing ship of the line, it languished on the stocks until being converted to a 54-gun razee frigate in the years 1850–53. It was converted again in 1860, to a screw frigate, then again in 1863, to a broadside ironclad.[26] During the 1860s Sweden and Norway each commissioned three monitors, but Denmark far surpassed their combined strength with an armored fleet of three broadside battery frigates, three small turret ships, and two small schooners, all of which were in service by 1870. Denmark was the last minor European naval power to fight a war against a great power, engaging Austria and Prussia in the war of 1864.[27]

THE WAR OF 1864

In 1863 King Christian IX incorporated Schleswig into the kingdom of Denmark, under the terms of a new constitution. This alteration of the status quo in Schleswig–Holstein led to a German-Danish war scare which could not be resolved by negotiation. As in 1848–49, Danish naval superiority over the German states allowed for such boldness. The country's wooden screw-propelled fleet included one ship of the line, four frigates, three corvettes, and ten schooners, supplemented by eight paddle steamers; its only north German rival, the Prussian navy, had a screw-propelled force of just three corvettes, one yacht, and 21 gunboats, with two paddle steamers. A fourth screw corvette under construction in Danzig joined the fleet in the summer of 1864. While Prussia had no ironclads at all, the Danish navy included the 3,100-ton armored frigate *Dannebrog*, converted in Copenhagen from a screw ship of the line, and three small British-built ironclads: the 1,350-ton Coles turret gunboat *Rolf Krake* and two armored schooners. Another pair of armored frigates, the 3,400-ton *Peder Skram* and 4,800-ton *Danmark*, were still under construction during 1864, the former in Copenhagen, the latter (originally laid down for the Confederate States) in Glasgow. After the Battle of Hampton Roads in 1862, Prussia had considered following the lead of its northern neighbors, Russia, Sweden, and Norway, in building a defensive ironclad force of monitors. But at the time, no north German shipyard was capable of constructing an ironclad of any size, and throughout the early 1860s a financial crisis kept Prussia from purchasing armored warships abroad. Prussia also imported most of the machinery for its larger unarmored warships from British firms and almost all of its naval artillery from Finspong of Sweden, in the latter case not yet trusting the guns produced in Prussia by Krupp.[28]

In January 1864 the new Prussian minister-president, Otto von Bismarck, persuaded the Austrian leadership to join him in demanding that the Danes rescind their constitution of 1863. When the Danes rejected the ultimatum, the German powers occupied Holstein and, in February, invaded Schleswig. Denmark retaliated by blockading the north German ports. In repeating their strategy from 1848–49, the Danes did not consider the fact that Austria had built a respectable navy in the meantime; at the least, Danish leaders did not think the Austrians would deploy their fleet in north German waters. But the Austrian navy was strong enough to hold the key to victory at sea for the German allies. By 1863 its unarmored screw-propelled fleet – 1 ship of the line, 5 frigates, 2 corvettes, and 21 gunboats – was roughly equal to its Danish counterpart, and its ironclad force, with 5 armored frigates, clearly superior. While legitimate fears of an Italian surprise attack in the Adriatic kept most of the Austrian navy in home waters, in February 1864 Captain Wilhelm von Tegetthoff left for the North Sea with the screw frigates *Schwarzenberg* and *Radetzky* and a screw gunboat, followed later by Rear Admiral Bernhard von Wüllerstorf with two armored frigates, one paddle steamer, and a screw-propelled force of one ship of the line, one corvette, and one gunboat.

The Prussians chose to attack the Danish blockade first, before the Austrian warships arrived. On 17 March 1864 Admiral Prince Adalbert sent Captain Eduard Jachmann on a sortie from Swinemünde against the Danish blockade at the mouth of the Oder River. Off Jasmund the Prussian force of two screw corvettes, six screw gunboats, and one paddle steamer met a Danish squadron consisting of the screw ship of the line *Skjold*, two screw frigates and three smaller steamers. Despite being outgunned by a wide margin, Jachmann engaged the enemy nevertheless, then withdrew to Swinemünde without losing a ship (see Plate 8). The indecisive Battle of Jasmund was the war's only action in the Baltic. Six weeks later, Tegetthoff arrived with the *Schwarzenberg* and *Radetzky* to challenge the Danish blockade in the North Sea. Joined by a Prussian contingent consisting of the paddle steamer *Preussischer Adler* and two screw gunboats, he left Cuxhaven on 9 May to engage a Danish squadron off Helgoland. The Danish force was commanded by Rear Admiral Edouard Suenson, a veteran of the 1848–49 war whose baptism of fire had come aboard a French brig at Navarino in 1827. His force included the screw frigates *Jylland* and *Niels Juel* and screw corvette *Heimdal*. With the small Prussian vessels adding little firepower to the German squadron, Tegetthoff's frigates bore most of the burden for the allies. Neither side sought a close action, but during a long-range artillery duel of several hours the Austrians sustained 138 casualties and serious damage to their ships. Their gunners inflicted some damage on Suenson's flagship *Niels Juel*, but casualties were much lighter on the Danish side. Afterward both commanders withdrew,

Tegetthoff to Cuxhaven, Suenson to the Skaggerak. The Austrian captain rather modestly claimed a draw, despite having broken the Danish North Sea blockade; in contrast, the Danes claimed victory.[29] After the battles of Jasmund and Helgoland, Jachmann and Tegetthoff were rewarded with promotions to rear admiral.

The Danes did not attempt to reimpose the North Sea blockade before late May, when Wüllerstorf arrived with the rest of the Austrian squadron. Prussian army leaders wanted him to attack Copenhagen or move into the Baltic Sea, but the Austrians, aware that pro-Danish sentiments were running high in Britain, were careful not to pursue the naval war with too much vigor. Meanwhile, the Danish ironclads played no role in the war aside from two summer sorties, by the *Rolf Krake* in the Baltic and *Dannebrog* in the North Sea, neither of which resulted in an encounter with enemy ships. In the end Austria employed its naval power in perfect measure, enough to rob Denmark of command of the sea without provoking Britain. The Danes sued for peace and in October 1864 surrendered the disputed duchies. Prussia took over the administration of Schleswig, and Austria took Holstein.

After the war Denmark tried to remain a regional naval power. Its ironclad fleet grew to eight units after the commissioning of the armored frigates *Peder Skram* and *Danmark*, and two more small turret ships built at Copenhagen. Meanwhile, in the spring of 1865 Prussia acquired its first armored warship, the 1,600-ton British-built turret ship *Arminius*. The Prussian navy also purchased three warships which French shipbuilders had laid down for the Confederate States, the 1,400-ton French-built ram *Prinz Adalbert* and two screw corvettes, and commissioned another pair of domestically built screw corvettes. In 1865 the navy followed the lead of the Prussian army in agreeing to purchase Krupp's revolutionary all-steel artillery.

THE WAR OF 1866

Following the occupation of Schleswig–Holstein, Austria's concessions to Prussia included granting the Prussian army transit rights across Holstein to Schleswig, and allowing the Prussian navy to move its Baltic base (formerly at Danzig) to Kiel. Prussia also secured rights to build a modern canal across Holstein, to replace the obsolete Eider Canal. At a time when the Austro–Prussian relationship was deteriorating over a proposed reform of the German Confederation, such provisions provided ample opportunity for clashes and misunderstandings. The two countries began to prepare for war, and in April 1866 Prussia concluded an alliance with Italy. Tensions finally boiled over in early June, when Prussia occupied Holstein, then seceded from the confederation, followed by most of the smaller north German states. Hanover joined the south German states in supporting Austria, and soon became a target for Prussian naval operations. Jachmann once again served as squadron commander, operating ships on the Elbe, Weser, and Ems rivers to help secure the surrender of Emden, Stade, and other cities. In the process he engaged no enemy naval forces, as the Austrians withdrew most of their fleet to the Adriatic late in 1864; their last warship left Kiel in March 1866, to avoid possible capture. Prince Adalbert himself confirmed the navy's insignificant role in the war by spending the summer with the army.[30] In late June, the Prussian army invaded Bohemia, and wrapped up a brief, decisive campaign by defeating the Austrians on 3 July at Königgrätz. Meanwhile, the Austrian army fared better against the Italians, beating back an invasion of Venetia with a victory on 24 June at Custoza.

Most of the naval action in 1866 came in the Adriatic, where Tegetthoff's Austrian fleet included seven armored frigates: the 5,100-ton *Habsburg* and *Erzherzog Ferdinand Max* (both completed 1865), the 3,600-ton *Kaiser Max*, *Juan d'Austria*, and *Prinz Eugen*, and the 2,800-ton *Drache* and *Salamander*. He faced a much stronger Italian fleet under Admiral Persano, including 12 ironclads: the 5,700-ton American-built frigates *Re d'Italia* and *Re di Portogallo*, the four 4,250-ton French-built frigates of the *Regina Maria Pia* class, the 4,100-ton British-built double-turret ram *Affondatore*, the 3,500-ton Italian-built frigate *Principe de Carignano*, the 2,700-ton French-built corvettes *Formidabile* and *Terribile*, and the gunboats *Palestro* (2,200 tons) and *Varese* (2,000 tons), also built in France. Whereas all of the Austrian ironclads were built at Trieste, of wood construction, the nine Italian ironclads built in Britain and France had iron hulls. While the Italian ironclads carried the latest imported ordnance, the Austrian ships were armed with guns from the Imperial-Royal Foundry at Mariazell.[31]

As the price of securing the neutrality of France, on the eve of the conflict Austria had accepted Napoleon III's demand that it cede Venetia to Italy after the war. The Austrians believed the cession would ensure Italian neutrality, too, but Italy went to war all the same, hoping to acquire more than Venetia. After the defeat at Custoza that decision appeared to have been taken in vain, but the Prussian victory at Königgrätz (which forced the Austrians to withdraw their southern forces from Venetia, to defend Vienna) restored Italian confidence. As their army occupied Venetia unopposed, Italian leaders began to fear that Austria would sue for peace before further conquests could be secured. On 12 July Prime Minister Bettino Ricasoli proposed landing troops on the coasts of Istria and Dalmatia, predominantly Slavic Austrian littoral provinces which Italy claimed because of their historical link to Venetia. To clear the way for the landings, Admiral Persano would have to defeat the Austrian navy. Four days later he steamed out of Ancona with his 12 ironclads and an unarmored fleet of 22 vessels, including transports carrying 3,000 troops. His first objective was to "take possession of an important station in the Adriatic," the island of Lissa.[32]

On 18–19 July the Italian fleet shelled the Austrian fortifications on Lissa, but Persano hesitated to put troops ashore out of concern that the Austrian fleet would attack during the landings. Tegetthoff put to sea from his base at Pola as soon as word arrived that Persano was off Lissa. Nearing the island on the morning of 20 July, he divided his ships into three groups for a line-abreast attack. The first of the V-shaped formations included the seven armored frigates, led by his flagship *Erzherzog Ferdinand Max*; the second, of seven larger screw-propelled warships, led by the ship of the line *Kaiser*; the third, of thirteen screw gunboats and paddle steamers. Persano stood between the Austrians and the island of Lissa with a line including his eleven foreign-built ironclads. He detached the Italian-built *Principe di Carignano* to serve as flagship for the unarmored vessels, which fell into line so far to the rear that they played no role in the subsequent battle. The Italians had adopted French ironclad tactics based upon Louis Bouët-Willaumez's *Tactique supplementaire à l'usage d'une flotte cuirassée* (1865), but Persano had done nothing to apply the new doctrine to an operational plan. He added to the confusion by shifting his flag from the *Re d'Italia* to the *Affondatore* as the battle was beginning, leaving his captains looking to the wrong ship for their admiral's signals. The battle was a melee in any event, from the moment the *Erzherzog Ferdinand Max* and the Austrian ironclads broke through the Italian line, followed by the two waves of unarmored ships.[33]

Owing to inferior guns on the Austrian side and incompetent gunners on the Italian, neither fleet inflicted serious damage on the other despite the close range of the fire. Tegetthoff's wooden ships were fully engaged, while Persano's were not, yet even an unarmored target the size of the *Kaiser* (the only screw ship of the line ever to fight in a battle between fleets of warships at sea, see Plate 9) remained afloat amid the chaos. When the flagship *Affondatore* attempted to ram the *Kaiser*, a broadside from the screw liner disabled one of its two turrets. Tegetthoff had planned to use ramming tactics to make up for his inferior artillery, and at the climax of the four hours of close combat, his *Erzherzog Ferdinand Max* rammed and sank the *Re d'Italia*. A second Italian ironclad, the *Palestro*, caught fire and exploded as Persano's fleet withdrew to Ancona. "The whole thing was chaos," Tegetthoff confided to a friend, "a melee in the fullest sense of the word. . . . It is a miracle that we did not lose a ship." After the battle, the Austrian ironclads lacked the speed to pursue the retreating Italians. They remained off Lissa until it became clear that Persano would not leave Ancona again, then returned to their own anchorage at Pola. Austrian losses included 38 men killed and 138 wounded. The Italians suffered 612 killed and

57 wounded or taken prisoner, the two sunken ships accounting for almost all of their casualties. The victory earned Tegetthoff a promotion to vice admiral, while in Italy, Persano became the scapegoat for the overall failure of the Italian war effort. The Treaty of Vienna (3 October 1866) gave the Italians only Venetia, which they would have received without going to war.[34]

Lissa was the first sea battle between fleets of armored warships, and – discounting Navarino (1827), where the Turco–Egyptian fleet was destroyed at anchor – the largest naval battle in the century between Trafalgar (1805) and Tsushima (1905). Not surprisingly, its "lessons" affected battle tactics as well as warship design. Europe's leading naval writers and tacticians, including Philip Colomb in Britain and Jurien de la Gravière in France, adopted Tegetthoff's ramming tactics and line-abreast attack, making the latter the favored battle formation for almost two decades.[35] Meanwhile, countless naval architects in all countries designed warships of all sizes with exaggerated ram bows, and continued to do so well into an era in which the range of naval artillery rendered fanciful any notion of one warship ramming another in battle.

THE FRANCO–PRUSSIAN WAR (1870–71)

The Prussian victory of 1866 led to the formation of the North German Confederation in 1867, after which the Royal Prussian navy became the North German Federal navy. In 1867 the navy acquired its first three armored frigates, all foreign-built: the 6,000-ton *Friedrich Carl*, delivered by La Seyne; the 5,800-ton *Kronprinz*, delivered by Samuda; and the 9,800-ton *Fatikh*, a Turkish warship under construction at the Thames Iron Works which entered North German service in 1869 as the *König Wilhelm*. All three were to be armed with all-steel Krupp muzzle-loading rifles, considered superior even to the latest Armstrong guns of the same type. The new "armored squadron" was supposed to cruise to the West Indies in the summer of 1869, but because the Krupp works was late delivering the ordnance, the voyage was cancelled. The following July, the three armored frigates and the ram *Prinz Adalbert* were at Plymouth, en route to Madeira for a cruise under the personal command of Prince Adalbert, when the prince received an urgent telegram from Bismarck warning of imminent hostilities with France. The ships made it back to the new North Sea base at Wilhelmshaven just before the French declared war on 19 July.[36]

Seeking a victory against France to complete the process of German unification, Bismarck had succeeded in baiting Napoleon III's government into declaring war first. While the Prussian army and its allies from the smaller German states invaded France, the North German navy braced itself for an attack by the French fleet. The three armored frigates joined the small turret ship *Arminius* in a squadron at Wilhelmshaven, under Vice Admiral Jachmann. Meanwhile, the *Prinz Adalbert* was assigned to Hamburg as harbor watch, and most of the navy's unarmored warships were dispersed to protect Kiel and the Baltic ports. The French had an overwhelming superiority over the North German navy in every type of warship, including an edge of 17 to 3 in larger armored frigates. Their leaders discussed assaults on Wilhelmshaven and Kiel, and amphibious landings of troops at various locations on the north German coast. Such plans were abandoned on the grounds that the fleet had insufficient numbers of screw gunboats and other small vessels which (as the Crimean War had shown) were indispensable for successful close coastal operations. The French also believed they could land troops successfully only on the north German Baltic beaches, where it would be extremely difficult to sustain a beach-head unless Denmark entered the war on France's side, securing the French line of supply. The Prussian army's early successes against the French sufficed to keep the Danes neutral.

In the first weeks of the war, Vice Admiral Bouët-Willaumez led the French Northern Fleet from the Channel into the Baltic, and Vice Admiral Martin Fourichon moved the Mediterranean Fleet into the North Sea. Lacking a clear plan of action, they limited their activity to seizing German merchant ships. Neither admiral attempted a close blockade of the coast, and the defeat and capture of Napoleon III at Sedan (2 September 1870), followed by the first signs of bad weather, prompted both to withdraw to Cherbourg. When the new Third Republic resolved to continue the war, over 30 warships were disarmed, and their manpower and artillery used to bolster the defenses of Paris and other cities threatened by the Prussian advance. Meanwhile, warships Fourichon had left behind in the Mediterranean evacuated the pope's French garrison from Rome, finally allowing Italy to annex the city. German naval weakness helped make it possible for France to continue to fight for another five months, as arms purchased by the republic in the United States flowed freely across the Atlantic. For the two navies the war all but ended in September 1870. The only ship-to-ship action occurred on 9 November 1870 off Havana, where the 350-ton German screw gunboat *Meteor* (commanded by future admiral Eduard Knorr) fought the 800-ton French dispatch steamer *Bouvet* to a draw. Bismarck hesitated to allow the North German navy to raid French commerce, granting his permission for such a campaign only after the French took several German merchantmen as prizes in the first weeks of the fighting. Ultimately only one German raider put to sea, in November 1870, long after the French navy had given up its blockade. Under the command of Captain Johannes Weickhmann, the corvette *Augusta* cruised around the northern tip of Scotland to the Atlantic coast of France, and in January 1871 seized three French ships off the mouth of the Gironde. The losses were inconsequential to the French, but the appearance of a German raider so near Bordeaux, then serving as temporary capital of the Third Republic, understandably alarmed French leaders. A number of armored frigates were dispatched to hunt down the *Augusta*, which Weickhmann prudently took to Vigo in neutral Spain, to await the end of the war. While the French navy captured over 200 German merchant ships during the war, bringing German overseas trade to a standstill for more than six months, the *Augusta*'s three prizes were the only French merchantmen taken by the North German navy.

The armored squadron tied up most of the North German navy's resources and manpower throughout the war, even though Jachmann took it out on just two sorties, one at the end of the first week of August 1870, before French warships arrived in the North Sea, and the other during the second week of September, after they had already left. In between, engine trouble kept at least one of the armored frigates idle at any given time. As in 1866, Prince Adalbert confirmed the navy's irrelevance to the overall war effort by spending the campaign with the army. As late as the First World War, senior commanders in the German army looked back with pride on their service as junior officers in the glorious wars of German unification; owing to the inconsequential role played by the navy, sea officers could not do the same. Indeed, the Franco–Prussian War had a lasting impact on the younger generation of the naval officer corps. For Lieutenant Alfred Tirpitz, then twenty-one years old, the humiliation of spending 1870–71 in Wilhelmshaven aboard the *König Wilhelm* helped form his belief that Germany must have a navy strong enough to engage any other fleet.

TRANSITIONS IN TECHNOLOGY AND TACTICS (1870s)

Compared to the ironclads of the 1860s, the battleships of the 1870s were much larger but also arguably weaker, vulnerable to new armor-piercing artillery and, by the end of the decade, the self-propelled torpedo. The casemate or central battery battleship design became increasingly common in the 1870s because it limited heavy plating to the waterline and central casemate, shielding the guns and the engines while leaving the rest of the ship virtually unprotected. In the first casemate ships, this strategy saved enough weight to allow for sufficient speed and maneuverability, but as the 1870s continued it became increasingly difficult to protect even the most vital parts of a ship with a sufficient thickness of wrought-iron armor without considerably reducing seaworthiness. Some ships were plated with "sandwich" (iron-and-wood) armor, which was abandoned in the late 1870s as soon as "compound" (iron-and-steel) armor was developed. Tests demonstrated that thicker plates of wrought iron were actually weaker than thinner plates of compound armor. Its introduction saved the armored battle-ship; nevertheless, the design crisis of the 1870s would make navies more receptive to alternatives to battleship-centered warfare.

Improvements in ordnance, armor, and basic construction condemned many battleships of the 1860s to short service lives. Several wooden-hulled ironclads were decommissioned during the 1870s; in France, these included two of the *Gloire*'s sister-ships (1871–72), followed by the *Gloire* itself (1879). In Spain, the armored frigate *Arapiles* was con-demned in 1873, after nine years in service; the same year a civil war in the country claimed another wooden-hulled ironclad, the *Tetuán*, blown up just a decade after its launching. In 1875, the British scrapped the armored frigate *Lord Clyde* after nine years of service, and the Italians decommissioned two armored frigates completed in 1864 and 1865. Iron-hulled ironclads survived much longer, the most extreme example being Britain's *Warrior*, which became a museum ship late in the twentieth century. But all-iron construction mattered little once a design became outdated. For example, it would have been suicidal for the *Warrior* or any other broadside battery frigate plated with just 4.5 inches of wrought iron to engage a casemate or turret battleship of the 1870s, as the latter were armed with pivoting or revolving guns and protected by thicker or stronger armor. Once an armored frigate became too weak to stand in the line of battle, it could always be employed as an armored cruiser; as late as the 1890s, the German navy renovated the *König Wilhelm* (commissioned 1869) for such duties. But cost alone kept more armored frigates from being converted into cruis-ers, as navies discovered that maintenance expenditures on large armored warships ran much higher than for their wooden predecessors. Indeed, the *Warrior*, which cost £377,000 to build, consumed another £121,000 for repairs in its first seven and a half years of service. In the end, the most cost-effective option for most broadside battery ironclads was to allow them to slowly rust at anchor as harbor watch ships.[37]

Technological changes strained the existing systems for the education of officers and the training of seamen, the latter being especially prob-lematic as every major European navy except the British still relied upon some form of conscription to fill its ranks. In addition to losing ironclads to obsolescence, some navies lost ships in accidents rooted in inexperience with the challenges of maintaining or maneuvering armored vessels. The Russian navy was the first to have one of its own armored warships accidentally sink one of its unarmored counterparts, in an accident in 1869 in which the armored frigate *Kreml* rammed and sank the wooden screw frigate *Oleg*. Five years after the *Captain* disaster of 1870, Britain lost the 6,010-ton casemate ship *Vanguard* after it was rammed in a heavy fog in Dublin Bay by its sister-ship *Iron Duke*. In

1875 France's 6,715-ton *Magenta* exploded and sank in harbor, and in 1878 Germany's brand-new 6,800-ton turret ship *Grosser Kurfürst* sank in the English Channel after it was rammed by the *König Wilhelm*.[38]

While the battleships of the 1870s were a heterogenous lot, the unarmored cruising warships of the decade featured even greater variety, including ships of wood, composite (wood-and-iron), and iron construction and, from the late 1870s, steel construction as well. Some early ironclads had composite hulls, but the Confederate raider *Shenandoah* and the Spanish *Tornado* (ex-Chilean *Pampero*), originally laid down for the Confederacy, were the only unarmored cruising warships of composite construction to serve during the 1860s. Among the great powers of Europe, Austria–Hungary pioneered the type with the composite frigates *Radetzky* (laid down in 1870) and *Laudon* (1871). France built its first composite ship in 1872, Britain in 1873, and Russia in 1876. The French and Russian navies constructed composite ships concurrently with iron-hulled unarmored cruisers, the British alongside iron-hulled and, later, steel-hulled cruisers. Only Germany and Italy built no composite warships at all. Most of the German navy's wooden screw steamers were completed in the 1860s and thus not due for replacement until after the introduction of the all-iron hull; the Italian navy had an even larger stock of wooden screw steamers, which it continued to use into the era of the steel cruiser.[39]

In the area of tactics, confusion reigned throughout the 1870s amid the continuation of a general trend toward the "militarization" of naval warfare which began in the 1850s, when naval writers first proposed tactics for formations of warships moving under steam. France's Admiral Bouët-Willaumez, in *Batailles de terre et de mer* (1855) and subsequent works, emphasized the flexibility steam provided to the individual ship captain and envisioned the future naval battle as a melee in which élan would be decisive. But most writers prophesied a less chaotic future. In Britain the works of retired general Sir Howard Douglas, in particular *Naval Warfare under Steam* (1858), theorized that steam propulsion would give admirals greater control over their fleets, making the basic principles of combat on land more applicable to combat at sea.[40] Such promoters of the conceptual "militarization" of naval warfare became increasingly influential in the ironclad age, even though their commonsense visions of the future remained unsupported by evidence that the steam engine would really bring military "order" to naval battles; indeed, Tegetthoff's victory at Lissa in 1866 clearly supported the "melee" hypothesis of Bouët-Willaumez. The development of ever more powerful naval ordnance contributed to the "militarization" trend, as commentators ranging from the exiled Prince de Joinville in the 1850s to future British admiral John Fisher in the 1870s speculated that fleets eventually would be reduced to little more

than artillery formations afloat. Nevertheless, naval writers from countries with large merchant fleets or colonial possessions understood the
limitations of the "military" theoretical rubric and tailored their works
accordingly. Britain's Captain John Colomb, author of *The Protection of
our Commerce and Distribution of our Naval Forces Considered* (1867), foreshadowed the "blue water" ideology of Alfred Thayer Mahan, though
without developing a comprehensive theory of command of the sea.[41]

During the 1870s torpedo technology remained primitive, but the
invention of the self-propelled torpedo had such an impact that, by the
1880s, many navies would question the future of the battleship and the
battle fleet concept. In the American Civil War, spar torpedoes had
sunk a US navy sloop and a Confederate ironclad, but in both cases the
attacking craft also sank. The first alternative to the spar torpedo, the
towed torpedo, was almost as dangerous for the attacking vessel, which
delivered the device by steaming straight for an enemy vessel, then
turning away at the last moment, unleashing the trailing torpedo to hit
its target. Robert Whitehead, a British expatriate with a factory at
Fiume (Rijeka) in Austria–Hungary, developed the self-propelled torpedo following its invention in 1864 by Johann Luppis, an Austrian
navy captain. Luppis's mechanical surface torpedo was transformed by
Whitehead into an underwater device equipped with a hydrostatic
depth regulator and propelled by compressed air. The Austro–
Hungarian navy bought its first Whitehead torpedoes in 1868, followed
by Britain in 1870, France in 1872, Germany and Italy in 1873, and
Russia in 1876. After international demand for the product outstripped
the capacity of Whitehead's own factory, he licensed a number of
foreign establishments to manufacture their own Whitehead torpedoes, starting in 1872 with Britain's Woolwich Arsenal. But because the
original Whitehead torpedoes were equipped with charges of less than
twenty pounds of dynamite and puttered along at a mere seven knots,
navies did not discard their spar torpedoes and towed torpedoes just
yet.[42] In the meantime, pending the development of more lethal self-
propelled torpedoes and a coherent concept for using them, few questioned the primacy of the battleship.

THE NAVIES OF EUROPE'S GREAT POWERS (1870s)

The sheer cost of maintaining a respectable fleet of armored warships
in a time of rapid technological change eliminated all but the great
powers from participation in the ironclad race. Aside from the
Netherlands' 5,315-ton *König der Nederlanden* (launched 1874) and
Denmark's 5,330-ton *Helgoland* (1878), during the decade of the 1870s
no minor European naval power built a battleship even approaching
the size of the newest types in the leading navies. Spain, after assem-

bling a respectable fleet of armored frigates in the 1860s, went eighteen years without adding a new battleship before commissioning the 9,745-ton *Pelayo* in 1888. For the first time in European history, the list of the great naval powers included the same countries as the overall list of great powers. Britain, France, Russia, Germany, Italy, and Austria–Hungary were the only countries with the resources and the resolve to continue to build ever larger and more powerful armored warships capable of high-seas operations.

Tegetthoff's victory at the Battle of Lissa in the war of 1866 temporarily made Austria the fourth naval power of Europe, trailing only Britain, France, and Russia. Yet even after losing two ironclads at Lissa, Italy still had ten to Austria's seven, and its acquisition of Venice in the peace settlement threatened the security of Trieste, the leading Austrian commercial port. Immediately after the war, General Carl von Franck, the Habsburg war minister, remarked that "under the circumstances" the further growth of the Austrian navy "appears to be of decisive importance."[43] But the constitutional reorganization of the empire in 1867, which made the navy "Austro–Hungarian," also gave delegates from the Hungarian parliament veto power over the naval estimates. While many Hungarian leaders considered the navy primarily an Austrian concern, at least initially the fleet continued to receive its fair share of defense expenditure, owing to the prestige of Tegetthoff, who took command of the service in 1868. In the late 1860s the navy laid down three casemate ships, the wooden-hulled *Lissa* and the iron-hulled *Erzherzog Albrecht* and *Custoza*, and began the conversion of the ship of the line *Kaiser* into a casemate ship. Austria–Hungary continued to build its battleships in domestic shipyards but relied on British firms for their armor and iron fittings, and until the turn of the century had to import all heavy naval ordnance. After 1866 obsolete domestic artillery was replaced by rifled muzzle loaders from Armstrong, which continued to supply the navy until the eventual warming of Austro–German relations brought a switch to Krupp.[44]

In the early 1870s, the Italian navy faced far greater problems than its Austro–Hungarian counterpart. By 1871 Italy had 16 ironclads built or building to Austria–Hungary's 11, but aside from the double-turret ram *Affondatore*, all were obsolete broadside battery warships. The addition of Venetians after 1866 further divided an officer corps already polarized between Piedmontese and Neapolitan factions, ironically making it less cohesive than its multinational Austro–Hungarian counterpart. The navy ministry compounded the problem by waiting until 1881 to replace the old naval academies at Genoa and Naples with a single academy at Livorno.[45] The Italian navy reached its low point in 1871, when the parliament granted the service its smallest budget ever (26.8 million lire, less than the same year's Austro–Hungarian naval outlay for the only time in history) and even considered deemphasizing the battle fleet in favor of a coastal defense system. Thereafter, the two navies were destined for different fates, for during 1871, Tegetthoff died at the age of forty-three, while in Italy, Benedetto Brin became chief of naval engineering.[46] The key figure in the subsequent Italian naval renaissance, Brin designed the largest, fastest, most heavily armored battleships yet built, the 11,100-ton *Duilio* (see Plate 10) and 11,200-ton *Dandolo*, both laid down in 1873. In contrast to the casemate or central battery ships then in vogue, Brin's new battleships had no masts or yards. The design featured four heavy guns paired in two centerline turrets, like the only other large mastless battleships of the time (Edward Reed's revolutionary *Devastation*, *Thunderer*, and *Dreadnought*, then under construction in Britain), but without the low freeboard which cast doubt over the credibility of those vessels as high seas warships.[47]

In many respects, the *Duilio* and *Dandolo* represented an important evolutionary step in the direction of the later "pre-dreadnought" capital ship design of the turn of the century. They were the first battleships fitted with all-steel armor, imported from the leading French producer, Schneider of Creusot. The unprecedented firepower of their four 17.7-inch guns, imported from Armstrong, also foreshadowed the eventual return to faith in artillery fire over ramming tactics. If they were less than a complete triumph from the Italian perspective, it was because the two projects depended so heavily upon imports from foreign firms. In addition to their guns and armor, their engines and the iron for their hulls had to be imported. The dependence on foreign suppliers continued for Brin's next battleship projects, begun in 1876. The 13,900-ton *Italia* and *Lepanto* were slightly larger versions of the *Duilio* and *Dandolo*, only with more powerful engines, lighter armor, and slightly lighter guns. The *Italia* had a hull made of both iron and steel, the *Lepanto*, entirely of steel. Each carried four 17-inch Armstrongs, and had engines capable of 18 knots. They were followed by three slightly smaller battleships of the 11,200-ton *Ruggiero di Lauria* class, laid down in 1881–82.[48] Meanwhile, for cruising duties, Italy employed its large fleet of wooden-hulled screw warships dating from the 1850s and 1860s until the completion of the 2,490-ton corvettes *Flavio Gioia* and *Amerigo Vespucci*, fully rigged steel-hulled vessels laid down in 1879.[49]

In contrast, in the wake of Tegetthoff's death the financially strapped Austro–Hungarian navy could make only modest improvements. After creative measures were taken to wring construction money from the politicians, additional casemate ships replaced some of the remaining broadside frigates. Starting in 1873 the navy received funding to "rebuild" the 3,600-ton broadside frigates *Kaiser Max*, *Prinz Eugen*, and *Juan d'Austria* as casemate ships, but these wooden-hulled ironclads were actually broken up and replaced by iron-hulled vessels of the same dimensions, with the old engines, guns, and armor plate salvaged and installed in the new ships. Another of Tegetthoff's original armored frigates was scrapped in 1875 and not replaced, while the remaining three served into the 1880s without renovation. The 7,550-ton casemate ship *Tegetthoff* (laid down in 1876) was the only completely new Austro–Hungarian battleship begun during the decade. Its commissioning in 1882 gave the navy a fleet of eight casemate ships completed within the past eleven years, six of which had iron hulls, all but one armed with the latest Krupp artillery. Owing to the slow pace of construction on Brin's new battleships, the Austro–Hungarian navy remained a credible rival to the Italian throughout the 1870s. The *Duilio* was not commissioned until 1880, seven years after it was laid down. The *Dandolo* (1882) took nine years to complete, the *Italia* (1885) nine, and the *Lepanto* (1887) eleven.[50] After 1866 Austria–Hungary also had to replace a deteriorating cruising fleet of wooden screw steamers; the composite frigates *Radetzky* and *Laudon* were joined by six composite corvettes, all laid down by 1876, before the unarmored iron-hulled cruiser gained popularity.[51] In May 1882 the Austro–Hungarian navy suffered its greatest setback since the death of Tegetthoff, when the Dual Monarchy joined Germany and Italy in the Triple Alliance, thus eliminating the service's anti-Italian *raison d'être*. Meanwhile, with Austria–Hungary as an ally in a German-led, anti-French bloc, Italy turned its attentions away from the Adriatic and dreamed of becoming a Mediterranean naval power on a par with France.

Britain would not view the Triple Alliance as a threat to its own security until the turn of the century, when Germany began its dramatic campaign of naval expansion under Admiral Tirpitz. Meanwhile, the fall of Napoleon III in 1870 calmed concerns about a naval threat from France, while Russia, the third naval power, did little to improve its fleet after abrogating the Black Sea clauses of the Treaty of Paris during the Franco–Prussian War. The London Conference of 1871 formally legalized this unilateral move, but the Russians waited a dozen years before laying down first-class battleships for their new Black Sea Fleet. Thus, for more than a decade the British enjoyed an unprecedented degree of security and maritime supremacy. As a consequence, the Admiralty kept fewer battleships in active service, by 1874 only four in the Mediterranean and four in home waters, the latter backed by ten coastal defense ironclads.[52] Lacking a foreign challenger to build against, experimentation in warship designs and technologies proceeded at an almost leisurely pace. The 9,490-ton *Alexandra* (built 1873–77) was the last true casemate ship constructed for the British navy. Experimentation resumed with the 8,540-ton *Temeraire* (1873–77), a central battery ship with no capability for end-on fire from the casemate, but with two heavy guns mounted on deck in two French-style barbettes, one forward and one aft.[53] These ships were followed by the 11,880-ton *Inflexible* (1874–81), the largest British capital ship built to date and a clear step toward a high-freeboard turreted battleship design.

Because the *Inflexible* looked like a two-masted version of Benedetto Brin's mastless *Duilio*, laid down one year earlier, some historians consider it a response to the Italian battleship. Nathaniel Barnaby, Reed's successor as chief constructor, made the *Inflexible* slightly larger than the *Duilio* but gave it a slightly lighter primary armament of four 16-inch guns. It was the first battleship to have electric power for interior lighting and searchlights, and the first fitted with fuel-efficient vertical compound engines. For a British battleship it took longer than usual to build, in part because it incorporated so much new technology, and in part because Reed (by then employed in the private sector) publicly criticized its design along with that of the *Duilio*, alleging that such ships would likely sink if their relatively unarmored bow or stern were to flood. The *Inflexible* weathered these storms and also survived a political battle over its cost (at £812,000, more than twice as much as the *Warrior*, laid down just fifteen years earlier) to become the general prototype for all British battleships begun in the late 1870s.[54] The 8,510-ton *Agamemnon* (built 1876–83) and *Ajax* (1876–83) and the 9,420-ton *Colossus* (1879–86) and *Edinburgh* (1879–87) were smaller versions of the *Inflexible* but with no sailing rig. The *Agamemnon* and *Ajax* had a shallower draught than the *Inflexible* (by 2 feet) or the *Temeraire* (by 3.5), for service in the Baltic or Black Sea, reflecting the fact that they were laid down during the Near Eastern crisis that preceded the Russo–Turkish War of 1877–78. The gun turrets of the *Inflexible*, *Agamemnon*, and *Ajax* were plated with compound (iron-and-steel) armor, developed by the firms of Cammell and John Brown. The *Colossus*, *Edinburgh*, and subsequent British battleships received compound plates for all of their armor needs. Reed's criticism of the design of these ships haunted them for two decades; the survival under heavy fire of similar units at the Battle of the Yalu during the Sino–Japanese War (1894–95) finally exonerated Barnaby.[55]

A pioneering capital ship in so many respects, the *Inflexible* was also the last British battleship built with a sailing rig. Its masts were removed during a renovation in 1885, but even after that the navy kept a few fully rigged older battleships on hand. At a time when concern for coal supply kept most European ironclads in European waters (even in the British navy, which had more coal depots worldwide than anyone else), the Admiralty wanted some of its capital ships to be capable of sailing at least part of the way to remote locations not easily served by coaling stations. The same concerns led navies to continue building their overseas cruising warships with masts and yards, throughout the 1870s and into the 1880s. Reed's iron-hulled unarmored cruising frigate and corvettes of 1869–70 were followed after his retirement by two frigates of similar design, the *Raleigh* (built 1871–74) and *Shah* (1870–76), supplemented by four iron corvettes. His successor, Barnaby, built three fully rigged armored cruisers for duty as overseas flagships: the 5,670-ton *Shannon* (1873–77), the 7,630-ton *Northampton* (1874–78), and the 7,470-ton *Nelson* (1874–81). These broadside armored frigates had a recessed freeboard near the bow, which allowed the forward gun in each broadside to fire ahead, as in most casemate ships. Constructed in response to the early ironclad cruisers of the French navy and the ironclad warships being acquired by some non-European navies, the first British armored cruisers proved to be a poor design, being too weakly armed and armored to engage enemy battleships, and too slow under either sail or steam to pursue commerce raiders or unarmored cruisers. Each served for less than a decade, the *Shannon* for just four years. Maintenance problems helped doom these and many other large iron-hulled cruisers, both armored and unarmored, to short careers, because their hulls had to be cleaned more frequently than wooden hulls, and no colonial naval bases had dry docks large enough to service them. Such considerations kept wooden-hulled corvettes and sloops in colonial service long after the introduction of iron-hulled cruising warships, and also made composite ships (built with wooden hulls covering an iron frame) a popular choice for showing the flag overseas.[56]

During the 1870s, the introduction of the self-propelled torpedo stimulated the construction of small torpedo craft. When the British navy held a competition for torpedo boat contracts, Thornycroft's *Lightning* (1876), a 32-ton boat capable of 19 knots, prevailed against larger and slower vessels. The *Lightning* owed its speed to a forced draught boiler, developed to solve the problem of how to draw more steam from an engine limited in size by the cramped dimensions of the boat. The forced draught system was so efficient that manufacturers soon applied it to boilers built for all other warship types.[57] By the end of the decade Thornycroft had constructed 12 of the British navy's first 18 torpedo boats and several more for foreign navies. During the 1880s, the major and minor naval powers alike commissioned large numbers of boats of various modified *Lightning* types.

In light of the fact that France led the way in emphasizing torpedo warfare in the 1880s, it is ironic that, during the 1870s, the French, too, ordered most of their first torpedo craft from Thornycroft and developed no innovative torpedo boat designs of their own. Reflecting the priority given to rebuilding the French army, the navy's share of the French defense outlay fell from 32 percent in 1870 to 23 percent in 1872; in the latter year the British navy received almost twice as much funding as the French.[58] With the government in no position to continue its tradition of subsidizing breakthrough technologies, the much-maligned industrial private sector filled the void. After adopting the Siemens Martin open-hearth process to produce steel strong enough for use in warship construction, Schneider of Creusot pioneered the manufacture of all-steel armor plate. The French were poised to become leaders in all-steel warship construction as well, but production setbacks and the Third Republic's financial problems ultimately left them behind other naval powers in both areas. In the 1870s French capital ship design followed its own unique path, as heavy guns in barbettes atop a battery in an armored casemate gave way to heavier barbette guns on deck and no battery in the hull below.[59] The first battleship laid down under the republic, the 9,220-ton central battery ship *Redoutable* (built 1873–78), was the first capital ship in any navy to be built primarily of steel. It had four 10.8-inch guns, one at each corner of the casemate, all capable of end-on fire thanks to the exaggerated tumblehome of the hull. Another four 10.8-inch pivoting guns, two atop the casemate, one in the bow and one in the stern, were practically unprotected. The 10,450-ton *Courbet* (1875–86) and *Dévastation* (1876–82) were larger versions of the *Redoutable* and the last of ten central battery ships built for the French navy.[60]

The 11,030-ton *Amiral Duperré* (1877–83) was the first French battleship to carry its entire primary armament in barbettes: four 13.4-inch guns, each mounted in its own barbette, two abreast forward and two on the centerline, amidships and aft. By the time of its commissioning, the French navy had ordered another ten barbette battleships, experimenting with designs as large as the 11,720-ton *Amiral Baudin* and *Formidable,* and as small as the four units of the 7,530-ton *Terrible* class. During the same years, the French constructed two smaller barbette ships for coastal defense and four to serve overseas as armored cruisers. The French navy wanted to protect its barbette ships with compound iron-and-steel armor but Schneider of Creusot refused to fill the orders, insisting instead on providing all-steel armor of the type exported to Italy for the Italian *Duilio* and *Dandolo,* even after trials in 1880 raised doubts about its strength. In the end, however, Schneider proved incapable of manufacturing enough steel armor for all of the warships in the French program, and had to fulfill its contracts with compound armor imported from abroad. Thus, the protection of the French barbette ships included a mixture of both compound armor and all-steel plates.[61]

The new barbette cruisers begun in the 1870s, when added to the ten central battery cruisers laid down in the late 1860s, gave the French many more armored cruising ships than any other navy. To modernize its unarmored cruising fleet, the navy built 3 iron-hulled frigates, the 5,905-ton *Duquesne* (1873–78), the 5,700-ton *Tourville* (1873–77), and the 3,480-ton *Duguay-Trouin* (1873–79), and in the years 1874–80 laid down 28 composite corvettes, gunboats, and dispatch vessels. One of the dispatch vessels, the *Voltigeur* (1876–79), was the first warship fitted with a modern water-tube boiler manufactured by Belleville.

Thereafter, the Belleville boiler was adopted by almost all major navies for warships of all types. By the time of its eclipse at the turn of the century, it was being produced under license in several countries.[62]

After the unification of Germany in 1871, the navy of the North German Confederation became the Imperial German navy. General Albrecht von Stosch became head of the new German Admiralty early in 1872, as Prince Adalbert never returned to the navy before his death in 1873, and Vice Admiral Jachmann, the operational commander during 1870–71, saw his career ruined by the navy's negligible role in the Franco–Prussian War. Stosch was a political rival of Bismarck but agreed with the chancellor on the degree of importance of sea power to Germany, remarking in 1872 that the German navy should "not . . . have the task to proceed offensively against the great European states, but . . . extend our power only where we have to represent lesser interests and where we cannot otherwise bring to bear the actual power of our state, our power on land." Bismarck agreed with him, but observed that "we must surpass all sea powers of the second rank."[63]

Stosch inherited a battle fleet of three armored frigates and another four ironclads under construction: the 3,950-ton casemate ship *Hansa*, and the three fully rigged turret ships of the 6,800-ton *Grosser Kurfürst* class (see Plate 11). During his eleven years at the helm, the navy completed these battleships and added another six: the 7,600-ton casemate ships *Kaiser* and *Deutschland*, designed by Edward Reed and built in Britain, and the four barbette battleships of the 7,600-ton *Sachsen* class, built in German shipyards (see Plate 12). In size and in speed (a mere 13.5 knots), the latter were no match for the British *Inflexible*, French *Redoutable*, Italian *Duilio*, and other new foreign battleships of their time, but Stosch defended them on the grounds that their primary purpose was coastal defense. At its birth the new German Empire had the world's third-largest merchant marine, trailing only Britain and the United States, and thus needed cruising warships to show the flag worldwide. Stosch supplemented the dozen wooden screw corvettes he inherited with eight large iron-hulled corvettes and three iron gunboats.[64] Under Stosch, the German navy appeared well on the way to achieving Bismarck's goal of surpassing all naval powers of the second rank, until the scandal and crisis following the accidental sinking of the new turret battleship *Grosser Kurfürst* in May 1878 overshadowed his last five years in office. Between 1878 and 1883 the Reichstag authorized no new battleships and reduced the naval outlay by a third.[65]

Owing to the completion of battleships laid down earlier in his tenure, by the time Stosch left office Germany had the third-largest armored fleet, trailing only Britain and France. With no construction starts after 1878, the German navy had no hope of maintaining such a high rank for long into the next decade; nevertheless, Stosch's achievements were far from ephemeral. Indeed, his insistence upon the use of domestic resources whenever possible was crucial to the establishment of the naval-industrial complex that later made Germany a first-class naval power. After the *Kaiser* and *Deutschland* (delivered from Britain in 1875), all German battleships were built in German shipyards. It took longer for Stosch to end the navy's dependence on British armor imports. Karl Stumm's foundry at Dillingen on the Saar provided "sandwich" armor (of alternating layers of iron and teak) for the *Sachsen* class battleships, before purchasing a license from a British firm, in 1880, to produce compound armor. The 870-ton gunboats *Brummer* and *Bremse*, laid down in 1883, were the first to receive the new product.[66]

As of the 1870s Krupp did not yet produce armor, but the Essen firm supplied all of the naval artillery for Germany as well as Austria–Hungary, Russia, and a number of smaller countries. Having earlier pioneered the all-steel rifled muzzle loader, Krupp introduced all-steel breech-loading ordnance ahead of the leading British and French manufacturers. During the 1870s the Royal Gun Factory at Woolwich and the leading British private manufacturer, Armstrong, both produced muzzle loaders made of steel reinforced by iron hoops. Starting in 1870 the French navy's ordnance factories at Ruelle and Nevers produced steel-tube breech loaders encased in cast iron; in 1875 both began to manufacture all-steel breech-loading artillery. Armstrong's first breech-loading guns, produced in 1878, were exported to Italy for Brin's new battleships but rejected as unsafe by the British navy. The Admiralty began to change its mind following an accident in January 1879 involving a Woolwich muzzle loader aboard the battleship *Thunderer*, which raised similar doubts about the older technology, and demonstrations that spring and summer of Krupp's latest steel breech loader, which impressed British representatives. Armstrong received orders for breech-loading guns for the new battleships *Colossus* and *Edinburgh*, and filled most of the orders for subsequent British battleships after it outperformed the navy's own Woolwich factory in the production of breech-loading ordnance.[67] By the 1880s Armstrong was Krupp's primary competitor in the export of heavy naval ordnance, but the German firm remained the clear leader of the industry.

The German navy achieved the status of Europe's third naval power largely because the battleship program that ended in 1878 coincided with a long hiatus in armored warship construction in Russia, which laid down no seagoing ironclads between 1870 and 1881, while those begun in the Baltic shipyards during the 1860s inched toward completion. The five largest iron-hulled warships took an average of eight years to complete, the armored cruiser *Minin* (built 1866–78) the longest of all. In the late 1870s the 6,140-ton *Minin*, the 5,030-ton *General Admiral* (1870–75), and the 4,840-ton *Gerzog Edinburski* (1870–77) were the most highly regarded ships in the Russian navy, but they were distinguishable from broadside armored frigates only in that they carried some of their guns in sponsons, which allowed for some radius of fire. The rest of the Russian cruising fleet consisted of wooden screw frigates, corvettes, and clippers (sloops) built in the late 1850s and early 1860s. After constructing no composite ships, Russia laid down eight small iron-hulled clippers after 1873, but just two were in service by 1877. The circular ironclads *Novgorod* and *Popov*, constructed at Nikolaiev for use in the Black Sea, were the only armored warships laid down by Russia during the 1870s. The strangest-looking ships ever built by any navy, the 2,490-ton *Novgorod* (1872–74) had a diameter of 101 feet, the 3,550-ton *Popov* (1874–77) 120 feet. Each drew only 13.5 feet of water. Envisaged as formidable floating fortresses, in service they did not handle well even in relatively calm waters, as their unique shape left them susceptible to an uncontrollable spinning motion.[68]

CONCLUSION

During the first generation of the armored warship, no country developed a new doctrine of naval warfare, then designed its ironclads accordingly; instead, all navies concentrated on the mere acquisition of ironclads regardless of type. Long after the introduction of the turret ship in 1862 and the casemate ship in 1864, navies continued to add broadside battery ironclads. Even the British navy commissioned one as late as 1873 (HMS *Triumph*), and throughout the 1870s other navies employed the type as armored cruisers.[69] Thus most fleets included a variety of ironclads, from broadside frigates and monitors to casemate ships, barbette and turret battleships, making it difficult to compare the strength of one fleet with another. By the late 1870s only ironclads of less than 2,000 tons, along with some larger monitors, were considered coastal defense vessels and not included in the battle fleet.

Britain ended 1878 with 61 armored warships built or building, of which 16 were for coastal operations. France had 59, including 17 for coastal defense. Russia was a distant third with 29, of which 19 were for coastal operations. Germany had 20, including 8 for coastal defense. Italy, with 18, and Austria–Hungary, with 11, had no ironclads of under 2,000 tons or suitable only for coastal operations. The greatest of Europe's minor naval powers, Spain, had just 7 ironclads, including 2 for coastal defense. While displacement alone was no gauge of fighting value, the sheer size of most of Britain's high seas battleships reflected the qualitative gap between the British battle fleet and those of the other leading navies. In armored warships of 6,000 tons or more,

Britain had 39, France 18, Germany 10, Italy 4, Russia 4, Austria–Hungary 3, and Spain 3. No other European navy had a warship so large and, indeed, cost alone sufficed to slow the proliferation of ironclads. The Greeks purchased two small armored warships in the late 1860s and the Portuguese one in 1876. Once Portugal joined the ironclad club, every country in the world that would own an armored warship before the First World War already had one.[70] But naval experts soon would no longer measure the strength of a fleet in terms of battleships, for naval combat in the late 1870s demonstrated both the lethal nature of the self-propelled torpedo and the vulnerability of wrought-iron armor to the latest armor-piercing shells. The possibility that an inexpensive torpedo boat might sink a battleship made naval leaders wonder if large armored warships were worth their cost. Advocates of alternative naval warfare would have their day in the era of the Jeune École, at least temporarily dislodging the traditional battle fleet from its central position in naval strategy.

NOTES

[1] Napoleon III to Théodore Ducos, Paris, 16 November 1854, text in Baxter, *Introduction of the Ironclad Warship*, 342–4. Lyons quoted in Lambert, *The Crimean War*, 260; Lambert considers the performance of the batteries to have been "much exaggerated." See also Lyons to Secretary of the Admiralty Thomas Phinn, *Royal Albert*, 18 October 1855, in Dewar (ed.), *Russian War, 1855, Black Sea*, 346–7; Lambert, "Iron Hulls and Armour Plate," 53.

[2] Lambert, "Iron Hulls and Armour Plate," 53.

[3] Lambert, "The Screw Propeller Warship," 41, 46; *idem, Battleships in Transition*, 65, 122–47. During the Crimean War, the Spanish navy commissioned two 86-gun ships of the line, but plans to give them engines were never carried out, leaving the Spanish fleet with the last two sailing ships of the line ever built but no screw liners. See Harbron, *Trafalgar and the Spanish Navy*, 173n.

[4] Lambert, *Battleships in Transition*, 101, 122–43 *passim; idem*, "Iron Hulls and Armour Plate," 53–4; *Conway's All the World's Fighting Ships, 1860–1905* (London, 1979), 286–7 [hereafter cited as *Conway, 1860–1905*].

[5] Lambert, "Iron Hulls and Armour Plate," 54; *Conway, 1860–1905*, 4; Campbell, "Naval Armaments and Armour," 158–9.

[6] Lambert, *Battleships in Transition*, 92–3, 114; *idem*, "The Screw Propeller Warship," 43; *Conway, 1860–1905*, 45, 284. In the abortive big frigate race of the late 1850s the French were less imaginative than the British or the Americans, launching a homogeneous class of six 3,765-ton frigates in 1856–57, each equipped with a conventional armament of 56 guns. They were the largest wooden screw frigates ever built by the French, but were considerably weaker than their British and American counterparts.

[7] David K. Brown, *Warrior to Dreadnought: Warship Development, 1860–1905* (London, 1997), 12–13; Lambert, "The Screw Propeller Warship," 43; *idem*, "Iron Hulls and Armour Plate," 55–7; *Conway, 1860–1905*, 7.

[8] Lambert, "Iron Hulls and Armour Plate," 57–8; *Conway, 1860–1905*, 7–13.

[9] Sondhaus, *The Habsburg Empire and the Sea*, 192, 202, 205; Mariano Gabriele, *La politica navale italiana dall'unità alla viglia di Lissa* (Milan, 1958), 29–30.

[10] Sondhaus, *The Habsburg Empire and the Sea*, 209–13; Gabriele, *La politica navale italiana*, 89, 129; Franco Bargoni, *Le prime navi di linea della marina italiana, 1861–1880* (Rome, 1976), *passim*; *Conway, 1860–1905*, 380.

[11] Tomitch, *Warships of the Imperial Russian Navy*, 98–9; *Conway, 1860–1905*, 173, 380.

[12] Watts, *The Imperial Russian Navy*, 14; Tomitch, *Warships of the Imperial Russian Navy*, 101; Gromov *et al.*, *Tri Veka Rossiiskogo Flota*, 1:211.

[13] Watts, *The Imperial Russian Navy*, 14.

[14] Lambert, *Battleships in Transition*, 113–14.

[15] Busk, *Navies of the World*, 41; Lambert, "Iron Hulls and Armour Plate," 53.

[16] Stanley Sandler, *The Emergence of the Modern Capital Ship* (Newark, DE, 1979), 177–233; Brown, *Warrior to Dreadnought*, 41–52; *Conway, 1860–1905*, 19–25, 111. On the Laird rams, see Warren F. Spencer, *The Confederate Navy in Europe* (Tuscaloosa, AL, 1983), 111, 116; on the *Captain*, see Arthur Hawkey, *Black Night off Finisterre: The Tragic Tale of an Early British Ironclad* (Annapolis, MD, 1999).

[17] David K. Brown, "The Era of Uncertainty, 1863–1878," in *Steam, Steel and Shellfire: The Steam Warship 1815–1905*, ed. Robert Gardiner (London, 1992), 76–8; *Conway, 1860–1905*, 4–5, 12–18. On Reed's opposition to Coles on the construction of the *Captain* see Beeler, *British Naval Policy*, 110–23.

[18] Sandler, *Emergence of the Modern Capital Ship*, 24, 171–2, 234–49; Brown, *Warrior to Dreadnought*, 58–63; idem, "The Era of Uncertainty, 1863–1878," 80–3; *Conway, 1860–1905*, 22–4, 111; Griffiths, "Warship Machinery," 175.

[19] Dupont and Taillemite, *Les guerres navales françaises*, 249–50; *Conway, 1860–1905*, 286, 320.

[20] Baxter, *Introduction of the Ironclad Warship*, 330; *Conway, 1860–1905*, 288–9.

[21] *Conway, 1860–1905*, 298, 301–2.

[22] Campbell, "Naval Armaments and Armour," 159.

[23] Brown, "The Era of Uncertainty, 1863–1878," 89; idem, *Warrior to Dreadnought*, 14, 20; *Conway, 1860–1905*, 47, 50.

[24] *Conway, 1860–1905*, 45–6.

[25] Watts, *The Imperial Russian Navy*, 14; Tomitch, *Warships of the Imperial Russian Navy*, 96 and *passim*; Campbell, "Naval Armaments and Armour," 168. The Russians even hired the former Bavarian artilleryman Wilhelm Bauer, inventor in 1850 of the *Brandtaucher*, a 26-foot manually powered submarine designed for use against the Danish blockade of Kiel during the war over Schleswig–Holstein. In St Petersburg he built a much larger (56-foot) submarine, known to history by the French name *Le Diable Marin*. Bauer's "sea devil" made over 130 dives in trials conducted after its completion in 1856, too late to be used in the Crimean War. Russian naval and engineering officers likewise experimented with submarine designs during and after the Crimean War. During the same years several primitive submarines were built in other countries, and there remain many competing claims to undersea breakthroughs and accomplishments. Even Spain had a submarine pioneer, Narcisso Monturiol, who built the steam-powered submarine *Ictineo* at Barcelona in 1859–60. See Michael Wilson, "Early Submarines," in *Steam, Steel and Shellfire: The Steam Warship 1815–1905*, ed. Robert Gardiner (London, 1992), 148–52.

[26] *Conway, 1860–1905*, 374.

[27] Ibid., 360–77 *passim*.

[28] Unless otherwise noted, the sources for this section are Sondhaus, *The Habsburg Empire and the Sea*, 239–41, 277; idem, *Preparing for Weltpolitik*, 73, 76–82, 259 n.8; Robert Steen Steensen, *Vore Panserskibe, 1863–1943* (Copenhagen, 1968), 137–8, 146, 148–9, 160–8, 178–83; idem, *Vore Krydsere* (Copenhagen, 1971), 37; Erich Gröner, *Die deutschen Kriegsschiffe, 1815–1945*, 8 vols (Coblenz, 1989), 1:68–9, 107, 113–14, 160–2; and Gert Laursen, "Kontraadmiral Edouard Suenson," http://www.milhist.dk/soldiers/Suenson/suenson.html (accessed 25 June 2001). There is no recent comprehensive Danish account of the navy's role in 1864. Otto Georg Lütken, *Søkrigsbegivenhederne i 1864* (Copenhagen, 1896), remains the most detailed study.

[29] The Danes apparently still claim Helgoland as a victory. The frigate *Jylland* is preserved in Copenhagen as a national historic monument. See F. H. Kjølsen, "The Old Danish Frigate," *The Mariner's Mirror* 51 (1965): 27–33.

[30] Sondhaus, *Preparing for Weltpolitik*, 82–4.

[31] Lawrence Sondhaus, *The Naval Policy of Austria–Hungary: Navalism, Industrial Development, and the Politics of Dualism, 1867–1918* (West Lafayette, IN, 1994), 6; Bargoni, *Le prime navi di linea della marina italiana, passim*.

[32] Instructions to Persano summarized in Depretis to Ricasoli, Florence, 17 July 1866, in Sergio Camerani and Gaetano Arfè (eds), *Carteggi di Bettino Ricasoli*, vol. 22: *20 giugno-31 luglio 1866* (Rome, 1967), 298, no. 421, which confirms that the Lissa campaign was intended only as a prelude to a direct assault on Istria and Dalmatia.

[33] Sondhaus, *The Habsburg Empire and the Sea*, 254–5; Luigi Donolo, "The History of Italian Naval Doctrine," in *A Doctrine Reader: The Navies of United States, Great Britain, France, Italy, and Spain*, ed. James J. Tritten and Luigi Donolo (Newport, RI, 1995), 102–3.

[34] Sondhaus, *The Habsburg Empire and the Sea*, 255–8; Tegetthoff to Baroness Emma Lutteroth, 22 July 1866, text in Maximilian Daublebsky von Sterneck zu Ehrenstein, *Admiral Max Freiherr von Sterneck: Erinnerungen aus den Jahren 1847 bis 1897*, ed. Jerolim Benko von Boinik (Vienna, 1901), 149–50.

[35] James J. Tritten, "Doctrine and Fleet Tactics in the Royal Navy," in *A Doctrine Reader: The Navies of United States, Great Britain, France, Italy, and Spain*, ed. James J. Tritten and Luigi Donolo (Newport, RI, 1995), 21; idem, "Navy and Military Doctrine in France," 54. On Philip Colomb see D. M. Schurman, *Education of a Navy: The Development of British Naval Strategic Thought, 1867–1914* (Malabar, FL, 1984), 36–59.

[36] The sources for this section are Sondhaus, *Preparing for Weltpolitik*, 91–100; Dupont and Taillemite, *Les guerres navales françaises*, 251–4; Campbell, "Naval Armaments and Armour," 160.

[37] Lambert, "Iron Hulls and Armour Plate," 53; *Conway, 1860–1905*, 13, 286, 338, 380–1; Sondhaus, *Preparing for Weltpolitik*, 190; Beeler, *British Naval Policy*, 91.

[38] *Conway, 1860–1905*, 15, 287; Sondhaus, *Preparing for Weltpolitik*, 123–4.

[39] *Conway, 1860–1905*, 51, 56, 198, 317, 321; Sondhaus, *The Naval Policy of Austria–Hungary*, 26.

[40] Tritten, "Navy and Military Doctrine in France," 54; Hamilton, *Anglo–French Naval Rivalry*, 108–9, 115–16; Lambert, *Battleships in Transition*, 109.

[41] Hamilton, *Anglo–French Naval Rivalry*, 117, 138, 143. On John Colomb see Schurman, *Education of a Navy*, 16–35.

[42] David Lyon, "Underwater Warfare and the Torpedo Boat," in *Steam, Steel, and Shellfire: The Steam Warship, 1815–1905*, ed. Robert Gardiner (London, 1992), 136; Campbell, "Naval Armaments and Armour," 166; Antonio Casali and Marina

Cattaruzza, *Sotto i mari del mondo: La Whitehead, 1875–1990* (Rome, 1990), 12–13; Brown, "The Era of Uncertainty, 1863–1878," 92.

[43] Franck to Wüllerstorf, 4 September 1866, Haus- Hof- und Staatsarchiv, AR, F44-Marinewesen, Carton 3: Generalia 1860–70, quoted in Sondhaus, *The Naval Policy of Austria–Hungary*, 9.

[44] Sondhaus, *The Naval Policy of Austria–Hungary*, 9–10, 16–26, 44–5.

[45] Donolo, "The History of Italian Naval Doctrine," 105.

[46] Sondhaus, *The Naval Policy of Austria–Hungary*, 26–7; Franco Micali Baratelli, *La marina militare italiana nella vita nazionale, 1860–1914* (Mursia, 1983), 237–8; Lucio Ceva, *Le forze armate* (Turin, 1981), 103.

[47] Sondhaus, *The Naval Policy of Austria–Hungary*, 49.

[48] Franco Bargoni, *Corazzate italiane classi Duilio–Italia–Ruggiero di Lauria, 1880–1892* (Rome, 1977), *passim*; *Conway 1860–1905*, 341–2; John Roberts, "Warships of Steel, 1879–1889," in *Steam, Steel and Shellfire: The Steam Warship 1815–1905*, ed. Robert Gardiner (London, 1992), 97.

[49] *Conway, 1860–1905*, 345.

[50] Sondhaus, *The Naval Policy of Austria–Hungary*, 45–7; Bargoni, *Corazzate italiane classi Duilio–Italia–Ruggiero di Lauria, passim*.

[51] Sondhaus, *The Naval Policy of Austria–Hungary*, 26, 392.

[52] Beeler, *British Naval Policy*, 10–11, 19, 202, 209.

[53] Brown, "The Era of Uncertainty, 1863–1878," 78; *Conway, 1860–1905*, 17–18.

[54] Brown, *Warrior to Dreadnought*, 203; *idem*, "The Era of Uncertainty, 1863–1878," 84–6; *Conway, 1860–1905*, 26; Griffiths, "Warship Machinery," 176.

[55] Roberts, "Warships of Steel, 1879–1889," 96–7; Brown, *Warrior to Dreadnought*, 167. On the Battle of the Yalu see Sondhaus, *Naval Warfare, 1815–1914*, 170–2.

[56] Beeler, *British Naval Policy*, 21, 215, 218; *Conway, 1860–1905*, 47–52, 56–8, 63–4; Brown, *Warrior to Dreadnought*, 70.

[57] Brown, "The Era of Uncertainty, 1863–1878," 92; Griffiths, "Warship Machinery," 176.

[58] Ray Walser, *France's Search for a Battle Fleet: Naval Policy and Naval Power, 1898–1914* (New York, 1992), 3; Beeler, *British Naval Policy*, 193, 205; *Conway, 1860–1905*, 330–1.

[59] Brown, "The Era of Uncertainty, 1863–1878," 86.

[60] Ibid., 86; Roberts, "Warships of Steel, 1879–1889," 96; *Conway, 1860–1905*, 289–90, 299.

[61] Roberts, "Warships of Steel, 1879–1889," 97–100; *Conway, 1860–1905*, 290–2, 300, 302–3.

[62] John Roberts, "The Pre-Dreadnought Age, 1890–1905," in *Steam, Steel and Shellfire: The Steam Warship 1815–1905*, ed. Robert Gardiner (London, 1992), 114; Griffiths, "Warship Machinery," 177; *Conway, 1860–1905*, 284, 314–21, 323.

[63] Stosch quoted in Ivo Nikolai Lambi, *The Navy and German Power Politics, 1862–1914* (Boston, MA, 1984), 4, and Ekkard Verchau, "Von Jachmann über Stosch und Caprivi," in *Marine und Marinepolitik im kaiserlichen Deutschland, 1871–1914*, ed. Herbert Schlottelius and Wilhelm Deist (Düsseldorf, 1972), 59; Bismarck quoted in Wilhelm Gerloff, *Finanz- und Zollpolitik des Deutschen Reiches* (Jena, 1913), 79.

[64] Sondhaus, *Preparing for Weltpolitik*, 113–15; Gröner, *Die deutschen Kriegsschiffe*, 1:28–33, 70–1, 117, 164–6.

[65] Sondhaus, *Preparing for Weltpolitik*, 125–35.

[66] Ibid., 136, 140.

[67] Roberts, "Warships of Steel, 1879–1889," 97–8.

[68] Watts, *The Imperial Russian Navy*, 15; Woodward, *The Russians at Sea*, 110; *Conway, 1860–1905*, 174–7, 186, 198.

[69] James J. Tritten, "Revolutions in Military Affairs, Paradigm Shifts, and Doctrine," in *A Doctrine Reader: The Navies of United States, Great Britain, France, Italy, and Spain*, ed. James J. Tritten and Luigi Donolo (Newport, RI, 1995), 145.

[70] *Conway, 1860–1905*, 378, 387.

4

TORPEDO WARFARE, CRUISERS, AND THE JEUNE ÉCOLE, 1878–89

The technological developments of the mid-1870s laid the foundation for the Jeune École, the French "Young School" promoting a strategy of cruiser and torpedo warfare. The international campaign against the battleship gained momentum after aggressive Russian torpedo operations paralysed a Turkish armored fleet during the Russo–Turkish War of 1877–78. The influence of the school grew through the early 1880s and peaked in 1886–87, when its founder, Admiral Théophile Aube, served as French navy minister. For the previous quarter-century Aube had considered the capabilities of ironclads overrated. A veteran of years of service on overseas stations, his vision of naval warfare naturally centered around colonies and sea lanes. He considered the British Empire particularly vulnerable to an aggressive campaign of commerce raiding, and saw in the modern steel cruiser, the self-propelled torpedo and the torpedo boat a combination that would give France the means to challenge British naval power worldwide. By the mid-1880s the Jeune École had a near-universal impact, as most of the great powers built many more cruisers and torpedo boats, and fewer battleships. But the ideas of the school were controversial, even in the French navy itself, where alternating administrations supporting and opposing Aube's ideas caused havoc in the construction program. Within Europe, the Jeune École had its most dramatic impact in Austria–Hungary, which considered the strategy a cost-effective deterrent to Italy's battleship buildup, and in Germany, where its adoption caused the fleet to fall from third place to fifth in armored tonnage.

THE BIRTH OF THE STEEL CRUISER

Within a few years of the development of the self-propelled torpedo, the British *Lightning* (1876) provided a general model for the torpedo boat which all other navies soon copied. In contrast, the modern cruiser had a much slower progression. Twenty years after the capital ship changed from a wooden ship of the line to an armored battleship, navies had yet to reconceptualize the cruising warship, continuing instead to build fully rigged screw frigates and corvettes, albeit with new materials. Thus the composite and iron cruisers of the 1870s, and the first steel cruisers, still had the general appearance and capabilities of cruising warships of the past.[1] The Jeune École finally provided the impetus for change, as the new strategy demanded the redefinition of the cruiser as a modern warship. As a result, within a dozen years the masts and yards and light armament disappeared, in favor of powerful engines, heavy guns capable of firing armor-piercing ordnance, and torpedo tubes for self-propelled torpedoes. The older cruisers of Europe's navies continued to serve throughout the 1880s, indeed, providing the muscle behind the so-called "new imperialism," in which Germany and Italy established their colonial empires and Britain and France added to their overseas possessions. But by the 1890s, even in distant waters, fully rigged cruisers were no longer taken seriously as warships once countries deployed their first modern steel cruisers.

While the French navy came to view the modern steel cruiser as the key to challenging British maritime supremacy, the type was first developed in Britain. After 1874 the Landore works in Wales became the first in Britain to produce steel using the same Siemens Martin open-hearth process as Schneider of Creusot, in a quantity and quality sufficient to support steel warship construction. Nathaniel Barnaby used Landore steel for his 3,730-ton all-steel cruisers *Iris* and *Mercury*, laid down in the winter of 1875–76 and completed in 1879. The two ships had a traditional appearance but modern capabilities, and thus represent a transition from the old to the new in cruiser construction. They were graceful three-masted vessels, and the *Iris* even had a clipper bow, but both ships had engines capable of unprecedented speeds; the *Mercury* made 18.5 knots in its trials, and for almost a decade no warship its size or larger equalled its speed. The *Iris* and *Mercury* were rated as second-class cruisers, yet their purpose remained unclear. Nevertheless, the British remained the leaders in developing the type. They constructed their last wooden-hulled cruiser in 1875 and their last iron hull in 1878, thereafter employing steel-hulled vessels to replace most older cruising warships as they were decommissioned. The dozen steel corvettes of the *Comus* and *Calypso* classes (completed 1878–84) were built alongside the thirteen composite corvettes of the *Emerald* and *Satellite* classes (completed 1876–84), but the latter were the last British warships of their size not constructed of steel. The sloops and gunboats employed as the smallest overseas cruisers likewise evolved from wood to composite to steel construction, losing more sailing rig with each new design. The thirteen modern steel cruisers of the *Leander*, *Mersey*, and *Medea* classes, begun between 1880 and 1887, were rated as second-class cruisers. By 1889 22 third-class steel cruisers had been laid down.[2]

Of all the shipbuilders involved in steel cruiser construction, Armstrong made the greatest breakthrough, and for the export market rather than the British navy. In 1881 the firm's Elswick shipyard laid down the cruiser *Esmeralda* for Chile, which at the time was fighting the War of the Pacific (1879–84) against Peru. George Rendel designed this first "Elswick cruiser" intending to make a clean break with the past. The 3,000-ton warship was built entirely of steel, with two military masts, no sailing rig, engines capable of 18 knots, a primary armament of two 10-inch pivoting guns (one fore and one aft), a secondary armament of six 6-inch pivoting guns (three in each broadside), and three torpedo tubes. The *Esmeralda* was history's first "protected" cruiser, featuring some armor around its gun mountings and two inches of deck armor, but no hull armor even at the waterline. At the time of the ship's delivery to Chile in 1884 (too late to see action against Peru), the British navy had no second-class steel cruiser of comparable strength. Rendel soon designed Elswick cruisers for Austria–Hungary (two, completed 1885–86), Italy (three, 1885–89), and Romania (one, 1888), as well as for Japan, China, Argentina, and Brazil. Armstrong had already established itself as the industry leader in steel cruiser construction by the time the British navy finally ordered its first Elswick cruisers, the first two of nine units of the 2,575-ton *Pearl* class, in 1888.[3] By then, Rendel's designs were being copied by a number of foreign shipbuilders. Notwithstanding its relatively small size and lack of armor, the heavily armed protected cruiser was hailed by proponents of the Jeune École as "the battleship of the future."[4]

THE RUSSO–TURKISH WAR (1877–78)

While the steel cruiser design emerged in Britain in the late 1870s and early 1880s, the concepts of torpedo warfare central to the Jeune École received their first primitive test in the Russo–Turkish War of 1877–78. In April 1877 a two-year-old Balkan crisis culminated in a Russian declaration of war against the Turks. At that time, Russia had 29 ironclads built or building, but 19 were designed for coastal operations and all except the circular *Novgorod* and *Popov* were in the Baltic. In contrast, the Ottoman Empire had 13 seagoing ironclads, 2 coastal ironclads, and 7 small river monitors. This impressive fleet, assembled during the recent reign of Sultan Abdul Aziz (1861–76), included the largest case-mate ship ever built, the 9,120-ton *Mesudiye*. Designed by Edward Reed and built by the Thames Iron Works, it had wrought-iron casemate and belt armor as thick as twelve inches. Because Russia had done little to build up the Black Sea Fleet since its restoration in 1871, the Ottoman Empire enjoyed a superiority at sea in the war zone rivaling that of the Western powers during the Crimean War. Indeed, the British and French considered the Turks strong enough to defend themselves and did not intervene.[5]

While the Russian army marched southward around both sides of the Black Sea, Russian naval leaders opted not to stand on the defensive despite the overwhelming superiority of the Ottoman fleet. Instead, the Black Sea Fleet prepared to wage a campaign of torpedo warfare, sup-plemented by nineteen fast merchant steamers of 1,000–1,500 tons, requisitioned for duty as tenders for small steam launches. The launches were armed with spar torpedoes, towed torpedoes, and ulti-mately self-propelled torpedoes. The Ottoman Danube flotilla became their first target, as it blocked the way for Russia's Balkan army to cross the great river from Romania into Turkish Bulgaria. To prevent the rein-forcement or retreat of the flotilla's two armored corvettes and seven small monitors, the Russians laid mines at the mouth of the river. As their troops neared the Danube, Russian field artillery joined the navy's torpedo attacks in putting the Turks on the defensive. On 11 May 1877 at Iriali, Russian army guns sank the 2,540-ton armored corvette *Lüft-ü Celil*, and two weeks later at Maçin, a steam launch equipped with a spar torpedo sank the 400-ton river monitor *Seyfi*. The latter attack marked the first time in history that a torpedo craft had sunk its target without also sinking; nevertheless, the attacks by the torpedo launches often bordered on suicidal, and the lieutenants commanding them (including two future admirals of the Russo–Japanese War, Stepan Makarov and Zinovy Rozhestvensky) showed considerable courage as well as resourcefulness, devising their tactics as the campaign unfolded. Early in the war the launches almost always failed to damage or destroy their targets, usually because they could not steam close enough to deliver their spar or towed torpedoes. The Turks also devised counter-measures such as deploying surface booms around their ironclads. On 10 June, such a device thwarted an attack by launches from the tender *Veliki Kniaz Konstantin* against four Ottoman ironclads at Sulina; on 23 June, anti-torpedo nets saved a Turkish monitor during an attack at Nikopol, where the Russian army was preparing to cross the Danube. In the end, the army's artillery proved more lethal to the Ottoman flotilla than the navy's torpedo attacks, damaging two monitors on 28 June during the barrage covering the crossing by the troops. On 16 July the Russians captured another two monitors, leaving just two of seven Ottoman river monitors still in service undamaged. At that stage, the

Turks withdrew their flotilla downstream. The Russian mine barrage laid earlier at the mouth of the Danube proved ineffective; it sank a Turkish wooden gunboat, but only months later, in October.

The end of the campaign on the Danube and in the western Black Sea freed the Russians to redeploy several of their tenders and torpedo launches to the eastern Black Sea, where the Ottoman navy had operated virtually unopposed since the onset of the fighting. The Russians suffered their greatest defeat of the war on 14 May 1877, when an Ottoman armored squadron of five casemate corvettes and one battery corvette shelled Sochi, then landed troops which secured the city for the Turks. In preparation for the eastern campaign, the Russians painted their torpedo launches sea-green, the first known case of warships being camouflaged in a color approximating that of the surrounding waters. The first action of their counterattack came on the night of 23–24 August, when launches from two different tenders attacked the casemate ship *Asar-i Şevket* at Sukkum Kale and the battery corvette *Asar-i Tevfik* at Sochi. While the former survived unscathed, the latter was damaged by a spar torpedo which detonated below its waterline, and had to withdraw to Batum for repairs. In late summer the Russian army took Sochi, then advanced on Batum. Russian torpedo launches first used self-propelled torpedoes on 27 December 1877, in an attack on the port of Batum. In another raid on the port on the night of 25–26 January 1878, two launches successfully targeted the wooden screw gunboat *Intikbah*, which became the first warship ever sunk by the new weapon. Less than a week later, the Russians occupied Batum under the terms of the armistice which ended the war.

Concerned that Russia still intended to deal a fatal blow to the Ottoman Empire, Britain belatedly intervened in the conflict. On 13 February a reinforced British Mediterranean Fleet passed through the Dardanelles, after which the Russian Balkan army advanced to San Stefano, six miles from Constantinople. In anticipation of war with Britain, Russia sent a squadron of the Baltic Fleet to Sveaborg, led by the turret ship *Petr Veliki*, the armored frigates *Petropavlovsk* and *Sevastopol*, and the casemate ship *Kniaz Pozharski*. Most of the navy's monitors and screw gunboats were mobilized to defend the Baltic coast, and Russian agents negotiated with German and American companies to purchase, arm, and fuel a fleet of raiders to attack British commerce. Britain responded by increasing the superiority of its battle fleet through the seizure and purchase of foreign warships under construction in British shipyards, a tactic used in future crises, especially on the eve of the First World War. Vessels seized during the Anglo–Russian war scare of 1878 included the 9,120-ton *Hamidiye*, sister-ship of the *Mesudiye*, under construction at the Thames Iron Works for the Ottoman navy, which entered service as *Superb* (1880); two 4,870-ton armored rams being built by Samuda for the Ottoman navy, which were commissioned as *Belleisle* (1878) and *Orion* (1882); and the 9,130-ton masted turret ship *Independencia*, built at Millwall for Brazil, which entered service as *Neptune* (1881). Bismarck's diplomacy averted war, and Germany subsequently hosted the Congress of Berlin, which reversed the draconian Treaty of San Stefano (3 March 1878). Russia kept all of its territorial gains but agreed to more modest borders for an independent Bulgaria and accepted Austria–Hungary's occupation of the rebellious Ottoman province of Bosnia–Hercegovina. Britain also occupied Turkish territory, adding Cyprus to its empire in order to further safeguard its Eastern Mediterranean interests. While a general European war was avoided, the confrontation of February–March 1878 strained the Anglo–Russian relationship for the remainder of the century and beyond. Having stopped the Russians from taking Constantinople, British strategists considered it crucial that the navy should be able to repeat the operation, not so much to save the Ottoman capital from the Russian army, but to prevent a strengthened Russian Black Sea Fleet from forcing the straits and entering the Eastern Mediterranean, where it would imperil the Suez Canal and Egypt, which Britain made a protectorate in 1882.[6]

In the Black Sea Fleet's makeshift campaign of 1877–78, the traditionally cautious Russian naval leadership took advantage of the heroic efforts of bold and imaginative junior officers to neutralize a superior Ottoman battle fleet. Fearful of losing the giant new *Mesudiye* and other large armored warships, the Ottoman navy simply kept them in port. Indeed, aside from the battery frigates *Mahmudiye* and *Osmaniye*, which saw duty mostly as troop transports, the Turks fought the war at sea with ironclads displacing 3,000 tons or less. Skeptics could point to the fact that few Turkish warships were actually sunk: a small monitor and a wooden screw gunboat by torpedoes, an armored corvette and another wooden screw gunboat by other means.[7] Nevertheless, to supporters of the Jeune École in the 1880s, the Russian torpedo campaign provided conclusive evidence that inexpensive torpedo boats could paralyse a fleet of expensive enemy battleships, and that torpedo flotillas constituted a more effective deterrent than a vulnerable battle fleet. Fearing that this might be the case, the leading battleship power, Britain, hedged its bets later in 1878 by commissioning its first torpedo boat tender, the *Hecla*, a 6,400-ton converted merchant liner.[8]

EUROPEAN NAVIES AND THE JEUNE ÉCOLE STRATEGY

While the Russo–Turkish War demonstrated the psychological impact the torpedo threat could have against a superior ironclad fleet, the following year a conflict far from European waters cast further doubt over the feasability of armored warships. Early in the War of the Pacific

(1879–84), Chilean ironclads fired armor-piercing shells of a type designed by British general Sir William Palliser, which penetrated eight inches of wrought-iron armor on the turret of the Peruvian ironclad *Huáscar*. Most armored warships with wrought-iron protection did not have armor thicker than that, and those that did – such as the Turkish *Mesudiye* and British *Superb*, with their twelve inches of casemate armor – had to displace over 9,000 tons in order to bear the weight of their protection, which in any event was limited to the casemate and waterline. Naval ordnance had advanced to the point where no battleship could be fitted with wrought iron thick enough to assure its safety without compromising its seaworthiness. The problem could be solved by the introduction of thinner and lighter yet stronger armor, but most navies remained skeptical of the newly developed all-steel and compound iron-and-steel plates. To make matters worse for the battleship, the power of the self-propelled torpedo received further confirmation in the sinking of two Chilean warships by Peruvian torpedo boats during 1880. Self-propelled torpedoes had yet to sink an armored warship, but almost every year witnessed advances in their speed and range, as well as in the size of explosive charge carried. Most experts doubted that primitive anti-torpedo devices such as the surface booms improvised by the Turks in 1877–78 would be able to protect battleships from the mounting danger.[9]

Thus, by the early 1880s the general technological factors that provided the framework for the Jeune École were all in place: the advent of the fast steel cruiser, the emergence of the self-propelled torpedo, and rising doubts about the feasability of large armored warships. The new school of thought arose in France because of the French inclination, since the time of Paixhans, to embrace new technologies as a means to redress the naval balance of power, and because of the tradition of the *guerre de course*, which predisposed many French naval thinkers to favor cruiser-based commerce raiding as an anti-British strategy. Vice Admiral Baron Richild Grivel, author of *De la guerre maritime avant et depuis les nouvelles inventions* (1869), was the ideological forefather of the Jeune École, recognizing late in the reign of Napoleon III that the emperor's long quest to match Britain in capital ships (first wooden screw liners, then armored warships) was doomed to fail. Admiral Aube, leader of the new school of thought, further developed its concepts in *La guerre maritime et les ports française* (1882), *A terre et à bord, notes d'un marin* (1884), and *De la guerre navale* (1885). Thereafter, the most significant French works were by journalist Gabriel Charmes, *La reforme de la marine* (1886), and by Commander Gabriel Fontin and Lieutenant Paul Vignot, *Essai de stratégie navale* (1893). Because the Third Republic gave the navy less generous funding than the imperial government had before 1870, most French officers embraced the new paradigm of naval warfare as an alternative to despair over the fact that

France would never equal Britain in capital ship strength. Yet through-out the period a number of senior officers and politicians opposed the strategy, a fact reflected in the frequently reshuffled cabinets of the republic. Between 1870 and 1900 the navy ministry changed hands thirty times, with advocates of the *guerre de course* and, from the early 1880s, the Jeune École typically alternating with traditional blue-water navy proponents. For a country with a weak industrial base, suffering from financial problems, the added burden of political instability all but guaranteed that other countries would take the lead in the intro-duction of modern cruisers and torpedo boats, despite the fact that Aube and his followers were responsible for devising the comprehen-sive strategy for their use.[10]

The founder of the Jeune École actually belonged to the older gener-ation. Born in 1826, he had spent most of his career on colonial or overseas stations, in the process developing a perspective more global than European. At heart he believed that, especially in a war against Britain, the ability to wage a worldwide *guerre de course* was much more important than having a large battle fleet in home waters, where forces designed specifically for coastal defense would suffice. He had been skeptical of ironclads from the time of their introduction and, after the advent of the steel cruiser and the self-propelled torpedo, felt that bat-tleships had outlived their usefulness. Assigned to Toulon in 1883, Aube became a great advocate of torpedo boats, and soon converted the journalist Charmes to the cause. Later that year, during maneuvers of the French Mediterranean Fleet, a pair of 46-ton torpedo boats sur-vived a heavy storm in better shape than some larger warships; after-ward, Charmes authored several articles promoting Aube's notion that torpedo boats could be used as autonomous seagoing commerce raiders. A school of thought evolved around the idea that in a modern *guerre de course*, hosts of torpedo boats would join steel cruisers in ruth-less attacks against enemy merchantmen. The Jeune École soon won a following not just among younger French naval officers, but among French Anglophobes in general, who were heartened by Aube's convic-tion that the self-propelled torpedo already had rendered Britain's superior battle fleet worthless. In addition to attacking its large and vulnerable merchant marine, Aube sought to take advantage of Britain's relatively weak coastal and harbor defenses by including in his strategy torpedo boat raids on ports and indiscriminate shelling of the enemy coastline, in the latter case to spread panic among the civilian population.[11]

Especially in the late Victorian era, a strategy encouraging such wanton destruction of lives and property understandably drew heavy criticism. In defending the Jeune École, Aube employed the language of Darwinism, arguing that "war is the negation of law.... Everything is therefore not only permissible but legitimate against the enemy."[12]

Protests over the immorality of the strategy did not prevent Aube from serving a term as navy minister in 1886–87; indeed, by then his ideas were having an impact on most navies. Torpedo-boat construction assumed a feverish pace, amid near-universal skepticism over the future of the battleship. The British naval estimates for 1886 included money to lay down the 12,590-ton battleships *Nile* and *Trafalgar*, prompting an extensive debate in Parliament in which even some of their defenders agreed they would be the last large armored warships ever built.[13] In 1887 no country laid down a battleship, the only year between the onset of work on the *Gloire* in 1858 and the beginning of international naval disarmament in 1922 for which that was the case. In France the suspension of battleship construction starts lasted for six years, from the onset of work on the last barbette battleship, the *Magenta*, in January 1883, to the first turret battleship, the *Brennus*, in January 1889. French battleship building continued throughout the intervening years, however, as the eleven barbette ships begun between 1877 and 1883 averaged nine years on the stocks.[14]

France laid down its first steel cruiser in 1882, seven years after the British *Iris* and *Mercury*. Like those ships, the 1,705-ton *Milan* included traditional design elements but also featured a plough bow that became a characteristic of future French cruisers (see Plate 13). By the time of its commissioning in 1885, Britain and the countries that had done business with Armstrong's Elswick shipyard already had steel cruisers of more modern design in service. France's first larger steel cruiser, the 4,560-ton protected cruiser *Sfax* (see Plate 14), was laid down in 1882 and completed in 1887, by which time another thirteen protected cruisers were under construction in French shipyards, from the 1,920-ton *Cosmao* to the 7,470-ton *Tage*. In contrast to the early Elswick cruisers, the French protected cruisers carried 6.4-inch guns as their primary armament. Four 1,270-ton *Condor* class torpedo cruisers and eight 400-ton *Bombe* class torpedo gunboats, laid down in 1883–84, were also tailored to serve the Jeune École strategy, as were the torpedo boats designed to function on the high seas.[15] As a general prototype for the latter, the French navy adopted Normand's 63-ton *Poti*, built in 1883 for the Russian navy. The nine boats of the 58-ton *Balny* class (built 1884–86) were followed by another nine, ranging from 104 to 117 tons, launched by 1889. In the years 1882–90 the French navy commissioned 70 coastal torpedo boats, most of which displaced either 45 or 53 tons, supplementing 58 smaller boats built during and immediately after the Russo–Turkish War. Other relatively small vessels designed specifically for coastal defense included eight armored gunboats, four of the 1,100-ton *Fusée* class and four of the 1,690-ton *Achéron* class.[16]

During the decade the navy saw action in the brief Franco–Chinese War (1884–85), which secured Indochina for the French colonial empire. The conflict came just after the ideas of the Jeune École had taken hold but long before any of the new warship types had been deployed. Vice Admiral A. A. P. Courbet destroyed China's Fukien fleet with a French force of 5 fully rigged casemate and barbette cruisers, supplemented by 26 unarmored wooden- and iron-hulled steamers. At the decisive Battle of the Min River (23 August 1884) Courbet copied the Russian tactic of 1877–78, using four steam launches as torpedo boats.[17]

In contrast to the French, throughout the era of the Jeune École the British navy never stopped building new battleships. Of the six barbette ships of the *Admiral* class (laid down 1880–83, completed 1887–89), four displaced 10,600 tons and carried four 13.5-inch guns paired in two barbettes. The first of the class, the 9,500-ton *Collingwood*, had a lighter primary armament of four 12-inch guns, and the last, the *Benbow*, two 16.25-inch guns, each in its own barbette. The *Admirals* shared some of the worst characteristics of the foreign battleships of their time, lacking adequate protection for their hulls, like Brin's Italian battleships, and for their guns, like the French barbette ships. Their successors were sounder in both respects, the 10,470-ton *Victoria* and *Sans Pareil* (built 1885–91) and the 12,590-ton *Nile* and *Trafalgar* (built 1886–91), all of which featured turrets rather than barbettes. While the *Victoria* and *Sans Pareil* carried their two 16.25-inch Armstrongs in a lone forward turret, the *Nile* and *Trafalgar* had a less novel arrangement of four 13.5-inch guns in two centerline turrets fore and aft. The *Sans Pareil* was the first battleship with triple expansion engines, introduced in merchant steamers in the 1870s and first applied in naval construction in the torpedo gunboat *Rattlesnake* (1885–87). Two 6,200-ton turret rams built alongside these ten battleships reflected some concern for coastal defense, but the *Conqueror* (built 1879–86) and *Hero* (1884–88) were larger than necessary for such duties, yet, at the same time, too small to function as battleships. The 8,500-ton armored cruisers *Imperieuse* (1881–86) and *Warspite* (1881–88) were far more useful. The *Imperieuse* was the last large British warship designed with a sailing rig, which it lost in an early renovation. From the start the *Warspite* had a single military mast. While Britain had not attempted to match France in armored cruiser construction during the 1860s and 1870s, it responded to the 14 French protected cruisers of the mid-1880s with the 7 armored cruisers of the 5,600-ton *Orlando* class (laid down 1885–86, completed in 1888–89), and the 9,150-ton first-class protected cruisers *Blake* (1888–92; see Plate 15) and *Blenheim* (1888–94). The latter pair, designed by William White, were capable of over 21 knots and able to carry 1,800 tons of coal, facilitating their mission of "long-range trade protection." Like the armored cruisers, they carried a formidable armament of two 9.2-inch and ten 6-inch guns (in contrast to other British protected cruisers, which typically had 6-inch guns as their primary armament). While they were built to deal with a threat to Britain specific to the Jeune École, down to the turn of the century several other navies built first-class cruisers modeled on their design. Thirty-seven second- and third-class steel cruisers laid down in the years 1875–89 gave the British navy a clear advantage over the French in those categories as well. Even in the torpedo craft that formed the heart of the Jeune École, Britain remained ahead of France, following the *Lightning* (1876) and the torpedo boat carrier *Hecla* (1878) with 159 torpedo boats and 17 torpedo gunboats, all in service by 1889. The first annual British naval maneuvers, held in 1885 against the backdrop of an Anglo–Russian war scare over Afghanistan, practiced an attack on a Russian Baltic port, a Jeune École scenario in which torpedo boats attempted to enter a harbor protected by a minefield and anti-torpedo boom.[18]

The strategy of the Jeune École may have come from France, but the French navy left it to others to work out the tactics of torpedo warfare. In this area the Austro–Hungarian navy established itself as a leader, and in turn was copied by the French. Under Admiral Max von Sterneck, who assumed command in 1883, the Austro–Hungarian navy hosted a number of French naval officers and politicians at its base in Pola and at the Whitehead torpedo factory in Fiume, building a relationship despite the fact that the Triple Alliance (1882) had committed Austria–Hungary to an anti-French diplomatic bloc. After visiting officers observed maneuvers in the Adriatic involving torpedo boats in simulated actions with battleships, the French navy adopted the Austro–Hungarian tactic of "hiding" a torpedo boat alongside each battleship until the smoke from heavy artillery exchanges provided cover for their attacks.[19] Since the Dual Monarchy did not yet have a naval attaché assigned to France, Sterneck maintained contact with Gabriel Charmes and French Jeune Écolist officers through his nephew, who served in Austria–Hungary's Paris embassy. He often found that his own navy had already tested many of the tactics the French were still debating on a theoretical plane. "It appears as if we have had the same ideas simultaneously, with the difference that I can put them into action immediately."[20]

Owing to Sterneck's enthusiasm for the Jeune École, the school of thought made a lasting impression in Austria–Hungary, despite the fact that the commanding admiral was not a "true believer" but had adopted its views purely on pragmatic grounds. A proponent of the armored battleship since his days as Tegetthoff's flag captain at Lissa, Sterneck recognized that with Austria–Hungary now an ally of Italy, his navy could not justify (and the government of the Dual Monarchy would never fund) a program designed to match Benedetto Brin's giant battleships. After laying down the casemate ship *Tegetthoff* (1876), the navy received authorization to start just two battleships, the 6,900-ton *Kronprinz Rudolf* (1884) and 5,100-ton *Kronprinzessin Stephanie* (1884), before the resumption of a systematic program of construction with the *Monarch* class (1893). Meanwhile, Austro–Hungarian naval construction focused on warship types that fit the strategy of the Jeune École. By 1891 Sterneck had added 53 torpedo boats to the 10 he inherited from his predecessor, and also built 6 torpedo gunboats. After ordering two small "Elswick" cruisers from Armstrong, he had another ship of the same type built in Trieste. His program culminated in two "ram cruisers," the 4,000-ton *Kaiser Franz Joseph I* (built 1888–90) and *Kaiserin Elisabeth* (1888–92), protected cruisers intended for service as flotilla leaders for torpedo boats. Their features included a heavy primary armament (two 9.4-inch Krupp guns) and no side armor, but also an anachronistic ram bow. Like the *Esmeralda* and other Elswick cruisers fitted with battleship guns, the ram cruisers were designed to provide long-range covering fire during torpedo boat attacks against enemy battleships. Because they cost half as much as the *Kronprinz Rudolf* and *Kronprinzessin Stephanie*, they were appealing to Austro–Hungarian politicians, who accepted Sterneck's contention that, as "battleships of the future," they could replace the navy's obsolete casemate ships. Thus Austria–Hungary all but abandoned battleship construction for seventeen years, and by the early 1890s had the weakest navy, by far, of any of the six great powers of Europe.[21]

Germany's contribution to the Jeune École came primarily in coastal defense, where Admiral Aube adapted many of the ideas of General Stosch, who headed the Imperial Admiralty until 1883. Aube recommended shallow-draught battleships similar to the German "sortie corvettes" of the 7,600-ton *Sachsen* class, which would be protected by fortified coastal bases until needed for sorties against an enemy blockade or to disrupt enemy troop landings.[22] Like Stosch, Aube felt that such ships would not be too weak to operate on the high seas, if needed, against larger enemy battleships. He seemed unaware of the problems the Germans experienced with the *Sachsen* class. With a profile dominated by four funnels arranged at the points of a square rather than on the centerline, these odd-looking ships earned the derisive nickname "cement factories," appropriate enough, considering they were also slow and hard to maneuver.[23]

The failure of warships designed specifically for a coastal defense mission in harmony with the Jeune École did not discourage its German supporters, in particular General Leo von Caprivi, who followed Stosch as chief of the Imperial Admiralty (1883–88). Caprivi presided over the construction of Germany's first five modern steel cruisers, of which the 4,300-ton protected cruisers *Irene* (built 1886–88) and *Prinzess Wilhelm* (1886–89) were the largest. Because neither of Germany's most likely adversaries, France and Russia, depended heavily on overseas trade, Caprivi gave little consideration to the cruiser warfare aspect of the Jeune École. Colonial considerations also mattered little to him, until the establishment of the first German colonies in Africa and the western Pacific in 1884–85. Unlike Aube, Caprivi valued torpedo boats not as autonomous high seas warships but for their defensive capabilities in the Baltic and in the coastal waters of the North Sea. He expanded their numbers dramatically, adding 65 to the 7 he inherited from Stosch. Most German torpedo boats were ordered from Schichau of Elbing, after two Schichau boats performed well in a storm in September 1884, at the end of annual maneuvers (see Plate 16). In 1886 Caprivi appointed Captain Alfred Tirpitz head of the new Torpedo Inspection at Kiel; the following year, he created separate torpedo divisions for the Baltic and North Sea stations. To supplement the production of Whitehead's German licensee, Schwartzkopf of Berlin, the navy also built its own torpedo factory at Friedrichsort.[24]

During his posting to the German Admiralty, Caprivi remained a soldier at heart. He refused to countenance the unnecessary diversion of resources away from the army, and was famous for his observation that the question should be one of "how small our fleet can be, not how large."[25] Seeking to improve the navy's chances against larger rivals without adding to its battle fleet, in 1883 Caprivi revived a plan for a canal across Holstein, to enable the fleet to concentrate rapidly in either the Baltic or North Sea, a capability he considered essential in the event Germany went to war with a Franco–Russian alliance. The Reichstag finally authorized this "Kiel Canal" in 1886, and it opened nine years later. Before leaving office Caprivi finally conceded that the German navy needed new armored warships, but only for coastal defense: the eight ships of the 3,500-ton *Siegfried* class, which carried three 9.4-inch Krupp guns in single turrets, two abreast on the foredeck and one aft (see Plate 17). Work began on the *Siegfried* in 1888, the year Caprivi left the Admiralty and naval enthusiast William II became emperor. Over the previous twelve years, the 5,200-ton casemate ship *Oldenburg* (built 1883–86) had been the only new battleship laid down in Germany. In 1883 Germany ranked third in armored tonnage, behind only Britain and France; thanks to the influence of the Jeune École, by 1893 Germany trailed all European powers except Austria–Hungary in both armored tonnage and total warship tonnage.[26]

Italy and Russia passed Germany in armored tonnage because they continued to build battleships during the era of the Jeune École. Both countries suspended their battleship programs for significant periods of time, yet the hiatus in construction starts came earlier in Russia (1870–81) and later in Italy (1885–93). The Russian naval campaign of 1877–78 may have inspired other countries to build scores of torpedo boats, but the Russians came away from the war regretting the fact that the Black Sea Fleet had included no battleships. While the Ottoman navy had kept its larger ironclads in port for fear of losing them to torpedoes, the Black Sea Fleet had been unable to provide fire support for

Russian armies advancing along the coasts. Lacking cover from battle-ship guns, the Russian Balkan army was far less secure before Constantinople in February 1878, and after the British fleet appeared, naval weakness had forced Russia to back down.[27]

The subsequent expansion of the Russian navy focused on providing heavy units for the Black Sea Fleet. Under a fleet plan promulgated in 1882, 15 battleships and 10 cruisers were to be built over the next twenty years. The Jeune École cruiser programs of other navies later led to a revision of the goals, to 20 battleships and 24 cruisers. The first nine battleships were laid down during the years 1883–89: the four units of the 10,200-ton *Ekaterina II* class at Nikolaiev and Sevastopol, for the Black Sea Fleet, and five smaller units at St Petersburg, for the Baltic Fleet. Building times averaged less than six years per ship, reflect-ing considerable improvements in the Russian shipyards. They were armed with artillery from Krupp's Russian licensee. All were barbette ships except the 9,480-ton *Navarin* and the 8,440-ton *Imperator Nikolai I*, which carried their guns in turrets. The *Ekaterina II* class had a pri-mary armament of six 12-inch guns paired in three barbettes; the smallest of the nine, the 6,590-ton *Gangut*, had one 12-inch gun in a forward barbette. All of the battleships had compound armor except the *Georgi Pobiedonosets* (built 1889–94), the last ship of the *Ekaterina II* class, which had all-steel armor. Among the cruisers, the 8,520-ton armored *Admiral Nakhimov* was the most formidable unit built in the early years of the program. Similar in design to Britain's *Warspite* and *Imperieuse*, it carried eight 8-inch and ten 6-inch guns, and could steam at 17 knots. After building Russia's first unarmored steel cruiser, the 3,000-ton *Pamiat Merkuria* (1878–81), France's Le Havre shipyard deliv-ered the 5,860-ton commerce raider *Admiral Kornilov* (1886–88). It was the largest of three protected cruisers commissioned by the Russian navy during the 1880s, with engines capable of 18.5 knots.[28]

The Russians did not aspire to build a navy capable of taking on the British, but the expansion program did have a clear anti-British motive, and Russian leaders hoped their fleet would someday combine with the French or others to wrest command of the sea away from Britain. While their improvised Black Sea effort of 1877–78 did not inspire the Russians to adopt a torpedo-centered naval strategy, the successful use of armed merchantmen against the Turks led to the creation of a "vol-unteer fleet" to supplement their battle fleet. By 1898 the volunteer list grew to include 25 merchant liners, which in case of war were to be armed with 8-inch and 6-inch guns stockpiled at Vladivostok and Sevastopol, then turned loose on the high seas as commerce raiders. Ironically, owing to the fact that Britain built so many merchantmen for export, all of the vessels designated for the Russian "volunteer fleet" were built in Britain. The British firm of Yarrow also provided the Russian navy with its first modern torpedo boat, the 43-ton *Batum*

(1880). Of another 26 boats added by 1889, half were were built in Russia, the rest imported from abroad. Meanwhile, the navy scrapped the torpedo boats and launches built during 1877–78, all of which were obsolete by the mid-1880s. Thus, after doing so much to inspire other countries to embrace torpedo warfare, by the end of the era of the Jeune École Russia had less than half as many torpedo boats as Austria–Hungary. They added another 61 boats between 1890 and 1904.[29]

In the early 1880s Italian shipyards finished Benedetto Brin's *Duilio* and *Dandolo*, continued to build his two *Italia* class battleships, and laid down the three *Ruggiero di Lauria* class battleships. The latter, at 11,200 tons slightly smaller than their predecessors, were begun after Brin was temporarily forced out of office in 1880. He wrote *La nostra Marina Militare* (1881) to justify his larger battleship designs, and after he returned to power in 1883 Italian battleship displacements increased again. The three units of the 13,900-ton *Re Umberto* class (laid down 1884–85) featured four 13.5-inch Armstrongs paired in two barbettes, and steel armor from Schneider of Creusot. While such imports, though expensive, compensated for the weaknesses of Italy's own armaments industry, Brin could do little to improve Italian shipyards. Indeed, their inefficiency grew worse, as construction times for the *Ruggiero di Lauria*s averaged almost eight years, the *Re Umberto*s almost ten.[30] As these six battleships inched toward completion, the Italian navy shifted its focus to adding cruisers and torpedo boats, and did not lay down another battleship until 1893. Brin ironically presided over this somewhat delayed reaction to the Jeune École, taking delivery of the 3,280-ton *Giovanni Bausan* (built 1882–85) and two other protected cruisers built by Armstrong, and laying down another 11 of the type in Italian shipyards in the years 1883–93. A further 15 protected cruisers of under 1,000 tons, most of them designated "torpedo cruisers," were laid down in the years 1885–91.[31] The Italians had four torpedo boats in 1881, then built another 159 by 1888, finishing the decade with a torpedo force roughly equal in size to the British and French.[32]

During the 1880s Italy, like Germany, claimed its first overseas colonies. The Italian navy facilitated the conquests of Eritrea, beginning in 1882, and Somalia, beginning in 1889. Other missions beyond the Mediterranean included over twenty circumnavigations of the globe.[33] Thus the focus of Italian naval activity shifted to cruising duties, but the battle fleet still took most of the navy's budget, while the large crews required by Brin's battleships accounted for most of its man-power. In any event, the battle fleet was needed to challenge France in the Mediterranean and North Africa, especially after the French annex-ation of Tunis in 1881 had strained Franco–Italian relations to breaking point. Italy subsequently alienated France by adhering to Bismarck's anti-French diplomatic system, first the Triple Alliance (1882) with

Nyack College Library

Germany and Austria–Hungary, then the Mediterranean Agreements (1887) with Britain, Austria–Hungary, and Spain. Tensions peaked after Italy's leading Francophobe, Francesco Crispi, became prime minister in 1887. Early the following year, when Franco–Italian trade talks collapsed just as the French Mediterranean Fleet was testing a new mobilization scheme, Crispi assumed France was preparing a surprise attack on Italy. With Anglo–French relations coincidentally strained by the Jeune École, Britain decided to dispatch a squadron to Genoa in a gesture of solidarity with Italy. The episode led to rumors of future Anglo–Italian naval cooperation and an expansion of the Triple Alliance to include Britain.[34] It also revealed the extent to which Italy's alliance with Germany was based on the assumption that Britain and France would remain rivals. As soon as Britain and Germany became rivals and Britain and France friends, Italy would seek to distance itself from its Triple Alliance partners.

Spain's inclusion in the Mediterranean Agreements of 1887 showed a measure of respect for its recent naval revival, which ensured its leading position in the second rank of European naval powers at least for the rest of the century. Aside from the 9,745-ton barbette battleship *Pelayo*, built at La Seyne (1885–88), the Spanish program reflected the influence of the Jeune École. Three armored cruisers ordered in 1889 and another three begun the following year helped lay the foundation for the fleet that would fight in the Spanish–American War of 1898. Three protected cruisers and a torpedo gunboat launched by British shipyards in 1886–87 provided the models for another three cruisers and seven gunboats built in Spain. Between 1883 and 1887, thirteen torpedo boats were purchased from shipyards in Britain, France, and Germany.[35]

The far more modest modernization programs of the other minor European navies likewise reflected the spirit of the times. Elsewhere in southern Europe, Greece built no protected cruisers but ordered its three *Spetsai* class armored cruisers (launched 1889–90) from French shipyards; the Greek navy commissioned seventeen torpedo boats, all by 1885. Portugal added four torpedo boats in the 1880s but waited until the late 1890s to order its first protected cruisers. In northern Europe, the Dutch and Scandinavian navies laid up most of the monitors and other small ironclads they had commissioned in the 1860s and 1870s, and turned to torpedo boats for their coastal defense. The Danes added 18 torpedo boats (1880–89), the Dutch 15 (1881–89), the Swedes 11 (1882–87), and the Norwegians 7 (1882–88). Like the southern European navies, the Danish navy ordered all of its torpedo boats abroad, while the others built most of theirs at home. The northern navies all built their own protected cruisers, the Danes launching their first in 1888, the Dutch following in 1890, the Norwegians in 1891. Sweden built no protected cruisers but launched the first of three small *Svea* class coastal-defense battleships in 1886, the same year that Denmark launched a similar ship. The Dutch followed suit in the mid-1890s with three armored coastal-defense ships. These miniature battleships of 3,000 to 3,500 tons, comparable to the German *Siegfried*s, reflected the fact that the countries building them had no intention of competing with the leading naval powers in armored warships.[36]

THE BIRTH OF THE SUBMARINE

During the First and Second World Wars, campaigns focusing on enemy shipping would be conducted not by torpedo boats and cruisers, as envisaged by the Jeune École, but by submarines. As the torpedo boat reached its peak of popularity during the 1880s, a few realists among torpedo warfare advocates acknowledged the weaknesses of the type and helped spark a renewed interest in the submarine as a torpedo-delivery vehicle. Ultimately, the undersea technology developed too slowly to breathe new life into the Jeune École, leaving submarine enthusiasts wondering "what might have been" as the battleship experienced a renaissance in the years after 1889.

Russia's leaders were not the only ones to doubt the conventional wisdom that torpedo boats had been a great success during the Russo–Turkish War. While they lamented their lack of Black Sea battleships on strategic grounds, at least some observers considered the Russian torpedo campaign a failure on tactical grounds. George Garrett of Liverpool, a British visitor to Russia during 1877–78, noted that Turkish anti-torpedo netting and surface booms had foiled countless Russian torpedo boat attacks; as such defensive devices became more common, torpedo attacks by surface vessels would be doomed to fail. He began to experiment with submarine designs and in 1879 launched the 30-ton *Resurgam*, a steam-powered vessel vastly superior to its many manually powered predecessors. After the *Resurgam* sank in an accident in 1880, Garrett went to Sweden to support submarine pioneer Thorsten Nordenfelt in the construction of another steam-powered undersea boat, the 60-ton *Nordenfelt I* (built 1882–85), the first submarine to carry self-propelled torpedoes. A Greco–Turkish war scare during the Bulgarian crisis of 1885–86 gave the two inventors the opportunity to sell the *Nordenfelt I* and take orders for another two submarines. Five of the great naval powers of Europe (France abstaining) demanded that the Greeks demobilize and used a blockade (January–June 1886) to force them to do so. As insurance against future blockades, Greece subsequently purchased the *Nordenfelt I* for £9,000, ignoring the fact that it had never run submerged for more than five minutes at a time. The boat was delivered to Piraeus but was never commissioned before being scrapped fifteen years later. Nevertheless, Greece's purchase of the

Nordenfelt I inspired Turkey to contract with Nordenfelt and Garrett for two submarines, both of which were built in Britain, then dismantled and shipped to Constantinople for reassembly. Garrett (ironically, a Protestant clergyman by training) was granted an Ottoman naval commission and, with a British crew, conducted trials for the first of the two submarines. After Garrett and his men returned home, the Turks abandoned both boats. A British shipyard subsequently built the *Nordenfelt IV* for the Russian navy, but en route to St Petersburg in November 1888 the 245-ton boat ran aground on the Danish coast, a total loss. Garrett then gave up the submarine business, while Nordenfelt constructed another pair of submarines, both for the German navy, both also failures.[37]

Meanwhile, in France, the submarine cause benefited from Dupuy de Lôme's lifelong openness to new ideas. The influential designer conducted experiments with undersea boats and, after his death in 1885, the effort continued under Gustave Zédé. In September 1888 Zédé completed the 30-ton *Gymnote*, history's first truly successful submarine (see Plate 18). In contrast to the steam-driven *Nordenfelts*, the *Gymnote* was powered by an electric battery. During two decades of service in the French navy, it made roughly 2,000 dives without a mishap. Zédé died three years after the launching of the *Gymnote*, before most French naval leaders fully understood the significance of his accomplishment, but during the last decade of the century other French designers established their country as the leader in submarine development. Former disciples of Aube provided at least some link between the Jeune École and the dawning era of submarine warfare; among those rising to admiral's rank, François Fournier became the most vocal proponent of a prominent place for submarines in French naval strategy.[38]

CONCLUSION

In January 1890 the French navy conceded that the nine *Balny* class torpedo boats were not fit for high seas service and relegated them to the coastal *défense mobile*.[39] The decision came one year after France resumed its program of battleship construction, at a time when even the country's most diehard Jeune Écolists had turned to the submarine as their weapon of the future. Far from succumbing to a senseless revival of battleship-centered "naval tradition,"[40] the Jeune École strategy simply could no longer be sustained, at least under its original premises. While some torpedo boats had been able to function in heavy storms (such as during the French maneuvers of 1883 and the German maneuvers of 1884), navies learned that the torpedo boats of the era could not be counted upon as autonomous high seas warships. By the end of the 1880s warships tailored for the strategy also no longer enjoyed a technological advantage over larger types. The break-throughs in medium-range artillery and propulsion technology, first applied to torpedo vessels and light cruisers, spread quickly to heavy cruisers and battleships, giving them the medium-range firepower and speed needed to respond to the torpedo threat at sea. A new Armstrong 4.7-inch gun introduced in 1887 fired ten rounds in 47.5 seconds, a revolutionary improvement over the standard 5-inch breech-loading rifle then in use, which managed just one round per 40 seconds. The British torpedo gunboat *Sharpshooter* (built 1888–89) and the Italian Elswick cruiser *Piemonte* (1887–89) were the first vessels equipped with the medium-caliber quick-firing gun; by the early 1890s it was the common secondary armament for battleships and large cruisers. Meanwhile, the French Belleville boiler technology, which had helped increase the speed of torpedo boats and smaller cruisers during the early 1880s, was applied to larger types, ensuring that the newest bat-tleships would not be the slow-moving targets that their predecessors had been. More benign defensive measures such as hull-mounted tor-pedo netting and electric searchlights also played a role in the death of the Jeune École by making even stationary battleships less susceptible to torpedo attacks.[41]

The spread of Belleville boiler technology was not the only area in which the French contributed to the decline of their own Jeune École. In 1886 they introduced nitro-cellulose smokeless powder, four years before the British developed their nitro-glycerine smokeless powder, cordite. While smokeless powder, in fact, produced some smoke when fired, the artificial "fog of war" which the Jeune École had taken for granted quickly disappeared, robbing torpedo boats of the smokescreen they would have used in close attacks on battleships. In the same year, the French shell manufacturer Holtzer introduced chrome steel shells, which were followed quickly by armor-piercing shell caps and the gen-eral manufacturing of shells clearly superior to the 1870s Palliser type. The new steel shells enhanced the destructive power of heavy naval ordnance, which could be employed most efficiently by battleships.[42] In the late 1880s Jeune École supporters could claim, with justification, that the same shells made battleships more vulnerable than ever, but a revolution in armor production in 1890–92 soon solved that problem, removing the last serious technological obstacle to a battleship renais-sance.

In addition to the many technological considerations, strategic factors ultimately worked against the Jeune École. No one wanted to trust tor-pedo flotillas to defend home waters, owing to the same vulnerability to bad weather that cast doubt upon their effectiveness as offensive forces. Furthermore, given the pervasive offensive martial spirit of the times, fear of the torpedo alone could not be counted upon to keep an enemy's largest battleships in port, as it had for the Ottoman navy in

1877–78. Deterrence has always been based upon intimidation, and in the late nineteenth century, battleships still served this purpose better than any other warship type. Finally, the Jeune École was primarily an anti-British strategy, and made sense only for countries which viewed Britain as a potential enemy. Most other countries did not depend enough on seaborne commerce to make commerce raiding justifiable as a primary strategy for their enemies. Thus Germany (in 1888), France (in 1889), Italy (in 1893), and Austria–Hungary (in 1893) resumed the systematic construction of battleships. Along with Britain and Russia, they continued to lay down ever larger battleships, competing in a general naval arms race that contributed considerably to European tensions in the years before the First World War.

NOTES

[1] Roberts, "Warships of Steel, 1879–1889," 105.

[2] Ibid., 106; Brown, "The Era of Uncertainty, 1863–1878," 89–90; Conway, 1860–1905, 51–82 passim.

[3] Roberts, "Warships of Steel, 1879–1889," 107; Conway, 1860–1905, 82, 154, 226–9, 277, 348–9, 396–7, 402–3, 411, 419.

[4] E.g. Austro–Hungarian naval chief, Admiral Max von Sterneck; see Sondhaus, The Naval Policy of Austria–Hungary, 99.

[5] Unless otherwise noted, the sources for this section are Gromov et al., Tri Veka Rossiiskogo Flota, 1:245–6, 252–4; Clarke, Russia's Sea-Power, 103–4, 107; Langensiepen and Güleryüz, The Ottoman Steam Navy, 5–6, 135–40, 161; Woodward, The Russians at Sea, 110–15; Watts, The Imperial Russian Navy, 15–16; Jane, The Imperial Russian Navy, 180; Conway, 1860–1905, 18, 25, 391.

[6] Gromov et al., Tri Veka Rossiiskogo Flota, 1:255. On the British occupation of Egypt see Sondhaus, Naval Warfare, 1815–1914, 125–6.

[7] Langensiepen and Güleryüz, The Ottoman Steam Navy, 6–7.

[8] Brown, "The Era of Uncertainty, 1863–1878," 92; Conway, 1860–1905, 106.

[9] On the War of the Pacific and its significance to naval warfare see Sondhaus, Naval Warfare, 1815–1914, 128–32.

[10] Tritten, "Navy and Military Doctrine in France," 56–7.

[11] Theodore Ropp, The Development of a Modern Navy: French Naval Policy, 1871–1904, ed. Stephen S. Roberts (Annapolis, MD, 1987), 132, 155–6, 159–65; Arthur J. Marder, The Anatomy of British Sea Power: A History of British Naval Policy in the Pre-Dreadnought Era, 1880–1905 (New York, 1940), 86–7.

[12] Aube quoted in Ropp, The Development of a Modern Navy, 165.

[13] Marder, The Anatomy of British Sea Power, 125.

[14] Roberts, "Warships of Steel, 1879–1889," 95; Conway, 1860–1905, 290–2.

[15] Roberts, "Warships of Steel, 1879–1889," 96, 109; Conway, 1860–1905, 308–10, 320, 324.

[16] Conway, 1860–1905, 211, 300, 327–8, 330–2.

[17] Dupont and Taillemite, *Les guerres navales françaises*, 246–8, 255–60; *Conway, 1860–1905*, 395; Lyon, "Underwater Warfare and the Torpedo Boat," 141–2.

[18] Roberts, "Warships of Steel, 1879–1889," 101–3, 109–10; Griffiths, "Warship Machinery," 176; Brown, *Warrior to Dreadnought*, 84–5, 99; Marder, *The Anatomy of British Sea Power*, 134; *Conway, 1860–1905*, 28–31, 64–6, 88–9, 101–6.

[19] Sondhaus, *The Naval Policy of Austria–Hungary*, 97.

[20] Sterneck quoted in Max von Sterneck to Richard Sterneck, Vienna, 3 March 1886, in Sterneck, *Erinnerungen*, 232.

[21] Sondhaus, *The Naval Policy of Austria–Hungary*, 97–100.

[22] Ropp, *The Development of a Modern Navy*, 28–30, 157.

[23] Sondhaus, *Preparing for Weltpolitik*, 136; Gröner, *Die deutschen Kriegsschiffe*, 1:33.

[24] Sondhaus, *Preparing for Weltpolitik*, 153–9, 161–4; Campbell, "Naval Armaments and Armour," 167; Gröner, *Die deutsche Kriegsschiffe*, 1:120–3.

[25] Caprivi quoted in Verchau, "Von Jachmann über Stosch und Caprivi," 67.

[26] Sondhaus, *Preparing for Weltpolitik*, 165–6, 168.

[27] Clarke, *Russia's Sea-Power*, 108.

[28] Gromov et al., *Tri Veka Rossiiskogo Flota*, 1:259; Woodward, *The Russians at Sea*, 117; Watts, *The Imperial Russian Navy*, 16; Roberts, "Warships of Steel, 1879–1889," 103–4; *Conway, 1860–1905*, 178–9, 186–8, 192–3.

[29] Jane, *The Imperial Russian Navy*, 334–5; Watts, *The Imperial Russian Navy*, 16; Woodward, *The Russians at Sea*, 117; *Conway, 1860–1905*, 211–15.

[30] Donolo, "The History of Italian Naval Doctrine," 105; Bargoni, *Corazzate italiane classi Duilio–Italia–Ruggiero di Lauria*, *passim*; idem, *Corazzate italiane classi Re Umberto–Ammiraglio di Saint Bon, 1893–1901* (Rome, 1978), *passim*; Roberts, "Warships of Steel, 1879–1889," 100–1.

[31] *Conway, 1860–1905*, 346–50.

[32] Baratelli, *La marina militare italiana*, 259–60; Giorgio Giorgerini, *Almanacco storico delle navi militare italiane: La Marina e le sue navi dal 1861 al 1975* (Rome, 1978), 419–27.

[33] Donolo, "The History of Italian Naval Doctrine," 104–5.

[34] Ropp, *The Development of a Modern Navy*, 191–2.

[35] *Conway, 1860–1905*, 380–6.

[36] Ibid., 360–79, 387–8.

[37] Wilson, "Early Submarines," 149–51; *Conway's All the World's Fighting Ships, 1906–21* (London, 1985), 387, 393 [hereafter cited as *Conway, 1906–21*]. On the Greco–Turkish crisis of 1886 see Sondhaus, *The Naval Policy of Austria–Hungary*, 105–6.

[38] Wilson, "Early Submarines," 154; *Conway, 1906–21*, 206; Walser, *France's Search for a Battle Fleet*, 136.

[39] *Conway, 1860–1905*, 327.

[40] As asserted in Robert L. O'Connell, *Sacred Vessels: The Cult of the Battleship and the Rise of the US Navy* (Oxford, 1993), 142.

[41] Campbell, "Naval Armaments and Armour," 163; Griffiths, "Warship Machinery," 177.

[42] Roberts, "The Pre-Dreadnought Age, 1890–1905," 113.

5

THE BATTLESHIP RENAISSANCE, 1889–1906

In the battleship renaissance that began with Britain's Naval Defence Act of 1889, the battle fleet returned to its central place in naval strategy. The following year, an American naval officer, Alfred Thayer Mahan, published the first of a series of books providing battle fleet proponents with historical arguments to support their cause. Mahan's works were influential throughout Europe but especially in Germany, where Emperor William II and Admiral Tirpitz became his greatest disciples. Cruisers and torpedo boats did not suddenly lose their significance, but only diehard Jeune Écolists still considered them potential replacements for battleships. While protected cruisers built under the Jeune École played important roles in the Sino–Japanese War (1894–95) and Spanish-American War (1898), the Russo–Japanese War was decided in classic Mahanian fashion by a high seas encounter at Tsushima (1905) between fleets led by battleships.

Shortly after the introduction of the armored warship, the emergence of the *Monitor* had offered an alternative to the armored-frigate paradigm of the *Gloire* and *Warrior*, ushering in a quarter-century of confusion in capital ship design. But by the end of the 1880s the standard battleship model later called the "pre-dreadnought" finally emerged. In the early 1890s the German firm of Krupp led the way in the perfection of nickel-steel armor, which provided better protection than compound iron-and-steel armor twice as thick. This breakthrough led to further increases in battleship displacement, leading to the revolutionary HMS *Dreadnought* (built 1905–6), a warship of unprecedented size and speed with an all big-gun armament. By making all pre-dreadnoughts obsolete, the *Dreadnought* sparked a new battleship race in which all of the major powers of Europe would spend unprecedented sums to build "dreadnoughts" of their own.

FROM THE NAVAL DEFENCE ACT TO THE FRANCO–RUSSIAN ALLIANCE

Britain showed the way for naval powers then wavering in their allegiance to the Jeune École by making the eight 14,150-ton battleships of the *Royal Sovereign* class the centerpiece of the Naval Defence Act of 1889. In addition to authorizing eight capital ships larger than any built up to that time, the Act was unique in two other respects, funding Britain's first systematic peacetime naval expansion and also finally making official the traditional "two-power standard." After Lord Castlereagh first proposed the standard, the British navy had maintained it as long as ships of the line (first sailing, then screw) were the capital ships being measured, but not in the era of the armored warship. Thus, in the Naval Defence Act, Britain resolved to achieve a level of naval supremacy it had not enjoyed in three decades.

The Act culminated five years of rising anxiety about the strength of the British navy, touched off by the Jeune École threat from France and the concurrent Russian naval buildup. The concerns first expressed in a series of critical articles under the title "The Truth About the Navy," published in 1884–85 in the popular *Pall Mall Gazette*, gained currency over the years that followed. The indifference toward the navy shown in recent years by the leading politicians of both parties (Conservative leader Benjamin Disraeli criticizing "bloated armaments," Liberal leader William Gladstone lamenting that the design of warships changed as often as the style of ladies' hats) finally gave way in 1888, after the Franco–Italian war scare of that year sparked a brief Anglo–French war scare as well.[1] A number of factors contributed to the perception that the navy was in a state of decline. During the decade following the defeat of Napoleon III in 1870, Britain laid down less than half the number of armored battleships as it had during the 1860s. The pace of construction slowed still more the following decade, when a mere ten battleships were laid down in the years 1880–88. In December 1888, Lord Charles Beresford, a naval officer and member of Parliament, demanded that the British navy maintain "a definite standard ... against the fleets of two powers combined, one of which should be France."[2] During the hearings that followed, the First Sea Lord, Admiral Sir Arthur Hood, cited the two-power standard as the traditional measure of British naval strength. When Parliament passed the Naval Defence Act on 7 March 1889, it became official.[3]

The Act provided £21.5 million for the construction of 8 first-class battleships (the 14,150-ton *Royal Sovereign* class; see Plate 19), 2 second-class battleships (the 10,500-ton *Centurion* and *Barfleur*), 9 first-class cruisers (the 7,350-ton *Edgar* class), 29 second-class cruisers (the 3,400-ton *Apollo* and 4,360-ton *Astraea* classes), 4 third-class cruisers (the last four units of the 2,575-ton *Pearl* class), and 18 torpedo gunboats, in order to give Britain a fleet equal to the combined naval strength of France and Russia within five years. In addition to being the largest battleships yet built, the *Royal Sovereign*s set the standard for battleship construction for the next seventeen years, until the all big-gun *Dreadnought* made their design obsolete. Modified versions of the 12,590-ton *Nile* and *Trafalgar*, the class included the same layout of four 13.5-inch guns paired on the centerline fore and aft, only now backed by a secondary armament of ten 6-inch quick-firing Armstrong guns as protection against attacks from torpedo boats. They also carried their heavy guns in barbettes, which saved precious tonnage and permitted a higher freeboard. One of the eight, the *Hood*, built 1889–93, carried its guns in turrets and had a lower freeboard, but otherwise was identical to the rest of the ships of the class, also displacing 14,150 tons.[4] Thus the *Royal Sovereign*s did not embody all of the breakthroughs in design and technology required for the battleship renaissance. They had quick-firing guns for their secondary armament and, once completed, surpassed their designed speed, some making over 18 knots under forced draught, but none carried their heavy guns in modern turrets, and all still had compound armor. Over the five years in which the ships of the Naval Defence Act were constructed, a revolution in armor production would further strengthen the battleship cause.

The Naval Defence Act of 1889 was funded by borrowing as well as by taxation, a practice Britain would not repeat in peacetime until 1937. This fact alone attests to the sense of urgency Parliament felt at the time, and also the depth of the anxiety over the navy's alleged shortcomings. By the end of the five-year program, all of the other great powers of Europe had resumed battleship construction, and the explosion of turn-of-the-century popular navalism was soon to follow. But in other countries with representative governments (especially Germany and, beyond Europe, the United States), the phenomenon went hand in hand with a self-confident patriotism and rising national ambitions, features that made the naval cause popular across a wide social and political spectrum. In contrast, in Britain, navalism stemmed from a lack of confidence about the country's ability to maintain its nineteenth-century position into the twentieth century. Reflecting a faith in numbers alone, the First Lord of the Admiralty, Lord George Hamilton, hoped that the sheer size of the 1889 program would preserve the British position by deterring other navies from matching it.[5]

In this atmosphere of anxiety and self-doubt, the writings of the US navy's Captain Alfred Thayer Mahan reminded the British that they had got it right in the past. Mahan also affirmed the battleship-centered course Britain had just taken in the Naval Defence Act by providing a strong rebuttal to the overall strategy of the Jeune École. Mahan's influential work *The Influence of Sea Power upon History, 1660–1783* (1890) and his subsequent books were grounded in his reading of Theodor Mommsen's classic history of Rome, from which Mahan concluded that naval strength had been the key to Rome's defeat of Carthage. While serving on the faculty of the Naval War College in Newport between 1886 and 1889, he formulated a theory of the rise and fall of nations based on naval power. In his first book, Mahan applied his analysis to the early modern rivalry between Britain and France. The manuscript was near completion when Britain passed the Naval Defence Act, and Mahan consciously sought to use the book to express his approval of it. Hoping to inspire his own country to pass similar legislation, he added a lengthy introduction on the "Elements of Sea Power," distilling his ideas on the importance of naval power, with an eye toward their applicability to the United States.[6]

A strategist rather than a tactician, Mahan did not address the "militarization" of naval warfare that had preoccupied naval writers since the 1850s (though, like Britain's John and Philip Colomb, he was the son of an army officer). His work was unique in being the first to treat matters of naval policy and naval operations in the broader contexts of international relations, economics, and domestic politics. Addressing the last, he argued that a strong fleet needed the backing of a coalition of special interests, to counter the tendency (especially in countries with representative governments) to keep peacetime defense spending low.[7] In the mood of the 1890s such coalitions were formed in all major European countries. Particularly in Britain, Germany, and Austria–Hungary, peacetime naval appropriations came to be seen not as "wasteful spending" but as subsidies for the industrial sector of the domestic economy. Even in countries that were not traditional sea powers, pro-navy politicians were able to attract considerable support for naval construction programs.[8] In Germany, the merchant shipping interests came aboard only reluctantly, owing to their belief that naval expansion made more likely future wars that would devastate their commercial interests.[9] Mahan addressed such concerns by deemphasizing commerce raiding. While conceding that it was bound to occur, and that it might even be beneficial to some belligerents, he called instead for blue-water forces of battleships to engage other battle fleets in decisive warfare to achieve command of the sea. Indeed, he minimized the need for cruisers to the point of theorizing that armed merchantmen could easily serve the same purpose.[10]

At the time, Mahan's lack of appreciation for commerce protection struck few readers as a radical departure, because even in Britain the "militarization" of naval warfare had reached a level where the navy no longer accepted such duties as fundamental to its mission. As early as the 1870s some British navy leaders scoffed at the notion that a country with a large merchant marine could build enough cruising warships actually to "protect" its overseas commerce. During his years as chief constructor for the British navy, Nathaniel Barnaby foreshadowed Mahan's later view by arguing that, in case of war, fast merchantmen could be armed to defend themselves and their slower brethren. On his advice, British shipyards constructed more merchant ships with watertight compartments, machinery below the waterline, and the structural soundness to mount all but the heaviest artillery.[11] Thus, even in the midst of the Jeune École, no one at the Admiralty advocated convoys for the protection of trade. Later, when Germany pursued its submarine *guerre de course* against Britain during the First World War, the Admiralty would wait almost three years before introducing a convoy system.

The publication of Mahan's second book, *The Influence of Sea Power upon the French Revolution and Empire* (1892) was followed a year later by his return to sea, as captain of the protected cruiser *Chicago* on a European cruise. He received an especially warm welcome in Britain, where he dined at Buckingham Palace as a guest of Queen Victoria. Both Oxford and Cambridge awarded Mahan honorary degrees, reflecting the fact that the British appreciated him as a historian as well as a strategist.[12] For the British, Mahan vindicated a course already taken (in the Naval Defence Act), while for others, especially the Germans, he provided arguments to be used in securing future approval for a similar naval buildup. German readers of the original English edition of *The Influence of Sea Power upon History* included both William II and Alfred Tirpitz. While the emperor retained his fondness for cruiser warfare through the mid-1890s, Tirpitz (who had just left the torpedo service in 1889) embraced the battle fleet as early as 1891. Indeed, Tirpitz's evaluation of the German autumn maneuvers of 1893 encouraged the "study of naval history," recommending "the works of Captain Mahan" to his fellow officers.[13]

A German edition of *The Influence of Sea Power upon History* appeared in 1896, the same year as a Japanese edition. Tirpitz had requested the German translation during his tenure as chief of staff to Admiral Eduard Knorr, chief of the High Command, in 1892–95; later, the Imperial Navy Office distributed copies of the book to support Tirpitz's campaign for the First Navy Law in 1897–98.[14] By the turn of the century, Mahan's works also appeared in French, Russian, Italian, and Spanish editions. Such international exposure enabled Mahan to surpass in influence all other naval writers of the era, even one as important as retired British admiral Philip Colomb, instructor at the Royal Naval College in Greenwich. Colomb's *Naval Warfare: Its Ruling Principles and Practice Historically Treated* (1891) also made a case for the battle fleet, defining concepts of command of the sea in much the same way as Mahan. Along with contemporary theorists of land warfare, Mahan and Colomb subscribed to the "cult of the offensive" and believed that future wars would be won in big, decisive battles.[15]

But the battle fleets that would wage such campaigns could not be built until armor manufacturers answered the question of how better to protect larger battleship types. As with so many other recent innovations (in boiler technology, smokeless powder, and steel shells), the French were involved, although their leading armor manufacturer, Schneider of Creusot, could not achieve the breakthrough on its own. Schneider had introduced all-steel armor in the 1870s, and sold it to Italy for the *Duilio* and other battleships, but the French navy had adopted it only reluctantly; afterward, Schneider could not produce enough steel armor to fill its contracts, and had to resort to imports of foreign compound armor for the French battleships begun in the early 1880s. Following inconclusive trials of Schneider nickel-steel armor during the late 1880s, some of the plates were entered in a US navy experiment held at Annapolis in September 1890, but only after being hardened in a new process devised by an American, Hayward Augustus Harvey. The "Harveyized" nickel-steel armor, treated with carbon and hardened in cold water, outperformed the latest compound armor from Britain.[16]

In the ensuing competition to reproduce or better Harvey's achievement, the unlikely victor emerged in Germany. When the German navy solicited bids for the armor contracts for the four 10,000-ton battleships of the *Brandenburg* class (authorized in 1889), Karl Stumm's Dillingen foundry, which since 1880 had been licensed to manufacture compound armor under the British "Wilson system," expected to be granted all four contracts. Wishing to end Stumm's virtual monopoly on German armor production, the navy invited Krupp into the bidding, and each firm received two of the contracts. But as soon as the Krupp works entered the armor business, Stumm and Friedrich Krupp foiled the navy's hopes by concluding a corporate alliance under which prices were fixed and future contracts divided. Krupp assumed responsibility for experimentation with new types of armor, in the meantime manufacturing compound armor for the *Brandenburg*s under Stumm's license. In October 1890, one month after the Annapolis trials, researchers at the firm's Essen complex joined the international competition to develop a harder nickel-steel plate.[17] The Krupp works already had some experience with the material, which it had adopted earlier that year for the manufacture of naval artillery. Early in 1892, after producing nickel-steel plates 15 percent stronger than compound armor, the firm decided to abandon compound armor production immediately. The first Krupp nickel-steel plates were ready in time for the *Kurfürst Friedrich Wilhelm*, a sister-ship of the *Brandenburg* and the first of the class to be launched. Owing to the use of plates already manufactured at Essen and Dillingen, the first three *Brandenburg*s had a mixture of compound and nickel-steel

armor, but the last of the class and all subsequent German armored warships had Krupp nickel-steel plate, produced either at the Krupp works
or by its corporate allies. By the end of 1892 further experimentation
led to the development of the "gas cementing" process (using gas to
carburize the face of nickel-steel plates before hardening them in running water), then, by the summer of 1894, to a process in which nickel-
steel plates, including small amounts of chromium and manganese,
were carburized with gas and hardened by a high-pressure water spray.
The 11,100-ton *Kaiser Friedrich III* (laid down 1895) was the first ship to
receive the ultimate product, and after 1895 Krupp produced only
plates of this type. Facing the latest Holtzer steel shells, 5.75 inches of
Krupp armor had the same strength as 7.5 inches of Harvey armor, 12
inches of all-steel plate, 12 inches of compound armor, or 15 inches of
wrought-iron plate.[18]

The breakthroughs at Essen established Krupp as the world leader in
armor production, ending a brief period during which Harvey dominated the market. Between 1892 and 1895, the Harvey Steel Company
licensed its process for the treatment of nickel-steel plates to Vickers in
Britain, Dillingen in Germany, Witkowitz in Austria, Terni in Italy, and,
following some litigation, Schneider in France. In Britain, the *Royal
Sovereign*s were completed too early to be fitted with Harvey armor,
which the Admiralty first ordered for the 12,350-ton second-class
battleship *Renown* (laid down in February 1893), then for all subsequent battleships through the last vessel of the 14,560-ton *Majestic*
class (laid down in March 1895). Starting with the 13,150-ton *Canopus*
class (laid down from December 1896), British battleships had Krupp
armor, manufactured under license in Britain. Russia made the change
in 1898, France and Italy in 1901.[19]

Plates tested during the armor revolution of the 1890s faced the latest
guns firing the latest shells, and thus also reflected the state of the art
in naval ordnance. Armstrong, Vickers, Krupp, and Canet of France all
produced heavy breech-loading nickel-steel guns. Firing steel shells
with smokeless nitro-cellulose or nitro-glycerin propellants, all were
superior to the most potent artillery of the 1880s. The 12-inch gun
became the favored primary armament for battleships, adopted in
France (1891), Britain (1893), Russia (1898), and Italy (1898). Germany
continued to provide its battleships with a primary armament lighter
than the new norm, as the 11.1-inch Krupps of the *Brandenburg* class
(laid down 1890) were followed by 9.4-inch guns in the next two
classes of battleships before the 11.1-inch gun returned in the
Braunschweig class (1901–2). Germany finally adopted the 12-inch gun
in 1908, for its second class of dreadnoughts. Austria–Hungary also
used 9.4-inch Krupp guns as a primary armament for battleships from
the resumption of its program in 1893 until until 1901, when one of its
own firms, Skoda, began producing 9.4-inch guns. Skoda developed a

12-inch gun by 1907, in time for the *Radetzky* class begun that year. During the 1890s the most common secondary armament was the quick-firing 6-inch gun, the type mounted in British pre-dreadnoughts.[20] The leading navies soon saw the new ordnance perform in action, but the Sino–Japanese (1894–95) and Spanish–American (1898) wars revealed the serious weaknesses of contemporary range-finding methods and fire control. Nevertheless, by most estimates the maximum range of the heaviest naval guns, roughly 2,000 yards since early in the ironclad age, doubled to 4,000 yards during the 1890s, although as late as 1900 many considered the effective range to be half that distance.[21]

In the meantime, Lord George Hamilton's prediction did not come true, as the Naval Defence Act failed to discourage other navies from building battleships. Russia did not abandon the twenty-year program begun in 1882, and France resumed battleship construction in 1889. The twelve French battleships begun in the years 1889–99, starting with the 11,190-ton *Brennus*, all were significantly smaller than the British *Royal Sovereign*s, none displacing over 12,500 tons. After building thirteen copies of the *Gloire* early in the ironclad age, France did not construct another homogeneous class of battleships until the three 11,100-ton *Charlemagne*s (laid down 1894–96), which also were the first French battleships to mount a primary armament of four heavy guns paired in two centerline turrets fore and aft. Differences in design among the other French battleships of the 1890s included variety in the type and the layout of their heavy guns. For example, the *Brennus* had three 13.4-inch guns in a double turret forward and single turret aft, while the next three ships had two 12-inch and two 10.8-inch guns, in four single turrets. The *Brennus*, like the British *Royal Sovereign*s, had compound armor, but the next four ships were fitted with nickel-steel plate manufactured under Schneider's own process. For the seven ships laid down in the years 1893–99, Schneider used its license to produce Harvey armor. Reflecting the lingering influence of the Jeune École, during the same period France laid down 18 armored cruisers. From the 6,680-ton *Dupuy de Lôme* (begun 1888) to the 11,090-ton *Jeanne d'Arc* (begun 1896), they received high marks from foreign observers despite the fact that they did not always live up to the French navy's expectations. For example, the *Jeanne d'Arc* never achieved its projected speed of 23 knots, but, as the first French armored cruiser fitted with Harvey armor, it caused some alarm in Britain, which at the time had no cruiser with armament heavy enough to penetrate such protection. British concerns mounted when French armored cruisers, after the 9,860-ton *Gloire* class (begun 1899–1901), were fitted with the even lighter, stronger Krupp armor.[22]

France's alliance with Russia coalesced rapidly after the retirement of Bismarck in 1890, when Germany no longer attempted to keep Russia in its own system of alliances. In 1891 the French navy visited Kronstadt, and in 1893 the Russian navy returned the favor at Toulon. Meanwhile, the two countries signed a treaty of alliance and military convention in 1892 and 1894. The Russian navy let lapse its licensing arrangement to produce Krupp artillery, opting instead for Canet guns, likewise manufactured in Russia under license. In the years 1891–95 Russia laid down 11 battleships, to meet the goal of 20 in the fleet plan of 1882. Of seven first-class battleships, the largest were the first two units of the 12,680-ton *Peresviet* class, the smallest, the 10,400-ton *Sissoi Veliki*. The 8,880-ton *Rostislav* was a weakly armed second-class battleship, and the three 4,970-ton coastal battleships of the *Admiral Ushakov* class were intended for Baltic duty only, to counter Sweden's three *Svea* class coastal defense battleships. Armored cruisers included the 11,000-ton *Rurik*, obsolete by the time of its launch in 1895, followed by the more modern 13,675-ton *Rossia* (laid down 1894) and 13,220-ton *Gromoboi* (1897). The Russian naval outlay increased from £4.3 million in 1890 to £7 million in 1898, roughly one-third the British navy's budget of the same year. With the last warships of the 1882 fleet plan either built or building, in 1898 Russia committed to construct another 8 battleships, 17 cruisers, and more than 50 smaller vessels, to be completed over the next seven years at a cost of £27.5 million. Despite the fact that Russia had developed the ability to construct first-class battleships faster than either France or Italy (the last seven of the previous program taking an average of just over six years), for the first time since the 1860s the navy placed battleship contracts with foreign shipyards. William Cramp of Philadelphia built the 12,700-ton *Retvisan* (1898–1901), the first Russian battleship fitted with Krupp armor, while La Seyne built the 12,915-ton *Tsesarevich* (1899–1903), which became a prototype for four warships of the 13,520-ton *Borodino* class. The *Borodino*s were built in Russian shipyards, as were the 12,580-ton *Potemkin* and a third ship of the *Peresviet* class. The eight battleships of the 1898 program were intended to support Russia's Far Eastern ambitions, and all were completed in time for the Russo–Japanese War. The new program also included the world's first purpose-built mine-layers, the 3,010-ton *Amur* and *Yenisei*, built in 1898–99, and Russia's first modern submarines, ordered just after the turn of the century.[23]

The alignment of Russia with France caused considerable alarm in Britain, which throughout the era of the Pax Britannica had never faced a formal alliance of the second and third naval powers. With the last ships of the Naval Defence Act nearing completion and no first-class battleships begun since 1891, in December 1893 Parliament approved another five-year program for 1894–98, known as the "Spencer program" after John Poyntz Spencer, the First Lord of the Admiralty. Earl Spencer's plan initially called for 7 battleships, 30 cruisers, and 122 smaller vessels to be built at a cost of £31 million; in its ultimate form, revised to include 9 battleships and fewer cruisers, the Spencer program left no doubt about Britain's commitment to battleships. The first of the nine units of the 14,560-ton *Majestic* class was laid down as soon as the bill passed Parliament, the last just fifteen months later. They were fitted with Harvey nickel-steel armor and were the first British battleships to carry their heavy guns in modern turrets (a "turret" now being defined as a fully armored hood protecting guns in a barbette mounting). Their armament included four 12-inch guns in two fore-and-aft centerline turrets, backed by twelve 6-inch quick-firing guns. By the time the program was completed, annual appropriations for new battleships had become the norm in Britain, which felt the need to respond immediately to further battleship-building abroad. In the six years 1896 through 1901, another twenty battleships were laid down: the six units of the 13,150-ton *Canopus* class (1896–98), three 14,500-ton *Formidable*s (1898), five 14,500-ton *London*s (1898–1901) and six 13,270-ton *Duncan*s (1899–1900). All were modeled after the *Majestic*s, with the same armament but slightly lighter overall, thanks mostly to their Krupp armor. Belleville boilers made them capable of 18–19 knots (a knot faster than the *Majestic*s), an unprecedented speed for battleships. Thus Britain enjoyed a significant qualitative advantage while also maintaining better than a two-power standard in numbers of battleships. The same was true with cruisers, after the Naval Defence Act's nine *Edgar* class protected cruisers were followed by another ten first-class protected cruisers. The six first-class armored cruisers of the 12,000-ton *Cressy* class (laid down 1898–99) and four of the 14,150-ton *Drake* class (1899) more than sufficed to counter the French *Jeanne d'Arc* and the Russian *Gromoboi* and *Rossia*.[24]

The Spencer program included among its smaller vessels 36 "torpedo boat destroyers," a new warship type. In 1892–93 Britain had ordered its first six destroyers, vessels of around 275 tons, capable of 26 or 27 knots, armed with torpedo tubes and light deck guns. They were designed to escort larger warships on the high seas, as further insurance against the torpedo threat. Other countries soon copied the type, and by 1902 every major European navy had destroyers, as well as Spain, Portugal, Norway, and Sweden among the minor naval powers.[25] By the First World War the newest destroyers displaced around 1,000 tons and were capable of 35 knots, but older destroyers half as large were still in commission.

Britain's new naval war plans, like Germany's Schlieffen Plan, took for granted that France and Russia had a common plan of their own. The most significant change came in the Mediterranean where, ever since 1878, the greatest strategic imperative of the British navy had been to prevent the Russian Black Sea Fleet from breaking out through the Turkish straits. As early as March 1894 the prime minister, Lord Rosebery, told the Austro–Hungarian foreign minister that he would not deploy the British Mediterranean Fleet to block a Russian sortie through the straits, because under such circumstances the French Mediterranean Fleet was likely to attack it from the rear. Conceding that, in case of war, the Black Sea Fleet would pass through the straits, in October 1896 the Admiralty produced new war plans with distinctly defensive goals, calling for the British navy to hold Gibraltar, Malta, and Alexandria, and stop the French and Russian fleets from joining forces.[26] Britain had no way of knowing that France and Russia did little to coordinate their naval planning, at least until after 1900. Nevertheless, its naval programs of 1889 and 1893 ensured a continued numerical superiority over the Franco–Russian alliance, while, qualitatively, the British navy still had the best personnel and the best warships in every class. And yet Britain's confidence continued to fall as its naval strength rose. Spencer's successor at the Admiralty from 1895 to 1900, George Goschen, feared that even with the two-power standard the British navy "might be fatally crippled by a single great disaster." But even he appeared calm compared to Sir Charles Dilke and other alarmists in Parliament, for whom no degree of superiority seemed sufficient.[27] The decline of British naval hubris cast doubt over the future of the Pax Britannica, which for eight decades had been upheld by a self-confident fleet backed by a self-confident nation. The turn of the century rise of the German, Japanese, and American navies would further alter the balance of naval power, bringing on new, more legitimate anxieties.

LESSONS FROM ABROAD (1894–98)

In the absence of naval warfare involving the leading powers of Europe, European navies attempted to draw lessons from two conflicts in distant waters. The first of these, the Sino–Japanese War of 1894–95, featured the largest naval battle since Lissa in 1866, fought off the mouth of the Yalu River on 17 September 1894. The engagement matched a Japanese fleet of seven protected cruisers supported by a small armored cruiser, an old casemate ship, an armored corvette, and two small escorts against a Chinese fleet of two 7,220-ton battleships, three small armored cruisers, five protected cruisers, and one dispatch vessel. The Chinese navy's tactical backwardness was apparent from its opening line-abreast attack, which attempted to imitate Tegetthoff's tactics at Lissa in 1866. (Even the Austro–Hungarian navy had returned to the line-ahead formation a decade earlier, in 1884.) The Japanese force divided into two squadrons and fought in line ahead. The Chinese opened fire at 5,000 meters, the Japanese at 3,900 meters, but most of the six-hour battle was fought at a range of just over 2,000 meters. Most of the ships engaged suffered some damage, but the Japanese lost no ships while the Chinese lost one armored cruiser and four protected cruisers.[28]

The Battle of the Yalu demonstrated that the line ahead gave commanders a greater degree of tactical control in battle and at least the possibility of coordinated fire. The Japanese line had the advantage of relative homogeneity, all of its units being similar in speed and armament except for two obsolete ironclads at the rear of the column. The Japanese also clearly benefited from their decision to delegate authority within their line by subdividing it into two squadrons. The Battle of the Yalu yielded no clues about the durability of the latest armor, as neither side had a ship with Harvey or Krupp plates. Owing to the primitive state of fire control in 1894 (the Japanese scored around 10 percent hits, the Chinese 5 percent) there were also no clear lessons regarding artillery, although cruiser advocates noted that the medium-caliber quick-firing guns of the Japanese cruisers sank or damaged seven Chinese cruisers. Once the range closed to 2,000 meters, the same guns also wreaked havoc aboard the two Chinese battleships, which barely remained functional owing to heavy casualties. Battleship proponents took heart in the fact that this success came at a heavy price, as the 12-inch guns of the two ships inflicted heavy damage on the attackers, in particular the Japanese flagship *Matsushima*, which miraculously did not sink. Indeed, the mere survivability of the battleships was impressive enough, as one took 150 hits, the other 200, but neither came close to sinking. Built in Germany in the early 1880s, they were close copies of the German *Sachsen* class and shared the general characteristics of the battleships designed by Brin and Barnaby during those years, being heavily armored amidships but unarmored at the bow and stern. The design, roundly criticized at the time, was finally vindicated some fifteen years later.[29]

Most navies considered the successes of the big guns of the Chinese battleships and quick-firing guns of the Japanese cruisers justification for continuing to arm their pre-dreadnoughts with a mixed battery of both types of ordnance, usually four 12-inch guns and a dozen 6-inch quick-firing guns. For the Germans, however, the medium-caliber quick-firing guns made more of an impression. After nearly stumbling on to the concept of the all big-gun battleship in the *Brandenburg* class of 1890 (each armed with six 11.1-inch guns and six 4.1-inch guns), the Battle of the Yalu helped lead the Germans in the opposite direction for their next two classes of battleships, which were given a secondary armament of eighteen 5.9-inch quick-firing guns to support their weaker primary armament of four 9.4-inch guns. For Britain, the tactical lessons of the Sino–Japanese War mattered less than the strategic consequences of Japan's victory, which was bound to increase tensions in the region. Because the *Royal Sovereign*s and *Majestic*s drew too much water to pass through the Suez Canal under normal circumstances, the subsequent *Canopus* class battleships laid down in 1896–98 (the lightest of the twenty begun in the years 1896–1901) were given a slightly shallower draught. By 1898, the increasing likelihood of a Russo–Japanese conflict prompted the British to deepen the Suez Canal.[30]

Three years after the end of the Sino–Japanese War, the United States declared war on Spain after the battleship USS *Maine* exploded and sank while on a visit to Havana in Spanish Cuba. The revitalization begun in the mid-1880s gave Spain a respectable battle fleet by 1898, with five armored warships in service and another four nearing completion. The former were the 9,745-ton barbette battleship *Pelayo*, built in France; the 7,230-ton armored cruiser *Cristóbal Colón*, built in Italy; and the three 6,890-ton armored cruisers of the *Infanta Maria Teresa* class, built in Spain at Bilbao. The latter included the 9,090-ton armored cruiser *Emperador Carlos V* and three smaller armored cruisers of the *Princesa de Asturias* class, near copies of the *Infanta Maria Teresas*. These four ships, along with the old iron-hulled armored frigates *Numancia* and *Vitoria* (renovated 1897–98), were not ready in time for the war.[31] When the fighting began, the United States enjoyed advantages over Spain in armored warships (5 battleships and 2 armored cruisers to 1 battleship and 4 armored cruisers), protected cruisers (14 to 5), and unarmored cruisers or steel gunboats (20 to 13).

Two naval battles decided the Spanish–American War. On 1 May 1898 in Manila Bay, an American squadron of four protected cruisers and two steel gunboats defeated a Spanish squadron of six unarmored cruisers and two small protected cruisers. The Americans did not lose a ship, while all of the Spanish ships were either sunk or scuttled to avoid capture. In the Atlantic theater, on 3 July 1898 a Spanish force of four armored cruisers and two destroyers broke out of Santiago Bay and was pursued along the Cuban coast by an American force led by five battleships and two armored cruisers. All four Spanish cruisers were set ablaze by American gunfire, then run ashore by their own captains in an effort to save as many crew members as possible. One of the Spanish destroyers was sunk, the other driven aground. As in Manila Bay, the Americans did not lose a ship.[32]

At least in artillery fire, the naval battles of the Spanish–American War appeared to confirm the lessons of the Sino–Japanese War. Quick-firing medium-caliber ordnance was responsible for all of the hits at Manila Bay (where no warship had heavy guns) and most of those at Santiago. In each case, the ranges were similar to the Battle of Yalu but the fire control much worse. At Manila Bay the American warships scored 141 hits out of some 6,000 shells fired (2.3 percent), against stationary Spanish targets. At Santiago, against Spanish warships in full flight, the American success rate was even lower, at just 122 hits out of 9,433 shells fired (1.3 percent), but the 12- and 13-inch guns of the battle-ships scored 42 of the hits, out of roughly 1,300 shells fired (3.2 per-cent). It was of some consolation to the US navy that Spanish fire control had been even worse, reflected in the near-total lack of damage incurred by American warships in the two battles. In the only major change in naval construction resulting from the war, shipbuilders reacted to the fiery end of the Spanish cruisers at Manila Bay and Santiago by using much less wood in the decks and interiors of steel-hulled warships.[33] All countries continued to build their pre-dread-nought battleships with a mixed armament of heavy guns and medium-caliber quick-firing guns, as the debate over gun types gave way to a new focus on improving fire control. When even reasonably well-trained gun crews could hit their targets only 1 or 2 percent of the time, all of the major navies had to acknowledge the need for better range-finding devices and techniques.

GERMAN NAVAL EXPANSION AND THE TRIPLE ALLIANCE

In the spring of 1897, William II named Rear Admiral Alfred Tirpitz state secretary of the Imperial Navy Office. Ambitious and opportunis-tic, Tirpitz had taken advantage of the Jeune École to become head of the navy's torpedo service in the 1880s, then read Mahan and turned to the battleship in the early 1890s. In his first audience with the emperor after taking office in June 1897, Tirpitz characterized Britain as Germany's "most dangerous enemy ... against which we most urgently require a certain measure of naval force as a political power factor."[34] His Anglophobia touched a cord with William II, who subsequently endorsed Tirpitz's program for an armored fleet of 19 high seas battle-ships and 8 coastal battleships,12 large cruisers, 30 small cruisers, and 12 divisions of torpedo boats, to be built by 1905 at a cost of 58 mil-lion marks per year over seven fiscal years. The cost seemed reasonable, as the Reichstag had already budgeted 58 million for naval construc-tion for 1897–98. The real price would be diplomatic rather than financial, for the adoption of the Tirpitz plan brought a dramatic change in the Anglo–German relationship, which had been generally friendly since the unification of Germany. Indeed, as recently as 1889 Bismarck had called the British navy "the greatest factor for peace in Europe."[35]

The 19 battleships in the original Tirpitz plan included 12 already built or building: the four 7,600-ton *Sachsen*s (commissioned 1878–83), the 5,200-ton casemate ship *Oldenburg* (1886), the four 10,000-ton *Brandenburg*s (1893–94), and the first three battleships of the 11,100-ton *Kaiser Friedrich III* class (still under construction). The 3,500-ton *Siegfried* class (1890–96) filled the quota of 8 coastal battleships. The 12 large cruisers included 10 built or building: the old battleships *König Wilhelm*, *Kaiser*, and *Deutschland* (recently renovated for service as armored cruisers), the protected cruiser *Kaiserin Augusta* (1892), the 5 vessels of the 5,700-ton *Hertha* class (under construction), and the 10,700-ton armored cruiser *Fürst Bismarck* (under construction). The 30 small cruisers included 19 commissioned between 1883 and 1896, and four 2,650-ton *Gazelle*-class warships (under construction; see Plate 20). The debate over Tirpitz's navy law focused on the new warships needed to meet the goals of the plan – 7 battleships, 2 large and 7 small cruisers – which represented a 30 percent expansion in the size of the fleet. The fact that the real commitment came in the provision for the automatic replacement of the warships in the plan – battleships after twenty-five years, large cruisers after twenty years, and smaller cruisers after fifteen years – went almost unnoticed. On 6 December 1897 Tirpitz delivered a speech to the Reichstag, opening the campaign to pass the navy law. Reflecting his own social Darwinist sentiments, he called the expansion of the fleet a "question of survival" for Germany.[36] After the Reichstag passed the law on 10 April 1898, the last two units of the 11,100-ton *Kaiser Friedrich III* class (laid down 1898; see Plate 21) and five of the 11,800-ton *Wittelsbach* class (1899–1900) completed the category of battleships. The 8,900-ton armored cruiser *Prinz Heinrich* (1898) and the 9,100-ton *Prinz Adalbert* (1900) filled the quota for large cruisers, while most of the additional small cruisers were new units of the *Gazelle* class.

By the time the last major warships of the program were begun, the international situation had enabled Tirpitz to go back to the Reichstag with a request for an even greater commitment to German sea power. The Second Navy Law of June 1900 expanded the fleet to 38 battleships (including the 3,500-ton *Siegfried*s, now counted as full-sized battleships for replacement purposes), 14 large and 38 small cruisers. The bill passed on the strength of anti-British sentiment inspired by the Anglo–Boer War in South Africa (1899–1902) and pro-navy sympathies stemming from the situation in China, where the Boxer Rebellion (1900) had claimed the German ambassador and German missionaries among its victims.[37] Nevertheless, the new units authorized (11 battleships, compared to 2 large and 8 small cruisers) indicated that Tirpitz was building a battleship navy for home waters, which would not have enough cruisers to give Germany on-the-spot influence in such distant conflicts. The five 13,200-ton *Braunschweig*s (laid down 1901–2) and five 13,200-ton *Deutschland*s (1903–5; see Plate 22) had a primary armament of 11.1-inch guns, an improvement over the 9.4-inch guns of the *Kaiser Friedrich III* and *Wittelsbach* classes. The new large cruisers were the 11,600-ton armored cruisers *Gneisenau* (1904) and *Scharnhorst* (1905; see Plate 23). Meanwhile, in 1901–3 work began on another three armored cruisers, to replace the trio of renovated old battleships which Tirpitz had counted as large cruisers in his original plan.

Tirpitz had 37 of his 38 battleships and all 14 of his large cruisers built or building by 1906, when the Reichstag passed a supplementary law increasing the number of large cruisers to 20 and raising the tonnage ceilings for new battleships. Because the next large cruiser due for replacement was the *Kaiserin Augusta* (1892) in 1912, the 6 new large cruisers filled the gap of 1906–12 and, by giving Tirpitz a total of 20 (each guaranteed to be replaced after twenty years), established a building commitment of one large cruiser per year. This further triumph solidified Tirpitz's reputation as the Second Reich's most successful politician, after Bismarck. William II showed his gratitude by elevating Tirpitz to the nobility in 1900 and awarding him a number of other high honors. The automatic replacement of warships (after twenty-five years for battleships, twenty for large cruisers, fifteen for small cruisers) assured the navy that a future, more left-wing Reichstag could not undo Tirpitz's grand design – a crucial factor given the long-standing trend of the Social Democratic Party (SPD) making gains in every German national election.[38] By guaranteeing the size of the fleet, the Reichstag of 1898–1900 had also given the navy the right to replace smaller old ships with larger new ships, because it was assumed that the design of replacement ships would be determined by the international norms of the time in which they were ordered. Fortunately for Tirpitz, the oldest battleships counted in his 1898 plan, the four 7,600-ton *Sachsen*s, came up for replacement right after Britain's *Dreadnought* transformed the design of battleships; thus, the four 18,900-ton dreadnoughts of the *Nassau* class "replaced" them. The 3,500-ton *Siegfried* class coast defenders, redesignated as regular battleships under the Second Navy Law, were "replaced" by dreadnoughts of the 22,800-ton *Helgoland* class and 24,700-ton *Kaiser* class. The increases were just as dramatic for the first "large cruisers" due for replacement, since Tirpitz had assigned ships as small as the 5,700-ton *Hertha* to that category. The *Ersatz Hertha*, completed during the First World War, was the 27,000-ton battle cruiser *Hindenburg*.

Tirpitz's navy laws laid the groundwork for the German navy to become Europe's second largest behind the British; they also undermined the Triple Alliance, which made sense for Italy only as long as Britain remained a potential enemy of France and on friendly terms with Germany. The alliance was already in trouble even before Tirpitz introduced his plan, for a variety of reasons. Italy and Austria–Hungary remained incompatible as allies, and accepted friendship with each other only as the price for alliance with Germany. Italian leaders had hoped the Franco–Russian alliance would pressure the British either to join the Triple Alliance or form a separate Anglo–Italian Mediterranean pact, and were disappointed when neither happened. Finally, in 1896 Francophobe Prime Minister Francesco Crispi, the strongest advocate of the Triple Alliance among leading Italian politicians, saw his career ruined by Italy's defeat at Aduwa, in its first attempt to conquer Ethiopia. The ensuing deterioration of Anglo–German relations left more Italians doubting the wisdom of an alliance with Germany. When the great powers responded to the Greco–Turkish crisis over Crete (1897–98) with an international naval demonstration, Italy actively sought to cooperate with countries other than its allies. Then, in 1900, Italy secretly agreed to let France annex Morocco in return for French acquiescence in the future Italian annexation of Libya. Thereafter, Austria–Hungary once again was considered the greatest potential naval adversary of Italy, ironically just as Germany and Austria–Hungary finally agreed to a long-standing Italian demand for a Triple Alliance naval convention.[39]

The Jeune École years were a confusing time for the Italian navy, which adopted the strategy rather late, then embraced it wholeheartedly, only to reject it with equal resolve just a few years later. Italy commissioned more torpedo boats in the years 1885–88 than any other navy during the entire decade, then built none at all until 1897. Battleship construction resumed in 1893, and over the next eleven years eight were begun: two of the 10,080-ton *Ammiraglio di Saint Bon* class, two of the 13,215-ton *Regina Margherita* class, and four of the 12,550-ton *Regina Elena* class. All were built in Italian shipyards, the last six in an average of just under six years per ship. By the turn of the century Italian shipbuilders became competitive in the international market, building cruisers for export to South America and the Far East. They also did business with Spain, whose armored cruiser *Cristóbal Colón* was a copy of the highly regarded 7,230-ton *Garibaldi* class. During the 1890s the Italian navy ordered three *Garibaldi*s and three armored cruisers of other designs. In 1898 Italy became the first country to equip its warships with wireless telegraph, invented three years earlier by Guglielmo Marconi and first tested at sea in 1897, in transmissions between a receiving station ashore and the pre-dreadnought *Sardegna* (completed 1895), 12 miles (19 km) out to sea. After the British navy tested Marconi's wireless at its summer 1899 maneuvers, transmitting messages up to 90 miles (140 km), all other navies quickly adopted the new invention.[40]

Austro–Hungarian naval leaders naturally welcomed the deterioration of relations between the Dual Monarchy and Italy, knowing it would justify a future expansion of the fleet. But in the first years after Austria–Hungary resumed its battleship program in 1893, the buildup was intended to counter the threat of the Franco–Russian alliance in the Mediterranean. The likelihood that the Black Sea Fleet would appear in the Aegean or Eastern Mediterranean during a future Russian offensive in the Balkans increased considerably once the British gave up the idea of preventing it from passing through the Turkish straits. Austria–Hungary also had a strong interest in safeguarding the Suez

Canal and Eastern Mediterranean trade routes, since Trieste had grown to become Mediterranean Europe's leading entrepôt for commerce with South and East Asia. Over the next eleven years the Austro–Hungarian navy ordered nine battleships, for the most part smaller than the eight Italy laid down in the same years: three ships each of the 5,600-ton *Monarch* class, the 8,300-ton *Habsburg* class, and the 10,600-ton *Erzherzog* class. The navy also commissioned three armored cruisers, including the 7,400-ton *Sankt Georg*. Aside from one battleship and one armored cruiser laid down in the Pola navy yard, all units were built by the Stablimento Tecnico Triestino. Austro–Hungarian shipyards were the most efficient in Europe after the British and German, and construction times averaged just over four years per ship. Starting with the armored cruiser *Maria Theresia* (built 1891–95) the navy ordered all of its armor plate from Witkowitz of Moravia, and from 1901 Bohemia's Skoda works fulfilled the navy's needs in artillery. In 1901 the navy leadership won over traditionally anti-navy Hungarian leaders by promising to patronize Hungarian firms for a share of the naval budget equivalent to the Hungarian contribution to the joint budget of the Dual Monarchy. Thus, in a divided domestic political landscape a broad pro-navy coalition evolved which represented the interests of nationalities far from the Adriatic. Most important of all, Archduke Francis Ferdinand, heir to the Habsburg throne, became the empire's leading naval enthusiast after travelling to Japan in 1892–93 aboard the protected cruiser *Kaiserin Elisabeth*.[41]

FROM RIVALS TO PARTNERS: BRITAIN AND FRANCE AT THE TURN OF THE CENTURY

While many British leaders doubted that their massive naval buildup of the 1890s provided a clear margin of superiority over the Franco–Russian combination, across the Channel the 37 British battleships laid down between 1889 and 1901 were cause for despair. The French navy came to the sobering realization that, even in league with the Russians, it could not keep up with the British. During the Anglo–French war scare resulting from the Fashoda Crisis of 1898, a mobilization revealed the embarrassing condition of the French battle fleet, yet afterward relatively little was done to remedy the situation. Against the 20 battleships ordered in Britain after the *Majestic*s, France built only six: two of the 14,605-ton *République* class (1901–6) and four of the 14,490-ton *Liberté* class (1902–8), all of which were obsolete by the time they finally entered service. The *République*s and *Liberté*s conformed to the established norm of pre-dreadnought design, carrying four 12-inch guns in two centerline turrets fore and aft; the ten 7.6-inch guns of the *Liberté*s also reflected the general trend toward a heavier secondary armament. As in the 1890s, just after the turn of the century France's most impressive warships were its armored cruisers. Seven laid down between 1901 and 1906, ranging in size from the 12,350-ton *Léon Gambetta* to the 13,995-ton *Waldeck-Rousseau*, would still be useful during the First World War.[42] Fortunately for the French navy, after 1898 Britain and France gradually moved toward a rapprochement formalized in the Entente Cordiale of 1904. The naval war college (*École supérieure de guerre de la Marine*), established in 1895 under Admiral Gabriel Darrieus, led the way in redefining French naval strategy, as the improvement of Anglo–French relations further reduced the influence of the Jeune École.[43] Its remaining supporters, both in the navy and in the Chamber of Deputies, insisted that the fleet continue to add torpedo boats even after other navies had scaled back or stopped construction of the type. In the years 1890–1905 France built 202 of them, including thirty-seven of 100–150 tons, allegedly capable of high seas duty. By 1908 another seventy-five torpedo boats of 100 tons were commissioned.[44]

Submarines continued to be a bright spot amid the overall gloom, as France maintained its lead over other countries in undersea warfare after developing the electric battery-powered *Gymnote* (1888). In December 1898 the old Jeune Écolist Vice Admiral Fournier arranged for the *Gustave Zédé* (1893) to participate in the maneuvers of the French Mediterranean Fleet, during which it torpedoed and sank a target hulk while submerged, the first time an undersea boat had accomplished such a feat. In the years 1900–14 the French navy commissioned 76 submarines, most of them modified versions of the successful *Narval* (1900; see Plate 24).[45] By then, the invention of the torpedo gyroscope by Austro–Hungarian naval officer Ludwig Obry had made self-propelled torpedoes far more lethal. Their range increased from less than 1,000 yards at the time of the breakthrough in 1896 to 2,000 yards by 1900 and 3,000 yards by 1904, dramatically enhancing the combat potential of submarines. Indeed, the possibility that the effective range of torpedoes would equal, or outstrip, the range of battleship guns posed the greatest threat to the battleship renaissance. Britain's Admiral Fisher was among the doubters, in 1904 predicting that torpedo ranges would soon reach 5,000 yards.[46] Fisher numbered among the British navy men who worried about a revival of France's Jeune École strategy right up to the conclusion of the Entente Cordiale. Such fears were hardly irrational, given the evidence: the French navy's best larger ships were its cruisers; it continued to build large numbers of torpedo boats after other navies had stopped; and France was the world leader in the development of the submarine, which could join the torpedo boat as a means of delivering torpedoes that now had an extended range and accuracy. More famous for his later *Dreadnought* and battle cruiser designs, at the turn of the century Fisher was most concerned about submarines. He was impressed by the power of the submarine not only as an offensive weapon, but as a defender of harbors that would make it impossible for navies of the future to impose close blockades. A posting as British Mediterranean commander (1899–1902) gave Fisher the opportunity to observe the growth of the French undersea force at Toulon, after which an assignment as commander in Portsmouth (1903–4) allowed him to supervise the early growth of Britain's submarine service. The British waited until 1901 to launch their first submarine, designated simply as *No. 1*, built by Vickers after the American Holland design. After this late start, however, Britain commissioned a total of 88 undersea boats by the time war began in 1914, more than any other country. The British traditionally have claimed credit for at least one submarine innovation, the first periscope, introduced to *No. 1* by Captain Reginald Bacon, but other sources contend that the French *Narval* had a periscope from the time it entered service in 1900.[47]

Until Fisher became First Sea Lord, the central place of the battleship in British naval strategy remained unquestioned. After laying down twenty battleships roughly similar to the nine *Majestics* begun in 1893–95, Britain again sought a clear advantage over potential rivals with the eight vessels of the 15,585-ton *King Edward VII* class, begun in 1902–4. They were the largest and most formidable warships yet built, carrying a mixed secondary battery of four 9.2-inch guns and ten 6-inch guns to supplement their standard pre-dreadnought primary armament of four 12-inch guns. Before coming to terms with France in the Entente Cordiale, Britain also felt compelled to respond to the latest French armored cruisers with another twenty-two laid down after the *Drakes* of 1899: ten of the 9,800-ton *Monmouth* class (1899–1901), six of the 10,850-ton *Devonshire* class (1902), and six of the 13,550-ton *Duke of Edinburgh* and *Warrior* classes (1903–4). Fear of international isolation had fueled the atmosphere of near-panic in which Britain spent £56.5 million on 60 new large armored warships (28 battleships and 32 armored cruisers) in just eight years, an expenditure which, combined with the cost of the Anglo–Boer War, caused a dramatic rise in the British national debt. The Anglo–Japanese alliance of 1902, followed by the Entente Cordiale two years later, brought a somewhat calmer atmosphere. The 1904–5 naval outlay included construction starts for just two battleships, the 16,090-ton *Lord Nelson* and *Agamemnon*, the last laid down before the *Dreadnought*, and three armored cruisers, the 14,600-ton *Minotaur* class, the largest of the type ever built in Britain. The British navy also added two second-class battleships, the 11,800-ton *Swiftsure* (ex-*Constitución*) and *Triumph* (ex-*Libertad*), under construction for Chile in British shipyards, acquired on the eve of the Russo–Japanese War to block their possible sale to Russia.[48]

After avoiding peacetime alliances throughout the nineteenth century, Britain entered into a formal partnership with Japan in 1902, once it became clear that the Japanese would clash with the Russians in the Far East. The Anglo–Japanese treaty marked the end of the Pax Britannica, as the British conceded they could no longer safeguard their international interests on their own. After Japan's victory in the Russo–Japanese War, Britain recalled all of its battleships from the Far East; by then, the conclusion of the Entente Cordiale further enabled the redeployment of British capital ships closer to home. Even before the rising threat from Germany forced Britain's hand, concerns for economy and efficiency dictated the redeployment. When Fisher became First Sea Lord in October 1904, Britain had 16 active battleships in the Home Fleet and Channel Squadron, 12 in the Mediterranean, and 5 on the China station. After the latter returned home, an enlarged Home Fleet, shifted to the Channel, included 14 battleships, while the former Channel Squadron, operating out of Gibraltar as the Atlantic Fleet, had 9, and the Mediterranean Fleet 9. As of 1906 16 battleships were in the Channel, 8 in the Atlantic, and 8 in the Mediterranean. By then, 16 of the 22 active armored cruisers were under the Channel, Atlantic, and Mediterranean commands, 3 on the North Atlantic station, and the remaining 3 in the Far East. Thus, aside from the latter trio of armored warships, Britain defended its interests beyond European and North Atlantic waters with protected and unarmored cruisers. These included the last British warships built with a sailing rig, the six 1,070-ton steel-hulled sloops of the *Cadmus* class (completed 1902–4).[49]

THE RUSSO–JAPANESE WAR (1904–5)

Russia reacted with alarm to the decisive Japanese victory in the Sino–Japanese War (1894–95). Japan emerged with territorial gains including the Liaotung Peninsula with Port Arthur, and established itself as Russia's main rival for influence in Korea and Manchuria. A Russian diplomatic offensive managed to undo the damage, but also placed the two countries on a collision course. In 1895 France and Germany backed Russia in an international campaign which forced Japan to give the Liaotung Peninsula back to China. The following year China granted Russia permission to build the Trans-Siberian Railway (begun in 1891) across Manchuria, cutting several hundred miles off the route to Vladivostok. Then, in 1898, China leased the Liaotung Peninsula to Russia, and granted the Russians a further concession to link Port Arthur to the Trans-Siberian Railway via a spur from Harbin. The Russians then moved the base of their Pacific squadron to Port Arthur from Vladivostok, which, since its founding in 1860, had proven to be far from ideal as an anchorage owing to the winter ice that limited its utility for several months of the year. Japan responded to the challenge from Russia by building a new fleet in the years 1897–1904: 6

battleships, 8 armored cruisers, and 8 protected cruisers. The battleships were improved versions of the British *Royal Sovereign* and *Majestic* classes, ordered from British shipyards. The armored cruisers were also purchased from European builders (four in Britain, two in Italy, one in Germany and one in France), along with one of the protected cruisers (built in Britain). Smaller, older ships that had fought in the war against China (one small armored cruiser and nine protected cruisers) or had been captured from the Chinese and recommissioned as Japanese warships (one battleship and a second small armored cruiser) were relegated to supporting roles. The Russian navy of 1904 was much stronger, at least on paper, with 27 battleships, 8 armored cruisers, and 14 protected cruisers commissioned since 1880. At the beginning of 1904 the Russians had 7 battleships at Port Arthur with another due to arrive soon. Under the Straits Convention of 1841 the Russian Black Sea Fleet could not leave the Black Sea in wartime, but the ships of the Baltic Fleet (the largest Russian naval force) were free to be sent to the Pacific as needed.[50]

Japan broke diplomatic relations with Russia on 6 February 1904, then attacked Port Arthur on the night of 8–9 February without first issuing a formal declaration of war. Ten Japanese destroyers led the raiding force, which succeeded in torpedoing the battleships *Tsesarevich* and *Retvisan* and a Russian cruiser. On 9 February Japan's six new battleships participated in a bombardment of Port Arthur but did not attempt to enter the harbor. No Japanese ships were sunk in these initial actions, and the Russian units damaged by torpedoes were soon repaired. The only Russian warships lost in the first days of the war were the protected cruiser *Varyag* and a gunboat, both damaged beyond repair in a losing battle to prevent a Japanese landing on the Korean coast at Inchon. The Russian squadron did little to challenge the Japanese until March, when Vice Admiral Stepan Makarov took command at Port Arthur. The charismatic former torpedo boat commander of the 1877–78 war waged an aggressive campaign of battleship sorties, which came to a sudden end on 13 April, when his flagship *Petropavlovsk* struck a mine and sank with a loss of 635 lives, including Makarov. The Russians more than avenged the sinking of the *Petropavlovsk* on 15 May, when two of Japan's newest battleships sank in a minefield sowed by the minelayer *Amur*. Over the months that followed, the Russian armored cruisers *Rurik*, *Gromoboi*, and *Rossia*, and the protected cruiser *Bogatyr*, operating out of Vladivostok, sank three Japanese troop transports and eighteen merchantmen in the Sea of Japan. But on 14 August the Russian cruiser squadron suffered defeat at the hands of four Japanese armored cruisers in the Battle of the Sea of Japan (also known as the Battle of Ulsan), in the process losing the armored cruiser *Rurik*. The three remaining Russian cruisers did not venture out of Vladivostok for the rest of the war.

In the meantime, the Japanese army completed its conquest of Korea, invaded Manchuria, and advanced down the Liaotung Peninsula to besiege Port Arthur, complementing a Japanese naval blockade of the Russian base. On 10 August Makarov's successor, Rear Admiral V. K. Vitgeft, escaped the trap with the entire Russian Pacific squadron and steamed for Vladivostok, only to have his plan foiled later that day by defeat in the Battle of the Yellow Sea (also known as the Battle of Shantung). Assisted by the latest Barr and Stroud optics in range finders imported from Britain, the Japanese opened fire with their 12-inch guns at the unprecedented distance of 11,000 meters. Several ships were soon exchanging shots at 8,000 to 9,000 meters, ranges at which medium-caliber quick-firing guns were useless. During the battle Japan's Admiral Heihachiro Togo first tried "crossing the T," a tactic copied from the British, who had introduced it at maneuvers in 1901. Vitgeft responded to the concentrated fire against the head of the Russian column by turning away, after which Togo repeated the move, maneuvering the Japanese column across the path of Vitgeft's new course. The Russians turned away a second time, then fled southeast-ward for the Korea Strait. The battle resumed two hours later, when the superior speed of Togo's column brought its lead ships within 7,000 meters of the rear of Vitgeft's column. As the Japanese continued to close the distance, their gunners registered hits on the bridge of the flagship *Tsesarevich*, killing Vitgeft and most of his staff. The Russian warships then scattered, most returning to Port Arthur. The Japanese gave chase but managed to capture just one destroyer. The protected cruiser *Novik* nearly made Vladivostok but was scuttled by its crew after running aground off Sakhalin, thus becoming the only ship involved in the battle not to survive it. The Russians also lost the further services of several ships which put in at neutral harbors, where they were interned for the rest of the war: the *Tsesarevich* and three destroyers in the German base at Tsingtao, and two protected cruisers and a destroyer in other ports.

After the defeats of mid-August 1904 the Russians decided to send Admiral Zinovy Rozhestvensky to the Pacific with reinforcements from the Baltic. Even though two months passed before the ships departed for the Far East, news that they were on the way spurred hopes in Port Arthur that the base could be held. The heavy artillery and manpower of the remaining Russian warships was put ashore to reinforce the city's defenses, which held up well enough until early December, when the Japanese captured a piece of high ground with a commanding view of the harbor, where they placed a battery of 11-inch howitzers. In the days that followed, the guns sank four battleships, one armored cruiser, and one protected cruiser, accounting for all of the larger warships except the *Sevastopol*, which the Russians themselves scuttled, deliber-ately choosing a spot in the harbor where the water was deep enough to prevent the Japanese from raising her later. With Rozhestvensky's fleet still months away, Port Arthur capitulated on 2 January 1905. The disaster brought Russian naval losses in the war to six battleships, two armored cruisers, and four protected cruisers, not counting ships interned in neutral ports. Smaller Russian units lost at Port Arthur included the minelayer *Amur*, the only surviving ship of its type after the *Yenisei* fell victim to one of its own mines earlier in the war. Japan's greatest losses were the two battleships sunk by mines on 15 May. Otherwise, the only Japanese units lost in 1904 (or in the entire war) were a small armored cruiser and two protected cruisers, all of which struck mines, and a protected cruiser, accidentally sunk in a collision with another Japanese cruiser.

Rozhestvensky's relief force, designated the Second Pacific Squadron, in fact included most of the Russian Baltic Fleet. It departed Libau on 15 October amid high hopes, which waned under the weight of bad news reports from the war zone and various mishaps along the way. The worst of the latter came just one week into the voyage, on the night of 21–22 October, as the fleet passed Dogger Bank in the North Sea. Nervous Russian gunners fired on a group of "Japanese torpedo boats," actually British fishing trawlers, sinking one trawler and damaging six, after which only the most strenuous diplomatic efforts by France (which considered Britain and Russia natural future allies against Germany) kept Britain from declaring war. Rozhestvensky divided his fleet off the coast of Spain, sending the smaller units to the Indian Ocean via the Mediterranean and the Suez Canal while the battleships proceeded around the Cape of Good Hope. In January 1905 Rozhestvensky reunited his forces off Madagascar, where he received news of the surrender of Port Arthur. In an attempt to make up for the ships lost there, Rozhestvensky received as reinforcement the Third Pacific Squadron under Rear Admiral N. I. Nebogatov, a force consisting of older or smaller battleships and cruisers not included in Rozhestvensky's squadron owing to their lack of speed and firepower. Cruising via the Suez Canal, the Third Squadron joined the Second in April 1905, at Camranh Bay in French Indochina. The combined force of 11 battleships, 3 armored cruisers, 5 protected cruisers, and 19 destroyers or smaller vessels then steamed northward to meet the surviving units of the Russian cruiser squadron at Vladivostok.[51]

As the long Russian column neared the war zone, Admiral Togo planned to intercept it in the Straits of Tsushima.[52] He had two fewer armored warships than Rozhestvensky (four battleships and eight armored cruisers) but the oldest of the lot had been commissioned in 1897, and Togo had three battleships larger than any ship in the Russian fleet. Aside from the four 13,520-ton *Borodino*s and the 12,680-ton battleship *Osliabia*, Rozhestvensky's warships were either unimpressive or obsolete. His battleships included the three 4,970-ton

Admiral Ushakov class coast defenders, and his three armored cruisers were actually armored frigates over twenty years old. At 13:40 on 27 May 1905, Togo opened the battle by crossing the Russian "T" from east to west, then repeating the maneuver from west to east. Rozhestvensky turned away and tried to steam past the Japanese to the northeast, forcing Togo to give chase. At 14:08 Russian guns scored the first hits of the battle, against the Japanese flagship, the 15,140-ton *Mikasa*, at a range of 7,000 meters. Though the two fleets fought at closer distances than in the Battle of the Yellow Sea (at Tsushima, the Japanese finally opened fire at 6,400 meters), medium-caliber artillery again played little role. Once again, the Japanese advantage in speed doomed the Russian quest to reach Vladivostok, but, unlike Vitgeft's ships the previous summer, Rozhestvensky's fleet had nowhere else to go. The *Osliabia* was the first casualty, at 15:00. As the Japanese line pulled ahead of the Russian line, Rozhestvensky doubled back and attempted to steam due north across the wake of Togo's column, but the Japanese admiral quickly doubled back to the west to cut him off. Rozhestvensky then turned away to the south, and his column began to disperse. The large stocks of coal the Russian warships carried into the battle only hastened their destruction, as widespread fires left many of them unable to defend themselves further as the Japanese closed to sink them. Between 18:30 and 19:30 three of the *Borodino*s sank, including Rozhestvensky's flagship *Suvorov*. The last fighting Russian units exchanged fire with their attackers at just 2,500 meters, and at such close range medium-caliber artillery finally came into play. During the night of 27–28 May the Japanese sank or captured most of the remaining Russian warships. Rozhestvensky, severely wounded, was rescued from the *Suvorov* before it sank, only to be captured aboard a Russian destroyer. On the morning of the 28th his second in command, Nebogatov, surrendered the last of the *Borodino*s (the 13,520-ton *Orel*) along with three smaller battleships.

Tsushima was just the sort of decisive battle Mahan had prophesied. The Japanese sank 6 Russian battleships, 1 armored cruiser, and 1 protected cruiser, and captured another 4 battleships. The Russians scuttled 1 battleship, 2 armored cruisers, and 1 protected cruiser to prevent their capture; the 3 remaining Russian protected cruisers eventually made their way to Manila, to be interned by the United States. Just 1 Russian warship, the armed yacht *Almaz*, made it through to Vladivostok; the other 18 smaller units were either sunk, scuttled, or captured. The Japanese lost 3 torpedo boats, and 3 of their armored warships suffered moderate damages. While the Japanese lost 110 men killed, Russian casualties included 4,830 men killed and 5,917 captured. The disastrous outcome of the largest naval engagement since Trafalgar forced Russia to the peace table. Negotiations mediated by the United States concluded in September 1905 in the Treaty of

Portsmouth. Russia's loss in territory (the southern half of Sakhalin Island) was minimal compared to its loss of influence in northeast Asia. Russia had to agree to transfer its lease of the Liaotung Peninsula to Japan, giving the Japanese the naval base at Port Arthur and informal title to the former Russian sphere of influence in Manchuria. Japan also gained a free hand in Korea, which it annexed in 1910.

The postwar Russian navy had just 10 battleships, 3 armored cruisers, and 8 protected cruisers, including 8 battleships and 1 armored cruiser in the Black Sea Fleet, a force paralysed by mutiny in June 1905, as a consequence of the revolution that swept Russia after the fall of Port Arthur. The 12,580-ton *Potemkin*, the largest Black Sea battleship, supported local revolutionaries at Odessa before steaming for Constanza. There, it was scuttled by its crew, who then sought asylum from the Romanian government. After the end of the revolution, the *Potemkin* was refloated, repaired, and renamed *Panteleimon*, to remove the stigma of disloyalty. It served in the Russian navy until 1917. Other Russian warships succumbing to mutiny in 1905 – an armored cruiser, a protected cruiser, and four destroyers – were also redesignated afterward.[53]

Anyone attempting to draw lessons from the Russo–Japanese War faced a difficult task, for the conflict had included almost all warship types in a number of different settings. A torpedo attack opened the war, but neither side deployed a submarine. Mines sank two Japanese battleships and one Russian battleship, and concern for mines to some extent shaped the behavior of both navies. Both sides made effective use of destroyers, which (aside from two deployed by Spain in 1898) saw their first action ever. The relative lack of importance of the medium-caliber quick-firing guns mounted by battleships and armored cruisers attracted the most attention of all. After being so significant in the major battles of the Sino–Japanese and Spanish–American wars, medium-caliber ordnance had little impact at the Battle of the Yellow Sea or at Tsushima, actions in which the big guns of the largest warships had registered hits at extraordinary ranges. Indeed, the performance of the newest battleships at Tsushima, in both firepower and speed, reflected the fact that the recent improvements in submarine and torpedo technologies had been matched after 1900 by further advances favoring large armored warships. Improved fire control, thanks to new range finders and better gun sighting, once again increased the advantage in range of heavy artillery over torpedoes. At the same time, the Belleville boiler gave way to new Yarrow and Babcock boilers, first fitted in British warships in 1901, which helped increase the speed of larger units. All of the ships at Tsushima burned coal, but the introduction of oil as a more efficient fuel for capital ships (then under consideration in Britain, which had tried oil in smaller warships as early as 1898) promised to extend yet another advantage to the battleship.[54]

INNOVATION BY ACCIDENT: THE *DREADNOUGHT* REVOLUTION

By the autumn of 1905 Britain had in service or under construction 66 battleships, including all those commissioned since the *Dreadnought* of 1879. France remained second, with 40 battleships, the oldest dating from 1878. Germany now ranked third with 37, the oldest likewise in service since 1878. Britain's superiority appears even more impressive if one subtracts from these totals the smaller battleships or large monitors designed for coastal operations only, of which Britain had 2, France 7, and Germany 8. Italy ranked a distant fourth among Europe's naval powers, with 18 battleships built or building, including the *Duilio* of 1880. The Russo–Japanese War had plunged Russia to fifth, its lowest ranking in two centuries, but the 10 battleships that had survived the disaster (including the *Ekaterina II* class, in service since 1889) by the end of 1905 were joined by another 5 under construction. Austria–Hungary ranked sixth, with 12 battleships built or building, including the *Tegetthoff* of 1882. In numbers and in quality, the battle fleet of the weakest of the six European naval powers far surpassed the greatest of the minor powers. In 1905 Spain had just one battleship in commission, the *Pelayo*. It had been in service since 1888 and was the only battleship in any of the minor European navies with a displacement of over 5,400 tons.

Britain had touched off the battleship renaissance in 1889 with its first formal commitment to the two-power standard, but by the autumn of 1905 recent events had made the standard meaningless. France was no longer an enemy and Russia no longer a great naval power, while, beyond Europe, Japan was a British ally and war with the United States seemed highly improbable. Germany now appeared to be Britain's most likely naval challenger, but as of 1905 the British navy was clearly superior, in numbers and in quality, to all three navies of the Triple Alliance. At sea, if not in all other respects, Britain was as secure and dominant as ever, but having already conceded the end of the Pax Britannica, the country's political and naval leaders seemed incapable of acting the part. As a naval power Britain had established the model for the modern hegemon, from 1815 to the mid-1890s reacting to innovations originating elsewhere (usually in France) but never compromising its existing strategic advantages by taking the lead in introducing a new technology. If there were any doubt that the Britain of 1905 no longer behaved like a true hegemon, it would be dispelled by Admiral Sir John Fisher.

The father of the revolutionary *Dreadnought* entered office as First Sea Lord in October 1904 convinced of the need for a new type of capital ship with a uniform armament of heavy guns, no secondary armament, and some light guns to ward off torpedo boats. By then, the idea of such an "all big-gun" warship was already being discussed internationally. Vittorio Cuniberti, the chief engineer of the Italian navy, shortly after the turn of the century had designed an all big-gun battleship which his own navy rejected; in 1903 he published his ideas in an article in *Jane's Fighting Ships* under the title "An ideal battleship for the British navy." By then, the British, American, and Japanese navies all were moving toward a single-caliber battleship design in order to improve fire control, as range-finding systems based on splash-spotting could not distinguish between the plumes of water created by shells from 6-inch and 12-inch guns. The *Lord Nelson* and *Agamemnon*, the last British capital ships ordered before Fisher took office, would have had an all big-gun armament of 12-inch guns if the sea lords had not overruled the Admiralty's design section; instead, they were given the standard four 12-inch guns with a very heavy secondary armament of ten 9.2-inch guns. As of 1904, however, Fisher's ideal type was not a battleship at all, but a large armored cruiser with 9.2-inch guns, reflecting the fact that his analysis of the wars of the 1890s had led him to embrace the heaviest caliber of quick-firing gun.[55] To the extent that the major naval battles of the Russo–Japanese War had an influence on Fisher's concept, it was in the abandonment of the 9.2-inch quick-firing gun as the weapon for his new ships. The all big-gun battleship *Dreadnought*, laid down at Portsmouth in October 1905, had ten 12-inch guns, no secondary armament, and two dozen 3-inch guns.

The writings of naval historian Arthur J. Marder have led countless authors to characterize Fisher as a disciple of Mahan, a staunch battle fleet advocate who considered the fast, all big-gun design the inevitable result of the evolution of the battleship. By introducing the new design, Fisher gambled that Britain would gain more than it lost by forfeiting the great advantage in pre-dreadnought battleships it had built up since 1889. But the more recent studies of Jon Tetsuro Sumida and Nicholas Lambert have provided an alternative view of Fisher as a maverick strategist determined to tear down the naval paradigm of his age. Fisher may have quoted Mahan at times, when it was useful for him to do so, but in general he rejected the lessons of history the American officer held so dear.[56] Sixty-three at the time of his appointment, Fisher had risen through the officer corps over the last four decades of the nineteenth century, an experience which led him to believe that Britain's fundamental naval interests were global rather than European. He saw France or the Franco–Russian combination as the greatest threat to Britain at sea, and considered it likely that the anti-British Jeune École would rise again in some form. Intrigued by the notion that the effective range of torpedoes might surpass that of battleship gunfire, he became an advocate of the destroyer and, especially, the submarine as delivery systems for torpedo warfare. This combination of factors, strategic and technological, brought Fisher to the conclusion that the future British capital ship should be a "fusion" of a battleship and armored cruiser, the design ultimately called a battle cruiser. The battle cruiser would be larger and more heavily armed than a battleship or an armored cruiser, with turbine engines providing an unprecedented speed. First fitted in the destroyer *Viper* in 1899, turbine engines had the further advantage of weighing hundreds of tons less than reciprocating engines with similar power. Fisher's specifications for the battle cruiser design called for still more weight to be saved by a significant reduction in armor. He argued that the finished product would be fast enough and powerful enough to hunt down any existing armored cruiser; more important, with its uniform primary armament guided by an improved fire control system, it would be able to outduel any battleship from a range at which its own weaker protection would be irrelevant. As of 1904, Fisher foresaw battle cruisers as the future defenders of British interests on the world's oceans. The pre-dreadnought battleships they replaced would defend home waters along with flotillas of destroyers and submarines. Fisher made sure Britain had more undersea boats than any other navy, and ordered so many flotilla craft that by 1909 they accounted for almost a quarter of the construction outlay.

The revolution touched off by the *Dreadnought* came more by accident than by design. Drawing up plans for his first capital ships, to be laid down in 1905–6, Fisher appeased battleship advocates by including one battleship (18,110 tons, 527 feet long, ten 12-inch guns, eleven inches of armor, with a speed of 21 knots) along with the units he considered the heart of his program, three battle cruisers (17,370 tons, 567 feet long, eight 12-inch guns, six inches of armor, with a speed of 25 knots). The battleship, the *Dreadnought,* was to be built first, beginning in October 1905, as a test platform for the unprecedented size, all big-gun armament, and turbine engines that would also be features of the three battle cruisers of the *Invincible* class. Work on the latter was begun early in 1906, and proceeded more slowly in order to incorporate lessons from the *Dreadnought*'s sea trials. Far from seeking to reinvent the battleship, Fisher apparently wanted the *Dreadnought* to be Britain's last battleship and all subsequent capital ships built as battle cruisers. But before work even began on the first battle cruisers, changes in Britain's international situation undermined Fisher's strategic vision. The Entente Cordiale had survived the Moroccan crisis of 1905 and the Russo–Japanese War, the latter had all but destroyed the Russian navy, and the German navy (further bolstered by Tirpitz's supplementary law of 1906) rather suddenly emerged as the British navy's primary rival. The unlikely combination of Britain, France, and Russia would soon coalesce into the Triple Entente, motivated by their mutual fear of Germany. Thus the dreadnought battleship, better suited for a war against Germany in the North Sea, won out over the battle cruiser, whose global reach for a war against France and Russia became irrelevant. Fisher had never intended to replicate the *Dreadnought*, yet it became the new model capital ship for the navies of Europe and the rest of the world as well (see Plate 25).

The *Dreadnought*'s preliminary trials were held in early October 1906, almost exactly a year after its keel was laid, and it was commissioned in December 1906. Its official building time of fourteen months has never been equalled for a capital ship. Its first cruise, to the Caribbean during the winter of 1906–7, impressed even the skeptics. The ship's Parsons turbine engines performed as expected, and its improved 12-inch guns fired two rounds per minute, a rate three times faster than that of the 12-inch guns of a decade earlier. The *Dreadnought* eventually received one of the first of the new range finders so crucial to Fisher's capital ship plans; developed by Arthur Hungerford Pollen and eventually produced by Pollen's Argo company, they had a 1 percent accuracy at 7,000 yards, a dramatic improvement over the British range finders of the 1890s, which offered the same rate of accuracy at 3,000 yards. The British naval estimates for 1906–7 included three dreadnoughts of the 18,800-ton *Bellerophon* class, and for 1907–8, three of the 19,560-ton *St Vincent* class. Slightly heavier copies of the original *Dreadnought*, they featured the same combination of ten 12-inch guns (paired in five turrets, three on the centerline and two amidships, abreast of the superstructure), Parsons turbine engines and Pollen range finders. Fisher finally got a fourth battle cruiser in the 1908–9 program, the 18,500-ton *Indefatigable*, funded along with an eighth dreadnought, the 19,680-ton *Neptune*.

CONCLUSION

Not since the demise of the wooden screw ship of the line at the onset of the ironclad age, forty-five years earlier, had a new type of capital ship so completely doomed its predecessor. After the completion of the *Dreadnought* just eight pre-dreadnought battleships were laid down: the last five units of France's *Danton* class and the three of Austria–Hungary's *Radetzky* class. By 1913 all six of the great powers of Europe had dreadnoughts in service, as did Spain, while Greece and Turkey had dreadnoughts under construction in foreign shipyards. The ability to build dreadnoughts from one's own domestic resources became a measure of great power status. Not unlike nuclear weapons in a later era, owning dreadnoughts made a country a factor in the international arena.

Among the European naval powers only Germany joined Britain in eventually commissioning battle cruisers, and only because Tirpitz could count these lightly protected fast battleships as "large cruisers" under the navy laws already in effect. Yet the introduction of the battle cruiser, though limited in scope, led to a fifteen-year hiatus in construction for the armored cruiser, a popular warship type during the preceding quarter-century. After work began on the first of Britain's *Invincibles* in February 1906, four armored cruisers were laid down in 1906–7 – France's *Waldeck-Rousseau*, Germany's *Blücher*, Italy's *San Marco*, and Greece's *Georgios Averof* – then none until after the Washington Naval Treaty of 1922 restricted the construction of warships of over 10,000 tons with more than 8-inch guns, creating the phenomenon of "treaty cruisers" built up to the new tonnage and armament limits. During the same years, navies also stopped building larger unarmored or protected cruisers, after 1905 constructing these types only as light cruisers of 5,500 tons or less. Even then, few were built other than by Britain (which began 41 in the years 1905–14) and Germany (which responded with 26). Italy laid down six, Austria–Hungary four, and Russia four, while France and the minor European naval powers built none at all. The general decline of traditional larger cruiser construction contributed to a remarkable increase in the tonnage differential between capital ships (dreadnoughts and battle cruisers) and other new units in the years before the First World War.

NOTES

[1] Marder, *The Anatomy of British Sea Power*, 7, 120–35; Aaron L. Friedberg, *The Weary Titan: Britain and the Experience of Relative Decline, 1895–1905* (Princeton, NJ, 1988), 146.

[2] Beresford to House of Commons, 13 December 1888, quoted in Charles William de la Poer Beresford, *The Memoirs of Admiral Lord Charles Beresford*, 2 vols (Boston, MA, 1914), 2:360.

[3] Marder, *The Anatomy of British Sea Power*, 105–6.

[4] Jon Tetsuro Sumida, *In Defence of Naval Supremacy: Finance, Technology and British Naval Policy, 1889–1914* (Boston, MA, 1989), 13–16; Roberts, "The Pre-Dreadnought Age, 1890–1905," 116; Brown, *Warrior to Dreadnought*, 124–32; *Conway, 1860–1905*, 32–3, 76–7, 66, 82.

[5] Philip Pugh, *The Cost of Seapower: The Influence of Money on Naval Affairs from 1815 to the Present Day* (London, 1986), 16; W. Mark Hamilton, *The Nation and the Navy: Methods and Organization of British Navalist Propaganda, 1889–1914* (New York, 1986), 9.

[6] Jon Tetsuro Sumida, *Inventing Grand Strategy and Teaching Command: The Classic Works of Alfred Thayer Mahan Revisited* (Baltimore, MD, 1997), 22–5.

[7] Sumida, *Inventing Grand Strategy and Teaching Command*, 99–103.

[8] Marder, *The Anatomy of British Sea Power*, 30; Sondhaus, *The Naval Policy of Austria–Hungary*, 126, 150–1; *idem*, "The Imperial German Navy and Social Democracy, 1878–1897," *German Studies Review* 18 (1995): 51–64.

[9] Sondhaus, *Preparing for Weltpolitik*, 223–4.

[10] Sumida, *Inventing Grand Strategy and Teaching Command*, 45, 72.

[11] Brown, *Warrior to Dreadnought*, 109.

[12] William N. Still Jr, *American Sea Power in the Old World: The United States Navy in European and Near Eastern Waters, 1865–1917* (Westport, CT, 1980), 94–101; Schurman, *Education of a Navy*, 62.

[13] Sondhaus, *Preparing for Weltpolitik*, 189, 193, 196–8. Tirpitz quoted from "Relation über die Herbstmanöver der Marine im Jahre 1893," Bundesarchiv-Militärarchiv, RM 4/62, 104–84.

[14] Lambi, *The Navy and German Power Politics*, 66; David C. Evans and Mark R. Peattie, *Kaigun: Strategy, Tactics, and Technology in the Imperial Japanese Navy, 1887–1941* (Annapolis, MD, 1997), 24.

[15] Tritten, "Doctrine and Fleet Tactics in the Royal Navy," 21.

[16] Thomas W. Harvey (comp.), *Memoir of Hayward Augustus Harvey* (New York, 1900), 62–3; *Krupp: A Century's History, 1812–1912* (Essen, 1912), 289; Günther Leckebusch, *Die Beziehungen der deutschen Seeschiffswerften zur Eisenindustrie an der Ruhr in der Zeit von 1850 bis 1930* (Cologne, 1963), 35; Benjamin Franklin Cooling, *Gray Steel and Blue Water Navy: The Formative Years of America's Military-Industrial Complex*, 1881–1917 (Westport, CT, 1979), 96–7.

[17] Richard Owen, "Military-Industrial Relations: Krupp and the Imperial Navy Office," in *Society and Politics in Wilhelmine Germany*, ed. Richard J. Evans (London, 1978), 75; *Krupp: A Century's History*, 288–9; Leckebusch, *Die Beziehungen der deutschen Seeschiffswerften zur Eisenindustrie*, 36n; Gröner, *Die deutschen Kriegsschiffe*, 1:36–7. Gary E. Weir, *Building the Kaiser's Navy: The Imperial Navy Office and German Industry in the von Tirpitz Era, 1890–1919* (Annapolis, MD, 1992), 30, dates the Krupp–Dillingen alliance from 1893.

[18] Owen, "Military-Industrial Relations," 75; *Krupp: A Century's History*, 289–91; Leckebusch, *Die Beziehungen der deutschen Seeschiffswerften zur Eisenindustrie*, 36–7; Gröner, *Die deutschen Kriegsschiffe*, 1:36; Brown, *Warrior to Dreadnought*, 150–1; Weir, *Building the Kaiser's Navy*, 31, 224n.

[19] Harvey, *Memoir of Hayward Augustus Harvey*, 65–79; Roberts, "The Pre-Dreadnought Age, 1890–1905," 116; Campbell, "Naval Armaments and Armour," 162; *Conway, 1860–1905*, 34, 142–9, 180–2, 221–2, 294–7, 343–4.

[20] Campbell, "Naval Armaments and Armour," 162–3; *Conway, 1860–1905*, 34, 142, 182, 221, 273, 293, 343; Sondhaus, *The Naval Policy of Austria–Hungary*, 153, 180.

[21] Nicholas A. Lambert, *Sir John Fisher's Naval Revolution* (Columbia, SC, 1999), 78; Jon Tetsuro Sumida, "The Quest for Reach: The Development of Long-Range Gunnery in the Royal Navy, 1901–1912," in *Tooling for War: Military Transformation in the Industrial Age*, ed. Stephen D. Chiabotti (Chicago, IL, 1996), 49.

[22] Roberts, "The Pre-Dreadnought Age, 1890–1905," 118–9; *Conway, 1860–1905*, 292–6, 303–5; Lambert, *Sir John Fisher's Naval Revolution*, 21.

[23] George F. Kennan, *The Fateful Alliance: France, Russia, and the Coming of the First World War* (New York, 1984), 97–115, 220–3 and *passim*; Roberts, "The Pre-Dreadnought Age, 1890–1905," 120–1; Tomitch, *Warships of the Imperial Russian Navy*, 25–75 *passim*; Watts, *The Imperial Russian Navy*, 172; *Conway, 1906–21*, 312; Lambert, *Sir John Fisher's Naval Revolution*, 23, 31.

[24] Brown, *Warrior to Dreadnought*, 143–6; Roberts, "The Pre-Dreadnought Age, 1890–1905," 117; *Conway, 1860–1905*, 34–7.

[25] Brown, *Warrior to Dreadnought*, 137–41; *Conway, 1860–1905*, 90–1, 157, 205, 237–8, 264, 326, 355, 363, 370, 379, 385.

[26] Ropp, *The Development of a Modern Navy*, 205; see text of British naval intelligence office memorandum of 28 October 1896 in Marder, *The Anatomy of British Sea Power*, 578–80.

[27] Marder, *The Anatomy of British Sea Power*, 263; Friedberg, *The Weary Titan*, 157–9.

[28] Evans and Peattie, *Kaigun*, 41–7.

[29] Ibid., 47–8; Charles H. Fairbanks Jr "The Origins of the *Dreadnought* Revolution: A Historiographical Essay," *International History Review* 13 (1991), 261; Brown, *Warrior to Dreadnought*, 167.

[30] Patrick J. Kelly, "Strategy, Tactics, and Turf Wars: Tirpitz and the Oberkommando der Marine, 1892–1895," paper presented at the Thirteenth Naval History Symposium, Annapolis, MD, 2–4 October 1997, 10; Gröner, *Die deutschen Kriegsschiffe*, 1:37–40; Fairbanks, "The Origins of the Dreadnought Revolution," 267.

[31] Rodríguez González, *Politica naval de la Restauracion*, 233–305 *passim*; Conway, *1860–1905*, 380–4.

[32] Sondhaus, *Naval Warfare, 1815–1914*, 175–6.

[33] Ibid., 177; Brown, *Warrior to Dreadnought*, 168.

[34] Tirpitz quoted in Jonathan Steinberg, *Yesterday's Deterrent: Tirpitz and the Birth of the German Battle Fleet* (New York, 1965), 126. Unless otherwise noted, the sources for the following paragraphs are Sondhaus, *Preparing for Weltpolitik*, 220–5, and Gröner, *Die deutschen Kriegsschiffe*, volume 1, *passim*.

[35] Bismarck quoted in Beresford, *Memoirs*, 2:363. See also Tirpitz, "Allgemeine Gesichtspunkte bei der Feststellung unserer Flotte nach Schiffsklassen und Schiffstypen," July 1897, in Volker R. Berghahn and Wilhelm Deist, *Rüstung im Zeichen der wilhelminischen Weltpolitik: Grundlegende Dokumente, 1890–1914* (Düsseldorf, 1988), 122–7.

[36] Tirpitz quoted in Holger H. Herwig, *The German Naval Officer Corps: A Social and Political History* (Oxford, 1973), 11.

[37] Alfred von Tirpitz, *Erinnerungen* (Leipzig, 1919), 100n., notes that the coastal battleships of the *Siegfried* class formed a separate category under the First Navy Law but were "rechristened, on paper, as battleships (*Linienschiffe*)" in the Second Navy Law of 1900. See also Sondhaus, *Preparing for Weltpolitik*, 225–6.

[38] Volker R. Berghahn, "Naval Armaments and Social Crisis: Germany before 1914," in *War, Economy, and the Military Mind*, ed. Geoffrey Best and Andrew Wheatcroft (London, 1976), 66.

[39] Baratelli, *La marina militare italiana*, 148; Marder, *The Anatomy of British Sea Power*, 171–2; Sondhaus, *Preparing for Weltpolitik*, 195, 220; *idem, The Naval Policy of Austria–Hungary*, 132, 156–7, 210, 236; Christopher Seton-Watson, *Italy: From Liberalism to Fascism, 1870–1925* (London, 1967), 181–3, 212.

[40] Bargoni, *Corazzate italiane classi Re Umberto – Ammiraglio di Saint Bon, passim*; Conway, *1860–1905*, 342–4, 350–1; http://users.hunterlink.net.au/westlakes/pagemorse.htm (accessed 10 August 2001); http://www.marconi.com/media/6p14to15.pdf (accessed 10 August 2001); http://digilander.iol.it/i2mov/page8.htm (accessed 10 August 2001).

[41] Sondhaus, *The Naval Policy of Austria–Hungary*, 124–9, 147–56.

[42] Walser, *France's Search for a Battle Fleet*, 42–5; Roberts, "The Pre-Dreadnought Age, 1890–1905," 119–20; Conway, *1860–1905*, 297.

[43] Tritten, "Navy and Military Doctrine in France," 55–8.

[44] Conway, *1860–1905*, 332–3.

[45] Tritten, "Navy and Military Doctrine in France," 55; Wilson, "Early Submarines," 154; Lambert, *Sir John Fisher's Naval Revolution*, 27.

[46] Nicholas A. Lambert, "Admiral Sir John Fisher and the Concept of Flotilla Defence, 1904–1909," *Journal of Military History* 59 (1995): 647–51; *idem, Sir John Fisher's Naval Revolution*, 77–9; Roberts, "The Pre-Dreadnought Age, 1890–1905," 113. On Ludwig Obry see Sondhaus, *The Naval Policy of Austria–Hungary*, 48, 72n.42.

[47] Lambert, *Sir John Fisher's Naval Revolution*, 73–86; Wilson, "Early Submarines," 155–7; *Conway, 1906–21*, 86–9, 206.

[48] Brown, *Warrior to Dreadnought*, 146–9; Roberts, "The Pre-Dreadnought Age, 1890–1905," 117–18; Lambert, "Admiral Sir John Fisher and the Concept of Flotilla Defence," 651; *idem, Sir John Fisher's Naval Revolution*, 31–2; *Conway, 1860–1905*, 38–40, 70–3.

[49] Lambert, *Sir John Fisher's Naval Revolution*, 99, 115; Brown, *Warrior to Dreadnought*, 204; *Conway, 1860–1905*, 60.

[50] The sources for this and the following paragraphs are Gromov *et al., Tri Veka Rossiiskogo Flota*, 1:343–78; Evans and Peattie, *Kaigun*, 75–9, 93, 100–9; Watts, *The Imperial Russian Navy*, 19–21; Woodward, *The Russians at Sea*, 122–5, 131–42; *Conway, 1860–1905*, 204, 220–30.

[51] Gromov *et al., Tri Veka Rossiiskogo Flota*, 1:379–87; Richard Hough, *The Fleet That Had To Die* (London, 1958), 32–144 *passim*; Woodward, *The Russians at Sea*, 139–44.

[52] On the Battle of Tsushima and its aftermath see Gromov *et al., Tri Veka Rossiiskogo Flota*, 1:387–402; Hough, *The Fleet That Had To Die*, 156–86, 206–7; Watts, *The Imperial Russian Navy*, 22–3; Woodward, *The Russians at Sea*, 151–3; Evans and Peattie, *Kaigun*, 119–24; Brown, *Warrior to Dreadnought*, 173.

[53] Woodward, *The Russians at Sea*, 156–9; see also Richard Hough, *The Potemkin Mutiny* (London, 1960).

[54] Sumida, "The Quest for Reach," 57; Lambert, "Admiral Sir John Fisher and the Concept of Flotilla Defence," 650–3; Roberts, "The Pre-Dreadnought Age, 1890–1905," 113; Griffiths, "Warship Machinery," 177.

[55] Brown, *Warrior to Dreadnought*, 182; *Conway, 1906–21*, 21; Fairbanks, "The Origins of the *Dreadnought* Revolution," 262.

[56] On Fisher's quotations from Mahan see Friedberg, *The Weary Titan*, 143. Sources for the remainder of this section are Sumida, *In Defence of Naval Supremacy*, 50–100 *passim; idem*, "Sir John Fisher and the *Dreadnought*: The Sources of Naval Mythology," *Journal of Military History* 59 (1995): 619–38 *passim*; Lambert, *Sir John Fisher's Naval Revolution*, 93–157 *passim; idem*, "Admiral Sir John Fisher and the Concept of Flotilla Defence," 641–60; Brown, *Warrior to Dreadnought*, 180–204; *Conway, 1906–21*, 21–6; Campbell, "Naval Armaments and Armour," 165; Griffiths, "Warship Machinery," 178.

6

THE DREADNOUGHT ERA AND FIRST WORLD WAR, 1906–22

The commissioning of the *Dreadnought* in December 1906 caught Europe's other naval powers with their latest classes of pre-dreadnoughts either under construction or already funded. Each country had to decide whether to attempt to copy the new design immediately or follow through with existing plans in the short term. Germany, Russia, and Italy resolved to lay down no more pre-dreadnoughts, but still suffered long interruptions in their battleship programs: for the Germans, the last pre-dreadnought was begun in August 1905, the first dreadnought in June 1907, while in Russia the hiatus in construction starts lasted from April 1904 to June 1909, and in Italy, from October 1903 to June 1909. Austria–Hungary and France proceeded to lay down pre-dreadnoughts already approved before the end of 1906, delaying the construction starts of their first dreadnoughts to July 1910 and September 1910, respectively. Amid the general disruption in battleship programs, Britain took a commanding lead in the new capital ship types.

The battleship renaissance preceding the dreadnought era drew its ideological justification from authors such as Alfred Thayer Mahan and Philip Colomb, who reflected upon the strategic questions of their time in the light of past history. In the process they ignored the militarization of naval warfare which had begun early in the industrial revolution and continued to intensify in their own era. But by the turn of the century, the swift, timely application of technology had become an obsession in Europe's armies, as reflected by Germany's Schlieffen Plan and the corresponding war plans of the other great powers. The same was true in Europe's navies. By the time the dreadnought entered service, naval strategists were preoccupied with the need to mobilize quickly in order to strike the first decisive blow, while strategists and tacticians alike accepted the primacy of technology. Mahan's strategic lessons from the era of sailing ships continued to play well with politicians and the reading public, but were considered irrelevant by the generation of navy men who had made their careers during the battleship renaissance. Thus the leading prewar British writer on naval doctrine, Sir Julian Stafford Corbett, had relatively less influence than Mahan or Colomb precisely because his work *Some Principles of Maritime Strategy* (1911) used historical examples in the manner of his predecessors.[1]

THE ANGLO–GERMAN NAVAL RACE

The British navy first devised war plans against Germany during the Moroccan crisis of 1905, but the growing strength of the German fleet did not affect the peacetime deployment of the British navy until the end of 1906, by which time Tirpitz had his 16 newest pre-dreadnought battleships stationed on the North Sea at Wilhelmshaven, prompting a decision to maintain 16 battleships in the Channel Fleet, at the time Britain's only fleet based in home waters. In arguing for the creation of a new Home Fleet over the winter of 1906–7, Fisher initially held to his earlier sentiments regarding home defense, proposing that it include all of the destroyers, torpedo boats, and submarines not otherwise assigned, backed by older reserve battleships. But by the time the new fleet was created in March 1907, it had grown to include the navy's eight best capital ships. As it entered regular service the *Dreadnought* was assigned to the Home Fleet, as were the first battle cruisers and subsequent dreadnoughts.[2]

Germany's first dreadnoughts, the four units of the 18,900-ton *Nassau* class (laid down June–August 1907), had a displacement 43 percent greater than that of its last pre-dreadnoughts of the *Deutschland* class. Thus, for the Germans, the transition to dreadnought construction required a Herculean effort by the naval-industrial complex, against which the onset of Fisher's capital ship program in Britain (where the *Dreadnought* was a mere 13 percent larger than the pre-dreadnoughts of the *Lord Nelson* class) pales in comparison. Even then, there was not enough time to develop all of the requisite technologies; thus, the *Nassau*s had the same 11.1-inch primary armament of their predecessors and had triple-expansion engines capable of just 19.5 knots, making them inferior to the first British dreadnoughts in both firepower and speed. They carried their twelve heavy guns in six turrets, two fore and two aft on the centerline and two abreast of the superstructure, a layout (like that of their early British counterparts) which prevented them from training all of their guns for a broadside. By October 1909, when the *Nassau* was commissioned, Britain already had five dreadnoughts and three battle cruisers in service, but Germany promised to close the gap soon enough with a second group of four dreadnoughts, the 22,800-ton *Helgoland* class, all of which were under construction by March 1909, thanks to a supplementary law passed by the Reichstag in 1908, allowing Tirpitz to accelerate future battleship construction. In addition to being significantly larger than the *Nassaus*, the *Helgolands* matched the latest British dreadnoughts in firepower (mounting 12-inch guns) if not in speed (owing to their triple expansion engines). Meanwhile, after the 15,800-ton armored cruiser *Blücher* (laid down 1907), Tirpitz filled his annual "large cruiser" quota with battle cruisers, starting with the 19,400-ton *Von der Tann* (1908; see Plate 26) and 23,000-ton *Moltke* (1909), the first German capital ships with turbine engines. Fisher's invention of a cruiser type as big as a battleship provided a welcome windfall for Tirpitz, whose doubts about the design were overriden by the fact that, without getting another navy law through the Reichstag, he could now build 58 capital ships (38 dreadnoughts and 20 battle cruisers) rather than 38 capital ships (all battleships) and 20 armored cruisers. In the midst of the flurry of German construction starts, Parliament funded just two new capital ships (the dreadnought *Neptune* and battle cruiser *Indefatigable*) in 1908–9, causing the British navy to lose most of its early lead. By March 1909 Britain had 12 dreadnoughts and battle cruisers built or building to Germany's 10, a pace that would leave the British navy far short even of the 3:2 ratio of superiority which Tirpitz was willing to accept.

The accelerated rate of German naval construction alarmed the British, who took decisive action to stay ahead in the race. At the end of March 1909 Parliament approved the naval estimates for 1909–10, including six dreadnoughts and two battle cruisers. Work would start on three dreadnoughts and one battle cruiser by December 1909, with the rest to follow by April 1910 if Germany refused to end the competition. Extremists in Britain called for negotiations based on a "two-German" standard, which Germany was certain to reject. Cooler heads prevailed at the Admiralty, which abandoned the two-power standard in April 1909 in favor of a 60 percent capital ship advantage over Germany. At the time, however, Tirpitz held out for a 4:3 ratio of British superiority. Seeing no chance for a settlement, in July 1909 the House of Commons authorized the remainder of the program for the spring of 1910. The House of Lords held up the measure for months, to protest the fact that Britain's Liberal government planned to finance the so-called "four-plus-four" program by raising taxes on the wealthiest Britons. Nevertheless, by May 1910 Britain had under construction two 20,225-ton *Colossus* class dreadnoughts, four 20,220-ton *Orion* class dreadnoughts, and two 26,270-ton *Lion* class battle cruisers (see Plate 27). Seeking a qualitative advantage, designers gave additional firepower to the *Orions* and *Lions* (13.5-inch guns instead of 12-inch guns) and unprecedented speed to the *Lion*s (27 knots). The dominions also contributed to the cause, as Australia and New Zealand each paid for a battle cruiser of the 18,500-ton *Indefatigable* class, laid down in British shipyards in June 1910.

In gambling that Britain would lack the political will to build enough dreadnoughts and battle cruisers to retain its lead over Germany, Tirpitz committed one of the most fateful political blunders of the twentieth century. The tables were now turned, and after laying down six new capital ships to Britain's two in 1908–9, Germany began just three to Britain's ten in 1909–10: the first two dreadnoughts of the 24,700-ton *Kaiser* class and the 23,000-ton battle cruiser *Goeben*. As of June 1910 Britain had 22 battleships or battle cruisers built and building to Germany's 13, figures which led Tirpitz to doubt privately whether Germany still could win the race. He became much more willing to come to terms, by 1911 proposing acceptance of a 3:2 (15:10) British advantage in capital ships, close to Britain's goal of a 60 percent (16:10) superiority over Germany. The two sides failed to reach a settlement because Britain insisted that the battle cruisers *Australia* and *New Zealand*, along with any future "dominion ships," not be included in British totals, while Germany insisted that any naval treaty should be part of a general political understanding involving explicit British recognition of the status quo in Europe, including Germany's possession of Alsace–Lorraine. In 1910–11 and again in 1911–12, the Germans laid down four capital ships (three dreadnoughts and one battle cruiser) and the British, five (four dreadnoughts and one battle cruiser). Meanwhile, the quest for a qualitative advantage led to further increases in displacement. The Germans followed the last three 24,700-ton *Kaiser* class dreadnoughts and the 25,000-ton battle cruiser *Seydlitz* with the first three dreadnoughts of the 25,800-ton *König* class (see Plate 28) and the 26,600-ton battle cruiser *Derfflinger*. Britain responded with the four dreadnoughts of the 23,000-ton *King George V* class and the 26,770-ton battle cruiser *Queen Mary*, followed by the four dreadnoughts of the 25,000-ton *Iron Duke* class and the 28,430-ton battle cruiser *Tiger*.

During 1911 British banker Sir Ernest Cassel and German steamship magnate Albert Ballin opened a private channel of Anglo–German negotiations which resulted in Lord Richard Haldane's famous mission to Berlin in February 1912. Once again, Germany's insistence that any naval treaty include broader political conditions precluded a settlement, even before the numbers were debated. In the end, Chancellor Theobald von Bethmann Hollweg wanted blanket assurances of Britain's neutrality in any war Germany would fight on the continent, assurances Britain could not give without jeopardizing the Triple Entente. Political rhetoric then further poisoned relations, as the recently appointed First Lord of the Admiralty, Winston Churchill, called the German navy a "luxury" fleet. Germany subsequently rejected Churchill's appeal for a "naval holiday" of one year, and in March 1912 Tirpitz secured passage of another supplementary navy law raising the authorized strength of the German fleet to 61 capital ships (41 dreadnoughts and 20 battle cruisers). Churchill responded by withdrawing the British Atlantic Fleet from Gibraltar to home waters, and moving the battleships of the Mediterranean Fleet to Gibraltar from Malta, where a division of battle cruisers accounted for the largest remaining units. The redeployment reflected the growing bond between Britain and France, whose navy became the primary guardian of the Entente's Mediterranean interests. The moves increased the number of British capital ships in home waters from 22 to 33, henceforth organized as the Grand Fleet. By 1913, it included 41 capital ships.

The supplementary law of 1912 was Tirpitz's final political victory. In 1913 the Reichstag funded a significant expansion of the German army, ending the fifteen-year trend of the navy consuming an ever greater share of the defense outlay. Whereas the navy had accounted for an all-time high of just over 35 percent of German defense expenditure in 1911–12, by 1913–14 the navy's share (albeit of a larger pie) was just under 25 percent. Germany continued to fund one new battle cruiser per year (the 26,700-ton *Lützow* in 1912–13 and the 27,000-ton *Ersatz Hertha* in 1913–14) but authorized just one new *König* class dreadnought in 1912–13 and the first two 28,500-ton *Bayern* class dreadnoughts in 1913–14. Over the same period, Britain continued its recent pace of five capital ships per year, all built as dreadnoughts now that Fisher had retired. The five 27,500-ton *Queen Elizabeth*s and five 28,000-ton *Royal Sovereign*s featured eight 15-inch guns in four centerline turrets, and the *Queen Elizabeth*s were the first battleships fitted to burn oil only.[3] Fisher's legacy included a continued investment in flotilla craft and submarines; indeed, there is evidence that, in revising the estimates for 1914–15 on the eve of the First World War, the Admiralty was prepared to reduce the number of new capital ships from four to two, barely enough to maintain the 60 percent margin of superiority over Germany, in order to allocate the money saved to build twenty new submarines.[4] The onset of war forced a revision of the program in any event and, under the direction of Fisher, who returned to office as First Sea Lord in October 1914, five battle cruisers were laid down in the first six months of 1915. Meanwhile, in Germany, another two *Bayern* class dreadnoughts and a battle cruiser were included in the estimates for 1914–15; one of the dreadnoughts was laid down in the spring of 1914, the other two ships early in 1915.

The high stakes and high degree of secrecy made the Anglo–German naval race the first truly modern arms race. In the recent heyday of industrial capitalism, corporate profits had mattered more than attempting to give one's own country a monopoly over a technological breakthrough; thus, for example, most naval powers ended up producing their own Whitehead torpedoes, Belleville boilers, and Krupp armor under license. Even in the Anglo–German naval race, British dreadnoughts and battle cruisers had Krupp armor, while their German counterparts eventually were powered by Parsons turbine engines. Yet in the crucial area of fire control, Fisher saw to it that Britain retained a monopoly over Pollen's range finders. Under his September 1906 agreement with the Admiralty, Pollen agreed to sign over all of his patents, present and future, to the British government, and to apply for no patents in other countries. But haggling over specific terms prevented a definitive contract from being signed until February 1908, and did not bode well for Pollen's future relations with the Admiralty. He was a controversial figure in his own time, and historians remain divided over the trustworthiness of both the man and his inventions. Admiral Sir Arthur Wilson, who succeeded Fisher as First Sea Lord in 1910, had little faith in Pollen's system and saw to it that the navy continued to purchase competing products from other companies. In 1913 the Admiralty elected not to buy Pollen's latest range finder, the Argo Clock Mark V, considering its cost (£2,400 per unit) exorbitant and other, less expensive range finders more than adequate. Thus, British navy leaders may have rejected the best range finder available to them, but they did so believing that, in any event, they would enjoy a superiority over the Germans in fire control. Pollen's Argo products included a gyroscopic stabilizer lacking in German range finders, but the German equipment featured superior stereoscopic optics. This factor, plus better fire-control training methods, may have facilitated a faster reaction to changing ranges, accounting for the relative success of German gunfire at the Battle of Jutland in 1916.[5]

Like most arms races, the Anglo–German naval race included a spiral in expenses, which naturally rose as capital ship displacements increased. The *Dreadnought*, laid down in 1905, cost slightly less that £1.73 million, the *Queen Elizabeths*, begun in 1912, just over £2.68 million apiece. The *Nassau*, laid down in 1907, cost slightly less than 37 million marks, the *Ersatz Hertha*, begun in 1913 (and commissioned during the war as the *Hindenburg*), 59 million.[6] But with the increase in unit cost of capital ships, the number maintained by the leading navies fell accordingly. In order to maintain Europe's strongest navy, in 1815 Britain had 100 ships of the line, in the 1870s, 60 ironclads, and in 1914, 42 dreadnoughts or battle cruisers, counting warships still under construction. At the end of July 1914, Britain had 33 dreadnoughts and 9 battle cruisers built or building, including a total of 29 (21 dreadnoughts and 8 battle cruisers) in commission. Germany had 27 (20 dreadnoughts and 7 battle cruisers) built or building, including 18 (14 dreadnoughts and 4 battle cruisers) in commission. The British public paid dearly for this margin of superiority, but the First World War would demonstrate that the financial sacrifice had not been made in vain.

THE DREADNOUGHT REVOLUTION IN THE REST OF EUROPE

In the years before 1914 Europe's greatest naval race outside of the North Sea was centered in the Adriatic, where nominal allies Italy and Austria–Hungary renewed their old naval rivalry. Counting all battleships building or built in the past twenty-five years, at the end of 1905 Italy had 18 to Austria–Hungary's 12, but in battleships begun since 1893, Austria–Hungary had 9 to Italy's 8. Thus, even before dreadnoughts were a factor, the impending retirement of Brin's battleships of the 1880s jeopardized the Italian quantitative advantage. Italy's qualitative edge remained strong, however, as Austria–Hungary's nine newest pre-dreadnoughts included three each of the 5,600-ton *Monarch* class, the 8,300-ton *Habsburg* class, and the 10,600-ton *Erzherzog* class, while all eight of Italy's newer battleships displaced 10,000 tons or more. By 1905 Italy also had six armored cruisers in service to Austria–Hungary's three. The Dual Monarchy built no more armored cruisers after the *Sankt Georg* (commissioned 1905); Italy, in contrast, had four armored cruisers (ranging in size from 9,800 to 10,700 tons) under construction as late as 1907. But the Austro–Hungarian navy benefited from the patronage of the heir to the throne, Archduke Francis Ferdinand, and enjoyed the support of a broad domestic political coalition. The Dual Monarchy had also developed a first-rate naval-industrial complex, and could build battleships much faster than Italy (indeed, faster than any countries other than Britain and Germany).[7]

In November 1906, one month before the completion of the *Dreadnought*, Austro–Hungarian legislators approved the naval estimates for 1907, including funds to begin work on the 14,500-ton *Radetzky* class, three battleships 45 percent larger than the most recent class, the *Erzherzogs*. Navy leaders did not want to risk resubmitting the *Radetzkys* through the Dual Monarchy's convoluted budget process as more expensive dreadnoughts, and some also doubted the country's naval-industrial complex could handle a jump directly from the 10,600-ton *Erzherzogs* to dreadnought construction even if the funding were available. The decision was made to proceed with the *Radetzkys*, formidable battleships with four 12-inch guns backed by a heavy secondary armament of eight 9.4-inch guns, a firepower far superior to any Italian pre-dreadnought. In response, the Italian navy proposed starting a dreadnought program in the 1907–8 fiscal year, only to be rejected by Italian political leaders who pointed to the fact that the Austro–Hungarian and French navies had yet to lay down dreadnoughts of their own. But after Austria–Hungary's annexation of Bosnia–Hercegovina in 1908 caused a further worsening of its relations with Italy, in April 1909 the socialist press in Vienna broke the story that the Austro–Hungarian naval commander, Admiral Count Rudolf Montecuccoli, had proposed to Emperor Francis Joseph a new fleet plan including four 20,000-ton dreadnoughts. The Italian parliament promptly authorized a dreadnought, the 19,550-ton *Dante Alighieri*, which was laid down in June 1909. It was the first dreadnought designed to carry its heavy guns (twelve of 12-inch caliber) in triple-gun turrets, with all four turrets on the centerline. Meanwhile, across the Adriatic, a constitutional crisis in Hungary paralysed the Dual Monarchy's legislative process from April 1909 to May 1910, and the common budget, including naval appropriations and the new dreadnought program, could not be approved. In this political vacuum, Admiral Montecuccoli, Archduke Francis Ferdinand, and the Rothschild bank arranged a deal under which the Stabilimento Tecnico Triestino shipyard, Skoda gun factory, and Witkowitz armor works would build two dreadnoughts "at their own risk," on the assumption that the navy would take over the contracts upon resolution of the Hungarian crisis. The illegal scheme was kept secret until April 1910, by which time materials for the two 20,000-ton ships were already being delivered to Trieste. The *Viribus Unitis* was laid down in July 1910, and the *Tegetthoff*, for which the class was named, in September. Like the *Dante Alighieri*, the *Tegetthoff*s were armed with twelve 12-inch guns, divided among four centerline triple-gun turrets (see Plate 29).

Before work began on either of the *Tegetthoff*s, the Italian parliament approved the three 22,990-ton dreadnoughts of the *Cavour* class, which were laid down in June, July, and August of 1910. Their design included one more 12-inch gun than the *Dante Alighieri* and the *Tegetthoff*s, necessitating a configuration of three triple-gun and two double-gun turrets. Austro–Hungarian legislators subsequently gave retroactive approval to the first two *Tegetthoff*s in October 1910, then approved a second pair in March 1911, along with a long-term Austro–Hungarian fleet plan calling for 16 battleships, 12 cruisers, 24 destroyers, 72 torpedo boats, and 12 submarines, with ships to be replaced automatically after fixed terms of service. Admiral Montecuccoli's plan put the Dual Monarchy on course to build and maintain a modern battle fleet roughly half the size of the German and one-third the size of the British, but at an exorbitant cost: in the last fiscal year before the war, the navy received one quarter of the entire Austro–Hungarian defense outlay.

In January 1912 Austria–Hungary laid down its second pair of dreadnoughts, the *Prinz Eugen* at Trieste and the *Szent István* at Fiume, a port in the Hungarian half of the Dual Monarchy. Italy responded with its fifth and sixth dreadnoughts, the 22,960-ton *Andrea Doria* and *Duilio*, laid down in February and March. Technically a new class, they were almost identical to the *Cavour*s, including the same configuration of thirteen 12-inch guns. Thanks to its more efficient shipyards, in October 1912 Austria–Hungary became the third European naval power to have a dreadnought in commission, when the *Viribus Unitis* entered service after a building time of just twenty-seven months. The *Dante Alighieri* was commissioned in January 1913, forty-three months after it was laid down. The *Tegetthoff* entered service in July 1913, followed by the first two *Cavour*s in May 1914 and the *Prinz Eugen* in July 1914. Thus, each navy had three dreadnoughts in commission at the outbreak of the First World War.

By then, the tensions fueling the Adriatic naval race had subsided, at least temporarily, thanks to the Italo–Turkish War of 1911–12, which temporarily strained Italy's relations with each of the countries of the Triple Entente, leading to an unexpected extension of the Triple Alliance in December 1912. At the urging of Germany, in June 1913 Italy and Austria–Hungary renegotiated the Triple Alliance naval convention of 1900. Admiral Anton Haus (Montecuccoli's successor as Austro–Hungarian naval commander) was designated commander of a battle fleet to include the Italian and Austro–Hungarian dreadnoughts and newest pre-dreadnoughts, joined by any German warships that happened to be in the Mediterranean. In case of war the allied fleet would assemble at Messina, Sicily, then steam westward to engage the French fleet and block the transport of colonial troops from North Africa to France. A strong mutual suspicion clouded the interactions between the Austro–Hungarian and Italian navies throughout the life of the convention, which became a dead letter on 31 July 1914, when Italy condemned Austria–Hungary's declaration of war against Serbia as an act of aggression. Over the months that followed, Italy pursued a policy of neutrality increasingly favorable to the Entente, which it joined in May 1915.

The prewar naval planning of the Triple Alliance paid remarkably little attention to the Russian navy, which four years after its disastrous loss to the Japanese had four dreadnoughts under construction and was well on the way to recovery. In the intervening years, the Revolution of 1905 had forced Nicholas II to concede a constitution, providing for an elected Duma which first met in 1906. Organizational changes affecting the navy included the creation of the post of navy minister in place of the traditional "General Admiral" (a combined operational and administrative commander-in-chief), and the formation of a naval general staff. Russian shipyards completed five pre-dreadnoughts under construction when the Russo–Japanese War ended (the 13,520-ton *Slava*, the 12,840-ton *Evstafi* and *Ioann Zlatoust*, and the 17,400-ton *Andrei Pervosvanni* and *Imperator Pavel*), all of which were commissioned by 1910. The 15,190-ton *Rurik* and three smaller armored cruisers begun in 1905 joined the fleet by 1911. The decommissioning of two old battleships and an armored cruiser left the Russian fleet of

1911 with an active list of 13 battleships, 6 armored cruisers, and 10 protected cruisers. As of 1914, the Russian navy had 37 submarines and 11 large destroyers.[8]

The Italian engineer Cuniberti had a strong influence on the design of the four dreadnoughts of the 23,360-ton *Gangut* class, laid down in June 1909 in St Petersburg. Like the *Dante Alighieri*, they had twelve 12-inch guns in four centerline triple-gun turrets. After having so many battleships sunk by Japanese gunfire in 1904–5, the Russians insisted upon an almost complete plating of the hull above the waterline. All four *Gangut*s were launched in 1911, and were completed in time to enter service in the Baltic Fleet late in 1914. During 1911 the same St Petersburg shipyards laid down four 32,500-ton battle cruisers of the *Borodino* class, and the Duma authorized three dreadnoughts of the 22,600-ton *Imperatritsa Maria* class for the Black Sea Fleet, laid down at Nikolaiev. Like the *Gangut*s, the *Imperatritsa Maria*s were unusually heavily armored, and carried twelve 12-inch guns in four centerline turrets. The dreadnought program brought a dramatic rise in Russian naval expenditure, from 87 million rubles in 1908 to 247 million in 1913, but the money was not well spent. After the shocking losses of 1904–5 most Russian admirals adopted a defensive mentality, and became extraordinarily cautious in their deployment of big, expensive battleships. In 1909 the navy made improvements to the Baltic bases guarding the approaches to St Petersburg (Reval, Vyborg, and Kronstadt) but at the same time all but abandoned the forward base at Libau on the Latvian coast, developed at great cost in the 1890s. Under a naval general staff war plan of 1912, the larger units of the Baltic Fleet would be kept at anchor, under the guns of formidable shore batteries, with minefields providing further protection. In the years before the First World War, no measures were taken to improve the navy's Black Sea bases. After the loss of Port Arthur, Vladivostok again became the primary Russian Pacific base, but the 5,900-ton protected cruiser *Askold* was the largest unit assigned to the "Siberian flotilla" stationed there.[9]

The *Gangut*s were already under construction for more than a year before France laid down its first dreadnought. The French navy lost valuable time in the competition by proceeding with the six 18,320-ton *Danton*s, Europe's largest pre-dreadnoughts, armed with four 12-inch and twelve 9.4-inch guns, despite the fact that only the lead ship of the class was under construction by the time the *Dreadnought* entered service. Politics determined the decision, as the Chamber of Deputies had authorized the *Danton*s almost as an emergency measure in the wake of the Moroccan crisis of 1905; with the French army's buildup against Germany consuming ever greater sums of money, the navy could not assume that any *Danton*s not built would automatically be replaced by dreadnoughts. Further complicating matters, Vice

Admiral Fournier, the last surviving Jeune Écolist among senior officers, tried to delay the *Danton*s (the last of which was finally laid down
in July 1908), proposing a larger submarine force as an alternative. At
least one Jeune École sympathizer in the chamber subsequently
attempted to obstruct the first French dreadnoughts, which were
approved in April 1910 as the first step in a ten-year construction program devised by the minister of marine, Vice Admiral Augustin Boué
de Lapeyrère. By September 1910, when work began on the 22,190-ton
Courbet, ten other countries had dreadnoughts built or building (the
other five European naval powers plus Spain, the United States, Japan,
Argentina, and Brazil) and four had dreadnoughts in commission
(Britain, Germany, the United States, and Brazil).[10]

A second *Courbet* was laid down later in 1910 and two more in 1911.
They carried their twelve 12-inch guns in six turrets, two fore and two
aft on the centerline and two abreast of the superstructure, and thus
could not train all of their guns for a broadside. This flaw was not
repeated in the three 23,230-ton *Bretagne*s, begun during 1912, or the
five 25,230-ton *Normandie*s, laid down in 1913–14. While the *Bretagne*s
carried ten 13.4-inch guns in five centerline turrets, the *Normandie*s featured a revolutionary configuration of twelve 13.4-inch guns in three
centerline turrets of four guns each. The *Jean Bart* was the first of the
*Courbet*s to enter service, in June 1913. The last of the class was commissioned on 1 August 1914. Thus, despite its late start, the French
navy entered the First World War with four dreadnoughts in service
and another eight under construction. Between 1905 and 1914 France
dropped from second place to a distant third among Europe's naval
powers and, beyond Europe, was also passed by the United States and
Japan. Nevertheless, during the war the French dreadnoughts, backed
by the six *Danton*s (all commissioned during 1911), easily dominated
the Mediterranean, which Britain had practically conceded to France in
1912. As late as the summer of 1914 some British leaders denied that
the Entente was an alliance, but Anglo–French naval commitments
indicated otherwise. In exchange for France defending Anglo–French
interests in the Mediterranean against the possible combination of
Triple Alliance naval forces, Britain pledged to defend the French
Channel and Atlantic coast against the German navy.[11]

Spain managed to have a dreadnought under construction before
France, but the Spanish navy was too small to be a factor in the pre-
1914 balance of naval power. The only larger warships of the 1890s to
survive the Spanish–American War were those withheld from action or
not completed in time to be deployed: the 9,745-ton pre-dreadnought
Pelayo (commissioned 1888), the 9,090-ton armored cruiser *Emperador
Carlos V* (1898), and the three 6,890-ton armored cruisers of the
Princesa de Asturias class (1902–4). For a decade after the disastrous
defeat Spain laid down no new battleships or cruisers; to make matters

worse, one of its newest warships, the *Princesa de Asturias*'s sister-ship *Cardinal Cisneros*, was lost to shipwreck in 1905. The Spanish navy's fortunes improved after 1908, when the Cortes approved a naval program including three dreadnoughts to be built in the navy yard at Ferrol. A new Anglo–Spanish consortium of armaments firms improved the country's naval-industrial complex, provided the necessary imported materials, then oversaw the construction of the warships. The three units of the *España* class were the smallest and least heavily armed dreadnoughts ever built, displacing just 15,450 tons, armed with eight 12-inch guns. The *España* (built 1909–13) was followed by the *Alfonso XIII* (1910–15) and the *Jaime I* (1912–21), the last delayed considerably by Spain's decision to remain neutral during the First World War, which froze British support for the program for the years 1914–19. In 1914 the Spanish Cortes approved a second trio of dreadnoughts, designed at 21,000 tons, but the war caused the project to be abandoned.[12]

Among the minor naval powers of northern Europe, only the Netherlands considered building dreadnoughts, and only for the defense of the Dutch East Indies. The lone Dutch battleship built in the dreadnought era was the coast defender *De Zeven Provincien* (1908–10), at 6,530 tons very small by the standards of the time, but still the largest warship yet commissioned by the Netherlands. During the prewar years the Scandinavian navies likewise constructed only small battleships for coastal defense. Denmark built the 3,735-ton *Peder Skram* (launched 1908), while Armstrong laid down the 4,900-ton *Nidaros* and *Björgvin* for Norway (1913), which were completed for British wartime use as the large monitors *Gorgon* and *Glatton* (1915). Sweden built the largest coastal battleship of the lot, the 7,125-ton *Sverige* (1912–17). Along with two sister-ships completed in the early 1920s, it served until the 1950s.[13]

THE NEAR EASTERN AND BALKAN WARS (1911–13)

On the eve of the First World War, the Ottoman Empire suffered defeats at the hands of Italy and an alliance of Balkan states, bringing further instability to Europe's least stable flank. Unlike in earlier crises during the long, gradual crumbling of the Ottoman Empire, the naval forces of the great powers could not be brought to bear to mediate either conflict, owing to the arms races in the North Sea and Adriatic, along with the recent collapse of Russian naval power. Thus the Italian navy easily defeated the Turks in the Italo–Turkish War of 1911–12, and the Greek navy likewise triumphed in the First Balkan War of 1912–13.[14]

As of 1911 the Ottoman navy's most formidable warships were the 10,000-ton *Barbaros Hayreddin* and *Torgud Reis*, twenty-year-old *Brandenburg* class pre-dreadnoughts recently purchased from Germany, and the former casemate ship *Mesudiye*, which an Italian shipyard had transformed into a pre-dreadnought. They remained inactive throughout the thirteen-month conflict that began in September 1911, while an Italian fleet under the Duke of the Abruzzi seized Libya and the Dodecanese Islands, shelled Beirut and other Turkish Near Eastern ports, and ultimately took the war to the mouth of the Dardanelles. The Italians suffered no naval losses in the conflict, while the Turks, by refusing to fight at sea, lost only the Beirut harbor watch (an old casemate corvette), three torpedo boats, two armed yachts, and seven small gunboats. With the Balkan states poised to intervene in the conflict, the Turks concluded the Treaty of Lausanne (18 October 1912), surrendering Libya to the Italians in return for their evacuation of the Dodecanese Islands. Italy subsequently reneged on its part of the bargain and retained possession of the Dodecanese until its defeat in the Second World War.

On the day the Italo–Turkish War officially ended, an alliance of Greece, Bulgaria, Serbia, and Montenegro attacked the Ottoman Empire. Facing less formidable opposition, the Turkish navy assumed an active role, the *Barbaros Hayreddin* and *Torgud Reis* joining the protected cruisers *Hamidiye* and *Mecidiye* in shelling several forts on the Bulgarian Black Sea coast. In late November, Bulgaria retaliated with a torpedo boat attack which put the *Hamidiye* out of action for the rest of the year. Meanwhile, over the winter of 1912–13, Ottoman warships in the Sea of Marmara provided fire support for Turkish forces defending Constantinople and the straits against an advancing Bulgarian army. The Balkan alliance's most formidable warships were the Greek navy's four armored cruisers: the 9,960-ton Italian-built flagship *Georgios Averof* (commissioned 1911), named for a Greek millionaire who contributed £300,000 toward its purchase, and the three 4,810-ton French-built units of the *Spetsai* class (launched 1889–90, renovated 1908–10). In December 1912, January 1913, and April 1913, the three Turkish battleships sortied from the straits into the Aegean, engaged the Greek armored cruisers, then returned to port. On each occasion neither side lost a ship. As in the Italo–Turkish War, the Ottoman navy did not sink a single enemy vessel, but its own losses were also light: the Salonika harbor watch (an old casemate corvette) and two torpedo boats sunk by the Greeks, and an old armored frigate which ran aground while shelling a Bulgarian port. The Greek navy deployed the war's only submarine, the French-built *Delfin*, which on 22 December 1912 became the first undersea boat to fire a self-propelled torpedo in action. The *Delfin* crept to within just 800 meters of the Ottoman cruiser *Mecidiye* before firing, but failed to hit its target. Bulgaria came away from the conflict with a disproportionate share of the territorial gains, touching off the Second Balkan War (June–July 1913) in which the former Bulgarian allies Greece, Serbia, and Montenegro joined Romania and

Turkey in attacking Bulgaria. The Bulgarians surrendered quickly, before any naval action occurred.

During the years 1911–14 the Ottoman Empire and Greece engaged in a brief naval arms race of their own. The Ottoman navy contracted Vickers to lay down the 23,000-ton dreadnoughts *Reşadiye* (in August 1911) and *Fatih Sultan Mehmed* (in June 1914), while Brazil sold the Turks the 27,500-ton dreadnought *Sultan Osman-i Evvel* (ex-*Rio de Janeiro*), which Armstrong had begun in 1911. The Greeks countered by ordering one dreadnought from the German shipbuilder Vulcan (the 19,500-ton *Salamis*, begun in July 1913), another from the Saint-Nazaire shipyard in France (the 23,500-ton *Basileos Konstantinos*, begun in June 1914), and purchasing two pre-dreadnoughts from the United States, the 13,000-ton *Kilkis* (ex-*Mississippi*) and *Limnos* (ex-*Idaho*), in June 1914. With the Ottoman Empire soon to side with Germany, at the outbreak of war in August 1914 the British government seized the *Reşadiye* and *Sultan Osman-i Evvel*, which entered British service as the *Erin* and *Agincourt*. The *Fatih Sultan Mehmed* was never completed. Meanwhile, neutral Greece fared no better, as Vulcan launched the *Salamis* in November 1914 but never completed it, while Saint-Nazaire barely started work on the *Basileos Konstantinos* before abandoning the project. In mid-August 1914 the fortunes of war gave the Turks a formidable capital ship, as Germany transferred the 23,000-ton *Goeben* to the Ottoman navy after the battle cruiser and its escort, the protected cruiser *Breslau*, were trapped in the Mediterranean at the onset of the fighting. On 10 August the two ships reached Constantinople, where a week later the *Goeben* became the *Yavuz Sultan Selim*, the *Breslau*, the *Midilli*, and their commander, Rear Admiral Wilhelm Souchon, commander of the Turkish navy.

THE FIRST WORLD WAR: OUTBREAK TO JUTLAND (1914–16)

The Central Powers hailed the successful escape of the *Goeben* and *Breslau* as their first naval victory of the war, but the battle cruiser was of much less use in the Black Sea than it would have been in the North Sea, where every capital ship was precious to the German navy. The loss of the *Goeben*, combined with the addition to the British navy of the dreadnoughts *Erin* (ex-*Reşadiye*), *Agincourt* (ex-*Sultan Osman-i Evvel*), and *Canada* (ex-Chilean *Almirante Latorre*), seized or purchased in August 1914, gave Britain 45 dreadnoughts or battle cruisers built or building, compared to 26 for Germany. Among the other major European powers, France had 12, Russia 11, Italy 6, and Austria–Hungary 4. Counting only the dreadnoughts or battle cruisers in commission, Britain had 31, Germany 17, France 4, Italy 3,

Austria–Hungary 3, and Russia none. During the war, Britain, Italy, and Austria–Hungary finished all of the capital ships they had under construction as of August 1914, while Germany completed all but the *Bayern* class dreadnought *Sachsen*, laid down in the spring of 1914. Russia's three *Imperatritsa Maria* class dreadnoughts entered service during the war, but the four *Borodino* class battle cruisers were never completed. France's three *Bretagnes* were commissioned during the war, but the five *Normandies* were never completed, although one, the *Béarn*, eventually became the first French aircraft carrier. For projects begun during the war, the completion rate was much worse. Thanks to Fisher's influence after his return to office, Britain completed five battle cruisers during the war: the 27,650-ton *Renown* and *Repulse* (built 1915–16), the 19,230-ton *Courageous* and *Glorious* (1915–17), and the 19,500-ton *Furious* (1915–17). Of another four battle cruisers laid down after Fisher again left office, only the giant 42,670-ton *Hood* (1916–20) was completed. Meanwhile, Germany laid down one dreadnought and five battle cruisers during the war, none of which was completed. The same was true of four Italian dreadnoughts and an additional Russian Black Sea dreadnought. In May 1914 Austro–Hungarian legislators funded the first two of a projected class of four 24,500-ton dreadnoughts, but the outbreak of war brought the cancellation of the entire program.

After the assassination of Francis Ferdinand at Sarajevo on 28 June 1914, the Austro–Hungarian dreadnought *Viribus Unitis* transported the archduke's remains from southern Dalmatia to Trieste. One month later, on the night of 28–29 July, three monitors of the Austro–Hungarian Danube Flotilla fired the first shots by naval vessels in the First World War, bombarding Belgrade. After their unsuccessful pursuit of the *Goeben*, the British and French navies focused their Mediterranean efforts on preventing the Austro–Hungarian fleet from leaving the Adriatic, an easy task, since Admiral Haus kept all of his battleships at Pola, determined not to risk them so long as Italy's intentions remained unclear. An Anglo–French convention signed on 6 August formalized the prewar understanding that the French would safeguard British interests in the Mediterranean, and gave them the use of Malta and Gibraltar as bases. Ten days later the senior Allied commander in the Mediterranean, former French navy minister Vice Admiral Lapeyrère, led the dreadnoughts *Courbet* and *Jean Bart* and a dozen predreadnoughts on a sortie into the Adriatic, which dispersed a flotilla of Austro–Hungarian cruisers blockading Antivari (Bar), Montenegro, in the process sinking the light cruiser *Zenta*. French sorties into the Adriatic continued until 21 December, when the Austro–Hungarian submarine *U 12* torpedoed the *Jean Bart* off Antivari. The ship survived, making it back to Malta for repairs, but for the remainder of the war the French navy never again sent a battleship into the Adriatic. In early December the French suffered another setback when the 400-ton submarine *Curie* was stranded while attempting to enter Pola harbor. Because the Austro–Hungarians had no undersea boat of its size and range, they repaired and recommissioned it as their own *U 14*.[15]

With the *Goeben* in Constantinople, the Austro–Hungarian navy bottled up in the Adriatic, and Italy neutral, the Central Powers were unable to disrupt colonial troop convoys from North Africa to the French mainland. Meanwhile, in the North Sea, the British imposed a distant blockade on the Germans, from the Grand Fleet's main base at Scapa Flow in the Orkneys eastward to the southwestern coast of Norway, while also sealing the eastern approaches to the English Channel. German naval leaders considered it foolhardy to attempt to force the Channel defenses, and allowed the British Expeditionary Force to cross unmolested in mid-August, to reinforce the French army. The first British and German naval casualties followed quickly on the heels of Britain's declaration of war. On 5 August a British destroyer sank the German auxiliary minelayer *Königin Luise* off Harwich, but the following morning one of the mines it had laid sank the British light cruiser *Amphion*.[16]

The first Anglo–German naval action of the war, the Battle of Helgoland Bight (28 August 1914), resulted from a sweep of the bight by a force of British light cruisers and destroyers under Commodore Reginald Tyrwhitt, which encountered German light cruisers and destroyers under Rear Admiral Leberecht Maas. While both sides called in reinforcements, Vice Admiral Sir David Beatty's battle cruisers, operating out of Rosyth in the Firth of Forth, arrived in time to tip the balance in Britain's favor, while Rear Admiral Franz Hipper's German battle cruisers did not appear until after the battle had ended. The light cruiser *Mainz* was the battle's first casualty, sunk by gunfire and torpedoes at 14:10. Beatty's battle cruisers subsequently sank Maas's flagship *Cöln*, which went under with the admiral and nearly all hands (507 dead) at 14:35. The action ended after the battle cruisers sank a third German light cruiser, the *Ariadne*, at 16:00. The Germans also lost a destroyer. The British lost no ships, but one light cruiser and two destroyers were damaged badly enough to be towed back to port.[17] The Battle of Helgoland Bight had little practical significance, but as a clear British victory it did much to deflate German morale, and also made William II less willing to allow his admirals to take risks with the capital ships of the High Sea Fleet.

The next Anglo–German surface action, the Battle of Texel Island (17 October 1914), was equally insignificant but also demoralizing for the German navy. Captain Cecil Fox in the light cruiser *Undaunted* led four British destroyers against four small German destroyers, all of which were sunk. Once again, the British force lost no ships. Amid these setbacks, the Germans took heart in the fact that they lost far fewer ships to submarine warfare, mines, and mishaps than did the British. On

22 September the German *U 9* torpedoed and sank the 12,000-ton armored cruisers *Cressy*, *Aboukir*, and *Hogue* off the Dutch coast, killing 1,459 British seamen. On 27 October the British dreadnought *Audacious* sank after striking a mine off Lough Swilly. But a week later the German armored cruiser *Yorck*, returning with Hipper's battle cruisers from a bombardment of Yarmouth, accidentally steamed into a minefield off Wilhelmshaven and sank. Late in November a Russian mine laid off Memel in the Baltic claimed the German armored cruiser *Friedrich Carl*. Such losses caused the belligerents to adopt a more serious attitude toward minesweeping; over the last four years of the war, the British navy alone commissioned 726 minesweepers. The Allied navies also reduced their risk by employing expendable pre-dreadnought battleships for inshore operations where the danger from mines was greatest. The *Revenge* (later renamed *Redoubtable*), authorized by the Naval Defence Act of 1889 and built in 1891–93, was the oldest of 41 British pre-dreadnoughts to see action in the war. Along with other pre-dreadnoughts and old gunboats, it participated in an ineffective bombardment of the German-occupied Belgian coast during October 1914. The first British pre-dreadnought lost in the war, the *Formidable* of the Channel Fleet, was torpedoed and sunk on New Year's Day by *U 24* off Portland.[18]

In the autumn of 1914 the Admiralty came into possession of three German code books, a windfall which eventually enabled British intelligence to decipher most German naval wireless messages. One copy came from the wreckage of one of the German destroyers sunk off Texel Island, netted by a British trawler; another, from a German merchant steamer seized in Australia at the beginning of the war; the third, via the Russian navy, from the German light cruiser *Magdeburg*, which ran aground off the Estonian coast in late August 1914.[19]

The *Magdeburg*'s loss came on a rare early sortie within striking distance of the Russian Baltic Fleet, which the Germans, given their North Sea focus, for the most part were content to leave undisturbed. Indeed, until the dramatic events of 1917, the Baltic remained a relatively quiet front in the naval war, as Tsar Nicholas II at the onset of the war had admonished his Baltic Fleet commander, Admiral Nikolai O. Essen, to avoid "a second Tsushima." The Russians remained in a defensive mode even after the four *Gangut*s entered service late in 1914, keenly aware that, even though these dreadnoughts gave them superiority in the Baltic, at any time the High Sea Fleet could detach enough units from Wilhelmshaven via the Kiel Canal to overwhelm them. The Russians lost their first warship on 11 October, when the German *U 26* sank the armored cruiser *Pallada* in the Baltic. Russian submariners remained relatively timid, but during the same month the British navy sent its first submarines into the Baltic, where they continued to operate as long as Russia remained in the war. By the end of 1915 they had sunk the armored cruiser *Prinz Adalbert*, a German light cruiser, and several merchantmen. The Russian dreadnoughts did not sortie beyond the Gulf of Finland until July 1915; between then and the end of that year, they typically went out in pairs, to support minelaying operations, venturing as far as the waters south of the island of Gotland, some 350 miles southwest of their advance base at Helsinki. The Germans attempted no major operations in the Baltic until 8–20 August 1915, when Vice Admiral Hipper led eight dreadnoughts and three battle cruisers from the High Sea Fleet in an abortive attempt to secure the Gulf of Riga. The Russian dreadnoughts remained safely in port, but after a British submarine torpedoed and damaged the battle cruiser *Moltke*, fear of submarines and mines forced the Germans to abandon the operation. Riga remained in Russian hands for another two years.[20]

Well into 1915, Britain seriously considered launching a major naval campaign in the Baltic. As First Lord of the Admiralty, Churchill advocated operations around the periphery of Europe as a way of breaking the stalemate on the Western Front that had set in after the First Battle of the Marne. As of the end of October 1914 he had a First Sea Lord who shared his views, thanks to the retirement of Admiral Prince Louis of Battenberg in favor of Admiral Fisher. The father of the dreadnought and battle cruiser proved to be as imaginative as Churchill, but men with such similar personalities were bound to have a stormy relationship. Ultimately Fisher's plan for a drive into the Baltic lost out to Churchill's plan to force the Dardanelles, and amid the latter disaster both would leave office. In the meantime, however, Fisher made his mark in Britain's wartime shipbuilding program, which led to the construction of 5 battle cruisers, 2 light cruisers, 5 flotilla leaders, 56 destroyers, 65 submarines, 37 monitors, 24 anti-submarine sloops, 50 anti-submarine motor launches, and 260 amphibious landing craft, all completed by war's end.[21] Fisher's monitors were joined by another three constructed in British shipyards for Brazil, and purchased by the navy in 1914. All had relatively low freeboard and carried one or two guns in a single forward turret. Most were completed during 1915. They ranged in size from the five vessels of the *M-29* class (355 tons, two 6-inch guns) to *Marshal Ney* and *Marshal Soult* (6,700 tons, two 15-inch guns). The monitor program stemmed from the realization that shallow-draught warships were needed to provide effective inshore fire support for troops fighting in coastal regions, following the ineffective British bombardment of the Belgian coast in October 1914. The monitors saw action along the Belgian coast, in the upper Adriatic near the mouth of the Isonzo River, in the Dardanelles operation and, after its failure, in the force assigned to blockade the Dardanelles.[22]

The last months of 1914 featured the war's two greatest naval battles beyond European and Mediterranean waters, both off the coast of

South America: the German victory at Coronel (1 November 1914) and the subsequent British triumph at the Falklands (8 December 1914). After Japan entered the war on the side of the Allies (23 August 1914), Germany gave up hope of retaining its Asian and Pacific colonial possessions. The most formidable units of Admiral Count Maximilian von Spee's German East Asian squadron, the 11,600-ton armored cruisers *Scharnhorst* and *Gneisenau*, gradually made their way eastward across the Pacific, in October joining the light cruisers *Leipzig*, *Dresden*, and *Nürnberg* off the west coast of South America. Off the Chilean port of Coronel they met a British force under Rear Admiral Sir Christopher Cradock, which had rounded Cape Horn from its base at Port Stanley in the Falkland Islands after an intercepted German wireless message revealed that the *Leipzig* had called at Coronel. Cradock had two armored cruisers, the 14,150-ton *Good Hope* and 9,800-ton *Monmouth*, both somewhat older than their German counterparts, along with the light cruiser *Glasgow* and the armed merchant cruiser *Otranto*. The predreadnought battleship *Canopus* followed at a distance, escorting the British colliers. Approaching Coronel, Cradock encountered not just the *Leipzig*, but Spee's entire squadron except for the *Nürnberg*, which arrived later. Despite his clear disadvantage he decided to seek battle, without waiting for the *Canopus*. The engagement began just after 19:00 in the southern springtime dusk, and it soon became apparent that Cradock would pay dearly for his aggressiveness. Gunfire from the German armored cruisers pounded the *Good Hope* and the *Monmouth*, the former sinking around 20:00, the latter shortly thereafter. Just five men survived the sinkings, and Cradock was among the nearly 1,600 lost. The *Otranto*, sent off by Cradock before the battle began, survived to return to Port Stanley, as did the *Glasgow*, which witnessed the sinking of the two armored cruisers and fled the scene to warn off the *Canopus* and the colliers. After the victory, German officials gave Spee a free hand to run for home at his own discretion. In late November he rounded Cape Horn and entered the South Atlantic.[23]

The Battle of Coronel occurred the day after Fisher returned to office as First Sea Lord, and he responded to the disaster by sending two of his battle cruisers to intercept Spee's force. This was precisely the sort of task for which they had been designed, and would be the only time during the First World War that any vessel of the type undertook such a mission. The *Inflexible* and *Invincible*, the latter serving as flagship for Admiral Sir Doveton Sturdee, made the 8,400-mile voyage to the Falklands in twenty-six days, arriving on 7 December. By then, the *Canopus* and *Glasgow* had been reinforced by the armored cruisers *Carnarvon*, *Cornwall* and *Kent*, the light cruiser *Bristol*, and the armed merchant cruiser *Macedonia*. Sturdee did not have to wait long for Spee to appear, as the German squadron arrived off East Falkland at midday on 8 December. The *Scharnhorst*, leading Spee's column, fired the first shots into Port Stanley harbor, targeting the *Canopus* from a range of 14,000 yards. As soon as he realized that the British force included two battle cruisers, Spee fled to the southeast, breaking off with the *Scharnhorst* and *Gneisenau* to lure the *Invincible* and *Inflexible* away from his light cruisers. Sturdee gave chase with the two battle cruisers and the *Carnarvon*, and did not spare ammunition in the ensuing hot pursuit, during which the *Invincible* fired 513 12-inch shells and *Inflexible* 661. The *Scharnhorst* was sunk at 16:17 from a range of nearly 11,000 yards, followed by *Gneisenau* at 18:02 with fire from between 7,000 and 10,000 yards. Meanwhile, at the onset of the battle the light cruisers *Nürnberg, Leipzig,* and *Dresden* scattered, with the *Kent, Glasgow,* and *Cornwall,* respectively, chasing them, but around 15:00 the *Cornwall* broke off pursuit of the *Dresden* to help the *Glasgow* hunt down the *Leipzig,* which was sunk at 21:23. Meanwhile, gunfire from the *Kent* sank the *Nürnberg* at 19:27, and the *Macedonia* and *Bristol* sank Spee's colliers. The *Canopus* remained behind in Port Stanley, not participating in the battle after the opening rounds were fired. The Battle of the Falklands cost the German navy four cruisers plus the lives of Spee and 2,100 of his men; Sturdee's force emerged almost entirely unscathed, sustaining just 10 casualties. Mission accomplished, the *Invincible* and *Inflexible* left Port Stanley on 9 December and made Gibraltar by New Year's Day. The ships Sturdee left behind more than sufficed to hunt down the *Dresden,* which was sunk on 14 March 1915 by the *Kent* and *Glasgow* at Mas a Terra in the Juan Fernandez Islands, 400 miles west of the Chilean coast.

The destruction of Spee's squadron eliminated most of the surviving German warships outside of European waters. Those he left behind in the Far East in the first weeks of the war had succumbed much earlier. On 7 November 1914 the Germans surrendered their base at Tsingtao to the Japanese, but only after scuttling all the warships on hand: the light cruiser *Cormoran,* four gunboats, and one destroyer, plus the protected cruiser *Kaiserin Elisabeth,* the only Austro–Hungarian warship stationed beyond European waters at the onset of war. The light cruiser *Emden,* which left Tsingtao early in the war to raid Allied commerce in the East Indies and Indian Ocean, sank a number of merchantmen and the Russian protected cruiser *Zhemchug* (at Penang, on 28 October) before falling victim to a reef in the Cocos Islands on 9 November during a firefight with the Australian cruiser *Sydney.* Other German warships attempting to serve as commerce raiders likewise had short careers. The light cruiser *Karlsruhe,* assigned to represent Germany at the opening ceremonies of the Panama Canal, sank sixteen merchantmen (72,800 tons) in the Caribbean before sinking off the Lesser Antilles on 4 November 1914 following an accidental explosion on board. Meanwhile, the light cruiser *Königsberg,* on the German East African station when the war began, sank a number of merchantmen and the British protected cruiser *Pegasus* (off Zanzibar, on 20 September) before being blockaded by British warships in the Rufiji

River on 30 October 1914. It remained there, a local distraction, until sinking as a result of an attack on 11 July 1915. To supplement the efforts of these cruising warships, early in the war Germany employed a total of 16 passenger liners and merchantmen as commerce raiders. The largest was the 24,900-ton North German Lloyd liner *Kronprinz Wilhelm*, which claimed 15 ships (60,500 tons) in a brief career in 1914–15. The most successful was the 9,800-ton *Möwe* (ex-*Pungo*), which sank 41 ships (186,100 tons) before being converted to a minelayer. The most famous German raider was also the only sailing ship used for that purpose, the 4,500-ton *Seeadler* (ex-*Pass of Balmaha*), commanded by the colorful Count Felix von Luckner, which sank 16 vessels (30,100 tons) before being wrecked on 2 August 1917 in the Society Islands. Lacking a global network of bases (indeed, having none, after the early Allied conquest of its colonial possessions), Germany had great difficulty keeping its raiders supplied, especially the converted passenger liners, which consumed a considerable amount of coal and other supplies. Of the 16 vessels, 7 eventually were sunk or scuttled, 4 ended up interned in neutral ports, and 2 were lost to shipwreck.[24]

Between the outbreak of war and the end of 1914, there were no naval actions in which both forces included dreadnoughts or battle cruisers. The initial German strategy for the North Sea called for Hipper's battle cruisers to lure a portion of the British Grand Fleet into battle with the main body of the High Sea Fleet, in the hope of achieving a decisive victory that would seriously reduce the British capital ship advantage. Provocations such as the bombardment of Yarmouth in early November failed to result in an engagement, but early in the New Year, at the Battle of Dogger Bank (24 January 1915), capital ships of the two fleets finally met. An intercepted wireless message gave the British advance warning of a sortie by a German battle cruiser force to the rich fishing grounds in the central North Sea. Hipper departed Wilhelmshaven just after midnight and steamed to the northwest until shortly after daybreak, when his screen of light cruisers encountered British light cruisers screening for a force of five battle cruisers under Beatty, approaching from Rosyth. Hipper promptly turned for home, and after the British battle cruisers came within sight of the retreating Germans at 07:50, a furious pursuit ensued. By 09:05 the British had closed enough to commence firing, opening a battle that lasted for over four hours. Hipper's column included three battle cruisers and the armored cruiser *Blücher*, a late replacement for the battle cruiser *Von der Tann*, then undergoing a refit. At 15,800 tons the *Blücher* was a respectable warship, but its 8.3-inch guns were no match for the 12-inch guns of the British battle cruisers; the unfortunate ship also brought up the rear of Hipper's column and thus bore the brunt of the fire from Beatty's ships. Throughout the battle visibility was poor and British signals confused; to make matters worse, British fire control suffered from the fact that the battle cruisers, stationed at Rosyth, did not get as much gunnery practice as the dreadnoughts of the Grand Fleet. Beatty's flagship *Lion* fired 243 shells and scored just four hits: one on the *Blücher*, one on the *Derfflinger*, and two on the *Seydlitz*, all at a range of roughly 16,000 yards. At one stage the British *Indomitable* closed to within 6,000 yards of the *Blücher*, but a shell from the *Princess Royal*, fired from 19,000–20,000 yards, ultimately dealt the fatal blow to the armored cruiser, penetrating its deck and igniting ammunition below. The ship capsized and sank at 13:13, with almost all hands (792 dead). Among German battle cruisers the *Seydlitz* suffered the worst, sustaining three hits, one of which caused a fire disabling both aft turrets. Three hits on the *Derfflinger* caused little damage, and the *Moltke* came through completely unscathed. In contrast, Beatty's *Lion* took seventeen hits and had to be towed back to Rosyth by the *Indomitable*. The *Tiger* took six hits and had a turret disabled, while the *Princess Royal* and *New Zealand*, along with the *Indomitable*, were not damaged. Beatty came away from the victory feeling that he should have sunk Hipper's entire squadron, and chastized his captains for wasting so much fire on the *Blücher* after it was clearly doomed. In Germany, William II reacted to the defeat by sacking Hipper's superior, Admiral Friedrich von Ingenohl, faulted for keeping the main body of the High Sea Fleet too far away from Hipper to have come to his aid in any event. Under his successor, Admiral Hugo von Pohl, the fleet was doomed to inactivity by the emperor's deepening conviction that his capital ships should not be risked. Pohl would accomplish nothing before giving way to Vice Admiral Reinhard Scheer a year later.[25]

As administrative head of the German navy, Admiral Tirpitz had no control over the operations of the fleet he had worked so hard to build. Throughout the first months of the war he pressed consistently for a more aggressive policy and did not hesitate to criticize those in command, regardless of what they did. As early as November 1914 he advocated unrestricted submarine warfare and soon became a leading champion of it within the German hierarchy, in the process transforming his philosophy of naval warfare in a manner reminiscent of the opportunism of his rise to prominence, when he had been an advocate of torpedo warfare during the heyday of the Jeune École.[26] The early successes of U-boats against British warships (by February 1915, they had sunk one pre-dreadnought, three armored cruisers, and two light cruisers, compared to the two armored cruisers and one old protected cruiser sunk by German surface warships) called further attention to their offensive potential. For William II, a submarine campaign offered the attraction of an aggressive policy likely to cause serious harm to the Allied war effort, without risking the dreadnoughts and battle cruisers of the High Sea Fleet. On 4 February 1915, he approved a proclamation warning that all merchant vessels in the waters around the British Isles were liable to destruction. What followed was the first phase of unrestricted submarine warfare, culminating on 7 May 1915 in the sinking of the 30,400-ton Cunard liner *Lusitania* by *U 20* off the coast of Ireland, with the loss of 1,201 lives, including 128 United States citizens, a key event in turning American public opinion against Germany.[27]

Unrestricted submarine warfare forever linked the undersea boat with the German navy, obscuring the fact that before the war the Germans had trailed most other navies in developing the type. Indeed, before the outbreak of war in 1914 Germany had completed just three dozen submarines, fewer than each of the three navies of the Triple Entente. The German navy still had just thirty-seven U-boats on hand when the campaign began at the end of February 1915, and during the ensuing months rarely had more than six on patrol around the British Isles at any given time. Their effectiveness fluctuated wildly from month to month, but even in lean times the tonnage sunk was dramatically higher than it had been during the first seven months of the war. Over the next seven months, the Germans sank 787,120 tons of merchant shipping (89,500 in March 1915, 38,600 in April, 126,900 in May, 115,290 in June, 98,005 in July, 182,770 in August, and 136,050 in September) while losing just fifteen submarines. The campaign ended when Tirpitz's adversary, Admiral Henning von Holtzendorff, became operational chief of staff (chief of the *Admiralstab*) of the navy. Holtzendorff joined the chancellor, Bethmann Hollweg, and the chief of the army high command, General Erich von Falkenhayn, in persuading William II that unrestricted submarine warfare was needlessly antagonizing the United States and other neutrals, while not seriously harming Britain's overall war effort. Tirpitz lobbied in vain for a resumption of the policy, in the process poisoning his relations with almost everyone in the German hierarchy before finally retiring from the Imperial Navy Office in March 1916, at the age of sixty-six.[28]

Long before Tirpitz's resignation, the political policy side of the naval war had claimed a significant casualty in Britain, where Churchill was forced to leave the Admiralty following the failure of his Dardanelles campaign. As early as the autumn of 1914 Churchill's desire to employ naval power decisively around the periphery of Europe had focused on the Turkish straits. On 3 November, shortly after the Ottoman Empire joined the Central Powers, the British battle cruisers *Indomitable* and *Indefatigable* and the French pre-dreadnoughts *Suffren* and *Vérité* bombarded the outer forts of the Dardanelles. Over the weeks that followed, as Churchill's idea grew into a plan, he persisted in the notion that the forts could be subdued by naval gunfire alone, without landing troops. He underestimated not only the defenses ashore but also the Turkish minefields; his critics considered the latter impregnable, but were proved wrong when the British submarine *B 11* slipped safely through the Dardanelles to torpedo and sink the pre-dreadnought *Mesudiye* on 13 December. Under Churchill's scheme, a column of Allied warships would force the Dardanelles and anchor off Constantinople, where their appearance ideally would compel the sultan to sue for peace. At the least, Churchill calculated, the operation would force a concentration of the Ottoman army for the defense of the capital, alleviating the Turkish threat to the Russians in the Caucasus and the British in Egypt. The Allies had little to fear from the Ottoman navy. It had just one modern capital ship, Souchon's *Yavuz Sultan Selim*, which could not be repaired because the Turks lacked a dry dock large enough to accommodate a vessel of its size. This nagging problem became a crisis after 26 December, when the the battle cruiser struck three Russian mines while on a sortie off the Bosporus and barely made it back to Constantinople. Makeshift repairs further limited the *Yavuz Sultan Selim*'s effectiveness, but even before then the Russian fleet at Sevastopol, under the able leadership of Vice Admiral Andrei Eberhardt, easily commanded the Black Sea.[29]

Owing to the threat from the High Sea Fleet, the British navy could not afford to send dreadnoughts and battle cruisers to the Dardanelles. The presence of Austro–Hungarian dreadnoughts in the Adriatic likewise tied down the French navy's dreadnoughts in the central Mediterranean. Over the objections of Admiral Fisher, Churchill secured one dreadnought, the *Queen Elizabeth*, and one battle cruiser, the *Inflexible*, for the initial effort at the Dardanelles, which also included twelve British and four French pre-dreadnoughts, and countless smaller warships. Preliminary bombardment of the outer forts began on 19 February 1915 and continued sporadically for four weeks, until the attempt to force the Dardanelles began late on the morning of 18 March. Rear Admiral Sir John de Robeck commanded the Allied force, which deployed in three columns. The battleships entered the straits at 11:30 and moved forward at a crawl, three abreast, following in the wake of a host of minesweepers. Their fire silenced most of the outer fortress guns, and the operation proceeded smoothly until batteries of Turkish horse artillery, moving targets difficult for the battleship guns to counter, began to disrupt the efforts of the minesweepers. At 14:00, as the columns neared Eren Keui Bay, the French pre-dreadnought *Bouvet* struck a mine and sank in less than two minutes, with almost all hands. Mines soon claimed the British pre-dreadnoughts *Implacable* and *Ocean* as well, bringing the advance to a halt. The battle cruiser *Inflexible* also struck a mine but was towed to safety and later sent to Malta for repairs. The French pre-dreadnoughts *Suffren* and *Gaulois* likewise were saved after taking a heavy shelling from Turkish shore batteries. By early evening, when all of De Robeck's ships had withdrawn from the Dardanelles, another four pre-dreadnoughts (three British and one French) had sustained at least some damage.

Four days after the fiasco, De Robeck resolved not to try to force the straits again without first landing troops to threaten the Turkish positions from the land side. Meanwhile, efforts were made to improve coordination with the Russian Black Sea Fleet. A Russian force of five battleships, two cruisers, and ten destroyers shelled the outer forts of the Bosporus ten days after the Anglo–French attack at the Dardanelles.[30]

On 25 April, British and French warships provided fire support for a makeshift fleet of some 200 merchantmen, pressed into service to carry one French, two British, and two ANZAC (Australia–New Zealand) divisions to their beachheads. In lieu of purpose-built landing craft, men went ashore in columns of rowing boats towed by steam launches. While a French landing provided a diversion south of the mouth of the Dardanelles, the other four divisions disembarked to the north, on the coast of the Gallipoli peninsula. The same day, the Russian Black Sea Fleet conducted another sortie against the mouth of the Bosporus. The diversions did no good, however, as the Ottoman army held the high ground above the Gallipoli beachheads. The bloodiest fighting occurred in the first nine days after the landings and in a subsequent Allied offensive on 6–9 August. The Allies added another nine divisions to their original five, only to have the Turks commit an equal number of divisions to contain them in three narrow coastal enclaves. Throughout the Gallipoli campaign the Turkish forts on the Dardanelles remained secure, idling the Allied fleet at the mouth of the straits. Churchill's scheme to break the stalemate of the Western Front at the Dardanelles had only resulted in another stalemate.[31]

Meanwhile, the Allied navies suffered further losses off the Dardanelles, starting with the British pre-dreadnought *Goliath*, torpedoed and sunk by a Turkish destroyer on the night of 12–13 May. The sinking brought to a boil a dispute between Fisher and Churchill over whether the *Queen Elizabeth*, Britain's lone dreadnought at the Dardanelles, should be withdrawn to the Grand Fleet. For weeks Fisher had argued that a dreadnought should not remain on a station so vulnerable to enemy mines and torpedoes; he had already succeeded in having the battle cruiser *Inflexible* called home after its repairs at Malta. Fisher had his way and the *Queen Elizabeth* was ordered home, but the admiral resigned anyway just two days later after a clash with Churchill over whether more reinforcements should be sent to the Dardanelles. The shock of his departure almost brought down Prime Minister Herbert Asquith's Liberal government. Asquith saved himself by finally forming a war cabinet including the Conservatives, who demanded Churchill's resignation in return for their cooperation. Churchill left the Admiralty ten days after Fisher. Former prime minister Arthur Balfour became First Lord, while Admiral Sir Henry Jackson succeeded Fisher as First Sea Lord.[32]

On the day after the *Goliath* sank, the German *U 21* reached the Austro–Hungarian base at Cattaro, at the end of an eighteen-day cruise from the North Sea via the Strait of Gibraltar. After being refueled and resupplied, it proceeded to the Dardanelles, where it torpedoed and sank the British pre-dreadnought *Triumph* on 25 May 1915. Two days later it struck again, sinking the pre-dreadnought *Majestic*. Thus began an illustrious career during which the U-boat ranged from the Levant to the Black Sea; nine months later it sank another large Allied warship, the French armored cruiser *Amiral Charner*, off Beirut. The *U 21* was the first, and most successful, of the dozens of German submarines sent to the Mediterranean in the last three and a half years of the war. They were supplemented by others shipped overland from Germany and assembled at Austro–Hungarian bases on the Adriatic. The campaign was undertaken because the Austro–Hungarian navy (with just seven U-boats as of the spring of 1915) lacked the submarine force to help the Turks at the Dardanelles, and in any event would be focused on matters closer to home after 23 May 1915, when Italy declared war on the Dual Monarchy. Because Italy did not declare war on Germany until August 1916, in the meantime all German U-boats operating in the Mediterranean were double-numbered as Austro–Hungarian, typically operating with a German commander and crew and an Austro–Hungarian junior officer on board. Almost three months after the spectacular debut of *U 21*, another German submarine, *UB 14*, sank the British transport *Royal Edward*, en route to the Dardanelles from Alexandria, drowning nearly 1,000 troops. In early August the British submarine *E 11* exacted a small measure of revenge, slipping through the Dardanelles to sink the Turkish pre-dreadnought *Barbaros Hayreddin* in the Sea of Marmara. Ottoman naval operations were further limited by the continuing maintenance problems of the *Yavuz Sultan Selim* and by the commissioning of the first two Russian Black Sea dreadnoughts, the *Imperatritsa Maria* in late summer and *Ekaterina II* at the end of 1915.[33]

By then, the Allies had decided to abandon the Dardanelles campaign. After Bulgaria joined the Central Powers in September 1915, the pro-Allied Greek prime minister, Eleutherios Venizelos, secretly agreed to allow an Anglo–French landing at Salonika to support the Serbs against the Bulgarians. The operation used troops that could have been sent as reinforcements to the Gallipoli peninsula, a sign that the stalemate there would soon end in an Allied withdrawal. By autumn 1915, despite having added to his fleet a number of newly commissioned monitors and dozens of minesweepers, De Robeck concluded that the minefields in the Dardanelles were impassable. The decision to evacuate the troops came after the British war minister, Field Marshal Lord Kitchener, visited the peninsula in November 1915. Naval forces successfully evacuated two of the beachheads on the night of 19–20 December, and the third on the night of 8–9 January 1916. The eight months of bitter fighting left 265,000 Allied troops killed or wounded, and generated over 300,000 Turkish casualties. At sea, the British lost five of twenty pre-dreadnoughts deployed in the Dardanelles campaign; a sixth, the *Russell*, struck a mine and sank in April 1916, while returning to Malta. The French lost one of their five pre-dreadnoughts, the Turks, two of three. Allied submarines sank over 56,000 tons of Turkish shipping during the campaign, in the process losing eight boats (four British and four French), most of them to mines.[34]

The Allied failure at the Dardanelles coincided with Italy's entry into the war, under the terms of the Treaty of London (26 April 1915), signed the day after the initial Gallipoli landings. Under an Anglo–French-Italian naval convention concluded at Paris on 10 May, Admiral Luigi of Savoy, Duke of the Abruzzi, received command of the First Allied Fleet, predominantly Italian and based at Brindisi. Admiral Lapeyrère's existing force, designated the Second Allied Fleet, was still mostly French but received an advance base at Taranto. Italy's insistence upon control over its own dreadnoughts and the Adriatic command led to a convoluted arrangement under which Lapeyrère remained the overall Allied Mediterranean commander with Abruzzi as his subordinate, but if Lapeyrère took the Second Allied Fleet into the Adriatic, he would be under the command of Abruzzi. On the evening of 23 May, within hours of Italy's declaration of war against Austria–Hungary, Admiral Haus left Pola with his entire fleet to conduct a punitive bombardment of the Italian coastline, supplemented by bombing raids on Venice and Ancona by Austro–Hungarian seaplanes. The Italian navy offered little opposition to the sortie, as the small force at Venice, led by three old pre-dreadnoughts, remained in port. Light cruisers and destroyers steaming northward from Brindisi turned back after encountering an Austro–Hungarian reconnaissance screen, which sank one Italian destroyer off Pelagosa.[35]

Austria–Hungary had made it through the first nine months of the war losing just one light cruiser and one torpedo boat, while the vastly superior Allied force sent no capital ships into the Adriatic after the near-loss of the dreadnought *Jean Bart* in December 1914. After Captain Georg von Trapp's *U 5* torpedoed and sank the French armored cruiser *Léon Gambetta* off Cape Santa Maria di Leuca, the boot-heel of Italy, on 27 April 1915, Lapeyrère grew even more conservative, forbidding any French vessel larger than a destroyer from operating north of the parallel of the Ionian island of Cephalonia, 300 miles south of Cattaro, the nearest Austro–Hungarian base. The Italians entered the war supremely confident but likewise rarely operated larger warships in the Adriatic after July 1915, when they lost two armored cruisers to submarine attacks within a span of eleven days. On 7 July Austro–Hungarian *U 26* (actually German *UB 14*) torpedoed the *Amalfi* off Venice, then, on 18 July, Austro–Hungarian *U 4* torpedoed the *Garibaldi* off the lower

Dalmatian coast. On 27 September Italians learned that their warships were not necessarily safe even when anchored at Brindisi, when Austrian saboteurs blew up the pre-dreadnought *Benedetto Brin* (456 dead). Further Italian losses by the end of 1915 included two auxiliary cruisers, one destroyer, four submarines, and three torpedo boats, while Austria–Hungary lost just two destroyers and two submarines. Aside from one Austro–Hungarian U-boat sunk by a French destroyer, all of these losses resulted from mines or submarine torpedoes. Despite the succession of early victories, the year ended in disappointment for the Austro–Hungarian navy. After the Central Powers completed their conquest of Serbia in December 1915, the Allied navies began to evacuate Serbian troops and refugees to Corfu via various Albanian ports. The two-month operation involved nearly 250 individual steamer passages, well within range of Austro–Hungarian forces and German submarines based at nearby Cattaro, yet just four of the transports were sunk, all by mines. Two French submarines, sunk in December by Austro–Hungarian destroyers, were the only Allied warships lost. By February, 260,000 Serbian soldiers and civilians made it safely to Corfu. In the spring of 1916 some 130,000 Serbian troops were shipped on to Salonika, where they languished with the rest of the Allied force until playing a role in the liberation of Serbia during the last weeks of the war.[36]

Italy's entry into the war did not have the desired impact for the Allies, either on land or at sea. The Italian army made little headway against makeshift Austro–Hungarian forces along the Isonzo River and in the Alps, while the Italian navy seemed as willing as the French to concede the Adriatic to the enemy. Abruzzi kept all of his dreadnoughts at Taranto, well out of harm's way, and as early as December 1915 feuded with Vice Admiral Louis Dartige du Fournet, Lapeyrère's successor as French (and overall Allied) commander, over alleged lack of support. Dartige had to restore to Abruzzi's First Allied Fleet a group of French destroyers detached earlier to support the transport of troops to Salonika.[37] It was only the first of many cases in which the French and British would have to appease the Italians by sending more help to the mouth of the Adriatic, enabling the Austro–Hungarian "fleet in being" to tie down an ever greater number of Allied warships that could have been put to better use elsewhere.

Thus 1915 ended with the Allies frustrated at the mouth of the Adriatic as well as at the mouth of the Dardanelles. The failure of Britain and France to force open a supply line to Russia via the Turkish straits, combined with the sobering losses suffered by the Russian army during 1915, brought a major Allied effort to get supplies through to Russia via the Arctic in the new year. During 1916 Allied shipments to Russia via Murmansk and Archangel totaled 2.5 million tons. Unfortunately, because the normal annual peacetime volume of trade in the White Sea ports rarely surpassed 100,000 tons, the windfall swamped the local infrastructure, and supplies continued to pile up at the docks while very little trickled down the rail lines to the Russian interior. Aside from mines laid by a lone auxiliary cruiser, the Germans did nothing to stop the shipments. Fears that the munitions and supplies stockpiled in the Arctic ports would fall into German hands, or that the Germans might use the ports to send out U-boats brought overland from the Baltic, motivated the later Allied intervention after the Bolshevik Revolution. During 1916, shipments to Archangel included the Brown-Curtiss turbines for the new Black Sea dreadnought *Imperator Alexander III*, which were transported southward to Nikolaiev mostly by canal and river. Meanwhile, the Baltic remained largely quiet in 1916, aside from some ineffective Russian summer sorties (none involving the *Gangut*s) against German iron-ore convoys from Sweden, and a disastrous German destroyer raid into the Gulf of Finland on the night of 10 November 1916, in which seven of the eleven vessels involved were sunk by Russian mines.[38]

For the Russian navy, most of the action during 1916 came in the Black Sea, where Vice Admiral Eberhardt now had two dreadnoughts at his disposal. On 8 January the *Ekaterina II* encountered the *Yavuz Sultan Selim* off the Turkish coast, opening fire at 18,500 meters. The exchange continued for half an hour, but neither side registered a hit. The spring and summer of 1916 featured a major Russian army offensive from the Caucasus which reached Trebizond, followed by a vigorous Turkish counterattack in the direction of Batum. During the campaign the *Yavuz Sultan Selim* and its escort *Midilli* provided fire support for Ottoman troops, and afterward returned safely to Constantinople despite considerable Russian efforts to cut them off. Frustration over the Black Sea Fleet's failure to catch the battle cruiser led to the sacking of its commander in favor of Alexander Kolchak. At forty-one Russia's youngest rear admiral, Kolchak had spent the first two years of the war commanding destroyers in the Baltic. He experienced nothing but trouble after his promotion. The first setback came on 20 October 1916 when the *Imperatritsa Maria*, in service barely a year, capsized and sank at Sevastopol after a magazine explosion, leaving Kolchak with just one operational dreadnought.[39]

Meanwhile, in January 1916 the German High Sea Fleet awoke from its year-long slumber, after Vice Admiral Scheer succeeded Admiral Pohl as commander. Scheer persuaded William II to allow a return to the strategy pursued before the defeat at Dogger Bank, in which Vice Admiral Hipper's battle cruisers would be used to bait a portion of the British Grand Fleet into battle with the main body of the High Sea Fleet. Unlike Admiral Ingenohl during the Dogger Bank action, Scheer intended to place the German dreadnoughts in a position to intervene quickly once a battle began. He took the fleet out on 10–11 February, 5–6 March, and

24–25 April, each time encountering no units of the Grand Fleet. The first sortie resulted in the mining of the British light cruiser *Arethusa*, flagship of a force of light cruisers and destroyers operating out of Harwich. The second featured no action at all, while the third (in which the German battle cruisers shelled Lowestoft and Yarmouth) resulted in another skirmish with the Harwich force, which this time returned to port unscathed. The German sortie of 24–25 April prompted a redistribution of British resources to better defend the southeast coast, as the Grand Fleet (at Scapa Flow) and the battle cruisers (at Rosyth) were never able to respond fast enough to catch German warships that conducted such bombardments. The Third Battle Squadron, pre-dreadnoughts of the *King Edward VII* class, was assigned to the Thames estuary, only with the *Dreadnought* replacing the *King Edward VII*, which had sunk after striking a mine off Cape Wrath in January. Thus the ship whose construction had started the prewar international naval race was no longer with the Grand Fleet by late May 1916, when it steamed out to meet the High Sea Fleet in the Battle of Jutland.[40]

Scheer's fourth sortie with the High Sea Fleet began at 01:00 on 31 May, when Hipper's battle cruisers left Wilhelmshaven. Instead of steaming westward along the Dutch coast, toward the southeast coast of England, this time the Germans advanced northward, parallel to the coast of Danish Jutland, toward the Skaggerak. Scheer and the main body of the High Sea Fleet followed some fifty miles behind Hipper, significantly closer than the seventy miles that had separated the two forces on the April sortie. Lacking only the dreadnought *König Albert*, then being refitted, the German fleet included 16 dreadnoughts and 5 battle cruisers, supplemented by 6 pre-dreadnought battleships, 11 light cruisers, and 61 destroyers. British intelligence that the High Sea Fleet was preparing to leave Wilhelmshaven enabled them to put to sea before the Germans, late on the evening of 30 May. Beatty departed Rosyth with his battle cruiser force at 23:00, some thirty minutes after Admiral Sir John Jellicoe left Scapa Flow with the rest of the Grand Fleet. Their ships included 28 dreadnoughts and 9 battle cruisers, every British capital ship except the recently reassigned HMS *Dreadnought*, 3 other dreadnoughts then fitting out or being refitted, and 1 battle cruiser being repaired. The ships under Jellicoe's direct command included 24 dreadnoughts and 3 battle cruisers, the latter, under Rear Admiral Horace Hood, recently sent to Scapa Flow from Rosyth for badly needed gunnery practice. Beatty's 6 battle cruisers were supplemented by 4 new *Queen Elizabeth* class dreadnoughts, under Rear Admiral Hugh Evan-Thomas, sent to Rosyth in exchange for Hood's ships. The British fleet also included 8 armored cruisers, 26 light cruisers or flotilla leaders, 78 destroyers, and 1 minelayer.[41]

Light vessels screening for Beatty and Hipper first sighted one another at 14:20 GMT, at 56° 48' N, 5° 21' E, just over 100 miles west of the

Jutland coast. The first exchange of fire came eight minutes later, between British and German light cruisers. At the time the two battle cruiser forces were still almost fifty miles apart, delaying their first exchange until 15:48. After sighting the British battle cruisers, Hipper turned away to the south-southeast, running back toward Scheer in an effort to draw Beatty into a battle with the entire High Sea Fleet. At that point, Scheer was just under fifty miles south of Hipper, while Jellicoe was just over fifty miles northwest of Beatty. More significant was the gap that had opened up within Beatty's force as it raced to the point of contact, then began its pursuit of Hipper. Owing to a series of questionable turning instructions issued by Evan-Thomas, the four *Queen Elizabeth*s, which had been steaming just five miles from the British battle cruisers, fell roughly ten miles behind them. The superior speed of the battle cruisers caused the gap to widen after Beatty began to chase Hipper into the German trap. The first phase of the battle, known to history as the "run to the south," lasted roughly fifty minutes. The two columns of battle cruisers, on parallel courses steaming to the south-southeast, dueled at a range of between 12,000 and 16,000 yards. In the first twelve minutes of the exchange, the Germans registered fifteen hits, the British just four. At 16:00 a shell from Hipper's flagship *Lützow* destroyed a turret on Beatty's flagship *Lion*, which was saved from a likely magazine explosion by the timely application of safety procedures. The *Lützow* went on to score a total of thirteen hits on the *Lion*; meanwhile, the *Moltke* scored nine hits on the *Tiger* within a span of twelve minutes, taking four hits in return. The first casualty of the battle, the *Indefatigable*, sank at 16:02 (1,107 dead) after a horrific magazine explosion ignited by four shells from the *Von der Tann*. The *Queen Elizabeth*s, too far to Beatty's rear to score hits, at 16:08 began to fire nevertheless, at distances of 19,000 to 23,000 yards from Hipper's ships. At 16:26 two or three shells from the *Derfflinger* struck the battle cruiser *Queen Mary*, which exploded and sank (1,266 dead). Around 16:30 the destroyer escorts of Beatty and Hipper engaged, with each side sinking two destroyers. At this time the *Seydlitz* was hit by a British torpedo but not seriously damaged. At 16:38, the first of Beatty's ships sighted the main body of the High Sea Fleet steaming up from the south. Beatty promptly reversed course to the north, hoping to draw the entire German fleet on to Jellicoe's advancing force.

The second phase of the battle, the "run to the north," lasted from just before 17:00 (when all of Beatty's ships had reversed course) to 18:15. The 15-inch guns of the *Queen Elizabeth*s were finally brought to bear, overmatching the 11- and 12-inch guns of Hipper's battle cruisers, which were now at the head of the German column. The *Lützow*, *Derfflinger*, *Seydlitz*, and *Von der Tann* all suffered damage, the latter so severe that all of its heavy gun turrets were temporarily inoperable. The first contact between Jellicoe's force and the Germans came at 17:36, when a light cruiser attached to Hood's battle cruiser squadron (which Jellicoe had sent on ahead of the rest of his fleet) met light cruisers of Hipper's group. By the end of this phase, the German light cruiser *Wiesbaden* was dead in the water and a British destroyer damaged badly enough to be abandoned. No capital ships were sunk, but a steering problem aboard one of Evan-Thomas's dreadnoughts, the *Warspite*, forced it to withdraw from the action just as the two main fleets met.

By 18:15, the remaining three *Queen Elizabeth*s had fallen into line at the rear of Jellicoe's 24 dreadnoughts, while Beatty's four surviving battle cruisers raced to the front of the line, where they joined Hood's trio as the entire British force executed a crossing of the German "T," steaming eastward in an east–west line. At the onset of this phase of the battle the old armored cruisers *Defence* and *Warrior*, deployed with Beatty at the head of the column, came under heavy fire from the German capital ships at a range of barely 8,000 yards. At 18:20 a shell from the *Friedrich der Grosse* ignited the magazine of the *Defence*, which exploded and sank with all hands (893 dead). The *Warrior* survived fifteen hits to be towed from the scene at the end of the day, only to founder and sink the next morning. Meanwhile, Hipper's battle cruisers, still heading the German column, came within 9,000 yards of Hood's battle cruisers before turning away. The *Lützow* took eight hits in eight minutes, and the *Derfflinger* suffered as well. Moments later, however, a German salvo landed squarely on the deck of Hood's flagship *Invincible*, blowing off one of its turrets amidships and igniting the magazine below. At 18:32, a thunderous explosion tore the ship in two, killing Hood and most of his crew (1,026 dead). Between 18:33 and 18:45, Scheer's column executed a turn-away to the southwest, covered by a smokescreen from his destroyers. At 18:57 the dreadnought *Marlborough* was hit by a torpedo, most likely fired by the disabled light cruiser *Wiesbaden*, but continued to move under its own power. The British assumed Scheer was running for Wilhelmshaven, but just before 19:00 he ordered his column to double back to the northeast. Only the badly damaged *Lützow*, abandoned by Hipper and his staff, fell out of line to continue its homeward course. Scheer subsequently gave a variety of explanations for his decision to turn back toward the enemy, none of which seem very convincing to historians. Some have noted that Scheer's new course, if maintained, would have led him into the Baltic via the Skaggerak, but not before his line crossed the wake of Jellicoe's column (by this time steaming southeastward), enabling him to inflict more damage on the British.

The battle resumed around 19:05, and the ensuing fourth phase lasted some forty minutes. By slowing his column, Jellicoe, not Scheer, achieved the desired crossing of the "T", as the lead ships of Scheer's column headed directly into Jellicoe's starboard flank. By 19:15 the entire British line was concentrating fire on the approaching German column from a range of 11,000 to 14,000 yards. Shells rained down on the front half of Scheer's line, with hits being registered as far back as the eleventh ship, the dreadnought *Helgoland*. The *Derfflinger*, heading the column, was struck by fourteen shells; among the other battle cruisers, the *Seydlitz* took five hits, the *Lützow* (not yet safely away) five, and the *Von der Tann* one. The dreadnought *Grosser Kurfürst* sustained between five and seven hits, the *Kaiser* two, the *König* and *Markgraf* one apiece. Returning fire, the Germans managed just two hits against the British line, both on the dreadnought *Colossus*. In the thick of the fight, Scheer ordered the German battle cruisers to sacrifice themselves against Jellicoe's line, but minutes later he rescinded the order and his entire force again turned away to the southwest, this time in considerable disarray. Around 19:35, aware that Scheer was withdrawing, Jellicoe made his most fateful decision of the battle, opting not to pursue. When Scheer ordered a destroyer attack to cover his retreat, Jellicoe responded in kind, deploying destroyers as he continued to steam to the southeast. With sunset still thirty minutes away, fear that German torpedoes would claim still more of his capital ships swayed the British commander against trying for the decisive victory then within his grasp.

Jellicoe soon reconsidered and by 20:00 the Grand Fleet was turning to the west, in the general direction of where he thought Scheer's column would be. The fifth and final phase of the battle began with the High Sea Fleet already enjoying a ten-mile lead over its pursuer, but the British closed fast. By 20:30 the two fleets were steaming almost due south, the British between the Germans and the Jutland coast. Up to this point Scheer had kept his II Battle Squadron, comprising five predreadnoughts of the *Deutschland* class and the older pre-dreadnought *Braunschweig*, out of danger at the rear of his column; now, he sent them directly into harm's way to help his light cruisers and destroyers cover the retreat of the rest of his ships. In the misty twilight, the *Schleswig–Holstein* and *Pommern* each sustained a hit, but their return fire included one shell that struck the battle cruiser *Princess Royal*. Their exchange was the day's last between battleships or battle cruisers; in the confusion that set in after dark, the cruisers and destroyers inflicted and suffered most of the damage. At 23:35 the cruiser *Southampton* torpedoed the light cruiser *Frauenlob*, the first German warship larger than a destroyer to be sunk in the battle, some nine hours after the action began. Around midnight the Germans sank two more British warships, the armored cruiser *Black Prince* and the flotilla leader *Tipperary*, after they blundered into Scheer's dreadnoughts. The losses of 1 June were all German. At 00:30 the dreadnought *Posen* accidentally rammed and severely damaged the light cruiser *Elbing*. Between 02:45 and 03:00, the light cruiser *Wiesbaden* (dead in the water for eight hours) finally sank, the *Elbing* was scuttled, and the *Lützow* was finally abandoned. The crippled battle cruiser, struck by at least two dozen heavy shells during the course of the battle, was sent to the bottom by a torpedo from a German destroyer. At 03:13, a British destroyer torpedoed and sank the pre-dreadnought *Pommern* (839 dead). Finally, the light cruiser *Rostock*, abandoned after being disabled by a torpedo from another British destroyer, was sunk at 05:25 by two German destroyers. On the final approach to Wilhelmshaven, the dreadnought *Ostfriesland* struck a mine but was able to make it into port under its own power. During the long final phase of the battle, the British lost four destroyers, the Germans one. After giving up on the *Lützow*, the Germans successfully shepherded home two other battle cruisers damaged almost as badly. The *Seydlitz*, recipient of twenty-two hits, took on over 5,300 tons of water and ran aground twice, while the *Derfflinger*, struck by twenty-one heavy shells, took on over 3,300 tons of water and slowed to a crawl. The *Seydlitz* finally straggled into Wilhelmshaven a day late, on 2 June, with the help of salvage vessels.

Remarkably, the High Sea Fleet made it home despite the fact that, for several hours during the night of 31 May–1 June, the British fleet was actually closer to Wilhelmshaven. The Germans survived because Scheer ultimately steered a course much closer to the Jutland and Schleswig coasts than Jellicoe anticipated; steaming south-southeast, the main body of his fleet ultimately crossed the wake of the British force, which was steaming south-southwest. At Jutland, the Germans clearly inflicted more damage than they suffered, sinking the battle cruisers *Invincible*, *Indefatigable*, and *Queen Mary*, the armored cruisers *Defence*, *Warrior*, and *Black Prince*, one flotilla leader and seven destroyers, while losing the battle cruiser *Lützow*, the pre-dreadnought battleship *Pommern*, four light cruisers and five destroyers of their own. Seven British and nine German capital ships sustained damages serious enough to require dry-docking; of these, all but one British and two German vessels were back in service within two months of the battle. The British lost 6,097 dead, the Germans 2,551. The Germans claimed Skaggerak (their designation for the battle) as a great victory, even though afterward the British remained in command of the North Sea. Nevertheless, the disappointment was far greater on the British side, which had fully expected that the long-awaited big battle with the High Sea Fleet would be a second Trafalgar. Jellicoe and Beatty (or, more accurately, their supporters within the officer corps) each blamed the other for opportunities missed. At the end of 1916 Beatty became commander of the Grand Fleet, when Jellicoe was appointed First Sea Lord. Meanwhile, in Germany, William II rewarded Scheer with a promotion to full admiral and the Iron Cross *Pour le Mérite*, the country's highest military decoration. An officer corps historically fragmented by infighting rallied around Scheer, excusing his tactical errors at Jutland. He would finally turn over command of the High Sea Fleet to Hipper in August 1918, then spend the last months of the war in the new post of Chief of the Supreme Navy Command.

Aside from Scheer's good luck and Jellicoe's moments of caution, Jutland turned out the way that it did largely because of the sturdier construction of the German capital ships, the unsafe handling of unstable powder supplies aboard the larger British warships, and poor fire control especially on the British side. The durability of the German capital ships was impressive enough. Four of the five battle cruisers absorbed heavy punishment but only one was lost. Among the dreadnoughts, the newest vessels of the *König* class sustained the most hits (the *König* ten, *Grosser Kurfürst* eight, and *Markgraf* five) but none was seriously damaged. Regarding powder supplies, critics have noted the low quality of British cordite, the lack of flashtight doors below heavy gun turrets on the British battle cruisers, and the remarkably careless way in which propellants were moved from magazines to turrets. Catastrophic magazine explosions claimed the battle cruisers *Invincible*, *Indefatigable*, and *Queen Mary*, and the armored cruiser *Defence*, and the nature of their demise brought instant death to most of their crews. Indeed, the three battle cruisers accounted for over half of the British dead at Jutland (3,339), and just 28 men survived them. As for fire control, the outcome of the battle showed clearly that German range-finding devices were not as inferior as the British had assumed, and that the British battle cruisers, lacking adequate gunnery training, had performed very poorly. None fared worse than the battle cruiser *New Zealand*, which fired 420 shots during the battle, more than any other capital ship, and scored just four hits.

Ironically, within days of the battle the British war effort suffered a greater blow than the missed opportunity at Jutland. On 5 June 1916 the cruiser *Hampshire* left for Archangel, carrying Lord Kitchener on a mission to Russia. Shortly after its departure, the ship struck a German mine off the Shetland Islands and sank, drowning the war minister and all but twelve of the crew.[42]

THE FIRST WORLD WAR: JUTLAND TO THE ARMISTICE (1916–18)

For the German navy, the celebration of the "victory" at Jutland soon gave way to gloom, upon the realization that the battle had done nothing to alter the strategic situation in the North Sea. In a report to William II dated 4 July, Scheer stated his opinion that the only hope for victory at sea lay in a U-boat war against British commerce. Germany's geographic and material disadvantages in the capital-ship war meant that further surface actions, no matter how successful, would not force Britain to the peace table. He advocated a renewal of unrestricted submarine warfare and, in the meantime, planned to make better use of submarines in conjunction with future sorties by the surface fleet.

Plate 1 British ship of the line *Thunderer* (left) and Austrian frigate *Guerriera* (center) in the bombardment of Sidon (26 September 1840). *Naval Historical Center (US), Basic Collection.*

Plate 2 The German fleet of 1848–52. *Historische Sammlung der Marineschule Mürwik.*

Plate 3 British ship of the line *Agamemnon* in the bombardment of Sevastopol
(17 October 1854). *Naval Historical Center (US), Basic Collection.*

Plate 4 The Anglo-French Baltic fleet (1854). *Naval Historical Center (US), Basic
Collection.*

Plate 5 French armored frigate *Gloire* (1860). *Naval Historical Center (US), Basic Collection.*

Plate 6 British armored frigate *Warrior* (1861). *Naval Historical Center (US), Basic Collection.*

Plate 7 British turret ship *Captain* (1870). *Naval Historical Center (US), Basic Collection.*

Plate 8 Prussian paddle steamer *Loreley* (left) and screw corvette *Arcona* (center) engage Danish warships at the Battle of Jasmund (17 March 1864). *Historische Sammlung der Marineschule Mürwik.*

Plate 9 Austrian screw ship of the line *Kaiser*, the day after engaging Italian ironclads at the Battle of Lissa (20 July 1866). *Naval Historical Center (US), Basic Collection.*

Plate 10 Italian battleship *Duilio* (1880). *Naval Historical Center (US), Basic Collection.*

Plate 11 German turret ship *Preussen* (1876) of the *Grosser Kurfürst* class, with casemate ship *Hansa* (1875) in background. *Historische Sammlung der Marineschule Mürwik.*

Plate 12 German *Sachsen*-class battleship (1878; pictured in 1895). *Naval Historical Center (US), Basic Collection.*

Plate 13 French protected cruiser *Milan* (1885). *Naval Historical Center (US), Basic Collection.*

Plate 14 French protected cruiser *Sfax* (1887). *Naval Historical Center (US), Basic Collection.*

Plate 15 British protected cruiser *Blake* (1892). *Naval Historical Center (US), Basic Collection.*

Plate 16 German torpedo boat (mid-1880s) with battleship *Sachsen* and rigged warships in background. *Historische Sammlung der Marineschule Mürwik.*

Plate 17 German *Siegfried*-class coastal battleship (pictured in early 1890s). *Naval Historical Center (US), Basic Collection.*

Plate 18 French submarine *Gymnote* (1888). *Naval Historical Center (US), Basic Collection.*

Plate 19 British pre-dreadnought *Royal Sovereign* (1891). *Naval Historical Center (US), Basic Collection.*

Plate 20 German *Gazelle*-class light cruiser (pictured circa 1900). *Naval Historical Center (US), Basic Collection.*

Plate 21 German pre-dreadnought *Kaiser Wilhelm II* (1900), of the *Kaiser Friedrich III* class. *Historische Sammlung der Marineschule Mürwik.*

Plate 22 German pre-dreadnought of the *Deutschland* class (1906). *Naval Historical Center (US), Basic Collection.*

Plate 23 German armored cruiser *Scharnhorst* (1907). *Naval Historical Center (US), Basic Collection.*

Plate 24 French submarine *Narval* (1900). *Naval Historical Center (US), Basic Collection.*

Plate 25 HMS *Dreadnought* (1906). *Naval Historical Center (US), Basic Collection.*

Plate 26 German battle cruiser *Von der Tann* (1911). *Naval Historical Center (US), Basic Collection.*

Plate 27 British battle cruiser *Lion* (1912). *Naval Historical Center (US), Basic Collection.*

Plate 28 German dreadnought of the *König* class (1915). *Naval Historical Center (US), Basic Collection.*

Plate 29 Austro–Hungarian dreadnought *Tegetthoff* (1913). *Naval Historical Center (US), Basic Collection.*

Plate 30 British carrier *Argus* (1918). *Naval Historical Center (US), Basic Collection.*

Plate 31 Austro–Hungarian dreadnought *Viribus Unitis* sinking in Pola harbor
(1 November 1918) after being mined by Italian saboteurs. *Naval Historical Center (US),
Basic Collection.*

Plate 32 British battle cruiser *Hood* (1920). *Naval Historical Center (US), Basic Collection.*

Plate 33 German 'pocket battleship' *Admiral Graf Spee* (1936). *Naval Historical Center (US), Basic Collection.*

Plate 34 Soviet battleship *Oktyabrskaya Revolutsia* (ex-*Gangut*) in 1936, after modernization. *Naval Historical Center (US), Basic Collection.*

Plate 35 Italian battleships *Littorio* and *Vittorio Veneto* (1940). *Naval Historical Center (US), Basic Collection.*

Plate 36 German battleship *Bismarck* (1940). *Naval Historical Center (US), Basic Collection.*

Plate 37 German battleship *Tirpitz* (1941), on station in Norway. *Naval Historical Center (US), Basic Collection.*

AIRCRAFT FLYING OVER H.M.S. ARK ROYAL.

Plate 38 British carrier *Ark Royal* (1938). *Naval Historical Center (US), Basic Collection.*

Plate 39 German S-boat (1939). *Naval Historical Center (US), Basic Collection.*

Plate 40 British batttleship *Queen Elizabeth* in 1943, after repairs. *Naval Historical Center (US), Basic Collection.*

Plate 41 French carrier *Arromanches* (ex-British *Colossus*) off Vietnam. *Naval Historical Center (US), Basic Collection.*

Plate 42 British cruiser *Belfast* off Korea (1952). *Naval Historical Center (US), Basic Collection.*

Plate 43 French helicopter cruiser *Jeanne d'Arc* (1964). *Marine Nationale, France.*

Plate 44 Italian cruiser *Caio Duilio* flanked by two destroyers and two frigates, pictured in early 1970s. *Naval Historical Center (US), Basic Collection.*

Plate 45 Soviet *Sverdlov*-class cruiser, pictured in 1957 *Naval Historical Center (US), Basic Collection.*

Plate 46 Soviet submarine of the 'Golf' class, pictured in 1965. *Naval Historical Center (US), Basic Collection.*

Plate 47 Soviet carrier *Novorossiysk* (1982). *Naval Historical Center (US), Basic Collection.*

Plate 48 French carrier *Charles de Gaulle* (2001). *Marine Nationale, France.*

While it has been repeated often enough that the High Sea Fleet never came out again after Jutland, in fact Scheer attempted another sortie as soon as he could muster the strength to do so. By mid-August the refitting of the *König Albert* and the commissioning of the new *Bayern* left him with eighteen dreadnoughts, supplemented by the *Moltke* and *Von der Tann*, the only German battle cruisers not still in dry dock. On the evening of 18 August the fleet left Wilhelmshaven; within hours the British left their bases at Scapa Flow and Rosyth. This time, surface units of the two fleets never made contact, but German submarine traps, which had been completely ineffective in the sortie of 31 May–1 June, caught two light cruisers screening for Beatty's battle cruisers. On the morning of 19 August *U 52* torpedoed and sank the *Nottingham*, and that afternoon *U 66* torpedoed the *Falmouth*. The latter actually survived the attack, only to be torpedoed and sunk by *U 63* on the 20th, while being towed back to port. Ironically the only capital ship to fall victim to a submarine during the sortie was the German dreadnought *Westfalen*, which had to return to Wilhelmshaven for repairs after being torpedoed by the British submarine *E 23* on the morning of the 19th. In a strategic sense the battle that did not happen on 19 August was more significant than Jutland, in that it marked the last time that the Grand Fleet would be so aggressive in searching for its German counterpart. In a letter to Jellicoe on 6 September, Beatty cited the adage "when you are winning, risk nothing," and a week later the two admirals agreed that under normal circumstances, British dreadnoughts and battle cruisers would not be risked south of 55° 30'N, a line stretching across the North Sea from Newcastle to the German–Danish border.[43]

Coinciding with their decision not to risk their capital ships to U-boat traps, the British resolved to use submarines rather than lighter surface vessels in their offensive sweeps of the lower North Sea. The Germans encountered no British capital ships on cruises by the High Sea Fleet to the Dogger Bank in mid-October and by a smaller force up the Jutland coast of Denmark in early November. During the latter operation, the British submarine *J 1* torpedoed and damaged the dreadnoughts *Grosser Kurfürst* and *Kronprinz*, making William II ever more reluctant to risk his capital ships. Scheer abandoned his regime of regular sorties; meanwhile, in a prelude to the resumption of unrestricted submarine warfare in February 1917, Germany began a restricted submarine campaign in the autumn of 1916. Adhering (sometimes loosely) to internationally accepted prize rules, German U-boats sank 231,570 tons in September 1916; 341,360 in October 1916; 326,690 in November 1916; 307,850 in December 1916; and 328,390 in January 1917. Thanks to the fact that there were now many more submarines deployed, the tonnage sunk over these five months was roughly double the total claimed in the seven months of unrestricted submarine warfare during 1915. Almost all of the damage was done by surfaced U-boats, as 80 percent of the victims were warned before being sunk, and 75 percent were sunk by the deck gun rather than by torpedoes. Remarkably, during these five months just ten boats were lost. After taking office as First Sea Lord in December 1916, Jellicoe made anti-submarine warfare a priority, entrusting it to a new Anti-Submarine Division in the Admiralty. Germany's resumption of unrestricted submarine warfare soon added a greater sense of urgency to such efforts.[44]

The five months of restricted submarine warfare were an eventful time elsewhere in the naval war, with things generally going the way of the Central Powers. The Italian navy, which on 2 August 1916 lost a second battleship, the dreadnought *Leonardo da Vinci*, to Austrian sabotage at Taranto, on 11 December lost the pre-dreadnought *Regina Margherita* in a minefield off Valona, Albania. The French navy likewise lost two battleships: the pre-dreadnought *Suffren*, torpedoed by German *U 52* off Lisbon on 26 November, and the pre-dreadnought *Gaulois*, torpedoed by German *UB 47* in the Aegean on 27 December. The French also had the distinction of being the first to lose a submarine to air attack, when an Austro–Hungarian seaplane bombed and sank the *Foucault* on 15 September, off Cattaro. Meanwhile, increasingly heavy-handed attempts to coerce Greece into declaring war against the Central Powers caused further embarrassment for the Allies. From the beginning of the war the Allies had repeatedly violated the Greek neutrality which King Constantine, brother-in-law of William II, sought so hard to preserve. French forces guarding the mouth of the Adriatic had operated out of Corfu, and by the time of the Dardanelles operation the Aegean island of Lemnos had been seized for use as a British base. First British and French, then Serbian troops were based on the Greek mainland at Salonika, where the renegade Venizelos established a pro-Allied de facto government. Starting in the spring of 1916 the British actively recruited Greek irregulars for use in raids along the Turkish coast, and in the autumn the Allies demanded that the Greeks supply their Salonika force with batteries of mountain artillery. On 1 December the Allied Mediterranean commander, Dartige, led a naval demonstration to Piraeus which included the dreadnought *Provence* and four *Danton* class pre-dreadnoughts. In the course of a sporadic shelling of Athens a round from the pre-dreadnought *Mirabeau* almost struck the Greek royal palace. Loyal Greek troops drove Allied landing parties back to their ships, inflicting over 200 casualties, but the king finally conceded the mountain artillery to the Allies and, in January 1917, agreed to withdraw his entire army to the Morea, securing for the Allies a free hand to operate in the north of Greece. Dartige became the scapegoat for the bungled operation and at the end of 1916 gave way to Vice Admiral Dominique-Marie Gauchet. Greece finally entered the war on the Allied side in July 1917, after a French squadron landed 9,500 troops at Piraeus, this time unopposed, to force Constantine to abdicate.[45]

On 9 January 1917, at a meeting in his Schloss Pless headquarters with Field Marshal Paul von Hindenburg, General Erich Ludendorff, Chancellor Bethmann Hollweg, and the chief of the *Admiralstab*, Holtzendorff, William II formally approved the renewal of unrestricted submarine warfare, effective 1 February. Holtzendorff, instrumental in ending the initial unrestricted campaign in September 1915, supported the resumption, reflecting the consensus of Scheer, Hipper, and other leading German admirals. In mid-December William II had joined the new Habsburg monarch, Charles, on a tour of Pola, paving the way for Austria–Hungary's participation in the campaign. In a second conference at Schloss Pless on 26 January, Charles and Admiral Haus met with William II and German naval officials to work out the details. The Austro–Hungarian navy agreed to send its own submarines out of the Adriatic to prey upon Allied convoys between Malta and Salonika, and disarmed two old cruisers to free up more personnel to support the German U-boats operating out of Cattaro. For the German navy, the commitment to submarine warfare had a far greater effect on the surface fleet, as two dreadnoughts and five battle cruisers then under construction were abandoned, among them the *Sachsen*, already launched and very near completion. When the campaign resumed, the German navy had 105 U-boats, of which roughly one-third were at sea. The new campaign claimed 520,410 tons in February 1917, 564,500 tons in March 1917, and an astounding 860,330 tons in April 1917, three months during which just nine submarines were lost. Another 616,320 tons were sunk in May 1917, and 696,725 tons in June 1917.[46]

In resolving to renew unrestricted submarine warfare, the leaders of the Central Powers either discounted the danger of the United States intervening in the war or considered the campaign worth the risk. The American declaration of war against Germany on 6 April 1917 had little effect on the land war, as it would take the United States more than a year to conscript, train, and deploy significant forces on the Western Front. The US navy, the world's largest behind the British and German, had a more immediate impact, despite the fact that, in the changing circumstances of the naval war, its fourteen dreadnoughts were practically irrelevant. Rear Admiral William S. Sims USN, appointed special liaison officer to the British navy just before the American declaration of war, arrived in London on 10 April and, shortly afterward, sided with junior officers at the Admiralty in a debate with their superiors over whether to adopt a convoy system against the U-boat threat. While the convoying of troopships had been accepted from the start of the war, the Admiralty had not extended the practice to merchantmen, in part because many merchant mariners felt their ships were better off without it. Circumventing British navy leaders, Sims presented the pro-convoy case of the junior officers to the prime minister, David Lloyd George, who compelled his own admirals to drop their long-standing opposition. On 27 April, Jellicoe formally approved the development of a convoy system. One week later, the first US naval vessels arrived in European waters: a group of destroyers, which took up anti-submarine patrols out of Queenstown, Ireland. The first transatlantic convoys crossed safely in June 1917; thereafter, the toll taken by U-boats fell dramatically, to 555,510 tons in July 1917, 472,370 tons in August 1917, 353,600 tons in September, and 302,600 tons in November. The campaign to starve Britain into submission clearly had failed, but the tonnage sunk in October (466,540) and December (411,770) underscored the continuing danger. On the first anniversary of the resumption of unrestricted submarine warfare, the overall tonnage at the disposal of the Allies was still decreasing, even though new construction had accelerated and dozens of German ships interned in US ports in 1914 had been added to the American merchant marine.[47]

The Allies also introduced a convoy system to the Mediterranean, with the US navy contributing a force based at Gibraltar and the Japanese navy sending a cruiser and fourteen destroyers to Malta. In the Mediterranean the anti-submarine effort led to an increased British involvement as the war progressed, despite the fact that the French remained nominally in overall command there. Reflecting the improvement of Allied anti-submarine warfare in both the Atlantic and the Mediterranean, Germany lost 43 U-boats in the last five months of 1917 alone. Alongside the convoy system, the Allies invested heavily in anti-submarine mining operations, a tactic favored by Admiral Beatty after he took command of the Grand Fleet. Over the last four months of 1917, mines claimed 11 U-boats in the North Sea; during the same period, British submarines sank another 6 U-boats. Between September and December 1916 the British had established an anti-submarine barrage across the Channel at Dover, consisting of mines and nets, the latter dragged by armed trawlers and auxiliary steamers known as "drifters." The Dover Barrage was modeled after the Otranto Barrage, established at the mouth of the Adriatic in 1915–16, during the initial period of unrestricted submarine warfare. Both were vulnerable to attack, the former from German destroyers based at Ostend and Zeebrugge, the latter from Austro–Hungarian cruisers and destroyers based at Cattaro. The most successful anti-barrage raid of the war came on 15 May 1917, when Captain Miklós Horthy led an Austro–Hungarian force of 3 light cruisers, 2 destroyers, and 2 submarines, supplemented by a German U-boat, in an operation which sank 14 of the 47 Otranto drifters, along with 2 destroyers (one French and one Italian) and an Italian freighter, while losing no ships of his own. In the long run, neither barrage justified the expenditure of resources required for its maintenance. In over three years the Otranto Barrage had just two confirmed successes, netting Austro–Hungarian *U 6* in May 1916 and German *UB 53* in August 1918; it probably also caused the loss of

Austro–Hungarian *U 30* in March 1917. Meanwhile, the Dover Barrage likewise sank just two U-boats before being reinforced with a significant mining effort in December 1917, after which it claimed another seven in just four months. In April and May 1918, British light craft raided Ostend and Zeebrugge, temporarily rendering the latter port useless to German destroyers and submarines. By the end of the war almost all U-boats entered or returned from the Atlantic via the northern route, around Scotland. The Allies attempted to close this avenue as well by establishing the so-called Northern Barrage between the Orkney Islands and Norway; it featured over 70,000 mines laid by the British and American navies between March and October 1918. The results were meager in comparison to the massive effort, as the Northern Barrage claimed only six or seven U-boats by war's end.[48]

For the navies of the Central Powers, the shift away from large-unit surface operations affected more than just matériel and construction policies. The most highly regarded junior officers were given command of U-boats, and others went to the light cruisers and destroyers, leaving less capable men to take their places aboard the battleships and larger cruisers. During the last two years of the war, the inexperience or mediocrity of shipboard "middle management" exacerbated the problem of the social gulf between officers and seamen, at a time when the relative inactivity of the big ships would have caused increased tensions in any event. In July 1917 discontent over food shortages sparked the first demonstrations in the Austro–Hungarian fleet at Pola. Order was restored fairly easily, and Haus's successor as navy commander, Admiral Maksimilian Njegovan, was lenient toward the seamen involved. Three months later, the Austro–Hungarian navy suffered its first and only desertion of a vessel at sea when a Czech machinist and a Slovene boatswain's mate seized *Torpedoboot 11* during a patrol in the Adriatic and made for the port of Recanati, Italy. The peculiar behavior of the mutineers indicated that they defected out of war weariness alone, as they destroyed code books and other sensitive materials before reaching Italy.[49] Njegovan and Austro–Hungarian leaders considered the desertion of the torpedo boat an isolated incident, but coming in the wake of the demonstrations at Pola it raised fears, especially in Germany, that the Austro–Hungarian fleet would be infected by the political problems the Austrian home front had begun to experience after Emperor Charles, in May 1917, reconvened the Reichsrat and eased censorship. But the German navy, too, suffered unrest in the summer of 1917, likewise reflecting the war weariness of the home front. At Wilhelmshaven in early June, the crew of the dreadnought *Prinzregent Luitpold* used a hunger strike to receive better food; sailors subsequently organized to press similar demands aboard other ships. Later in the month the Reichstag authorized Tirpitz's successor, Admiral Eduard von Capelle, to create "food committees" aboard all ships of the fleet, but few captains did so until their crews forced them to. The situation deteriorated still more after the Reichstag's passage of the famous "Peace Resolution" in mid-July. Unrest in the fleet became increasingly politicized and, during the months of July and August alone, an estimated 5,000 sailors joined the newly formed Independent Social Democratic Party (USPD), an anti-war secession from the SPD. The first half of August was particularly tense, with some sailors refusing all orders. The *Prinzregent Luitpold* was again at the center of the strikes but four other dreadnoughts and a light cruiser were also affected. Scheer reacted decisively in breaking the strikes. Courts martial meted out a total of 360 years in prison terms to the mutineers, and two of their leaders were executed.[50]

The problems of social divisions, short rations, and general inactivity were greater for the Russian navy than for the German or Austro–Hungarian, and left the crews of the tsar's fleet increasingly susceptible to revolutionary agitation. Since their commissioning late in 1914, the Russian Baltic Fleet's four dreadnoughts had spent most of the war anchored at Helsinki. In May 1915 the navy's able Baltic commander, Admiral Essen, succumbed to a lung infection at age fifty-four; none of his successors would be as effective. In March 1917, shortly after the February Revolution ousted Nicholas II, unrest in the fleet culminated in the murder of its commander, Vice Admiral A. J. Nepenin, and several other officers. Revolutionary committees took over many of the ships, and by the summer of 1917 most were sympathetic toward V. I. Lenin and the Bolsheviks. It was against this much weakened foe that the German navy, in October 1917, launched its largest Baltic operation since August 1915, seeking, as then, to secure the Gulf of Riga. It helped matters considerably that the retreating Russian army had abandoned the city of Riga one month earlier. From the battle cruiser *Moltke*, Vice Admiral Erhard Schmidt commanded ten dreadnoughts, nine light cruisers, a host of smaller vessels and transports carrying almost 25,000 troops, against a defending force under Rear Admiral M. K. Bakhirev consisting of the pre-dreadnoughts *Slava* and *Grazhdanin* (ex-*Tsesarevich*), two armored cruisers, a protected cruiser and several lighter craft. On 12 October German troops were landed on Ösel Island, which commanded the northern approaches to the gulf. After four days the Germans secured the island, and their attentions turned to the Russian warships in Moon Sound, the body of water separating nearby Dagö Island from the Estonian coast. On the morning of 17 October Bakhirev's two pre-dreadnoughts joined the armored cruiser *Bayan* in a desperate defense of the sound. Fire from the German dreadnought *König* soon disabled the *Slava* and damaged the *Bayan*, while the guns of the *Kronprinz* scored two hits on the *Grazhdanin*. At midday a Russian submarine torpedoed and sank the abandoned *Slava*, while the rest of Bakhirev's force withdrew. By 20 October Dagö Island and Moon

Sound were in German hands and the Gulf of Riga secured. By the end of the month Schmidt's capital ships were en route back through the Kiel Canal to rejoin the High Sea Fleet at Wilhelmshaven. In addition to the *Slava*, the Russians lost one destroyer. The Germans lost one destroyer, three torpedo boats, and eight minesweepers, and temporarily lost the services of the dreadnought *Bayern*, badly damaged by a mine during the landings of 12 October.[51]

The defeat at Moon Sound was the last battle of the Imperial Russian Baltic Fleet. After the demise of Russia's Provisional Government three weeks later, the sailors devoted their energies to the new Bolshevik regime, becoming its most loyal followers.[52] Meanwhile, in the Black Sea Fleet, the fall of the tsar did not usher in the same sort of disorder. Because the fleet was maintaining a more active regimen, winning its own war against the Turkish navy and dominating the Black Sea, relations between officers and the revolutionary committees formed aboard the ships deteriorated more gradually. In June 1917 an exasperated Kolchak resigned his post, but the fleet remained capable of action right up to the eve of the Bolshevik Revolution, on 1 November 1917 leaving Sevastopol on its last major sortie against the mouth of the Bosporus. Commanded by Rear Admiral Nemits, the force included two dreadnoughts, the flagship *Svobodnaya Rossia* (ex-*Ekaterina II*) and the newly commissioned *Volya* (ex-*Imperator Alexander III*), supported by three pre-dreadnoughts and five smaller escorts. Before the operation was complete, the crew of the flagship mutinied, giving Nemits no choice but to return to port. The Soviet government suspended all offensive military and naval operations as soon as it took power, and in December 1917 concluded an armistice pulling Russia out of the war.[53] The end of the war in the Black Sea had immediate implications for the Turkish navy, as it freed the *Yavuz Sultan Selim* for a short-lived career in the Aegean. On 20 January 1918 Souchon's successor, Vice Admiral Hubert Rebeur-Paschwitz, took the battle cruiser and its escort *Midilli* on a sortie which resulted in the sinking of two British monitors, the 6,150-ton *Raglan* and the 540-ton *M 28*, off Imbros Island. The success came at a heavy cost, however, as the *Yavuz Sultan Selim* hit three mines and had to limp back to Constantinople, while the *Midilli* struck five and sank with almost all hands (330 dead). The battle cruiser was not repaired until after German troops seized control of Sevastopol, and its dry dock, four months later.[54]

The year 1917 certainly featured no naval developments more significant than unrestricted submarine warfare bringing the United States into the war and revolution driving Russia out of it. Otherwise, the war at sea continued to go the way of the Central Powers, at least in terms of enemy warships sunk, with German submarines now doing all of the damage. Britain and France each lost another pre-dreadnought battleship, as *U 32* torpedoed and sank the *Cornwallis* east of Malta on

9 January, and *U 64* torpedoed and sank the *Danton* south of Sardinia on 19 March. After sinking the British monitor *M 15* off Gaza on 11 November, *UC 38* also sank the 7,900-ton French protected cruiser *Châteaurenault* in the Ionian Sea on 14 December, only to be sunk, in turn, by two of the *Châteaurenault*'s destroyer escorts. The British armored cruiser *Drake*, torpedoed on 2 October off Northern Ireland by *U 79*, was the only larger warship the Western Allies lost to enemy action during 1917 outside of the Mediterranean. The most costly sinking of an Allied warship came in an accident which reflected the fact that the British navy was still having difficulty storing and handling munitions safely: on 9 July the dreadnought *Vanguard* blew up at anchor in Scapa Flow (804 dead). Meanwhile, the largest warship lost by the Central Powers during the year was the 5,600-ton Austro–Hungarian pre-dreadnought *Wien*, serving as Trieste harbor watch when torpedoed and sunk on 10 December by *MAS 9*, a small Italian motor torpedo boat.[55]

As the German submarine campaign progressed, the larger surface units of the High Sea Fleet remained inactive aside from periodic guard duty in the Helgoland Bight, where they would stand watch whenever minesweepers were sent out to clear channels for the U-boats to sortie. The war's last engagement between British and German capital ships came on 17 November 1917, when Beatty sent Vice Admiral T. W. D. Napier with the new battle cruisers *Courageous, Glorious*, and *Repulse*, eight light cruisers and a number of destroyers into the Helgoland Bight, in an attempt to engage German warships covering that day's minesweeping operations. It was the only time that British capital ships ventured south of the 55° 30'N "risk nothing" limit set in September 1916 by Jellicoe and Beatty, and the results were negligible. The British forces dueled with the dreadnoughts *Kaiser* and *Kaiserin* and German light cruisers before withdrawing, scoring five hits while sustaining seven. Three weeks after this "Second Battle of Helgoland Bight," five US navy dreadnoughts joined the Grand Fleet, further reinforcing its superiority over the High Sea Fleet. This made a major surface encounter in 1918 even less likely, despite the fact that Beatty, in April of the new year, moved the base of the Grand Fleet from Scapa Flow to Rosyth, 250 miles closer to the Germans. By then, Jellicoe had been ousted as First Sea Lord, replaced after just a year in office by Admiral Sir Rosslyn Wemyss. Jellicoe's earlier lack of enthusiasm for the convoy system had strained his relationship with Lloyd George, and in the autumn of 1917 the losses in one particular convoy – nine Scandinavian neutrals and two of their British destroyer escorts, sunk off the Shetlands on 17 October by two German light cruisers – had caused him considerable embarrassment. His critics also held him accountable for Napier's lack of success in the action of 17 November.[56]

In the midst of a hard winter, the Central Powers suffered unprecedented unrest on the home front. During January 1918 more than a million workers went on strike in Germany and Austria–Hungary. The German navy was affected only in that the strikes suspended U-boat construction for a week and resulted in a temporary torpedo shortage during the month of February. For the Austro–Hungarian navy the situation was far worse. For several days in late January, sailors of the fleet actively supported a strike by workers in the Pola arsenal; then, on 1–3 February, a mutiny temporarily paralysed the naval forces at Cattaro. The Cattaro mutiny started aboard the armored cruiser *Sankt Georg*, where the captain was shot in the head but, miraculously, not killed. Support for the rebels was strongest aboard the larger ships, weaker in the torpedo flotillas, and nonexistent aboard the submarines, reflecting the fact that morale was less of a problem in smaller, more active units. Along with better food and working conditions, the mutineers demanded an end to Austria–Hungary's dependence upon Germany and a good-faith response to Woodrow Wilson's Fourteen Points of 8 January 1918. Their manifesto also endorsed Bolshevik Russia's appeal for a peace without annexations or indemnities. The mutiny began to collapse after army artillery fired on the red-flagged harbor watch *Kronprinz Rudolf*, killing one sailor and wounding several others. The arrival of three *Erzherzog* class pre-dreadnoughts from Pola on the morning of 3 February caused the remaining mutineers to surrender. The uprising had included sailors of all nationalities of the empire, reflecting the fact that war weariness and socialist politics were its strongest influences. Four mutineers were executed and almost four hundred imprisoned. Afterward, Emperor Charles reorganized the naval command, promoting forty-nine-year-old Captain Miklós Horthy to rear admiral and placing him in command of the fleet.[57]

As was the case with Kolchak earlier in the war for the Russian Black Sea Fleet, the extraordinary promotion of Horthy brought a temporary revitalization of the Austro–Hungarian navy. Coincidentally, after the demise of the empires they served, both men became commanders of counterrevolutionary land forces, a role in which Horthy would have far greater success than Kolchak. Shortly after the Soviet government signed the Peace of Brest–Litovsk (3 March 1918) with the Central Powers, civil war erupted within Russia between Lenin's "Reds" and a disparate array of opponents collectively labeled as "Whites," the latter including a Siberian army led by Kolchak. Because the Germans had provided Lenin with transportation from Switzerland to Russia in 1917, and had received such tremendous territorial gains at Brest–Litovsk, many Allied leaders considered Soviet Russia, willingly or unwillingly, a satellite of Imperial Germany. These fears were not borne out in the Baltic, where each navy treated the other as a hostile force. Within days of Brest–Litovsk, a German task force including three dreadnoughts landed troops which occupied the Åland Islands, except for Eckerö, which was seized by Swedish forces landed by the *Sverige* and two older coastal battleships. On 5 April 1918 a German division landed at Hangö, to support the Finnish White Army against the Soviets. The dreadnoughts soon withdrew, but one of them, the *Rheinland*, ran aground in a fog en route to Danzig and sustained such heavy hull damage that it was never repaired. Later that month, as the Soviets lost control over Finland, they abandoned the Russian naval base at Helsinki and withdrew the four *Gangut* class dreadnoughts to Kronstadt. They also scuttled eight of the Baltic Fleet's best submarines, four at Hangö and four at Tallinn (Reval), Estonia, to keep them from falling into German hands. At the same time, the British navy ended its Baltic submarine campaign, scuttling seven boats which could not run for home.[58]

In numbers of warships the Soviet Baltic Fleet remained a formidable force, including four dreadnoughts, four pre-dreadnoughts, five armored cruisers, and four protected cruisers. But by May 1918 two of the pre-dreadnoughts had been hulked and the rest of the fleet laid up, with the exception of three vessels: the dreadnought *Petropavlovsk*, the pre-dreadnought *Andrei Pervosvanni*, and the protected cruiser *Oleg*. The deactivation of so many warships enabled the Bolshevik regime to assign the sailors to duties ashore, where they served loyally with the Red Army on various fronts in the civil war, and in raids of the countryside to confiscate grain from the peasantry. The Soviets also controlled the Russian navy's tiny Arctic force from December 1917, when the crew of the well-traveled protected cruiser *Askold* (flagship at Vladivostok from 1906–14 and Russia's representative in the Mediterranean from 1914 to 1916) declared its allegiance to Lenin's regime. Allied operations against Soviet Russia, which could not begin in earnest in the Baltic or Black Sea until 1919, opened in the Arctic in the summer of 1918, ostensibly to prevent supplies landed earlier at Archangel and Murmansk from falling into German hands. The Allied expeditionary force, primarily Anglo–American, included small contingents from France, Italy, and Serbia; at sea, the old French armored cruiser *Amiral Aube* was the largest Allied warship on hand. Soviet naval resistance collapsed in July, when the British captured the *Askold*. By November 1918 the Russian Arctic ports were in Allied hands, and Allied troops had advanced southward down the rail lines linking the ports to the Russian interior.[59]

In the Black Sea, the German–Soviet armistice of December 1917 required the Russian fleet to be disarmed pending a definitive peace treaty, but on 9 February 1918 the Central Powers recognized the independence of Ukraine, which then claimed the ships as its own. Many of them flew the Ukrainian flag during the spring of 1918, until German troops occupied Sevastopol on 14 May. The Black Sea Fleet left just as the Germans arrived, or at least those elements of it that chose to obey the orders of Vice Admiral N. P. Sablin, who in turn followed orders from Lenin's goverment in Moscow to take the ships to

Novorossisk. Both of the dreadnoughts and 18 destroyers went with Sablin, while the 6 pre-dreadnoughts and over 20 smaller warships, ranging in size from cruisers to submarines, remained behind. After the Germans demanded that Sablin's ships return to Sevastopol, the revolutionary councils of the fleet voted to decide the matter. With each ship free to determine its own fate, on 18 June the *Volya* and three destroyers steamed back to Sevastopol, while the *Svobodnaya Rossia* and the rest of the destroyers were scuttled at Novorossisk.[60]

The Central Powers quickly exploited their complete command of the Black Sea, recognizing that, along with the Ukrainian rivers and the Danube, it provided the most cost-effective route to ship the much-anticipated Ukrainian grain harvest of 1918 to the hungry home front of Germany and Austria–Hungary. The Austro–Hungarian navy detached monitors and patrol boats from its Danube Flotilla for service on the Dnieper, Dniester, and Bug, where they were joined by other small craft abandoned earlier by the Russians. At the same time, German naval leaders harbored far greater ambitions. Their most grandiose scheme called for adding a repaired *Yavuz Sultan Selim* to the captured units of the Russian Black Sea Fleet and taking the lot on a sortie through the Turkish straits and into the Eastern Mediterranean, coordinating the move with a breakout of the Austro–Hungarian fleet from the Adriatic. Such scenarios caused considerable concern for the Allies, whose fears of German–Soviet collusion in the Black Sea reflected their lack of reliable intelligence on the region. As it turned out, it was impossible for the Germans to repair and man enough of the former Russian Black Sea Fleet to launch an Aegean sortie that would be anything other than suicidal. Meanwhile, in the Adriatic, the Austro–Hungarian dreadnoughts attempted no further action after 10 June 1918, when the *Szent István* was torpedoed and sunk by *MAS 15* off Premuda Island, as it made its way from Pola down the Dalmatian coast with its three sister-ships for a carefully planned attack on Allied forces at the Otranto Straits. Rear Admiral Horthy had hoped to replicate the previous spring's successful raid by light cruisers and destroyers against the Otranto Barrage. This time, however, the dreadnoughts and the three *Erzherzog* class pre-dreadnoughts (based at Cattaro since the mutiny of February 1918) would be following close behind to annihilate the Allied cruisers sent out in response to the initial raid, and to take on any French or Italian dreadnoughts that might join the fight. The loss of the *Szent István* forced the cancellation of the entire operation, and afterward Austro–Hungarian morale plummeted, dashing Horthy's hopes to revitalize the fleet. The Germans fared no better in the Black Sea, activating just one of the captured Russian battleships, the dreadnought *Volya*. Commissioned on 15 October, it made one cruise to the Bosporus before the Armistice.[61]

To counter a breakout through the Dardanelles by the imagined German Black Sea force, in the summer of 1918 the Allies kept their best pre-dreadnoughts in the Aegean: four French *Dantons* plus the British *Lord Nelson* and *Agamemnon*. By autumn the British had added the dreadnoughts *Superb* and *Temeraire*, more in order to justify Admiral Sir Somerset Gough-Calthorpe wresting local Allied command there from the French than because the ships were really needed. They were the first British dreadnoughts stationed in the Mediterranean theater since the withdrawal of the *Queen Elizabeth* in May 1915. Calthorpe, rather than the Allied Mediterranean commander-in-chief, Admiral Gauchet, concluded the armistice with the Ottoman Empire, signed aboard the *Agamemnon* off Mudros on 30 October 1918. Calthorpe's flagship *Superb* subsequently led the Allied fleet through the Dardanelles, to anchor off Constantinople on 13 November. By then, the German officers and crew of the *Yavuz Sultan Selim* had left for home, leaving the battle cruiser in the hands of Turkish personnel. It went on to have the longest career of any capital ship of the First World War. Renamed the *Yavuz* after the fall of the Ottoman dynasty, it was finally decommissioned and sold for scrap in 1971.[62]

In the year between the inconclusive Second Battle of Helgoland Bight and the Armistice, the capital ships of the Grand Fleet and High Sea Fleet never again engaged one another and, aside from one aborted German sortie in April 1918, were never even at sea at the same time. On 23–24 April the High Sea Fleet ventured out for the last time, after Scheer learned that the British were detaching divisions of capital ships to escort convoys between the Orkney Islands and Bergen, Norway. Hipper and the 5 battle cruisers led the mission, followed some sixty miles behind by Scheer with the flagship *Baden* and 16 other dreadnoughts, a scouting group of light cruisers, and 4 flotillas of destroyers. The Germans missed by one day a westbound convoy whose escort included 4 older British battle cruisers, and were too early to intercept the next eastbound convoy. Hipper took his battle cruisers almost all the way to Bergen before turning back. By late morning on 24 April Beatty had 31 British and 4 American capital ships at sea, along with a host of light cruisers and destroyers, but the Grand Fleet left Rosyth too late to intercept the Germans on their run home. On the evening of 25 April the British submarine *E 42* torpedoed the *Moltke*, which had been slowed by a near-catastrophic engine failure suffered off the Norwegian coast. The battle cruiser took on 2,000 tons of water but managed to limp home to Wilhelmshaven.[63]

With the High Sea Fleet spending almost all of the last year of the war in port, U-boats continued to shoulder the burden of the German war effort at sea. The tonnage sunk was well off the alarming totals registered in the first months after the renewal of unrestricted submarine warfare in 1917, yet until the autumn of 1918 the campaign continued to inflict considerable damage on Allied shipping: 295,630 tons were sunk in January, 335,200 in February, 368,750 in March, 300,070 in

April, 296,560 in May, 268,505 in June, 280,820 in July, and 310,180 in August. Thereafter, the dramatic decline in U-boat activity reflected the collapse of the German war effort, as just 171,970 tons were sunk in September, 116,240 in October, and 10,230 in the first eleven days of November. The totals for 1918 included 166,910 tons sunk by six long-range U-boats dispatched to hunt off the eastern coast of the United States. One of them laid a mine off Long Island which, on 19 July, claimed the armored cruiser *San Diego*, the only larger US warship to sink during the First World War. In endorsing the resumption of unre-stricted submarine warfare in January 1917, the German High Command had calculated that, even if the United States responded by entering the war, U-boats would prevent significant numbers of American troops from being shipped to Europe. In this respect the German submarine force failed miserably, sinking just three troop transports on the transatlantic route, all during 1918: the *President Lincoln*, torpedoed on 31 May by *U 90* some 600 miles west of the French coast; the *Covington*, torpedoed on 1 July by *U 86* off Brest; and the *Mount Vernon*, torpedoed on 5 September by *U 57* around 200 miles west of the French coast. The latter made it to port before sinking, and in all three cases the overwhelming majority of the men aboard were saved. Indeed, the three sinkings combined claimed just 68 lives, while 2,079,880 American troops made it safely to Europe. The greatest loss of American servicemen at sea came on 5 February 1918, when 166 US and Canadian troops that had already made the Atlantic crossing were drowned when *UB 77* torpedoed the transport *Tuscania* off the Irish coast. Just over half of the US troops sailed to Europe aboard British ships, most of the rest aboard American ships. The US navy provided most of the escorts for troopship convoys, but the European Allied navies shared in the burden. The only Allied warship sunk while escort-ing a troopship convoy, the French armored cruiser *Dupetit-Thouars*, was torpedoed on 7 August 1918 by *U 62*, some 400 miles west of Brest.[64]

One day after the sinking of the *Dupetit-Thouars*, a British army break-through at Amiens on the Western Front marked the beginning of the end for the German war effort. As fresh US troops bolstered the British and French effort, Hindenburg and Ludendorff were unable to halt the Allied counteroffensive. The Central Powers soon experienced trouble on other fronts, as the Italian army began pushing Austro–Hungarian forces out of northern Albania, and the joint Anglo–French–Serbian–Greek army at Salonika launched an offensive against Bulgaria. In mid-September the Bulgarian front broke, and on 3 October the government in Sofia concluded a truce with the Allies. These reversals on land forced the navies of the Central Powers to abandon their most exposed stations. As Allied armies liberated Serbia and occupied Bulgaria, Austro–Hungarian river monitors withdrew from the Black Sea up the

Danube, giving up the water route to the grain harvest of Ukraine, little of which had made it to the home front of the Central Powers. As the Allies advanced into Belgium, the German navy abandoned its bases at Ostend and Zeebrugge (29 September–3 October), scuttling the destroyers and submarines that could not be moved. As the Italians advanced northward through Albania, the Austro–Hungarian navy evacuated a number of troops via Durazzo before losing the port following a battle on 2 October. That action matched an Austro–Hungarian force of 2 destroyers, 2 submarines, and 1 torpedo boat against an Allied strike force under Italy's Admiral Paolo Thaon di Revel consisting of 3 Italian armored cruisers, 5 British light cruisers, 14 British and 2 Italian destroyers, Italian torpedo boats and MAS boats, American submarine chasers (larger, slower versions of the MAS), submarines from the British, French, and Italian navies, and bombers from the British and Italian air services. All five Austro–Hungarian vessels survived to withdraw to Cattaro; U 31 inflicted the only casualty on the Allied force, damaging the British cruiser Weymouth with a torpedo hit.[65]

At the behest of the German High Command, which insisted that the Western Front would not hold much longer, on 3 October William II appointed a new chancellor, Prince Max of Baden, who attempted to negotiate an end to the war on the basis of Wilson's Fourteen Points. To appease the American president, on 21 October unrestricted submarine warfare was ended and all German U-boats were ordered home. In his capacity as Chief of the Supreme Navy Command, Scheer acquiesced in the return of the submarines but was not willing to have his capital ships finish the war without a fight. On 24 October, in connivance with Hipper (since August 1918 chief of the High Sea Fleet) and without consulting the emperor or the chancellor, he adopted the infamous Operations Plan 19, which would have sent Germany's remaining 18 dreadnoughts and 5 battle cruisers on a suicidal raid of the Thames estuary, to draw out the Grand Fleet for a final battle off the Dutch coast. The High Sea Fleet was scheduled to raise steam on 29 October, with the sortie to begin late that evening, but the sailors had caught wind of the insane scheme two days earlier, and by the 29th seven dreadnoughts and four battle cruisers had succumbed to varying degrees of mutiny. When the rebellion spread to two more dreadnoughts on 30 October, Scheer and Hipper gave up their plan. Hipper then made the fateful decision to disperse his mutinous capital ships, sending some up the Elbe and others through the Kiel Canal into the Baltic, unwittingly enabling the sailors to serve as the catalyst for the revolution which swept through most northern German ports in early November. In the end, the mutineers gained control of the fleet with little resistance; four officers were wounded and none killed.[66]

During the same days, the Austro–Hungarian navy likewise succumbed to mutiny. As in the High Sea Fleet, the first open unrest came on 27

October. Three days earlier, the Austro–Hungarian front against Italy had collapsed in the face of a major offensive, leaving Trieste and Pola vulnerable to conquest by land. At the same time, in the south, the Italian conquerors of Albania had advanced to within sixty miles of Cattaro. By 29 October most of the warships were in the hands of their crews. The Germans abandoned their Austro–Hungarian submarine bases, heading for home aboard twelve U-boats after scuttling another ten. In Pola, their departure brought the indiscipline to a new low, as gangs of mutineers looted the vacated German quarters. Acknowledging the impending dismemberment of his empire, on 30 October Emperor Charles decided to turn the fleet over to the Yugoslav national council. The following day, Horthy relinquished command of his ships to Slovene and Croatian officers loyal to the council, and all seamen not belonging to the South Slav nationalities received immediate furloughs. The scene was repeated at Cattaro on 1 November. Meanwhile, Charles assigned the navy's Danube Flotilla to Hungary. As a postscript to the collapse of the Austro–Hungarian navy, the twelve German U-boats that fled the Adriatic at the end of October all made it safely home, although not until after the collapse of their own country and its navy. En route, on 9 November off Cape Trafalgar, *UB 50* torpedoed and sank the pre-dreadnought *Britannia*, the last warship casualty of the conflict.[67] The same day, William II abdicated and went into exile in the Netherlands. Charles waited until 11 November to leave Austria for Switzerland. That morning, the Armistice went into effect on the Western Front, ending the First World War.

At sea, as on land, in a losing effort the Central Powers inflicted more damage and casualties than they sustained. This was especially true in the largest classes of warships. Germany lost 1 battle cruiser and Austria–Hungary 1 dreadnought, while Britain lost 2 dreadnoughts and 3 battle cruisers, Italy 1 dreadnought, and Russia (before leaving the war in December 1917) 1 dreadnought. In pre-dreadnought battleships, Germany and Austria–Hungary each lost 1, while Britain lost 11, France 4, Italy 2, and Russia 1. Thus the British navy lost not just more of the most modern capital ships (dreadnoughts and battle cruisers) than the navies of the Central Powers, but more than all other belligerents combined, and the same was true in pre-dreadnoughts. Fortunately for Britain and for the Allies in general, the British victory in the prewar naval arms race provided such a wide margin of material superiority that such losses could be sustained without seriously jeopardizing the war effort.

Ultimately, the greatest threat to British (and overall Allied) command of the sea came from German submarines, which sank 11.9 million tons of Allied shipping. These successes came at a high cost, as 178 of 335 U-boats were sunk (53 percent), 134 by anti-submarine operations, and 4,474 German submariners killed.[68] In the submarine war, as in the war on land, offensive strategies brought significantly higher casualties for the attacker than for the defender. Germany's junior partner in unrestricted submarine warfare, Austria–Hungary, lost 8 of its 27 U-boats (30 percent), while among the Allied navies, the British lost just 43 of 269 submarines (16 percent), the French, 13 of 72 (18 percent), the Italians, 8 of 75 (11 percent), and the Russians, through December 1917, 9 of 61 (15 percent).[69] In the end, the German undersea *guerre de course* made life miserable for the British but did not revolutionize naval warfare or even vindicate the earlier concepts of the Jeune École, as the survival of Britain's superior surface fleet ensured its national security and naval preeminence.

THE BIRTH OF NAVAL AVIATION

The aircraft carrier, like the submarine, first emerged as an important warship type during the First World War, but naval aviation had a later prewar start and developed at a slower pace than submarine warfare. In 1908, five years after their first successful flight, the Wright brothers brought their aircraft to Europe for a series of public demonstrations. Thereafter, France became the early center of European aviation, and the French army pioneered the military use of airplanes, including them in its 1910 maneuvers. By then, Louis Blériot's flight across the English Channel (1909) had alerted British military and naval leaders to the potential of the airplane, and in 1912 Britain established separate army and navy air services. In 1911 the German navy began experimenting with airplanes and dirigibles, favoring the latter owing to the prominence of Count Ferdinand von Zeppelin and other Germans among early airship pioneers. Prewar Italy likewise favored dirigibles over airplanes, even though Italian pilots were the first to fly airplanes in combat missions, in the 1911–12 war against Turkey. Austria–Hungary favored airplanes, and in 1912 established a seaplane station at Pola. In France, Italy, and Russia, the navy initially controlled no airplanes as the army enjoyed an early monopoly over air power. In 1910–11 the US navy was the first to launch and land aircraft from warships, in each case using temporary platforms, and the first to attempt to use aircraft for long-range artillery spotting.[70] In 1912 the British Admiralty rejected a proposal to build an aircraft carrier for wheeled aircraft, but on the eve of the First World War authorized a seaplane tender, the 7,080-ton *Ark Royal*, which was built on the hull of an unfinished merchantman. Other, smaller tenders were hastily converted after the outbreak of the war.[71]

The *Ark Royal* was commissioned in December 1914, too late to participate in the British navy's first air raid against a German target, the Cuxhaven Zeppelin base, on Christmas Day. In that operation, the tenders *Engadine*, *Riviera*, and *Empress* launched nine seaplanes, of which seven made it to the target. Their bombs caused minimal damage, and just three returned to be picked up by the tenders.[72] Throughout the rest of the war the British remained the leader in naval aviation, employing aircraft as bombers, fighters, and in reconnaissance roles. Tenders and primitive carriers were present at most major operations, starting in 1915 when the *Ark Royal* participated in the Gallipoli campaign. Seaplanes from another tender, the 3,900-ton *Ben-my-Chree*, in August 1915 conducted the first successful aerial torpedo attacks, against unarmed Turkish ships off the Dardanelles. British tenders converted after 1914 were fitted with deck platforms to permit the launching of airplanes equipped with both wheels and floats; in November 1915 the British achieved the first successful wartime deck launch, from the tender *Vindex*. The following year the *Engadine* was attached to the Grand Fleet at Jutland, where one of its seaplanes spotted the High Sea Fleet during a reconnaissance flight. While Admiral Jellicoe did not receive this news until after the battle was over, it heightened his fascination with naval aviation. After British experiments in September 1916 demonstrated that aircraft could land successfully after hooking an arrester cable, during Jellicoe's tenure as First Sea Lord the navy began to convert the unfinished liner *Conte Rosso* as the flush-deck carrier *Argus*, and refitted the new battle cruiser *Furious* for service as an aircraft carrier. The *Furious* entered service in March 1918 with separate launching and landing flight decks fore and aft of its centerline funnel and superstructure. It flew off seven Sopwith Camels on 19 July 1918 for a successful raid on the Tondern Zeppelin sheds in Schleswig–Holstein. Its afterdeck proved useless for landing, however, as a large net failed to prevent aircraft from crashing into the funnel. This was not a problem aboard the *Argus*, which had no superstructure at all; its first successful deck landings came on 1 October 1918, shortly after it entered service. This achievement, repeated routinely thereafter, made the odd-looking 14,550-ton ship the world's first truly operational aircraft carrier (see Plate 30). Admiral Beatty planned to use the *Argus* in a torpedo-bombing raid on Kiel, but the war ended before the operation took place.

By the end of the war the British navy had employed sixteen aircraft tenders and carriers, of which only two were lost: the converted cruiser *Hermes*, torpedoed and sunk by *U 27* in the Channel in October 1914, and *Ben-my-Chree*, victim of Turkish shore batteries in January 1917. Between 1914 and 1918 the Royal Naval Air Service grew from a force with 93 aircraft to one with 2,949 aircraft. By comparison, the French naval air service had 1,264 aircraft when the war ended. Other than the British, no navy had a ship capable of launching and landing wheeled aircraft, and only the French navy (with five) and the Russian Black Sea Fleet (with eight) had even commissioned seaplane tenders. At war's end, Britain had another two aircraft carriers under construction, the

10,850-ton *Hermes*, laid down in January 1918, and the 21,630-ton *Eagle* (ex-Chilean *Almirante Cochrane*), converted from March 1918. Shortly after the war, the decision was made to rebuild the *Furious* with a full flight deck; the battle cruisers *Glorious* and *Courageous* were also designated for conversion to aircraft carriers. While no battleship or larger naval vessel of any type had yet been sunk from the air, in 1919 Admiral Sir Charles Madden, commander-in-chief of the Atlantic Fleet and future First Sea Lord, called for the future British navy to be built around a force of twelve carriers.[73] Britain's leading military aviator, Air Marshal Hugh Trenchard, became famous for repeatedly stating "I do not claim to be able to sink a battleship,"[74] but his American counterpart, Colonel "Billy" Mitchell, was not so modest. In July 1921 Mitchell staged a demonstration in which airplanes from the United States Army Air Corps sank the former German dreadnought *Ostfriesland* near the mouth of Chesapeake Bay. The choreographed sinking became a watershed event, as Mitchell's critics in the US navy had claimed that even a defenseless stationary battleship could not be sunk by aircraft alone.[75] The battleship had withstood every previous technological breakthrough, from the steam engine to the submarine, but in the long run it would not survive the challenge from the air.

FROM THE ARMISTICE TO THE WASHINGTON NAVAL TREATY (1918–22)

On 20 November 1918, the German navy turned over the first of its U-boats to the British at Harwich; eventually 176 were surrendered there, including almost two dozen too new to have seen action during the war. The following day, Germany's 11 newest dreadnoughts (5 *Kaisers*, 4 *Königs*, and 2 *Bayerns*), all 5 battle cruisers, 8 light cruisers, and 50 destroyers steamed out into the North Sea under Allied escort, to be interned at Scapa Flow until the Paris Peace Conference determined their fate, along with that of Germany as a whole. Vice Admiral Ludwig von Reuter served as senior German officer at Scapa Flow. Throughout the winter months and into the spring, his skeleton crews lived an isolated existence, receiving little news as the victorious Allies deliberated in Paris and at the German constituent assembly in Weimar. The British did not even inform Reuter when the Armistice was extended beyond its original limit of 21 June 1919, to allow the Paris Peace Conference to conclude its work. Taking advantage of the fact that the British fleet was temporarily out of the harbor on exercises, on the afternoon of 21 June the German warships carried out Reuter's order to scuttle. In the confusion that followed, British guards inflicted 30 casualties on Germans abandoning the sinking ships. Afterward, the 1,860 survivors had to wait over seven months to be repatriated to Germany, where they were welcomed as heroes.[76]

Seven days after the scuttling of the High Sea Fleet, representatives of the new Weimar Republic signed the Treaty of Versailles. Its provisions limited the postwar German navy to six active and two reserve armored ships (the surviving newest pre-dreadnoughts of the 13,200-ton *Braunschweig* and *Deutschland* classes), 6 active and 2 reserve cruisers (of the 2,650-ton *Gazelle* and 3,300-ton *Bremen* classes), 12 active and 4 reserve destroyers, and 12 active and 4 reserve torpedo boats. Ultimately another 4 torpedo boats were substituted for the 4 reserve destroyers. All other warships not scuttled at Scapa Flow had to be turned over to the Allies or scrapped. No submarines were allowed and, owing to the general ban on German military aviation, no aircraft carriers. Future replacements for the armored warships were limited to 10,000 tons and 11.1-inch guns; future cruisers could displace no more than 6,000 tons. The treaty also limited the manpower of the navy to 15,000, including 1,500 officers, a blessing in disguise, as it would enable the service to be extraordinarily selective in recruitment. To avoid a future repetition of the mutinies of 1917–18, the interwar German navy introduced an iron discipline and vigilance against left-wing influences; indeed, a seaman had no chance of being promoted to petty officer if he or anyone in his family had any connection to the Social Democratic or Communist parties.[77] Issues of quality and cohesion aside, the material restrictions reduced Germany to a second-rate naval power, with an armored tonnage roughly equal to that of Spain and not much greater than that of Sweden.

After the scuttling of the German battle fleet, whose ships were coveted as reparations especially by France and Italy, attention shifted to the fate of the much smaller Austro–Hungarian navy. The Allies did not recognize Emperor Charles's eleventh-hour cession of the battle fleet to the Yugoslavs and the Danube Flotilla to Hungary. The Italians took unilateral action to keep the fleet out of Yugoslav hands, sending saboteurs into Pola harbor on 1 November 1918 to sink the dreadnought *Viribus Unitis* (see Plate 31). The British were sympathetic to subsequent Yugoslav appeals to keep the fleet, but the Italians insisted that it be divided among the victorious powers. The surviving dreadnoughts, pre-dreadnoughts, armored cruisers, and older lighter vessels all were scrapped, but Italy commissioned 2 of the light cruisers and 7 destroyers, while France commissioned 1 light cruiser, 1 destroyer and the submarine *U 14* (ex-*Curie*), which re-entered French service under its original name. The minor Allies also commissioned their share of the spoils: Greece, 1 destroyer and 6 torpedo boats; Romania, 7 torpedo boats and 3 river monitors; and Portugal, 6 torpedo boats. The new Yugoslav navy was left with just 12 torpedo boats and 4 river monitors. The successor states Austria and Hungary each received 4 small river patrol boats, but the Austrians subsequently sold 3 of theirs to the Hungarians, whose interwar leader, Admiral Horthy, took great pride in his tiny Hungarian riverine navy.[78] From among the German warships not scuttled at Scapa Flow or retained by the navy of the Weimar Republic, France ultimately commissioned 4 light cruisers, 9 destroyers, and 10 submarines; Italy, 3 light cruisers and 3 destroyers; Belgium, 14 torpedo boats; and Poland, 6 torpedo boats.[79]

Concurrent with the reduction of the German navy and the elimination of the Austro–Hungarian, the Russian navy also suffered heavy losses owing to the civil war of 1918–20 and Allied support for the White Russian cause. Britain shouldered the burden in the Baltic and the Arctic, in the latter supported by the United States. The only naval combat came in the Baltic, where the British dominated the Bolsheviks with a force of light cruisers and destroyers, supplemented by the dozen aircraft of the 9,750-ton carrier *Vindictive*, a modified cruiser completed just before the Armistice. Rear Admiral Edwyn Alexander-Sinclair provided fire support for Estonian and Latvian forces against the Bolsheviks late in 1918, but under his successor, Rear Admiral Sir Walter Cowan, the British became much more aggressive during 1919. Cowan harassed the Bolshevik fleet from his base at Bjorko, Finland, barely fifty miles west of Kronstadt. His coastal motor boats (CMBs), the British version of the highly successful Italian *MAS*, penetrated the formidable defenses there on two occasions, torpedoing and sinking the protected cruiser *Oleg* on the night of 17–18 June 1919, then claiming the dreadnought *Petropavlovsk*, the pre-dreadnought *Andrei Pervosvanni*, and the submarine tender (ex-armored cruiser) *Pamiat Azova* on the night of 17–18 August. The Bolsheviks later raised and repaired the *Petropavlovsk*, but elected not to salvage the *Andrei Pervosvanni*. Other Soviet losses during the campaign included three destroyers sunk and two surrendered. Even before losing the services of his only two operational battleships, Soviet commander A. P. Zelenoy challenged the British campaign primarily with destroyers and submarines, which, combined with minefields, made the British Baltic intervention anything but cost-free. A mine sank the light cruiser *Cassandra* on 5 December 1918, shortly after it arrived in the Gulf of Finland. On 4 June 1919 the Soviet destroyer *Gavriil* sank the submarine *L 55* off Kronstadt, and on the night of 31 August–1 September 1919 the Soviet submarine *Pantera* sank the British destroyer *Vittoria* off Seiskar Island. Other British losses included 2 destroyers, 2 minesweepers, 8 CMBs, and 3 auxiliary vessels. Late in the year the British force suffered a series of mutinies, fueled by war weariness, the harsh Baltic conditions, and the pro-Bolshevik sympathies of many of the seamen's families and friends at home. Britain left only a token naval force in the Baltic for 1920, but by then the blows inflicted against the Soviet Baltic Fleet had helped secure Finland and the Baltic states from a Russian reconquest. None of these newly independent countries participated in the anti-Bolshevik naval operations of 1918–20, but the postwar navies of Finland, Latvia, and Estonia were formed from smaller warships abandoned by the Bolsheviks, the largest of which were two destroyers commissioned by the Estonians.[80]

In the Black Sea the Allied navies more directly supported the White Russian cause, at one time or another occupying all of the major Russian ports. In contrast to the light forces assigned to the Baltic, dreadnoughts were sent to the Black Sea; those deployed during 1919 included the British *Ajax*, *Iron Duke*, and *Benbow*, and the French *Jean Bart* and *France*. After the Armistice, the Germans surrendered to the British all of the Russian Black Sea warships they had seized in May 1918. The British scuttled fifteen Russian submarines at Sevastopol in April 1919, during a Red Army offensive in the Crimea, and most of the surface warships were disarmed, their machinery removed or disabled, to render them useless in case they fell into Bolshevik hands. Those spared included the dreadnought *Volya* (renamed *General Alekseev*), the pre-dreadnought *Georgi Pobiedonosets*, the seaplane carrier *Almaz*, the protected cruiser *Ochakov* (renamed *Admiral Kornilov*), and two submarines, which were turned over to the White Russian leader, General Baron Peter Wrangel, in the autumn of 1919, to support the army he commanded. The protected cruiser *Pamiat Merkuria* (renamed *Komintern*) was the only significant repairable Russian Black Sea warship seized by the Bolsheviks following Wrangel's defeat in November 1920. Allied Black Sea mutinies affected the French more than the British, in the spring of 1919 temporarily crippling the *Jean Bart* and *France*, 4 pre-dreadnoughts, 2 armored cruisers, and 6 smaller warships. Far fewer French units were still on hand to help the British and Wrangel's navy evacuate White Russian refugees to Constantinople. After the end of the campaign Wrangel's ships became prizes of the Allies, who eventually sold them for scrap.[81]

In addition to breaking up most of their prizes of war, in the years 1919–22 the victorious navies also quickly scrapped dozens of their own older warships. Of the 45 British dreadnoughts and battle cruisers in commission at the Armistice, 3 were slated for conversion to aircraft carriers, 1 (*Canada*, ex-*Almirante Latorre*) was delivered, albeit belatedly, to Chile in 1920, and another 17 were stricken or sold for scrap, before the onset of postwar naval disarmament, and broken up starting in 1921. The latter included the *Dreadnought* itself, sold on 9 May 1921, obsolete after a service life of just fourteen and a half years. The thirty pre-dreadnoughts still on hand at the end of the war were all were disarmed, decommissioned, or scrapped in the years 1919–22. France kept its 7 dreadnoughts but disarmed or decommissioned 12 of its 16 remaining pre-dreadnoughts, scrapping most of them in the years 1920–22. Italy likewise kept its 5 surviving dreadnoughts but disarmed or decommissioned 7 of its 11 remaining pre-dreadnoughts, which were scrapped in the years 1920–23. Britain's *Hood* (built 1916–20; see

Plate 32) was the only European capital ship under construction at war's end, as its three sister-ships were ordered broken up on the slipways in October 1918. With the reduction in matériel came a dramatic discharge of manpower. For example, Britain, which had almost 450,000 naval personnel in 1918, was down to 100,000 by 1923, significantly fewer than the prewar peacetime stand of 150,000.[82]

With no serious rivals in Europe, the Admiralty sought only to keep the British navy equal to or larger than the US navy, no easy task, for by November 1921, the United States had laid down 15 of the 16 dreadnoughts and battle cruisers authorized in a naval program passed by Congress in 1916; during the same years, Britain had completed only the *Hood* and laid down no other capital ships. Because Britain had ended the war deeply in debt to the United States, it was in no position to challenge an American bid for absolute naval supremacy. Furthermore, Lloyd George hoped to strengthen the Anglo–American relationship in the postwar years and did not want a new naval race to foil his plans. When the Republican-dominated US Senate passed a resolution by one of the country's leading isolationists, William E. Borah of Idaho, calling for the world's three leading naval powers to conclude a naval arms reduction agreement, the British welcomed the news. Borah's resolution resulted in the United States hosting the Washington Naval Conference, convened on 12 November 1921.[83]

As the conference began, Britain's concern about American naval expansion was matched by American concern that Britain might continue its alliance with Japan, last renewed in 1911 for a period of ten years. Indeed, the growing Japanese–American animosity in the Pacific put the British in a difficult position, and made Lloyd George's government all the more eager to see the leading naval powers agree to an arms reduction treaty. The British delegation was led by Arthur Balfour, a former prime minister, foreign secretary, and First Lord of the Admiralty, who had been involved in the negotiation of the Anglo–Japanese alliance of 1902. Other members included the First Lord of the Admiralty, Viscount Lee, and the First Sea Lord, Admiral Beatty. Entering the conference, Britain wanted a 3:3:2 ratio of capital ships for Britain, the United States, and Japan, and serious discussion of the abolition of all submarines.[84] For the other European naval powers, France and Italy, the agenda was much simpler, as the French navy wanted to maintain its advantage over the Italian, while the Italian navy sought to gain on the French. The French delegation, led by Premier Aristide Briand and Vice Admiral Ferdinand de Bon, was willing to accept parity in capital ships with Japan and Italy, below Britain and the United States. France also wanted no limits on units smaller than capital ships, as it planned to center its postwar fleet around cruisers, destroyers, and submarines. Italy entered the conference dreaming of Franco–Italian naval parity but hoping for a quota 90 percent of France's strength, and willing to accept 80 percent. Whereas France wanted Franco–Italian limits on numbers or tonnage of warships placed higher, to force Italy to build more in order to achieve parity, Italy wanted Franco–Italian limits to be placed as low as possible, so that it could have parity or near-parity without further short-term investment in naval construction.[85]

US Secretary of State Charles Evans Hughes shocked the conference with his opening proposal that all capital ships then under construction should be scrapped and none laid down for a period of ten years. He called for the United States, Britain, Japan, France, and Italy to agree to a ratio of 5:5:3:1.75:1.75 for strength in all warship types. The proposal pleased the British, who wanted parity with the United States and had no capital ships under construction at the time. It also promised the Italians all they had hoped for. The French feigned offense at being treated as a minor power, and Briand left Washington by the end of the month. Nevertheless, France could still achieve its goals if the ratios only applied to capital ships. During the ensuing negotiations, Admiral de Bon first insisted on parity with Japan in capital ships (even though France had no intention of building more battleships anytime soon), then finally accepted parity with Italy on the condition that the ratios would not apply to cruisers, destroyers, or submarines. While the British and especially the Italians were in a cooperative mood in Washington, being self-conscious about their war debts to the United States, the French so exasperated Hughes that at one stage he reminded them that their financial situation did not square with their purported naval ambitions. Nevertheless, the French persisted, and once they got their way on submarines, the British joined them in insisting on no limits for destroyers, which everyone needed for anti-submarine warfare, and cruisers, which Britain felt it needed more of, to defend its global interests.[86]

The final agreement applied the ratios only to battleships and battle cruisers, with a modified scale of 5:5:3:2.2:2.2 devised for aircraft carriers. All five navies were allowed to add further side armor to their existing capital ships, up to a maximum of 3,000 tons per ship. France and Italy, whose dreadnoughts were acknowledged to be weaker than those of the leading naval powers, were given permission to strengthen deck armor as well, and to increase the caliber of guns in primary armament. New battleships were limited to 35,000 tons and 16-inch guns, with none to be laid down until 1931. Carriers were limited to 27,000 tons, but each of the three leading navies could have two of 33,000, and France and Italy one apiece of 33,000 tons, with no restrictions on when new units could be built. As with existing capital ships, an additional 3,000 tons of armor could be added to existing hulls designated for conversion to carriers. New cruisers were limited to 10,000 tons and 8-inch guns, but navies could build as many as they liked, effective immediately. Special provisions allowed Britain to lay down two new battleships immediately, the 33,300-ton *Nelson* and *Rodney* (built 1922–27), in recognition of the fact that its existing capital ships, on average, were several years older than their American or Japanese counterparts. France and Italy also received permission to lay down new battleships as early as 1927, for the same reason.[87]

The Washington Naval Treaty was signed on 6 February 1922. To get down to its prescribed number of 20 capital ships, the British navy had to scrap another 7 not already stricken. Upon the completion of the *Nelson* and *Rodney*, its battle fleet consisted of those ships plus the 14 battleships of the *Iron Duke*, *Queen Elizabeth*, and *Royal Sovereign* classes, and the battle cruisers *Tiger*, *Renown*, *Repulse*, and *Hood*. Its carriers included the *Argus*, the *Eagle* (commissioned 1920), the *Hermes* (under construction), and the three battle cruisers designated for conversion: the *Courageous*, *Glorious*, and *Furious*. France's four *Courbet* class and three *Bretagne* class battleships automatically met its quota of 7 allowed under the treaty. The *Béarn*, the only *Normandie* class battleship not abandoned during the war, was converted to an aircraft carrier in the years 1922–27. Meanwhile, Italy's *Dante Alighieri*, *Conte di Cavour*, *Giulio Cesare*, *Andrea Doria*, and *Caio Duilio* actually left it two short of its limit of 7 battleships. Capital ship parity with France proved to be largely symbolic, as Italy never built up to its treaty limit as long as the naval disarmament regime remained in place. Italy never used its aircraft carrier tonnage quota, did not exercise its right to lay down a new battleship in 1927, and in 1928 fell even farther behind France in battleships when it scrapped the *Dante Alighieri* without laying down a replacement. In France, the issue of capital ship parity with Italy toppled the Briand government and delayed ratification of the Washington Naval Treaty until July 1923. The right-wing nationalists were especially hard on the treaty, Action Française leader Charles Maurras branding it "Trafalgar II."[88] Yet France, like Italy, did not take full advantage of its limits under the treaty. The French also did not exercise their right to begin a new battleship in 1927, even though they lost one of the *Courbet*s, the *France*, to shipwreck in Quiberon Bay in August 1922. Over half of France's carrier allowance also remained unspent, as the *Béarn*, when completed, displaced just over 22,000 tons.

CONCLUSION

The world's navies commissioned 134 dreadnoughts and battle cruisers between December 1906 and November 1918. Subtracting the United States's 16, Japan's 12, Argentina's 2, Brazil's 2, and neutral Spain's 2, the six major European belligerents of the First World War accounted for exactly 100: Britain 50, Germany 26, France 7, Russia 7, Italy 6, and

Austria–Hungary 4. The automatic replacement provisions in Tirpitz's navy laws reflected the general assumption that capital ships would have a twenty-five-year service life, and yet, for these vessels, the average was just over thirteen years. Admittedly, the sudden demise of the German and Austro–Hungarian navies depresses this number, but it is of equal significance that the sinking of large numbers of units in battle does not. The relatively light overall losses of dreadnoughts and battle cruisers during the First World War – Britain 5, Russia 2, Germany, Italy, and Austria–Hungary 1 apiece, and France none – reflects the fact that most of these ships spent most of their relatively short service lives at anchor. Never before had so many ships that had cost so much money seen so little action during so few years in commission. The unprecedented naval races of 1906–14 were followed by the unprecedented destruction of so many of these ships in the scuttlings and scrappings of the immediate postwar years and under the naval disarmament regime of 1922. While new battleships and battle cruisers would be laid down in the 1930s and early 1940s, the postwar disposal of so many of them, and the creation of a new system which placed relatively fewer restrictions on the construction of aircraft carriers and none on submarines, pointed the way to the future.

NOTES

[1] Tritten, "Doctrine and Fleet Tactics in the Royal Navy," 22–3. On Corbett's career see Schurman, *The Education of a Navy*, 147–84.

[2] Unless otherwise noted, sources for this section are Arthur J. Marder, *From the Dreadnought to Scapa Flow: The Royal Navy in the Fisher Era, 1904–1919*, 5 vols (London, 1961), 1:136–79; Lambert, *Sir John Fisher's Naval Revolution*, 157–291 *passim*; Holger H. Herwig, *'Luxury' Fleet: The Imperial German Navy, 1888–1918*, rev. ed. (Atlantic Highlands, NJ, 1987), 59–80; *Conway, 1906–21*, 25–33, 145–55; Gröner, *Die deutschen Kriegschiffe*, 1:46–54, 80–5.

[3] Sumida, *In Defence of Naval Supremacy*, 192; Herwig, *"Luxury" Fleet*, 80. Despite their lower standard displacement, the *Queen Elizabeths* were actually slightly larger than the *Royal Sovereigns* and had a greater full-load displacement.

[4] Lambert, *Sir John Fisher's Naval Revolution*, 296–303.

[5] Sumida, *In Defence of Naval Supremacy*, 247, 252, 301–2, 316, 331; idem, "The Quest for Reach," 67–75; Correlli Barnett, *Engage the Enemy More Closely: The Royal Navy in the Second World War* (New York, 1991), 6. Sumida is the leading defender of Pollen and his system.

[6] Sumida, *In Defence of Naval Supremacy*, 358; Herwig, *"Luxury" Fleet*, 273–9.

[7] The source for this and the following paragraphs is Sondhaus, *The Naval Policy of Austria–Hungary*, 173, 180–3, 191–8, 203–4, 231–47, 274.

[8] René Greger, *The Russian Fleet, 1914–1917*, trans. Jill Gearing (London, 1972), 9–10; Evgenii F. Podsoblyaev, "The Russian Naval General Staff and the Evolution of Naval Policy, 1905–1914," *Journal of Military History* 66 (2002): 42–3; Gromov *et al.*, *Tri Veka Rossiiskogo Flota*, 2:10–11; Tomitch, *Warships of the Imperial Russian Navy, passim*; *Conway, 1906–21*, 309, 312–15.

[9] Greger, *The Russian Fleet*, 10–12; Podsoblyaev, "The Russian Naval General Staff," 62–5; Woodward, *The Russians at Sea*, 160–1; *Conway, 1906–21*, 296, 302–4.

[10] Walser, *France's Search for a Battle Fleet*, 144–6, 180–96; Paul G. Halpern, *The Mediterranean Naval Situation, 1908–1914* (Cambridge, MA, 1971), 54–7; Tritten, "Navy and Military Doctrine in France," 58.

[11] Halpern, *The Mediterranean Naval Situation*, 13–46, 86–110; Samuel R. Williamson Jr, *The Politics of Grand Strategy: Britain and France Prepare for War, 1904–1914* (Cambridge, MA, 1969), 264–83; *Conway, 1906–21*, 196–8.

[12] Halpern, *The Mediterranean Naval Situation*, 280–95; *Conway, 1906–21*, 374–5, 378, 381–2.

[13] *Conway, 1906–21*, 349, 352, 359, 366.

[14] The sources for this section are Langensiepen and Güleryüz, *The Ottoman Steam Navy*, 17–18, 20–5, 142, 151; Paul G. Halpern, *The Naval War in the Mediterranean, 1914–1918* (Annapolis, MD, 1987), 47–8; *idem*, *The Mediterranean Naval Situation*, 323–4; *Conway, 1906–21*, 383–7, 391; Donolo, "The History of Italian Naval Doctrine," 109.

[15] Sondhaus, *The Naval Policy of Austria–Hungary*, 245–6, 258–65; Halpern, *The Naval War in the Mediterranean*, 26–7.

[16] Paul G. Halpern, *A Naval History of World War I* (Annapolis, MD, 1994), 27; *Conway, 1906–21*, 53.

[17] Halpern, *A Naval History of World War I*, 31–2; Gröner, *Die deutschen Kriegsschiffe*, 1:128, 135.

[18] Halpern, *A Naval History of World War I*, 33–5, 39, 44; *Conway, 1860–1905*, 32, 265; *Conway, 1906–21*, 6; Gröner, *Die deutschen Kriegsschiffe*, 1:78. The German warships lost at the Battle of Texel Island were the 447-ton vessels *T-115*, *T-117*, *T-118*, and *T-119*. Some accounts refer to these ships, and other German vessels like them, as large torpedo boats.

[19] Halpern, *A Naval History of World War I*, 36–7.

[20] Ibid., 179–205; *Conway, 1906–21*, 296; Gröner, *Die deutschen Kriegsschiffe*, 1:78, 129, 131.

[21] Halpern, *A Naval History of World War I*, 34–6. On the drawbacks of Churchill's leadership style at the Admiralty see Tritten, "Doctrine and Fleet Tactics in the Royal Navy," 24.

[22] *Conway, 1906–21*, 42–50.

[23] The sources for this and the following paragraph are Geoffrey Bennett, *Coronel and the Falklands* (London, 1962); John Irving, *Coronel and the Falklands* (London, 1927); Halpern, *A Naval History of World War I*, 79, 89, 93, 96–100; *Conway, 1906–21*, 7, 12, 24–5; Gröner, *Die deutschen Kriegsschiffe*, 1:80, 131, 133.

[24] Sondhaus, *The Naval Policy of Austria–Hungary*, 262–3; Halpern, *A Naval History of World War I*, 79, 81–2; Gröner, *Die deutschen Kriegsschiffe*, 1:133, 137; *Conway, 1906–21*, 16, 143, 157, 160, 184–6, 296.

[25] Halpern, *A Naval History of World War I*, 44–7; Gröner, *Die deutschen Kriegsschiffe*, 1:80; *Conway, 1906–21*, 25, 29, 33, 151, 153–4.

[26] Sondhaus, *Preparing for Weltpolitik*, 229.

[27] Halpern, *A Naval History of World War I*, 39, 293–4, 298–9.

[28] Ibid., 295–9, 302–3; *Conway, 1906–21*, 174–6.

[29] Halpern, *The Naval War in the Mediterranean*, 53–5, 62, 68; *Conway, 1906–21*, 152.

[30] Halpern, *The Naval War in the Mediterranean*, 62–3, 76–7; idem, *A Naval History of World War I*, 114–15; *Conway, 1906–21*, 25, 34, 192.

[31] Halpern, *The Naval War in the Mediterranean*, 115; Keegan, *The First World War*, 234–49, provides the best concise account of the Gallipoli campaign.

[32] Halpern, *The Naval War in the Mediterranean*, 114–15; idem, *A Naval History of World War I*, 117; *Conway, 1906–21*, 25.

[33] Halpern, *The Naval War in the Mediterranean*, 110, 204; Halpern, *A Naval History of World War I*, 118–9, 236. The sinking of the *Majestic* and the *Triumph*, each of which had its anti-torpedo netting deployed when attacked, demonstrated the uselessness of such devices against the latest submarine-fired torpedoes. A total of 56 German submarines received Austro–Hungarian numbers. See Sondhaus, *The Naval Policy of Austria–Hungary*, 279.

[34] Casualty figures from Keegan, *The First World War*, 248; see also *Conway, 1906–21*, 7–10, 192; Halpern, *The Naval War in the Mediterranean*, 171, 183, 185, 188–9.

[35] Sondhaus, *The Naval Policy of Austria–Hungary*, 272–6.

[36] Ibid., 267, 276–85.

[37] Ibid., 283–4.

[38] Halpern, *A Naval History of World War I*, 134–6, 206–12, 249.

[39] Ibid., 237, 244–5, 249.

[40] Ibid., 310–13; *Conway, 1906–21*, 9, 22.

[41] The most recent of many English accounts of the battle is Keith Yates, *Flawed Victory: Jutland 1916* (London, 2000). See also V. E. Tarrant, *Jutland: The German Perspective* (Annapolis, MD, 1995), and H. W. Fawcett and G. W. W. Hooper (eds), *The Fighting at Jutland: The Personal Experiences of Sixty Officers and Men of the British Fleet* (Annapolis, MD, 2002). The best concise account is in Halpern, *A Naval History of World War I*, 315–28. On gunnery ranges at Jutland see Sumida, "The Quest for Reach," 77 and *passim*. Other sources for the following paragraphs include Andrew Gordon, *The Rules of the Game: Jutland and British Naval Command* (Annapolis, MD, 1996), 76–151, 433–99; Gröner, *Die deutschen Kriegsschiffe*, 1:46, 85, 129, 137, 139–40; *Conway, 1906–21*, 13, 22, 25, 27–36, 146, 148, 152, 154.

[42] Halpern, *A Naval History of World War I*, 329; *Conway, 1906–21*, 12.

[43] Halpern, *A Naval History of World War I*, 328–31; Tarrant, *Jutland: The German Perspective*, 250–1.

[44] Halpern, *A Naval History of World War I*, 332–6, 343.

[45] Halpern, *The Naval War in the Mediterranean*, 289–300, 367; Sondhaus, *The Naval Policy of Austria–Hungary*, 289; *Conway, 1906–21*, 192, 196, 256, 259.

[46] Halpern, *A Naval History of World War I*, 338–41; Sondhaus, *The Naval Policy of Austria–Hungary*, 293–4; Holger H. Herwig, "Innovation Ignored: The Submarine Problem – Germany, Britain, and the United States, 1919–1939," in *Military Innovation in the Interwar Period*, ed. Williamson Murray and Allan R. Millett (Cambridge, 1996), 229; idem, *"Luxury" Fleet*, 197–8.

[47] Halpern, *A Naval History of World War I*, 342, 354, 357–60; Herwig, "Innovation Ignored: The Submarine Problem," 229; Tritten, "Doctrine and Fleet Tactics in the Royal Navy," 25.

[48] Halpern, *A Naval History of World War I*, 344–51, 393, 399, 407–8, 411–16, 438–41; Sondhaus, *The Naval Policy of Austria–Hungary*, 287–92, 305–7.

[49] Sondhaus, *The Naval Policy of Austria–Hungary*, 309–12. The Italian navy subsequently commissioned the boat under the name *Francesco Rismondo*.

[50] Herwig, *"Luxury" Fleet*, 230–4.

[51] Gromov *et al.*, *Tri Veka Rossiiskogo Flota* 2:113–17, 128–33; Halpern, *A Naval History of World War I*, 181, 193, 212–20; *Conway, 1906–21*, 294. According to the Russian account, the dreadnought *Grosser Kurfürst* suffered mine damage along with the *Bayern*.

[52] Anatol Shmelev, "Mutiny in the Destroyer Division of the Baltic Fleet, May–June 1918," in *Rebellion, Repression, Reinvention: Mutiny in Comparative Perspective*, ed. Jane Hathaway (Westport, CT, 2001), 171.

[53] Halpern, *A Naval History of World War I*, 250–4.

[54] Herwig, *"Luxury" Fleet*, 237–8; *Conway, 1906–21*, 44, 48, 152, 160; Gröner, *Die deutschen Kriegsschiffe*, 1:137.

[55] Sondhaus, *The Naval Policy of Austria–Hungary*, 313; *Conway, 1906–21*, 8–9, 12–13, 23, 47–8, 194, 196, 330. In addition to the *Vanguard*, other British warships destroyed in similar accidents involving ammunition fires included the pre-dreadnought *Bulwark*, at Sheerness on 26 November 1914, the cruiser *Natal*, at Cromarty on 31 December 1915, and the monitor *Glatton*, at Dover on 16 September 1918.

[56] Halpern, *A Naval History of World War I*, 376–7, 403–4, 417; *Conway, 1906–21*, 39–40.

[57] Holger H. Herwig, *The First World War: Germany and Austria–Hungary, 1914–1918* (London, 1997), 361–2, 378–80; Sondhaus, *The Naval Policy of Austria–Hungary*, 318–28. At the time of his promotion, Horthy was eleventh in seniority among captains and twenty-ninth in seniority overall.

[58] Halpern, *A Naval History of World War I*, 221–2; Gröner, *Die deutschen Kriegsschiffe*, 1:47; *Conway, 1906–21*, 303, 312–17.

[59] Shmelev, "Mutiny in the Destroyer Division of the Baltic Fleet," 171; Halpern, *A Naval History of World War I*, 136–7; *Conway, 1906–21*, 294–6, 303. The *Askold* joined the British White Sea force as *Glory IV*. It was scrapped after being returned to the Soviet government in 1921.

[60] Halpern, *A Naval History of World War I*, 256–7.

[61] Sondhaus, *The Naval Policy of Austria–Hungary*, 331–6; *Conway, 1906–21*, 303–4.

[62] Halpern, *A Naval History of World War I*, 258, 401.

[63] Ibid., 418–20; Herwig, *"Luxury" Fleet*, 240–1.

[64] Halpern, *A Naval History of World War I*, 423, 432, 434–7; http://www.USMM.org/ww1navy.html (accessed 14 October 2001).

[65] Sondhaus, *The Naval Policy of Austria–Hungary*, 340; Halpern, *A Naval History of World War I*, 444.

[66] Herwig, *"Luxury" Fleet*, 247–51; Halpern, *A Naval History of World War I*, 444–5.

[67] Sondhaus, *The Naval Policy of Austria–Hungary*, 350–6; Halpern, *A Naval History of World War I*, 401.

[68] Herwig, "Innovation Ignored: The Submarine Problem," 231; *idem, "Luxury" Fleet*, 247, 291; *Conway, 1906–21*, 4. Some sources say 133 U-boats were sunk by anti-submarine operations. Only 320 U-boats actually sortied during the war.

[69] *Conway, 1906–21*, 86–94, 207–12, 274–8, 312–17, 342–4. Some sources have as many as 56 British submarines being lost during the war.

[70] John Buckley, *Air Power in the Age of Total War* (London, 1999), 31–9; Herwig, *"Luxury" Fleet*, 84–5; Sondhaus, *The Naval Policy of Austria–Hungary*, 200; Barry Watts and Williamson Murray, "Military Innovation in Peacetime," in *Military Innovation in the Interwar Period*, ed. Williamson Murray and Allan R. Millett (Cambridge, 1996), 387.

[71] Geoffrey Till, "Adopting the Aircraft Carrier: The British, American, and Japanese Case Studies," in *Military Innovation in the Interwar Period*, ed. Williamson Murray and Allan R. Millett (Cambridge, 1996), 192; Norman Friedman, *British Carrier Aviation: The Evolution of the Ships and their Aircraft* (Annapolis, MD, 1988), 28–30.

[72] Unless otherwise noted, the sources for the remainder of this section are Friedman, *British Carrier Aviation*, 32–67; *Conway, 1860–1905*, 205; *Conway, 1906–21*, 64–9, 201, 307–8; Till, "Adopting the Aircraft Carrier," 194–5.

[73] Geoffrey Till, *Airpower and the Royal Navy, 1914–1945: A Historical Survey* (London, 1979), 64; Halpern, *A Naval History of World War I*, 426.

[74] Till, "Adopting the Aircraft Carrier," 216.

[75] Buckley, *Air Power in the Age of Total War*, 91.

[76] Herwig, *"Luxury" Fleet*, 254–7; Halpern, *A Naval History of World War I*, 403, 448–9; *Conway 1906–21*, 139, 147–71 *passim*.

[77] Joseph A. Maiolo, *The Royal Navy and Nazi Germany, 1933–39: A Study in Appeasement and the Origins of the Second World War* (London, 1998), 20; Keith W. Bird, *Weimar, the German Naval Officer Corps, and the Rise of National Socialism* (Amsterdam, 1977), 8–13, 150–4, 198–204; *Conway's All the World's Fighting Ships, 1922–46* (London, 1980), 218, 222–3, 227 [hereafter cited as *Conway, 1922–46*].

[78] Sondhaus, *The Naval Policy of Austria–Hungary*, 359–60.

[79] *Conway, 1922–46*, 257–8, 286–7, 348, 385.

[80] Richard H. Ullman, *Anglo–Soviet Relations, 1917–1921*, volume 2: *Britain and the Russian Civil War, November 1918–February 1920* (Princeton, NJ, 1968), 55–8, 273, 289–93; Geoffrey Bennett, *Cowan's War: The Story of British Naval Operations in the Baltic, 1918–1920* (London, 1964), 35–6, 119, 125–6, 148–56, 162, 228–9; *Conway, 1906–21*, 61, 94, 295–6, 303, 316, 352–3, 364.

[81] Philippe Masson, *La Marine française et la mer Noire (1918–1919)* (Paris, 1982); *Conway 1906–21*, 30, 32, 197, 294, 296, 304, 312–17.

[82] John Wells, *The Royal Navy: An Illustrated Social History, 1870–1982* (London, 1994), 125.

[83] Erik Goldstein, "The Evolution of British Diplomatic Strategy for the Washington Conference," in *The Washington Conference, 1921–22: Naval Rivalry, East Asian Stability, and the Road to Pearl Harbor*, ed. Erik Goldstein and John Maurer (London, 1994), 10–11, 14, 23; B. J. C. McKercher, "The Politics of Naval Arms Limitation in Britain in the 1920s," in ibid., 38, 42; Thomas H. Buckley, "The Icarus Factor: the American Pursuit of Myth in Naval Arms Control, 1921–36," in ibid., 126.

[84] Erik Goldstein, "The Evolution of British Diplomatic Strategy," 7, 15, 17, 22, 24, 27.

[85] Joel Blatt, "France and the Washington Conference," in *The Washington Conference, 1921–22: Naval Rivalry, East Asian Stability, and the Road to Pearl Harbor*, ed. Erik Goldstein and John Maurer (London, 1994), 196–9, 201; Brian R. Sullivan, "Italian Naval Power and the Washington Disarmament Conference of 1921–22," in ibid., 227.

[86] Buckley, "The Icarus Factor," 131; Blatt, "France and the Washington Conference," 200–5; Sullivan, "Italian Naval Power and the Washington Disarmament Conference," 228, 236.

[87] Robert Jackson, *The Royal Navy in World War II* (Annapolis, MD, 1997), 7–8; Friedman, *British Carrier Aviation*, 97; Sullivan, "Italian Naval Power and the Washington Disarmament Conference," 233.

[88] Blatt, "France and the Washington Conference," 206–7.

7

THE INTERWAR PERIOD AND SECOND WORLD WAR, 1922–45

The demise or near-destruction of half of Europe's great-power navies, followed by the introduction of international naval arms control, made the interwar period a quieter time, in sharp contrast to the frenzied building of larger surface warships in the years between 1889 and 1914. For the three leading naval powers of Europe, the total number of battleships and battle cruisers laid down between the world wars (Britain nine, France five, Italy four) barely exceeded that of a single robust year of pre-1914 construction. Even before the Great Depression, financial considerations kept Britain from further modernizing its navy, while both France and Italy stayed below their legal limits in battleships and aircraft carriers, Italy building none of the latter. At least until the 1930s, most navies also built fewer destroyers and submarines, instead using the large numbers of these types constructed during the war or, in the case of France and Italy, acquired as reparations after the war. Significant expansion occurred only in cruiser forces, an unintended consequence of the Washington Naval Treaty limiting warships other than capital ships to 10,000 tons and 8-inch guns. In the new nomenclature those with tonnage and armament at or just below the new limits were classified as heavy cruisers (popularly known as "treaty cruisers"), while those smaller or more weakly armed were designated light cruisers.

THE 1920s

The combination of international naval arms limits and financial problems led to lapses in capital ship construction unprecedented in the modern era. After work started on the *Rodney* and *Nelson* in December 1922, Britain did not lay down another battleship until January 1937. The battleship hiatus lasted longer in France (from January 1914 to December 1932) and even longer in Italy (from June 1915 to October 1934). Meanwhile, France resumed cruiser construction in 1922, having begun none of the type since 1906; Britain laid down no cruisers between 1918 and 1924, and Italy, none between 1913 and 1925. There was no general pattern for smaller warship types. Britain launched no destroyers between 1919 and 1926, and no submarines between 1919 and 1923. France launched no destroyers between 1917 and 1923 but never stopped building submarines, launching at least one in every year except 1923. In contrast, Italy launched no submarines between 1919 and 1926 but never stopped building destroyers, launching at least one every year from 1913 through 1932.

In the 1920s the British navy reverted to its pre-1905 (pre-*Dreadnought*) strategic culture, waiting for other countries to introduce innovations in warship design. Such an approach had worked well enough in the nineteenth century, when Britain's industrial superiority had allowed it the luxury of letting others take the lead; by the interwar years, however, the British clearly lacked the ability to catch up with more innovative rivals. The renewed conservatism reflected the expectation of a "Long Peace," formalized in the so-called Ten Year Rule, imposed by the government in February 1919, under which British naval and military planners were instructed to assume that no major war would occur within ten years. The Ten Year Rule remained in effect until 1932, when Japan's aggression against China brought its abandonment. After the general election of 1922, the domestic political landscape offered little hope to the defense establishment. The fall of Lloyd George ushered in a new era of Conservative governments determined to restrain spending. At the same time, the decline of the Liberals left the leading opposition role to the Labour party, which opposed most military and naval expenditure on ideological grounds.[1]

After leading all other navies in the early development of the aircraft carrier, the interwar British navy consciously allowed the American and Japanese navies to refine the type further. Britain chose not to exercise its treaty right to build two 33,000-ton carriers or to build replacements for the 14,550-ton *Argus*, the 21,630-ton *Eagle*, and the 10,850-ton *Hermes* (the latter completed in 1924), three unique designs each of which could carry no more than 20 aircraft and usually operated with less. The converted light battle cruisers *Furious* (1922–25), *Courageous* (1924–28), and *Glorious* (1924–30) emerged as carriers of roughly 22,500 tons, the former, like the *Argus*, with no superstructure, the latter pair, like the *Eagle* and *Hermes*, with the starboard island superstructure adopted by all navies except the Japanese. The *Furious* carried 36 aircraft, *Courageous* and *Glorious* 48 apiece; all were capable of 30 knots, a great improvement over their predecessors, which steamed in the 20–25 knot range. Thus, by the late 1920s Britain still had the largest carrier force, yet none of its carriers measured up to their foreign counterparts in size, speed, or complement of aircraft. Even the newest trio were outclassed by the American *Lexington* and *Saratoga* (63 aircraft apiece, 33 knots) and the Japanese *Akagi* and *Kaga* (90 aircraft apiece, 27–31 knots), completed in 1927–28 on full-sized battle cruiser or battleship hulls, displacing the maximum 36,000 tons (33,000 plus the 3,000-ton supplemental armor allowance permitted under the treaty). The British navy also rarely got the aircraft it wanted, procurement being controlled by the Royal Air Force under a policy dating from the creation of the RAF in 1918. Rather than admit their inferiority, British naval aviators developed a faith in smaller carriers with smaller numbers of aircraft, insisting that the American and Japanese navies could never effectively operate so many planes from a single carrier in any event.[2]

Britain may have chosen not to compete with the United States and Japan in constructing large carriers, but cruisers were another matter. In the 1920s a resurgent Anglo–American naval rivalry centered around the "treaty cruiser" programs of the two countries, as both fleets added 10,000-ton cruisers armed with 8-inch guns, as allowed under the Washington Treaty. In the years 1924–28, Britain laid down 13 such heavy cruisers, all of which were in service by 1931: 5 of the *Kent* class, 4 of the *London* class, and 2 of the *Norfolk* class, all armed with eight 8-inch guns, and the slightly smaller 8,250-ton *York* and 8,390-ton *Exeter*, with six 8-inch guns. By 1928 the United States had laid down just 8 new heavy cruisers but planned to build 15 more starting in 1930. The British buildup actually was more dramatic in smaller types, as 20 destroyers and 9 sloops were launched in the years 1926–30; the United States, in contrast, launched no destroyers until 1934 and no sloops at all. In addition to its responsibilities for the defense of the colonies and dominions of the empire, Britain justified the buildup with the traditional argument that the ships were needed to keep sea lanes open, and added the observation that, as the strongest naval power in the League of Nations, it would bear much of the burden of maintaining maritime sanctions against future violators of the League Covenant. In calling the Geneva Conference of 1927, President Calvin Coolidge hoped to apply the Washington Treaty ratios for capital ships to cruisers, destroyers, and other smaller warships, but the conference failed when France and Italy refused to attend, and when the British insisted upon a common Anglo–American limit of 70 cruisers and 500,000 total cruiser tons, significantly higher than the American proposal of 50 cruisers and 400,000 tons. The Americans viewed the British cruiser program as a violation of the spirit, if not the letter, of the Washington Treaty, and were offended that Britain, France, or Italy would consider building new warships of any type at a time when they still owed war debts to the United States. The failure of the Geneva Conference left Stanley Baldwin's Conservative government vulnerable to criticism from the Labour party, whose leader, Ramsay MacDonald, argued for acceptance of the American figures in the interest of good Anglo–American relations. As prime minister following the general election of 1929, MacDonald took a personal interest in resolving the cruiser dispute, playing the leading role in bringing about the London Naval Conference of 1930.[3]

Historians are divided on the matter of whether the British navy learned much from its experiences in the First World War, aside from the need for a convoy system. As a whole, the interwar officer corps was open enough to innovative or unconventional thinking, enabling non-conformists such as John Cunningham, Bertram Ramsay, and James Somerville to rise to senior rank by the late 1930s. The Naval Staff College, opened at Greenwich in 1919, and the Tactical School, opened at Portsmouth in 1924, typically receive credit for laying the foundation for British successes in the Second World War. The Anti-Submarine Warfare School was clearly less successful. Opened in 1920, it suffered from understaffing and from a tactical outlook that placed too much faith in asdic, the predecessor of sonar. The RAF compounded the problem by providing little help in developing aircraft types and aerial tactics for use against submarines at sea. To some degree the British hoped the submarine question would simply go away. The navy which, in 1914, had more submarines than any other, pushed for their abolition at the Washington Naval Conference and would do so again in 1930, at the London Naval Conference. Just twenty new submarines were added by 1930. In the mid-1920s Britain briefly became the world leader in torpedo technology, developing a model capable of delivering a 750-pound charge at a range of 5,500 yards, but production of the weapon received a low priority. As late as 1939 the British torpedo industry turned out a mere 80 torpedoes per week.[4]

The French navy, in contrast, embraced the submarine as a key element of its postwar revitalization. At the Washington Conference the French had insisted that naval powers weak in capital ships needed submarines to defend themselves at sea. They persisted in this view throughout the 1920s, taking advantage of the absence of treaty limits to commission 10 former German U-boats and, by 1929, launch 42 new submarines. The French cruiser program included three 7,250-ton ships of the *Duguay-Trouin* class (built 1922–26), then, under the Washington Treaty, seven heavy cruisers laid down in the years 1924–31: two of the *Duquesne* class, four of the *Suffren* class, and the *Algérie*, all of which were in service by 1934. Other surface ships laid down by 1930 included two light cruisers and fifty destroyers. While the post-1922 political situation in Britain favored naval retrenchment, the opposite was true in France, where the establishment of the fascist regime in Italy prompted the French left to support naval expenditure on anti-fascist grounds, while the right supported it on nationalist grounds.[5]

The interwar French navy produced the country's most prolific naval writer of all time, Admiral Raoul Castex, whose magnum opus, the five-volume *Théories stratégiques* (1929–35), combined the Mahanian and Jeune École traditions. Castex argued for a doctrine seeking decisive battle at sea but recognized that such battles were rare, and that commerce raiding, blockades, and amphibious landings were important as well. He rebutted the arguments of interwar critics of the battleship, contending that the French navy and other navies of the second rank must maintain battle fleets strong enough to attack a superior enemy. Castex had the greatest international influence of any naval writer since Mahan, reflected in the number of languages into which his writings were translated. His entire five-volume work was translated into Japanese and Spanish (in the latter case, for the Argentinian navy), and summaries or sections of it appeared in English, Russian, Greek, and Serbo–Croatian.[6]

Meanwhile, the Italian navy suffered from the fact that Italy's leading interwar military theorist, General Giulio Douhet, was the world's foremost advocate of air power. Douhet believed that future wars, at sea as well as on land, would be won by aircraft alone; like Mitchell in the United States, he doubted any surface warship could defend itself against an air attack. Douhet's theories, plus the experience of the Adriatic war of 1915–18, led some Italian naval officers to embrace strategies based around aircraft, submarines, and torpedo boats. Admiral Thaon di Revel led another faction which stood by the battle-ship and the theories of Mahan; not surprisingly, their domestic supporters included Italy's leading steelmakers and shipbuilders. At least one of the battleship admirals, Angelo Iachino, opposed the construction of aircraft carriers, but he was much less influential than Admiral Romeo Bernotti, the navy's leading advocate of carriers, who headed the Italian naval war college at Livorno after 1922 and was the most prolific Italian naval writer of the 1920s. The carrier debate became moot in 1923, when Benito Mussolini founded the Italian air force and gave it control over all military aircraft. A law dating from that year (which remained in effect until 1992) actually prohibited the Italian navy from operating aircraft carriers, reflecting the fact that most Italian strategists believed aircraft from bases in Italy and its colonies (Libya, Somalia, Eritrea, and the Dodecanese Islands) could easily cover any waters in which the Italian navy was likely to operate.[7]

In addition to defending the Italian coast, the interwar navy counted among its future wartime missions the protection of the sea routes to Italian possessions in Africa, convoying troops or supplies to or from those colonies, and the disruption of the operations of an enemy's fleet or convoys in the Mediterranean. Anti-French sentiments dominated the Italian navy, reflecting the reemerging Franco–Italian naval rivalry; the anti-British sentiments common in the Italian army and diplomatic service were hard to find in the navy, which had long considered the British navy its role model. Owing to Italy's chaotic political situation and financial weakness, in the immediate postwar years the navy added no surface vessels larger than destroyers and no new submarines. After Mussolini consolidated his power and, over the winter of 1925–26, secured a restructuring of Italy's war debts to Britain and the United States, warship construction resumed in earnest. Almost $200 million in foreign bank loans in the years 1926–28 helped sustain the program. Under the Washington Treaty Italy matched France's heavy cruiser program by laying down 7 of its own in the years 1925–30: 2 of the *Trento* class, 4 of the *Zara* class, and the *Bolzano*, all of which were in service by 1933. During the same years, Italy also laid down 6 light cruisers, 36 destroyers, and 24 submarines.[8]

The postwar German navy operated no larger warships until 1921, when 2 of the 6 pre-dreadnought battleships allowed under the Versailles Treaty were reactivated. By the winter of 1925–26 5 were in commission, and through the remainder of the decade at least 4 were in service at any given time. The 15,000-man ceiling on German naval personnel limited operations, and the number of battleships in service fell to 2 by the end of 1932, to free personnel for new light cruisers constructed as replacements for the six old *Gazelles* and *Bremens* retained under the Versailles Treaty. The 5,300-ton *Emden* (built 1921–25) was followed by the 6,000-ton *Königsberg* (1926–29), *Karlsruhe* (1926–29), and *Köln* (1926–30), the 6,310-ton *Leipzig* (1928–31), and the 7,150-ton *Nürnberg* (1933–35), the last two exceeding the Versailles limit for German cruisers. Under the leadership of Admiral Erich Raeder, appointed commander of the navy in 1928, the Germans showed great ingenuity in designing replacements for their pre-dreadnought battleships. Faced with the fact that the Versailles Treaty limited their new armored warships to 10,000 tons and 11.1-inch guns, the Germans designed the *Deutschland* class of 28-knot heavy cruisers to conform to these limits. The British called them "pocket battleships," but officially they were simply "armored ships (*Panzerschiffe*)" until their reclassification as heavy cruisers in 1939. Thus, while Germany was forbidden to have modern battleships, it would have heavy cruisers far more capable than the 10,000-ton, 8-inch gun ships other navies were building under the limits of the Washington Treaty, a pact to which it was not a party. Raeder successfully defended the program against criticism in the Reichstag, and ensured its long-term continuation by cultivating ties with Adolf Hitler long before January 1933, indeed, as soon as it became clear he was the rising star in German politics. The *Deutschland* (built 1929–33), *Admiral Scheer* (1931–34), and *Admiral Graf Spee* (1932–36; see Plate 33) all were actually heavier than their official 10,000 tons; the *Admiral Graf Spee*, completed long after Hitler took power, displaced 12,340 tons. Under the Nazis, the rest of the program of "pocket battleships" was cancelled in favor of larger designs.[9]

Most veteran U-boat commanders responded to the postwar ban on German submarines by quitting the navy, yet under the Weimar Republic, covert experimentation with submarines continued. Under a government with serious financial troubles, in a country paralysed by depression, the German navy accumulated 100 million Reichsmarks in the years 1919–22 thanks to the victorious Allies, who allowed it to keep money from the sales of ships scrapped under the Versailles Treaty. The navy used this supplementary fund to establish a submarine construction company in the Netherlands and torpedo factories in Spain. The Dutch firm of IvS (Ingenieurskantoor voor Scheepsbouw) built submarines in the Netherlands for the Finnish, Swedish, Spanish, and Turkish navies, and in partnership with Kawasaki, in Japan for the Japanese navy. German engineers designed the submarines, which were equipped with German engines. German personnel gained valuable experience by operating the submarines during their trials and delivering them from the Netherlands to their new owners. Officially, the German navy had nothing to do with submarine research and development, although an anti-submarine warfare section created in 1925 was a thinly veiled submarine section for a navy without submarines.[10]

While the Versailles Treaty limited the size of the German navy, a lack of means and desire to maintain a larger fleet limited the size of the Soviet navy. In the years 1922–25 the Soviets scrapped all of the surviving pre-dreadnoughts and armored cruisers of the old Imperial fleet. In 1925 they also deactivated the battleship *Poltava* (by then renamed *Frunze*), keeping it on hand as a source of spare parts for the remaining three units of the *Gangut* class, which formed the core of the Soviet fleet: the *Oktyabrskaya Revolutsia* (ex-*Gangut*; see Plate 34), *Marat* (ex-*Petropavlovsk*), and *Parizhkaya Kommuna* (ex-*Sevastopol*). The protected cruisers *Komintern* (ex-*Pamiat Merkuria*) and *Aurora* were the only former Imperial navy cruisers commissioned in the Soviet navy, the latter serving mostly as a training ship before being placed in reserve and eventually converted to a museum ship, in commemoration of its role in the Bolshevik Revolution. Smaller units included 25 destroyers, 9 torpedo boats, and 10 submarines, which were supplemented by projects laid down by the Imperial navy before or during the First World War, and eventually completed by the Soviets: the 6,830-ton light cruisers *Profintern* (ex-*Svetlana*) and *Chervona Ukraina* (ex-*Admiral Nakhimov*) and the 7,650-ton light cruiser *Krasnyi Kavkaz* (ex-*Admiral Lazarev*), commissioned in 1927, 1928, and 1932, respectively, and 4 submarines, completed in 1920–21. The Soviet navy's only new build-ing projects during the decade were 6 submarines authorized in 1926 and launched in 1928–29.[11]

The interwar Soviet navy, like the Imperial navy before it, kept most of its forces in the Baltic. All three battleships were there until 1929, when the *Parizhkaya Kommuna* was transferred to the Black Sea. But for a navy with a purely defensive focus, the smaller units were the most sig-nificant. During the 1920s these were linked to a central command ashore in an integrated coastal defense system similar in concept to those of Aube and Stosch during the era of the Jeune École, only with the addition of land-based aircraft, and made more effective by the modern technology of radio. This system had the added advantage of eliminating individual initiative for warship commanders, problematic in a Soviet navy which, initially, relied heavily on former Imperial offi-cers. At first the sailors of the fleet could be counted upon to keep their officers in line, but this changed when personnel of the Baltic Fleet rose up against Lenin's regime in the tragic Kronstadt rebellion of 1921. Afterward the communist regime no longer trusted the navy any more than the army, and Leon Trotsky introduced the army's system of pol-itical commissars into the fleet. His successor as commissar for war, Mikhail Frunze, abolished the political commissars in 1924, but they were reintroduced again from 1937 to 1940 and permanently after the German invasion of the Soviet Union in June 1941. Former Imperial officers faced a difficult life in the Soviet naval officer corps, yet after Josef Stalin restored the rank of admiral in 1937, two of the first three men to attain it, I. S. Isakov and L. M. Geller, were former Imperial officers.[12]

Beyond the ranks of the great powers, only three European countries – Spain, the Netherlands, and Sweden – launched a warship larger than a destroyer during the interwar years. The Spanish navy led the way. In 1921 Spain commissioned the last of the three *España* class battleships, the *Jaime I*, but two years later lost the *España* to shipwreck off the Moroccan coast. The third battleship, the *Alfonso XIII*, assumed the name *España* in 1931, when Spain became a republic. Three light cruis-ers launched in 1920–23 were followed by the 7,475-ton *Principe Alfonso* (renamed *Libertad* in 1931) and its sister-ships *Almirante Cervera* and *Miguel de Cervantes* (launched 1925–28), then the 10,000-ton *Canarias* (1931) and *Baleares* (1932), the latter pair copies of the "treaty cruisers" of the British *Kent* class. Nineteen destroyers were launched in the years 1922–33, and six submarines completed in 1921–23 joined four built during the First World War. The Netherlands launched five light cruisers during the interwar years, two of the 6,670-ton *Sumatra* class (1920–21), the 6,000-ton *De Ruyter* (1935), and two of the 3,790-ton *Tromp* class (1937–39), supplemented by eight destroyers (1926–30) and twenty-six submarines (1921–40). Sweden launched the 4,700-ton light cruiser *Gotland* (1933), eight destroyers (1926–39), and ten sub-marines (1925–38) in the interwar years.[13] In the relative calm of the 1920s, neither these navies nor those of the great powers fired a shot in anger.

FROM THE LONDON NAVAL TREATY TO THE OUTBREAK OF WAR (1930–39)

After Ramsay MacDonald became British prime minister, his desire to resolve the Anglo–American cruiser debate led to the London Naval Conference. As the Great Depression spread from the United States worldwide, other naval powers came to the conference in a mood to fur-ther reduce and restrict the size of their fleets. In the London Naval Treaty, signed on 22 April 1930, Britain, the United States, and Japan maintained their 5:5:3 ratio of capital ships but pledged to reduce their actual num-bers from 20:20:12 to 15:15:9, and to lay down no new capital ships until after 31 December 1936, extending the Washington Naval Treaty's orig-inal construction "holiday" which was to end on 31 December 1931. The Anglo–American cruiser debate was resolved when Britain abandoned its 1927 argument for 70 cruisers in favor of the American ceiling of 50; in return, the United States agreed to allow the British navy a total cruiser tonnage 50,000 greater than the US navy. The 10,000-ton ceiling on indi-vidual cruiser displacement was retained, but those laid down after the London Treaty were to be limited to 6-inch guns; the United States, how-ever, would be allowed to lay down 10 more cruisers with 8-inch guns by 1935. To assuage neutralist American concerns about British blockades limiting the freedom of American merchants to trade with all belligerents during a future European war, the British agreed to limit their use of blockades. Further concessions had to be made in order to get France and Italy to sign the London Treaty. Under the Washington Treaty each could have built two battleships at any time since 1927 but had not done so; in the London Treaty, they received exemptions from the extended building ban to allow these ships to be laid down in the years 1931–36. When France and Italy refused, as before, to limit their numbers or overall ton-nage of cruisers, Britain insisted that the London Treaty include an "esca-lator clause" allowing it to exceed the new Anglo–American cruiser limits if French or Italian cruiser construction posed a threat to its security. As it had at Washington, Britain raised the issue of banning submarines entirely, but the proposal attracted no support.[14]

For Britain, the five ships decommissioned under the new treaty were the battle cruiser *Tiger* and the four battleships of the *Iron Duke* class; all were scrapped except *Iron Duke* itself, which survived as a training ship. France used its battleship exemptions to lay down the 26,500-ton *Dunkerque* (December 1932) and *Strasbourg* (November 1934), each of which carried its eight 13-inch guns in the unique configuration of two centerline four-gun turrets on the foredeck, and had no heavy guns aft of the superstructure. Italy responded with the 40,725-ton *Littorio* and *Vittorio Veneto*, both laid down in October 1934, armed with nine 15-inch guns in three centerline triple-gun turrets, two fore and one aft of the superstructure (see Plate 35); when completed, they would be Europe's largest warships after Britain's *Hood*. Among the leading European navies, the so-called "6-inch cruisers" allowed under the London Treaty were popular only with the British, who laid down nineteen in the years 1931–36, ranging in size from the 10,000-ton *Edinburgh* class to the 5,220-ton *Arethusa* class. These, plus the thirteen 8-inch cruisers built earlier, gave Britain a cruiser force slightly larger but perhaps qualitatively weaker than that of the United States, which had eighteen 8-inch and nine 6-inch cruisers built or building by 1936. France laid down seven 6-inch cruisers in the years 1931–33, six of the 7,600-ton *Galissonnière* class and one of a smaller design. Italy began six during the same years, ranging in size from the 9,440-ton *Abruzzi* class to the 7,405-ton *Montecuccoli* class.[15]

While the Great Depression inspired a greater willingness to further limit naval armaments, its economic repercussions in some cases led to furloughs and reductions in pay, which in turn had a devastating impact on morale and readiness. Among the leading navies the British suffered the worst. In September 1931, the Admiralty announced pay cuts of 11 percent for officers and 25 percent for most seamen. Within days the crews of seven capital ships and four cruisers mutinied in protest; aside from one cruiser, on the North American and West Indies station, all of the units involved belonged to the Atlantic Fleet. The First Lord of the Admiralty, Austen Chamberlain, took no action other than ordering all ships to return to their home ports, and within a day the protests ended. Afterward, Chamberlain refused to allow any of the mutineers to be punished. Under the circumstances his policy may have been the most prudent and the most humane, but the news of the mutiny, reported worldwide, only served further to diminish the reputation of the British navy.[16]

Within days of the British naval mutiny, the Japanese invasion of Manchuria signaled the onset of the international tensions that would result in a general war by the end of the decade. At least initially, the economic situation compelled the leading navies to continue to honor the regime of arms limitations, and to restrict expansion to the smaller, unregulated unit types. In the years 1931–39 Britain launched 88 destroyers, 23 sloops, and 36 submarines. France added little to its large destroyer program of the 1920s, completing just 16 more by 1939, along with 9 sloops; submarines were another matter, as a further 45 were launched in the 1930s. Italy added 24 more destroyers by 1939 and just one sloop, but dramatically expanded its submarine force, launching another 84 by 1939.[17] Measured against the French navy, the

Italian navy was on course to achieve a qualitative superiority in battleships and cruisers and an overwhelming advantage in numbers of destroyers and submarines. Italy's post-London construction program clearly reflected Mussolini's intention to act upon his ambitions to dominate the Mediterranean, eventually, if necessary, taking on the British navy. In this quest he enjoyed the full support of his pro-Fascist chief of the naval staff, Admiral Domenico Cavagnari, in overcoming the navy's traditional pro-British sentiments. Like Tirpitz in the North Sea before the First World War, Cavagnari felt that by building up to a 2:3 ratio of inferiority to its enemy, Italy would have a fighting chance in a future Mediterranean naval war.[18]

The Italians calculated that a German naval buildup would draw a significant share of Anglo–French naval forces away from the Mediterranean and, even before 1933, speculation about such a buildup was not unfounded. Indeed, France felt threatened enough by the construction of the "pocket battleships" to use its treaty exemptions to build the *Dunkerque* and *Strasbourg*. In the last months of the Weimar Republic, conservative leaders planned for an outright violation of the naval clauses of the Versailles Treaty. In July 1932 the defense minister (later chancellor), General Kurt von Schleicher, initiated the stockpiling of materials for the construction of submarines totaling 5,000 tons over a five-year period. As soon as Hitler became chancellor, the navy received a supplemental grant of 115.7 million Reichsmarks to its existing budget of 186 million for that fiscal year. By the end of 1933 the decision was made to double the tonnage of Schleicher's submarine plan to 10,000, but through 1934 preparations continued to be shrouded in secrecy. The Nazi regime also took a cautious approach to surface warship construction, initially only completing those projects it inherited from the Weimar Republic. During 1934 the first four of an eventual 22 prewar destroyers were laid down. After deciding to build no more "pocket battleships" Germany waited until May 1935 to lay down the 35,540-ton fast (32-knot) battleships *Scharnhorst* and *Gneisenau*. Theoretically built in response to the 29.5-knot *Dunkerque* and *Strasbourg*, they displaced almost 10,000 tons more than their French counterparts yet were armed with nine 11.1-inch guns, the same type carried by the "pocket battleships." They were supposed to carry 15-inch guns but Raeder did not want to delay their commissioning until the ordnance was ready, and the change was never made.[19]

In an effort to shore up the deteriorating interwar naval arms control regime, in the spring of 1935 Britain opened negotiations intended to bring Germany into the existing system of the Washington and London treaties. The Anglo–German Naval Treaty (18 June 1935), an early milestone on the road of Britain's appeasement of Hitler, conceded to the Third Reich a fleet equal to those of France and Italy under the 1922 quotas. The agreement also allowed the Germans to build a submarine force 45 percent the size of the British. By the end of June, the Deutsche Werke at Kiel had launched *U 1*, and the German navy's "anti-submarine" school established a decade earlier had been redesignated as a submarine school. Raeder appointed Captain Karl Dönitz to oversee the dramatic expansion of the new submarine service. During the last six months of 1935, Germany launched U-boats at the rate of almost one per week. By 1938 three dozen were in service and 82 more on the stocks, but roughly half were in the 250–300 ton range, no larger than the submarines of 1914–18, and would be of limited utility after 1939. The first Type VII submarines, displacing around 700 tons, were launched in 1936–37.[20]

Following the general logic of appeasement, Britain conceded Germany the right to build U-boats in the belief that the Versailles Treaty had been a mistake. Britain was convinced that Nazi Germany was going to resume submarine construction, was not prepared to use force to stop it, and thus sought to control it by treaty. Most British leaders considered the matter more symbolic than real, doubting Germany would again attempt a submarine strategy that had, in fact, failed during the First World War. Amid the deepening American isolationism of the 1930s, another German campaign of unrestricted submarine warfare appeared to be just about the only thing that would prompt the United States to intervene in a future European war, and surely Germany would not be foolish enough to repeat that mistake.

Britain concluded the Anglo–German Naval Treaty without consulting the other Washington and London signatories, but in the end it mattered little, as the regime of naval limits was already dying. Japan was the first to break ranks, announcing in 1934 that it would not renew the agreements made at London after they expired at the end of 1936. Early in 1935 France likewise announced its intention to quit the regime, and in October of that year laid down the 35,000-ton *Richelieu*, a larger version of the *Dunkerque* and *Strasbourg* armed with 15-inch guns, as a response to Italy's *Littorio* and *Vittorio Veneto* and Germany's *Scharnhorst* and *Gneisenau*.[21] In a last-ditch effort to prevent a new naval arms race, the British convened the Second London Naval Conference (December 1935–January 1936). At the outset Japan dashed hopes for a meaningful agreement by demanding parity with Britain and the United States. Countering a proposal for qualitative restrictions, the Japanese proposed the elimination of all battleships and aircraft carriers, a position they knew no one would accept. Its rejection served as the pretext for Japan to quit the conference, after which the remaining powers (Britain, France, Italy, and the United States) joined Germany and the Soviet Union in a new treaty. The agreement imposed qualitative limits for individual warship types, for example, reducing the maximum size of all new aircraft carriers from 27,000 tons to 23,000 tons, but included no system of overall tonnage quotas. Thus, a country could build as many new aircraft carriers as it wished, so long as each carrier did not exceed 23,000 tons displacement. Escape clauses further weakened the agreement, as the signatories reserved the right to exceed the qualitative limits in response to the building projects of others, including countries outside the agreement, namely Japan. Thus, when the Japanese failed to respect the qualitative limits of a treaty they did not sign, the treaty became a dead letter for everyone else. After preexisting treaty limits expired on 31 December 1936, the interwar experiment in naval arms limits came to an end.[22]

The Second London Naval Conference took place in an atmosphere of heightened tension for the three leading naval powers of Europe, owing to Mussolini's invasion of Ethiopia. The British Mediterranean Fleet remained on a war footing from August 1935 to July 1936, reinforced after September 1935 by units from the Home Fleet, but did nothing to enforce League of Nations sanctions against the Italians. Indeed, Britain actually facilitated the conquest of the East African country (October 1935–May 1936) by allowing Italian troopships and their naval escorts to transit the Suez Canal unhindered. France also joined Britain's appeasement policy, agreeing in the Hoare–Laval Pact of December 1935 to offer half of Ethiopia to Mussolini. Britain enjoyed a great superiority over Italy in every warship type except submarines but was more interested in avoiding war at all costs than in preserving Ethiopia or the broader concept of collective security. Meanwhile, the general war scare stemming from the Ethiopian campaign prompted the Italian navy to lay plans for an "escape fleet (*flotta d'evasione*)" consisting of 9 or 10 battleships, 4 aircraft carriers, 36 cruisers, and several dozen new submarines. Such a fleet would be strong enough to seize control of both the Suez Canal and the Strait of Gibraltar, enabling Italian warships to "escape" the Mediterranean and cooperate on the high seas with the Germans or other naval allies. But Mussolini was not inclined to lift Italy's 1923 ban against carrier aviation, and in August 1936 Admiral Cavagnari deleted the carriers from the plan. Germany provided Italy with diplomatic support throughout the crisis of 1935–36 and was the first country to recognize its conquest of Ethiopia. Afterward, Italian naval planners took for granted that any future war against the Anglo–French combination would be fought in alliance with Germany. At the same time, the German navy made no plans involving the Italians, and the two navies held no staff talks until June 1939, one month after the "Pact of Steel" formalized the German–Italian Axis partnership of 1936.[23]

In the intervening years, Germany and Italy deepened their ties in the common cause of supporting General Francisco Franco's Nationalist forces against the Spanish Republic in the Spanish Civil War (July 1936–March 1939).[24] Within the Spanish navy most officers sympathized with Franco and most sailors with the Republic, leaving the ships that fell into Nationalist hands short of common manpower and those retained by the Republic lacking in experienced commanders. As soon as the civil war began, minister of marine and future prime minister José Giral authorized the men of the fleet to seize their ships if their officers tried to join the Nationalists. In the resulting bloodbath dozens of officers were murdered as the Republicans retained the battleship *Jaime I*, the cruisers *Libertad* and *Miguel de Cervantes*, two light cruisers, and almost all of the navy's destroyers and submarines. Meanwhile, early in the war the Nationalists gained control of the installations at Vigo and Ferrol, seizing the battleship *España* along with the cruisers *Canarias*, *Baleares*, and *Almirante Cervera*. In September 1936 the Republicans withdrew most of the ships under their control to the northern coast of Spain, leaving just two destroyers to guard the Strait of Gibraltar. Late that month the cruisers *Canarias* and *Almirante Cervera* sank one of these destroyers and damaged the other, securing the route for Franco to ship Nationalist troops from Spanish Morocco to the mainland. Until that time, Franco had relied upon aircraft provided by Hitler and Mussolini to ferry his troops from Morocco to Nationalist strongholds in Spain.

The civil war eventually destroyed the largest units of the Spanish navy. The Nationalists lost the battleship *España* to a mine off Cape Penas in April 1937 and the heavy cruiser *Baleares* to a torpedo attack by Republican destroyers off Cape Palos in March 1938. An Italian submarine torpedoed but failed to sink the Republican cruiser *Miguel de Cervantes* off Cartagena in November 1936, but the following June the Republicans lost the battleship *Jaime I* to a magazine explosion while the ship was under repair in the Cartagena dockyard, after being damaged earlier in a Nationalist air attack. The Republicans also lost six submarines during the war. Over the opposition of Admiral Cavagnari, Mussolini had the Italian navy transfer four destroyers and six submarines to the Nationalist navy, to compensate for its disadvantage in these types; four of the submarines were returned when the war ended.[25]

German and Italian aid to the Nationalists, and subsequent Soviet aid to the Republicans, continued throughout the war despite a non-intervention agreement concluded by the five major European powers. A non-intervention committee met at London from September 1936 to July 1938. Warships from Britain, France, Italy, and Germany patrolled zones along the Spanish coast starting in April 1937, ostensibly to stop arms shipments from reaching either side, and Britain, France, and Italy patrolled the Mediterranean sea lanes starting in September 1937, to stop the sinking of non-Spanish ships by "unidentified" submarines. The latter were Italian, serving in an on-again, off-again campaign of unrestricted submarine warfare against merchantmen suspected of carrying supplies to the Republicans. As in the Ethiopian crisis, Britain sought to avoid war at all costs and declined to use its naval power to prevent Germany and Italy from bringing about a Nationalist victory. In any event, British naval leaders, appalled by the massacre of Spanish naval officers at the onset of the civil war, were overwhelmingly pro-Nationalist and disinclined to enforce a blockade that might hurt Franco's forces. The appeasement policy only deepened after May 1937, when Neville Chamberlain replaced Stanley Baldwin as prime minister. Foreign warships of note involved in the patrols of the Spanish coast included the battle cruiser *Hood*, sent to the Bay of Biscay in the spring of 1937 over the objections of the First Lord of the Admiralty, Sir Samuel Hoare, and the "pocket battleship" *Deutschland*, bombed by Republican planes in late May 1937 while docked at Ibiza in the Balearics. The latter incident, in which 31 men were killed and 74 wounded, accounted for the war's only non-Spanish naval casualties.

During the Spanish Civil War, Germany led the way in exploiting the end of naval arms limits. The 45,950-ton battleship *Bismarck* (laid down July 1936; see Plate 36) and its 42,900-ton half-sister *Tirpitz* (October 1936; see Plate 37), each armed with eight 15-inch guns, formed the heart of Hitler's program. They were followed by two unnamed 52,600-ton battleships (July–August 1939). The 23,200-ton aircraft carrier *Graf Zeppelin* (December 1936) and a second unnamed carrier (during 1938) were begun over the objections of Hermann Göring, who did not want to see resources diverted from his Luftwaffe into naval aviation. Meanwhile, the 14,050-ton heavy cruiser *Admiral Hipper* (July 1935) was followed by its sister-ship *Blücher* and the slightly larger half-sisters *Prinz Eugen*, *Seydlitz*, and *Lützow* (March 1936–August 1937), all armed with eight 8-inch guns. Counting the three "pocket battleships" as heavy cruisers, these projects gave Germany six battleships, two carriers, and eight heavy cruisers built or building when the Second World War began. Hopelessly inferior to Britain in all of these warship types, the Germans sought a qualitative advantage, in 1936 pioneering a radar set aboard the "pocket battleship" *Admiral Graf Spee*, to detect enemy warships and aircraft, and serve as a range finder. The British navy did not introduce a similar system until 1938. Hitler agreed to the buildup of the surface fleet against his better judgement, as he considered the Tirpitz plan to have been a great mistake. Admiral Raeder had no such doubts; indeed, since the dark early years of the Weimar Republic he had lived for the day when he could recreate the High Sea Fleet. Raeder acquiesced in the resumption of U-boat construction but was too much of a Mahanian traditionalist to consider submarines the centerpiece of his navy.[26]

Like Raeder, Italy's Admiral Cavagnari was a Mahanian traditionalist. His plans for the "escape fleet" reflected his faith in powerful surface forces. The large, first-rate Italian submarine force may have caused potential rivals a great deal of concern, but the navy's own leading admiral viewed it as a secondary branch. Cavagnari considered the Italian submarine campaign during the Spanish Civil War a waste of his navy's resources, and feared it would provoke a war against the British and French before his surface fleet was ready. The four surviving battleships of the First World War were thoroughly renovated during the decade, the *Conte di Cavour* and *Giulio Cesare* in 1933–37, the *Andrea Doria* and *Caio Duilio* in 1937–40. Meanwhile, after the new *Littorio* and *Vittorio Veneto* were launched in Genoa and Trieste, respectively, their sister-ships *Impero* (May 1938) and *Roma* (September 1938) were laid down on the same slips. Amid the focus on the battleship program, cruiser construction on the eve of the war was limited to the dozen light cruisers of the 3,690-ton *Capitani Romani* class, all laid down in 1939. These projects gave Cavagnari 8 battleships and 31 cruisers built or building by the end of 1939, close to the goals of his "escape fleet" plan of 1935–36. But inadequate funding kept his dream from being realized, as the navy never received more money than the army, and the fiscal year 1935–36 was the last in which it was given more than the air force. In 1939–40, as Italy made its final preparations for war, the navy took just 19 percent of the defense outlay. The same navy which forty years earlier had been the first to introduce the wireless telegraph went into the Second World War without radar, and apparently was not even aware of its existence until 1941.[27]

Britain responded to the German and Italian battleship programs with the five units of the 36,725-ton *King George V* class (laid down January–July 1937), armed with ten 14-inch guns. They were followed by the 40,550-ton *Temeraire* (June 1939) and *Lion* (July 1939), designed for nine 16-inch guns. At the same time, the carrier force was modernized with the 22,000-ton *Ark Royal* (September 1935; see Plate 38), the four units of the 23,000-ton *Illustrious class* (April–November 1937), and the 23,450-ton *Implacable* (February 1939) and *Indefatigable* (November 1939). They were a dramatic improvement over the navy's six older carriers, all being capable of over 30 knots and, aside from the *Ark Royal*, all built with 3-inch armored flight decks. Otherwise, the design remained faithful to the British preference for carriers smaller than their American and Japanese counterparts: *Ark Royal*, *Implacable*, and *Indefatigable* could carry 60 aircraft apiece, the *Indomitable* 45, the remaining three units of the *Illustrious* class just 33 apiece. A smaller new carrier, the 14,750-ton *Unicorn* (June 1939), for political purposes was designated an aircraft maintenance ship; it was designed to function as such but also for emergency use as a light fleet carrier. Britain's prewar construction program also included another eleven 6-inch cruisers of the 8,350-ton *Fiji* class and eleven light cruisers of the 5,600-ton *Dido* class. These additions gave Britain 20 capital ships (17 battleships and 3 battle cruisers), 13 carriers, and 54 modern cruisers built or building by the end of 1939, but 12 of the capital ships were old

enough to have seen action in the First World War, and the 6 oldest carriers were of limited value. The battleships and carriers laid down in
1937–39 ultimately formed the core of the wartime fleet, but none was
ready before 1940.[28]

In France, the deepening interwar political polarization afflicting the
country as a whole began to affect the fleet following the election of a
Popular Front government in 1936. Communist cells were uncovered
aboard eight warships, including the cruiser *Montcalm*, a victim of sabotage late in the year. More important, the change in governments
brought a temporary hiatus in new naval construction, as France laid
down no warship larger than a destroyer in 1936 or 1937. Thereafter,
under its prewar chief of staff, Vice Admiral François Darlan (from
January 1937), the French navy belatedly began to prepare for war. Son
of a radical socialist politician, the progressive Darlan proved to be a
unifying figure within the navy. Under his direction, shipyards started
work on the 6-inch cruiser *De Grasse* (November 1938), the 18,000-ton
aircraft carrier *Joffre* (December 1938), and two sister-ships of the battleship *Richelieu*, the *Jean Bart* (January 1939) and *Clemenceau* (January
1939). These projects gave France a total of 11 battleships, 2 carriers,
and 19 cruisers built or building when the Second World War began,
but none of the major projects laid down in 1938–39 would be ready
in time to see action. Nevertheless, thanks to Darlan's efforts, in
September 1939 the navy was not as unprepared as the French army
and air force. On paper the French navy remained the fourth largest in
the world and the second largest in Europe, trailing only the US,
Japanese, and British navies in overall tonnage, but both Germany and
Italy had newer, more capable fleets than France. The prewar navy gave
a higher priority to the defense of overseas colonies than to naval aviation or anti-submarine warfare, in part because the latter weaknesses
made the former more important, at least in Africa. Fear of Italy's submarine force and its substantial fleet of land-based bombers led French
and British war planners to assume that in the event of hostilities, the
Mediterranean would be closed to their merchantmen; thus, new bases
were established in French and British possessions on the west and east
coasts of Africa to support the diversion of mercantile traffic around the
Cape of Good Hope, and these colonial bases, in turn, had to be
defended. Despite its qualitative inferiority to the Italian navy, in 1939
the French navy was committed to defend British interests in the
Mediterranean, as it had been at the onset of the First World War, this
time not to facilitate a British concentration in the North Sea against
Germany, but the possible redeployment of the British Mediterranean
Fleet to Singapore in case of war against Japan.[29]

After consolidating his power as Lenin's successor, Joseph Stalin
approved a massive expansion of the Soviet navy. A program drafted in
1936 called for 24 battleships and battle cruisers, 20 cruisers, 17

destroyer flotilla leaders, 128 destroyers, and 533 submarines, goals which the Soviet Union lacked the means to achieve. Few of the capital ships were ever begun and none completed. The three 59,150-ton battleships of the *Sovyetskiy Soyuz* class (laid down 1938–39), designed for nine 16-inch guns, were intended as flagships for the Baltic, Black Sea, and Northern fleets. Work also started on the first pair of 35,240-ton battle cruisers of the *Kronstadt* class (1939), designed for nine 12-inch guns. All five projects were suspended in October 1940. The cruiser program fared better. The 7,880-ton *Kirov* and *Voroshilov* (already under construction since 1935) were followed by four 8,180-ton half-sisters of the *Maxim Gorkiy* class (laid down 1936–39), all armed with nine 7.1-inch guns, and five units of the 11,500-ton *Chapayev* class (1938–39), armed with a dozen 6-inch guns. All 11 ships eventually were completed, the *Chapayev* class after the Second World War. Ironically, given the Soviet–Italian animosity of the Spanish Civil War years, the Soviet battleships and cruisers were designed with the help of Italian firms. A Livorno shipyard also built the 2,890-ton flotilla leader *Tashkent* for the Soviet navy, delivering it in February 1939, while Soviet shipyards in the late 1930s built six slightly smaller flotilla leaders of the *Leningrad* class. These ships were intended to head the large force of destroyers, 70 of which were launched between 1935 and the German invasion in June 1941. But the centerpiece of Stalin's naval program was his submarine force, expanded dramatically to become the world's largest. At the beginning of the 1930s the Soviets had just 20 submarines, most of them old enough to have been inherited from the Imperial Russian navy; in the years 1931–41 they launched around 275 more, of which 130 were in service in the Baltic, Black Sea, and Northern fleets by June 1941. At least early in the program the Soviet submarine buildup benefited from Weimar-era German technology, accessed via the Dutch firm of IvS. From the onset of Nazi rule in January 1933 until the conclusion of the Nazi–Soviet Pact in August 1939, direct and indirect German–Soviet naval cooperation ceased. Contact resumed between August 1939 and June 1941, the most significant transaction being the sale of the incomplete heavy cruiser *Lützow* to the Soviet Union early in 1940. It was towed to Leningrad that spring and renamed *Petropavlovsk*, but never completed. In the area of personnel, Stalin's 1937 purge of the Soviet armed forces took its toll on the naval hierarchy. The elimination of dozens of senior officers cleared the way for Nikolai G. Kuznetsov to become naval commissar in 1939, at age 34.[30]

After the outbreak of the Second World War the Soviet navy was the only one to suspend construction of all capital ships then on the stocks, but after September 1939 a number of other major European warship projects were cancelled as well. Britain never completed the battleships *Lion* and *Temeraire*; France, the battleship *Clemenceau* and carrier *Joffre*; and Italy, the battleship *Impero*. Germany ultimately cancelled its two unnamed 52,600-ton battleships, the carrier *Graf Zeppelin* and a second unnamed carrier. After the sale of the *Lützow* to the Soviet Union, its sister-ship *Seydlitz* was slated for conversion to an 18,000-ton aircraft carrier but was never completed. For the larger warships of the 1930s that were completed, construction times reflected the fact that Britain no longer enjoyed an advantage over its European rivals in shipbuilding capability. Of the major British navy projects begun during 1937, the four carriers took an average of three years, seven months to complete, the five battleships four years, seven months. In comparison, the four German battleships begun in 1935–36 were completed in an average of three years, nine months, the three French battleships laid down in 1932–35, four years, five months. Of the Italian battleships laid down in the 1930s the three eventually completed took an average of almost six years to build. Britain also was no longer self-sufficient in basic warship construction materials. Indeed, because the British had to import some of their armor from Czechoslovakia (whose Witkowitz works earlier had provided armor plate for the Austro–Hungarian navy), the Czech crisis of 1938 affected the construction of the carrier *Indomitable*.[31]

THE ATLANTIC WAR, 1939–41

During the last two weeks of August 1939, Hitler ordered the "pocket battleships" *Admiral Graf Spee* and *Deutschland* into the Atlantic along with several U-boats, to raid British and French commerce should the Western powers remain faithful to their April 1939 pledge to defend Poland if it were attacked by Germany. At 04:45 on the morning of 1 September, the old pre-dreadnought battleship *Schleswig–Holstein*, employed since 1932 as a cadet training ship, shelled the Polish garrison at Gdynia from the Bay of Danzig, where it had anchored a week earlier ostensibly on a routine port call. The bombardment was timed to coincide with a manufactured incident on the German–Polish frontier which Hitler used as the pretext to invade. It was no small irony that the first warship engaged in the Second World War had survived the Versailles Treaty because of its obsolesence, and thus was a symbol of the German navy's humiliation at the end of the First World War. On 3 September both Britain and France declared war on Germany. Later that day, a pessimistic Raeder privately conceded that his navy faced certain defeat in the war at sea. His hopes were dashed just as those of Tirpitz had been a quarter-century earlier, as once again, the outbreak of war found the German surface fleet in a position of hopeless inferiority vis-à-vis the British. Hitler's submarine buildup notwithstanding, the German navy was also in no position in September 1939 to unleash an effective campaign of unrestricted submarine warfare. Since the resumption of U-boat construction 57 submarines had been commissioned, but at the onset of the war Dönitz had just 26 large enough to operate effectively in the Atlantic, including only 15 Type VII boats specifically designed for that purpose.[32]

Hours after the declarations of war on 3 September, Churchill became First Lord of the Admiralty in the Chamberlain cabinet, returning to the office he had left in disgrace twenty-four years earlier, in the wake of the disastrous Gallipoli campaign. As both a maverick and a micro-manager, he was unpopular at the Admiralty; as a man of action, he was beloved in the British navy as a whole. The first naval action of the war occurred the same day, when the British light cruiser *Ajax* hunted down two German freighters in the South Atlantic, both of which were scuttled by their captains to avoid capture. Later on 3 September *U 30* torpedoed the British passenger liner *Athenia* off Rockall Bank, drowning 112 of the 1,400 people aboard. Assuming a German campaign of unrestricted submarine warfare to be in effect, on 6 September the British navy escorted its first convoys of the war. In the first days of the war Britain's aggressive anti-submarine campaign included extensive use of carrier-based aircraft, a practice which ended abruptly on 17 September, when *U 29* torpedoed and sank the carrier *Courageous* off the western approach to the English Channel (518 dead). Another dramatic U-boat success followed four weeks later, when *U 47* slipped into the harbor at Scapa Flow on the night of 13–14 October to torpedo and sink the battleship *Royal Oak* (833 dead). Meanwhile, British submarines were just as bold, operating against German commerce right into the Helgoland Bight until January 1940, when three were lost there within a single month.[33]

As dramatic as these torpedoings were, German submarines did their greatest damage by laying mines. Minefields sown by U-boats claimed over 180,000 tons of British coastal shipping in the first three months of the war alone. By the end of the year the British were developing the so-called "degaussing girdle" for ships' hulls, a demagnetization device which made them far less vulnerable to mines. Eventually degaussing girdles were fitted to the undersides of Wellington bombers, which flew low over mine-infested coastal waters, detonating German mines by generating an electromagnetic field.[34] Losses to mines declined dramatically over the next four months of the war, totaling just over 100,000 tons of Allied shipping for December 1939 through March 1940.

Of the "pocket battleships" dispatched to the Atlantic sea lanes prior to the outbreak of war, the *Deutschland* hunted for Allied targets in the North Atlantic and the *Admiral Graf Spee*, commanded by Captain Hans Langsdorff, headed for the South Atlantic. While the *Deutschland* sank less than 7,000 tons of shipping before returning home, the *Admiral Graf Spee* sank over 50,000 tons during a three-month cruise ranging from the coast of South America to the coast of southern Africa. Its career as a raider came to an end on the morning of 13 December off the mouth of the River Plate, when Langsdorff blundered into a battle with Commodore Henry Harwood's heavy cruiser *Exeter* and light cruisers *Ajax* and *Achilles*, which, from a distance, he had mistaken for a convoy of merchantmen. From the start of the war German raiders were under a standing order not to engage enemy warships, but Langsdorff could not bring himself to run from smaller ships with smaller guns. He commenced firing at 06:17, at a distance of 11 miles. Aware that the *Admiral Graf Spee*'s 11.1-inch guns outranged his heaviest ordnance (the 8-inch guns of the *Exeter*) by over four miles, Harwood made the decision to close as quickly as possible, even though his cruisers would take a pounding in the process. To force Langsdorff to divide his fire, he ordered the three ships to approach their prey from different directions. During the ninety-minute battle Langsdorff finally chose to concentrate on the *Exeter*, which took seven hits, had all of its 8-inch gun turrets disabled, and almost sank. Harwood's flagship *Ajax* suffered one hit which put two of its four 6-inch gun turrets out of action, while the *Achilles* sustained little damage. The *Admiral Graf Spee* took seventeen hits, which damaged or destroyed the ship's radar and range finder, communication systems, reconnaissance seaplane, kitchen, and bakery, forcing Langsdorff to put in at nearby Montevideo at the close of the battle, for provisions and to attempt repairs. After ordering the battered *Exeter* to Port Stanley, Harwood followed Langsdorff to Montevideo with the *Ajax* and *Achilles* and, with the help of the heavy cruiser *Cumberland*, blockaded him there. Informed that the carrier *Ark Royal* and battle cruiser *Renown* had been dispatched to the South Atlantic to further reinforce Harwood, on 17 December Langsdorff scuttled the *Admiral Graf Spee* and, afterward, committed suicide. The Battle of the River Plate was significant not only as the first Allied victory of the war, but as the first sea battle in which radar played an important part (enabling the *Admiral Graf Spee* to hit the *Exeter* accurately, from a range of over nine miles), and the first instance during the Second World War in which British disinformation influenced German actions. At the behest of the Admiralty, the BBC had deliberately beamed false reports that the *Ark Royal* and *Renown* were nearing Montevideo, when in fact they were still 1,000 miles away, off the coast of Brazil.[35]

From September 1939 through March 1940, U-boats sank 753,800 tons of Allied shipping. In terms of monthly average, the totals fell far short of the toll taken by German unrestricted submarine warfare during the First World War. Supplementing their efforts, surface raiders sank 63,000 tons, most of it sunk by the *Admiral Graf Spee* before its demise. On 21 November 1939 the *Scharnhorst* and *Gneisenau* left on their first sortie as commerce raiders but found no victims before being spotted, not far from

Iceland, by the British armed merchantman *Rawalpindi*, which alerted Scapa Flow. The *Scharnhorst* and *Gneisenau* destroyed the *Rawalpindi* but wisely aborted their cruise, and were back in Wilhelmshaven just six days after they departed. En route home they had to evade almost the entire British Home Fleet plus a French force of three battleships, two cruisers, and eight destroyers. The employment of larger German warships as raiders forced the Allies to use capital ships and carriers to hunt for them, and to escort Atlantic convoys. By December 1939 the French battleships *Dunkerque* and *Lorraine* and the carrier *Béarn* had contributed to this effort, safeguarding the transit of Canadian troops as well as American supplies purchased under the "cash and carry" policy. The French also contributed the battleship *Strasbourg* to the hunt for the *Admiral Graf Spee*.[36]

Britain sent troops to France in September 1939, where they joined the French army in waiting for the Germans to initiate a Western European campaign. Labeled the "phony war" by journalists, the period of relative inactivity extending through the winter of 1939–40 had its counterpart at sea, where the *Courageous*, *Royal Oak*, and *Admiral Graf Spee* were the only larger surface vessels sunk during the first seven months of the war. Aside from submarines, the only other warships lost were destroyers. The French suffered no losses at all until March and April 1940, when accidental explosions sank two of their destroyers.[37]

During the months of the "phony war" Hitler consolidated his gains in the east and plotted his strategy for the spring. A planned strike through Denmark to conquer Norway owed much to the influence of Raeder's old friend and navy school classmate, Wolfgang Wegener, whose *Maritime Strategy of the Great War* (1929) argued that if Germany had occupied Norway in the First World War, it could not have been blockaded successfully by the British navy. Hitler also wanted to secure his supply of Swedish iron ore, which for five months of the year reached Germany primarily via the ice-free Norwegian port of Narvik. Both Hitler and Raeder feared Britain would occupy Norway if Germany did not do so first. When the time came, the Wehrmacht rolled through Denmark in a single day, but the operation against Norway posed greater difficulties, as all troops not transported by air had to go by sea. The Germans divided their invasion force into five groups, bound for Narvik, Trondheim, Bergen, Christiansand, and Oslo. Their escorts included the battleships *Scharnhorst* and *Gneisenau*, "pocket battleship" *Deutschland* (by this time rerated as a heavy cruiser and renamed *Lützow*), heavy cruisers *Admiral Hipper* and *Blücher*, and several destroyers and torpedo boats. Most of the force was already at sea on 7 April, two days before the invasions of Denmark and Norway actually began. The first naval encounter followed on 8 April, when the *Admiral Hipper*, protecting the Trondheim group, sank a British destroyer. That afternoon, the Polish submarine *Orzel* torpedoed and sank a German troop transport off Lillesand. Convinced until the evening of 8 April that the German navy was attempting a breakout into the North Atlantic rather than escorting an invasion of Norway, the British navy responded too slowly to stop the five landings. Around dawn on 9 April the battle cruiser *Renown* attacked the escorts of the Narvik group, exchanging fire with *Scharnhorst* and *Gneisenau* and scoring several hits on the latter; otherwise, no Home Fleet capital ships engaged the enemy, and by that evening the Germans had secured their objectives. The only larger German units lost were the *Blücher*, which fell victim to Norwegian shore batteries and torpedoes on the approaches to Oslo, and the light cruiser *Karlsruhe*, sunk in the Kattegat by the Germans after being crippled by torpedoes from the British submarine *Truant*.[38]

The British counterattack began the following day, when Skua dive bombers based in the Orkneys sank the light cruiser *Königsberg* at Bergen. Subsequent engagements at Narvik on 10 April and 13 April sank a number of destroyers. In a series of landings beginning on 14 April, Allied warships put ashore an Anglo–French force of 11,000 to retake Trondheim, but they met with stiff resistance and by 3 May all were evacuated. The Allies concluded that their chances would be better farther to the north, where the Germans were weaker. On 21 May the carriers *Furious* and *Glorious* provided air cover for the landing of an Anglo–French force of 25,000 near Narvik, which was taken a week later. Meanwhile, after 10 May the German invasion of the Low Countries and France relegated the Norwegian campaign to a peripheral operation. With France nearing collapse, on 7 June Allied troops were evacuated from Narvik. The *Scharnhorst* and *Gneisenau* arrived to harass the operation and, the following day, intercepted the *Glorious* as it steamed home to Scapa Flow. Opening fire at 16:30 at a range of 28,000 yards, they used salvoes from their 11.1-inch guns to sink the carrier and two escorting destroyers (1,429 dead). The *Glorious* thus earned the dubious distinction of being the only aircraft carrier ever sunk by battleship gunfire. The heavy cruiser *Effingham* (wrecked on 17 May, and later scuttled) and light cruiser *Curlew* (bombed and sunk on 26 May) were the only other British warships larger than destroyers lost in the Norwegian campaign. Aside from the *Glorious*, the two cruisers were also the largest British warships sunk in all of 1940. In defeat, the British navy lost 1 carrier, 1 heavy cruiser, 2 light cruisers, 5 destroyers, and 1 sloop, while the French lost 1 destroyer. In victory, the German navy lost 1 heavy cruiser, 2 light cruisers, and 10 destroyers (almost half of their prewar stock), while assorted damages would keep the *Scharnhorst*, *Gneisenau*, *Lützow*, and *Admiral Hipper* in port for the rest of the year.[39]

Ironically, the bungled, indecisive Norwegian campaign, for which Churchill was largely responsible in his capacity as First Lord of the Admiralty, helped bring about the fall of Neville Chamberlain on 10 May 1940 and the appointment of Churchill as prime minister.

Churchill relinquished the portfolio of First Lord but, as prime minister, continued to direct the naval war in consultation with the Admiralty.[40] As early as 19 May, nine days after Germany invaded the Low Countries and France, the campaign was going badly enough for the Admiralty to begin planning a mass evacuation of the British Expeditionary Force from the European mainland. The withdrawal began a week later and lasted until 4 June. A total of 224,686 men of the BEF were evacuated from Dunkirk, along with 141,445 other Allied troops, most of them French. Of the 693 British ships of all sizes (including ferries, private yachts, and old paddle steamers) participating in the evacuation, 226 were sunk, of which 56 were naval vessels, most of them minesweepers or transports. Dunkirk was not the only evacuation site. On 24 May British and French destroyers carried troops from Calais and Boulogne to Britain, and between 4 June and 25 June, another 191,870 Allied troops and 35,000 civilians were evacuated from ports ranging from Le Havre to Saint-Jean de Luz near the Spanish border. The biggest loss during this phase was the troopship *Lancastria*, which the Germans bombed and sank at Saint-Nazaire, killing 3,000 of the 5,800 men packed aboard. On 16 June Marshal Philippe Pétain became French premier, with a mandate to seek an armistice with the Germans. The following day Admiral Darlan became his navy minister. On 18 June, the same day that General Charles de Gaulle, already in Britain, urged the French people via radio to continue the struggle, Darlan issued similar instructions to his captains to continue to "resist to the utmost" and, if necessary, either scuttle their ships or take them to the safety of North Africa. On the eve of the German occupation of the French Atlantic ports, the French scuttled four submarines and broke up another four that were still under construction. During the evacuations the British and French navies limited their losses by employing no warships larger than destroyers. By the time the Pétain government concluded an armistice with the Germans on 22 June, ending the Battle of France, the French navy had lost eight destroyers and two submarines to enemy action. Between 10 May and 25 June the British lost a total of eleven destroyers in operations along the French coast.[41]

After France left the war, Britain fully expected Germany to launch a cross-Channel invasion in the near future. Destroyer losses during the recent evacuation operations made it difficult for the British to organize their defenses; it helped them considerably that so many German destroyers had been lost during the Norwegian campaign. As early as 19 June German motor torpedo boats or S-boats (*Schnellboote*; see Plate 39) began to operate against British merchant shipping in the Channel. In July the Luftwaffe joined the fray, concentrating its efforts along the east coast of Britain, where convoys suffered 75,700 tons of losses in July alone. By August the Luftwaffe was sowing mines in harbors as distant as Belfast and Liverpool. During September the British finally counterattacked, using destroyers and motor torpedo boats to raid the French and Belgian coasts, in particular targeting German convoys entering Ostend.[42]

Meanwhile, on 16 July Hitler issued a directive to his armed forces to prepare for an invasion of Britain. He envisaged a series of landings all along the Channel coast, perhaps after preliminary operations to secure the Isle of Wight or Cornwall. To prepare the way for the invasion, the Luftwaffe was to destroy the RAF and secure air superiority, while the Luftwaffe and the German navy were to wear down the strength of the British Home Fleet. Hitler counted upon Italy, which had entered the war on 10 June, to use its navy to keep the British Mediterranean Fleet occupied.[43] While Hitler and his generals wanted a broad beachhead or series of beachheads, Raeder realized that under such a plan the German navy would have to secure most, if not all, of the Channel to facilitate the crossings and sustain the troops once they landed, an impossibility given the resources at hand. He argued for a single smaller beachhead, which would require the navy to hold only a small sector of the Channel. In late August the army and navy agreed to a compromise plan, and the invasion was scheduled for the last ten days of September, contingent upon the Luftwaffe first securing air superiority. Meanwhile, the navy began sowing two extensive minefields across the Channel, from the French coast to the British, in an attempt to seal the eastern and western flanks of the projected invasion route. The invasion force was to consist of between 100,000 and 150,000 troops. To transport them and their supplies across the Channel, the Germans assembled 567 steamers and tugs, each of which was to tow two barges. With a total of 1,939 barges prepared, most of the towboats were expected to make two crossings; some barges, however, were equipped with engines and could have moved under their own power. Large ferries were requisitioned to carry tanks and heavy equipment. To supplement the efforts of larger surface vessels, the navy assembled a force of 994 motorboats to help escort the barges and support the landings. When the Luftwaffe failed to accomplish its mission before 1 October, deteriorating weather conditions in the Channel forced the postponement of the operation until the spring of 1941, by which time Hitler had resolved to invade Russia instead.[44]

From the first collection of invasion equipment until the onset of bad weather made it clear the operation would not take place during 1940, the British navy and RAF did what they could to disrupt the German preparations. The Channel skirmishes of July–October 1940 were primarily actions by destroyers, torpedo boats, and land-based aircraft, but Britain also used the monitor *Erebus*, which bombarded Calais on 30 September and 16 October, and the battleship *Revenge*, which bombarded Cherbourg on 10 October, in each case escorted by destroyers.

These attacks destroyed a number of German barges and other invasion craft. In the meantime, the German minefields laid in the Channel took a heavy toll. Between July and December the British lost another 11 destroyers; overall, 28 of the 42 small British naval vessels sunk in the Channel between September and December 1940 were claimed by German mines.[45]

With the British concentrating their destroyers in the Channel to cover the evacuation of troops from France and, subsequently, in anticipation of a German invasion, U-boats met with little opposition in the Atlantic shipping lanes, where an early wartime high of almost 300,000 tons was sunk during June 1940. Allied convoys were especially vulnerable in the central North Atlantic "Air Gap," waters which could not be covered by land-based Allied aircraft operating from eastern Canada, Iceland, the Azores, or the British Isles. Without ever having more than 15 U-boats at sea at any given time, during the autumn of 1940 the German submarine campaign caused the greatest crisis to British security since the summer of 1917. Still, the sinking totals never approached those of the most deadly months of the First World War and, in any event, success came at a high price. In the first fifteen months of the war 31 U-boats were lost, leaving Germany with just 22 in service by the end of 1940. With submarine construction not yet a priority item, the German navy was losing U-boats faster than they were being replaced. Furthermore, like aircraft, submarines could be built much faster than crews could be trained; this was especially true in the German navy, which required nine months of rigorous training in the relative safety of the Baltic before a crew was sent out into the Atlantic. The Germans were able to maintain their challenge only because the British anti-submarine effort suffered from a lack of destroyers. In an effort to address the shortage, in September 1940 Britain struck a destroyers-for-bases deal with the United States, granting 99-year leases and lease options on bases in Newfoundland, Bermuda, the British West Indies, and British Guiana in exchange for 50 surplus US navy destroyers (launched 1917–20), 7 of which were assigned to the Canadian navy for convoy escort duties in the western Atlantic. At least on paper the remaining 43 more than compensated for the 34 destroyers Britain had lost during 1940, but in fact the ships took a while to refurbish and, even then, were poor substitutes for the larger, newer units they replaced. In the long run their value to the British war effort was more symbolic than real.[46]

During the last eight months of 1940 the German navy deployed seven armed merchantmen as raiders, to prey upon undefended Allied merchantmen cruising alone. The most successful, the *Atlantis*, sank 145,700 tons between April 1940 and December 1941. Unable to detach warships to deal with the threat, the British navy commissioned 50 armed merchantmen of its own, but these did not fare well against their more heavily armed German counterparts and even worse against conventional German warships. During the first six months of 1941 land-based aircraft based in Norway and France did more damage than U-boats to Allied shipping in the Atlantic and North Sea. The longest-range Luftwaffe planes, four-engine Fw 200 Kondors, were able to attack Atlantic convoys west of Ireland from bases at Stavanger and Bordeaux. In April 1941 the Luftwaffe sank a wartime peak of 116 ships (323,000 tons).[47]

After staying in port for most of 1940, recovering from the Norwegian campaign, late in the year the largest German surface ships again put to sea as commerce raiders. Between October 1940 and March 1941, the *Admiral Scheer* cruised in both the Atlantic and Indian oceans. Between November 1940 and April 1941, the *Admiral Hipper* conducted three sorties: from the Baltic into the central North Atlantic by way of the Arctic (passing between Iceland and Greenland via the Denmark Strait), then into Brest; out of Brest to the vicinity of the Azores; and from Brest via the Denmark Strait to return to the Baltic. In January 1941 Vice Admiral Günther Lütjens took the battleships *Scharnhorst* and *Gneisenau* out of the Baltic for a cruise via the Denmark Strait into the central North Atlantic. On 8 February he engaged the British battleship *Ramillies* and, on 7 March, while hunting for merchantmen between the Cape Verde Islands and Canary Islands, his ships dueled with the battleship *Malaya*. The sortie ended when the *Scharnhorst* and *Gneisenau* put in at Brest two weeks later. Victims of the four raiders included 48 Allied merchantmen either sunk or captured (totaling 270,000 tons) and one enemy warship sunk, the British armed merchant cruiser *Jervis Bay* (by the *Admiral Scheer*, 5 November 1940). Considering the material assets placed at risk, and the manpower and operating costs involved, the results were meager indeed, yet Raeder considered the sorties a success worth repeating. From Brest, Lütjens returned to Germany overland to receive command of the battleship *Bismarck* and heavy cruiser *Prinz Eugen*, both commissioned in August 1940, neither of which had yet ventured out into the Atlantic. Plans called for Lütjens to take them on the same general course as the raid of January–March 1941. The sortie out of the Baltic by the *Bismarck* and *Prinz Eugen* was supposed to coincide with a sortie from Brest by the *Scharnhorst* and *Gneisenau*, but the former required such extensive engine repairs that it could not put to sea again that soon, while the latter suffered heavy damage during an air raid on 6 April 1941, at the hands of an RAF torpedo bomber. Rather than postpone the operation, Raeder decided to have Lütjens proceed with the *Bismarck* and *Prinz Eugen* alone.[48]

The *Bismarck* had spent its first nine months in commission either in port or working up on brief cruises in the Baltic. It left the Baltic on 19 May, passed through the Kattegat and Skaggerak, then hugged the coast of Norway while steaming northward, before heading westward into the Atlantic, setting a course to the north of Iceland. In addition to the *Prinz Eugen*, its group included a supply ship, six tankers, two patrol ships, and three weather ships, which scattered into the Arctic and North Atlantic. Until the *Bismarck* was safely out into the Atlantic, three destroyers and three minesweepers provided an escort. The big battleship made it all the way to the Denmark Strait before being sighted on the evening of 23 May by the British heavy cruisers *Norfolk* and *Suffolk*, part of a large force under Vice Admiral Lancelot Holland dispatched to hunt it down. At 05:35 the following morning, Holland's flagship, the battle cruiser *Hood*, sighted the *Bismarck* from a distance of 17 miles and closed to engage. At 05:53 the *Hood* fired the first salvo of the battle, at a range of 26,500 yards. The *Bismarck* soon responded, and at 06:00 its third salvo of shells, fired from 20,000 yards, landed directly on *Hood*'s deck, causing a catastrophic explosion. The ship went down with almost all hands (3 of 1,419 men aboard survived). The *Prinz Eugen* emerged from the brief engagement unscathed. The *Hood*'s escort, the new battleship *Prince of Wales*, sustained damage to its bridge and one gun turret, but managed to score three hits on the *Bismarck*, causing it to leak oil. As the ships disengaged, Admiral Lütjens ordered the *Prinz Eugen* to proceed with the commerce raiding mission on its own, while he took the *Bismarck* to Saint-Nazaire on the Atlantic coast of France, the nearest German-controlled port with a dry dock that could accommodate such a large ship. Admiral Sir John Tovey then pursued the *Bismarck* with elements of the Home Fleet, joined by Admiral James Somerville's Gibraltar task force (Force H), formed the previous summer and normally deployed against the Italian navy in the western Mediterranean.[49]

By 26 May the British armada closing in on the *Bismarck* included five battleships, two carriers, and nine cruisers. That morning, British aerial reconnaissance sighted the *Bismarck* 700 miles due west of Brest. During the day Somerville's carrier *Ark Royal* drew within striking range, and around 21:30, its Swordfish torpedo bombers succeeded in torpedoing the *Bismarck*, seriously damaging its propellers and rudder. The ship came to a halt, dead in the water, still over 300 miles from the French coast. On the morning of 27 May Tovey's battleships *King George V* and *Rodney* closed to finish off the *Bismarck*. The stationary target took a tremendous beating but remained afloat, a smouldering wreck. The heavy cruisers *Norfolk* and *Dorsetshire* eventually joined the attack, firing torpedoes into the *Bismarck*'s hull. It finally sank at 10:40. To this day German sources persist in claiming that the ship went down only after being scuttled by its own crew, while British sources insist with equal vigor that the ship was sunk by British action. Just 115 men survived the disaster, picked up by the British cruisers before they departed the scene, fearful that a U-boat might torpedo them during their rescue operation. The German dead, either in the water or aboard the *Bismarck*, numbered 1,977, including Admiral Lütjens. The death toll remains the greatest ever suffered by a European navy in the destruction of a single warship.[50]

Within a week British warships also captured or sank the *Bismarck's* supply ship and four of its tankers, leaving the *Prinz Eugen* unable to function as a raider. The cruiser made it safely to Brest where, along with the *Scharnhorst* and *Gneisenau*, it remained pinned down for the rest of 1941 thanks to frequent RAF bombing raids. Two weeks after the loss of the *Bismarck* the heavy cruiser *Lützow* left Kiel with a destroyer escort, on a mission to raid the North Atlantic sea lanes, but on 12 June it was sighted off Lindesnes, Norway, and torpedoed by RAF aircraft. The *Lützow* returned safely to Kiel two days later, then remained out of action for six months while being repaired. The aborted sortie of the *Lützow* was the last German attempt to send a battleship or heavy cruiser into the Atlantic sea lanes as a commerce raider.[51]

The British navy celebrated the sinking of the *Bismarck* as its greatest victory of the Second World War. In the long run, however, a far less celebrated engagement earlier the same month had a far greater impact on the course of the conflict at sea. On 8 May 1941, while escorting an Atlantic convoy, the destroyer *Bulldog* forced *U 110* to the surface with depth charges. The German crew set explosive charges to scuttle the boat, but after they abandoned ship the charges failed to detonate. A British boarding party captured *U 110's* Enigma code machine intact, and by the summer of 1941 the British were able to decipher virtually all coded messages sent by the German navy. The Germans knew the Enigma machine had been lost but had such faith in the indecipher-ability of their own coding system that they assumed the intelligence leaks must be coming from elsewhere, and wasted considerable resources for the remainder of the war trying to resolve the problem. By October 1941 the Germans had 40 U-boats in the Atlantic, but in November they sank just 62,000 tons, the lowest total for any month since May 1940. By then, the British had registered another coup in the anti-submarine war, as aircraft in August 1941 forced *U 570* to surface and surrender southwest of Iceland. The damaged boat was towed to Iceland, first to be repaired and recommissioned as HMS *Graph*, then decommissioned for use in depth-charge tests which provided valuable data on the structural strength of U-boat hulls.[52]

During the summer and autumn of 1941 the United States moved closer to direct involvement in the Atlantic war. Following the destroyers-for-bases deal of September 1940, the US Congress in March 1941 passed the Lend-Lease Act, granting President Franklin Roosevelt $7 billion for war matériel which he could then sell, loan, or trade to any country whose security he considered vital to the security of the United States. On 10–12 August Churchill and Roosevelt held a series of meetings aboard the *Prince of Wales* and heavy cruiser USS *Augusta* off the coast of Newfoundland, where they signed the Atlantic Charter. The United States committed to escort fast convoys between Newfoundland and Iceland, while the Canadian navy continued to protect slower convoys on the same western segment of the transatlantic route. The US navy took up these duties on 17 September, almost three months before the United States entered the war against Germany. The United States further supported the anti-submarine war by building escort carriers for the British navy. The 10,220-ton *Archer* (16 aircraft, 16.5 knots) was the first delivered, in November 1941. By then, Britain already had one escort carrier in service, the *Audacity* (6 aircraft, 15 knots), built between January and June 1941 on the hull of a captured German merchantman. British shipyards converted another 5, commissioned between October 1942 and March 1944, while American shipyards provided another 37 after the United States entered the war, commissioned between March 1942 and November 1944. Most escort carriers displaced just over 10,000 tons, carried between 15 and 24 aircraft, and steamed at 15–18 knots, too slow to be useful in most combat situations but fast enough to serve as convoy defenders. Some eventually saw duty in anti-submarine warfare operations, in amphibious landings, and as aircraft ferries. As luck would have it, the first British escort carrier to enter service was also the first to be sunk. On 22 December 1941, *U 751* torpedoed and sank the *Audacity* during an attack on a convoy in the North Atlantic. During the rest of the war the British navy lost just 4 of the other 43 escort carriers it commissioned: another 3 to U-boats, 1 to an accident in harbor.[53]

THE MEDITERRANEAN WAR (1940–43)

When Italy entered the war on 10 June 1940, its navy included 6 battleships, 7 heavy and 12 light cruisers, while the British Mediterranean Fleet had 5 battleships, 1 aircraft carrier, 4 heavy and 10 light cruisers, with another pair of capital ships and a second carrier at Gibraltar in Somerville's Force H. Meanwhile, the French navy in the Mediterranean had 5 battleships, 3 heavy and 7 light cruisers. Mussolini delayed Italy's entry into the war as long as he could, but not quite long enough to please Admiral Cavagnari. The new 40,725-ton battleships *Vittorio Veneto* and *Littorio*, just commissioned in the spring of 1940, would not be ready until August, and the renovation of the battleships *Andrea Doria* and *Caio Duilio* would not be completed until July and October, respectively. The British navy, focusing on the evacuation operations along the French coast, then on defending against the expected German cross-Channel invasion, was in no position to take advantage of Italy's temporary weakness. A Franco–Italian armistice signed on 24 June, two days after the

Franco–German armistice, removed the French navy from the equation, leaving the British alone in the Mediterranean to face an Italian navy superior in all warship types except battleships and aircraft carriers, and vastly superior in destroyers (with over 50) and submarines (with over 100).[54]

Once all six Italian battleships were in service and the Italian air force was fully engaged, the British would lose their only advantages. But when faced with the prospect of waging war, Cavagnari forgot his bravado of the mid-1930s, his eagerness to take on the Anglo–French combination from a 2:3 disadvantage, and his plans for an "escape fleet" capable of dominating the Mediterranean and operating outside of it. Like all other Italian naval leaders, he favored a conservative strategy. The chief of the general staff, Marshal Pietro Badoglio, valued the navy primarily as a fleet-in-being, and in September 1940 ordered it to limit its operations to protecting Axis convoys and attacking Allied convoys. The Italian navy would take few risks, always refusing battle when outnumbered or outgunned and never engaging the enemy at night.[55] Nevertheless, the Italians remained strong enough, and aggressive enough, to require the British to use capital ships and fleet carriers to keep their Gibraltar–Malta–Alexandria supply line open.

Throughout the Mediterranean war, the British base at Malta remained a thorn in the side of the Axis. On the day Italy declared war, Britain had only 4,000 troops and eight naval aircraft stationed on the island. Taking advantage of its overwhelming superiority, the Italian air force bombed the island seven times between 10 June and 20 June. The British soon reinforced Malta and, thereafter, kept just enough air and naval assets there to make it prohibitively costly for the Italians to take it. By July 1941 Britain's Malta forces included 30,000 troops and 180 aircraft.[56]

The day after Italy entered the war, a British force shelled Tobruk in Italian Libya. On 14 June, in the only significant French naval action against Italy before the fall of France, a force from Toulon shelled Genoa. During the first three weeks of the war, the Italian navy lost a destroyer and ten submarines, four of the latter in the Red Sea. The British seized Italian code books from the submarine *Galileo*, captured after a malfunction in its cooling system forced it to surface. Meanwhile, on 12 June, the Italian submarine *Bagnolini* torpedoed and sank the British light cruiser *Calypso* off Crete. In the first week of the Mediterranean war, Italian destroyers and torpedo boats also sank three British submarines.[57]

As the Mediterranean campaign entered its second month, Britain's attentions temporarily shifted away from the Italian navy to the French navy, which, under Article Eight of the Franco–German armistice of 22 June, was to retain in commission only those warships necessary to defend the French colonial empire, and to disarm the rest under the control (*contrôle*) of the Axis powers. The Germans guaranteed that they would not seek to use the French navy in their own war effort and would claim no French ships as war booty in an eventual permanent peace treaty. As recently as 11 June Admiral Darlan had personally assured Churchill that the French fleet would never be surrendered to the Axis; he accepted the armistice because it left the French navy anchored in French ports, manned by French crews. But Churchill recognized that a mere promise from Hitler was the only thing now keeping the French navy out of Axis hands; he also understood *contrôle* to have the same meaning as "control" in the English language, rather than its proper French meaning indicating a right of oversight or supervision. Churchill responded with an ultimatum to French navy leaders offering them the following options: to defy the armistice and continue to fight alongside the British; to turn their warships over to Britain; to "demilitarize" or scuttle their ships where they were; or to cruise to the French West Indies where their ships would be either "demilitarized" or entrusted to the United States for the remainder of the war. At the time of the armistice the main body of the French Mediterranean Fleet was anchored at Oran (Mers-el-Kébir), Algeria, under the command of Admiral Marcel Gensoul. To support the ultimatum, the British navy sent Admiral Somerville from Gibraltar to Oran with the newly formed Force H, including the carrier *Ark Royal*, the battleships *Valiant* and *Resolution*, and the battle cruiser *Hood*. Somerville personally opposed the operation, but after Gensoul rejected all of the options offered in the British ultimatum, on 3 July he ordered his ships to open fire on their former allies. Gunfire all but destroyed the battleship *Bretagne* and sank two destroyers, while the battleships *Dunkerque* and *Provence* sustained heavy damage. After nightfall on 3 July the battleship *Strasbourg* and five destroyers slipped out of port and made it safely to Toulon, surviving attacks by Swordfish from the *Ark Royal*. The following day, Swordfish from the carrier finished off *Bretagne* with torpedoes and also sank the auxiliary ship *Terre Neuve*. French dead totaled 1,297.[58]

Elsewhere, the Anglo–French confrontations of 3 July were less dramatic and less tragic. At Alexandria, Admiral René Godfroy agreed to a peaceful deactivation of the rest of the French Mediterranean Fleet, a squadron which included the battleship *Lorraine*, four cruisers, three destroyers and a submarine that had been operating in the Eastern Mediterranean alongside the main body of the British Mediterranean Fleet, under Admiral Sir Andrew Cunningham. At Plymouth and Portsmouth, units of the French Atlantic Fleet were boarded without warning, but the battleships *Paris* and *Courbet*, ten destroyers, and a host of smaller warships surrendered peacefully along with six submarines. Aboard a seventh submarine, the *Surcouf*, the crew's resistance resulted in one French and three British deaths. Meanwhile, the new battleship *Richelieu*, launched at Brest in January 1939 and 95 percent complete, and its sister-ship *Jean Bart*, launched at Saint-Nazaire in March 1940 and 75 percent complete, got under way just before the armistice and steamed for Dakar and Casablanca, respectively. The *Jean Bart* remained in the French Moroccan port, unmolested, while the *Richelieu* withstood two British attacks, in July 1940 by aircraft from the carrier *Hermes*, and in September 1940 by aircraft from the *Ark Royal*, the latter during a failed British and Free French attempt to seize Senegal. The aircraft carrier *Béarn* was at Halifax at the time of the armistice, preparing to transport new aircraft to France. It steamed for the West Indies but did not comply with the British ultimatum until May 1942, when it was demilitarized at Martinique along with two cruisers.[59]

The attack at Oran had a sequence of unintended consequences. The dramatic act of British hostility against France helped legitimize the decision of Marshal Pétain to collaborate with the Germans after the armistice. Governing unoccupied France from its capital at Vichy, the Pétain regime subsequently used Oran as the cornerstone of an anti-British propaganda campaign. Though personally neither an Anglophobe (he was married to an Englishwoman) nor a fascist, Darlan became a symbol of defiance to the British and the leading Vichy political figure under the octogenarian Pétain. The admiral retained his portfolio as navy minister while also being entrusted at various times with the ministries of foreign affairs, war, the interior, and information. A significant share of French public opinion remained staunchly opposed to the Allied cause even after the United States entered the war, and at least until 1943 De Gaulle would have difficulty recruiting for the Free French, owing to the fact that Churchill and the British were his primary benefactors. Meanwhile, Hitler moved quickly to capitalize on the impact of the attack on the French public and within the French navy: on 4 July 1940 he suspended Article Eight of the armistice, allowing Vichy France to keep all of its remaining warships in commission. This, in turn, guaranteed that most of what remained of the French navy would stay loyal to Pétain. More to defy the British than to help the Germans, the French made an extraordinary effort to salvage the *Provence* and *Dunkerque* (the latter after it was further damaged, again by Swordfish from the *Ark Royal*, in a second, limited British strike against Oran in October 1940). Ultimately both battleships steamed from Oran to Toulon, to join the *Strasbourg* and other remnants of the Mediterranean Fleet. France's colonies likewise remained loyal to Pétain, securing, for the time being, the *Jean Bart* at Casablanca, the *Richelieu* at Dakar, and the *Béarn* at Martinique. In addition to its larger warships, the navy of Vichy France included 13 cruisers, 42 destroyers, 61 submarines, and 11 armed merchantmen. Thus, a British operation intended to deny the use of the French navy to the Axis resulted in the destruction of just one French battleship, the *Bretagne*, and the seizure of another three, all of which had been built before the First World War. The newest French battleships remained out of Allied hands, along with France's only carrier and most of its cruisers and smaller warships.[60]

The attack at Oran also made it all but impossible for the Free French to form a navy. Initially the only senior naval officer to collaborate with De Gaulle was Vice Admiral Emile Muselier, whom Darlan had forced to retire in October 1939. His colorful band of followers included Captain Georges Thierry d'Argenlieu, a veteran of the First World War who had spent the interwar years as a Catholic priest before returning to active duty. Their task would have been hopeless if not for the patronage of Churchill, who considered a Free French navy the key to rallying the French colonies behind the Allied cause. Muselier used the old battleship *Courbet* as a stationary headquarters and, with British help, repaired and manned several of the smaller French units interned in British ports. Along with Thierry d'Argenlieu, he persuaded De Gaulle to add the Cross of Lorraine to the flag of the resistance, to distinguish Free French vessels from those of Vichy France. By November 1940 the navy had enlisted 3,100 men, many of them from the French merchant marine. Early surface units reactivated included the large destroyers *Triomphant* and *Léopard*, which Thierry d'Argenlieu, armed with the rank of rear admiral, took to the Pacific in 1941 on a "political mission" to French possessions there. Before falling out with De Gaulle in the spring of 1942, Muselier personally led the "political mission" which secured for the Free French the islands of Saint-Pierre and Miquelon, off the Canadian coast. Between 1941 and 1943, the British gave the Free French nine newly constructed corvettes, antisubmarine patrol craft displacing around 1,000 tons (generally smaller than the sloops and frigates built for the same purpose), a modest contribution from a program of 170 such vessels built for their own navy in the years 1940–44.[61] Until it commissioned its first battleships and cruisers in 1943, the Free French navy remained a negligible force in the war at sea. The Vichy French navy played no role other than to defend Toulon and the colonial ports where its active warships remained. Pétain's government, though collaborating with the Axis, remained technically neutral, and in any event neither the German nor the Italian navies trusted the French as allies.

Less than one week after the British attack at Oran, the first significant Anglo–Italian sea battle of the war occurred in the Ionian Sea, off Punta Stilo on the Calabrian coast. On 9 July 1940, while escorting a convoy from Alexandria to Malta, the main body of Cunningham's British Mediterranean Fleet, including the battleships *Warspite*, *Malaya*, and *Royal Sovereign*, the carrier *Eagle*, five cruisers, and several destroyers, engaged a force under the Italian fleet commander, Admiral Inigo

Campioni, consisting of the battleships *Giulio Cesare* and *Conte di Cavour*, the heavy cruisers *Trento* and *Bolzano*, and a number of light cruisers and smaller vessels, supported by land-based Italian aircraft. Neither side lost a ship but the *Warspite*, at a range of 26,000 yards, scored hits on the *Giulio Cesare*, reducing its speed to 18 knots and forcing Campioni to break off the action. Italian air attacks during the battle and after Cunningham's arrival at Malta ultimately left the *Eagle* so badly damaged that it had to spend four months in dry dock. Ten days later, in the Aegean Sea off Cape Spada, the Australian light cruiser *Sydney* and five British destroyers engaged the Italian light cruisers *Bartolomeo Colleoni* and *Bande Nere*. Gunfire from the *Sydney* disabled the *Bartolomeo Colleoni*, which the destroyers then sank.[62]

The British more than made good on the temporary loss of the *Eagle* by sending Cunningham the new 23,000-ton fleet carrier *Illustrious*, which arrived at Malta in late August. On the night of 11 November twenty-one Swordfish from the *Illustrious* attacked the Italian fleet at Taranto, where five of Italy's six battleships were anchored. Their torpedoes hit the *Conte di Cavour*, the *Caio Duilio* and the *Littorio*, badly damaging all three. The *Littorio* was out of action for four months, the *Caio Duilio* for six months. The *Cavour*, which sank completely, was later raised and refitted to serve as a harbor watch at Trieste, where it was sunk for good by RAF bombers on 17 February 1945. Thirteen months before Pearl Harbor, the British navy had demonstrated that a fleet of battleships could be crippled by air attack alone. The Italians, still without radar at the time, were caught completely by surprise. The operation seriously discredited Admiral Cavagnari, who had assured Mussolini that such a thing could not happen at Taranto.[63]

After the Taranto raid, the Italian navy concentrated its three remaining undamaged battleships at Naples, considered a safer anchorage owing to its distance from Malta. On 27 November Campioni took 2 of these battleships, the *Vittorio Veneto* and *Andrea Doria*, along with 7 heavy cruisers and 14 destroyers on a sortie against the Gibraltar–Malta convoy route. At the Battle of Cape Teulada (also called the Battle of Cape Spartivento), southwest of Sardinia, he encountered Somerville's Force H, including the battleships *Renown* and *Ramillies*, the carrier *Ark Royal*, 1 heavy cruiser, 4 light cruisers, and 14 destroyers, escorting a convoy to Malta. Under standing orders not to risk his battleships, Campioni reversed course for Italian waters shortly after sighting the British force. The Italian battleships survived Swordfish attacks from the *Ark Royal*, but the tables were turned once Somerville pursued Campioni within range of Italian air bases on Sardinia; the *Ark Royal* then became the target of Italian bombers, escaping with minor damage. The indecisive battle, coming on the heels of the debacle at Taranto, prompted Mussolini to sack both Cavagnari and Campioni. Admiral Arturo Riccardi became naval chief of staff, while Admiral

Angelo Iachino became fleet commander. The new Italian command team faced an immediate crisis owing to four British air raids on Naples (14 December 1940–8 January 1941) which damaged the battleships *Vittorio Veneto* and *Giulio Cesare*, along with the heavy cruiser *Pola*.[64] As the year drew to a close, the Italian navy faced the new task of supporting the army's invasion of Greece, launched in late October from Italian-occupied Albania. Operations included securing a supply line across the Otranto Straits and harassing British attempts to aid the Greeks.

During its first seven months as a belligerent, Italy owed all of its successes to air and submarine attacks, the audacity of which contrasted sharply with the conservatism of Italian generals in their handling of ground forces, as well as Italian admirals in their direction of surface warships. Italian bombers struck British oil refineries at Haifa in Palestine several times during the summer of 1940, and on 19 October four Italian bombers conducted the longest-distance air raid of the European theater of the Second World War, striking oil fields in Bahrain on the Persian Gulf in a further effort to disrupt British oil supplies. Such long-distance raids were rarely undertaken by the Italians, who had few bombers with that sort of range; indeed, for that very reason the Italian air force rarely attacked Gibraltar. In the undersea campaign, as early as July 1940 Italy sent submarines through the Strait of Gibraltar and into the Atlantic sea lanes. By late October, 17 Italian submarines were operating from bases on the German-occupied Atlantic coast of France. They scored their first successes during November, against convoys on the route between Britain and West Africa.[65]

As the new year began, the ebb and flow of the North African campaign turned decidedly against the Italian army. The Italians had invaded Egypt in September 1940, but in early December a British counteroffensive drove them back into Libya, where they were pursued to Tobruk, which fell on 22 January 1941. The only Italian naval vessel lost in the campaign was the old armored cruiser *San Giorgio*, employed as a floating battery at Tobruk, where it was scuttled on the day of the surrender. The defeat was far more costly for the Italian army, which in barely six weeks lost over 100,000 prisoners. As the British counteroffensive rolled westward, Hitler decided to intervene. In early January, over a month before Field Marshal Erwin Rommel's Afrika Corps deployed in Libya, Luftwaffe aircraft arrived in Sicily to reinforce the Italian effort against the British navy and convoys in the Mediterranean. The Germans never sent as many dive bombers to Italian airfields as the Italians requested, but at this stage those deployed tipped the balance in the air war decisively in favor of the Axis. On 10 January, west of Malta, Stukas attacked and seriously damaged the carrier *Illustrious*, which survived largely because of its armored deck. The same day, bombs damaged the cruiser *Southampton* so badly that it had to be scuttled. Over the next two weeks, the *Illustrious* endured several more German air raids at Malta before being withdrawn to Alexandria. The patched-up carrier then steamed via the Suez Canal and Cape of Good Hope to the increasingly less neutral United States, where the Norfolk Navy Yard repaired the bomb damage. Meanwhile, in late March the newly completed *Formidable* replaced the *Illustrious* in Cunningham's Mediterranean Fleet, ending a period of two and a half months during which the British navy, lacking adequate air cover, had been unable to resupply Malta, which the Luftwaffe had subjected to daily bombings. As Rommel's Afrika Corps prepared to deploy in Libya, Admiral Raeder tried to persuade Hitler that Malta should be taken first, but to no avail. Rommel considered the island insignificant relative to the numbers of troops that would have to be sacrificed in order to secure it. On 14 February the first elements of the Afrika Korps landed in Libya; six weeks later, Rommel launched his first offensive against the British. The Italian navy convoyed Rommel's force safely across the central Mediterranean without the loss of a single transport to British action. The achievement came against the expectations of the British army commander, Field Marshal Sir Archibald Wavell, who had assured Churchill that "the inefficiency of the Italian navy" would prevent the deployment of large numbers of German troops in North Africa. The only warship sinkings during those weeks came in late February, when the British submarine *Upright* torpedoed and sank the Italian light cruiser *Armando Diaz* off Kerkenah Island, while the Luftwaffe sank the British monitor *Terror* and a destroyer off the North African coast.[66]

As Rommel stood poised to turn the North African campaign back in favor of the Axis, the Italian navy suffered a serious defeat in the Battle of Cape Matapan (28 March 1941) off the southern tip of Greece. In the daylong action, Admiral Iachino's force consisting of the battleship *Vittorio Veneto*, 8 cruisers and 13 destroyers, attempting to disrupt British convoys between Alexandria and Greece, engaged the main body of Cunningham's Mediterranean Fleet, including the just-arrived carrier *Formidable*, the battleships *Warspite*, *Barham*, and *Valiant*, 4 cruisers, and 13 destroyers. Aircraft from the *Formidable* torpedoed and damaged the *Vittorio Veneto* and the cruiser *Pola*, forcing the Italians to scuttle the latter. Meanwhile, as the action continued after dark, gunfire from the *Warspite* and *Valiant* sank the cruiser *Fiume*, and fire from all three British battleships damaged the cruiser *Zara* so badly that it had to be scuttled. Cape Matapan marked the last time that a British fleet would ever meet an enemy fleet in battle on the high seas. Cunningham directed his forces brilliantly, taking full advantage not only of the *Formidable*'s aircraft but of his ships' radar, the existence of which the Italians finally discovered, thanks to an intercepted radio transmission during the battle. In addition to the *Pola*, *Fiume*, and *Zara* – all heavy cruisers with 8-inch guns – the Italians lost two destroyers, while the British lost no ships at all. Nevertheless, Cunningham was disappointed at not having sunk the *Vittorio Veneto*, which made it safely home, damaged badly enough to require four months of repairs. The impact of the British victory at Cape Matapan would have been greater if not for Italian successes the same week in the waters off Crete, where an MAS boat sank the cruiser *York* (26 March) and the submarine *Ambra* sank the cruiser *Bonaventure* (31 March).[67]

A week after Rommel launched his first offensive in North Africa, Germany also intervened to support Italy in the Balkans, on 6 April 1941 attacking both Yugoslavia and Greece. The Yugoslavs capitulated in eleven days, the Greeks in eighteen. The unexpected sudden collapse of Greece trapped some 53,000 British and Commonwealth troops only recently sent there. Under constant pressure from Luftwaffe attacks, Cunningham's cruisers and destroyers joined Allied merchantmen in rescuing 41,000 of the troops plus several thousand Greek and Yugoslav refugees. Unfortunately for the Allies, many of the troops evacuated from Greece were sent to Crete, which the Germans invaded a month later. In the Battle of Crete (20–31 May) the Germans used paratroopers for their initial assault, then flew most of the rest of their troops across from Greece in transport aircraft. Cunningham kept his heavy units to the west of the island, to guard against an intervention by the Italian battle fleet which never came, primarily because the Germans had hardly bothered to involve their allies in the operation. The British navy's only success of the battle came on 21 May, when the Germans attempted to reinforce the island by sea, sending a convoy of small troop transports over from the Greek mainland, escorted by a single Italian destroyer. British cruisers and destroyers sank most of the transports, killing 4,000 German troops, but in turn suffered heavily at the hands of the Luftwaffe. Air power decided the battle, as the Germans and Italians had more land-based aircraft stationed closer to the island (on the Greek mainland and at Rhodes, in the Dodecanese Islands) than the RAF (in Egypt) and easily secured control of the skies. For the British, the battle reinforced the hard lesson learned a year earlier in Norway, that superiority in surface warships mattered little without air superiority. Axis air attacks inflicted some 2,000 casualties in sinking the British cruisers *Fiji*, *Gloucester*, and *Calcutta* and six destroyers, and damaging the battleships *Warspite* and *Barham*, another six cruisers, seven destroyers and the carrier *Formidable*, the latter badly enough to require six months of repairs. Meanwhile, the Italian navy lost a destroyer and a gunboat. By the end of the battle Cunningham had managed to evacuate 17,000 troops from Crete to Egypt, but over 15,000 were killed on the island or captured by the Germans.[68]

During the Balkan Blitzkrieg the Greek navy lost its two largest warships, the pre-dreadnought battleships *Kilkis* (ex-USS *Mississippi*) and

Limnos (ex-USS *Idaho*), sunk by Luftwaffe bombers on 23 April off Salamis. German air attacks also claimed five Greek destroyers. Greek warships escaping to Alexandria included the old armored cruiser *Georgios Averof*, nine destroyers, and five submarines. The destroyer *Vasilefs Georgios*, scuttled at Salamis, was later raised, repaired and operated by the Germans under the name *Hermes*.[69] While much of the Greek navy was saved to continue to fight on the Allied side, most of Yugoslavia's tiny navy ended up in Italian hands. Following the dismemberment of the country, former Yugoslav naval vessels recommissioned by the Italians included three destroyers, six torpedo boats and two submarines. The only Yugoslav units resisting the Axis takeover were a submarine and two torpedo boats based at Sebenico (Šibenik), which made a harrowing escape to Malta under the command of Captain Ivan Kern, a Slovene and former Austro–Hungarian officer.[70]

Coinciding with the loss of Yugoslavia, Greece, and Crete, developments in the Middle East caused Britain further concern. A pro-Axis regime came to power in Iraq in March 1941, and fighting against British troops (stationed there under a 1930 treaty) broke out on 2 May. A Luftwaffe detachment operating out of Mosul supported the Iraqi war effort, but only briefly. By the end of the month the British had secured control over the country, thanks to the timely arrival of the British East Indies Squadron under Vice Admiral G. S. Arbuthnot, which secured Basra for a pro-Allied Iraqi faction until troops arrived from India. The abortive German attempt to provide air cover for pro-Axis Iraqis would have been impossible in the first place if the Vichy French regime had not granted the Luftwaffe the use of airfields in Syria for transit. Having already lost Greece and Crete, and with Rommel advancing into western Egypt, Britain could not afford a further weakening of its position in the Middle East. Churchill ordered the occupation of Syria and Lebanon by British and Commonwealth forces based in Palestine, Jordan, and Iraq, supplemented by Free French troops. Cunningham detached two cruisers and ten destroyers to support the campaign. The Vichy French navy had nothing larger than a destroyer stationed in the Levant, and lost a destroyer to a British air attack on 16 June, eight days after the campaign began. More formidable Vichy resistance on land prevented the territories from being completely occupied until 12 July.[71]

Once Syria and Lebanon were secured for the Allies, the British navy's Mediterranean efforts focused on supporting an Anglo–Australian force at Tobruk, which found itself besieged by Rommel starting on 8 April, just eleven weeks after it had taken the city from the Italians. Between April and November the British navy ferried over 34,000 reinforcements with tanks, artillery, and supplies into the port. Between June and September 1941, British submarines jeopardized Axis efforts to keep Rommel supplied and reinforced, sinking 49 transports and

supply ships (roughly 150,000 tons). For the year, Italy lost 79 merchantmen totaling 356,420 tons on convoys to North Africa; in terms
of ships lost September (nine) was the costliest month, in terms of tonnage, November (54,990). In contrast, air attack continued to be the
cause of most British losses, at least until June 1941, when the demands
of the German invasion of Russia forced the Luftwaffe to withdraw its
planes from Sicily; they did not return until late in the year. In their
absence the pressure eased on Malta and on the British convoys reinforcing it. By the autumn of 1941, the British had more aircraft based
on Malta alone than the Italians had in all of Sicily. Fearing the loss of
Axis air superiority in the central Mediterranean, Mussolini authorized
the conversion of the passenger liner *Roma* into a 23,000-ton aircraft
carrier, eventually named the *Aquila*. Work on the project began at
Genoa in November.[72]

Meanwhile, during October 1941, the German navy did its part to
increase pressure on the Malta convoys by deploying U-boats in the
Mediterranean for the first time in the war. They soon made their presence felt in a series of dramatic warship sinkings that seriously jeopardized British naval operations in the region. On 13 November, *U 81*
torpedoed the *Ark Royal* while it was en route from Malta to Gibraltar.
Listing heavily to starboard, the carrier almost made it back to
Gibraltar, sinking while under tow just twenty-five miles from the base.
On 25 November *U 331* torpedoed and sank the battleship *Barham* off
Alexandria, then on the night of 14–15 December *U 557* torpedoed and
sank the light cruiser *Galatea*, also off Alexandria. To make matters
worse, on 18 December mines claimed the light cruiser *Neptune* and a
destroyer. The Italians also did their share of damage. On the night of
18–19 December saboteurs from the submarine *Scire* infiltrated
Alexandria harbor and attached timed charges to the hulls of the
battleships *Queen Elizabeth* and *Valiant*. The resulting explosions caused
both ships to sink; both were eventually raised and repaired, but the
damage to the *Queen Elizabeth* was so extensive that it did not re-enter
service until June 1943 (see Plate 40). These disasters, coinciding with
the onset of the war in the Pacific, stretched British resources to the
limit. As the year ended, Britain could take consolation in the relief of
Tobruk (27 November) by a British army counterattack from Egypt, the
sinking of the Italian light cruisers *Albercio da Barbiano* and *Amberto di
Giussano* off Cape Bon (13 December) by a force of one Dutch and three
British destroyers, and the inability of Admiral Iachino to damage,
much less destroy, an inferior British force under Rear Admiral Philip
Vian in the First Battle of Sirte Gulf (17 December). In the latter engagement, Iachino's force included the battleships *Littorio*, *Andrea Doria*,
and *Giulio Cesare*, 2 heavy cruisers, and 10 destroyers, against Vian's 6
cruisers and 14 destroyers. Neither side lost a ship as both commanders remained cautious, the British naturally avoiding closing with a

superior Italian force, the Italians believing that the British force included battleships.[73]

During 1941 the British losses in the Mediterranean included 1 battleship, 1 carrier, 8 cruisers, 14 destroyers, 7 submarines, 1 sloop, and 1 corvette sunk, and another 2 battleships and 2 carriers heavily damaged. The Italian navy suffered considerably less, losing 7 cruisers, 10 destroyers, and 18 submarines. With sufficient land-based air cover, the Italian fleet was more than capable of securing the Axis supply line to North Africa and seriously disrupting any British operation in the Mediterranean. The sinking of the *Ark Royal*, coming while the *Illustrious* and *Formidable* were still being repaired, left the British navy woefully short of carriers and at an even greater disadvantage in the air war. After the United States entered the war, the US navy deployed the light (14,700-ton) carrier *Wasp* to the British Mediterranean Fleet for several weeks in the spring of 1942, but its duties were limited to ferrying aircraft to Malta. The Axis continued to enjoy air superiority in the region.[74]

Until the autumn of 1942, when the buildup for Operation Torch, the Allied landings in French North Africa, altered the Mediterranean balance of power, the British navy continued to take a beating at the hands of the Luftwaffe and Italian air force, the Italian surface fleet, German and Italian submarines, and even a flotilla of German S-boats operating out of a base at Derna, Libya. Owing to its losses of carriers and battleships late in 1941, the British navy tried well into the summer of 1942 to keep Malta supplied with convoys escorted by cruisers and destroyers alone. In the Second Battle of Sirte Gulf (22 March 1942) a convoy bound from Alexandria to Malta, escorted by four light cruisers and sixteen destroyers, was fortunate to survive an attack by Iachino with the battleship *Littorio*, three cruisers and ten destroyers. Aside from two Italian destroyers sunk in a storm after the battle ended, neither side lost a ship. The convoy made it through, only to lose most of its ships and cargo to Luftwaffe air raids on Malta in the days that followed. The German High Command belatedly conceded that the island should be taken, and in April 1942 approved an invasion plan in which the Italian navy would have played a prominent role. Italian morale rose in anticipation of the operation, only to be dashed in mid-June, when Hitler decided that the 70,000 tons of fuel oil budgeted for the conquest of Malta would be better spent in North Africa, where Rommel was preparing for his final push into Egypt. From January through June, Italian convoys successfully landed 805 tanks in Libya which, along with supplies and reinforcements, enabled Rommel to launch his offensive. In sharp contrast to the heavy losses suffered by the convoys in 1941, especially late in the year, during the first six months of 1942 the British sank only 15 Italian merchantmen (76,980 tons) on the route to North Africa. During the first six months of 1942 British losses in the Mediterranean included the light cruisers *Naiad*, torpedoed on 11 March by *U 565*, and *Hermione*, torpedoed on 16 June by *U 205*, along with 16 destroyers and 9 submarines. During the same period Italian losses were much lighter, including the light cruiser *Bande Nere*, torpedoed on 1 April by the British submarine *Urge*, the heavy cruiser *Trento*, torpedoed on 16 June by the British submarine *Umbra*, 4 destroyers and 6 submarines. On 11–13 August 1942 the British suffered their last major defeat of the Mediterranean campaign, when Axis naval and air forces destroyed most of a convoy bound from Gibraltar to Malta. During the battle *U 73* torpedoed and sank the old carrier *Eagle*, an Italian torpedo boat sank the cruiser *Manchester*, and Italian submarines sank the cruiser *Cairo* and one destroyer; Axis losses were limited to two Italian submarines. The British extracted a measure of revenge against Axis convoys in the central Mediterranean, sinking 11 ships (59,970 tons) in August 1942 alone, the highest monthly total since September 1941.[75]

In preparation for Operation Torch, the first large-scale Allied amphibious landing of the war, on 19 August the British navy supported a disastrous "reconnaissance in force" by 5,000 Canadian troops and 1,000 British commandos at Dieppe on the French Channel coast. Eight destroyers and nine infantry landing ships (LSI) were the principal units in an operation that included 257 vessels of various types. The 4-inch guns of the destroyers could provide little in the way of fire support, and, in the interest of surprise, no attempt had been made to soften the area's defenses beforehand by bombing from the air. From the fiasco the Allies came to understand that fire support from the heavy guns of battleships and cruisers, along with preparatory bombing raids, would be crucial to the success of future, more ambitious amphibious assaults.[76] Three months later, Operation Torch had the naval artillery and aerial support that Dieppe had lacked. Cunningham served as Allied naval commander, under the overall leadership of General Dwight D. Eisenhower. His Anglo–American armada included 6 battleships, 5 fleet carriers, 7 escort carriers, 15 cruisers, and 81 destroyers convoying 216 transports, landing craft, and supply ships to facilitate the landing of almost 75,000 troops on the coast of French North Africa on 8 November 1942. Aircraft massed at Gibraltar supplemented the carriers to control the skies over the landing zones. Vichy French armed forces resisted until Admiral Darlan, their chief, agreed to a ceasefire on 10 November. At Algiers the British lost one destroyer and at Oran, two sloops. The US navy suffered no losses in taking Casablanca. Vichy French warships suffered heavily in the defense, their losses including the cruiser *Primaguet*, nine destroyers, and eight submarines. Another six submarines were scuttled, while three escaped to Toulon. The battleship *Jean Bart*, still unfinished but with one heavy gun turret operational, was badly damaged at Casablanca in a duel with the battleship USS *Massachusetts*.[77]

Geography and an acute fuel shortage helped keep German and Italian air and sea forces away from the Torch landing zones. Algiers, 900 miles from Taranto, was also far enough from Sardinia to be out of range of most land-based Axis aircraft, leaving even the easternmost of the landings unopposed by Axis naval or air power. To make matters worse, by October 1942 the Italian navy was getting one-third of the fuel oil it needed, just 20,000 tons per month, all of which came from the Germans. Iachino's battleships and cruisers were kept in port to save fuel for the smaller units, but by November only the submarines were running on a regular basis. These played no role in opposing the Torch landings, as the Axis navies were duped by Allied disinformation that the convoys were headed for Dakar. Thus, while dozens of German U-boats and Italian submarines combed the waters southeast of the Azores, the Torch convoys, totaling 1.3 million tons of shipping, made it to the North African coast without losing a single vessel.

Darlan's ceasefire agreement with the Allies prompted Hitler to order the immediate occupation of Vichy France, Corsica, and French Tunisia, the latter a move long advocated by the Italians. Pétain's regime would survive until the liberation of France in 1944 but lost all credibility after November 1942, as it could no longer pretend to be an independent government safeguarding French national interests. Darlan, in North Africa at the time of the armistice, was recognized by the Allies as French High Commissioner there. Presenting himself to Vichy loyalists as Pétain's legitimate successor, he "invited" the French fleet at Toulon to steam for Dakar, assuring its commander, Admiral Jean de Laborde, that the Allies would allow the ships to pass unmolested. After the Vichy government disavowed Darlan's actions, Laborde chose to keep the fleet at Toulon, but on 27 November, when German troops finally stormed the naval base there, Laborde honored Darlan's standing order of 18 June 1940 and promptly scuttled his ships. These included the battleships *Dunkerque*, *Strasbourg*, and *Provence*, 4 heavy cruisers, 3 light cruisers, 32 destroyers, 16 submarines, 18 sloops and smaller warships. After the sinkings, the Allies opened negotiations with the commanders of the larger French warships that had been idled elsewhere since the summer of 1940. In May 1943 the battleship *Lorraine* and rest of the force interned at Alexandria went over to the Free French, followed in June 1943 by the carrier *Béarn* and the cruisers that had sought refuge in the French West Indies. Meanwhile, France's largest surviving battleship, the 35,000-ton *Richelieu*, left Dakar for a refit in the United States, and entered Free French service in October 1943. The amalgamation of warships proved less problematic than the integration of personnel, which grew from less than 6,000 to over 40,000 during 1943. A strong mutual hostility continued to divide the Vichy French veterans from the officers and seamen who had been loyal to the Free French since 1940. The process was made easier by the death of the enigmatic Darlan, assassinated at Algiers on 24 December 1942, and by the fact that most senior admirals withdrew to private life rather than change masters; those who did not were forced to retire by the end of 1943. De Gaulle's new chief of naval staff, Rear Admiral André Lemonnier, ultimately kept peace between the two groups by keeping them apart: the original Free French ships and personnel served primarily in the Channel and North Atlantic, while the former Vichy French ships and personnel served primarily in the Mediterranean and central Atlantic.[78]

After the occupation of Vichy France, the Germans allowed the Italian navy to raise a number of the smaller warships scuttled there, but ultimately only 2 destroyers, 2 corvettes, and 3 torpedo boats were repaired and recommissioned in Italian service. In December 1942 the Germans gave the Italians 9 former Vichy French submarines and 4 corvettes seized at Bizerta, Tunisia, but of the lot only one submarine ever entered Italian service. After November 1942 the Italians also seized 535,000 tons of French merchant shipping, much of which had been idle and was in no condition to be used immediately. Bizerta in Axis hands shortened Rommel's sea supply line considerably; for the moment, the port was also far more secure than the Libyan ports used previously, which came under increasing pressure after Field Marshal Bernard Montgomery defeated Rommel at the Battle of El Alamein (23 October–4 November 1942) and launched a British offensive westward out of Egypt. During the last eighteen days of November alone, the Italians shipped 695 tanks to Bizerta, with reinforcements and supplies, some destined for Rommel, the rest to defend the new Tunisian foothold against the Anglo–American forces advancing from the west following the Torch landings. The Italian navy was far from dead, but its ever worsening fuel shortage continued to keep even the smaller surface units in port, and also weakened the navy's commitment to complete larger units still under construction. The fourth *Littorio* class battleship, the *Impero* (launched November 1939) and the aircraft carrier *Aquila* (converted after November 1941) were never finished. Of the twelve *Capitani Romani* class light cruisers laid down in 1939, only three were completed in time to serve in the war and eight were never finished. Meanwhile, the third *Littorio* class battleship, the *Roma*, saw no action after its commissioning in June 1942. The naval war in the central Mediterranean became static after Operation Torch, as the Italians sought to compensate for their inability to escort convoys properly by laying heavy mine barrages on either side of their convoy route to Tunis and Bizerta. The Allies responded by laying thousands of their own mines across the same route. In a sign of things to come, on 4 December 1942 the Italian cruiser *Museo Attendolo* was sunk at Naples during an Allied air raid. The British and American air forces, enjoying better than a 3:1 margin of superiority in aircraft in the Mediterranean theater as of January 1943, launched over 200 air raids on Axis ports in the first five months of the year. Between March and May, 118 Axis merchantmen were sunk, almost all of them in port. The raids also claimed the *Trieste*, sunk on 10 April at La Maddalena, leaving the Italian navy with just two heavy cruisers.[79]

Over the winter of 1942–43 it became clear that the Allies would soon push the Axis powers out of North Africa, making Italy the obvious next target for invasion. Hitler's fears that Italy would somehow quit the war led to a series of heavy-handed measures by which Germany took control of the Italian war effort. In February 1943 Vice Admiral Friedrich Ruge arrived to assume command of the Tunisian convoy route; under an agreement made on 17 March the German navy also took control of Italian bases at Bizerta, Naples, and on Sicily. Personnel exchanges sent some Italian seamen to the North Sea and Baltic; by the summer of 1943 Italian naval detachments had also seen action in support of the Germans on the Russian front, in the Black Sea and on Lake Ladoga. Meanwhile, German officers and crews were sent to the Mediterranean to assume control of some of the merchantmen and escort craft on the convoy route, but, with the Allies now firmly in control of the skies, Ruge could do nothing to salvage the situation. The Axis stock of merchantmen and escort vessels continued to dwindle, with losses averaging almost 18 ships per week in March 1943 and 23 per week in April.[80]

After the Axis surrender in Tunisia (13 May 1943) left all of North Africa in Allied hands, preparations began for Operation Husky, the Allied invasion of Sicily. Between May and July, British submarines sank another 30 Axis merchantmen in the Mediterranean, and Allied air raids continued to harass the Italian navy in its ports; warships sunk included the old light cruiser *Bari*, at Livorno on 28 June. The British force covering Husky included the carriers *Indomitable* and *Formidable*, 8 battleships, 2 cruisers, and 24 destroyers. The overall Allied force, the largest ever assembled to date, totaled 2,590 vessels of all types, of which 1,614 were British, 945 American, and 31 from other countries. Starting on 10 July, 115,000 British and Commonwealth troops were landed, along with 66,000 US troops. During and after the operation the Allies lost just two landing craft and a dozen supply ships. Among the Allied warships the most significant casualty did not sink: the *Indomitable*, torpedoed by a Luftwaffe bomber, was damaged so seriously that it had to be sent to Norfolk, in the United States, where repairs were not completed until April 1944. The Italian navy's surface ships were blockaded in port for the duration of the operation, limiting the Axis opposition at sea to submarines, of which the Italians lost seven (including one captured) and the Germans three. During the first half of August the Axis abandoned Sicily, successfully withdrawing 62,000 Italian and 40,000 German troops from the island while leaving behind 162,000 prisoners, mostly Italian.[81]

On 25 July, in the midst of the Battle of Sicily, a cabinet coup in Rome deposed Mussolini in favor of the former chief of the general staff, Marshal Badoglio. As the new regime in Italy sought a way out of the war, the navy, lacking the fuel to put to sea or the air cover to stay safely in port, shifted as many ships as possible to northern Italian harbors, out of easy range of Allied air strikes.[82] On 3 September British and Canadian troops crossed the Straits of Messina to Calabria, the tip of the Italian boot. British naval support included the carriers *Illustrious* and *Formidable*, joined by the new light carrier *Unicorn* (completed March 1943), 4 escort carriers, 3 cruisers, and 7 British and 2 Polish destroyers. Five days later, on the eve of an Anglo–American landing at Salerno, the Badoglio government formally agreed to an armistice with the Allies. On 9 September, coinciding with the Salerno landings, Cunningham secured Taranto without firing a shot, landing 6,000 troops from warships of the British Mediterranean Fleet. As the armistice took effect, all Italian navy units proceeded to Malta for internment. En route to Malta on 9 September, the battleships *Roma* and *Littorio* (the latter renamed *Italia* after the overthrow of Mussolini) were struck by a new German weapon, the FX-1400 radio-controlled glider bomb, dropped by Luftwaffe aircraft. The *Roma* suffered a magazine explosion, broke in half and sank; the *Italia* limped onward to Malta with serious hull damage. The navy's two surviving heavy cruisers, the *Gorizia* and the *Bolzano*, remained behind at La Spezia and were captured by the Germans; they would remain idle there until June 1944, when Italian navy saboteurs, fighting for the Allies, sank both of them. In the days after the armistice, 12 destroyers and 10 submarines were scuttled by their crews or sunk by the Germans, while another 7 destroyers and 7 submarines passed into German service, along with a number of torpedo boats. The rest of the navy's smaller units fell into Allied hands along with the *Italia*, the *Vittorio Veneto*, the older battleships *Caio Duilio*, *Andrea Doria*, and *Giulio Cesare*, and 7 light cruisers. In terms of tonnage, roughly two-thirds of the Italian navy surrendered intact.[83] Meanwhile, on 19 September a British force took Sardinia unopposed, and at the end of the month 2 cruisers, 4 destroyers, and 3 submarines of the Free French navy facilitated the occupation of Corsica by French troops. It was the first Free French operation involving former Vichy French warships and personnel.[84]

In the Mediterranean war through 8 September 1943, the British navy lost 1 battleship, 2 aircraft carriers, 14 cruisers, 49 destroyers, 41 submarines, 5 sloops, 5 corvettes, and 1 monitor. In comparison, Italy lost 1 battleship, 12 cruisers, 44 destroyers, 84 submarines, and 197 smaller craft and auxiliaries. Italian navy dead numbered 28,937. The Italian merchant marine paid a high price for keeping German and Italian troops in North Africa supplied and reinforced; 1,278 Italian merchantmen were sunk, and 3,520 merchant mariners killed. It is not surprising that almost all Italian battleships survived, to account for a significant share of the warship tonnage passing into Allied hands on and after 9 September. During Italy's three years and three months in the war, the battleships had been used very conservatively, had fired their heavy guns in only five engagements, and failed to register a hit on an enemy warship other than with their secondary armament.[85]

After Badoglio, on behalf of the rest of Italy, declared war on Germany, the Allies used the surrendered ships of the Italian navy only selectively, but as early as November 1943 the cruisers *Duca degli Abruzzi* and *Duca d'Aosta* were escorting Allied convoys across the central Atlantic. Three days after the armistice, the Germans rescued the imprisoned Mussolini and subsequently installed him as ruler of German-occupied northern Italy, but the navy of his puppet state consisted only of *MAS* boats and other small vessels, which operated under German command along the Riviera and in the upper Adriatic. When the former Italian destroyers and torpedo boats passing into German service were quickly sunk or pinned down in port by Allied bombing raids, the Germans used air attacks, glider bombs, U-boats, and mines to harass the British navy. Between October 1943 and October 1944 these means accounted for not inconsiderable further British losses: 3 cruisers, 10 destroyers, 1 frigate, and 3 submarines. Axis naval operations in the Mediterranean did not cease completely until the last active MAS boats and their German counterparts were scuttled on the Italian Riviera in late April 1945.[86] Nevertheless, the surrender of the main body of the Italian navy in September 1943 enabled the Allied European navies to reassign their assets elsewhere, especially to the Pacific.

EUROPEAN NAVIES IN THE WAR AGAINST JAPAN (1941–45)

Unlike the European powers and the United States, Japan took full advantage of its allowances under the interwar naval arms limits and, by the early 1930s, had arguably the world's most modern navy, having built more than double the tonnage of the United States since 1922. Thereafter, Japan had been the first naval power to break with the arms control regime, announcing in 1934 that it would not renew existing agreements when they expired at the end of 1936. Between 1937 and 1941 the Japanese further enhanced their capabilities by adding the 62,315-ton battleship *Yamato*, another 11 aircraft carriers, 7 cruisers, 37 destroyers, and 22 submarines, in the process surpassing the British in numbers and capability to become the world's second naval power after the United States.[87]

The collapse of France in 1940 foiled Britain's plan to deal with the eventuality of a war against Japan by reinforcing the British East Indies

Squadron with ships from the Mediterranean, which would then be left to the French navy to defend. Fighting for survival against Germany and Italy, Britain did little to reinforce the East Indies Squadron at Singapore until Japan's occupation of French Indochina (July 1941) placed the rest of Southeast Asia in imminent danger. In October, Rear Admiral Sir Tom Phillips was designated commander of the new Eastern Fleet and sent to Singapore with the battleship *Prince of Wales*, the old battle cruiser *Repulse*, and four destroyers, with further reinforcements to follow. Proceeding via the Cape of Good Hope, the ships arrived on 2 December 1941.[88]

The vast Dutch East Indies were even more vulnerable than British Malaya. Dutch naval forces there, under the operational control of the British navy since the German conquest of the Netherlands in May 1940, initially included 3 light cruisers, 7 destroyers, and 15 submarines. Of the Dutch warships in home waters at the time of the German invasion, only two submarines were captured, along with several warships still on the stocks. The rest of the navy – 2 light cruisers, a destroyer, a sloop, and 9 submarines – escaped to Britain. All of these vessels remained in European waters, attached to the British Home or Mediterranean fleets, except for the light cruiser *Java*, sent to reinforce the squadron in the East Indies.[89]

The Netherlands joined Britain in declaring war on Japan on 8 December 1941. The previous day, coinciding with its attack on the United States at Pearl Harbor, Japan had bombed both Hong Kong and Singapore without warning, invaded Malaya, and attacked the Dutch East Indies. Phillips attempted to challenge the Japanese landings on the Malayan coast, a suicide mission given his lack of air cover. On 10 December Japanese torpedo bombers attacked his force, sinking the *Prince of Wales* at 12:33 and the *Repulse* at 13:20. The 840 dead included Phillips; British destroyers rescued another 2,101 men. The heavy losses in the Mediterranean in the last weeks of 1941 made the immediate replacement of these ships impossible and, after the sinkings, the British concentrated on merely holding Singapore. At the same time they all but abandoned Hong Kong, losing only a sloop and smaller craft there before it fell to the Japanese on 25 December. On 2 January 1942 the surviving British and Dutch naval forces in the East Indies joined American and Australian units in the joint "ABDA" command, under the overall command of an American admiral. The Allies kept Singapore supplied from Java until its surrender on 15 February, taking care not to risk their remaining naval assets. Only two small warships, both British sloops, were lost when the city fell. The Japanese then focused on Java, which had survived thus far only because of a lifeline from Darwin, cut when a carrier air raid on 19 February severely damaged the northern Australian port.[90]

In the cluster of engagements known as the Battle of the Java Sea (27 February–1 March), an ABDA force of 5 cruisers (the Dutch *Java* and *De Ruyter*, HMS *Exeter*, one American and one Australian) and 10 destroyers (four American, three British, three Dutch), initially under the command of Rear Admiral Karel Doorman of the Dutch navy, attempted to foil further Japanese landings in the Dutch East Indies. The Japanese forces opposing them included 4 cruisers and 13 destroyers, ultimately reinforced by an aircraft carrier and other units. Aside from one Dutch and three American destroyers, Doorman's entire force was sunk. The Dutch navy alone suffered a loss of 984 dead, including the admiral, who went down with his ship on the evening of the battle's first day. Meanwhile, the Japanese lost no warships and just two troop transports, and completed their conquest of Java on 9 March. In attempting to defend the Dutch East Indies, the Dutch navy ultimately lost its entire Pacific force except for four submarines.[91] It remained a negligible factor in the war until 1944–45, when reinforcements from European waters again enabled it to play a minor role.

The loss of the *Prince of Wales* and *Repulse* convinced the British navy that it needed more fleet carriers to provide air cover for battleships in situations where they were vulnerable to land-based bombers. Unfortunately new carriers the size of the *Illustrious* and its sisters could not be completed in time to see action during the war; while the four laid down in 1937 had taken an average of forty-three months to complete, wartime shortages in labor and materials would delay the pair begun in 1939 to fifty-four months (for the *Indefatigable*, commissioned May 1944) and sixty-five months (for the *Implacable*, commissioned August 1944). In contrast, the 14,750-ton light fleet carrier *Unicorn*, also laid down in 1939, took forty-five months to complete (in March 1943). The Admiralty concluded that light fleet carriers were the answer and laid down ten (the 13,190-ton *Colossus* class) between June 1942 and January 1943. Six units of the 14,000-ton *Majestic* class followed between April and November 1943, and four of the 18,310-ton *Centaur* class betweeen March 1944 and May 1945. Of the lot, only five carriers of the *Colossus* class were completed in time to see action in the war, but for these ships, building times averaged an impressive twenty-nine months.[92]

After the loss of the East Indies, the Admiralty again attempted to form the new Eastern Fleet, this time under Admiral Somerville, reassigned from the Mediterranean. By late March 1942 the ships assembled at his base at Colombo, Ceylon, included the *Formidable* (newly repaired from the damage suffered off Crete in May 1941), the *Indomitable*, and a third carrier, the old *Hermes*, with 5 battleships of First World War vintage, 7 cruisers (one Dutch), 15 destroyers (one Dutch, one Australian), and 7 submarines. Somerville soon faced an attack by the victor of Pearl Harbor, Vice Admiral Chuichi Nagumo, whose force of 5 carriers,

4 battleships, 3 cruisers and 9 destroyers steamed for Ceylon with the goal of destroying the new British fleet. During a four-day battle (5–9 April 1942), aircraft from the Japanese carriers sank the heavy cruisers *Cornwall* and *Dorsetshire*, the carrier *Hermes*, and two destroyers (one Australian), along with an armed merchant cruiser and a corvette. Nagumo's warships also sank 93,000 tons of Allied shipping during the battle. The Japanese suffered no losses. Coinciding with the conquest of Burma (completed May 1942), a Japanese landing on Ceylon would have further imperiled India. Fearing the worst, Somerville withdrew half of its fleet to Bombay in the hope of retaining control over the Arabian Sea and sent the other half to the coast of East Africa to guard the convoy route between the Cape of Good Hope and the Red Sea. But Japan's priorities lay elsewhere, and after giving the British navy a beating Nagumo withdrew from the Indian Ocean. The Japanese navy never threatened India again. Of the five carriers used in Nagumo's attack, four were sunk by the US navy two months later at Midway.[93]

As soon as it became apparent that the Japanese were not going to follow up on Nagumo's success off Ceylon, the British turned their attention to the conquest of Madagascar, the last remaining Vichy French stronghold in the Indian Ocean. In early May 1942, Somerville sent the *Indomitable* to join the carrier *Illustrious* in providing air cover for Operation Ironclad, the largest British amphibious landing since Gallipoli in 1915. In addition to the two carriers, the supporting fleet included the battleship *Ramillies*, 2 cruisers, 11 destroyers, 7 corvettes, and a number of minesweepers. The Vichy loyalists defending the island had at their disposal 2 armed merchant cruisers, 2 sloops, and 5 submarines. In heavy fighting for Diego Suarez (5–8 May), the British sank one armored merchant cruiser, one sloop, and three submarines while losing just one corvette of their own. British forces quickly took the northern part of the island, then faced a protracted struggle against guerrilla resistance to secure the rest of it. The last Vichy forces in Madagascar finally surrendered on 6 November 1942, ironically just days before the German occupation of Vichy France. Long before then, the *Indomitable* returned to the Mediterranean, where the *Formidable* soon joined it. By August 1942 the *Illustrious* was the only carrier remaining in the Indian Ocean. In January 1943 it left as well, returning to the Home Fleet. Not a single European warship was lost in the Indian Ocean during 1943, and not a single one to Japanese action anywhere during the year. With the Japanese threat to his command area diminished and major Allied offensives under way in the Mediterranean and the Pacific, Somerville continued to lose ships until by the end of 1943 he had just the battleship *Ramillies*, 10 cruisers, two dozen destroyers, frigates, sloops, or corvettes, and 6 submarines. He had no aircraft carriers from January until October 1943, when the escort carrier *Battler* arrived to head a new anti-submarine warfare group.[94] That month, Acting Admiral Lord Louis Mountbatten arrived in Delhi as head of the newly created South-East Asia Command (SEAC), signaling the intention of the Allies to take the offensive against the Japanese in Southeast Asia during 1944. Fresh resources sent to the theater included British warships freed from Mediterranean duty following the demise of the Italian navy. The changes were a mixed blessing for Somerville, who would resent taking orders from a man almost twenty years younger, whose extraordinary promotion owed much to his connection to the royal family.[95]

By the end of January 1944 the British Eastern Fleet had been reinforced by the battleships *Queen Elizabeth* and *Valiant*, battle cruiser *Renown*, carrier *Illustrious*, light carrier *Unicorn*, 2 cruisers and 7 destroyers. They were followed by the Free French battleship *Richelieu*, reassigned from the British Home Fleet, and carrier USS *Saratoga*, on loan for the spring of 1944. In the first weeks of the new year, two of Somerville's submarines sank a Japanese light cruiser and destroyer, the first Japanese surface warship losses to British naval action after over two years of hostilities. During April and May Somerville used most of his fleet in a series of attacks against the Japanese-occupied East Indies. The *Illustrious*, *Queen Elizabeth*, *Valiant*, 5 cruisers and 7 destroyers were supported by the *Saratoga*, the *Richelieu*, the Dutch cruiser *Tromp*, and 9 Allied destroyers (one Dutch, three American, and five Australian). On 19 April aircraft from the two carriers heavily damaged the Japanese airfield and harbor on Sabang Island. On 17 May the battleships joined carrier aircraft in targeting the Japanese fuel depot and harbor at Surabaya. After the *Saratoga* rejoined US forces in the Pacific, the fleet carriers *Victorious* and *Indomitable* and four escort carriers arrived in July 1944, more than compensating for the loss. The new escort carriers joined the *Battler* in anti-submarine warfare, while the fleet carriers spearheaded further attacks on Sabang between 22 July and 27 July, supported by the battleships *Queen Elizabeth*, *Valiant*, and *Richelieu*, battle cruiser *Renown*, 5 cruisers (including the Dutch *Tromp*), and 5 destroyers (including three Australian). In August 1944 the Eastern Fleet grew to include 11 cruisers and 32 destroyers; it gained the battleship *Howe* but temporarily lost the carrier *Illustrious*, sent to Simonstown, South Africa, for repairs. By then repeated clashes with Mountbatten had forced Somerville to give way to Admiral Sir Bruce Fraser. During the late summer the *Victorious* and *Indomitable* launched further air strikes on Japanese positions in the East Indies, then on 17–19 October 1944 against the Nicobar Islands, in the latter case in an operation designed as a diversion for the concurrent US operation against Leyte in the Philippines. Meanwhile, between July and December 1944 26 British and Dutch submarines operating from Ceylon ranged eastward to the East Indies and even into the South China Sea, sinking 16 merchantmen (35,000 tons) along with 2 German U-boats and 1 Japanese submarine.[96]

In November 1944 the ever expanding British Eastern Fleet was sub-divided into the Pacific Fleet, under Fraser, and the East Indies Fleet, under Vice Admiral Sir Arthur Power. Fraser, operating out of Sydney from January 1945, kept the best larger units of the old Eastern Fleet, including the fleet carriers *Illustrious, Indomitable*, and *Victorious*, and the battleships *Richelieu, Howe*, and *King George V*, the last just arrived from the Home Fleet. Fraser also had 7 British cruisers and 3 (mostly British) destroyer flotillas. The *Queen Elizabeth*, the *Renown*, and the 5 escort carriers spearheaded Power's force, which continued to operate out of the Eastern Fleet's old base at Trincomalee, Ceylon. Power's 8 cruisers and two dozen destroyers included several Australian and Dutch units. In December 1944 and January 1945, the East Indies Fleet supported the British army's offensive against the Japanese in Burma. Meanwhile, en route to their new base at Sydney, Fraser's carriers launched strikes against Japanese oil refineries in the East Indies. Following its redeployment, the British Pacific Fleet was organized along the lines of a US navy fast carrier task force and integrated into the US Pacific command structure. Its operations during 1945 would reflect the extent to which the British navy had adopted American doctrine for carrier operations. Meanwhile, Power's East Indies Fleet remained under the overall command of Mountbatten's SEAC.[97]

After the relocation of the British Pacific Fleet, the East Indies Fleet assumed primary responsibility for attacking Japanese positions in the East Indies. During the first months of 1945 four more escort carriers joined Power's force, which in April and May 1945 supported Allied landings near Rangoon. During the operation the *Queen Elizabeth* and British cruisers provided fire support, joined by the Dutch cruiser *Tromp* and the French *Richelieu*, the latter recently returned from Fraser's fleet. On 15 May destroyers from the East Indies Fleet sank the Japanese cruiser *Haguro* southwest of Penang, and on 8 June the British submarine *Trenchant* torpedoed and sank its sister-ship, the *Ashigara*, near the Banka Strait. These 10,000-ton heavy cruisers were the largest Japanese warships sunk by the British during the Second World War; each was attempting to evacuate an isolated island garrison at the time of its demise. During June and July the ships and aircraft of the East Indies Fleet harassed Japanese outposts and convoys in the Andaman Islands, Sumatra, southern Burma and southern Thailand. The only kamikaze attack against the fleet came on 26 July 1945 in the Bay of Bengal, when one of the suicide pilots almost struck the escort carrier *Ameer*.[98]

When it came to kamikaze attacks, the ships of the British Pacific Fleet were not so lucky. After setting up headquarters at Sydney early in 1945, Fraser remained there while his ships, under the operational command of Vice Admiral Sir Bernard Rawlings, cruised some 6,000 miles northward to join the US Fifth Fleet in supporting the American landings at Okinawa in late March. By then Fraser's fleet had received a fourth carrier, the *Indefatigable*, which on 1 April 1945 became the first British ship to be struck by a kamikaze. It would have been lost if not for its armored deck. On 6 April a kamikaze crashed into the sea after clipping the superstructure of the carrier *Illustrious*, which suffered considerable damage to its hull after the plane's bomb exploded underwater. The ship had to be sent home to Britain for repairs and remained out of action for the rest of the war. Aircraft from the British carriers subsequently bombed Japanese airfields on Taiwan, source of many of the kamikazes appearing over Okinawa and the rest of the Ryuku Islands. On 4 May kamikazes struck the decks of the *Formidable* (just arrived in the Pacific as a replacement for the *Illustrious*) and the *Indomitable*; like the *Indefatigable* earlier, they would have been put out of action if not for their armored decks. On 9 May the *Formidable* was struck again, and two kamikazes hit the *Victorious*, the last British carrier previously unscathed. The *Formidable* lost a number of aircraft in the attack but both carriers continued to operate once fires were extinguished. During the two-month battle for Okinawa, the five British fleet carriers launched 5,335 aircaft sorties, losing 160 planes. Their survival in the face of kamikaze attacks vindicated the concept of the armored deck, once criticized by the Americans because it made them considerably slower than unarmored carriers of similar size and capacity.[99]

In late June 1945 the carrier *Implacable* joined the British Pacific Fleet at its anchorage at Manus in the Admiralty Islands, replacing the *Indefatigable*. En route, on 12–14 June 1945 it had joined the escort carrier *Ruler*, 4 cruisers, and 5 destroyers in attacking Japanese targets on Truk in the Carolines. In July the fleet joined American warships in attacking the Japanese home islands. On 17 July the British carriers launched air strikes against targets in northern Honshu while the *King George V* joined American battleships in a long-range shelling of Tokyo. On 9–10 August, as Japan reeled from the effects of the atomic bombs on Hiroshima (6 August) and Nagasaki (9 August) and the Soviet Union's entry into the Pacific war (8 August), Rawlings led his 4 fleet carriers, 2 battleships, 6 cruisers, and 17 destroyers in attacks on Japanese shipping in the Onagawa Wan. The following day the Japanese agreed to surrender terms, but the carriers continued to launch sorties over Tokyo until the definitive suspension of offensive operations on the morning of 15 August. The next day Fraser arrived to resume operational command of the fleet, which by then included the new light fleet carriers *Colossus*, *Glory*, *Vengeance*, and *Venerable*, none of which saw much action before the Japanese capitulation. Meanwhile, far to the south, in the last days of the war the British East Indies Fleet focused on preparations for the reconquest of Singapore. The British navy launched a midget submarine raid on Singapore harbor on 30 July, as a preliminary step to Operation Zipper, an amphibious landing on the western Malayan coast commanded by

Mountbatten. Zipper was cancelled after the Japanese accepted Allied surrender terms. When the East Indies Fleet finally landed the troops starting on 2 September, they occupied Malaya without resistance. On the same day, the warships of the British Pacific Fleet joined American and other Allied warships in Tokyo Bay, to witness the surrender ceremony aboard the USS *Missouri*. On 12 September Mountbatten formally accepted the surrender of all Japanese forces in Southeast Asia and the East Indies.[100]

The Japanese–Soviet non-aggression pact of April 1941 idled the Soviet Pacific Fleet for all but the last days of the war. The respite allowed 147,000 men from the fleet to be sent overland to the European theater, to help the Red Army turn back the German invasion of the Soviet Union. In August 1945 Soviet naval forces in the Pacific theater included the cruisers *Kaganovich* and *Kalinin*, 13 destroyers, 95 submarines, a host of smaller vessels, and 1,829 land-based aircraft. After 8 August these warships and planes supported a series of amphibious landings, for the most part unopposed, on the Korean coast, Sakhalin, and the Kurile Islands.[101]

THE ATLANTIC WAR (1941–45)

Along with freeing up Soviet Pacific naval personnel to fight in the European theater, the Soviet–Japanese non-aggression pact also secured Vladivostok, the eastern terminus of the Trans-Siberian Railway, as an entrepôt for Allied aid shipments to the Soviet Union. Ultimately 8.24 million tons of American aid flowed in through the port, more than the total entering through the Arctic (3.96 million) and Iran (4.16 million) combined. Meanwhile, the navy's two largest fleets, in the Baltic (2 battleships, 2 cruisers, 21 destroyers, and 71 submarines) and in the Black Sea (1 battleship, 5 cruisers, 17 destroyers, and 44 submarines), were of no use to the Soviet Union in its quest to establish lifelines to the outside world after the German invasion of 22 June 1941. The Northern Fleet, upgraded from flotilla status only in 1937, had just 8 destroyers, 15 submarines, and 7 patrol ships to keep open the Arctic route into Archangel and Murmansk. The Soviet Union's three European fleets, like its Pacific force, depended upon land-based naval aircraft for its air cover, but in 1941 the Northern Fleet's air arm included just 116 planes. As German troops pushed deep into the Soviet Union, the Northern Fleet remained out of easy reach of enemy air raids, but the Luftwaffe repeatedly pounded the Soviet Baltic and Black Sea fleets, sinking almost all of their destroyer and submarine forces: 31 destroyers and 103 submarines in all, over half of them between June and December 1941. Ironically, most of the largest targets emerged unscathed. Air attacks damaged all three Soviet battleships but only one (the *Marat*, at Kronstadt on 23 September 1941) beyond repair. The *Chervona Ukraina* (13 November 1941) and *Komintern* (16 July 1942) were the only cruisers sunk, both in the Black Sea.[102]

To strengthen the Soviet Northern Fleet, the United States eventually provided 28 anti-submarine frigates and 465 smaller vessels (minesweepers, PT boats, and landing craft) under Lend-Lease. As advance compensation for the Soviet Union's share of the surrendered Italian navy, in 1944 the Northern Fleet received on loan the British battleship *Royal Sovereign* (renamed *Arkhangelsk*), the American light cruiser *Milwaukee* (renamed *Murmansk*), 9 old British (former US navy) destroyers, and 4 British submarines. In the summer of 1941, however, the Soviet navy had to fight with the meager Arctic forces already at its disposal, and was far from equal to the task. The need to secure the supply route into the Soviet Arctic ports brought the British navy to the coast of Norway in force for the first time since June 1940. The first convoy from Iceland to Archangel made the passage unmolested on 21–31 August 1941, escorted by the carriers *Argus* and *Victorious*, the cruisers *Devonshire* and *Suffolk*, and six destroyers. Between September and December 1941, another eight Allied convoys made it safely from Iceland to Archangel or Murmansk. The Germans did not attempt to attack an Arctic convoy either from the air or sea until 2 January 1942, when *U 134* sank one British freighter making the run. On 17 January *U 454* sank a British destroyer escorting a convoy, the first Allied warship lost in the Arctic. After his invasion of the Soviet Union fell just short of Moscow in December 1941, Hitler finally recognized the need for decisive measures to close the Arctic convoy route. He planned to concentrate the German navy's largest warships in Norwegian waters, starting with the *Tirpitz*, which had not left the Baltic since its commissioning in February 1941. In mid-January 1942 the 42,900-ton ship was relocated to Trondheim.[103]

On 11–13 February 1942, Vice Admiral Otto Ciliax took the battleships *Scharnhorst* and *Gneisenau* and the heavy cruiser *Prinz Eugen* back to Germany from Brest, where they had been idled since the spring of 1941. Ciliax caused the British navy considerable embarrassment by successfully running the gauntlet of the Channel, aided in his passage by bad weather and considerable help from minesweepers, S-boats, and Luftwaffe planes based along the northern French coast. Days after its arrival in Germany the *Prinz Eugen* was ordered to Norwegian waters with the heavy cruiser *Admiral Scheer* and an escort of three destroyers, only to be torpedoed en route on 27 February by the British submarine *Trident*. The ship survived but had to undergo extensive repairs, after which it became a training vessel in the Baltic. Following his return from Brest, Ciliax received command of the *Tirpitz* at Trondheim. On 6–9 March he took the big battleship out on its first sortie against an Allied convoy, accompanied by three destroyers and four U-boats. The destroyers sank one Russian freighter before the group returned to Trondheim, under air attack by planes from the British carrier *Victorious*. Shortly thereafter, Ciliax received the heavy cruiser *Admiral Hipper*, three destroyers, and three torpedo boats as reinforcements. Meanwhile, to deny the *Tirpitz* or any other German capital ship the ability to be repaired while on an Atlantic sortie, on 28 March the British launched a raid on the dry dock at Saint-Nazaire, where the *Bismarck* would have been repaired ten months earlier had it not been sunk en route to its destination. The old destroyer *Campbeltown* (ex-USS *Buchanan*), loaded with timed explosives, rammed the lock gates and exploded several hours later, rendering the dry dock useless for the remainder of the war.[104]

In addition to their increased interest in challenging convoys on the Arctic route to Russia, the Germans sought to take their submarine campaign across the Atlantic once the United States entered the war. At the start of 1942 Admiral Dönitz had 91 operational U-boats at his disposal, enough to sustain Operation Drumbeat (*Paukenschlag*) which began with five U-boats hunting for targets along the east coast of the United States in mid-January. Over the next six months they and their eventual reinforcements sank an astounding total of 397 Allied merchantmen. Aside from an American destroyer which *U 578* torpedoed and sank off Cape May on 28 February, the U-boats had few encounters with US navy warships because, at least initially, so few were assigned to coastal anti-submarine warfare. The Germans benefited greatly from the fact that the US chief of naval operations, the Anglophobe Admiral Ernest King, initially showed little interest in cooperating with the British and Canadian navies, and even less in adopting their improved anti-submarine warfare methods. Over a period of six months only six of the U-boats assigned to the aggressive campaign were lost and none until 14 April, when an American destroyer sank *U 85* off Nags Head. During May the US navy started to convoy merchantmen along the Atlantic coast, and in mid-July Admiral Dönitz called off the campaign, once again focusing the attentions of his U-boats on Allied convoys passing through the central North Atlantic "Air Gap." The Allies attempted to bridge this gap with escort carriers, but these, too, were liable to be sunk by U-boats, as demonstrated in the torpedoing of the British *Avenger* by *U 155* on 14 November. Despite improved Anglo–American cooperation, superior intelligence, and better anti-submarine warfare methods, in November 1942 U-boats sank approximately 700,000 tons of Allied shipping, their greatest monthly total of the war (though still well below the total for April 1917, the best U-boat month in the First World War). For the year 1942, almost 8 million tons (1,664 merchantmen) were sunk. In the process, the German navy lost 58 U-boats in the last six months of 1942 alone; during the same period German shipyards (which had all but stopped working on larger surface vessels) better than doubled the replacement rate, completing another 121 submarines.[105] At a time of disastrous German setbacks on the Eastern Front at Stalingrad and in North Africa after El Alamein and Torch, the Atlantic remained a bright spot.

The toll taken by U-boats off the Atlantic coast of the United States during the first half of 1942 might have been even greater if not for Hitler's repeated insistence that more of Dönitz's forces be assigned to Norwegian waters, to disrupt the Arctic convoys to Russia. Starting in April the US navy joined the British in escorting the convoys, yet German surface warships, U-boats, and aircraft based in Norway continued to sink merchantmen attempting the passage. Of the 58 Allied merchantmen lost on the Arctic route during the entire war, 24 were sunk on a single day, 5 July 1942, when the Germans attacked convoy PQ-17, destroying 144,000 tons of shipping along with cargoes including 430 tanks and 210 aircraft. Meanwhile, between late March and late December 1942, skirmishes on the Arctic convoy route claimed remarkably few warships. The Germans lost one destroyer and three U-boats, all to British surface warships, while British losses included the cruiser *Edinburgh* (5 May), one destroyer and one minesweeper, all sunk by U-boats. Accidents claimed another British destroyer, rammed in a snow squall by the battleship *King George V*, and the Polish submarine *Jastrzab*, a victim of friendly fire. The year ended with the Battle of the Barents Sea (31 December), which began after Vice Admiral Oskar Kummetz conducted a sortie from the German base at Altenfjord–Kåfjord with the heavy cruisers *Lützow* and *Admiral Hipper* and six destroyers, against an Arctic convoy escorted by the cruisers *Sheffield* and *Jamaica*, with several destroyers and smaller craft. Despite its advantage in firepower (from the 11.1-inch guns of the *Lützow* and 8-inch guns of the *Admiral Hipper*, against the 6-inch guns of the *Sheffield* and *Jamaica*), the German force lost one of its destroyers while sinking one British destroyer and one minesweeper, and failed to sink a single merchantman in the convoy. Afterward the *Admiral Hipper* and *Lützow* were recalled to the Baltic, where they spent the rest of the war in relative inactivity.[106]

As 1943 began, the Germans clung to the notion that their largest warships, operating out of Norwegian fjords, could make a difference against the Arctic convoys. They eventually sent the battleship *Scharnhorst* to join the *Tirpitz* in Norwegian waters, and would have sent the *Gneisenau*, too, if it had not been badly damaged in an RAF raid on Kiel (26 November 1942). Nevertheless, the German defeat in the Battle of the Barents Sea prompted Hitler to summon Raeder to his headquarters at the Wolfsschanze. According to the admiral, Hitler spent an hour "attack[ing] the navy in a vicious and impertinent way," alleging that "except for the submarines the entire history of the German navy had been one of futility." Raeder responded to this withering criticism of his surface fleet by submitting his resignation, which Hitler accepted on 30 January 1943. Dönitz, head of the German submarine service since its revival in 1935, succeeded him as fleet commander. The appointment of a U-boat man to head the navy signaled a change in focus, as Hitler belatedly decided to give U-boat construction a clear priority. During 1943 Dönitz cancelled a reconstruction plan for the *Gneisenau*, which would have given the ship a heavier primary armament of 15-inch guns; instead, it remained unrepaired and never saw action again. Other projects cancelled included the carrier *Graf Zeppelin*, a second unnamed carrier, and the project of converting the unfinished heavy cruiser *Seydlitz* into a carrier.[107]

At the start of 1943 Dönitz had 212 operational U-boats, more than twice as many as a year earlier. As late as March 1943 the Germans were still sinking Allied merchantmen faster than they could be replaced, and building U-boats faster than the Allies could sink them. During the first three weeks of that month the German submarine service sank 97 merchantmen at a cost of 7 U-boats, while commissioning another 14 new boats. At that rate, the Battle of the Atlantic could still have gone Germany's way. Following an "Atlantic convoy conference" held in Washington in March 1943, the Canadian navy assumed greater responsibility for convoy protection in the western North Atlantic, absolving the British navy of any responsibility west of a line 47° W longitude. A redoubled Allied anti-submarine effort included land-based long-range bombers (equipped with improved searchlights and radar) and the increased use of escort carriers to provide convoys with further protection in the "Air Gap." Thanks to such measures, the war in the Atlantic turned around rather abruptly. During May 1943 alone the Germans lost 41 U-boats, and the following month passed without a single Atlantic convoy being attacked by submarines. During September and October 1943, U-boats sank just 9 of the 2,468 merchantmen convoyed across the Atlantic; in the process another 25 U-boats were lost. Meanwhile, during all of 1943 the British lost only one escort carrier, the *Dasher*, and to an accident rather than a U-boat: on 27 March, the ship caught fire and burned while anchored in the Clyde.[108]

The Arctic convoy route remained relatively quiet from the Battle of the Barents Sea at the end of 1942 until 6–9 September 1943, when the *Tirpitz*, the *Scharnhorst*, and an escort of nine destroyers went on a sortie to the southern tip of the island of Spitsbergen, 400 miles north–northwest of Norway's North Cape. There, they destroyed a weather station at Barentsburg which serviced the Arctic convoys. The raid took the battleships to a latitude of 76.5° N, the farthest north that any surface capital ships have ever attempted to operate. Two days after the ships returned to Altenfjord–Kåfjord, the British launched the first of a series of attempts by midget submarines to penetrate the base and sink the *Tirpitz*. None of the submarines involved survived, but on 23 September one of them succeeded in planting timed charges on the battleship's hull, which caused damage severe enough to put the ship out of action for six months.[109]

The *Scharnhorst*, meanwhile, remained idle until Christmas Day, when Admiral Erich Bey took it out with an escort of five destroyers in an attempt to intercept an Allied convoy rounding the North Cape. British intelligence immediately alerted Admiral Sir Bruce Fraser, then Home Fleet commander, and a trap was quickly set. Owing to the fact that a westbound convoy returning from Murmansk was passing the eastbound convoy the *Scharnhorst* planned to attack, the British navy had plenty of warships in the area. Rear Admiral Robert Burnett's cruisers *Belfast*, *Norfolk*, and *Sheffield* joined 8 destroyers (one of them Norwegian) in screening the vulnerable convoys while Fraser, some 200 miles to the west with the battleship *Duke of York* and cruiser *Jamaica*, steamed to the scene. As the *Scharnhorst* raced northward through heavy seas it outran its destroyers, which played no role in the subsequent action. The Battle of North Cape started at 09:30 on 26 December. In the predawn darkness of the Arctic winter, the *Belfast* and *Norfolk* intercepted the *Scharnhorst* thirty miles south of the passing convoy. They opened fire, scoring two hits almost immediately, one of which destroyed the German battleship's radar. Bey broke off the action but continued to search for the convoy until just after noon, when he finally headed back for Altenfjord–Kåfjord. This delay enabled Fraser to position his flagship between the *Scharnhorst* and its base, after which he used radar to locate and target his prey. The *Scharnhorst* was roughly the same size as the 36,725-ton *Duke of York*, a battleship of the *King George V* class, but the nine 11.1-inch guns of its main battery were no match for the ten 14-inch guns of its British adversary. Night had fallen by the time the *Duke of York* opened fire on the *Scharnhorst* at 16:50, scoring two hits in its first salvo. Bey then attempted to use his ship's superior speed (32 knots, to the *Duke of York*'s 28) to race Fraser to the Norwegian coast, but at 18:20 a third 14-inch shell from the *Duke of York*, in a salvo fired at a range of some 18,000 yards, destroyed the *Scharnhorst*'s starboard boiler room and reduced its speed to just over 20 knots. Thereafter, Burnett's cruisers joined the *Duke of York* in pounding the crippled battleship at an ever closer range; finally, Fraser ordered the cruisers and destroyers to unleash their torpedoes, several of which hit the stricken ship. The *Scharnhorst* sank at 19:45, taking with it almost all hands. Only 36 survivors were rescued from the icy waters, and the 1,803 dead (including Bey) remain the greatest number lost in the sinking of a European warship after the 1,977 who perished with the *Bismarck*.[110]

The Battle of North Cape ended the last high seas sortie by a German capital ship, as the only one remaining, the *Tirpitz*, was destined never to fight again. Theoretically ready for sea as of March 1944, the *Tirpitz* remained at Altenfjord–Kåfjord, where it was damaged on 2 April by aircraft from a British task force led by the carriers *Victorious* and *Furious*. On 17 July a larger force including the carriers *Furious*, *Formidable*, and *Indefatigable* repeated the operation, but the Germans received enough advance warning to hide the battleship in a smoke-screen, and none of the bombs hit their target. A third sustained assault against the *Tirpitz* included 247 carrier aircraft sorties between 22 August and 29 August, during which the British inflicted further damage on the ship but at a heavy cost, as *U 354* torpedoed the escort carrier *Nabob* on the first day of the operation, leaving it damaged beyond repair. A fourth attack, on 15 September, employed RAF Lancasters, flying home from northern Russia, to drop 12,000-pound "Tallboy" bombs, one of which hit the bow of the *Tirpitz*. By rendering the big battleship unfit to operate on the high seas, the cumulative effects of the British raids posed a dilemma for the Germans: either they could leave the ship at Altenfjord–Kåfjord, where it would be of no further use to their war effort, or move it down the coast to a some-what less spartan port where it would be properly repaired but even more vulnerable to British air attack while those repairs were under way. Dönitz chose the latter course, and the *Tirpitz* made its way 250 miles down the Norwegian coast to Tromsø. The gamble did not pay off. On the morning of 12 November 1944, six "Tallboys" dropped by Lancasters flying from Scotland hit the *Tirpitz* in rapid succession. The ship sank at 08:45, taking with it 1,204 members of the crew.[111]

During 1944 the increasing frequency of British air attacks made the Norwegian fjords less secure for German U-boats. By the end of the year nine Allied convoys totaling 304 merchantmen had made the trip into Murmansk or Archangel, with a loss of just four ships to submarine attack. By the end of the war, 720 Allied merchantmen had completed the Arctic voyage, with another 58 lost to enemy action and 33 turned back for other reasons. During the final buildup of forces in Britain for the Normandy invasion, the growing volume of traffic on the Atlantic convoy route likewise crossed virtually unmolested. Between January and March 1944, just three of the 3,360 Allied merchantmen convoyed across the Atlantic were sunk. The Allies entrusted naval planning for the cross-Channel invasion to Admiral Sir Bertram Ramsay, who had been appointed "Naval Commander Expeditionary Force" in June 1942. After orchestrating the Torch landings in North Africa and the subsequent invasion of Sicily, Ramsay turned his attentions to the Normandy invasion. By June 1944 he had assembled a "bombardment force" of 107 battleships, cruisers, and monitors, and an escort force of 286 destroyers, frigates, sloops, and corvettes. Landing craft included 4,216 vessels of various types. Other ships included dozens of tugs to tow two "Mulberry" artificial harbors and breakwater blockships (including the old French battleship *Courbet*) across the Channel and into place after the initial beachheads were secured. Dozens of merchantmen and obsolete warships were assembled to be scuttled in the creation of the two artificial ports on the Normandy coast. To disrupt Allied preparations the Luftwaffe flew hundreds of sorties over the British ports of the Channel, concentrating on Portsmouth, but inexperienced bomber crews failed to do significant damage while many were shot down. During the first five months of 1944 these raids cost the Germans over 300 aircraft, losses which virtually eliminated the Luftwaffe as a factor by the time of the invasion. During the same months, the German navy intensified its S-boat activity in anticipation of the forthcoming Allied attack, using flotillas of the small craft to lay mines and attack coastal convoys in the Channel and North Sea. The only serious disruption came on the night of 27 April 1944, when nine S-boats stumbled on to a group of unescorted American tank landing ships (LSTs) designated for the D-Day force at Utah Beach, which were en route from Plymouth and Brixham to practice landings on the South Devon coast. Two of the LSTs were sunk and over 600 lives lost, enough for the Allies to suppress news of the fiasco until long after the war ended. The Channel skirmishes of January–May 1944 involved no warships larger than destroyers, aside from a handful of cruisers eventually deployed by the British. Losses among these warships were limited to one British and two German destroyers.[112]

When Operation Overlord and its naval corollary, Operation Neptune, were launched on 6 June 1944, Rear Admiral Vian commanded a British task force including the battleships *Warspite* and *Ramillies*, the monitor *Roberts*, and 11 cruisers which bombarded the British beaches of Sword, Gold, and Juno. The battleships *Nelson* and *Rodney* were held in reserve along with one cruiser. The British contributed the monitor *Erebus*, six cruisers, and several destroyers to support the US navy off Utah Beach and Omaha Beach, where the Free French navy contributed the cruisers *Montcalm* and *Georges Leygues*, a destroyer, and a number of smaller vessels, under the command of Rear Admiral Robert Jaujard. Four German destroyers, 36 U-boats, and a number of S-boats left their French Atlantic ports and attempted to enter the Channel to disrupt the Normandy invasion, but few made it through thanks to the British escort carriers *Activity*, *Tracker*, and *Vindex*, which led a force of destroyers, frigates, and sloops guarding the western approach to the Channel. On 6 June S-boats sank the Norwegian destroyer *Svenner* and a few landing craft, but the massive Allied fleet escorting the transports easily fended off the attacks. British aircraft and destroyers sank five U-boats between 7 June and 9 June and another six by 29 June, by which time U-boat attacks had claimed one LST, four supply ships, and three small British warships (two frigates and one corvette) in the Channel. One Canadian and two German destroyers were sunk in a destroyer battle off Brest on the night of 8–9 June.[113]

At the end of July 1944 the German navy had 180 operational U-boats and another 252 on trials or with crews in training. Over half (95) of the operational boats were based in the French Atlantic ports, and another third (60) in Norway. By the end of September the German collapse in France left just 5 U-boats operating from French ports and raised to 120 the number operating out of Norway. The withdrawal of the U-boats left the tiny S-boats as the only German warships based in France; their attacks in the Channel continued but achieved no significant successes, especially after US navy destroyers and PT boats were deployed to reinforce British patrols. During the summer of 1944 the S-boats were supplemented by a variety of small craft developed for sabotage operations, an initiative inspired by the disabling of the *Tirpitz* by British midget submarines in September 1943. They were organized into *Kleinkampfverbände* (*K-Verbände*), "small battle units" under the command of Rear Admiral Helmut Heye. After D-Day the Germans deployed over two dozen Italian-style manned torpedoes along the Normandy coast, where they sank one British destroyer, the Polish-manned British cruiser *Dragon*, and three minesweepers during July 1944. Exploding boats called *Linsen* ("Lentils"), modeled after the Italian navy's disposable one-man assault boats, were used to sink the destroyer *Quorn* and an anti-submarine trawler on the night of 2–3 August. These modest successes notwithstanding, the program as a whole was a colossal waste of money. The Italians embraced similar operations with great ingenuity and bravado, and the Japanese, with a stoic willingness to die; in these respects, the Germans were not the equals of their allies. In the end, Heye's *K-Verbände*, operating in seas teeming with enemy warships, under skies dominated by enemy aircraft, were successful only in the rare cases when they achieved absolute surprise.[114]

With the invasion of northern France proceeding successfully, on 15 August 1944 Allied naval attention shifted temporarily to the Mediterranean, where the British and Free French navies joined the US navy in supporting Operation Dragoon, a landing in the south of France primarily by American and Free French troops. The British force consisted of the battleship *Ramillies*, 7 escort carriers, 10 cruisers, and almost 30 destroyers and smaller warships; the French force included the battleship *Lorraine*, 5 cruisers, and over 20 destroyers and smaller warships. In September 1944, the same seven British escort carriers supported the Allied reconquest of Crete and German-occupied islands in the Aegean, an operation completed by early November. Meanwhile, in the North Sea, the battleship *Warspite* and monitors *Erebus* and *Roberts* provided fire support for an Anglo–Canadian assault on Walcheren Island. The landings helped open a supply route via the Scheldt to Antwerp, taken recently by Allied troops advancing into the Low Countries from France. Ships using the new route had to run a gauntlet of German mines between the mouths of the Scheldt and Thames, laid during nighttime sorties by S-boats based on the Dutch coast. These operations finally ended in late March 1945, when Allied forces completed the liberation of the Netherlands; during that month alone, eight merchantmen (31,745 tons) fell victim to mines sown by S-boats.[115]

In contrast to the continued activity of the S-boats, the largest surviving German surface vessels were usually at anchor during the last months of the war, relegated to harbor defense duties and frequently targeted by Allied bombers. At Danzig the Germans scuttled the bomb-damaged pre-dreadnought *Schleswig–Holstein* (21 March) and battleship *Gneisenau* (27 March), just days before the city fell to the Soviets. On 9 April RAF bombers sank the heavy cruiser *Admiral Scheer* at Kiel. Warships scuttled on 2–4 May at Wilhelmshaven, Kiel, and Swinemünde included the heavy cruisers *Lützow* and *Admiral Hipper*, the light cruisers *Emden* and *Köln*, and the pre-dreadnought *Schlesien*, all of which had been damaged in air raids. Only three surface vessels larger than destroyers survived to be taken by the Allies after the war: the heavy cruiser *Prinz Eugen*, sunk by the United States in 1946 in the Bikini Atoll atomic bomb test; the light cruiser *Leipzig*, scuttled by the British in 1946 in the North Sea; and the light cruiser *Nürnberg*, commissioned by the Soviet navy in 1946 as the *Admiral Makarov*.[116]

Over the winter of 1944–45 the final phase of the German U-boat war focused on the waters around the British Isles. Between mid-November and late January, around 30 merchantmen were sunk at a cost of 12 U-boats. The campaign also claimed two frigates and the escort carrier *Thane*, torpedoed on 15 January 1945 by *U 482* off the mouth of the Clyde. During the final submarine onslaught against the British Isles, lasting from 5 April to 7 May, the odds were much worse for the Germans, as 8 ships were sunk at a cost of 15 U-boats. Because these efforts were based almost entirely out of Norway, the British navy countered by taking the war aggressively into the fjords, at little risk because most Luftwaffe aircraft had been called home for the defense of Germany. The British navy's last action of the war in Europe came on 4 May 1945, four days before the German surrender, when aircraft from the escort carriers *Trumpeter*, *Searcher*, and *Queen* sank *U 711* and a submarine depot ship in the harbor of Kilbotn. The last U-boat sunk by the British was bombed off Bergen on 7 May by aircraft from RAF Coastal Command. The last action by a German U-boat against British shipping had come hours earlier, when *U 2336* sank the merchantman *Avondale Park* in the Firth of Forth. The last two U-boats lost in the war sank on 8 May (V-E Day), one wrecked accidentally off the coast of Portugal and another striking a mine off the coast of Denmark. As late as 4 May 1945 Germany still had 126 operational U-boats (120 based in Norway, five in the Baltic, and one cruising off the French Atlantic coast) with 267 more working up or with crews in training. Fears that "Nazi fanatics" would pursue a submarine guerrilla war inspired the Allies to continue to escort convoys for several days after the surrender.[117] The victors held Raeder and Dönitz accountable for the navy's role in the war, trying them at Nuremberg along with leaders of the German army and the Nazi party. Their sentences, to life (eventually commuted to nine years) and ten years imprisonment, respectively, remain the most controversial decisions of the War Crimes Tribunal.

CONCLUSION

In the Second World War, as in the First, submarine warfare ultimately became the centerpiece of the German navy's war effort, but the U-boat campaign of 1939–45 was relatively less successful than that of 1914–18. Just 22 percent more Allied shipping was sunk (14.6 million tons) in a war that lasted 30 percent longer, while four times more U-boats were lost (at least 754) and six times more submariners killed (27,491, with 5,000 taken prisoner). A staggering 70 percent of all German submariners seeing action in 1939–45 were killed, the majority of them aboard the 429 U-boats sunk with all hands. The changing balance of submarine and shipping losses reflected the dramatic wartime improvements in Allied anti-submarine warfare. From May 1944 to May 1945 the Germans lost 342 U-boats while sinking just 138 Allied merchantmen (687,790 tons). By comparison, two years earlier, from May 1942 to May 1943, the Germans lost 168 U-boats while sinking 1,169 Allied merchantmen (6,320,650 tons). Britain again withstood the onslaught, but this time the wartime damage to its merchant marine proved to be permanent. In contrast to the First World War, during which most British shipping lost to U-boats was replaced by British wartime construction, in the Second World War American wartime construction filled the void, leaving the British merchant marine of 1945 just 70 percent as large as it had been in 1939, in no position to remain a leader in the carrying trade in a postwar world glutted with American-built merchantmen flying a variety of flags.[118]

Of the five British carriers lost during the war, three fell victim to U-boats, yet to a remarkable degree air power (if not exclusively carrier-based air power) trumped the undersea threat, as more German submarines were sunk by Allied aircraft than by Allied surface vessels. Roughly half of the battleships and battle cruisers sunk in the Second World War fell victim to carrier-based aircraft, reflecting the emergence of the carrier as the capital ship of the second half of the twentieth century. Unlike in the First World War, when the British lost more dreadnoughts and battle cruisers than all other belligerents combined, in the Second World War Britain lost 5 of its 20, the other European powers

12 of their 23. Among the Allies, France lost five (one sunk by the British at Oran, the rest scuttled) and the Soviet Union one; on the Axis side, Germany lost four and Italy two (one by German action, after the September 1943 armistice). Of course, the balance of large-unit losses is less lopsided if one counts carriers as capital ships, because only Britain employed carriers in combat roles during the war, and the five lost by the British navy were the only European carriers to be sunk (the French *Béarn*, active only in the years 1939–40 and 1943–45, had served primarily as an aircraft transport). In the postwar world carrier operations would become the hallmark of a great naval power, no less significant than having one's own dreadnoughts before 1914. But it remained to be seen whether any European navy other than the British would have the will or the means to acquire and maintain aircraft carriers after 1945.

NOTES

[1] Till, "Adopting the Aircraft Carrier," 198–9; Friedman, *British Carrier Aviation*, 95; McKercher, "The Politics of Naval Arms Limitation in Britain," 41.

[2] Watts and Murray, "Military Innovation in Peacetime," 398, 403–4; Till, "Adopting the Aircraft Carrier," 207–8; Friedman, *British Carrier Aviation*, 69, 98, 102–9; *Conway, 1906–21*, 67, 70–1; *Conway, 1922–46*, 101,179–80.

[3] McKercher, "The Politics of Naval Arms Limitation in Britain," 43–50; Buckley, "The Icarus Factor," 136; *Conway, 1922–46*, 26–9, 37–8, 55–6, 113–15; 125.

[4] The Anti-Submarine Warfare School had an earlier existence, from 1917 to 1919. On British torpedo production see Kenneth Poolman, *The Winning Edge: Naval Technology in Action, 1939–1945* (Annapolis, MD, 1997), 6. In general, Arthur J. Marder, *From the Dardanelles to Oran* (London, 1974), 35–7, 42, and Tritten, "Doctrine and Fleet Tactics in the Royal Navy," 26, give the British navy high marks for the interwar years. Barnett, *Engage the Enemy*, 24–5, and Herwig, "Innovation Ignored: The Submarine Problem," 243, 248, are far more critical.

[5] Richard Dean Burns, "Regulating Submarine Warfare, 1921–41: A Case Study in Arms Control and Limited War," *Military Affairs* 35 (1971): 57–8; Legohérel, *Histoire de la Marine française*, 105–6; Blatt, "France and the Washington Conference," 208; *Conway, 1906–21*, 212–13; *Conway, 1922–46*, 262–8, 272–4.

[6] Tritten, "Navy and Military Doctrine in France," 59–60.

[7] Sullivan, "Italian Naval Power and the Washington Disarmament Conference," 225; Donolo, "The History of Italian Naval Doctrine," 113–14; James J. Sadkovich, *The Italian Navy in World War II* (Westport, CT, 1994), 1; *Conway's All the World's Fighting Ships, 1947–95* (London, 1995), 204 [hereafter cited as *Conway, 1947–95*].

[8] Sullivan, "Italian Naval Power and the Washington Disarmament Conference," 226, 240; Donolo, "The History of Italian Naval Doctrine," 114–15; *Conway, 1922–46*, 291–4, 298–300, 304–8.

[9] Erich Raeder, *My Life*, trans. Henry W. Drexel (Annapolis, MD, 1960), 146–65; Bird, *Weimar, the German Naval Officer Corps, and the Rise of National Socialism*, 260–97; Maiolo, *The Royal Navy and Nazi Germany*, 20–1; Gröner, *Die deutschen Kriegsschiffe*, 1:87–91, 145–52; *Conway, 1922–46*, 222. Raeder, 165, is careful to note that his first

meeting with Hitler took place three days after the Nazi leader became chancellor; previous contacts were through intermediaries.

[10] Herwig, "Innovation Ignored: The Submarine Problem," 231–3.

[11] *Conway 1906–21*, 302–17 *passim*; *Conway 1922–46*, 322–7, 332.

[12] Norman Polmar, *The Naval Institute Guide to the Soviet Navy*, 5th edn (Annapolis, MD, 1991), 72–3; Norman Friedman, *Seapower and Space: From the Dawn of the Missile Age to Net-Centric Warfare* (Annapolis, MD, 2000), 129.

[13] *Conway, 1922–46*, 371–4, 387–91, 399–401.

[14] Jackson, *The Royal Navy in World War II*, 8; McKercher, "The Politics of Naval Arms Limitation in Britain," 52; Buckley, "The Icarus Factor," 139–40.

[15] Jackson, *The Royal Navy in World War II*, 8; *Conway, 1922–46*, 30–2, 259–60, 265–6, 289–90, 295–6.

[16] Wells, *The Royal Navy*, 141–4.

[17] *Conway, 1922–46*, 38–41, 49–50, 56–7, 268–70, 273–7, 300–1, 304–10, 316.

[18] Robert Mallett, *The Italian Navy and Fascist Expansionism* (London, 1998), 2–3, 11, 102. Sadkovich, *The Italian Navy in World War II*, 3, characterizes Italy's naval buildup as purely defensive, in response to France's program.

[19] Herwig, "Innovation Ignored: The Submarine Problem," 235–6; *Conway, 1922–46*, 225–7, 232–3; Gröner, *Die deutschen Kriegsschiffe*, 1:55–8; Poolman, *The Winning Edge*, 3. Gröner reflects standard German practice in calling the *Scharnhorst* and the *Gneisenau* battleships; many English-language works categorize these fast battleships, along with their French counterparts *Dunkerque* and *Strasbourg*, as battle cruisers.

[20] Maiolo, *The Royal Navy and Nazi Germany*, 11–37; Herwig, "Innovation Ignored: The Submarine Problem," 236, 242; *Conway, 1922–46*, 240–1.

[21] *Conway, 1922–46*, 260.

[22] Stephen E. Pelz, *Race to Pearl Harbor: The Failure of the Second London Naval Conference and the Onset of World War II* (Cambridge, MA, 1974), 59–64; Friedman, *British Carrier Aviation*, 109, 130.

[23] Marder, *From the Dardanelles to Oran*, 64–104; Mallett, *The Italian Navy and Fascist Expansionism*, 50, 54, 62, 103, 192.

[24] Unless otherwise noted, sources for this and the following paragraph are Lawrence Sondhaus, "The Non–Intervention Committee During the Spanish Civil War: A Study in the Failure of Diplomacy" (MA thesis, University of Virginia, 1982), and *Conway, 1922–46*, 398–404.

[25] Mallett, *The Italian Navy and Fascist Expansionism*, 97.

[26] Raeder, *My Life*, 230–54; Herwig, "Innovation Ignored: The Submarine Problem," 231, 262; Murray, "Innovation," 321; Poolman, *The Winning Edge*, 8–9; Gröner, *Die deutschen Kriegsschiffe*, 1: 58–62, 93–6, 98–101.

[27] Mallett, *The Italian Navy and Fascist Expansionism*, 60, 101; *Conway, 1922–46*, 289–90, 297.

[28] Friedman, *British Carrier Aviation*, 15, 110–54, 362; Till, "Adopting the Aircraft Carrier," 217; *Conway, 1922–46*, 15–6, 19–22, 33–4.

[29] Philippe Masson, *La Marine française et la guerre, 1939–1945* (Paris, 1991), 20–1; Hervé Coutau–Bégarie and Claude Huan, *Darlan* (Paris, 1989), 117–18, 159; George E. Melton, *Darlan: Admiral and Statesman of France, 1881–1942* (Westport, CT, 1998), 5–6, 30; Jackson, *The Royal Navy in World War II*, 8–10; *Conway, 1922–46*, 260–1, 266.

[30] Tobias R. Philbin III, *The Lure of Neptune: German–Soviet Naval Collaboration and Ambitions, 1919–1941* (Columbia, SC, 1994), 23–37; Polmar, *The Naval Institute Guide to the Soviet Navy*, 423; Gromov *et al.*, *Tri Veka Rossiiskogo Flota*, 2:345, 350, 3:12; Conway, *1922–46*, 318–38.

[31] Friedman, *British Carrier Aviation*, 143.

[32] Jackson, *The Royal Navy in World War II*, 11; Raeder, *My Life*, 280–1; Poolman, *The Winning Edge*, 16; Axel Niestlé, *German U-Boat Losses during World War II: Details of Destruction* (Annapolis, MD, 1998), 4; Michael Gannon, *Operation Drumbeat* (New York, 1990), 75.

[33] Barnett, *Engage the Enemy*, 66–71; Marder, *From the Dardanelles to Oran*, 107, 171.

[34] Jackson, *The Royal Navy in World War II*, 16, 18.

[35] Dudley Pope, *Graf Spee: The Life and Death of a Raider* (Philadelphia, PA, 1956), *passim*; Derek Howse, *Radar at Sea: The Royal Navy in World War II* (Annapolis, MD, 1993), 45; Poolman, *The Winning Edge*, 23–6; Conway, *1922–46*, 29–30, 227.

[36] Barnett, *Engage the Enemy*, 73–8; Paul Auphan and Jacques Mordal, *The French Navy in World War II*, trans. A. C. J. Sabalot (Annapolis, MD, 1959), 33–4.

[37] Conway, *1922–46*, 38–40, 232, 268, 270.

[38] Barnett, *Engage the Enemy*, 102–18; Raeder, *My Life*, 300–16.

[39] Barnett, *Engage the Enemy*, 119–39; Poolman, *The Winning Edge*, 33–8; Auphan and Mordal, *The French Navy in World War II*, 50–3; Conway, *1922–46*, 10, 267.

[40] Marder, *From the Dardanelles to Oran*, 171–2.

[41] Barnett, *Engage the Enemy*, 140–67; Auphan and Mordal, *The French Navy in World War II*, 54–95, 108; Conway, *1922–46*, 12–13, 38–46, 267–70, 272–3.

[42] Jackson, *The Royal Navy in World War II*, 40–1.

[43] "Directive No. 16, On the Preparation of a Landing Operation Against England," text in Egbert Kieser, *Hitler on the Doorstep: Operation Sea Lion, the German Plan to Invade Britain, 1940*, translated by Helmut Bögler (Annapolis, MD, 1997), 274–5.

[44] Raeder, *My Life*, 321–31; Kieser, *Hitler on the Doorstep*, 223–4, 228, 264–5.

[45] Jackson, *The Royal Navy in World War II*, 41–2.

[46] Ibid., 53–4; Barnett, *Engage the Enemy*, 184; Conway, *1922–46*, 12–13, 38–46.

[47] Jackson, *The Royal Navy in World War II*, 55–6.

[48] Raeder, *My Life*, 349–54; Graham Rhys-Jones, *The Loss of the Bismarck: An Avoidable Disaster* (Annapolis, MD, 1999), 33–70, 79–80; Barnett, *Engage the Enemy*, 278–80.

[49] Rhys-Jones, *The Loss of the Bismarck*, 119; Poolman, *The Winning Edge*, 40–2.

[50] Rhys-Jones, *The Loss of the Bismarck*, 178–208. Gröner, *Die deutschen Kriegsschiffe*, 1:59, reflects the standard German contention that the ship was scuttled, not sunk.

[51] Jackson, *The Royal Navy in World War II*, 62–3.

[52] Ibid., 64–6.

[53] Ibid., 125, 163; Friedman, *British Carrier Aviation*, 179, 182–201, 363–4.

[54] Mallett, *The Italian Navy and Fascist Expansionism*, 197, and Sadkovich, *The Italian Navy in World War II*, 53, give slightly different figures for the strengths of the Mediterranean navies in the summer of 1940.

[55] Sadkovich, *The Italian Navy in World War II*, 12, 82, 84; Donolo, "The History of Italian Naval Doctrine," 116.

[56] Jackson, *The Royal Navy in World War II*, 81; Sadkovich, *The Italian Navy in World War II*, 70, 78.

[57] Jackson, *The Royal Navy in World War II*, 43–4; Sadkovich, *The Italian Navy in World War II*, 55.

[58] Marder, *From the Dardanelles to Oran*, 214, 228–75; Masson, *La Marine française et la guerre*, 114–66; Auphan and Mordal, *The French Navy in World War II*, 111–23, 126–35. For text of Article Eight of Franco–German armistice see Masson, 440.

[59] Marder, *From the Dardanelles to Oran*, 258–9; Masson, *La Marine française et la guerre*, 429–30; Auphan and Mordal, *The French Navy in World War II*, 123–6, 135–9, 272; *Conway, 1922–46*, 257–66.

[60] Marder, *From the Dardanelles to Oran*, 276–80; Masson, *La Marine française et la guerre*, 167–96; Auphan and Mordal, *The French Navy in World War II*, 144–9.

[61] Auphan and Mordal, *The French Navy in World War II*, 154–69; *Conway, 1922–46*, 62–3, 277.

[62] Sadkovich, *The Italian Navy in World War II*, 14, 58–9; Jackson, *The Royal Navy in World War II*, 46–8.

[63] Sadkovich, *The Italian Navy in World War II*, 90–2; Poolman, *The Winning Edge*, 100–1; Mallett, *The Italian Navy and Fascist Expansionism*, 194.

[64] Sadkovich, *The Italian Navy in World War II*, 94–9; Jackson, *The Royal Navy in World War II*, 51.

[65] All other warship losses in the Mediterranean between July and December 1940 not accounted for in the paragraphs above resulted from air or submarine attack: four Italian destroyers, two British destroyers, and one British submarine. See Jackson, *The Royal Navy in World War II*, 46–7, 55, 63; Sadkovich, *The Italian Navy in World War II*, 59, 67, 88–9, 100.

[66] Jackson, *The Royal Navy in World War II*, 67–8, 81; Sadkovich, *The Italian Navy in World War II*, 12, 14, 70, 125; Raeder, *My Life*, 364–5, 367; *Conway, 1906–21*, 262; *Conway, 1922–46*, 38, 50, 294. Wavell to Churchill, 27 March 1941, quoted in Winston S. Churchill, *The Second World War*, 6 vols (Boston, MA, 1948–52), 3:203.

[67] Barnett, *Engage the Enemy*, 335–45; Sadkovich, *The Italian Navy in World War II*, 125–34; Howse, *Radar at Sea*, 75–6; Tritten, "Doctrine and Fleet Tactics in the Royal Navy," 28. While Italian sources contend the *Pola* was scuttled, British sources insist it was sunk by British action.

[68] Barnett, *Engage the Enemy*, 252–65; Jackson, *The Royal Navy in World War II*, 71–2; Sadkovich, *The Italian Navy in World War II*, 155–6; *Conway, 1922–46*, 19.

[69] *Conway, 1906–21*, 386; *Conway, 1922–46*, 236, 404–5. The Greek navy lost two vessels before the German intervention, the light cruiser *Helle* (sunk 15 August 1940 by an Italian submarine, two months before Italy declared war on Greece) and the submarine *Proteus* (sunk 19 December 1940 by an Italian torpedo boat).

[70] Jerko Kačić-Dimitri, "Das Ende der königlich jugoslawischen Flotte," *Marine – Gestern, Heute* 15 (1988): 9–11; Sadkovich, *The Italian Navy in World War II*, 38.

[71] Jackson, *The Royal Navy in World War II*, 72; Auphan and Mordal, *The French Navy in World War II*, 197–201. Churchill, *The Second World War*, 3:253–67, 321–32, remains the most accessible detailed English-language account of these rather obscure campaigns.

[72] Jackson, *The Royal Navy in World War II*, 72–3, 83–4; Sadkovich, *The Italian Navy in World War II*, 186, 189; Mallett, *The Italian Navy and Fascist Expansionism*, 112; *Conway, 1922–46*, 290–1.

[73] Friedman, *British Carrier Aviation*, 125–7; Jackson, *The Royal Navy in World War II*, 73, 83–4; Sadkovich, *The Italian Navy in World War II*, 14, 213–14; *Conway, 1922–46*, 294.

[74] Jackson, *The Royal Navy in World War II*, 85.

[75] Ibid., 84–8, 163–7; Sadkovich, *The Italian Navy in World War II*, 79, 229, 237, 242–6, 248, 272, 274, 288–99; *Conway, 1922–46*, 291–309 *passim*.

[76] The best recent works on Dieppe are John Campbell, *Dieppe Revisited: A Documentary Investigation* (London, 1993) and Brian Loring Villa, *Unauthorized Action: Mountbatten and the Dieppe Raid* (Oxford, 1994). For a brief account see Jackson, *The Royal Navy in World War II*, 94–5.

[77] On Operation Torch see Norman Gelb, *Desperate Venture: The Story of Operation Torch, the Allied Invasion of North Africa* (New York, 1992); William Breuer, *Operation Torch: The Allied Gamble to Invade North Africa* (New York, 1985). See also Auphan and Mordal, *The French Navy in World War II*, 209–37 *passim*; Barnett, *Engage the Enemy*, 551–69; Sadkovich, *The Italian Navy in World War II*, 316; *Conway, 1922–46*, 260–75 *passim*.

[78] Masson, *La Marine française et la guerre*, 373–413; Auphan and Mordal, *The French Navy in World War II*, 238–89; *Conway, 1922–46*, 257–76. France's other two surviving battleships, the *Paris* and *Courbet*, interned in Britain since July 1940, were deemed too old to be of any use and never saw action again. On the assassination of Darlan see Coutau-Bégarie and Huan, *Darlan*, 682–728, and Melton, *Darlan*, 207–28.

[79] Sadkovich, *The Italian Navy in World War II*, 14, 38, 314–19, *Conway, 1922–46*, 289–91, 296, 301, 304, 312, 317. In Sadkovich's calculations, the two corvettes are counted as destroyers.

[80] Sadkovich, *The Italian Navy in World War II*, 324–6; Donolo, "The History of Italian Naval Doctrine," 117.

[81] Jackson, *The Royal Navy in World War II*, 109–10; Friedman, *British Carrier Aviation*, 127, 151–2; *Conway, 1922–46*, 286.

[82] Sadkovich, *The Italian Navy in World War II*, 329.

[83] Barnett, *Engage the Enemy*, 666–9; Jackson, *The Royal Navy in World War II*, 112–15; *Conway, 1922–46*, 236, 283–312 *passim*; Donolo, "The History of Italian Naval Doctrine," 117. The glider bombs first used against the *Roma* and *Italia* were employed again a week later against British warships providing fire support off Salerno; on 16 September the battleship *Warspite* had to be towed back to Malta for repairs after being struck by one of the bombs.

[84] Auphan and Mordal, *The French Navy in World War II*, 294–6; Legohérel, *Histoire de la Marine française*, 117.

[85] Jackson, *The Royal Navy in World War II*, 163–8; Sadkovich, *The Italian Navy in World War II*, 329, 338; Sullivan, "Italian Naval Power and the Washington Disarmament Conference," 242.

[86] Jackson, *The Royal Navy in World War II*, 163–8; Auphan and Mordal, *The French Navy in World War II*, 292, 348.

[87] Evans and Peattie, *Kaigun*, 353, 365.

[88] Edwyn Gray, *Operation Pacific: The Royal Navy's War against Japan, 1941–1945* (Annapolis, MD, 1990), 17–26; Evans and Peattie, *Kaigun*, 467–8. The first Japanese troops entered French Indochina in September 1940, under a Franco–Japanese agreement to provide bases and allow transit rights. The Vichy French land and naval forces were tolerated by the Japanese until March 1945, when their leaders refused a demand to join in active combat against the Allies. See Auphan and Mordal, *The French Navy in World War II*, 194–6, 355–63.

[89] *Conway, 1922–46*, 386–92.

[90] Gray, *Operation Pacific*, 27–94 *passim*. See also Martin Middlebrook and Patrick Mahoney, *Battleship: the Sinking of the Prince of Wales and the Repulse* (New York, 1979).

[91] Gray, *Operation Pacific*, 96–103, 107; *Conway, 1922–46*, 388–91.

[92] Friedman, *British Carrier Aviation*, 221–9, 362–3.

[93] Gray, *Operation Pacific*, 111–23, 128.

[94] Ibid., 124–7, 145–6; Auphan and Mordal, *The French Navy in World War II*, 203–5; *Conway, 1922–46*, 273–9 *passim*.

[95] Philip Ziegler, *Mountbatten* (New York, 1985), 238–40.

[96] Ibid., 285; Gray, *Operation Pacific*, 160–75. The first Japanese naval vessel sunk by British action was the submarine *I 34*, by the submarine *Taurus*, off Penang on 13 November 1943. The first surface vessel sunk was the light cruiser *Kuma*, by the submarine *Tally Ho*, off Penang on 11 January 1944. *Conway, 1922–46*, 174, 176, 200.

[97] Gray, *Operation Pacific*, 170–1, 175; Jackson, *The Royal Navy in World War II*, 121–2; Tritten, "Doctrine and Fleet Tactics in the Royal Navy," 28.

[98] Gray, *Operation Pacific*, 201–3, 238–9; Jackson, *The Royal Navy in World War II*, 121–4.

[99] Gray, *Operation Pacific*, 203–35; Friedman, *British Carrier Aviation*, 148, 151.

[100] Gray, *Operation Pacific*, 233–4, 243–57; Friedman, *British Carrier Aviation*, 229.

[101] Gromov *et al.*, *Tri Veka Rossiiskogo Flota*, 3:188; Polmar, *The Naval Institute Guide to the Soviet Navy*, 20.

[102] Gromov *et al.*, *Tri Veka Rossiiskogo Flota*, 3:12; *Conway, 1922–46*, 322–38. Aid tonnage figures from Paul Kemp, *Convoy! Drama in Arctic Waters* (London, 2000), 235.

[103] Jackson, *The Royal Navy in World War II*, 89, 97–9; *Conway, 1922–46*, 322, 325, 328, 332, 338.

[104] Jackson, *The Royal Navy in World War II*, 89–94, 99.

[105] Ibid., 129, 163; Gannon, *Operation Drumbeat*, 309–10, 380–1, 388–9, 395, and *passim*.

[106] Jackson, *The Royal Navy in World War II*, 100–6.

[107] Raeder quoted in *My Life*, 370. The two 52,600-ton battleships laid down in 1939 had been cancelled earlier and were broken up starting in November 1941. See *Conway, 1922–46*, 225; Gröner, *Die deutschen Kriegsschiffe*, 1:58, 62, 101, 106.

[108] Jackson, *The Royal Navy in World War II*, 131–5, 163; Gannon, *Operation Drumbeat*, 393–6.

[109] Jackson, *The Royal Navy in World War II*, 137, 139; V. E. Tarrant, *The Last Year of the Kriegsmarine, May 1944–May 1945* (Annapolis, MD, 1994), 34–5. The Allies evacuated Spitsbergen's 3,000 Norwegian and Russian inhabitants in August 1941. Within weeks the Germans established a weather station there, which remained in operation until the Allies returned in the summer of 1942, to retake the island.

[110] John Winton, *The Death of the Scharnhorst* (New York, 1983). See also Howse, *Radar at Sea*, 187–90.

[111] Barnett, *Engage the Enemy*, 745–7; Jackson, *The Royal Navy in World War II*, 139–43.

[112] Barnett, *Engage the Enemy*, 694, 753–80 *passim*; Jackson, *The Royal Navy in World War II*, 136, 146, 149, 151–2.

[113] Barnett, *Engage the Enemy*, 814–32; Auphan and Mordal, *The French Navy in World War II*, 318–24.

[114] Tarrant, *The Last Year of the Kriegsmarine*, 35–9, 205–6, 223; Jackson, *The Royal Navy in World War II*, 155.

[115] Auphan and Mordal, *The French Navy in World War II*, 328–40; Tarrant, *The Last Year of the Kriegsmarine*, 220–1; Jackson, *The Royal Navy in World War II*, 155–6.

[116] Gröner, *Die deutschen Kriegsschiffe*, 1:46, 90–1, 96, 145, 149, 152.

[117] Tarrant, *The Last Year of the Kriegsmarine*, 206, 235; Jackson, *The Royal Navy in World War II*, 144–6, 156, 163.

[118] Gannon, *Operation Drumbeat*, xxi, 417; Niestlé, *German U-Boat Losses during World War II*, 4, 303; Tarrant, *The Last Year of the Kriegsmarine*, 180; Pugh, *The Cost of Seapower*, 18–19. Historians disagree over the number of U-boats that actually sortied during the war and the number of those lost. Gannon contends that 754 of 863 were sunk; Niestlé, 757 of 859. Herwig, "Innovation Ignored: The Submarine Problem," 231, gives higher figures, 784 of 940.

8

EUROPEAN NAVIES IN THE ERA OF THE COLD WAR, 1945–91

Britain lost a total of 379 warships during the Second World War, including 5 battleships and battle cruisers, 5 aircraft carriers, 5 escort carriers, 27 cruisers, 142 destroyers, and 75 submarines.[1] Nevertheless, in 1945 its fleet was significantly larger than it had been in 1919, with personnel numbering 863,500 and a navy list of just over 1,000 warships, including 11 aircraft carriers, 39 escort carriers, and 131 submarines, a force second only to the US navy in size and capability.[2] The First World War reduced the ranks of European naval powers from six to three; Britain, France, and Italy were subsequently rejoined by Germany thanks to Hitler's naval buildup, only to have the Second World War reduce the number again, to Britain alone. As Europe entered the postwar era, the onset of the Cold War and decolonization raised new questions about the future role of all of its navies, large and small.

FRANCE AND BRITAIN: FROM SAIGON TO SUEZ

In the summer of 1945 France was in no position to function as a European naval power, or as a great power in any sense of the word. Yet, as provisional president, Charles de Gaulle made the recovery of France's former status his highest priority. At his insistence the French emerged with a permanent seat on the United Nations Security Council and a zone of occupation in Germany. He also sought to reestablish control over France's colonial empire, a quest in which the French navy was to play a central role.

By the end of the war the Free French had secured the allegiance of the entire French empire except for Indochina, which after the withdrawal of Japanese troops was divided into two occupation zones along the parallel of 16°N, with Britain assuming responsibility for the south and Nationalist China for the north. In anticipation of a French return to the colony, on 14 August 1945 De Gaulle appointed Admiral Thierry d'Argenlieu to the office of High Commissioner of French Indochina, but on 2 September the Vietnamese communist wartime resistance leader, Ho Chi Minh, proclaimed a republic at Hanoi. The first British troops reached Saigon on 11 September. Thereafter, under Clement Attlee's Labour government, Britain gladly deferred to a France eager to assume responsibility for the Southeast Asian quagmire. The first French troops were airlifted into Saigon the day after the British arrived, and on 3 October naval transports landed the first elements of an armored division, escorted to Vietnam by the battleship *Richelieu* and the large destroyer *Triomphant*. Over the weeks that followed, De Gaulle sent every available French warship to the Far East; between 15 and 27 October alone, the carrier *Béarn*, the cruisers *Gloire* and *Suffren*, and five smaller warships arrived. By the end of 1945 the navy had convoyed some 50,000 French troops to Vietnam. After De Gaulle left office in January 1946, the new government of the Fourth Republic continued his Indochina policy. The British supported French operations against the communist Viet Minh until 15 January; meanwhile, the Nationalist Chinese forces briefly occupied northern Indochina before agreeing, on 29 February, to give way to the French. One week later, on 6 March, France accepted the Hanoi regime as a member of the new French Union, opening the way for a French garrison to enter the north. This force arrived by sea in six transports, escorted by a squadron under Vice Admiral Philippe Auboyneau consisting of the *Béarn*, the cruisers *Emile Bertin*, *Tourville*, and *Duquesne*, and eight smaller warships. After Ho Chi Minh left Hanoi for further negotiations in Paris, Thierry d'Argenlieu, on his own authority, made the fateful decision to recognize a rival southern Vietnamese republic based at Saigon. Months of mounting tension culminated in the admiral's decision to have the cruiser *Suffren* shell Haiphong on 23 November, in retaliation for the death of French soldiers in a skirmish with the Viet Minh. Within a month, the French were embroiled in a full-scale war in Indochina. The peculiar naval career of Thierry d'Argenlieu, the admiral–priest, ended with his recall from Saigon in February 1947; upon returning to France, he reentered the Catholic priesthood.[3]

The French navy of the immediate postwar years lacked the resources to fulfill the ambitious mission of supporting a major war effort in Southeast Asia while also safeguarding the interests of France in Europe and the rest of the colonial empire. The *Richelieu*, the *Béarn*, and nine cruisers formed the core of the fleet, but the latter averaged fifteen years of service by 1947 and the oldest three, dating from the late 1920s, were no longer of any use. Four large destroyers of the *Fantastique* class were rerated as light cruisers, while two others served as tenders for a force of nine former German destroyers and torpedo boats awarded to France after the war. By 1947 the French navy's large submarine force of the interwar years had dwindled to just seven boats, supplemented by five former German U-boats. Over 100 smaller vessels, from frigates to patrol boats, were a hodgepodge of wartime acquisitions from Britain and the United States, and vessels acquired after the war as reparations from Germany. In lieu of a coherent programme, impossible in any event given the circumstances of the late 1940s, France rebuilt its navy through a series of stopgap measures. The *Richelieu's* incomplete sister-ship *Jean Bart*, idle at Casablanca since being damaged there in 1942, was moved to Brest during 1946 and finally completed in 1949, a decade after being laid down. To supplement the *Béarn*, the 12,850-ton escort carrier *Dixmude* (ex-*Biter*) and the 13,190-ton light fleet carrier *Arromanches* (ex-*Colossus*; see Plate 41) were acquired from Britain in 1945 and 1946 respectively, followed by the 11,000-ton light fleet carriers *Lafayette* (ex-*Langley*) and *Bois Belleau* (ex-*Belleau Wood*) from the United States in 1951 and 1953. In 1948, Italy ceded two light cruisers and four destroyers to France as compensation for the Italian salvaging of ships scuttled at Toulon in 1942. France laid down no new warships until after 1950, but work resumed on the 9,380-ton cruiser *De Grasse* (laid down 1938, completed 1956) and five submarines (laid down 1937–39, completed 1949–54) that had survived the German occupation still on the stocks.[4]

In the late 1940s and early 1950s the same foreign and domestic issues dividing France as a whole also left their mark on the navy. Problems avoided during 1943–45 arose after the war, when the first complete integration of Vichy and Free French veterans occurred. The treason trials of retired French admirals, some held as late as 1955, divided the officer corps; these usually resulted in verdicts of at least partial guilt, but no death sentences were carried out and most imprisonments suspended. Meanwhile, the memory of Oran caused the navy to be more Anglophobe than the French population in general, and left its leaders looking to the US navy, rather than the British, as its model for the future. The French navy adapted American doctrine on carrier and amphibious operations to its war in Indochina, where many Viet Minh targets for bombing or ground attack were within reach of the coast. Four of the five French carriers saw action in the war (the *Bois Belleau* did not receive its French commission until 30 April 1954, just three days before the surrender at Dien Bien Phu). The *Dixmude* was the first to be involved in combat operations, on 2 April 1947 launching the first air strikes ever flown from a French carrier. After the *Dixmude* left for home, the *Arromanches* arrived in November 1948 for the first of four tours of duty off Southeast Asia. At the onset of its first tour, the *Arromanches* steamed up the Mekong River to become the largest warship ever to dock at Saigon.[5]

Between 1947 and 1951 the navy also supported a number of troop landings on the coast of Vietnam; the experience gave rise to a formal *Force Amphibie d'Intervention*, which remained in existence until 1969. The 4,500-ton dock landing ship *Foudre* (ex-*LSD 12*) and six LSTs, transferred to France by the US navy under the Mutual Defense Assistance Program (MDAP) of the North Atlantic Treaty Organization (NATO), initially formed the core of the French amphibious force. MDAP also provided eight former US destroyer escorts along with patrol boats and other small craft useful in the waters of Southeast Asia. The ongoing war helped justify a construction program, begun in 1951 under the direction of a new naval chief of staff, Admiral Henri Nomy. Ironically, none of the ships were completed before the defeat at Dien Bien Phu (3 May 1954) drove France out of Indochina. The largest projects were the 9,085-ton cruiser *Colbert* (laid down 1953) and the 22,000-ton carriers *Clemenceau* (1955) and *Foch* (1957), each of which took six years to complete. Smaller units included 18 destroyers, 23 frigates, and 17 submarines (all laid down 1951–59, completed 1955–64). By the end of the decade the French navy included 110 warships of all sizes and 90,000 personnel. Another 10,800 were in naval aviation, which grew to include 850 mostly land-based aircraft.[6]

Even with its rebuilding program well under way, the French navy remained significantly smaller than the British, despite the fact that, under Attlee, the strength of the British fleet declined dramatically. In sharp contrast to postwar France, Britain under the Labour government recognized that it could no longer afford to be a world power of the first rank, on a par with the United States and its emerging Cold War rival, the Soviet Union. The navy, historically the foundation of Britain's great-power status, consequently suffered a severe reduction in size. Of the 15 battleships and battle cruisers on the navy list as of 1945, all but the 4 surviving *King George V*s were sent to the scrapyard in 1948–49, along with the oldest carriers, the *Argus* and *Furious*, which had been withdrawn from service before the end of the war. The only British battleship under construction at the end of the war, the 44,500-ton *Vanguard* (laid down 1941), had the distinction of being the largest, and last, battleship ever completed by a European navy. Commissioned in 1946, it was destined never to fire a shot in anger during its ten-year service life. The carriers clearly were destined to be the core of the postwar fleet, but navy leaders recognized that, with the United States a permanent ally and the empire shrinking, the force was much larger than Britain needed. In the years 1953–56 three of the four units of the 23,000-ton *Illustrious* class were scrapped, along with the 23,450-ton *Implacable* and *Indefatigable*. The lone surviving member of the *Illustrious* class, the *Victorious*, was rebuilt (1950–57) as a 30,530-ton carrier capable of handling jet aircraft. When recommissioned, it joined the 45,720-ton *Eagle* (built 1942–51) and 43,340-ton *Ark Royal*

(1943–55) to form the operational heart of the British fleet. Of the 20 light fleet carriers of the *Colossus*, *Majestic*, and *Centaur* classes, all laid down during the war, 12 eventually served in the British fleet, 2 were completed as aircraft maintenance ships, 5 were transferred to Commonwealth countries (Canada, Australia, and India), and 1 was never completed. Of the dozen commissioned as British warships, four eventually were sold to foreign countries (the *Colossus* to France as the *Arromanches*, and others to the Netherlands, Argentina, and Brazil). The four units of the *Centaur* class were kept on the stocks until needed as replacements for other carriers; the *Hermes* (laid down 1944, completed 1959) was the longest delayed and the last commissioned. Meanwhile, only 1 of the 39 British escort carriers in commission at the end of the war (HMS *Campania*) remained on the navy list after 1948. One (HMS *Biter*, as *Dixmude*) went to France, another to the Netherlands, and the rest were converted or reconverted to merchantmen. The British navy used the *Campania* for a variety of postwar missions, including that of transport and observation platform for scientists and others witnessing Britain's first nuclear tests in the Monte Bello Islands in 1952. The ship was scrapped three years later.[7]

As with some of the light fleet carriers, the British cruisers under construction at war's end remained on the stocks for years before being completed as replacements for other cruisers. The 9,550-ton *Tiger* (laid down 1941, completed 1959) and its sister-ships *Lion* (1942–60) and *Blake* (1942–61) had the distinction of being under construction longer than any other warships built during the twentieth century. Of the nine British heavy cruisers in service at the end of the Second World War, eight were broken up in the years 1948–55 and the last in 1959. Of the 36 less heavily armed cruisers on the navy list in 1945, 5 were sold or scrapped in the late 1940s, 16 during the 1950s. Modernization extended the service lives of the remaining 15 into the 1960s. Owing to insufficient fire control and air defense systems, most of the smaller surface vessels in the fleet of 1945 had short postwar lives. All of the sloops and corvettes were sold or scrapped, as were many of the destroyers and frigates. Sixteen destroyers and 33 frigates laid down during the war were modernized in the 1950s. The 8 destroyers of the 2,830-ton *Daring* class (laid down 1945–49, completed 1952–54) were the largest new surface vessels begun for the British navy before 1959; frigates (46 laid down in the years 1952–59) accounted for most of the rest, as Britain reconfigured its fleet for a Cold War anti-submarine warfare role. Most of the large British submarine force of 1945 likewise did not last long into the postwar era. Twenty-seven submarines laid down during the war were completed by 1948, after which new construction did not resume until 1955, with a dozen new boats laid down by 1959.[8]

While the postwar British navy was far from the leading edge in submarine or surface warship design, in the area of carrier aviation most of the breakthroughs were British in origin. On 3 December 1945 a British navy pilot landed a jet fighter on the deck of the light fleet carrier *Ocean*, the first successful carrier landing of a jet aircraft. The dawn of the jet age posed unique challenges for naval aviation. The hydraulic catapults employed aboard many carriers of the Second World War were inadequate for the launching of jets, which were heavier than the propeller planes they replaced. The introduction of jet aircraft also posed problems in takeoff-and-landing traffic control, and their speed rendered obsolete the traditional signal-flag system of communication between the flight deck and a landing pilot. In their search for solutions the British seized upon the idea of a steam catapult, and on 1 July 1951 the light fleet carrier *Perseus* became the first to launch a plane using the new technology. The British were also the first to consider an angled deck to improve traffic control; the initial test of the idea came on 8 February 1952, in landings on an angled deck template painted on the deck of the light fleet carrier *Triumph*. Finally, the mirror landing system, invented by the British navy's Commander H. C. Goodhart, had its first demonstration on 14 March 1953. The six British carriers commissioned during the 1950s (the *Eagle*, the *Ark Royal*, and the four light fleet carriers of the *Centaur* class), as well as the rebuilt *Victorious*, all used the mirror landing system and had some degree of angled deck. Except for two of the *Centaurs*, all had steam catapults as well. The US navy showed its appreciation for these British innovations by introducing them in American carriers. As early as April 1952 the USS *Hancock* had steam catapults. The world's first supercarrier, the 61,000-ton *Forrestal* (commissioned October 1955), incorporated the steam catapult, angled deck, and mirror landing system, as did all subsequent American carriers.[9]

The late 1940s and early 1950s were less eventful for the British navy than for the French, but the ships of the fleet saw their share of action. From 1946 to 1948 the light fleet carrier *Ocean* supported British forces in Palestine, its aircraft eventually helping to cover their withdrawal. The old heavy cruiser *London* led the Far East squadron from 1947 to 1949, and on 20 February 1949 ascended the Yangtze with the destroyer *Consort* to rescue the frigate *Amethyst*, trapped upriver by Communist Chinese artillery fire. Before withdrawing to the coast all three ships sustained damage in exchanges with Chinese batteries, the *Amethyst* being hit 53 times. Later the same year the British navy found itself involved in another Cold War confrontation, as the light fleet carrier *Triumph* supported British troops attempting to put down a communist guerrilla movement in Malaya.[10]

These skirmishes paled in comparison to the navy's subsequent involvement in the Korean War, during which Britain played the role of loyal second to the United States, waging war against North Korea and, eventually, Communist China under a United Nations mandate.

On 29 June 1950, just four days after North Korean troops invaded South Korea, a force under Rear Admiral Sir William Andrewes, led by the *Triumph*, arrived at Okinawa and was attached to the US Seventh Fleet. On 2 July, the cruiser *Jamaica* and frigate *Black Swan* were involved in the war's first naval engagement, fending off an attack by North Korean torpedo boats. The following day, the *Triumph* and an American carrier launched the first air strikes against North Korean positions. On 13 September the cruisers *Kenya* and *Jamaica* joined two American cruisers and six destroyers in bombarding Wolmi-do Island. Four days later, anti-aircraft fire from the *Jamaica* shot down two North Korean Yak-3s attacking one of the American cruisers in the group. In late September, the *Triumph* was replaced by its sister-ship *Theseus*, which went on to head the new British-led Task Force 95.1, initially consisting of the cruisers *Belfast* (see Plate 42), *Kenya*, and *Ceylon*, along with a carrier and two cruisers from the US navy. Andrewes initially served as commander of the force, giving way in 1951 to Rear Admiral A. K. Scott-Moncrieff. The British navy kept one light fleet carrier in service off the Korean coast until an armistice ended the war in May 1953. In addition to the *Triumph* and *Theseus*, the *Ocean* and *Glory* also saw action, the latter leading the way with three tours of duty. To prevent fatigue to men and matériel the ships were rotated frequently, none serving more than seven months at a time. A fifth light fleet carrier, the *Vengeance*, was used to transport British troops to South Korea in 1952. Carrier-based British aircraft flew 23,000 sorties over Korea during the three years of fighting, and pilots accounted for most of the navy's 42 combat deaths.[11]

The British reduced their naval presence in the Far East after the Korean War but, at least initially, kept one carrier on the station most of the time. In the summer of 1953, just weeks after the end of the Korean War, the *Glory* steamed for Malaya to support British troops against the ongoing communist insurgency there. The light fleet carrier *Warrior* arrived off Korea in February 1954, for UN duty in the naval force helping to supervise the Korean armistice. Months later, after the collapse of French rule in Indochina, the *Warrior* assisted in the evacuation of refugees from communist North Vietnam. In the wake of the French defeat in Indochina, Britain and France joined the United States, Australia, New Zealand, the Philippines, Thailand, and Pakistan in signing the Treaty of Manila (6 September 1954), forming the Southeast Asia Treaty Organization (SEATO). The American effort to employ the NATO model to contain communist aggression outside of Europe was reflected again in the Baghdad Pact (24 February 1955), which established the Central Treaty Organization (CENTO), including Britain, Pakistan, Iran, Iraq, and Turkey, with the United States as an associate member. British naval and amphibious forces theoretically had a critical role to play, in particular in CENTO; ironically, that alliance would not hold its first joint naval exercise until 1974, just a few years before its demise.[12]

The next instance of Anglo–French cooperation occurred not in the new cause of containing communism but in the defense of a traditional interest, during the Suez Crisis of 1956. In 1952 Colonel Gamel Abdel Nasser led an Arab nationalist coup which overthrew the Egyptian monarch, Farouk. Two years later he negotiated the end of the British military presence in Egypt, which dated from 1882. In the summer of 1956, six weeks after the withdrawal of the last British troops, Nasser nationalized the Suez Canal, which had been owned by an Anglo–French consortium since its opening in 1869. To Anthony Eden, prime minister since April 1955, Nasser's actions made him the Hitler or Mussolini of his time, and he rejected as "appeasement" anything other than a firm stand against him. Meanwhile, the leaders of the French Fourth Republic welcomed the opportunity to strike a blow against Nasser, who since 1954 had caused them no end of trouble by supplying arms to the Arab independence movement in Algeria. But it was Eden who embraced the Suez Crisis as a defining moment, both personally and for postwar Britain, only to have it turn into a debacle that forced him to resign after less than two years as prime minister, and exposed the myth that Britain and France were still great powers, capable of acting without the support of the United States.[13]

Eden's decision to use force against Nasser came against the advice of Lord Mountbatten, First Sea Lord since 1955, and most other British military and naval leaders. Only reluctantly did they join their French counterparts in planning an operation to seize the Suez Canal. The British naval force, under Admiral Sir Guy Grantham, included the fleet carrier *Eagle* and the light fleet carriers *Bulwark*, *Albion*, *Ocean*, and *Thesus*, the last two re-equipped as marine assault ships, carrying helicopters. Meanwhile, the French organized a task force around the battleship *Jean Bart* and the carriers *Arromanches* and *Lafayette*. The British contingent included no battleships, the *Vanguard* having been withdrawn from service in March 1956, after just a decade in commission; thus, the *Jean Bart* would have the honor of being the last European battleship in combat. To provide a rationale for the operation, Britain and France struck a deal under which Israel would invade Egypt, after which the Anglo–French force would take the canal under the pretext of keeping it open for international shipping. The arrangement was kept secret from the United States, whose president, Dwight D. Eisenhower, was up for reelection on 6 November and wanted to keep the crisis in check for the time being. On 29 October 1956 Israeli troops crossed the border into the Sinai Peninsula; the Anglo–French operation began two days later, when RAF bombers based in Cyprus struck Egyptian targets along the canal. On 1 November, aircraft from the *Eagle*, *Albion*, *Bulwark*, *Arromanches*, and *Lafayette* joined RAF planes in sorties over the canal. On 5 November some 1,100 British and French paratroopers were dropped on Port Said, but later that day Israel, under heavy pressure from the UN to halt its campaign, did so after achieving its military objectives. Britain and France, robbed of their pretext for intervention, proceeded nevertheless, at least for another day. On 6 November their warships shelled Egyptian strong-holds in Port Said, and 22 helicopters from the *Ocean* and *Theseus* landed 415 marines with 23 tons of supplies, while a conventional beach landing brought ashore many more troops, along with tanks. That evening the British and French governments agreed to a ceasefire proposed by the UN and supported by both the United States and the Soviet Union. The troops were withdrawn and, in January 1957, Eden left office. The brief Suez campaign was a fiasco from a diplomatic, mili-tary, and naval perspective, yet the 90-minute helicopter airlift on 6 November, the first of its kind in naval history, provided evidence of the potential of carrier-based helicopter operations and, as a result, would have a profound impact on the future of amphibious warfare.

The Suez crisis marked the last time that either Britain or France would launch a major military operation without first consulting the United States. While France, under De Gaulle again after 1958, often super-ficially behaved as an independent great power, by the mid-1960s the French navy had disposed of most of its larger warships. The decom-missioning of the *Richelieu* (in 1959) and *Jean Bart* (in 1960) left France with no battleships. After the Indochina war, the old carrier *Béarn* served as an accommodation hulk before being scrapped in 1967; by then, the *Bois Belleau* (1960), *Lafayette* (1963), and *Dixmude* (1966) had been returned to the US navy for disposal. After a modernization (1957–58) gave it an angled deck and mirror landing system, the *Arromanches* embarked helicopters in 1962 and thereafter spent most of its last dozen years in commission as a helicopter carrier.[14] Meanwhile, under the leadership of Harold Macmillan (1957–63) following Eden's downfall, Britain's Conservative party acquiesced in the international realities that Labour had accepted a decade earlier. Cost-saving measures implemented in 1957 included a further reduction in naval personnel to just 88,000 (compared to 195,000 in 1947, after the initial postwar reduction), and the sale for scrap of the four surviving battle-ships of the *King George V* class. Three years later the *Vanguard* met a similar fate, leaving the British navy with no battleships. The remain-ing light fleet carriers of the *Colossus* class left service by 1958; the *Ocean*, *Glory*, and *Theseus* went into reserve (to be broken up in 1961–62) and the *Triumph* was converted to a maintenance ship. Mountbatten secured permission to convert the light fleet carriers *Bulwark* (in 1959–60) and *Albion* (in 1961–62) to "commando" (heli-copter) carriers. As such, they lost their angled-deck markings and mirror landing systems, and became the only two units of the *Centaur* class never to be fitted with steam catapults. After their reconfiguration, each carried eight helicopters and four light landing craft, and could accommodate 700–900 marines. After serving as First Sea Lord from 1955 to 1959, Mountbatten went on to become Chief of the Defence Staff under Macmillan, and implemented the absorption of the Admiralty by the Defence ministry, effective in April 1964.[15] The British navy remained Europe's largest and the world's second largest only until 1959, when the growing Soviet fleet passed it in overall tonnage.

EUROPEAN NAVIES, NATO, AND THE COLD WAR

After the Suez crisis, the Soviet Union was the only European naval power truly functioning as an independent great power. The North Atlantic Treaty Organization (established 1949) provided western Europe with a permanent peacetime alliance with the United States, against the threat of invasion from the massive Soviet army in eastern Europe, but the postwar growth of the Soviet fleet added a naval dimension to the NATO mission. Ultimately NATO provided the framework within which the postwar navies of Britain and France were reduced in size and reconfigured for specific regional roles. The minor naval powers of western Europe, as well as Italy and, after 1955, West Germany likewise had modest naval forces with regional missions in NATO.

After the formal establishment of the NATO command structure for ground forces in Europe (SACEUR) in April 1951, the focus shifted to finalizing command arrangements at sea. In December 1950, during preliminary negotiations over the structure of the Atlantic naval command (SACLANT), the North Atlantic Council agreed to the appointment of an American admiral to the position, mirroring the provision that an American general would always head SACEUR. This set off a political row in Britain, where it became one of a number of issues which toppled the Attlee government in February 1951. Back in power as prime minister, Churchill harbored illusions of Britain still playing a "Big Three" role on the international stage, alongside the United States and the Soviet Union. He tried to get NATO to agree to let a British admiral head SACLANT, and when the other eleven alliance members all reaffirmed their belief that an American should have the post, he questioned whether SACLANT should even be created. In a January 1952 meeting with President Harry Truman in Washington, Churchill asked that the United States "make room for Britain to play her historical role" in the Atlantic. When he finally agreed to an American SACLANT, formally on 30 January, he considered it a surrender, but as part of the bargain the United States agreed to grant the British navy four important consolation prizes. Under SACLANT, the subordinate eastern Atlantic (EASTLANT) command went to a British admiral. Command of Channel forces likewise went to a British admiral. CHAN-COM, formally established in February 1952, was further subdivided into British, French, and Dutch area commands; until its abolition in 1991, it was directly subordinate to the North Atlantic Defense Council, and thus on a par with SACLANT and SACEUR. A British admiral (head-quartered at Gibraltar) likewise headed IBERLANT, a subunit of EAST-LANT, until the 1970s, when it passed to an American admiral and IBERLANT was elevated to equal status with EASTLANT, immediately under SACLANT. A British admiral also headed SACEUR's Allied Forces North (AFNORTH) subcommand, including Norway, Denmark, and their coastal waters, in recognition of the essential naval dimension to the land defense of Scandinavia. The other important subcommand under SACLANT went to an American admiral, when NATO's Atlantic "strike fleet" was established in 1952. The United States would not allow STRIKFLTLANT to be commanded by a non-American flag officer or have a non-American flag officer in its operational chain of command, since it included nuclear assets aboard ships of the US Second Fleet. This arrangement was a bitter pill for the British navy to swallow, as STRIKFLTLANT inherited the strategic mission of the Grand Fleet of the First World War and Home Fleet of the Second. Because STRIKFLT-LANT would only assemble for maneuvers or in a crisis that threatened war, an Atlantic "standing naval force" (STANAVFORLANT) was established in 1967. NATO created an analagous STANAVFORCHAN under CHANCOM in 1973, responsible for countermeasures against possible Soviet mining of the Channel and North Sea.[16]

The definition of Anglo–American command arrangements in the Mediterranean proved to be far more difficult. Alliance leaders established an Allied Forces South (AFSOUTH) command, under an American admiral, mirroring AFNORTH, under a British admiral. The authority of AFSOUTH extended over all of Italy and Italian waters, while responsibility for the rest of the Mediterranean went to the Allied Forces Mediterranean (AFMED) command, under a British admiral. The AFSOUTH commander, headquartered at Naples, had beneath him an Italian general and a US Air Force general, responsible for land and air operations, respectively, while the AFMED commander, based at Malta, had beneath him the commanders of the British and French Mediterranean fleets and of the navies of Italy, Greece, and Turkey. With an eye toward expanding the role of AFMED at the expense of AFSOUTH, Churchill chose Britain's most prominent admiral, Lord Mountbatten, as its first head. Mountbatten had already been serving as commander of the British Mediterranean Fleet since May 1952; over American objections he continued in that role after formally opening his NATO headquarters at Malta in March 1953. From the start

Mountbatten clashed frequently with his American counterpart at Naples. The establishment of NATO's Mediterranean "strike force" posed a further complication. Because STRIKFORSOUTH included nuclear assets aboard ships of the US Sixth Fleet, the United States would not allow it to be commanded by a non-American flag officer or have a non-American flag officer in its operational chain of command. Even though STRIKFORSOUTH logically should have been subordinated to Mountbatten's AFMED, instead it came under the jurisdiction of AFSOUTH, in order to give it an all-American chain of command. The same would be true later of the Mediterranean "standing naval force" (STANAVFORMED) established in 1969 as a counterpart to STANAVFORLANT. Mountbatten remained at Malta until his appointment as First Sea Lord in 1955, but was powerless to change the situation to Britain's advantage.[17] In his quest, he was not helped by the fact that the fall of King Farouk in 1952 caused the United States to build a new NATO naval base at Iskenderun, Turkey, as a hedge against the loss to the alliance of Britain's Egyptian bases. The subsequent Suez fiasco of 1956 poisoned the Anglo–American naval relationship enough to weaken further the British position within the alliance. SACLANT Admiral Jerauld Wright complained that, in the weeks before the intervention, the British did not consult him before moving a substantial number of warships, including four aircraft carriers, from the Atlantic to the Mediterranean. In the first days of November 1956 the US Chief of Naval Operations, Admiral Arleigh Burke, ordered the commander of the US Sixth Fleet, Vice Admiral Charles R. 'Cat' Brown, to "keep clear" of the Anglo–French fleet "but take no guff from anybody," instructions which inspired Brown to be less than accommodating to the British task force commander, Admiral Robin Durnford-Slater.[18] Of course, it was not in Britain's interest to see its relations with the United States deteriorate over such incidents. Amid the post-Suez reduction of British naval forces, the Americans grew to dominate NATO as much at sea as on land.

On Trafalgar Day, 21 October 1960, the British navy staged two events which set the tone for its future: the launching of its first nuclear-powered submarine, aptly named *Dreadnought*, and the first flight of the Hawker P.1127 Kestrel vertical/short takeoff and landing (VSTOL) aircraft, the forerunner of the Hawker Harrier. The *Dreadnought* (4,000 tons submerged), laid down in June 1959, entered service in April 1963, the first of a series of 12 British nuclear attack submarines. The five units of the 4,900-ton *Valiant* class (laid down 1962–68, completed 1966–71) were followed by six of the 4,900-ton *Swiftsure* class (laid down 1969–77, completed 1973–81). Concurrent with the *Valiant*s, the British navy built its first nuclear-powered submarines capable of firing ballistic missiles, long-range strategic nuclear weapons developed in the 1950s on the general model of the wartime German V-2 rockets. The

8,500-ton *Resolution*, laid down February 1964, entered service in October 1967. Another three units of the class, laid down in 1964–65, were completed in 1968–69. They remained in service until the 1990s. Britain trailed the United States and Soviet Union in developing both types of nuclear submarine, and would have been even farther behind if not for the pragmatism of Mountbatten, who in the late 1950s struck a deal with Admiral Hyman Rickover that allowed the British to purchase an American power plant for the *Dreadnought*. The move saved the navy millions in research and development costs, as did the subsequent purchase of Polaris submarine-launched ballistic missiles (SLBMs) for the *Resolutions*, first proposed by Mountbatten before he left office in 1959. Nevertheless, the *Dreadnought* still cost £18.5 million, each of the four boats of the *Resolution* class roughly £40 million, reflecting the high value Cold War Britain placed on having its own undersea nuclear deterrent.[19] As these projects proceeded, Britain compensated by reducing its carrier force. In 1966 the new Labour government of Harold Wilson cancelled CVA-01, the first of two projected 53,000-ton fleet carriers, citing the potential of VSTOL aircraft and helicopters based aboard smaller platforms. Following the decision, the existing carriers were gradually withdrawn from service, over the objections of Britain's NATO allies. The light fleet carrier *Centaur* became an accommodation ship in 1966, the renovated fleet carrier *Victorious* was sold in 1969, the light fleet carrier *Hermes* was converted to a helicopter carrier in 1971–73 (to replace the *Albion*, decommissioned in 1973), and the fleet carrier *Eagle* went into reserve in 1972 (to be broken up in 1978). This left the *Ark Royal* as the only active British aircraft carrier, and when it left service at the end of 1978, the British navy had just the helicopter carriers *Bulwark* and *Hermes*. After trials in 1977–78 with VSTOL Harrier aircraft, in 1980–81 the *Hermes* was fitted with a 12.5-degree "ski jump" bow ramp to facilitate their short takeoffs. In the meantime, the new 16,000-ton VSTOL carrier *Invincible*, laid down in July 1973, entered service in July 1980, ending a period of 19 months during which the British navy had no carrier-based aircraft. The *Bulwark* was never given VSTOL capability before being laid up in reserve in 1981, shortly before the *Hermes* reentered service; it was broken up in 1984. Notwithstanding its modest size, and the fact that it was the first British carrier laid down in 28 years, the *Invincible* was approved by Parliament largely because the navy marketed the ship as a "through-deck cruiser" rather than an aircraft carrier. Only in 1975 did the navy reveal that the ship, fitted with a 7-degree "ski jump" bow ramp, would carry five Sea Harriers along with nine Sea King helicopters. Two sister-ships followed, the *Illustrious* (built 1976–82) and *Ark Royal* (1978–85).[20]

The suspension of conventional carrier construction was only one manifestation of the further downsizing of the British navy. No new cruisers were ordered after the Second World War, and between 1949 and 1959 Britain laid down no surface warships larger than frigates. The hiatus ended with the onset of construction on eight "County" class guided missile destroyers, 6,200-ton cruiser-sized warships labeled destroyers for political purposes. Their primary armament consisted not of guns but of guided missiles, developed after 1945 on the model of the wartime German V-1 and earlier, smaller rockets. The first units, *Devonshire* and *Hampshire*, were laid down in 1959 and completed in 1962; the last of the class were built in 1966–70. A ninth oversized destroyer, the 6,700-ton *Bristol* (built 1967–73), was followed by the ten units of the 3,850-ton *Sheffield* class (laid down 1970–78) and four of the 4,750-ton *Manchester* class (laid down 1978–80). The navy continued to invest heavily in frigates, replacing those laid down in the 1940s and 1950s with another 40 begun in the years 1960–80. These ranged in size from the last units of the 2,100-ton "Tribal" class to the first of the 4,100-ton *Boxer* class, the latter as large as the light cruisers of the Second World War. Like the new destroyers, all were fitted with missile launchers, which fired Seaslug, Sea Dart, Seacat and, eventually, Sea Wolf surface-to-air missiles (SAMs), all developed in Britain.[21]

While VSTOL aircraft became the centerpiece of British naval aviation, France remained committed to conventional carrier operations. The angled-deck carriers *Clemenceau* (completed 1961) and *Foch* (1963) each could accommodate 40 jet aircraft; thanks to careful maintenance and periodic overhauls, both remained in service until the end of the century. For helicopter operations the French supplemented the reconfigured *Arromanches* (retired in 1974) with the 10,000-ton *Jeanne d'Arc* (laid down 1960, completed 1964; see Plate 43), a cruiser designed to carry eight helicopters which it launched from a flight deck aft of the centerline superstructure. Other new surface warships modernized the fleet for the missile age. Of 15 guided missile destroyers (laid down 1962–86, completed 1967–91) the largest were the first pair, the 5,090-ton *Suffren* and *Duquesne*, equipped with French Masurca SAMs. The three units of the *Tourville* class (laid down 1970–72) were the first to have Exocet surface-to-surface missiles (SSMs). All subsequent French destroyers and a class of 17 corvettes (laid down 1972–81, completed 1976–86) were equipped with Exocets, along with 4 slightly older frigates (laid down 1960–62, completed 1963–70) which received theirs in refits. To modernize warships built in the 1950s the French navy used a mixture of French and American missile technology. While several *Surcouf* class destroyers (completed 1955–57) were fitted with the US navy's Tartar SAMs, the cruiser *Colbert* received Masurca SAMs in a 1970–72 refit, after which it served as France's Mediterranean flagship until being decommissioned in 1991. Even after the demise of the formal *Force Amphibie d'Intervention* in 1969, the French still had the strongest amphibious capability of any western European navy, led by the 5,800-ton dock landing ships *Ouragan* (launched 1963) and *Orage* (1967).[22]

The highly successful Exocet established France as the world leader in SSM development. While the British imported American Polaris SLBMs for their *Resolution* class submarines and, for frigates completed after 1975, supplemented their Sea Wolf SAMs with Exocets, early on De Gaulle committed France to achieve self-sufficiency in missile technology. From the start the navy had a role in the development of France's own nuclear deterrent, the *force de frappe*, which De Gaulle considered the key to French independence in world affairs.[23] Unlike the United States, the Soviet Union, and Britain, France built a nuclear-powered ballistic missile submarine long before it built a nuclear-powered attack submarine. The *Redoutable* (8,940 tons submerged), laid down March 1964, completed December 1971, was the first of a class of six boats, the *Inflexible* (built 1980–85) the last. They remained the largest French submarines until the late 1990s. French SLBM technology improved gradually, from the M-1 (range 1,500 miles) of the *Redoutable*'s initial armament to the M-5 (range 3,600 miles) installed in the *Inflexible* at the turn of the century. France built another eight diesel-electric patrol and attack submarines (laid down 1961–74, completed 1966–78) before work began on its first nuclear-powered attack submarine, the 2,670-ton *Rubis*, the first of six boats of the type (laid down 1976–87, completed 1983–93).[24]

In the quest for an independent foreign and defense policy, France deliberately distanced itself from NATO. Upon returning to power in 1958, De Gaulle began to agitate for a greater role for France in NATO's command structure, to no avail. His break with the alliance began the following year, when he withdrew the French Mediterranean Fleet from active participation in AFMED. In April 1964, one month after the *Redoutable* was laid down, De Gaulle withdrew French naval officers from the AFMED and CHANCOM commands. Early in 1967, just before NATO headquarters moved to Brussels from Paris, the US Sixth Fleet moved to Gaeta, Italy, from Villefranche, which had been its home port since 1956. The removal of the French Mediterranean Fleet seriously weakened British-led AFMED, which NATO abolished later in 1967, leaving its powers to be assumed by the American-led AFSOUTH command at Naples.[25]

The Italian navy formed an important component of AFMED up to 1967, and of AFSOUTH thereafter, albeit in a form reduced by the postwar peace settlement. Italy finished the Second World War fighting on the side of the Allies and in 1949 was among NATO's charter members, yet the country still had to pay for its earlier Axis affiliation. Under the naval terms of the peace, Italy lost the battleships *Italia* (to the United States), *Vittorio Veneto* (to Britain), and *Giulio Cesare* (to the Soviet Union), of which only the latter ever served under its new master. The Italians retained the old battleships *Andrea Doria* and *Caio Duilio*, which served until 1956. Of the nine cruisers on hand in 1945, two were ceded to France, one to the Soviet Union, and one to Greece; another was scrapped in 1951. Of ten destroyers, four were ceded to France and one to the Soviet Union. Italy was barred from building any new warships until 1950, and could have no aircraft carriers, new battleships, submarines, or torpedo boats. Of Italy's large interwar and wartime submarine force just two boats survived to be recommissioned in 1952, when the Western Allies agreed to drop the ban on submarines and torpedo boats. Under a US-funded program begun in 1950, the remaining four cruisers were modernized and a fifth (the *San Marco*, ex-*Giulio Germanico*, laid down in 1939) completed in 1956; these remained the principal warships of the Italian navy into the 1960s and 1970s. Two destroyers and three frigates provided in 1951 by the US navy were supplemented by four destroyers and eight frigates laid down between 1952 and 1960 in Italian shipyards; of these, the destroyers *Impavido* (built 1957–63) and *Intrepido* (1959–64) were Italy's first warships equipped with missiles, Tartar SAMs from the United States. Subsequent new construction reflected the navy's NATO roles in coastal defense, mine countermeasures and anti-submarine warfare. The 5,000-ton helicopter cruisers *Andrea Doria* (1958–64) and *Caio Duilio* (1958–64; see Plate 44) eventually replaced the battleships of the same names, and were followed by the 7,500-ton *Vittorio Veneto* (1965–69). All three were fitted with extensive afterdecks; the former pair each carried four helicopters, the latter nine. All three also served through the end of the Cold War, by which time they were supported by 4 destroyers (laid down 1968–89), 18 frigates (laid down 1963–83), and 8 corvettes (laid down 1983–87). Starting in the 1970s all Italian destroyers and frigates were armed with Otomat SSMs, produced by a consortium of the Italian firm OTO-Melara and the French Engins Matra. The revival of the Italian submarine service began in 1954–55, with two boats transferred from the United States. These and another 7 former US navy submarines acquired during the 1960s and 1970s were all out of service by the late 1980s, replaced by 12 boats laid down in Italy between 1965 and 1991. Under the republic (established 1946) Italy became notorious for its political instability and frequent changes of government, but within the defense establishment the primacy of the air force remained a constant, keeping Mussolini's 1923 ban on air-craft carriers in effect. In 1978 the navy finally secured permission to build a helicopter carrier, the 10,000-ton *Giuseppe Garibaldi*. Laid down in 1981 and completed in 1985, it was the largest warship built for the Italian navy since the battleship *Roma* (1938–42). The final design pro-vided the *Garibaldi* with a "ski jump" bow ramp for VSTOL aircraft, but initially it was equipped with 12 Sea King helicopters. After the Italian parliament finally revoked the 1923 law in 1992, the *Garibaldi* became Italy's first operational aircraft carrier, equipped with ten aircraft and one helicopter.[26]

For more than two decades after the end of the Second World War the Netherlands was the only western European country other than Britain and France to operate an aircraft carrier. In 1946 the British loaned the Dutch navy the 13,825-ton escort carrier *Nairana*, which was recommissioned as the *Karel Doorman* in honor of the admiral killed in the Battle of the Java Sea. It was returned to Britain in 1948, when the British sold the Dutch navy the 13,190-ton light fleet carrier *Venerable*, which subsequently assumed the name *Karel Doorman*. It remained in service until 1968, when the Netherlands abandoned carrier-based naval aviation and refurbished the ship for sale to Argentina. The British also provided most of the rest of the postwar Dutch navy, which had a decidedly makeshift character. Just two *Tromp* class light cruisers and six submarines had survived the Second World War; all were out of commission by 1958. Ships acquired from Britain after the war included seven destroyers and four submarines, all of which left service by 1964. Under MDAP the US navy provided six destroyer escorts and two submarines; delivered in 1950–53, these vessels served until 1967–71. MDAP also funded the construction in the United States of six small frigates. Dutch shipyards revived after the war, as work resumed on the 9,530-ton cruisers *De Ruyter* and *De Zeven Provincien* (both laid down 1939, completed 1953), which had survived the German occupation still on the stocks. Further domestic construction included 12 destroyers (laid down 1950–55, completed 1954–58), 30 frigates (laid down 1963–90, completed 1967–95), and 10 submarines (laid down 1954–88, completed 1960–94). After 1982 the Dutch operated no surface warships larger than frigates, having sold both of their cruisers and eight destroyers to Peru in the years 1973–82 and scrapped the remaining destroyers during the 1970s. In the years 1985 to 1988 the Dutch also decommissioned their 12 oldest frigates, selling half of them to Indonesia. The remaining frigates, equipped with American and British SSMs and SAMs, led a fleet which occupied a well-defined niche within NATO, responsible for anti-submarine operations in the North Sea and at the eastern approach to the Channel. Indeed, 1949 was a watershed year in Dutch naval history, as the creation of NATO coincided with the loss of the Dutch East Indies, the country's last substantial overseas colony. A navy which, since the 1700s, had not been equal to its sweeping responsibilities suddenly had goals that were within reach, and fulfilled them admirably.[27]

The remaining European naval states in the original NATO lineup – Norway, Denmark, Belgium, and Portugal – maintained no warships larger than frigates during most of the Cold War era. Greece, which joined the alliance in 1951, finally decommissioned the 9,960-ton armored cruiser *Georgios Averof* that year, after four decades in service. The light cruiser *Helle* (ex-Italian *Eugenio di Savoia*) was delivered in 1951 as compensation for the ship of the same name sunk by an Italian submarine in 1940, before Greece entered the Second World War; it served until 1964. Aside from the *Georgios Averof*, the entire Greek navy of 1945, from destroyers to minesweepers, consisted of warships loaned or given to Greece by Britain. As a NATO member, Greece transferred its dependence to the United States, between 1951 and 1992 commissioning 22 destroyers, 4 destroyer escorts, 3 frigates, and 5 submarines discarded by the US navy. In the years 1971–92 Greece also acquired 2 frigates and 8 submarines built in West Germany, and 2 frigates built in the Netherlands. Among the minor European naval powers Greece maintained one of the largest Cold War forces, but its utility was compromised by the age and condition of its matériel, a chronic shortage of skilled personnel, and most of all by the fact that Greece considered Turkey – which also joined NATO in 1951 – as its principal naval rival.[28]

Four years after Greece entered NATO, the Federal Republic of Germany rearmed as a member of the alliance. West Germany's navy initially could have no warships larger than 3,000 tons, and prominent personnel had to be untainted by Nazism or wartime atrocities. Vice Admiral Ruge, best known for his service in the Mediterranean during 1943, became the first commander. In 1956 the navy commissioned its first vessels, patrol boats reassigned from the Federal Frontier Guard. The first substantial warships were 6 US navy destroyers, acquired under MDAP in the years 1958–60, and 7 British frigates, acquired in 1958–59. Thereafter, aside from the navy's first guided-missile destroyers (three vessels of the *Lütjens* class, built in the United States in 1966–70), all subsequent warships were built in German shipyards: 4 *Hamburg* class destroyers (built 1959–68), as well as 6 *Köln* class frigates (1957–64) and their eventual replacements, 8 *Bremen* class frigates (1979–90). Other than French Exocets ordered for the *Hamburg*s in the mid-1970s, all SSMs and SAMs were imported from the United States. The first West German submarines were three former Nazi German U-boats sunk off the German coast in the last days of the Second World War, which were raised and repaired in the years 1956–58. New construction included 30 small coastal submarines (launched 1961–74), the largest of which displaced just 500 tons submerged. Like its army and air force, West Germany's navy operated entirely within the framework of NATO, as a "forward defense" force in northern waters. By 1970 it accounted for three-fourths of NATO's standing naval strength in the Baltic.[29]

Thanks to its neutrality during the Second World War, in the late 1940s Spain had the largest fleet among the minor European naval powers, including 6 cruisers and 16 destroyers built in the interwar years. Western European disdain for Francisco Franco kept Spain out of NATO until 1982, seven years after the dictator's death, but after 1953 a bilateral treaty with the United States linked Spain to the Cold War West. To replace aging warships built in the 1920s and 1930s, in the years

1957–74 the Spanish navy acquired 10 destroyers, 5 submarines, and a host of amphibious vessels from the United States under MDAP. In the years 1945–51 Spanish shipyards laid down 12 destroyers which took an average of over 15 years to complete, the last entering service in 1970. Improvements in the country's industrial capacity were reflected in the construction of 8 submarines (laid down 1968–81) and 17 frigates (laid down 1969–92), which were completed in an average of just four years. In 1967 Spain became only the fourth European country to operate an aircraft carrier, acquiring the 13,000-ton light carrier *Cabot* from the United States under MDAP. Renamed *Dedalo*, initially it carried twenty jet aircraft, but eventually embarked seven VSTOL aircraft and twenty helicopters. It was returned to the United States in 1989, after the commissioning of the 16,700-ton *Principe de Asturias* (laid down 1979, completed 1988), a VSTOL carrier with a 12-degree "ski jump" bow ramp, capable of operating as many as two dozen VSTOL aircraft and helicopters at a time. The *Principe de Asturias*, built at Ferrol from an American design, became fleet flagship after its commissioning and remained the pride of the Spanish navy into the twenty-first century. The incorporation of the Spanish navy into NATO was eased considerably by measures taken in the 1970s (the transfer of IBERLANT's command from a British admiral at Gibraltar to an American admiral, and its elevation to coequal status with British-led EASTLANT, immediately under American-led SACLANT), which left no British flag officers in the Spanish chain of command. Its role within IBERLANT required the Spanish navy to adopt a pronounced Atlantic focus, basing more warships at Ferrol and Cadiz, and fewer at Cartagena in the Mediterranean.[30]

Spain's strategic location made it a welcome addition to NATO. The near-worst-case scenarios of the late Cold War also considered the country the likely place for the alliance to make a "last stand" in the event of a Soviet invasion of western Europe, in which case Spanish ports would be the most secure entrepôts for American reinforcements and supplies. Such grim assumptions were a standard feature of NATO maneuvers throughout the Cold War. During September 1952 NATO conducted "Mainbrace," its first major naval maneuver, in the EAST-LANT waters around the British Isles. It included over 160 warships, led by the British carriers *Eagle*, *Illustrious*, and *Theseus* and battleship *Vanguard*, along with two carriers and one battleship from the US navy. The exercise simulated NATO's naval response to a Soviet invasion of Denmark and Norway, following a successful Soviet conquest of West Germany. As the Soviet surface and submarine fleets grew, NATO naval maneuvers shifted their focus from European coastal waters to the high seas. In "Teamwork," held in September 1964, the US navy joined seven European NATO navies in simulating STRIKFLTLANT convoying merchant ships across the Atlantic and conducting defensive mining operations. As the center of gravity of the expanding Soviet navy shifted to its Northern Fleet, NATO became increasingly self-conscious about its ability to fight at sea in Arctic conditions. As a result, the August 1966 exercise "Straightlaced" took place in the Norwegian Sea, involving 31 ships and 15,000 men from the US, Britain, Norway, the Netherlands, and France, the last participating even while in the process of leaving active membership in the alliance. As of 1970, NATO's naval strategy in the event of a war against the Soviet Union called for the British navy to sweep the Norwegian Sea of Soviet surface vessels, enabling the ships of STRIKFLTLANT to take up positions there and, along with the US Sixth Fleet in the Mediterranean and the US Seventh Fleet in the northern Pacific, launch air strikes and SLBMs to destroy as many Soviet bomber bases as possible. This would neutralize the Soviet air-based nuclear capability which, at the time, was considered the greatest threat to the West. Soviet submarines sent out to sink the carriers would be destroyed by the carrier escorts in the individual battle groups. The Soviet surface fleet was still largely discounted in these calculations.[31]

In the early 1970s NATO suffered internal tensions which threatened its ability to conduct naval operations in the event of war. In May 1973 an Anglo–Icelandic fishing dispute led Iceland to ban British warplanes from landing at the NATO airfield at Keflavik. Iceland considered closing the base altogether until an election brought a change in government and, in August 1974, confirmation that the base would stay open. The dispute flared up again in January 1976, at which time Iceland threatened to leave NATO altogether. Meanwhile, in the wake of the Arab–Israeli War of 1973 and the subsequent Arab oil embargo of the West, European NATO members were less willing than before to follow the lead of the US in its pro-Israeli Middle East policy. When the US rushed over $2 billion in emergency military aid to Israel during October 1973, Portugal (which allowed the use of the Azores) was the only NATO country willing to allow fighter aircraft ferried to Israel by US pilots to land for refueling. In August 1974 Greece responded to the Turkish occupation of northern Cyprus by withdrawing its armed forces from the military and naval structure of NATO, becoming the first country other than France ever to do so. Greece did not return to active membership until 1981 but, like France, made exceptions to its "inactivity" in the meantime. As early as September 1977, Greek naval and air forces participated in the NATO exercise "Display Determination," held in the Eastern Mediterranean. In May 1979 Greece and France both contributed to the 100 ships and 400 aircraft in AFSOUTH's exercise "Dawn Patrol 79," which also involved the United States, Britain, Italy, the Netherlands, Portugal, and Turkey. Greece subsequently boycotted "Display Determination 79," an exercise in September 1979 involving 50 ships and 400 aircraft from

Britain, Portugal, the United States, Italy, and Turkey, with the last three countries providing 7,000 troops for an amphibious landing on the Turkish coast.[32]

In addition to these tensions within NATO, by the 1970s the alliance was affected by the further weakening of Britain and its navy. As late as 1961 British marines from the helicopter carrier *Bulwark* deterred Iraq from invading Kuwait; during a ten-week period in 1964, the carrier *Eagle* alone flew air cover over the Straits of Malacca during a crisis in Indonesia, then steamed for the East African coast to provide air cover for Zambia when Rhodesia threatened it with invasion. But in 1968 the Wilson government announced its intention to end Britain's "east of Suez" commitments, and amid economic hard times subsequent prime ministers did nothing to reverse this policy. As late as November 1974 Britain sent warships to the Arabian Sea to participate in the CENTO naval exercise "Midlink 74," but afterward a US aircraft carrier entered the Persian Gulf, the first such deployment since 1948, reflecting the fact that the United States, rather than Britain, henceforth would have the responsibility for policing the Gulf. Farther east, in 1976 the British withdrew their last forces from Singapore, ending a presence dating from 1819, and in 1977 the dissolution of SEATO ended Britain's last formal commitment to the defense of the Far East. The British did not pretend to be able to defend Hong Kong, the last remnant of their once extensive Asian empire, and ten years later the Thatcher government would negotiate its return to China. Much closer to home, by the end of the 1970s there was little evidence that the British navy intended to maintain its "west of Suez" commitments, either. Within NATO, the abolition of AFMED and the transfer of IBERLANT to American leadership deprived the British of two of their original five commands, and reduced the significance of both Malta and Gibraltar. For several years after 1976, British warships were not regularly assigned to NATO duties in the Mediterranean, and in 1979 the British withdrew their last forces from Malta, which they had owned since 1800. The same year, the navy decommissioned HMS *Blake*, its last active cruiser. In the autumn of 1980 British warships made a rare Indian Ocean appearance, participating in "Beacon Compass," a joint exercise with the US navy involving 25 ships, 170 aircraft, and 18,000 men. Otherwise, British naval activity was limited to the NATO commands led by British admirals (AFNORTH, CHANCOM, and EASTLANT) and the assignment of warships to STANAVFORLANT.[33]

THE SOVIET NAVY AND THE COLD WAR

The re-emergence of Russian sea power ranks as the most dramatic development of post-1945 European naval history. A Cold War buildup, accelerating after 1956 under the direction of Admiral Sergei Georgiyevich Gorshkov, gave the Soviet Union a navy second only to that of the United States, ultimately with a global presence, designed not to achieve command of the sea but to deny it to the US navy.[34] But the postwar rise of Soviet naval power was not a smooth one, as an initial buildup centered around large surface units, begun by Stalin in the late 1940s, was ended after his death in 1953. Only years later, after a long and persistent struggle, would Gorshkov succeed in adding such ships to the Soviet fleet.

The Soviet navy of 1945 included three battleships and nine cruisers. Fifty-three destroyers survived the war, but eight loaned by the British navy were returned in the years 1949–52. The Soviets had 176 submarines in 1945, over half of them in the Pacific Fleet. In 1946 they received a tenth cruiser, the German *Nürnberg* (renamed *Admiral Makarov*) and, over the winter of 1948–49, returned the battleship *Arkhangelsk* (ex-*Royal Sovereign*) to Britain and cruiser *Murmansk* (ex-*Milwaukee*) to the United States upon receipt of the Italian battleship *Giulio Cesare* (renamed *Novorossiysk*) and cruiser *Duca d'Aosta* (renamed *Stalingrad*, later *Kerch*). Smaller prizes alloted from the defeated Axis navy included 10 destroyers and 10 submarines.[35]

As with his abortive prewar program of naval expansion, Stalin wanted a postwar Soviet fleet centered around battleships and battle cruisers. Planning for a class of eight giant 75,000-ton battleships, designed to carry nine 16-inch guns, continued until 1952. Meanwhile, in 1951 and 1952, work began on the 36,500-ton battle cruisers *Stalingrad* and *Moskva*, for the Black Sea and Baltic fleets, respectively, to be armed with nine 12-inch guns. Navy commander Admiral Kuznetsov, whom Nikita Khrushchev later characterized as "too outspoken and stubborn for Stalin's taste," returned to Moscow in 1951 after a four-year exile as head of the Pacific Fleet, and promptly sought to cancel the battle cruiser projects and the proposed class of battleships. Kuznetsov favored a balanced fleet, including aircraft carriers and a heavier investment in submarines, while Stalin was skeptical of the value of carriers and a large submarine force.[36] They agreed on the need for a large program of cruisers, which became the centerpiece of the Soviet surface fleet of the 1950s. After the war, work resumed on five 11,500-ton *Chapayev* class cruisers laid down in 1939; four were completed in 1950, the fifth delayed until 1959. In 1949 the first of a projected twenty-five cruisers of the 13,600-ton *Sverdlov* class was laid down; like the *Chapayev*s, they were armed with twelve 6-inch guns (see Plate 45). Two classes of destroyers dominated the program of smaller surface warships: 70 of the *Skorij* class (laid down 1948–52, completed 1949–53) and 31 of the *Spokoiniy* (NATO "Kotlin" and "Kildin") class (laid down 1953–57, completed 1955–58). [In the mid-1950s the US and NATO started giving K-series code names to classes of Soviet warships, but from the late 1960s they were usually called by their Soviet names. Classes of Soviet submarines were labeled alphabetically and randomly (starting with "Whiskey") until the letters A–Z had been used. In 1985 the US and NATO began a new series, starting with "Akula" ("shark" in Russian). See Polmar, *The Naval Institute Guide to the Soviet Navy*, 5, 94.] By the time of Stalin's death, plans had been devised to fit the *Skorij* and *Spokoiniy* class destroyers with missiles. Building upon captured German technology, starting in the late 1940s the Soviet Union developed a wide variety of guided (cruise) and ballistic missiles. The first Soviet anti-ship missiles, developed for aircraft, were deployed by 1955, but as of the mid-1950s no Soviet warship was fitted with missiles of any type. Through the Stalin era the Baltic Fleet remained the largest of the four Soviet naval forces. Maneuvers were limited to coastal operations and foreign port visits to eastern European communist countries.[37]

Shortly after Stalin's death in March 1953, work stopped on the battle cruisers *Stalingrad* and *Moskva*, and plans for the 75,000-ton battleships were cancelled. The navy's older battleships also soon left service: the *Oktyabrskaya Revolutsia* was decommissioned and scrapped after its name went to a *Sverdlov* class cruiser commissioned in November 1954; the *Novorossiysk* was sunk in October 1955, after striking an old German mine in the Black Sea; finally, the *Parizhkaya Kommuna* (which had reverted to its original name *Sevastopol*) was scrapped starting in 1957. Confusion over the future direction of the Soviet navy continued as Stalin's successor, Khrushchev, consolidated his power. Work continued on the *Sverdlov*s, with the twenty-first cruiser being laid down during 1955, but none of the units begun after January 1953 was completed, and ultimately only 14 were commissioned, the last in September 1955.[38] A formal review of the navy's future began a year after Stalin's death, but the Soviet leadership rejected two revised naval programs proposed during 1954. By October 1955 Kuznetsov's insistence upon a balanced fleet (which earlier had caused him to oppose Stalin's focus on battleships and battle cruisers) had poisoned his relationship with Khrushchev, who condemned him for "demonstrating . . . the same obstinacy and arrogance that had gotten him into trouble with Stalin." Khrushchev used the accidental sinking of the *Novorossiysk* as an excuse to sack Kuznetsov, ironically just seven months after he had promoted the navy commander to the new rank of fleet admiral, the equivalent of marshal. Later that month Khrushchev convened a conference at Sevastopol, attended by the minister of defense, Marshal G. K. Zhukov, a staunch opponent of a large surface fleet. With Kuznetsov out of the way, a majority of the political, military, and naval leaders present supported Khrushchev's position that the future Soviet navy should be based around submarines and land-based naval aircraft, both armed with missiles.[39]

In January 1956 Khrushchev passed over several senior admirals to appoint 45-year-old Vice Admiral Sergei Georgiyevich Gorshkov as new navy commander. Gorshkov's views on the material needs of the fleet actually did not differ dramatically from those of Kuznetsov, but in his early years in office he remained faithful to Khrushchev's vision for the navy, which allowed room for new smaller surface warships provided that they were armed with missiles. After years of experimentation, in October 1958 the *Spokoiniy* (NATO "Kildin") class destroyer *Bedoviy* became the first Soviet surface ship in regular commission to be armed with missiles. It carried the first Soviet naval SSM, the Korabelnye Snaryad Shchuka or KSShch (NATO SS-N-1 "Scrubber"), a shipboard version of the air-launched Shchuka missile developed by Vladimir N. Chelomey and already in use at the time. [As with warship types, the United States and NATO developed a series of code names for Soviet missile systems. They were numbered in sequence, starting with an abbreviation indicating missile type (SS for surface-to-surface, SA for surface-to-air, etc.) and also given a nickname.] The range of the KSShch extended beyond the ship's horizon, but because the Soviets at the time had no reliable system of over-the-horizon (OTH) targeting, its practical range was limited to targets within sight of the ship. The next Soviet destroyers, eight Project 57B (NATO "Krupny") class vessels (laid down 1958–59, completed 1960–61) carried a dozen KSShch missiles apiece. The horizon range of the next Soviet ship-launched SSM, the P-15 (NATO SS-N-2 "Styx"), sufficed to give a powerful striking potential to the flotillas of Project 205 (NATO "Osa") class fast attack craft which began to enter service in 1959. Conceptually the equivalent of the coastal torpedo boats of the Jeune École, these 172-ton boats, each equipped with four missiles, were intended to defend Soviet territorial waters against an enemy's larger surface warships. The Soviet navy commissioned almost 300 "Osa" boats in the years 1959–70, and eventually exported another 200 to clients abroad, mostly communist countries. In October 1967 the P-15 became the first missile to sink a ship in combat, when one of ten "Osa" boats sold to Egypt successfully targeted the Israeli destroyer *Eilat*.[40]

As the KSShch and P-15 entered service, the M-1 (NATO SA-N-1) surface-to-air missile, the first Soviet SAM, made its debut in Gorshkov's next destroyers, the Project 61 (NATO "Kashin") class. The 20 "Kashins," designed to provide other vessels with defense against air attack, carried 32 M-1s. The first ship of this successful class was built 1959–62, the last 1970–73. While work was under way on the first "Kashin," Chelomey developed the first practical OTH missile for the

Soviet navy, guided by radar video data relayed from the fired missile via an airplane to the firing ship, which thus could retain control over the missile after it passed beyond the ship's horizon. The P-35, a modified version of the P-5 (NATO SS-N-3 "Shaddock"), was tested in 1961 and introduced late the following year aboard the *Grozny*, the first of four 4,400-ton Project 58 (NATO "Kynda") class guided missile cruisers. The "Kynda" class ships carried 16 P-35s and, for defensive purposes, 24 M-1 SAMs. Though classified as cruisers, these ships (laid down 1960–61, completed 1962–65) were considerably smaller than the British "County" class destroyers built during the same years.[41] Nevertheless, they were the largest surface warships commissioned in the Soviet navy between 1955 and 1967, and, for Gorshkov, an important break in Khrushchev's ban against the construction of surface vessels larger than destroyers. By the time the *Grozny* was completed, the admiral had secured permission for the construction of two 14,590-ton helicopter carriers, the *Moskva* (built 1962–67) and *Leningrad* (1965–69), designed specifically for anti-submarine warfare, to counter the threat of the US navy's new Polaris missile submarines. A somewhat larger version of the type introduced in the French navy's helicopter cruiser *Jeanne d'Arc*, the ship could carry up to 20 helicopters, which it launched from a flight deck aft of its centerline superstructure. Each unit had an armament of 18 anti-submarine (NATO SUW-N-1 "Hormone") missiles and, for air defense, 44 M-11 (NATO SA-N-3 "Goblet") SAMs. The *Leningrad* was laid down the day after the *Moskva* was launched, on the same slip at Nikolaiev, which Gorshkov intended to make the construction site for future, larger surface warships.[42]

Even though Gorshkov's heart may have been in the construction of larger surface warships, he prudently satisfied Khrushchev's desire for a submarine-heavy fleet. Production of the first postwar design, the Project 613 (NATO "Whiskey") class attack submarine, displacing 1,340 tons submerged, began in 1950–51 and continued until 1957–58, by which time 215 boats of the type had been commissioned. Over half of the "Whiskeys" were built on the Volga at the "closed" city of Gorky, allowing a considerable degree of secrecy especially in the days before satellite reconnaissance. Gorshkov also inherited two other attack submarine programs, the 2,350-ton Project 611 (NATO "Zulu") class, including 18 units completed 1952–55, and the 540-ton Project 615 (NATO "Quebec") class, including 30 units completed 1954–57. The latter, owing to their small size, were limited to operating in the Baltic and Black Sea. After assuming command, Gorshkov introduced a series of new attack submarine types. The 1,700-ton Project 633 (NATO "Romeo") class included 21 units completed 1957–62, all at Gorky, while other submarine shipyards started work on units of the 2,485-ton Project 641 (NATO "Foxtrot") design, a class of 62 boats produced from 1957 until 1971. Gorshkov also inherited the first unit of the 5,300-ton

Project 627 (NATO "November") class of nuclear-powered attack submarines. The *K 3*, later named *Leninskiy Komsomol*, was laid down in the covered Arctic submarine yard at Severodvinsk in May 1954 and completed in March 1959, four and a half years after the *Nautilus*, the first US navy submarine of the same type. By 1963 another 13 "Novembers" had entered service. Meanwhile, at the end of 1957 work began on the first of five units of the 5,500-ton Project 659 (NATO "Echo I") class, nuclear-powered guided missile submarines. After entering service in 1961–62, they were armed with a submarine version of the P-5 "Shaddock" SSM. The 29 boats of the 6,000-ton Project 675 (NATO "Echo II") class, completed 1962–67, received a modified "Shaddock," the P-6. While building the "Novembers" and "Echos" the Soviet navy did not abandon diesel-powered submarines, producing 16 units of the 3,750-ton Project 651 (NATO "Juliett") class guided missile submarine in the years 1963–68. The "Julietts" likewise were armed with "Shaddock" missiles, as were several modified units of the older "Whiskey" class. In order to take advantage of the air-based OTH targeting technology of the 1960s, Soviet submarines armed with the "Shaddock" had to remain surfaced while guiding the missile to its target. This left them vulnerable to attack, but their speed at least partially compensated for the liability. Amid the initial Soviet submarine buildup of the 1950s the US navy took comfort in the fact that the slowest American aircraft carrier could still outrun the fastest Soviet submarine; by the early 1960s the margin of safety had narrowed, and the 23–25 knot submerged speed of the "Echos" caused considerable concern in the West. The 30-knot speed of the "Novembers" likewise worried the US navy, as it was only two knots slower than the first American nuclear-powered carrier, the *Enterprise* (commissioned 1961). The quest for speed led Gorshkov to lay down the 5,200-ton Project 661 (NATO "Papa") class nuclear-powered guided missile submarine in 1963. Armed with ten P-120 Ametist (NATO SS-N-9 "Siren") missiles when finally completed six years later, it achieved a record submerged speed of 44.7 knots while on patrol in 1970–71. Fortunately for the United States and its NATO allies, the "Papa" was too expensive to reproduce.[43]

The overwhelming majority of Soviet submarines commissioned during the Khrushchev era were armed with torpedoes or guided missiles, but experimentation with submarine-launched ballistic missiles progressed throughout the period. The first breakthrough predated Gorshkov's appointment as navy commander. On 16 September 1955 "Zulu" class submarine *B 67* of the Northern Fleet, modified to launch an adapted Soviet army R-11 (NATO "Scud") missile, conducted the first-ever launch of a ballistic missile from a submarine. Starting in 1958, five "Zulus" were converted to fire R-11s, which had a range of 80 miles. After 1961 they were armed with the R-13 (NATO SS-N-4

"Sark") missile, the first genuine Soviet SLBM, which had a range of 350 miles. The first purpose-built Soviet ballistic missile submarines were diesel-powered, the 23 units of the 2,900-ton Project 628 (NATO "Golf") class, completed 1959–62 (see Plate 46). They were built concurrently with the navy's first nuclear-powered ballistic-missile submarines, eight units of the 6,000-ton Project 658 (NATO "Hotel") class, which were completed 1960–64. The first of the "Hotels," *K 19*, entered service in November 1960, just eleven months after the first US navy ballistic missile submarine, the nuclear-powered *George Washington*, but their design and capability, as well as that of their diesel-powered counterparts, was primitive by comparison. The "Zulus," "Golfs," and "Hotels" each carried just three R-13 missiles, which had to be launched from the surface, in a process that took at least ten minutes per missile. In comparison, the *George Washington* carried 16 Polaris SLBMs, which it could fire while submerged. Their shortcomings aside, the variety of attack and ballistic missile submarines entering service in the 1950s and early 1960s gave Khrushchev what he wanted for the Soviet navy, the largest submarine force in history. Because scores of submarines launched in the 1940s remained in commission through the 1950s, in sheer numbers of boats the Soviet submarine fleet reached its peak strength in 1958, with 475 units. The overall size of the fleet declined thereafter, as obsolete submarines leaving service outnumbered new ones being commissioned.[44]

While the growth of the submarine fleet remained shrouded in secrecy, the surface fleet became increasingly visible. Starting in 1956 Gorshkov expanded the regimen of overseas cruises and foreign port calls begun after Stalin's death, using the fourteen *Sverdlov* class cruisers and escorting destroyers to show the flag abroad. After *Sverdlov*s visited Helsinki and Stockholm in 1954, two *Sverdlov*s and four destroyers called at Portsmouth in 1955, in the first visit of Soviet warships to a NATO country. In April 1956 the cruiser *Ordzhonikidze*, escorted by two destroyers, carried Khrushchev on a state visit to Britain; twenty years passed before the next Soviet warships called at a British port, in the era of détente. Later in the spring of 1956 the Black Sea Fleet commander, Admiral V. A. Kasatonov, led the cruiser *Mikhail Kutuzov* and two destroyers through the Turkish straits to visit ports in Albania and Yugoslavia. Ever since these countries became communist in 1945, the Soviet Union had sought submarine bases on their Adriatic coasts, to circumvent the Montreux Convention's restrictions on the passage of submarines through the Turkish straits. The quest took on a greater urgency after Turkey joined NATO in 1951. Ultimately eight "Whiskey" class submarines operated out of a base on Albania's Gulf of Valona in 1960–61, in an arrangement brought to an abrupt end by a rupture of relations between the Soviet and Albanian governments. The Soviet navy also supported Khrushchev's Middle East policy by sending ships to call at Arab ports, starting with the cruiser *Zhdanov*, which visited Latakia, Syria, in 1957. Far beyond Europe and the Mediterranean, Khrushchev used the navy and its assets in an effort to lure Indonesia into the Soviet orbit. In 1959 a cruiser and two destroyers called at Djakarta; later that year, the Soviet Union delivered the first of 14 "Whiskey" class submarines, 8 destroyers, and dozens of smaller craft to Indonesia, in a series of transfers culminating in 1962 with the sale of the cruiser *Ordzhonikidze*, which served for another decade as the Indonesian navy flagship *Irian*. President Sukarno's shift to a pro-Chinese attitude before his ouster in 1965 ended the brief Soviet–Indonesian flirtation.[45]

Gorshkov's quest to make the Soviet Union a leading naval power reached an important milestone in 1959, when the Soviet navy passed the British in overall tonnage to become Europe's largest and the world's second largest, behind the US navy. The achievement owed much to the submarine buildup, as the British remained ahead of the Soviets in surface warship tonnage into the 1960s. In his campaign to build a formidable blue-water navy for a traditional land power, Gorshkov had much in common with Tirpitz and Raeder. Unlike his earlier German counterparts, he dismissed the concepts of Mahan as outdated or irrelevant, yet his overall vision of sea power reflected the Mahanian tradition. Concern for access to the open seas prompted Gorshkov to redeploy his forces. In a step considered provocative in the West, in 1956 the main base of the Baltic Fleet was moved from Kronstadt to the ice-free port of Baltiysk (formerly Pillau) near Kaliningrad (formerly Königsberg), in the Soviet part of what once was East Prussia. More significant, Gorshkov built up the Northern Fleet (based at Severomorsk, a White Sea port near Murmansk, on the Kola Peninsula) from the smallest of the Soviet fleets to the largest.[46]

During the Cuban Missile Crisis of October 1962, the Soviet Union paid dearly for the weakness of its surface fleet. No Soviet warship had visited Cuba at any time since Fidel Castro's takeover there (and none would visit until 1969), and during the US naval blockade of Cuba, the only Soviet naval vessels in the Caribbean or western Atlantic were non-nuclear submarines, none of which escaped detection by the US navy. Khrushchev's withdrawal of Soviet missiles from Cuba marked the beginning of the end of his dictatorship, but the fact that he had been forced to back down by a US naval blockade did much to strengthen the hand of Gorshkov in his quest for a balanced fleet including significant surface units. Shortly before he gave way to Leonid Brezhnev, Khrushchev approved four 6,000-ton Project 1134 (NATO "Kresta I") class cruisers (laid down 1964–66, completed 1967–69). Compared to their predecessors of the "Kynda" class, they carried fewer "Shaddock" SSMs (4) but many more M-1 SAMs (42) and had considerable anti-submarine warfare capability. The same was true of their half-sisters of the Project 1134A (NATO "Kresta II") class, which at 5,600 tons were slightly smaller, but carried a greater number of more modern missiles: 8 RPK-3 (NATO SS-N-14) anti-submarine missiles, and 48 M-11 SAMs. The class had 10 units, the first built 1966–69, the last 1975–77. Production of the design overlapped with the next Soviet cruisers, the seven 6,700-ton Project 1134B (NATO "Kara") class ships, the first built 1968–71, the last 1975–79. They, too, carried 8 RPK-3s but had far greater anti-aircraft capability than their predecessors, provided by 72 M-11 and 40 RZ-13 (NATO SA-N-4 "Gecko") SAMs.[47]

As of the summer of 1970 Gorshkov's surface fleet was led by 2 helicopter carriers and 19 cruisers, but the latter included 10 *Sverdlovs* (only three of which had been modernized to fire missiles). The big slip at Nikolaiev, where the helicopter carriers *Moskva* and *Leningrad* were built, remained empty for two years after the launching of the *Leningrad* in July 1968. That hiatus ended in July 1970, when work began on the 36,000-ton *Kiev*, the first of a class of four ships (two for the Northern Fleet, two for the Pacific Fleet) that were aircraft carriers in all but name. The decision to call the ships "tactical aviation cruisers" apparently stemmed from a desire to avoid violating the Montreux Convention, which restricted the right of passage through the Turkish straits of aircraft carriers (as well as submarines), and might have prevented the completed ships from leaving the Black Sea for their intended stations. The unique designation was also justified by the fact that the *Kievs* resembled no other warships ever built, before or since. They had a profile not unlike a battleship of the Second World War, with an extensive superstructure rather than a carrier island; but, like a carrier island, the superstructure was offset to starboard, to allow for an angled flight deck which extended from the stern of the ship to the port side of the superstructure. The flight deck did not extend forward, where the ship had a graceful bow reminiscent of a battleship. They carried 31 Yak-38 (NATO "Forger") VSTOL attack aircraft, which typically had to take off vertically because the *Kievs* (unlike western European VSTOL carriers) did not have a "ski jump" ramp to aid in takeoffs. The *Kiev* was completed in 1975, followed in rapid succession by its sister-ships *Minsk* (built 1972–78) and *Novorossiysk* (1975–82; see Plate 47), each of which was laid down as soon as the previous vessel was launched. Work began on the *Baku* in 1978, as soon as the *Novorossiysk* was launched, but modifications during construction delayed its completion until the end of 1987. In addition to their aircraft, the *Kievs* carried 24 Bazalt (NATO SS-N-12 "Sandbox") guided missiles and had formidable air defenses, provided by 72 M-11 and 40 RZ-13 SAMs.[48] Upon its completion the *Kiev* was the largest warship yet built in the Soviet Union, but it had less than half the displacement and only one-third the number of aircraft carried by the US navy's nuclear-powered *Nimitz*, commissioned the same year. The purpose of the class was never clearly defined, as the ships were not large enough to function effectively as conventional aircraft carriers, yet lacked the flexibility of much smaller contemporary VSTOL carriers, such as the British *Invincible*s, and were less formidably armed than much smaller guided-missile cruisers.

The other major Soviet surface warship class of the Brezhnev years was just as unique but had a far clearer purpose. The four 24,000-ton *Kirov* class missile cruisers, all built at Leningrad, were intended to serve as fleet flagships. They were the Soviet Union's first nuclear-powered surface warships and the largest non-aircraft carrying ships completed by any navy after the commissioning of the British battleship *Vanguard* in 1946. Their formidable armament included 20 P-500 Granit (NATO SS-N-19 "Shipwreck") missiles and 16 RPK-3 anti-submarine missiles, with air defense provided by 96 S-300 (NATO SA-N-6 "Grumble") and 40 older RZ-13 SAMs. The *Kirov* was laid down in 1974 and completed in 1980, followed by its sister-ships *Frunze* (built 1978–84) and *Kalinin* (1983–88). The fourth unit, laid down in 1986, remained incomplete at the end of the Cold War. Upon entering service, the *Kirov*s replaced aging *Sverdlov* class cruisers that had been modernized to serve as flagships. To replace the rest of the *Sverdlov*s, Gorshkov ordered the more conventional *Slava* class cruisers, a 10,000-ton design armed with 16 Bazalt SSMs, as well as 64 S-300 and 40 RZ-13 SAMs. Meanwhile, two classes of 6,200-ton destroyers, reproductions of the *Sovremenniy* (built 1976–80) and *Udaloy* (1977–80), were built as eventual successors to the small missile cruisers that entered service in the 1960s. Twenty *Sovremenniy*s were laid down by 1989, 14 *Udaloy*s by 1990; the former, designed as a land-attack destroyer, carried P-80 Moskit (SS-N-22 "Sunbeam") missiles as their primary offensive armament, the latter, intended for anti-submarine warfare, carried RPK-3 missiles. In the event of an amphibious assault by the Soviet armed forces, the *Sovremenniy*s would have supported a landing force led by the 11,000-ton assault ship *Ivan Rogov* (completed 1978) and two sister-ships (1982, 1989), each of which could accommodate 550 troops, 10 tanks, and 30 armored personnel carriers.[49]

As the Soviet Union joined the United States and its NATO allies in building cruiser-sized destroyers, it also followed the lead of the West in replacing aging destroyers with destroyer-sized frigates. The Soviet navy's first missile frigates, of the 3,300-ton Project 1135 (NATO "Krivak") class, included 39 units completed 1970–90. The first three units of the subsequent 3,500-ton *Neustrashimy* class were laid down 1986–90 but none was completed before the end of the Cold War. As successors to the "Osa" class and earlier small missile-launching surface combatants, the Soviet navy built several types of corvettes and fast attack craft, the most notable of which were the Project 1234 (NATO

"Nanuchka") and Project 1241 (NATO "Tarantul") class missile corvettes. The "Nanuchkas," produced from 1967, and the "Tarantuls," produced from 1970, both had a ducting radar system of fire control installed later in the *Sovremenniy* class destroyers.[50]

Early in the Brezhnev era, the capabilities of all missile-launching Soviet warships were enhanced by the development of satellite-based OTH targeting to replace the navy's initial air-based system. The project began in 1961 and the first satellite test launch occurred in 1965; the system was fully operational by 1973, just one year after the US navy achieved satellite-based OTH targeting capability through its new Ocean Surveillance Information System (OSIS). Of course, satellite-based missile fire control was worthless unless the submarines or surface ships firing the missiles knew their own precise location. The Soviets recognized this fact from the start, and in 1962 began work on a navigational satellite. Some "Whiskey" and "Zulu" class submarines used satellite navigation on an experimental basis as early as 1969, but the system was not fully operational until 1971. While all of the Soviet navy's vessels benefited from these new space-based technologies, they were much more important for Soviet submarines which, unlike the surface vessels, normally cruised worldwide. Notwithstanding Gorshkov's increasing focus on larger surface warships, the Soviet navy of the Brezhnev era continued to maintain the world's largest submarine fleet, including some 409 boats by the mid-1970s, of which 95 were nuclear-powered.[51]

The nuclear-powered share of the Soviet undersea fleet grew dramatically in the Brezhnev era, as few new classes of submarines were diesel-powered. Seventeen nuclear-powered guided-missile submarines of the 4,900-ton Project 670A (NATO "Charlie") class, completed 1968–80, were armed with eight P-20 (NATO SS-N-7) missiles or older P-120s. They were built concurrently with three versions of the Project 671 (NATO "Victor") class nuclear-powered attack submarine, completed 1968–91; the 48 "Victors" displaced 5,100–6,000 tons, and were armed with 82R (NATO SS-N-15 "Starfish") anti-submarine missiles plus torpedoes. The seven 3,680-ton Project 705 (NATO "Alfa") class nuclear-powered attack submarines completed 1972–83 were also armed with 82R anti-submarine missiles plus either torpedoes or mines. Thanks to an advanced lead-bismuth reactor plant, the "Alfas" had a submerged speed of over 40 knots; their innovative titanium hulls also allowed them to dive deeper than steel-hulled submarines of the time. They were followed by the largest non-ballistic missile submarines ever built for the Soviet navy, the 10 14,600-ton Project 949 (NATO "Oscar") class nuclear-powered guided-missile submarines, completed 1980–94, which carried a formidable armament of 24 P-500 Granit SSMs. Three smaller classes of nuclear attack submarines were built concurrently with the "Oscars": the single unit of the 8,500-ton Project 685 (NATO

"Mike") class, completed 1983, the four units of the 7,900-ton Project 945 (NATO "Sierra") class, completed 1984–93, and the six units of the 9,100-ton Project 971 (NATO "Akula") class, completed 1984–89. All fired torpedoes, although the "Akulas" also tested the S-10 (NATO SS-N-21 "Sampson") strategic guided missile. Another three "Akulas" were laid down in the 1990s. The Soviet navy also commissioned two classes of diesel-powered attack submarines during and after the Brezhnev years: 19 units of the 3,900-ton Project 641 BUKI (NATO "Tango") class, completed 1972–81, and 28 units of the 3,075-ton Project 877 (NATO "Kilo") class, completed 1982–93. Soviet shipyards built at least 16 more "Kilos" for export.[52]

To the end of the Cold War the Soviet Union continued to base the overwhelming majority of its ballistic missiles on land, while the United States based an increasing share of its ballistic missiles aboard submarines. Nevertheless, during and after the Brezhnev era the Soviet Union commissioned ever more powerful nuclear ballistic missile submarines, starting with the 34 units of the 9,600-ton Project 667A (NATO "Yankee") class, completed 1967–72. While the earlier Soviet ballistic missile submarines of the "Golf" and "Hotel" classes had been armed with just three missiles, the boats of the "Yankee" class carried 16 R-27 (NATO SS-N-6 "Sawfly") missiles. They finally gave the Soviet navy an equivalent of the US navy's Polaris/Poseidon ballistic missile submarines, in service since 1959, but the first "Yankee" was commissioned the same year as the last Poseidon submarine, reflecting just how far ahead the United States remained in the undersea arms race. But in their quest to close the gap the Soviets benefited from the fact that the US navy went fourteen years (1967–81) without commissioning a new ballistic missile submarine. During that time the Soviet navy completed all of the "Yankees" and most of the Project 667 (NATO "Delta") class, 43 submarines in four subgroups ranging in size from the 11,750-ton "Delta I" to the 13,500-ton "Delta IV", commissioned 1972–92. The "Delta Is" were armed with 12 R-29 (NATO SS-N-8 "Mod 1 Sawfly") ballistic missiles, which had a range of 4,000 miles, long enough to hit any target in the United States from the relative safety of the Barents Sea (for Northern Fleet units) or the Sea of Okhotsk (for Pacific Fleet units). The introduction of the "Delta" and the R-29 missile forced the United States and its NATO allies to abandon their old anti-submarine warfare strategies, as they could no longer count on their navies catching Soviet submarines en route from their bases to mid-ocean launching grounds. Subsequent modified versions of the "Delta" were armed with modified versions of the R-29 missile, the R-29U (NATO SS-N-18 "Stingray") and the R-29RM (NATO SS-N-23 "Skiff"), and carried 16 missiles rather than 12. Concurrently with the "Delta IVs" and the US navy's Trident missile submarines of the *Ohio* class (commissioned from 1981), the Soviet navy added six Project 941

(NATO "Typhoon") class nuclear-powered ballistic missile submarines, the first built 1977–81, the last 1987–89. Designed by Sergey N. Kovolev, these remarkable vessels each carried 20 R-39 (NATO SS-N-20 "Sturgeon") missiles, which had a range of just under 4,500 miles. At 18,500 tons surfaced (25,000 tons submerged) and 562 feet in length, they were the largest submarines ever built, larger than the battleship *Dreadnought* of 1906 (and, at 25 knots submerged, also faster). They were also considerably larger than the American *Ohio*s (18,700 tons submerged) but may have had less destructive capacity, as the *Ohio*s carried 24 Trident SLBMs. The "Typhoons" all were built in great secrecy at Severodvinsk, and upon completion all joined the Northern Fleet. In case of nuclear war with the West they would have operated under the Arctic ice, guided by satellite to breaks in the icecap through which they would fire their missiles.[53]

In the Brezhnev era the growth of the Soviet surface fleet brought an increase in the visibility and frequency of the navy's overseas operations. Starting in 1964 the Soviet navy always had at least a nominal representation in the Mediterranean, which expanded dramatically during crises in the Middle East. The most impressive showing to date came during the Arab–Israeli war of 1967, when 70 Soviet warships assembled in the Eastern Mediterranean. The display prompted a change in behavior by the US navy, which no longer had the luxury of focusing exclusively on Soviet submarines, taking for granted that the surface fleet, lacking carriers for air cover, would rarely leave home waters in force. Starting in 1967 Gorshkov assigned Soviet destroyers to shadow American aircraft carriers, raising fears in the US navy that, in case of war, the Soviet navy would attempt to disable the carriers via some sort of coordinated preemptive strike carried out by these shadow vessels. Tensions heightened in 1968, when the Soviet navy conducted exercise "Sever," a maneuver involving ships in the North Atlantic as well as the Baltic, Norwegian, and Barents seas, including units from the Polish and East German navies. The largest Soviet naval exercise to date, it featured a simulated high seas encounter against an enemy fleet. During the crisis following North Korea's seizure of the intelligence ship USS *Pueblo* in 1968, the Soviet navy responded to an American show of force led by the carrier *Enterprise* by intercepting it en route across the Pacific with a "November" class nuclear attack submarine, then by massing 16 ships (including auxiliary and surveillance vessels) off the Korean coast, to harass the operations of the American carrier group. The force was far weaker than its American counterpart but sufficed to demonstrate Soviet resolve to defend North Korea. In contrast to the boldness of this episode, the Soviet navy generally steered clear of Southeast Asia during the American military intervention in Vietnam (1965–73). After Singapore became independent in 1965, the Soviets opened negotiations with the city-state for docking rights and repair facilities, but by the time the last British forces left Singapore in 1976, the Soviet navy had secured access to Camranh Bay, thanks to the communist victory in the Vietnam war.[54]

The Soviet navy opened the 1970s by conducting one of the most ambitious exercises ever attempted by any navy, stretching the limits of a force which, like its Imperial Russian predecessor, still relied on conscripted manpower from inland regions. The maneuver "Okean," held in the spring of 1970, included around 200 ships and submarines in the Barents, Norwegian, and Baltic seas, in the Mediterranean, and in both the Philippine Sea and the Sea of Japan. (In comparison, the largest NATO naval maneuver ever held, "Ocean Safari 85," in the summer of 1985, included 157 ships from the US navy and nine European navies). The "Okean" simulations included anti-submarine and anti-carrier warfare as well as amphibious landings. Underscoring their global reach, the Soviets maintained naval forces in the Indian Ocean during the exercise that were not a part of it, and while it was still under way sent a naval task force to Cuba. The triumph of "Okean" was marred only by the loss of *K 8* of the "November" class off Cape Finisterre (12 April 1970), the first of four known accidental sinkings of Soviet nuclear submarines during the Cold War. In 1973 the helicopter carrier *Leningrad* conducted the navy's first circumnavigation of Africa, finishing at the Suez Canal where its helicopters, outfitted for minesweeping duties, participated in an international effort to clear the waterway, which had been blocked since the 1967 Arab–Israeli war. Later that year the next major Middle East conflict brought a far larger Soviet contingent to the area. The navy's Eastern Mediterranean show of force during the Yom Kippur War of October 1973 grew to 96 warships, including 5 cruisers, 14 frigates and destroyers, 2 "Nanuchka" class corvettes, 8 amphibious ships, 38 intelligence and support ships, and 23 submarines. The Soviet representation was considerably larger than the 60 warships serving with the US Sixth Fleet at the peak of the crisis. Unfortunately for the Soviet Union, after Egypt's face-saving performance against Israel, Anwar Sadat shifted his country's Cold War allegiances to the United States, expelling Soviet advisers and, in 1976, cancelling Soviet docking rights in Egyptian ports.[55]

In the spring of 1975 the Soviet navy conducted another multi-ocean 200-ship simulation, the exercise "Vesna" (called "Okean 75" in the West). Compared to "Okean" five years earlier, this time amphibious operations were more central to the program, as the Northern Fleet in the Barents Sea and the Pacific Fleet in the Sea of Japan both practiced escorting amphibious groups and supply convoys. "Vesna" also allowed the Soviet navy to conduct the first thorough test of the satellite-based missile fire-control system introduced in 1973, in targeting exercises involving ships in the Atlantic, Pacific, and Indian oceans as well as the Mediterranean.[56] That May, reflecting the easing of

East–West tensions in the brief era of détente, for the first time the Soviet navy exchanged visits with the US navy, sending two destroyers to Boston while the United States sent a destroyer and a frigate to Leningrad. In November 1975 the Soviet frigate *Storozhevoy* of the Baltic Fleet attempted an unauthorized visit to a Western port, after mutineers seized the ship and steamed for neutral Sweden. Once other Baltic Fleet units intercepted the ship, order was restored and the leaders of the uprising later executed. This embarrassing incident was not indicative of broader serious problems within the navy; indeed, in the late 1970s the frequency and ambition of surface operations only increased. In February 1976, while deployed off the coast of Angola, the "Kresta II" class cruiser *Admiral Makarov* provided fire support for the Marxist MPLA in the local civil war. Months before the final collapse of détente in the wake of the December 1979 Soviet invasion of Afghanistan, the Soviet navy made a series of provocative port calls in Vietnam. In March 1979 a cruiser, a frigate, and a minesweeper visited the former US naval base at Camranh Bay, which the Soviet navy had not used in the years since 1975 to avoid antagonizing the United States. That November, on the first anniversary of a new Soviet–Vietnamese friendship treaty, a Soviet cruiser and two destroyers called at Haiphong.[57]

In the early 1980s Soviet naval activity reflected the re-chilling of the Cold War. In 1980 and 1981, the Soviet Baltic Fleet held exercises in the North Sea involving warships from East Germany and Poland. In the spring of 1981 the Soviet Mediterranean squadron conducted a joint maneuver with the armed forces of Syria, during which 1,000 Soviet troops were landed on the Syrian coast. That autumn, in the midst of the Solidarity crisis in Poland, the Soviet navy's "Zapad" exercise brought ships of the Northern and Black Sea fleets to the Baltic. VSTOL aircraft from the *Kiev* and helicopters from the *Leningrad* supported troop landings on the Soviet Baltic coast, near the Polish border. Meanwhile, in the early 1980s the Soviet naval presence in the Indian Ocean, provided by ships and submarines from the Pacific Fleet, grew to include 20–25 vessels, serviced at Ethiopia's Dehalak Island in the Red Sea, Yemen's Socotra Island east of the Gulf of Aden, and various ports in India. The Soviet–Indian naval relationship, which began after Gorshkov personally led the first Soviet naval visit to Bombay and Madras in 1968, included a series of arms sales by which the Soviet Union surpassed Britain to become the leading supplier of warships to the Indian navy. The Soviet navy's spring maneuver of 1984 was the third largest ever, including over 180 surface warships and submarines from the Northern, Baltic, and Black Sea fleets. A contingent sent to the Caribbean was led by the helicopter carrier *Leningrad*, which (at 14,590 tons) became the largest Soviet warship ever deployed to Cuban waters. Later that year the *Leningrad* visited Yemen, escorted by a cruiser, a destroyer, and smaller warships. The Soviet navy also showed the flag in the Persian Gulf throughout the Iran–Iraq war of 1980–88, drawing upon its Indian Ocean squadron for escorts for Soviet-flagged tankers and freighters. The warships usually stayed outside of the Gulf, off the coast of Oman, and entered only to carry out specific missions. All of these missions and exercises combined to make the years 1984–85 the busiest ever for Soviet naval operations beyond coastal waters.[58]

The death of Brezhnev late in 1982 ushered in the brief reign of Yuri Andropov (1982–84), followed by the even shorter tenure of Konstantin Chernenko (1984–85). Amid the uncertainty the big slip at Nikolaiev remained empty for over a year and a half after the launching of the last unit of the *Kiev* class, until November 1983, when work began there on the largest Soviet warship ever, a 60,000-ton aircraft carrier named *Leonid Brezhnev* in honor of the man whose patronage had enabled Gorshkov to build a respectable surface fleet. The angled-deck design featured a 12-degree "ski jump" at the bow, to compensate for the fact that it had no launching catapults. In contrast to American carriers, it had its own formidable defenses, including 16 P-500 Granit SSMs and 144 SAMs (NATO SA-N-7 "Gauntlet"), but it could accommodate a combination of just 30 jets and helicopters (18 to 24 aircraft, with 6 to 12 helicopters). After its commissioning, it would fly Su-27 (NATO "Flanker"), MiG-29 (NATO "Fulcrum"), and Su-25 (NATO "Frogfoot") aircraft. As with the earlier *Kiev* class, the Soviet navy maintained the fiction that the ship was not an aircraft carrier, as late as 1989 calling it a "heavy aircraft-carrying cruiser." As soon as the *Leonid Brezhnev* was launched late in 1985, work began on the *Riga*, a second unit of the class. By then Mikhail Gorbachev was in power, but the new Soviet leader did not formally change his country's foreign and domestic policies until over a year after he took office. In the meantime he allowed the *Riga* to be laid down and, the following spring, the last missile cruiser of the *Kirov* class, named *Yuri Andropov* after his late mentor.[59]

Gorbachev recognized that the Soviet Union would not survive without sweeping economic changes, and that the country could no longer afford to sustain its Cold War competition with the United States. In six years he held ten summit conferences with American presidents, and in the years 1988 to 1991 signed the arms reduction and peace agreements which ended the Cold War and the East–West division of Europe. In a symbolic gesture, in 1989 the *Slava* class cruiser *Marshal Ustinov* and its escorts called at Norfolk, Virginia, in only the second visit by Soviet warships to the United States and the first since 1975. But for the Soviet navy, the changes were more real than symbolic, as arms reduction treaties and overall cost-cutting had a profound effect on the fleet. In December 1985 Gorbachev laid the foundation for his future naval policies by forcing the 75-year-old Gorshkov to retire, just weeks short of his thirtieth anniversary in office. His successor, former submariner Admiral of the Fleet Vladimir N. Chernavin, cooperated fully with Gorbachev's policies, first saving money by reducing the number of ships at sea and decommissioning older warships, then by decommissioning newer warships, and finally, by all but stopping new construction. When Gorbachev's anti-corruption campaign exposed abuses in the Brezhnev era, the new aircraft carrier bearing the former leader's name became the *Tblisi*. After his policy of openness (*glasnost*) provided the opportunity for separatist movements to arise in the country's non-Russian republics, the names of their capitals were removed from warships: thus, during 1990 the *Kiev* class carrier *Baku* became the *Admiral Gorshkov*, the carrier *Tblisi* was renamed again, as *Admiral Kuznetsov*, and its sister-ship *Riga*, under construction at Nikolaiev, became the *Varyag*. Notwithstanding the imminent end of the Cold War, late in 1988 Gorbachev allowed construction to begin on the 65,000-ton aircraft carrier *Ulyanovsk*, on the big slip at Nikolaiev just cleared by the launching of the *Varyag*. The *Admiral Kuznetsov* was finally completed early in 1991; by the end of that year the *Varyag* was nearly finished and the *Ulyanovsk* 40 percent complete and almost ready to launch. The latter two were destined never to serve.[60]

At the time of its demise in 1991, the Soviet Union had the largest navy ever assembled by any European country, with more personnel than the British, French, Italian, and German navies combined. Its warships included 62 ballistic missile submarines armed with 940 SLBMs, 147 other nuclear-powered submarines, and 100 non-nuclear submarines. In comparison, the US navy had 34 ballistic and guided missile submarines and 80 other submarines, all nuclear-powered. The Soviet navy enjoyed a narrow advantage over the US navy in amphibious ships (75 to 66) but dominated in smaller types, with far more frigates (206 to 121), corvettes (162 to 19), and minesweepers (205 to 23), as well as 115 patrol torpedo boats and missile boats, and three minelayers, categories in which the US navy had none. Analysts considered the Soviet navy superior to the US navy in most aspects of submarine warfare as well as mine warfare, anti-ship missile development, and amphibious assault capabilities, albeit in the latter case not for long-distance operations. But the US navy dominated in larger surface warships, with more carriers (13 to 5), helicopter carriers or assault ships (13 to 2), guided missile cruisers (45 to 31) and destroyers (51 to 40). While most American carriers were nuclear-powered, the largest nuclear-powered warships in the Soviet navy were the *Kirov* class cruisers.[61] The Soviet navy had no equivalent to the deterrent provided by the big American carriers and their battle groups; the same vessels, along with the assault ships, gave the United States a global intervention capability the Soviet Union could not match. The six "Typhoon" class ballistic missile submarines were the Soviet navy's greatest technological achievement and its most potent warships, yet by 1991 their American counterpart, the *Ohio* class, already included 12 units and, within six years, another six would be completed. In its naval-industrial complex as in so many other areas, the Soviet Union simply lacked the resources to compete with the United States; compounding the problem, it had no equivalent to the US's NATO allies to supplement its strength. Despite its periodic internal problems, NATO functioned far better than the Warsaw Pact, within which the Soviets only reluctantly armed their eastern European satellites. When communism collapsed in these states, ending their alliances with the Soviet Union, Poland and Romania (with one destroyer apiece) were the only Warsaw Pact countries with ships larger than frigates. Poland, Romania, and Bulgaria collectively had just eight submarines and East Germany none, reflecting the fact that the Soviets, unlike the NATO allies, never trusted "their" Germans to operate U-boats again.[62]

FROM THE FALKLANDS TO THE PERSIAN GULF (1982–91)

It was no small irony that the navies of the NATO countries, once reconfigured for specific Cold War roles within the alliance, in the last years of the Cold War were called upon to serve very different purposes. The most dramatic case came in 1982, when the British navy, dramatically downsized for a specific mission in the North Sea and North Atlantic, had to fight a war 8,000 miles from home after Argentina occupied the Falkland Islands, one of Britain's last remaining colonial possessions.[63]

Argentina had long claimed the Falklands (also known as the Malvinas), 350 miles east of the southern tip of Patagonia, but under the rule of a military dictatorship established in 1976 the Argentinians became more aggressive in pressing the issue. Finally, on 1–2 April 1982, the Argentinian navy landed troops on the islands and easily defeated their tiny garrison of British marines. On 3 April Argentinian forces also seized South Georgia Island (Isla San Pedro), 900 miles east of the Falklands, and the South Sandwich Islands, an archipelago 400–500 miles southeast of South Georgia, all of which had been administered by Britain as part of its Falklands territory. Prime Minister Margaret Thatcher responded by ordering the navy to mount an operation to reconquer the islands. Fleet commander Admiral Sir John Fieldhouse entrusted Rear Admiral Sandy Woodward with operational command. The VSTOL carriers *Invincible* and *Hermes* spearheaded a force of 35 warships, while the luxury liner *Queen Elizabeth II*, converted to a troopship, led 22 auxiliary vessels. Argentina's small, antiquated navy was led by two ships that had seen action in the Pacific theater of the Second World War, the 15,890-ton aircraft carrier *25 de Mayo* (ex-British *Venerable*, ex-Dutch *Karel Doorman*), completed in 1945, and the 9,770-ton cruiser *General Belgrano* (ex-USS *Phoenix*), dating from 1938, supported by 6 destroyers, 3 corvettes, and 3 submarines. Argentina had recently purchased Super Etendard attack aircraft from France, but the *25 de Mayo* had not yet been refitted to operate them and thus was a negligible factor in the war. The destroyers and corvettes, rearmed in the late 1970s with Exocet missiles, were the most formidable warships of the lot.

The British force first retook South Georgia (21–26 April), in the process forcing the Argentinians to evacuate the South Sandwich Islands as well. On 25 April the first casualty of the war, the Argentinian submarine *Santa Fe* (ex-USS *Catfish*), was beached by its commander on the coast of South Georgia after being damaged by a missile fired by a helicopter from the destroyer *Antrim*. The turning point of the war at sea came at 16:00 on the afternoon of 2 May, when the 4,900-ton nuclear attack submarine *Conqueror* intercepted the *General Belgrano* 220 miles south of the Falklands and sank it with two torpedoes, killing 321 of the 1,201 men aboard. Thereafter the Argentinian navy attempted no further operations, while the British landed troops on the Falklands on 21 May and completed their reconquest by 14 June. The victors paid a price for their triumph, with air-launched Exocet missiles and bombs dropped by the Argentinian air force posing the greatest threat to British vessels. On 4 May an Exocet set afire the 3,850-ton destroyer *Sheffield*, which was abandoned and later scuttled, and on 26 May conventional bombs sank its sister-ship *Coventry*. In between, an air attack with older-generation unguided rockets sank the 3,100-ton frigate *Ardent*, and the accidental detonation of an unexploded Argentinian bomb during a defusing attempt sank its sister-ship *Antelope*. The British also lost a supply ship and a landing ship. The Falklands War revealed both the promise and the perils of the dawning age of high-tech warfare, demonstrating the striking power of Exocets and other recently developed missile systems, and also the ability of ships to confuse the targeting of these "smart" weapons by rather simple methods, such as firing clouds of metal "chaff" or deploying a "hot" hovering helicopter off their stern. The loss of the *Sheffield* revealed how narrow a ship captain's margin of error had become. At the time it was hit by an air-launched Exocet, the destroyer was escorting the carrier *Hermes*. To avoid revealing the position of the *Hermes* by an enemy signal intercept, the *Sheffield* communicated via a satellite link. Electronic spillover from the ship's satellite dish caused its ESM (electronic support measures) receiver to set off false alarms whenever the dish was in use, so the ESM receiver was routinely turned off whenever a message was being sent or received. As luck would have it, an Argentinian pilot sighted and targeted the *Sheffield* during one of these brief blackouts, before the ship (with its ESM receiver down) could sight and target his aircraft. The result was disaster for the British.

The war demonstrated the versatility of the British VSTOL carriers, which employed their Sea Harriers and Sea King helicopters effectively in a campaign very different from their intended Cold War mission of anti-submarine warfare in northern waters. The Thatcher government dropped a 1981 plan to sell one of the three *Invincibles* to Australia, but the old *Hermes* (commissioned 1959) was sold to India in 1986, the year after the last of the *Invincibles*, the *Ark Royal*, entered service. During the years 1982–91 the British continued to modernize their fleet of smaller surface warships, laying down another 17 frigates while retiring their oldest destroyers and frigates. Meanwhile, the seven nuclear attack submarines of the 5,200-ton *Trafalgar* class (completed 1983–91) strengthened the undersea force, and in 1986 work began on the first of four 16,000-ton *Vanguard* class Trident ballistic-missile submarines, intended eventually to replace the Polaris missile submarines of the *Resolution* class. Four *Upholder* class patrol submarines (laid down 1983–90) were the first non-nuclear submarines built for the British navy since the mid-1960s; intended for training purposes, they were a poor investment and would be transferred to Canada at the turn of the century.[64]

In the late Cold War years no other European naval power faced a test as daunting as Britain's Falklands War, but in 1983–84 both France and Italy followed the United States in its ill-conceived intervention in Lebanon. The operation had the short-term goal of restoring order in Beirut, a city in chaos following almost a decade of civil war and an Israeli attack during the Arab–Israeli war of 1982. Super Etendards from the French carrier *Clemenceau* joined aircraft from the USS *Dwight D. Eisenhower* in patrolling the skies over Beirut, and other French and Italian warships served alongside the *Eisenhower*'s battle group for the duration of the operation. French and Italian troops joined US Marines in establishing bases ashore, and in October 1983 the French troops, like their American counterparts, saw their quarters destroyed in a terrorist attack. Despite the cost and uncertain long-term purpose of the mission, the French and Italians stayed on until the end; indeed, the French warships did not carry away the last of their country's troops until late March 1984, five weeks after the last US troops were withdrawn. In the wake of the intervention both France and Italy sought to enhance their amphibious warfare capabilities by ordering new dock-landing ships. The French built the 4,200-ton *Bougainville* (completed 1988), which carried 2 helicopters and could accommodate 500 troops, while the Italians built the three vessels of the 5,000-ton *San Giorgio* class (completed 1988–94), each of which carried 5 helicopters and could accommodate 345 troops and 36 vehicles.[65]

The East German navy's large amphibious force became the property of the German Federal navy following the reunification of Germany in October 1990, but all of these vessels were immediately decommissioned. The 14 1,770-ton *Frosch* class landing ships were the largest units of the East German navy at the time of its demise; other warships included 3 small (1,440-ton) frigates, 16 corvettes, 39 fast attack craft, and over 2 dozen minesweepers. During 1990–91 2 frigates, 6 corvettes, and 6 minesweepers served briefly in the German Federal navy, but in 1993–94 the 14 landing ships and 16 corvettes were all sold to Indonesia, along with 9 minesweepers. Lithuania, Latvia, and Estonia divided a dozen of the fast attack craft (ex-Soviet "Osa" class boats), while Latvia and Uruguay purchased some of the remaining minesweepers. One corvette (an ex-Soviet "Tarantul" class missile ship) was turned over to the US navy. One of the fast attack craft, taken over by the Federal Border Patrol, became the only former East German naval vessel to remain in the service of the reunified Germany after 1991.[66]

In the late Cold War years, the western European countries took important steps toward improving the satellite-based command and control systems of their navies. At Northwood, England, headquarters of EASTLANT, the British navy built a Fleet Command Centre which, from 1985, was equipped with the OPCON computer information system, designed to receive and disseminate satellite information on Soviet ship movements. In 1988 the Dutch built a version of OPCON, and in 1992 the French navy began using SYCOM, integrated with the French Syracuse military satellite system. Meanwhile, the Joint Operational Tactical System (JOTS) installed aboard US navy carriers and command ships from 1981 eventually was introduced aboard the three *Invincible* class carriers and other British vessels functioning as flagships. Dutch warships helping to enforce the embargo of Iraq during and after the Persian Gulf War of 1990–91 were also fitted with JOTS.[67]

In the Persian Gulf War, the navies of Europe mounted their largest operation (in numbers of ships deployed and numbers of countries involved) since the Second World War. The conflict began in August 1990, when Iraq invaded and subsequently annexed Kuwait. The UN ultimately gave Iraq until 15 January 1991 to withdraw from Kuwait, by which time the United States assembled an international coalition for a military campaign in the event that the Iraqis ignored the deadline. Just after midnight on 17 January, the United States and its coalition partners initiated Operation Desert Storm. An air campaign lasting 37 days included sorties by planes from 6 US navy carriers, as well as cruise missile launches from surface warships and submarines. Kuwait was finally liberated during a brief ground campaign (23–27 February). While the US navy accounted for the majority of the naval forces in

Desert Storm (over 130 ships of all types), every European NATO country with a coastline contributed at least one warship. France sent the strongest contingent (the carrier *Clemenceau*, the cruiser *Colbert*, 4 destroyers, 2 minehunters) while Britain sent the largest (3 destroyers, 4 frigates, 3 minehunters, 2 submarines), along with 11 auxiliary and landing ships to support 43,000 troops, the largest ground force in the coalition other than that of the United States. Others making contributions included Italy (1 destroyer, 2 frigates, the amphibious ship *San Marco*, 3 minehunters), Spain (6 frigates and the 10,710-ton amphibious transport *Aragon*), the Netherlands (4 frigates, 1 minehunter), Portugal (2 frigates), Greece (1 frigate), Denmark (1 corvette), Norway (1 patrol vessel), Belgium (3 minehunters), and Germany (2 minehunters). Several countries also sent supply vessels of various types, and among the former Soviet bloc countries, Poland sent a hospital ship.[68] The coalition's armada spent the war supporting the ground and air campaigns, launching missile strikes, and defending itself against Iraqi missile attacks. In one instance of the latter, the British destroyer *Gloucester* on 25 February fired Sea Dart interceptor missiles that destroyed an Iraqi Silkworm missile aimed at the battleship USS *Missouri*. Most of Iraq's small fleet of patrol boats, minesweepers, and fast attack craft was destroyed piecemeal, British navy helicopters alone accounting for 15 vessels. Most Iraqi warships that survived the war saved themselves only by defecting to neutral Iran.[69]

CONCLUSION

During the forty-six years of the Cold War era, as the US navy dominated the world's oceans, the navies of Europe remained the driving force in the evolution of warfare at sea. Britain pioneered most innovations in naval aviation, from the angled flight deck, steam catapult, and mirror landing system essential to conventional carrier operations, to the assault helicopters, VSTOL aircraft, and "ski jump" bow ramps of the small carriers of the late twentieth century. The Soviet Union, meanwhile, built the largest navy ever assembled by a European power, including more submarines of all types than any other navy in history. The Soviet navy became the world's best in most aspects of submarine warfare, mine warfare, anti-ship missile development, and short-range amphibious operations. Beyond these areas, simply by posing a credible threat to the US navy's command of the seas, the Soviet fleet forced its superior rival to become even better. The global nature of the Soviet challenge provided the rationale for the United States to maintain a surface fleet based around a dozen or more carrier battle groups, and the formidable Soviet undersea force compelled the US navy and its NATO allies to develop ever more sophisticated strategies, tactics, and means of anti-submarine warfare.

The British and French navies survived their countries' post-1945 decline in great-power status to remain significant forces and valued allies of the US navy into the 1990s. The British navy resumed a continuous presence in the Mediterranean, and would be a frequent visitor to the waters around the Arabian Peninsula as well. During the Persian Gulf War, France began a quiet reintegration into NATO and would participate in all NATO deployments through the following decade, while remaining uncommitted to permanent operational structures such as standing naval forces. As the century entered its last decade the Italian and German navies had reached their greatest levels of strength since 1945, while, among the smaller navies of Europe, the Dutch and Spanish were arguably more relevant in the broader scheme of things than at any other time in the past 200 years. But for Europe's largest navy, the future appeared bleaker than ever. On 25 December 1991 the Soviet Union officially came to an end, and plans for the superpower's armed forces to remain intact under the Russian-led "Commonwealth of Independent States" proved illusory. Ultimately post-communist Russia would keep only a small fraction of the former Soviet navy afloat. With their Cold War challenger no longer a threat, the navies of the United States and its European NATO allies faced an uncertain future as well.

NOTES

[1] Jackson, *The Royal Navy in World War II*, 163–9. In comparison, the US navy in four years lost 2 battleships, 5 carriers, 6 escort carriers, 10 cruisers, 71 destroyers, and 52 submarines. The US navy lost a total of 696 vessels in 1941–45, the overall figure inflated by heavy losses in PT boats and amphibious support craft. See Norman Polmar, *Chronology of the Cold War at Sea, 1945–1991* (Annapolis, MD, 1998), 2.

[2] Paul M. Kennedy, *The Rise and Fall of British Naval Mastery* (London, 1976), 302, 333.

[3] Auphan and Mordal, *The French Navy in World War II*, 365–8; Spencer C. Tucker, "Shelling of Hai Phòng," in *Encyclopedia of the Vietnam War*, ed. Spencer C. Tucker, 3 vols (Santa Barbara, CA., 1998), 1:260–1; *idem*, "Georges Thierry d'Argenlieu," ibid., 1:147.

[4] Legohérel, *Histoire de la Marine française*, 119; Auphan and Mordal, *The French Navy in World War II*, 314; Friedman, *British Carrier Aviation*, 362–3; *Conway, 1922–46*, 260–79; *Conway, 1947–95*, 98–120. The American-built *Biter* technically was acquired from the US navy after being returned to the United States by Britain. All four carriers were loaned, rather than sold, to France, but in 1951 the French navy purchased the *Arromanches* outright.

[5] Legohérel, *Histoire de la Marine française*, 121; Auphan and Mordal, *The French Navy in World War II*, 373–80; Tritten, "Navy and Military Doctrine in France,"61–2; Polmar, *Chronology*, 9, 16, 46.

[6] Legohérel, *Histoire de la Marine française*, 120–1; *Conway, 1947–95*, 103–31 *passim*.

[7] Friedman, *British Carrier Aviation*, 153, 229, 245–67 *passim*, 327, 362–4; *Conway, 1922–46*, 7, 9, 14–16; *Conway, 1947–95*, 486–7. Friedman calls the *Centaur* class the

Hermes class, after the last ship completed among the four. *Conway, 1947–95*, designates the first three as the *Centaur* class and classifies the *Hermes* separately, citing extensive design changes during the 15 years it was under construction which made it a different ship from its original sisters.

[8] *Conway, 1922–46*, 26–63 *passim; Conway, 1947–95*, 504–30 *passim*.

[9] Friedman, *British Carrier Aviation*, 256, 267; Polmar, *Chronology*, 3, 32, 35, 46.

[10] Friedman, *British Carrier Aviation*, 230–1; Polmar, *Chronology*, 17.

[11] Friedman, *British Carrier Aviation*, 230–2; Polmar, *Chronology*, 24, 26–7, 37; Sean M. Maloney, *Securing Command of the Sea: NATO Naval Planning, 1948–1954* (Annapolis, MD, 1995), 200–1; Wells, *The Royal Navy*, 216; http://www.britains-smallwars.com/korea/ships.html (accessed 25 March 2002).

[12] Friedman, *British Carrier Aviation*, 230–1; Polmar, *Chronology*, 48, 64, 154.

[13] Hugh Thomas, *Suez* (New York, 1966) remains the most accessible account of the crisis. Other sources for this and the following paragraph are Ziegler, *Mountbatten*, 537–47; Friedman, *British Carrier Aviation*, 231; Polmar, *Chronology*, 53, 55.

[14] *Conway, 1922–46*, 261; *Conway, 1947–95*, 98–102.

[15] Friedman, *British Carrier Aviation*, 267, 346, 362; Ziegler, *Mountbatten*, 548, 553; Wells, *The Royal Navy*, 211, 248; *Conway, 1922–46*, 15–16.

[16] Maloney, *Securing Command of the Sea*, 112, 121, 123, 125, 134–5, 147, 156, 168; Tritten, "Doctrine and Fleet Tactics in the Royal Navy," 29; Polmar, *Chronology*, 125; Michele Cosentino, "Multinationality: The Way Ahead for Western Maritime Power," *US Naval Institute Proceedings* 124/3 (March 1998): 65.

[17] Ziegler, *Mountbatten*, 508–24; Maloney, *Securing Command of the Sea*, 191, 194–5; Polmar, *Chronology*, 41, 133. The "standing naval force Mediterranean" was known as the "naval on-call force Mediterranean" (NAVOCFORMED) until 1992, when it officially became STANAVFORMED.

[18] Polmar, *Chronology*, 43; Maloney, *Securing Command of the Sea*, 199; Thomas, *Suez*, 141. Burke to Brown, 1 November 1956, quoted in "Suez Crisis," http://www.fas.org/man/dod-101/ops/suez.htm (accessed 9 January 2002).

[19] Mountbatten, *Ziegler*, 558–60; *Conway, 1947–95*, 529–31; Polmar, *Chronology*, 68; "Submarines of the Royal Navy," http://www.argonet.co.uk (accessed 28 October 2000). The US navy's first nuclear powered attack submarine, the *Nautilus*, was commissioned in September 1954, the Soviet navy's first, *K 3*, in March 1959. The first US nuclear-powered ballistic missile submarine, the *George Washington*, was commissioned in December 1959, the Soviet navy's first, *K 19*, in November 1960.

[20] Friedman, *British Carrier Aviation*, 256–7, 347, 354, 363; Polmar, *Chronology*, 181–2.

[21] *Conway, 1947–95*, 482, 508–11, 518–24.

[22] Ibid., *1947–95*, 100–18, 125.

[23] Tritten, "Navy and Military Doctrine in France," 62.

[24] *Conway, 1947–95*, 122–4.

[25] Maloney, *Securing Command of the Sea*, 201; Polmar, *Chronology*, 84, 118, 122.

[26] *Conway, 1947–95*, 195, 197–9, 204–13, 216; Donolo, "The History of Italian Naval Doctrine," 119.

[27] Friedman, *British Carrier Aviation*, 362–3; *Conway, 1947–95*, 269–80.

[28] *Conway, 1947–95*, 24–8, 73–82, 158–67, 289–96, 317–22.

[29] David R. Snyder, "Arming the *Bundesmarine*: The United States and the Build-up of the German Federal Navy, 1950–1960," *Journal of Military History* 66 (2002): 477–500; *Conway, 1947–95*, 140–7.

[30] *Conway, 1947–95*, 427–40.

[31] Maloney, *Securing Command of the Sea*, 155; Polmar, *Chronology*, 37, 87, 109; Friedman, *Seapower and Space*, 174, 232.

[32] Polmar, *Chronology*, 148, 150, 154, 161, 167, 174, 176.

[33] Eric Grove and Geoffrey Till, "Anglo–American Maritime Strategy in the Era of Massive Retaliation, 1945–60," in *Maritime Strategy and Balance of Power: Britain and America in the Twentieth Century*, ed. John B. Hattendorf and Robert S. Jordan (New York, 1989), 286–99 *passim*; Joel J. Sokolsky, "Anglo–American Maritime Strategy in the Era of Flexible Response, 1960–80," in ibid., 311–12, 317; *Conway, 1947–95*, 497; Polmar, *Chronology*, 154, 162, 167, 174, 184; http://britishwarships.cjb.net (accessed 12 January 2002).

[34] George E. Hudson, "Soviet Naval Doctrine and Soviet Politics, 1953–1975," *World Politics* 29 (1976): 107–8.

[35] Gromov *et al.*, *Tri Veka Rossiiskogo Flota*, 3:214–15.

[36] Nikita Seigeyevich Khrushchev, *Khrushchev Remembers: The Last Testament*, trans. and ed. Strobe Talbot (Boston, MA, 1974), 20; *Conway, 1947–95*, 341, 376–7. According to *Conway*, a third postwar battle cruiser, the *Kronstadt*, was laid down in 1955 for the Northern Fleet, ostensibly as a platform for missiles, but little work was ever done on it. At the time, Western intelligence agencies were confused over whether this hull, in the Arctic shipyard at Molotovsk (later Severodvinsk), was a new one or the incomplete hull of the *Sovyetskiy Soyuz* class battleship *Sovyetskaya Byelorussiya*, laid down in 1939. Polmar does not mention this ship at all; he also has the *Stalingrad* being laid down in 1949 rather than 1951. There is some confusion over whether the hull of the *Moskva* reportedly seen on the slip in Leningrad in 1952 was really the surviving hull of the prewar battle cruiser *Kronstadt*, laid down in 1939. See Polmar, *The Naval Institute Guide to the Soviet Navy*, 78–9, 164.

[37] Polmar, *The Naval Institute Guide to the Soviet Navy*, 18, 37, 80; Friedman, *Seapower and Space*, 135, 137; *Conway, 1947–95*, 368, 379, 386–9.

[38] *Conway, 1947–95*, 367, 379. Five *Sverdlovs* were launched but never completed, and two were never launched. Ten served into the 1980s. According to Polmar, *The Naval Institute Guide to the Soviet Navy*, 164, 20 (not 21) *Sverdlovs* were laid down, of which 3 were launched but never completed and 3 never launched. Polmar has 12 *Sverdlovs* serving into the 1980s.

[39] Hudson, "Soviet Naval Doctrine," 98; Gromov *et al.*, *Tri Veka Rossiiskogo Flota*, 3:224–6; Friedman, *Seapower and Space*, 140–1; Polmar, *The Naval Institute Guide to the Soviet Navy*, 79; *Conway, 1947–95*, 342–3. Khrushchev quoted in *Khrushchev Remembers: The Last Testament*, 27. Kuznetsov, though just 51 years old at the time, had suffered a heart attack in May 1955 and most likely would have had to retire in any event.

[40] Friedman, *Seapower and Space*, 141–2; Khrushchev, *Khrushchev Remembers: The Last Testament*, 28–34; *Conway, 1947–95*, 351, 389, 417. During this period the only new Soviet surface warships not armed with missiles were four classes of small frigates (NATO "Kola," "Riga," "Petya," and "Mirka"), armed with conventional artillery, torpedoes, and mines. The "Grisha" class frigates of the 1960s were armed with SAMs but carried no SSMs. See *Conway, 1947–95*, 392–3, 395–6.

[41] Friedman, *Seapower and Space*, 141–2; *Conway, 1947–95*, 349–50, 353, 380, 390.

[42] Polmar, *The Naval Institute Guide to the Soviet Navy*, 83, 144–5; *Conway, 1947–95*, 375–6.

[43] Gromov *et al.*, *Tri Veka Rossiiskogo Flota*, 3:254; *Conway, 1947–95*, 396–402, 405; Friedman, *Seapower and Space*, 99, 209–10, 219. The first US navy guided missile, the Regulus, was introduced in 1958. To counter the threat from the faster Soviet submarines of the 1960s, the US navy sought to develop a submarine of its own fast enough to escort a carrier battle group, armed with an SSM with greater OTH range than the "Shaddock." The result was the *Los Angeles* class (completed from 1976), eventually armed with the satellite-guided Tomahawk cruise missile (operational from 1983).

[44] Gromov *et al.*, *Tri Veka Rossiiskogo Flota*, 3:254; *Conway, 1947–95*, 356, 398–9, 401; Polmar, *The Naval Institute Guide to the Soviet Navy*, 80–1. In addition to the types mentioned in the paragraphs above, the 1958 total also included one 1,200-ton Project 617 (NATO "Whale") class attack submarine, built in 1951–52, which left service following an accident in 1959.

[45] Polmar, *The Naval Institute Guide to the Soviet Navy*, 37–9, 43, 446; *Conway, 1947–95*, 178, 379, 396.

[46] Polmar, *The Naval Institute Guide to the Soviet Navy*, 15–17, 25.

[47] Ibid., 41, 155–62; Hudson, "Soviet Naval Doctrine," 102–3; *Conway, 1947–95*, 381–2.

[48] Polmar, *The Naval Institute Guide to the Soviet Navy*, 49, 137, 141–3; *Conway, 1947–95*, 374–5.

[49] Polmar, *The Naval Institute Guide to the Soviet Navy*, 148–50, 152–3; *Conway, 1947–95*, 382–4, 413. The *Kirov* was commissioned twenty-one years after the completion of the 15,750-ton icebreaker *Lenin*, the world's first nuclear-propelled surface ship, and nineteen years after guided-missile cruiser USS *Long Beach*, the first nuclear-powered surface warship.

[50] Friedman, *Seapower and Space*, 153; *Conway, 1947–95*, 394–5, 414–15.

[51] Friedman, *Seapower and Space*, 155–9, 163, 166, 175; Kennedy, *Rise and Fall of British Naval Mastery*, 333.

[52] Polmar, *The Naval Institute Guide to the Soviet Navy*, 81; *Conway, 1947–95*, 399, 405–10.

[53] Polmar, *The Naval Institute Guide to the Soviet Navy*, 83, 91, 96–100; Friedman, *Seapower and Space*, 206; *Conway, 1947–95*, 403–4, 408.

[54] Polmar, *The Naval Institute Guide to the Soviet Navy*, 38–9, 43–4; Friedman, *Seapower and Space*, 173, 230.

[55] Polmar, *The Naval Institute Guide to the Soviet Navy*, 40–1, 44, 93; *idem, Chronology*, 136, 162.

[56] Polmar, *The Naval Institute Guide to the Soviet Navy*, 26, 40; Friedman, *Seapower and Space*, 159.

[57] Polmar, *Chronology*, 158, 160, 173; *Conway, 1947–95*, 381.

[58] Polmar, *The Naval Institute Guide to the Soviet Navy*, 17, 38–9, 41–2, 44–5, 461; *idem, Chronology*, 189.

[59] Polmar, *The Naval Institute Guide to the Soviet Navy*, 135–7; *Conway, 1947–95*, 373–4, 382.

[60] Polmar, *The Naval Institute Guide to the Soviet Navy*, 2, 45, 135–7; *idem, Chronology*, 216; *Conway, 1947–95*, 372–4.

[61] Gromov *et al.*, *Tri Veka Rossiiskogo Flota*, 3:311; Polmar, *The Naval Institute Guide to the Soviet Navy*, 3–4. Gromov identifies the 62 ballistic-missile submarines of 1991 as 13 "Yankees," 43 "Deltas," and 6 "Typhoons." Polmar gives a figure of 63 but does not account for them by class.

[62] Polmar, *The Naval Institute Guide to the Soviet Navy*, 445–54.

[63] On the Falklands War see David Brown, *The Royal Navy and the Falklands War* (London, 1987). Other sources for the following paragraphs include Friedman, *British Carrier Aviation*, 362; idem, *Seapower and Space*, 84; *Conway, 1947–95*, 6–11, 510, 522.

[64] Friedman, *British Carrier Aviation*, 354–5, 363; *Conway, 1947–95*, 524–5, 532–3; A. D. Baker III, "World Navies in Review," *US Naval Institute Proceedings* 127/3 (March 2001): 33.

[65] Polmar, *Chronology*, 199–202 *passim*; Donolo, "The History of Italian Naval Doctrine,"121; *Conway, 1947–95*, 126, 214.

[66] *Conway, 1947–95*, 135–9, 141–2, 180–2.

[67] Friedman, *Seapower and Space*, 189–90, 221, 227–8.

[68] "Coalition Units of the Gulf War," http://www.homepage.jefnet.com/gwvrl/coalition.html (accessed 9 January 2002); see also http://www.desert-storm.com/War/nations.html (accessed 9 January 2002).

[69] Polmar, *Chronology*, 223; *Conway, 1947–95*, 188–9; http://britishwarships.cjb.net (accessed 13 January 2002).

9

THE PRESENT AND FUTURE OF EUROPEAN NAVIES

Russia's post-communist fleet raised the flags and reintroduced the warship names from pre-1917 Imperial Russia, but the country's severe political and economic problems prevented it from filling the role of the former Soviet Union in world affairs, and precluded a revitalization of the Russian navy. As the 1990s progressed it became increasingly clear that the United States would be the world's only superpower for the foreseeable future. NATO, robbed of its anti-Soviet raison d'être, came to be viewed by some as a relic of the Cold War, an alliance whose time had passed. But in the decade after the demise of the Soviet Union, crises from Somalia to Haiti, from Bosnia and Kosovo to Afghanistan, provided plenty of evidence that relatively small conflicts, if allowed to run unchecked, could have broader negative consequences for world stability. The United States somewhat reluctantly filled the vacuum, ushering in a Pax Americana in which the US navy played a central role in policing the world. But under the post-1991 Pax Americana, as under the post-1815 Pax Britannica, the hegemonic power did not limit itself to the occasional intervention in regional conflicts. By the dawn of the twenty-first century the United States had deployed its armed forces to stamp out international terrorism and drug trafficking, crusades against general evils which mirrored the British navy's post-1815 efforts against piracy and the slave trade. Both the post-1815 British navy and the post-1991 US navy undertook these ambitious campaigns while also tasked with keeping the world's sea lanes open and conducting or supporting interventions in troubled areas. Like the post-1815 British government, which expected its navy to meet the demands of its new policies with a fleet dramatically smaller than the one deployed against France during the Napoleonic Wars, the post-

1991 American government expected the US navy to handle its new missions with barely half the number of ships of its Cold War fleet of the 1980s. Just as the British navy of the nineteenth century often resorted to cooperation with the smaller navies of friendly states to enforce the Pax Britannica, the US navy of the twenty-first century required the help of the navies of Europe, in particular of the NATO countries, to enforce the Pax Americana.

The end of the Cold War naturally brought changes to NATO's command structure. In 1991 Allied Forces North (AFNORTH) absorbed the Channel Command (CHANCOM), and in 1998 Standing Naval Forces Channel (STANAVFORCHAN) was redesignated Mine Countermeasures Force North (MCMFORNORTH), a more accurate description of its role. AFNORTH remained under permanent British command until a further restructuring in 2000 eliminated NATO's German-based Allied Forces Central (AFCENT), formerly the alliance's largest command for ground forces. Thereafter, AFNORTH had responsibility for all of Europe north of neutral Switzerland and Austria, and a British general or admiral alternated with a German general as head of the command. A British admiral headed the Naval Forces North (NAVNORTH) subcommand under AFNORTH, while command of MCMFORNORTH rotated among the British and other northern European navies. The situation in the Mediterranean remained relatively unchanged, as Allied Forces South (AFSOUTH) and Strike Fleet South (STRIKFLTSOUTH) continued to be commanded by American admirals. An Italian admiral headed the new Naval Forces South (NAVSOUTH) subcommand under AFSOUTH. In 1998 NATO created a Mine Countermeasures Force Mediterranean (MCMFORMED) as a counterpart to MCMFORNORTH. In the Atlantic, the Supreme Allied Command Atlantic (SACLANT) remained under an American admiral and its EASTLANT subcommand under a British admiral. IBERLANT disappeared, replaced by a small SOUTHLANT under a Portuguese admiral. An American admiral continued to head Strike Fleet Atlantic (STRIKFLTLANT) but command of Standing Naval Forces Atlantic (STANAVFORLANT) was delegated to the commander of EASTLANT, once the end of the Cold War brought an end to the routine assignment of nuclear-armed US warships to the force, and thus the requirement that an American admiral command it. The same was true of Standing Naval Forces Mediterranean (STANAVFORMED), which during the 1990s and into the new century typically consisted of one destroyer or frigate apiece from the United States, Turkey, and six European NATO countries (Britain, Germany, Italy, the Netherlands, Spain, and Greece), with the command rotating among the participating countries under the general direction of NAVSOUTH's Italian admiral. The British navy consolidated its command structure and responsibilities by having the commander-in-chief of the British fleet also head all of Britain's NATO naval commands: NAVNORTH,

EASTLANT, and STANAVFORLANT. In 2000 these roles were filled by highly decorated Falklands War veteran Admiral Sir Alan West, who thus ranked as the most prominent European admiral at the turn of the century.[1]

At the beginning of the twenty-first century the heart of the British surface fleet consisted of the three VSTOL carriers of the *Invincible* class (completed 1980–85), 11 destroyers of the *Sheffield* and *Manchester* classes (completed 1979–85), and 16 "Duke" class frigates (completed 1990–2002). At 3,500 tons, the last were somewhat smaller than earlier classes of British frigates; with a crew of just 170, they were considered by some US navy officers to be a model for the "lean manning" sought for the DD-21 (ultimately cancelled late in 2001) and other American surface combatants designed for the new century.[2] The assault helicopter carrier *Ocean* (completed 1998) led the amphibious force; roughly the same size as the *Invincibles*, it had a full flight deck but no "ski jump" bow ramp to facilitate easy takeoffs by Harriers or other VSTOL aircraft. The *Ocean* typically carried 12 Sea King helicopters along with 6 Lynx or Apache attack helicopters, and could accommodate 700 troops. In 1998 Britain announced plans to replace the three *Invincibles* by 2010 with two larger carriers (at least 40,000 tons standard displacement; perhaps as much as 60,000 full load) rather than a new class of small VSTOL carriers. Initial debate focused on whether they would carry conventional aircraft or short takeoff/vertical landing (STOVL) planes similar to the American Joint Strike Fighter then in development. For much of the 1990s Britain, France, and Italy were partners in Project Horizon, a scheme to co-produce a large air defense frigate which would replace older destroyers and frigates in all three navies. After Britain quit the consortium in the late 1990s, it filled the void in its own program with a projected twelve 6,500-ton *Daring* class destroyers, designed with formidable air defense capabilities. The first three were ordered in 2001, and plans called for the last of the class to be operational by 2014. At the turn of the century four new dock landing ships were under construction, scheduled to enter service in the years 2003–5: the 16,980-ton *Albion* and *Bulwark* and the 16,160-ton *Largs Bay* and *Lyme Bay*, the latter pair based on the highly acclaimed Dutch *Rotterdam* design (see below). Another pair of *Largs Bay* class ships was ordered late in 2001. These vessels, along with the *Ocean*, promised to give Britain a rapid overseas intervention capability second only to that of the United States. The 4 16,000-ton nuclear-powered ballistic missile submarines of the *Vanguard* class (laid down 1986–93, completed 1993–99), each armed with 16 Trident II missiles, replaced the 4 Polaris missile submarines of the *Resolution* class to become the centerpiece of the British undersea fleet. They were backed by 12 nuclear attack submarines of the *Trafalgar* and *Swiftsure* classes, all due for eventual replacement by a projected 9 7,200-ton units of the *Astute* class, the first of which was laid down in 2001.[3]

The French navy ushered in the new century by finally commissioning the 34,500-ton aircraft carrier *Charles de Gaulle* (built 1989–2001; see Plate 48), the largest nuclear-powered warship ever built by any country other than the United States. At $2.7 billion, it was also the most expensive ship ever commissioned in any European navy. The retirement of the *Clemenceau* (1997) and sale of the *Foch* to Brazil (2000) brought a temporary hiatus in French carrier-based aviation, as delays in the development of the Rafale-M fighter jet initially left the *Charles de Gaulle* without its intended air group. Aside from the new carrier, the largest warship in the fleet was the 10,000-ton helicopter cruiser *Jeanne d'Arc*, nearing forty years in service. While 13 older destroyers and frigates and 10 corvettes (completed 1967–91) remained in commission at the turn of the century, the French surface fleet of the future had begun to take shape. The five 3,280-ton frigates of the *Lafayette* class (completed 1994–2001), armed with Exocet SSMs and Crotale SAMs, were well suited to support amphibious operations, while the six 2,600-ton corvettes of the *Floreal* class (completed 1992–94) were lightly armed vessels designed for coastal and overseas patrol duties. In October 2000 France ordered its first two 6,700-ton Project Horizon guided missile frigates, the *Forbin* and *Chevalier Paul*, to be completed in 2006 and 2008. By 2002, speculation concerning future projects centered around another pair of Horizons and as many as 17 modified *Lafayette* class frigates. France, like Britain, also enhanced its amphibious warfare capabilities. In 1990 and 1998 the French navy commissioned *Foudre* class dock landing ships (9,300 tons standard displacement, 11,880 tons full load). Another pair of *Foudres* were cancelled in favor of two units of the much larger *Mistral* class (21,000 tons full load); these ships, scheduled for completion in 2005–6, would be more accurately described as helicopter carriers, as their designed capacity included 20 helicopters and 450 troops, compared to the 4 helicopters and 1,200 troops of the *Foudres*. France also followed Britain's lead in introducing a new class of large nuclear ballistic missile submarines. The 14,120-ton *Triomphant* (built 1989–97), armed with 16 French M-4 ballistic missiles, had a sister-ship in commission by 1999. Pending the completion of another two *Triomphants*, scheduled for 2004 and 2010, two ballistic-missile submarines of the older *Redoutable* class remained in service. Plans called for all four *Triomphants* to carry an improved strategic missile, the M-51. Meanwhile, the six nuclear attack submarines of the *Rubis* class (completed 1983–93) were slated to be replaced by six units of the *Barracuda* class, to be completed between 2010 and 2020. The French navy, again following the British example, decommissioned the last of its non-nuclear submarines in 2001.

At the start of the twenty-first century the VSTOL carrier *Giuseppe Garibaldi* (completed 1985) remained the largest unit of the Italian navy and its fleet flagship. The helicopter cruiser *Vittorio Veneto* (1969) remained in service but the two older, smaller helicopter cruisers of the *Andrea Doria* class were decommissioned in the early 1990s. After going through the entire decade of the 1990s without ordering a single new surface warship, in June 2001 the Italian navy laid down a 26,500-ton vessel with the ambiguous label "New Major Unit (*Nuova Unita Maggiore*)." Initially designated the *Luigi Einaudi* before being renamed *Andrea Doria*, the ship was conceived as a VSTOL carrier with amphibious assault capability. The design initially included a docking well for landing craft which was deleted as construction commenced, amid revisions made to have the ship accommodate future STOVL aircraft such as the Joint Strike Fighter. Italy remained a partner in Project Horizon after Britain dropped out, but lagged behind France in planning for its first pair of the 6,700-ton frigates. By 2002 they were projected to be completed in 2007 and 2009, by which time the ships they were to replace (two destroyers of the *Audace* class) would have seen 35 years of service. At the turn of the century another 2 newer destroyers, 16 frigates, and 8 corvettes rounded out the surface fleet, while the submarine force included just 7 small diesel-electric units, with 2 German-designed Type 212A boats scheduled to enter service in 2005–6. Italy did not join in the general trend of building larger amphibious warships, instead renovating the three vessels of the 5,000-ton *San Giorgio* class (completed 1988–94).

At the beginning of the new century the four 3,660-ton *Brandenburg* class frigates (laid down 1992–93, completed 1994–96) joined eight older *Bremen* class frigates to form the core of the German surface fleet. Two of the three old *Lütjens* class destroyers remained in service, destined to be replaced by three 5,100-ton *Sachsen* class guided missile frigates (laid down 1999–2001). During 2000, plans were made to replace 28 small missile boats (completed 1974–84) with a class of 6 1,580-ton corvettes, and to acquire 2 large dock landing ships. In 2001–2 the navy further enhanced its amphibious and intervention capabilities by commissioning the "Deployment Group Support Ships (*Einsatzgruppe Versorgungsschiffe*)" *Berlin* and *Frankfurt*, large unarmed auxiliary vessels marketed for political purposes as enhancing Germany's international disaster relief response capability. Each carried two helicopters and displaced 20,400 tons full load.[4] After 1974 the German navy went almost thirty years without launching a new submarine; at the end of the Cold War the active U-boat force was reduced from 24 units to 12, all of them small Type 206 boats (500 tons submerged). Between the 1970s and 1990s German shipyards, especially Kiel's Howaldtswerke and Emden's Thyssen Nordseewerke, became world leaders in the construction of small diesel-electric patrol and attack submarines for export to smaller European countries and to the Third World, producing 122 units for 16 navies over a 30-year period.[5] Finally, the German navy contracted the two firms for a class of four Type 212A boats (1,840 tons), to be completed in the years 2003–6.

Owing to its large number of small attack craft, the German navy had long been larger than the Dutch, but if one counts only ocean-going surface warships (corvettes and larger) and submarines, the Dutch navy remained larger than the German until the late 1990s, when its post-Cold War decommissionings outstripped new construction. By the start of the twenty-first century the Dutch fleet had been reduced to 13 frigates and 4 submarines, but the construction of 4 6,040-ton *De Zeven Provincien* class frigates (roughly the equivalent of the British *Daring* class destroyers and the Franco–Italian Project Horizon frigates) promised to reverse the decline. The first ship of the class (built 1997–2002) was the largest warship completed for the Dutch navy in 49 years. The Netherlands started the 1990s with no amphibious warfare capability but soon became a world leader in the design of dock landing ships, thanks to the construction of a single highly regarded vessel, the *Rotterdam* (12,000 tons full load), laid down in 1994 and completed in 1998. The *Rotterdam* carried 4–6 helicopters, and could embark 600 troops with either 30 tanks or 170 armored personnel carriers. Plans called for a larger unit of the same general type, the *Johan de Witt*, to be built in 2002–7. By the time it was laid down, Spain (a partner in the original *Rotterdam* project) had two similar ships in service, Britain had copied the design for its four *Largs Bay* class dock landing ships, and both Germany and Portugal were considering the acquisition of their own *Rotterdam*s. The Dutch navy also enhanced its operational capabilities through unprecedented cooperation with the much smaller Belgian navy. In 1995 Belgium and the Netherlands established a joint peacetime naval command at Den Helder, the main base of the Dutch navy, led by a so-called "Admiral Benelux (ABNL)" and Deputy ABNL, with admirals from the two navies alternating in each role.[6] Belgium, which at the turn of the century had a navy of just 3 frigates and 6 mine-hunters, planned to build a 19,200-ton dock landing ship on the model of an enlarged *Rotterdam* or the French *Mistral*, to provide an amphibious capability for its own troops and those of landlocked Luxembourg.

The Spanish navy entered the twenty-first century with a fleet consisting of the VSTOL carrier *Principe de Asturias*, 15 frigates, and 8 small submarines. Four 5,800-ton frigates of the *Alvaro de Bazán* class were under construction in the state-owned Izar shipyard; upon completion in the years 2002–5, they would be Europe's only warships with the American Aegis anti-air combat system (of the same type fitted in destroyers of the *Arleigh Burke* class) and, therefore, the only ones with the potential to be upgraded for an anti-ballistic missile role.[7] The *Rotterdam*'s Spanish sister-ships *Galicia* (completed 1998) and *Castilla*

(2001) gave Spain a respectable amphibious and intervention capability. After cooperating with the Dutch in the *Rotterdam* project, in 2000 Spain's Izar contracted with a Norwegian firm to coproduce five *Fridtjof Nansen* class frigates for Norway. These ships, at 5,100 tons (full load), had triple the displacement of the *Oslo* class frigates (completed 1966–67) they would replace starting in 2005. The cost of the *Nansens* was a factor in Norway's decision to scale back production of copies of the *Skjold* (completed 1999), a 260-ton patrol boat armed with eight SSMs and one SAM, capable of 57 knots. The boat's design drew international acclaim, and in February 2002 the US navy, considering construction of a similar type, leased the *Skjold* for further trials.

Sweden decommissioned the last of its destroyers in 1985, thereafter limiting its navy to small submarines and attack craft, yet in both of these types the Swedes maintained their reputation for shipbuilding excellence. The firm of Kockums achieved a breakthrough with the three submarines of the 1,490-ton *Gotland* class (completed 1996–97), the first ever to implement successfully an air independent propulsion (AIP) system using a combination of liquid oxygen and diesel fuel. As early as the Second World War both Nazi Germany and the Soviet Union had experimented with AIP technology; the postwar Soviet navy's "Quebec" class of small (540-ton) submarines also used the system, but a number of fires and explosions aboard the boats brought an end to the program. The AIP system of the *Gotlands* enabled them to operate submerged for extended periods of time, like nuclear submarines, but the type could be built and maintained at a far lower cost. After Germany's Howaldtswerke purchased Kockums in 1999, it joined its partner Thyssen Nordseewerke in incorporating AIP technology into their new Type 212A boats built for the German and Italian navies and in three Type 214 boats ordered in 2000 by the Greek navy. In international maneuvers during 2000 the *Gotlands* proved to be the world's best non-nuclear submarines. In September of that year the *Gotland* class unit *Halland* became the first Swedish submarine to participate in NATO maneuvers in the Mediterranean. Two months later, it outperformed its Spanish and nuclear-powered French counterparts in war games in the Atlantic.[8] At the turn of the century Sweden also took the lead in developing a new concept for small surface warships, as Kockums' subsidiary Karlskronavarvet attracted worldwide attention for the June 2000 launching of the 620-ton, 38-knot corvette *Visby*, a revolutionary vessel with a low-weight, high-strength hull made of plastic and carbon fiber. The low magnetic signature of these materials, along with a no-right-angles design, made the *Visby* the first operational model of a "stealth" surface warship, and thus had implications for the construction programs of all other navies. The Swedish navy originally planned to order 20 *Visbys*, but the high cost of the ship forced the program to be scaled back to a class of five.[9]

During the Cold War it would have been unthinkable for scrupulously neutral Sweden to conduct any sort of joint maneuvers with NATO navies, but the alliance's Partnership for Peace (PfP) launched in 1994 allowed former Cold War neutral states, former east bloc communist countries, former non-Russian republics of the Soviet Union, and Russia itself to develop formal ties to NATO. Three of the 29 PfP countries – Hungary, the Czech Republic, and Poland – became members of NATO in 1999, raising its membership to 19, including 12 European countries with coastlines and navies. NATO membership sparked efforts to upgrade the matériel of the Polish navy, which included one old "Kashin" class destroyer and a few obsolete submarines and patrol boats, most of them former Soviet navy vessels acquired before 1991. In June 2000 the Polish navy commissioned a US navy *Oliver Hazard Perry* class frigate as the *General Pulaski*. The United States planned to transfer a sister-ship in 2003, to be named *General Kosciuszko*. Meanwhile, Germany offered Poland two of its Type 206 submarines, already a quarter-century old, as replacements for the Polish navy's two "Foxtrot" class submarines, which were even older. In October 2001 a Gdynia shipyard began work on the first of a projected seven small German-designed frigates; plans called for the class to enter service over the years 2004–17.

Russia's declining military and naval strength enabled the West to disregard its strong objections to the incorporation of former Warsaw Pact countries into NATO. The decline of Soviet naval power in the late Gorbachev years accelerated for the Russian fleet under Boris Yeltsin. By the turn of the century Europe's largest navy had experienced a near-total peacetime collapse unparalleled in modern history. The independence of the fourteen non-Russian republics of the former Soviet Union directly affected only the Black Sea Fleet, which Russia and Ukraine ultimately divided, the former receiving most of the warships, the latter most of the shore installations, including the base at Sevastopol and shipyard at Nikolaiev. Ukraine received three "Krivak" class frigates, one old "Foxtrot" class submarine, and a number of corvettes and patrol boats. A fourth "Krivak" taken over at Kerch while still under construction entered service in 1993. In 1999 the government of Ukraine announced its intention to complete the 10,000-ton *Slava* class cruiser *Ukrayina* (ex-*Admiral Lobov*, laid down at Nikolaiev in 1985), but in 2001 offered the ship as partial payment of Ukrainian debts owed to Russia, only to have the Russian government reject the proposal early in 2002. Far more significant than the loss of these Black Sea warships, the loss of the Nikolaiev shipyard spelled the end of the Russian carrier program. The Ukrainians broke up the incomplete *Ulyanovsk* on the slip, sold the nearly complete *Varyag* to China, and let the only facility in the former Soviet Union capable of repairing the *Admiral Kuznetsov* fall into disrepair, dooming the lone operational Russian carrier to a short service life.[10]

In the post-communist Russian navy, shortages of trained manpower, fuel, and money for routine maintenance kept even the small number of technically active warships in port most of the time. The navy's largest warship, the carrier *Admiral Kuznetsov*, was a case in point. Officially in commission from 1991, when it left the Black Sea to join the Northern Fleet, it finally became fully operational in 1994, after completion of sea trials and flight training. Its first deployment outside the Arctic came in the winter of 1995–96, when it went on a three-month cruise in the Mediterranean. It then returned to the Arctic and remained inactive for over four years before participating in maneuvers in August 2000, in preparation for another Mediterranean cruise during the winter of 2000–1, subsequently cancelled after the accidental loss of the nuclear guided missile submarine *Kursk*. The navy's other large surface units fared even worse. The first three *Kiev* class carriers (completed 1975, 1978, and 1982) and the older helicopter carriers *Moskva* (1967) and *Leningrad* (1969) were out of service by 1990. All were scrapped later in the decade except for the *Kiev*'s sister-ship *Minsk*, which suffered the indignity of becoming the centerpiece of "Minsk World," an amusement park near the Chinese city of Shenzhen.[11] The *Varyag* appeared headed for the same destination when it finally left the Black Sea late in 2001. The last of the four *Kiev*s, the *Admiral Gorshkov* (built 1978–87), was saved for possible sale to the Indian navy, but as of early 2002 no deal had been struck. The first three 24,000-ton *Kirov* class missile cruisers (completed 1980, 1984, and 1988) were out of service by the early 1990s. The *Admiral Ushakov* (ex-*Kirov*), disabled in 1990 by a nuclear accident, finally entered a dockyard for repairs in 1999, only to have the work halted by lack of funds. The turn of the century found the *Admiral Nakhimov* (ex-*Kalinin*) in a similar predicament, while the *Admiral Lazarev* (ex-*Frunze*) was idled at Vladivostok after the early 1990s, for want of repairs. The fourth and last unit of the class, the *Petr Veliki* (ex-*Yuri Andropov*), in 1995 became the largest new warship commissioned by the post-communist Russian navy. Laid down in 1986, it finally joined the Northern Fleet in 1998, when funding for its operation became available. The *Petr Veliki* was the largest Russian warship to put to sea during 2001. Lower manning and maintenance costs spared at least some of the navy's smaller surface vessels from sharing the fate of the larger warships. Active units of the early twenty-first century included the *Slava* class cruisers *Moskva* (ex-*Slava*) and *Marshal Ustinov*, 17 destroyers of the *Sovremenniy* and *Udaloy* classes, 12 "Krivak" class frigates, and the frigate *Neustrashimiy* (commissioned 1993), the only completed unit of a class under construction at the end of the Cold War. When two *Udaloy*s based in Vladivostok visited India and Vietnam early in 2001, it marked the first time since 1994 that any ships of the Pacific Fleet had ventured so far from home. It appeared likely that the navy would continue to use destroyers and frigates to show the flag in the future.[12] With Russia's large coastal flotillas gradually falling into disrepair, in 2000 the Rybinsk shipyard completed the *Molnaya*, a 550-ton boat armed with four P-80 Moskit anti-ship missiles. Ostensibly the prototype for fast attack craft to replace the "Tarantul" class, the *Molnaya* was more likely a demonstration vessel for the export market.[13]

Aside from the *Molnaya*, during the 1990s Russia laid down no new surface vessels except for export. Meanwhile, submarine construction continued both for export and for the Russian navy.[14] In 1996 the Severodvinsk shipyard began work on the nuclear ballistic missile submarine *Yuriy Dolgorukiy* (19,400 tons submerged), which by 2000 was roughly 50 percent complete; supposedly the lead ship of a new class, it had no sisters under construction as of 2002. During the 1990s the Russians laid down 11 nuclear attack submarines, 10 more units of the "Akula" class and one of a new design, the 11,800-ton *Severodvinsk*. The latter, begun in 1993, remained incomplete nine years later, but four of the new "Akulas" were in service by 2001. As a general rule all new submarines constructed for export were diesel-electric, while all those built for the Russian navy were nuclear-powered except the 2,700-ton *Sankt Petersburg* (laid down 1997, still unfinished 2002), designed to run on liquid oxygen and diesel fuel like the new generation of small AIP submarines built in the West. Even though the *Sankt Petersburg* was not ordered by a foreign navy, like the *Molnaya* it served the purpose of an export demonstrator, built to show that Russia could compete with Sweden and Germany in the construction of small submarines for export. Ten years after the collapse of the Soviet Union, the Russian navy had 24 nuclear ballistic and guided missile submarines at least nominally in commission, backed by 21 nuclear attack submarines and 18 diesel-electric submarines, but, by the turn of the century, the Northern Fleet typically kept just 3 submarines on patrol at any given time. Only two giant "Typhoons" remained with the fleet, and a combination of poor maintenance and inactivity in harsh Arctic conditions left them in no shape to leave port. Russian navy leaders also estimated that none of the "Oscars" (the last of which was commissioned in 1994) would remain serviceable past 2004. The accidental sinking of the "Oscar" class guided missile submarine *Kursk* during maneuvers in August 2000 underscored doubts about the effective condition of vessels which, for financial reasons, spent most of their time at anchor.[15] The lost of the *Kursk* was only the most serious of a number of embarrassing mishaps that plagued the navy after 1991. Chernavin's successor as navy commander, Admiral Feliks Gromov, lost his post in 1997, after five years in office, following a series of accidents and allegations of corruption. Shortly after taking office, his replacement, Admiral Vladimir Kuroyedov, conceded that "Russia does not need its fleet to provide the same kind of balance with the US navy as the leadership of the USSR once strived for."[16] Even if the Russian navy had been able to keep more submarines and surface warships in service, it would not have had the same warfighting capability as the Soviet fleet of the late Cold War, for by the late 1990s the old Soviet satellite-based global surveillance system had ceased to function, leaving Russian naval vessels unable to fire ballistic or cruise missiles at any target over the horizon with any degree of precision.[17]

Thus, at least on paper, post-Cold War Russia still had Europe's largest navy and the world's second largest, but its capabilities were so diminished that it hardly counted in the international balance of power. In the first years of the new Pax Americana, Russia learned that its overall military weakness left it in no position to object effectively to the interventionism of the United States and its European allies. This was especially true in the breakup of Yugoslavia, which began in the summer of 1991 but took an especially violent turn after the secession of Bosnia in the spring of 1992. Over the persistent protests of Russia, which supported Serbian leader Slobodan Milošević's quest to hold together the Yugoslav union by force, the United States and NATO gradually became more involved in pressuring the Serbs to accept a peace deal. From July 1992 until June 1996, the six European navies represented in STANAVFORMED patrolled the Adriatic Sea to enforce a UN arms embargo on the former Yugoslavia. Warships from STANAV-FORLANT joined them briefly during September 1992, and after June 1993 they combined forces with other European naval vessels assigned to the Adriatic by the Western European Union (WEU). In the four years of operations, NATO and WEU warships boarded more than 7,000 vessels.[18] During the summer of 1995 Croatian and Bosnian counteroffensives, combined with US and NATO air strikes against Serbian targets in Bosnia, forced Milošević to the peace table, and by the end of the year the fighting had come to an end. European naval forces played no role in these air attacks, which were launched from the USS *Theodore Roosevelt* and the NATO air base at Aviano, Italy.[19]

Under the leadership of Prime Minister Tony Blair (from 1997), Britain's "special relationship" with the United States became stronger than in recent years, while under the leadership of President Jacques Chirac (from 1995), France's post-Cold War reintegration into NATO slowed considerably. After 1996 Britain was the only American ally still providing aircraft to patrol the "no fly zones" over northern and southern Iraq, imposed after the Persian Gulf War. Following the collapse of the regime of UN arms control inspections in Iraq in 1998, Britain alone supported the United States in Operation Desert Fox (16–19 December 1998), with the RAF joining in punitive strikes against suspected chemical and biological warfare manufacturing sites, and military targets in general. During the operation the British frigates *Boxer* and *Cumberland* helped provide air defense for the carrier USS *Enterprise*, which launched bombing raids while the ships in its battle group fired dozens of cruise missiles at targets inside Iraq. The British navy sent the VSTOL carrier *Invincible* to the Persian Gulf on three separate occasions in the years 1996–99, but it happened not to be on station in December 1998 to participate in Desert Fox.[20]

Within weeks of its return to the Gulf in January 1999, the *Invincible* was ordered to the Adriatic to support Operation Allied Force, a NATO air campaign against Serbian forces in the predominantly Albanian Kosovo territory of Yugoslavia. After three years of relative calm, warfare in the former Yugoslavia had resumed during 1998, when Serbian leader Milošević began a campaign to drive ethnic Albanians out of Kosovo. As international tensions waxed and waned, NATO sent STANAVFORMED to the Adriatic in October 1998, then again in January 1999. During Operation Allied Force (24 March–10 June 1999), the *Invincible* and the French carrier *Foch* joined the USS *Theodore Roosevelt* in launching sorties against targets in Kosovo and Serbia. Other European NATO warships deployed in the Adriatic and Ionian seas during the campaign included 15 destroyers and frigates from Britain, France, Italy, Greece, the Netherlands, Germany, and Spain, along with the British submarine *Splendid*, which became the first European warship to launch Tomahawk land-attack cruise missiles (TLAMs) in combat. Britain also had on hand the new helicopter carrier *Ocean* and the 11,060-ton assault ship *Fearless*, a veteran of the Falklands War, but the marines they carried did not go ashore until after Serbian forces withdrew from Kosovo, giving way to a NATO-led international occupation force. The need for vigilance against mines led NATO to assign both MCMFORNORTH and MCMFORMED to the war zone; this brought Belgian, Danish, and Portuguese vessels into the action as well. Because the small Yugoslav navy remained in port and did not use the mines it had stockpiled at Bar and Kotor, the MCM forces spent most of their time locating and detonating unexploded ordnance dropped in the water by NATO warplanes en route home to their bases in Italy.[21]

The next deployment of European forces in support of the Pax Americana came after the Afghanistan-based terrorist group al Qaeda launched attacks on the World Trade Center in New York and the Pentagon in Washington on 11 September 2001. At the time, the British navy and marines were already deployed to the Middle East for the previously scheduled exercise "Saif Sareea (Swift Sword)" with the armed forces of Oman. From the VSTOL carrier *Illustrious*, Rear Admiral James Burnell-Nugent commanded a force including the nuclear attack submarines *Trafalgar* and *Superb*, while ashore, marines under Brigadier Roger Lane joined the Omani army in joint maneuvers which conveniently served to train them for subsequent deployment in Afghanistan. After 11 September Britain rushed a third nuclear attack submarine, the *Triumph*, to the region for a three-month tour of duty.

By the time the United States opened its war against the Taliban government of Afghanistan on 7 October, Burnell-Nugent's force had taken up station in the Gulf of Oman, off the Iranian coast. On the first night of the campaign the initial strikes included TLAMs fired from the *Trafalgar* and *Triumph* while the *Superb* stood guard nearby. With the navy's new landing ships still under construction, the British marines once again were based on the assault ship *Fearless*. The initial force assigned to Operation Veritas (the British corollary to the US Operation Enduring Freedom) also included the destroyer *Southampton*, frigate *Cornwall*, and seven auxiliary vessels. During October NATO ordered STANAVFORMED to the Eastern Mediterranean, but none of its eight frigates and destroyers transited the Suez Canal to cruise closer to the war zone. In November both France and Italy committed warships to the allied force in the Arabian Sea, the Italians sending the VSTOL carrier *Giuseppe Garibaldi* and two escorts, the French their new carrier *Charles de Gaulle* and five escorts, but by the time the ships arrived in mid-December, al Qaeda had been routed from Afghanistan and the Taliban regime replaced by a pro-Western provisional government. As the focus of the campaign against terrorism widened to include possible targets in Somalia and Yemen, in January 2002 Germany sent two frigates and four support ships carrying marines, to be joined later by five fast attack craft, to help patrol the waters at the mouth of the Red Sea.[22]

After 11 September 2001 the American war on terrorism overshadowed the campaign against international drug trafficking, but the latter continued throughout the 1990s and into the twenty-first century with the navies of Europe assisting the US navy and US coast guard. For example, during the spring of 1999 Operation Snow Boat involved warships from the British, French, and Dutch navies as well as the US navy and US coast guard, patrolling the Caribbean in search of merchantmen smuggling cocaine. On 27 May 1999 the British frigate *Marlborough*, with US coast guard agents aboard, stopped and boarded a cargo ship south of Puerto Rico, seizing 8,800 pounds of cocaine. Four days later, the same ship stopped a second merchantman off the coast of Venezuela and seized another 8,700 pounds of cocaine. At the time, the two incidents ranked among the dozen all-time most significant high seas interdictions of illegal drugs, and led to the collapse of an international cocaine-smuggling network directed from Greece, which used cargo ships manned by Ukrainians to transport tons of the drug for dealers in Colombia.[23] Cooperation came in chance encounters as well as planned operations. During a NATO MCM exercise 150 miles off the coast of Portugal in January 1997, a Dutch naval vessel spotted a suspicious speedboat near a shallow reef; after further investigation, a minesweeper recovered a cache of narcotics buried there. During the pursuit of another suspicious speedboat, in September 2001 off the coast of Belize, the British frigate *Coventry* dispatched a Lynx helicopter which forced aground a vessel found to be carrying £40 million worth of cocaine.[24]

Like the wooden sailing frigates of the years after 1815, the destroyers, frigates, and smaller surface warships deployed by Europe's navies in the early twenty-first century had to be both durable and versatile, able to deploy for a variety of missions at relatively short notice. In the dawning era of the Pax Americana, the navies and shipyards of Europe, constructing smaller ships in smaller classes, were responsible for many more technological innovations than the United States. As evidenced by the destroyers of the British *Daring* class, the frigates of the Spanish *Alvaro de Bazán* class, the German *Sachsen* class, the Dutch *De Zeven Provincien* class, the Norwegian *Nansen* class, and the Franco–Italian Project Horizon, as well as the smaller surface combatants of the Swedish *Visby* class and Norwegian *Skjold* class, the navies of Europe ranked with the best in the world in warship design and construction. When one considers that all of the destroyers and most of the frigates of 2000 were large enough to have been rated as cruisers during the Second World War, the European naval powers lagged behind the United States only in the construction of the largest types of surface warships. Even here, the design of the Soviet navy's *Kiev* class carriers and *Kirov* class missile cruisers were innovative enough, though fated never to be copied, while the western European navies made their mark in the development of versatile VSTOL carriers, helicopter carriers, and amphibious assault ships. In the construction of nuclear ballistic missile submarines and attack submarines, only the Soviet Union ever matched the United States, but the *Vanguard* and *Triomphant* classes and their smaller attack submarine counterparts bore witness to the willingness of Britain and France to spend enormous sums of money to maintain a respectable level of strength in all aspects of sea power. In the construction of smaller, non-nuclear submarines, the shipbuilders of northern Europe were responsible for the breakthroughs in AIP technology which, owing to its lower cost and greater safety, could lead to the reduction or elimination of the use of nuclear propulsion for submarines. All things considered, with the notable exception of the Russian fleet, the navies of Europe entered the new century on a positive note, with their generally smaller fleets of technologically impressive warships facing a challenging array of missions.

NOTES

[1] Maloney, *Securing Command of the Sea*, 201; Cosentino, "Multinationality," 65; http://www.nato.int/structur/struc-mcs.htm (accessed 18 January 2002).

[2] Clint Johnson, "Manning DD-21," *US Naval Institute Proceedings* 127/5 (May 2001): 28.

[3] Unless otherwise noted, this and the following paragraphs are based upon A. D. Baker III, "World Navies in Review," *US Naval Institute Proceedings* 128/3 (March 2002): 32–44 *passim*; Baker, "World Navies in Review" (2001), 32–45 *passim*; and Andrew Toppan, "World Navies Today," http://www.hazegray.org/worldnav/ (accessed 12–14 January 2002).

[4] A. D. Baker III, "World Navies in Review," *US Naval Institute Proceedings* 126/3 (March 2000): 36.

[5] The figure includes "kits" provided by the two firms for assembly elsewhere. See Don Walsh, "The AIP Alternative: Air-Independent Propulsion, an Idea Whose Time Has Come?," http://www.navyleague.org/seapower/aip_alternative.htm (accessed 14 January 2002).

[6] Cosentino, "Multinationality," 66.

[7] Juan Carlos Campbell-Cruz, "Spain Wants to Play Big," *US Naval Institute Proceedings* 128/3 (March 2002): 77–9.

[8] Walsh, "The AIP Alternative: Air-Independent Propulsion, an Idea Whose Time Has Come?," http://www.navyleague.org/seapower/aip_alternative.htm (accessed 14 January 2002); "HMS Halland Triumphs in Naval Duels," 15 November 2000, http://www.seawaves.com/News/Articles/Europe/November%202000/00111612.htm (accessed 13 January 2002).

[9] Thomas E. Engevall, "Swedish Navy Mixes Evolution and Revolution to Launch Stealth Multimission Corvette," *US Naval Institute Proceedings*, 125/3 (March 1999): 60–2; "Talks Between FMW, HDW and Kockums Lead to Constructive Result," 24 October 2001, http://www.karlskronavarvet.se/ (accessed 14 January 2002).

[11] Unless otherwise noted, this and the following paragraphs are based upon Toppan, "World Navies Today," http://www.hazegray.org/worldnav/ (accessed 19 January 2002), and Baker, "World Navies in Review" (2002), 44.

[11] Jonathan Holburt, "Cold War, Hot Rides: The Chinese Relive the Heyday of Soviet Military Power," *Wall Street Journal* (6 September 2001).

[12] Richard Scott, "Russia's Navy Looks to Show the Flag Again," 10 April 2001, http://www.janes.com/defence/naval_forces/news/ (accessed 19 January 2002).

[13] Baker, "World Navies in Review" (2001), 42–3.

[14] By 2000 Russian shipyards had built two *Sovremenniy* class destroyers for China and ten "Kilo" class submarines for India. Baker, "World Navies in Review" (2001), 34, 36.

[15] Ian Traynor, "Putin's Stock May Sink with Fleet," 16 August 2000, http://www.guardian.co.uk/Print/ (accessed 19 January 2002); Baker, "World Navies in Review" (2001), 35. On 7 October 2001 the Dutch firm Mommoet-Smit International raised the *Kursk* and carried it 100 miles from the site of its sinking to Murmansk. Its nuclear reactors and 22 Granit anti-ship missiles were secured. See Norman Polmar, "The *Kursk* is Salvaged," *US Naval Institute Proceedings* 127/11 (November 2001): 28.

[16] "Russian Navy Celebrates Despite Cutbacks, Scandals," 26 July 1998, http://www.cdi.org/russia/johnson/2283.html (accessed 24 January 2002).

[17] Friedman, *Seapower and Space*, 170.

[18] http://www.afsouth.nato.int/factsheets/STANAVFORMED.htm (accessed 18 January 2002).

[19] http://www.navyhistory.com/CVN70TR.html (accessed 20 January 2002).

[20] "The Royal Navy and the Gulf," http://www,btinternet.com/~warship/Feature/gulf.htm (accessed 20 January 2002); http://www.defenselink.mil/specials/desert_fox/ (accessed 18 January 2002).

[21] Richard Cobbold, "Kosovo: What the Navies Did," *US Naval Institute Proceedings*

125/10 (October 1999): 87; http://www.afsouth.nato.int/factsheets/
STANAVFORMED.htm (accessed 18 January 2002);
http://www.defenselink.mil/specials/kosovo/index.html (accessed 20 January 2002).

[22] Marc Champion, "Is the British Military Feeling Frustrated?" *Wall Street Journal* (30
October 2001); John D. Gresham, "Forces Fighting for Enduring Freedom," *US Naval
Institute Proceedings* 127/11 (November 2001): 45; http://britishwarships.cjb.net
(accessed 12 January 2002); http://www.afsouth.nato.int/factsheets/
STANAVFORMED.htm (accessed 21 January 2002); "Italy Pledges Troops to US," 7
November 2001, www.cnn.com/2001/WORLD/europe/11/07/gen.italy.military/
(accessed 20 January 2002); "Powell Enlists British, French," 11 December 2001,
www.cbsnews.com/now/story/0,1597,320827–412,00shtml (accessed 20 January 2002);
"German Navy Ships Set Off to Patrol Horn of Africa in Biggest Deployment since
World War II," 3 January 2002, www.krem.com/war/archive/html (accessed 20 January
2002).

[23] http://www.uscg.mil/d8/99REL/99REL107.htm (accessed 21 January 2002);
http://www.usdoj.gov/usao/txs/initiatives/drugs.html (accessed 21 January 2002).

[24] http://www.hri.org/docs/USSD-INCSR/97/Europe/Portugal.html (accessed 21 January
2002); http://britishwarships.cjb.net (accessed 12 January 2002).

BIBLIOGRAPHY

MEMOIRS, PUBLISHED DOCUMENTS, AND CONTEMPORARY PUBLICATIONS

Beresford, Charles William de la Poer, *The Memoirs of Admiral Lord Charles Beresford*, 2 vols. Boston, MA, 1914.

Bianchini, Lodovico, *Della storia delle finanze del regno di Napoli*. Naples, 1859.

Bonner-Smith, D. (ed.), *Russian War, 1855, Baltic: Official Correspondence*. London, 1944.

Bonner-Smith, D. and A. C. Dewar (eds), *Russian War, 1854, Baltic and Black Sea: Official Correspondence*. London, 1943.

Busk, Hans, *The Navies of the World; Their Present State, and Future Capabilities*. London, 1859.

Camerani, Sergio and Gaetano Arfè (eds), *Carteggi di Bettino Ricasoli*, vol. 22: *20 giugno–31 luglio 1866*. Rome, 1967.

Churchill, Winston S., *The Second World War*, 6 vols. Boston, MA: Houghton Mifflin, 1948–52.

Clarke, George Sydenham, *Russia's Sea-Power Past and Present, or The Rise of the Russian Navy*. London, 1898.

Dewar, A. C. (ed.), *Russian War, 1855, Black Sea: Official Correspondence*. London, 1945.

Fawcett, H. W. and G. W. W. Hooper (eds), *The Fighting at Jutland: The*

Personal Experiences of Sixty Officers and Men of the British Fleet. Annapolis, MD, 2002.

Hall, W. H., *Narrative of the Voyages and Services of the Nemesis, from 1840 to 1843,* 2nd edn. London, 1845.

Harvey, Thomas W. (comp.), *Memoir of Hayward Augustus Harvey.* New York, 1900.

Jane, Fred T., *The Imperial Russian Navy,* 2nd edn. London, 1904; reprint, London, 1983.

——, *The British Battle Fleet,* 2 vols. London, 1915; reprint, London, 1990.

Joinville, François Ferdinand d'Orléans, Prince de, *De l'état des forces navales de la France.* Frankfurt, 1844.

——, *Essais sur la marine française.* Paris, 1853.

Khrushchev, Nikita Sergeievich, *Khrushchev Remembers: The Last Testament,* trans. and ed. Strobe Talbot. Boston, MA, 1974.

Krupp: A Century's History, 1812–1912. Essen, 1912.

Raeder, Erich, *My Life,* trans. Henry W. Drexel. Annapolis, MD, 1960.

Randaccio, Carlo, *Le marinerie militari italiane nei tempi moderni, 1750–1850.* Turin, 1864.

Sterneck zu Ehrenstein, Maximilian Daublebsky von, *Admiral Max Freiherr von Sterneck: Erinnerungen aus den Jahren 1847 bis 1897,* ed. Jerolim Benko von Boinik. Vienna, 1901.

Tirpitz, Alfred von, *Erinnerungen.* Leipzig, 1919.

BOOKS, ARTICLES, PAPERS, BOOK CHAPTERS

Auphan, Paul and Jacques Mordal, *The French Navy in World War II,* trans. A. C. J. Sabalot. Annapolis, MD, 1959.

Baker, A. D., III, "World Navies in Review," *US Naval Institute Proceedings* 126/3 (March 2000): 30–42.

——, "World Navies in Review," *US Naval Institute Proceedings* 127/3 (March 2001): 32–45.

——, "World Navies in Review," *US Naval Institute Proceedings* 128/3 (March 2002): 32–44.

Baratelli, Franco Micali, *La marina militare italiana nella vita nazionale, 1860–1914.* Mursia, 1983.

Bargoni, Franco, *Le prime navi di linea della marina italiana, 1861–1880*. Rome, 1976.

——, *Corazzate italiane classi Duilio–Italia–Ruggiero di Lauria, 1880–1892*. Rome, 1977.

——, *Corazzate italiane classi Re Umberto–Ammiraglio di Saint Bon, 1893–1901*. Rome, 1978.

Barnett, Correlli, *Engage the Enemy More Closely: The Royal Navy in the Second World War*. New York, 1991.

Battesti, Michèle, *La Marine au XIXe siècle: Interventions extérieures et colonies*. Paris, 1993.

Baxter, James Phinney, *The Introduction of the Ironclad Warship*. Cambridge, MA, 1933.

Beeching, Jack, *The Chinese Opium Wars*. New York, 1975.

Beeler, John F., *British Naval Policy in the Gladstone–Disraeli Era, 1866–1880*. Palo Alto, CA, 1997.

Bennett, Geoffrey, *Coronel and the Falklands*. London, 1962.

——, *Cowan's War: The Story of British Naval Operations in the Baltic, 1918–1920*. London, 1964.

Berghahn, Volker R., "Naval Armaments and Social Crisis: Germany before 1914," in *War, Economy, and the Military Mind*, ed. Geoffrey Best and Andrew Wheatcroft. London, 1976, 61–88.

Berghahn, Volker R. and Wilhelm Deist, *Rüstung im Zeichen der wilhelminischen Weltpolitik: Grundlegende Dokumente, 1890–1914*. Düsseldorf, 1988.

Bird, Keith W., *Weimar, the German Naval Officer Corps, and the Rise of National Socialism*. Amsterdam, 1977.

Blatt, Joel, "France and the Washington Conference," in *The Washington Conference, 1921–22: Naval Rivalry, East Asian Stability, and the Road to Pearl Harbor*, ed. Erik Goldstein and John Maurer. London, 1994, 192–219.

Breuer, William, *Operation Torch: The Allied Gamble to Invade North Africa*. New York, 1985.

Brown, David, *The Royal Navy and the Falklands War*. London, 1987.

Brown, David K., "The Era of Uncertainty, 1863–1878," in *Steam, Steel and Shellfire: The Steam Warship 1815–1905*, ed. Robert Gardiner. London, 1992, 75–94.

——, *Paddle Warships: The Earliest Steam Powered Fighting Ships, 1815–1850*. London, 1993.

——, *Warrior to Dreadnought: Warship Development, 1860–1905*. London, 1997.

Buckley, John, *Air Power in the Age of Total War*. London, 1999.

Buckley, Thomas H., "The Icarus Factor: the American Pursuit of Myth in Naval Arms Control, 1921–36," in *The Washington Conference, 1921–22: Naval Rivalry, East Asian Stability, and the Road to Pearl Harbor*, ed. Erik Goldstein and John Maurer. London, 1994, 124–46.

Burns, Richard Dean, "Regulating Submarine Warfare, 1921–41: A Case Study in Arms Control and Limited War," *Military Affairs* 35 (1971): 56–63.

Campbell, John, "Naval Armaments and Armour," in *Steam, Steel and Shellfire: The Steam Warship 1815–1905*, ed. Robert Gardiner. London, 1992, 158–69.

——, *Dieppe Revisited: A Documentary Investigation*. London, 1993.

Campbell-Cruz, Juan Carlos, "Spain Wants to Play Big," *US Naval Institute Proceedings* 128/3 (March 2002): 77–9.

Canney, Donald L., *The Old Steam Navy*, 2 vols. Annapolis, MD, 1993.

Casali, Antonio and Marina Cattaruzza, *Sotto i mari del mondo: La Whitehead, 1875–1990*. Rome, 1990.

Ceva, Lucio, *Le forze armate*. Turin, 1981.

Champion, Marc, "Is the British Military Feeling Frustrated?" *Wall Street Journal*, 30 October 2001.

Cobbold, Richard, "Kosovo: What the Navies Did," *US Naval Institute Proceedings* 125/10 (October 1999): 87.

Conway's All the World's Fighting Ships, 1860–1905. London, 1979.

Conway's All the World's Fighting Ships, 1906–21. London, 1985.

Conway's All the World's Fighting Ships, 1922–46. London, 1980.

Conway's All the World's Fighting Ships, 1947–95. London, 1995.

Cooling, Benjamin Franklin, *Gray Steel and Blue Water Navy: The Formative Years of America's Military-Industrial Complex, 1881–1917*. Westport, CT, 1979.

Cosentino, Michele, "Multinationality: The Way Ahead for Western Maritime Power," *US Naval Institute Proceedings* 124/3 (March 1998): 64–6.

Coutau-Bégarie, Hervé and Claude Huan, *Darlan*. Paris, 1989.

Dakin, Douglas, *British and American Philhellenes during the War of Greek Independence, 1821–1833*. Thessaloniki, 1955.

——, *The Greek Struggle for Independence*. Berkeley, CA, 1973.

Daly, John C. K., *Russian Seapower and "the Eastern Question", 1827–41*. Annapolis, MD, 1991.

Donolo, Luigi, "The History of Italian Naval Doctrine," in *A Doctrine Reader: The Navies of the United States, Great Britain, France, Italy, and Spain*, ed. James J. Tritten and Luigi Donolo. Newport, RI, 1995, 91–123.

Dupont, Maurice and Étienne Taillemite, *Les guerres navales françaises: du Moyen Age à la guerre du Golfe*. Paris, 1995.

Engevall, Thomas E., "Swedish Navy Mixes Evolution and Revolution to Launch Stealth Multimission Corvette," *US Naval Institute Proceedings*, 125/3 (March 1999): 60–2.

Evans, David C. and Mark R. Peattie, *Kaigun: Strategy, Tactics, and Technology in the Imperial Japanese Navy, 1887–1941*. Annapolis, MD, 1997.

Fairbanks, Charles H., Jr, "The Origins of the *Dreadnought* Revolution: A Historiographical Essay," *International History Review* 13 (1991): 246–72.

Friedberg, Aaron L, *The Weary Titan: Britain and the Experience of Relative Decline, 1895–1905*. Princeton, NJ, 1988.

Friedman, Norman, *British Carrier Aviation: The Evolution of the Ships and their Aircraft*. Annapolis, MD, 1988.

——, *Seapower and Space: From the Dawn of the Missile Age to Net-Centric Warfare*. Annapolis, MD, 2000.

Gabriele, Mariano, *La politica navale italiana dall'unità alla viglia di Lissa*. Milan, 1958.

Gannon, Michael, *Operation Drumbeat*. New York, 1990.

Gelb, Norman, *Desperate Venture: The Story of Operation Torch, The Allied Invasion of North Africa*. New York, 1992.

Gerloff, Wilhelm, *Finanz- und Zollpolitik des Deutschen Reiches*. Jena, 1913.

Giorgerini, Giorgio, *Almanacco storico delle navi militare italiane: La Marina e le sue navi dal 1861 al 1975*. Rome, 1978.

Gogg, Karl, *Österreichs Kriegsmarine, 1848–1918*. Salzburg, 1967.

Goldstein, Erik, "The Evolution of British Diplomatic Strategy for the Washington Conference," in *The Washington Conference, 1921–22: Naval Rivalry, East Asian Stability, and the Road to Pearl Harbor*, ed. Erik Goldstein and John Maurer. London, 1994, 4–34.

Gordon, Andrew, *The Rules of the Game: Jutland and British Naval Command*. Annapolis, MD, 1996.

Gray, Edwyn, *Operation Pacific: The Royal Navy's War against Japan, 1941–1945*. Annapolis, MD, 1990.

Greger, René, *The Russian Fleet, 1914–1917*, trans. Jill Gearing. London, 1972.

Gresham, John D., "Forces Fighting for Enduring Freedom," *US Naval Institute Proceedings* 127/11 (November 2001): 45–7.

Griffiths, Denis, "Warship Machinery," in *Steam, Steel and Shellfire: The Steam Warship 1815–1905*, ed. Robert Gardiner. London, 1992, 170–8.

Gromov, F. N., Vladimir Gribovskii and Boris Rodionov, *Tri Veka Rossiiskogo Flota*, 3 vols. St Petersburg, 1996.

Gröner, Erich, *Die deutschen Kriegsschiffe, 1815–1945*, 8 vols. Coblenz, 1989.

Grove, Eric and Geoffrey Till, "Anglo–American Maritime Strategy in the Era of Massive Retaliation, 1945–60," in *Maritime Strategy and Balance of Power: Britain and America in the Twentieth Century*, ed. John B. Hattendorf and Robert S. Jordan. New York, 1989, 286–99.

Halpern, Paul G., *The Mediterranean Naval Situation, 1908–1914*. Cambridge, MA, 1971.

——, *The Naval War in the Mediterranean, 1914–1918*. Annapolis, MD, 1987.

——, *A Naval History of World War I*. Annapolis, MD, 1994.

Hamilton, C. I., *Anglo–French Naval Rivalry, 1840–1870*. Oxford, 1993.

Hamilton, W. Mark, *The Nation and the Navy: Methods and Organization of British Navalist Propaganda, 1889–1914*. New York, 1986.

Harbron, John D., *Trafalgar and the Spanish Navy*. London, 1988.

Harding, Richard, *Seapower and Naval Warfare, 1650–1830*. London, 1999.

Hawkey, Arthur, *Black Night off Finisterre: The Tragic Tale of an Early British Ironclad*. Annapolis, MD, 1999.

Herwig, Holger H., *The German Naval Officer Corps: A Social and Political History.* Oxford, 1973.

——, *"Luxury" Fleet: The Imperial German Navy, 1888–1918,* rev. ed. Atlantic Highlands, NJ, 1987.

——, "Innovation Ignored: The Submarine Problem Germany, Britain, and the United States, 1919–1939," in *Military Innovation in the Interwar Period,* ed. Williamson Murray and Allan R. Millett. Cambridge, 1996, 227–64.

——, *The First World War: Germany and Austria–Hungary, 1914–1918.* London, 1997.

Holburt, Jonathan, "Cold War, Hot Rides: The Chinese Relive the Heyday of Soviet Military Power," *Wall Street Journal* (6 September 2001).

Hough, Richard, *The Fleet That Had To Die.* London, 1958.

——, *The Potemkin Mutiny.* London, 1960.

Howse, Derek, *Radar at Sea: The Royal Navy in World War II.* Annapolis, MD, 1993.

Hudson, George E., "Soviet Naval Doctrine and Soviet Politics, 1953–1975," *World Politics* 29 (1976): 90–113.

Irving, John, *Coronel and the Falklands.* London, 1927.

Jackson, Robert, *The Royal Navy in World War II.* Annapolis, MD, 1997.

Johnson, Clint, "Manning DD-21," *US Naval Institute Proceedings* 127/5 (May 2001): 28.

Kačić-Dimitri, Jerko. "Das Ende der königlich jugoslawischen Flotte," *Marine–Gestern, Heute* 15 (1988): 4–11.

Kelly, Patrick J., "Strategy, Tactics, and Turf Wars: Tirpitz and the Oberkommando der Marine, 1892–1895," paper presented at the Thirteenth Naval History Symposium, Annapolis, MD, 2–4 October 1997.

Kemp, Paul, *Convoy! Drama in Arctic Waters.* London, 2000.

Kennan, George F., *The Fateful Alliance: France, Russia, and the Coming of the First World War.* New York, 1984.

Kennedy, Paul M., *The Rise and Fall of British Naval Mastery.* London, 1976.

Kieser, Egbert, *Hitler on the Doorstep: Operation Sea Lion, The German Plan to Invade Britain, 1940,* trans. Helmut Bögler. Annapolis, MD, 1997.

Kjølsen, F. H., "The Old Danish Frigate," *The Mariner's Mirror* 51 (1965): 27–33.

Lambert, Andrew, *Battleships in Transition: The Creation of the Steam Battlefleet, 1815–1860*. Annapolis, MD, 1984.

——, *The Crimean War: British Grand Strategy against Russia, 1853–56*. Manchester, 1991.

——, *The Last Sailing Battlefleet: Maintaining Naval Mastery, 1815–1850*. London, 1991.

——, "Introduction of Steam," in *Steam, Steel, and Shellfire: The Steam Warship, 1815–1905*, ed. Robert Gardiner. London, 1992, 14–29.

——, "Iron Hulls and Armour Plate," in *Steam, Steel and Shellfire: The Steam Warship 1815–1905*, ed. Robert Gardiner. London, 1992, 47–60.

——, "The Screw Propeller Warship," in *Steam, Steel and Shellfire: The Steam Warship 1815–1905*, ed. Robert Gardiner. London, 1992, 30–46.

Lambert, Nicholas A., "Admiral Sir John Fisher and the Concept of Flotilla Defence, 1904–1909," *Journal of Military History* 59 (1995): 639–60.

——, *Sir John Fisher's Naval Revolution*. Columbia, SC, 1999.

Lambi, Ivo Nikolai, *The Navy and German Power Politics, 1862–1914*. Boston, MA, 1984.

Langensiepen, Bernd and Ahmet Güleryüz, *The Ottoman Steam Navy, 1828–1923*, ed. and trans. James Cooper. Annapolis, MD, 1995.

Leckebusch, Günther, *Die Beziehungen der deutschen Seeschiffswerften zur Eisenindustrie an der Ruhr in der Zeit von 1850 bis 1930*. Cologne, 1963.

Legohérel, Henri, *Histoire de la Marine française*. Paris, 1999.

Lewis, Michael, *A Social History of the Navy, 1793–1815*. London, 1960.

——, *The Navy in Transition, 1814–1864: A Social History*. London, 1965.

Lubbock, Basil, *Cruisers, Corsairs & Slavers: An Account of the Suppression of the Picaroon, Pirate & Slaver by the Royal Navy during the 19th Century*. Glasgow, 1993.

Lütken, Otto Georg, *Søkrigsbegivenhederne i 1864*. Copenhagen, 1896.

Lyon, David, "Underwater Warfare and the Torpedo Boat," in *Steam, Steel, and Shellfire: The Steam Warship, 1815–1905*, ed. Robert Gardiner. London, 1992, 134–46.

McKercher, B. J. C., "The Politics of Naval Arms Limitation in Britain in the 1920s," in *The Washington Conference, 1921–22: Naval Rivalry, East Asian Stability, and the Road to Pearl Harbor*, ed. Erik Goldstein and John Maurer. London, 1994, 35–59.

Maiolo, Joseph A., *The Royal Navy and Nazi Germany, 1933–39: A Study in Appeasement and the Origins of the Second World War*. London, 1998.

Mallett, Robert, *The Italian Navy and Fascist Expansionism, 1935–1940*. London, 1998.

Maloney, Sean M., *Securing Command of the Sea: NATO Naval Planning, 1948–1954*. Annapolis, MD, 1995.

Marder, Arthur J., *The Anatomy of British Sea Power: A History of British Naval Policy in the Pre-Dreadnought Era, 1880–1905*. New York, 1940.

——, *From the Dreadnought to Scapa Flow: The Royal Navy in the Fisher Era, 1904–1919*, 5 vols. London, 1961.

——, *From the Dardanelles to Oran*. London, 1974.

Masson, Philippe, *La Marine française et la mer Noire (1918–1919)*. Paris, 1982.

——, *La Marine française et la guerre, 1939–1945*. Paris, 1991.

Melton, George E., *Darlan: Admiral and Statesman of France, 1881–1942*. Westport, CT, 1998.

Middlebrook, Martin and Patrick Mahoney, *Battleship: the Sinking of the Prince of Wales and the Repulse*. New York, 1979.

Niestlé, Axel, *German U-Boat Losses during World War II: Details of Destruction*. Annapolis, MD, 1998.

O'Connell, Robert L., *Sacred Vessels: The Cult of the Battleship and the Rise of the US Navy*. Oxford, 1993.

Owen, Richard, "Military-Industrial Relations: Krupp and the Imperial Navy Office," in *Society and Politics in Wilhelmine Germany*, ed. Richard J. Evans. London, 1978, 71–89.

Pelz, Stephen E., *Race to Pearl Harbor: The Failure of the Second London Naval Conference and the Onset of World War II*. Cambridge, MA, 1974.

Philbin, Tobias R., III, *The Lure of Neptune: German–Soviet Naval Collaboration and Ambitions, 1919–1941*. Columbia, SC, 1994.

Podsoblyaev, Evgenii F., "The Russian Naval General Staff and the Evolution of Naval Policy, 1905–1914," *Journal of Military History* 66 (2002): 37–69.

Polmar, Norman, *Chronology of the Cold War at Sea, 1945–1991.* Annapolis, MD, 1998.

——, *The Naval Institute Guide to the Soviet Navy,* 5th edn. Annapolis, MD, 1991.

——, "The *Kursk* is Salvaged," *US Naval Institute Proceedings* 127/11 (November 2001): 28.

Poolman, Kenneth, *The Winning Edge: Naval Technology in Action, 1939–1945.* Annapolis, MD, 1997.

Pope, Dudley, *Graf Spee: The Life and Death of a Raider.* Philadelphia, PA, 1956.

Pugh, Philip, *The Cost of Seapower: The Influence of Money on Naval Affairs from 1815 to the Present Day.* London, 1986.

Radogna, Lamberto, *Storia della Marina Militare delle Due Sicilie, 1734–1860.* Turin, 1978.

Rasor, Eugene L., *Reform in the Royal Navy: A Social History of the Lower Deck, 1850 to 1880.* Hamden, CT, 1976.

Rhys-Jones, Graham, *The Loss of the Bismarck: An Avoidable Disaster.* Annapolis, MD, 1999.

Ridley, Jasper, *Lord Palmerston.* New York, 1971.

Roberts, John, "The Pre-Dreadnought Age, 1890–1905," in *Steam, Steel and Shellfire: The Steam Warship 1815–1905*, ed. Robert Gardiner. London, 1992, 112–33.

——, "Warships of Steel, 1879–1889," in *Steam, Steel and Shellfire: The Steam Warship 1815–1905*, ed. Robert Gardiner. London, 1992, 95–111.

Rodríguez González, Agustín Ramón, *Politica naval de la Restauracion, 1875–1898.* Madrid, 1988.

Ropp, Theodore, *The Development of a Modern Navy: French Naval Policy, 1871–1904,* ed. Stephen S. Roberts. Annapolis, MD, 1987.

Sadkovich, James J., *The Italian Navy in World War II.* Westport, CT, 1994.

Sandler, Stanley, *The Emergence of the Modern Capital Ship.* Newark, DE, 1979.

Schurman, D. M. *The Education of a Navy: The Development of British Naval Strategic Thought, 1867–1914.* Malabar, FL, 1984.

Seton-Watson, Christopher, *Italy: From Liberalism to Fascism, 1870–1925.* London, 1967.

Shmelev, Anatol, "Mutiny in the Destroyer Division of the Baltic Fleet, May–June 1918," in *Rebellion, Repression, Reinvention: Mutiny in Comparative Perspective*, ed. Jane Hathaway. Westport, CT, 2001, 169–94.

Snyder, David R., "Arming the *Bundesmarine*: The United States and the Build-up of the German Federal Navy, 1950–1960," *Journal of Military History* 66 (2002): 477–500.

Sokolsky, Joel J., "Anglo–American Maritime Strategy in the Era of Flexible Response, 1960–80," in *Maritime Strategy and Balance of Power: Britain and America in the Twentieth Century*, ed. John B. Hattendorf and Robert S. Jordan. New York, 1989, 300–24.

Sondhaus, Lawrence, "The Non-Intervention Committee During the Spanish Civil War: A Study in the Failure of Diplomacy," MA thesis, University of Virginia, 1982.

——, *The Habsburg Empire and the Sea: Austrian Naval Policy, 1797–1866*. West Lafayette, IN, 1989.

——, *The Naval Policy of Austria–Hungary: Navalism, Industrial Development, and the Politics of Dualism, 1867–1918*. West Lafayette, IN, 1994.

——, "The Imperial German Navy and Social Democracy, 1878–1897," *German Studies Review* 18 (1995): 51–64.

——, *Preparing for Weltpolitik: German Sea Power before the Tirpitz Era*. Annapolis, MD, 1997.

——, *Naval Warfare, 1815–1914*. London, 2001.

Spencer, Warren F., *The Confederate Navy in Europe*. Tuscaloosa, AL, 1983.

Steensen, Robert Steen, *Vore Panserskibe, 1863–1943*. Copenhagen, 1968.

——, *Vore Krydsere*. Copenhagen, 1971.

Steinberg, Jonathan, *Yesterday's Deterrent: Tirpitz and the Birth of the German Battle Fleet*. New York, 1965.

Still, William N., Jr, *American Sea Power in the Old World: the United States Navy in European and Near Eastern Waters, 1865–1917*. Westport, CT, 1980.

Stolz, Gerd, *Die Schleswig-Holsteinische Marine, 1848–1852*. Heide in Holstein, 1978.

Sullivan, Brian R., "Italian Naval Power and the Washington Disarmament Conference of 1921–22," in *The Washington*

Conference, 1921–22: Naval Rivalry, East Asian Stability, and the Road to Pearl Harbor, ed. Erik Goldstein and John Maurer. London, 1994, 220–48.

Sumida, Jon Tetsuro, *In Defence of Naval Supremacy: Finance, Technology and British Naval Policy, 1889–1914*. Boston, MA, 1989.

——, "Sir John Fisher and the *Dreadnought*: The Sources of Naval Mythology," *Journal of Military History* 59 (1995): 619–38.

——, "The Quest for Reach: the Development of Long-Range Gunnery in the Royal Navy, 1901–1912," in *Tooling for War: Military Transformation in the Industrial Age*, ed. Stephen D. Chiabotti. Chicago, IL, 1996.

——, *Inventing Grand Strategy and Teaching Command: The Classic Works of Alfred Thayer Mahan Revisited*. Baltimore, MD, 1997.

Tarrant, V. E., *The Last Year of the Kriegsmarine, May 1944–May 1945*. Annapolis, MD, 1994.

——, *Jutland: The German Perspective*. Annapolis, MD, 1995.

Thomas, Hugh, *Suez*. New York, 1966.

Till, Geoffrey, *Airpower and the Royal Navy, 1914–1945: A Historical Survey*. London, 1979.

——, "Adopting the Aircraft Carrier: The British, American, and Japanese Case Studies," in *Military Innovation in the Interwar Period*, ed. Williamson Murray and Allan R. Millett. Cambridge, 1996, 191–226.

Tomitch, V. M., *Warships of the Imperial Russian Navy*. London, 1968.

Tritten, James J., "Doctrine and Fleet Tactics in the Royal Navy," in *A Doctrine Reader: The Navies of United States, Great Britain, France, Italy, and Spain*, ed. James J. Tritten and Luigi Donolo. Newport, RI, 1995, 1–36.

——, "Navy and Military Doctrine in France," in *A Doctrine Reader: The Navies of United States, Great Britain, France, Italy, and Spain*, ed. James J. Tritten and Luigi Donolo. Newport, RI, 1995, 37–75.

——, "Revolutions in Military Affairs, Paradigm Shifts, and Doctrine," in *A Doctrine Reader: The Navies of United States, Great Britain, France, Italy, and Spain*, ed. James J. Tritten and Luigi Donolo. Newport, RI, 1995, 125–51.

Tucker, Spencer C., "Shelling of Hai Phòng," in *Encyclopedia of the Vietnam War*, 3 vols, ed. Spencer C. Tucker. Santa Barbara, CA, 1998, 1:260–1.

——, "Georges Thierry d'Argenlieu," in *Encyclopedia of the Vietnam War*, 3 vols, ed. Spencer C. Tucker. Santa Barbara, CA, 1998, 1:147.

Ullman, Richard H., *Anglo–Soviet Relations, 1917–1921*, volume 2: *Britain and the Russian Civil War, November 1918–February 1920*. Princeton, NJ, 1968.

Verchau, Ekkard, "Von Jachmann über Stosch und Caprivi," in *Marine und Marinepolitik im kaiserlichen Deutschland, 1871–1914*, ed. Herbert Schlottelius and Wilhelm Deist. Düsseldorf, 1972, 54–72.

Villa, Brian Loring, *Unauthorized Action: Mountbatten and the Dieppe Raid*. Oxford, 1994.

Walser, Ray, *France's Search for a Battle Fleet: Naval Policy and Naval Power, 1898–1914*. New York, 1992.

Watts, Anthony J., *The Imperial Russian Navy*. London, 1990.

Watts, Barry and Williamson Murray, "Military Innovation in Peacetime," in *Military Innovation in the Interwar Period*, ed. Williamson Murray and Allan R. Millett. Cambridge, 1996, 369–415.

Weir, Gary E., *Building the Kaiser's Navy: The Imperial Navy Office and German Industry in the von Tirpitz Era, 1890–1919*. Annapolis, MD, 1992.

Wells, John, *The Royal Navy: An Illustrated Social History, 1870–1982*. London, 1994.

White, Colin, *Victoria's Navy: The End of the Sailing Navy*. Annapolis, MD, 1981.

Williamson, Samuel R., Jr, *The Politics of Grand Strategy: Britain and France Prepare for War, 1904–1914*. Cambridge, MA, 1969.

Wilson, Michael, "Early Submarines," in *Steam, Steel and Shellfire: The Steam Warship 1815–1905*, ed. Robert Gardiner. London, 1992, 147–57.

Winton, John, *The Death of the Scharnhorst*. New York, 1983.

Wong, J. Y., *Deadly Dreams: Opium, Imperialism, and the Arrow War (1856–1860) in China*. Cambridge, 1998.

Woodward, David, *The Russians at Sea: A History of the Russian Navy*. New York, 1966.

Yates, Keith, *Flawed Victory: Jutland 1916*. London, 2000.

Ziegler, Philip, *Mountbatten*. New York, 1985.

INTERNET SOURCES

Laursen, Gert, "Kontraadmiral Edouard Suenson," http:/www.milhist.dk/soldiers/Suenson/suenson.html (accessed 25 June 2001).

Scott, Richard, "Russia's Navy Looks to Show the Flag Again," 10 April 2001, http://www.janes.com/defence/naval_forces/news/ (accessed 19 January 2002).

Toppan, Andrew, "World Navies Today," http://www.hazegray.org/worldnav/ (accessed 12–19 January 2002).

Traynor, Ian, "Putin's Stock May Sink with Fleet," 16 August 2000, http://www.guardian.co.uk/Print/ (accessed 19 January 2002).

Walsh, Don, "The AIP Alternative: Air-Independent Propulsion, an Idea Whose Time Has Come?," http://www.navyleague.org/seapower/aip_alternative.htm (accessed 14 January 2002).

"Coalition Units of the Gulf War," http://www.homepage.jefnet.com/gwvrl/coalition.html (accessed 9 January 2002).

"German Navy Ships Set Off to Patrol Horn of Africa in Biggest Deployment since World War II," 3 January 2002, www.krem.com/war/archive/html (accessed 20 January 2002).

"HMS Halland Triumphs in Naval Duels," 15 November 2000, http://www.seawaves.com/News/Articles/Europe/November%202000/00111612.htm (accessed 13 January 2002).

"Italy Pledges Troops to US," 7 November 2001, www.cnn.com/2001/WORLD/europe/11/07/gen.italy.military/ (accessed 20 January 2002).

"Powell Enlists British, French," 11 December 2001, www.cbsnews.com/now/story/0,1597,320827–412,00shtml (accessed 20 January 2002).

"The Royal Navy and the Gulf," http://www,btinternet.com/~warship/Feature/gulf.htm (accessed 20 January 2002).

"Russian Navy Celebrates Despite Cutbacks, Scandals," 26 July 1998, http://www.cdi.org/russia/johnson/2283.html (accessed 24 January 2002).

"Submarines of the Royal Navy," http://www.argonet.co.uk/ (accessed 28 October 2000).

"Suez Crisis," http://www.fas.org/man/dod-101/ops/suez.htm (accessed 9 January 2002).

"Talks Between FMW, HDW and Kockums Lead to Constructive Result," 24 October 2001. http://www.karlskronavarvet.se/ (accessed 14 January 2002).

http://britishwarships.cjb.net (accessed 12–13 January 2002).

http://digilander.iol.it/i2mov/page8.htm (10 August 2001).

http://users.hunterlink.net.au/westlakes/pagemorse.htm (accessed 10 August 2001).

http://www.afsouth.nato.int/factsheets/STANAVFORMED.htm (accessed 18–21 January 2002).

http://www.britains-smallwars.com/korea/ships.html (accessed 25 March 2002).

http://www.defenselink.mil/specials/desert_fox/ (accessed 18 January 2002).

http://www.defenselink.mil/specials/kosovo/index.html (accessed 20 January 2002).

http://www.desert-storm.com/War/nations.html (accessed 9 January 2002).

http://www.hri.org/docs/USSD-INCSR/97/Europe/Portugal.html (accessed 21 January 2002).

http://www.marconi.com/media/6p14to15.pdf (accessed 10 August 2001).

http://www.nato.int/structur/struc-mcs.htm (accessed 18 January 2002).

http://www.navyhistory.com/CVN70TR.html (accessed 20 January 2002).

http://www.uscg.mil/d8/99REL/99REL107.htm (accessed 21 January 2002).

http://www.usdoj.gov/usao/txs/initiatives/drugs.html (accessed 21 January 2002).

INDEX